CONGRESS RECONSIDERED

CONGRESS RECONSIDERED

Eighth Edition

✧ ✧ ✧

Edited by

LAWRENCE C. DODD

University of Florida

BRUCE I. OPPENHEIMER

Vanderbilt University

A Division of Congressional Quarterly Inc.
Washington, D.C.

CQ Press
1255 22nd Street, N.W., Suite 400
Washington, D.C. 20037

202-729-1900; toll-free: 1-866-4CQ-Press (1-866-427-7737)

www.cqpress.com

Cover design by Circle Graphics

Printed and bound in the United States of America

08 07 06 05 04   5 4 3 2 1

∞ The paper used in this publication exceeds the requirements of the American National Standard for Information Sciences–Permanence of Paper for Printed Library Materials, ANSI Z39.48-1992.

Library of Congress Cataloging-in-Publication Data

Congress reconsidered / edited by Lawrence C. Dodd,
Bruce I. Oppenheimer Vanderbilt University.—8th ed.
p. cm.
Includes bibliographical references and index.
ISBN 1-56802-859-8 (pbk. : alk. paper)
1. United States. Congress. I. Dodd, Lawrence C. II. Oppenheimer, Bruce Ian.

JK1021.C558 2004
328.73—dc22   2004026308

Contents

✧ ✧ ✧

Tables and Figures

✧ ✧ ✧

Tables

Figures

Contributors

✧ ✧ ✧

John H. Aldrich is the Pfizer–Pratt University Professor at Duke University. He had taught at Michigan State University and the University of Minnesota before joining the Department of Political Science at Duke, where he has served as chair. For his research in American politics, positive theory, and methodology, Aldrich has received the Gladys M. Kammerer, Heinz Eulau, Pi Sigma Alpha, and CQ Press awards. His current projects involve the role of political parties in the U.S. Congress, the impact of economic globalization on political preferences, the emergence of electoral competition in the southern United States, and strategic voting in Israel. Aldrich is currently the president of the Midwest Political Science Association. He received his Ph.D. from the University of Rochester in 1975.

Sarah A. Binder is associate professor of political science at George Washington University and a Brookings Institution Senior Fellow in Governance Studies. She is the author or coauthor of three books on Congress: *Politics or Principle? Filibustering in the United States Senate* (1997), with Steven S. Smith; *Minority Rights, Majority Rule: Partisanship and the Development of Congress* (1997); and *Stalemate: Causes and Consequences of Legislative Gridlock* (2003). Her work on judicial selection is supported by a grant from the Carnegie Corporation of New York. She received her Ph.D. from the University of Minnesota in 1995.

Joseph Cooper is professor of political science at Johns Hopkins University. He has served as the Autrey Professor of Social Sciences and dean of social sciences at Rice University; staff director of the U.S. House Commission on Administrative Review, or Obey Commission; and provost at Johns Hopkins University. He is currently a member of the U.S. Advisory Committee on the Records of Congress. His publications include several books and articles on the development of congressional structures and processes, party voting in Congress, presidential power, changing patterns of congressional leadership, and the decline of trust in Congress.

Lawrence C. Dodd holds the Manning J. Dauer Eminent Scholar Chair in Political Science at the University of Florida. His books include *Coalitions in Parliamentary Government* (1976), *Congress and the Administrative State* (1979), *Congress and Policy Change* (1986), and *New Perspectives on American Politics* (1994). A student of comparative politics as well as of the U.S. Congress, Dodd is the coauthor with Leslie E. Anderson of *Learning Democracy* (2005), which examines the advent of democratic elections in Nicaragua. Dodd has been an American Political Science Association Congressional Fellow (1974–1975), Hoover National Fellow (1984–1985), University Fellow (Colorado, 1993–1994), and Woodrow Wilson Center Fellow (2003–2004). He also was the recipient of the 1997–1998 Superior Faculty Service Award for his leadership and program-building efforts at the University of Florida. He received his Ph.D. from the University of Minnesota in 1972.

Robert S. Erikson is professor of political science at Columbia University. He has written numerous articles on congressional elections and is the coauthor of *Statehouse Democracy: Public Opinion and Policy in the American States* (1993); *The Macro Polity* (2002); and *American Public Opinion: Its Origin, Contents, and Impact* (7th ed., 2005). The former editor of the *American Journal of Political Science,* he currently edits the journal *Political Analysis.* He received his Ph.D. from the University of Illinois in 1969.

C. Lawrence Evans is professor of government at the College of William & Mary and coeditor of *Legislative Studies Quarterly.* A former American Political Science Association Congressional Fellow and Brookings Research Fellow, he is the author of *Leadership in Committee* (1997), *Congress under Fire* (1997), and numerous articles about legislative politics. He has received the CQ Press and Patrick J. Fett awards for his research. During 1992 and 1993, he served as an associate staff member for Chairman Lee H. Hamilton on the Joint Committee on the Organization of Congress. He earned his Ph.D. from the University of Rochester in 1988.

Morris P. Fiorina is the Wendt Family Professor of Political Science and a Senior Fellow of the Hoover Institution at Stanford University. Fiorina has written widely on American government and politics, with special emphasis on representation and elections. His ten books include *Retrospective Voting in American National Elections* (1981); *Congress—Keystone of the Washington Establishment* (1989); *The Personal Vote: Constituency Service and Electoral Independence* (1990), coauthored with Bruce Cain and John Ferejohn; *Home Style and Washington Work* (1991), coedited with David Rohde; *Civic Engagement in American Democracy* (1999), coedited with Theda Skocpol; and *Culture War? The Myth of a Polarized America* (2005), coauthored with Samuel Abrams and Jeremy Pope. Fiorina has served on the editorial boards of a dozen journals in the fields of political science, economics, law, and public policy and was chairman of the Board of Overseers of the American National Election Studies from 1986 to 1990. He is a member of the American Academy of Arts and Sciences and the National Academy of Sciences. He earned his Ph.D. from the University of Rochester in 1972.

Gerald Gamm is chair of the Department of Political Science and associate professor of political science and history at the University of Rochester. He is the author of *The Making of New Deal Democrats* (1989), *Urban Exodus: Why the Jews Left Boston and the Catholics Stayed* (1999), and a forthcoming book with Steven S. Smith on the rise of party leadership in the Senate. He received his Ph.D. from Harvard University in 1994.

Joshua B. Gordon is senior policy analyst at the Concord Coalition, a nonpartisan, grassroots organization dedicated to educating the public about federal budget issues. He received his Ph.D. in political science from the University of Florida in 2002. His dissertation was on the budget process and the House Appropriations Committee, and he conducted much of his research in the office of committee chairman C. W. Bill Young, R-Fla. Gordon earned an M.A. from the University of Florida and his B.A. from Emory University.

Kerry L. Haynie is associate professor of political science at Duke University, where he also is associate director of the Center for the Study of Race, Ethnicity, and Gender in the Social Sciences. His articles have appeared in the *Journal of Politics, Legislative Studies Quarterly,* and the *International Journal of Africana Studies,* and he is the author of *African American Legislators in the American States* (2001). He is coeditor of *New Race Politics: Understanding Minority and Immigrant Voting* (forthcoming 2005). Haynie earned his Ph.D. from the University of North Carolina, Chapel Hill, in 1994.

Paul S. Herrnson is director of the Center for American Politics and Citizenship and professor of government and politics at the University of Maryland. He is the author of *Party Campaigning in the 1980s* (1988) and *Congressional Elections: Campaigning at Home and in Washington* (4th ed., 2004). He is the coauthor or coeditor of several books, including *Responsible Partisanship? The Evolution of American Political Parties since 1950* (2002); *The Financiers of Congressional Elections: Investors, Ideologues, and Intimates* (2003); and *War Stories from Capitol Hill* (2004). He has written numerous articles on Congress, campaign finance, political parties, and elections and has served as an American Political Science Association Congressional Fellow. Herrnson has received several teaching awards, including the Excellence in Teaching Award from the College of Behavioral and Social Sciences at the University of Maryland.

John R. Hibbing is the Foundation Regents University Professor of Political Science at the University of Nebraska, Lincoln. He is the author of *Congressional Careers* (1991) and *Congress as Public Enemy* (1995), for which he won the American Political Science Association's 1996 Richard F. Fenno Jr. Prize for the best book on legislative politics, and coauthor of *Stealth Democracy* (2002). Hibbing has served as editor of *Legislative Studies Quarterly* and has been a NATO Fellow in Science, a Senior Fulbright Fellow, and president of APSA's organized section on legislative politics. His current research pursuits involve the extent to which evolutionary biology and environmental factors influence political attitudes and behaviors. He received his Ph.D. from the University of Iowa in 1981.

Christopher W. Larimer is currently pursuing a Ph.D. in political science at the University of Nebraska, Lincoln. His dissertation concerns the application of experimental research methods to political behavior. His other primary interests include American politics, state politics, and public administration. Larimer received his B.A. from the University of Northern Iowa in 2001 and an M.A. from the University of Nebraska, Lincoln, in 2003.

Daniel Lipinski was elected to Congress as a Democrat in 2004 to represent the Third Congressional District of Illinois. He previously had taught at the University of Notre Dame and the University of Tennessee. He is the author of *Congressional Communication: Content and Consequences* (2004) and of numerous articles and chapters focusing on Congress and political communication. Lipinski is a past recipient of the Carl Albert Dissertation Award for the best dissertation in the area of legislative studies and was an American Political Science Association Congressional Fellow. He received his Ph.D. from Duke University in 1998.

Forrest Maltzman is professor of political science at George Washington University. He is the author of *Competing Principles: Committees, Parties, and the Organization of Congress* (1997) and coauthor with James Spriggs and Paul Wahlbeck of *Crafting Law on the Supreme Court: The Collegial Game* (2000). His work on judicial and legislative politics has appeared in numerous journals, including the *American Journal of Politics, American Political Science Review, Journal of Politics,* and *Legislative Studies Quarterly.* He earned his Ph.D. from the University of Minnesota in 1993.

Bruce I. Oppenheimer is professor of political science at Vanderbilt University. He has been a Brookings Fellow in Governmental Studies (1970–1971) and an American Political Science Association Congressional Fellow (1974–1975). His book *Sizing Up the Senate: The Unequal Consequences of Equal Representation* (1999), cowritten with Frances Lee, was awarded the Lyndon Baines Johnson Foundation's D. B. Hardeman Prize for the best book on Congress. Oppenheimer is also the editor of *U.S. Senate Exceptionalism* (2002). He received his Ph.D. from the University of Wisconsin.

Kathryn Pearson is an assistant professor of political science at the University of Minnesota. Her dissertation, "Party Discipline in the Contemporary Congress," analyzes the extent to which party leaders in the House of Representatives exert discipline when they allocate scarce legislative, committee, and campaign benefits to their members. Her research also includes work on women's representation in Congress, public opinion on language policy and immigration, campaign finance, and women and congressional elections. Pearson was a Brookings Institution Research Fellow (2002–2003), and from 1993 to 1998 she worked as a legislative assistant on Capitol Hill.

David W. Rohde is the University Distinguished Professor of Political Science at Michigan State University. He has served as chair of the Michigan State Department of Political Science, editor of the *American Journal of Political Science,* and chair of the Legislative Studies Section of the American Political Science Association. He is the author of several books and articles on aspects of American national politics, including *Parties and Leaders in the Postreform House* (1991). He received his Ph.D. from the University of Rochester in 1971.

Catherine E. Rudder is professor and associate dean for academic affairs in the School of Public Policy at George Mason University. She previously had been executive director of the American Political Science Association for fourteen years. Rudder also served as director of APSA's Congressional Fellowship

Program and chief of staff for a member of the U.S. House Ways and Means Committee.

Eric Schickler is professor of government at Harvard University. He is the author of *Disjointed Pluralism: Institutional Innovation and the Development of the U.S. Congress* (2001), which received the American Political Science Association's Richard F. Fenno Jr. Prize, and coauthor with Donald Green and Bradley Palmquist of *Partisan Hearts and Minds* (2002). Schickler has written or cowritten numerous articles that appeared in the *American Journal of Political Science, American Political Science Review, Comparative Political Studies, Legislative Studies Quarterly, Polity, Public Opinion Quarterly,* and *Social Science History.*

Barbara Sinclair is the Marvin Hoffenberg Professor of American Politics at the University of California, Los Angeles. Her many articles and books on the U.S. Congress include *Majority Leadership in the U.S. House* (1983); *Legislators, Leaders, and Lawmaking: The U.S. House of Representatives in the Postreform Era* (1995); and *Unorthodox Lawmaking: New Legislative Processes in the U.S. Congress* (2nd ed., 2000). Her *Transformation of the U.S. Senate* (1989) won the American Political Science Association's Richard F. Fenno Jr. Prize for outstanding book on legislative studies and the Lyndon Baines Johnson Foundation's D. B. Hardeman Prize for outstanding book on the U.S. Congress. She received her Ph.D. from the University of Rochester in 1971.

Steven S. Smith is Kate M. Gregg Professor of Social Sciences and director of the Murray Weidenbaum Center on the Economy, Government, and Public Policy at Washington University. He is the author of *Call to Order: Floor Politics in the House and Senate* (1989) and *The American Congress* (1999). He is the coauthor of *Managing Uncertainty in the U.S. House of Representatives* (1988); *Committees in Congress* (3rd ed., 1995); *Politics or Principle? Filibustering in the Senate* (1997); and *The Politics of Institutional Choice: The Formation of the Russian State Duma* (2000). He received his Ph.D. from the University of Minnesota in 1980.

Donald R. Wolfensberger is director of the Congress Project at the Woodrow Wilson International Center for Scholars. He is the author of *Congress and the People: Deliberative Democracy on Trial* (2000) and coauthor of *Democracy and the Internet: Allies or Adversaries?* (2002). From 1969 to 1997 he worked as a staff member of the U.S. House of Representatives, culminating his career in an appointment as chief of staff of the House Rules Committee in the 104th Congress. Wolfensberger received an M.A. in political science at the University of Iowa in 1966.

Gerald C. Wright is professor of political science at Indiana University and was formerly director of the political science program at the National Science Foundation. He is the author of *Electoral Choice in America* (1974); coeditor of *Congress and Policy Change* (1986); and coauthor of *Statehouse Democracy: Public Opinion and Policy in the American States* (1993) and *Keeping the Republic: Power and Citizenship in America* (3rd ed., forthcoming 2005). He received his Ph.D. from the University of North Carolina, Chapel Hill, in 1973.

Preface

✧ ✧ ✧

As we prepare this preface, we realize that it has been thirty years since we first met as APSA Congressional Fellows, following the 1974 elections. It was during that year that we sensed how much Congress had changed and how different it was from the institution about which we were teaching at our respective universities. That experience provided the impetus for the first edition of *Congress Reconsidered.*

At the time there was no reason to anticipate that there would be more than a single edition. (As junior faculty, we were overjoyed that someone was willing to publish our edited manuscript.) We learned, however, that political institutions were constantly changing, sometimes only in modest ways but frequently in major ones. Moreover, with an ever-growing community of active legislative scholars, it made sense to provide a timely and accessible vehicle through which their research on Congress could reach undergraduates, graduate students, and those teaching Congress and legislative process courses. With the cooperation of an exceptionally talented group of contributors and a young CQ Press, we have been able to produce a new edition of *Congress Reconsidered* every four years since the first edition appeared in 1977. As kibitzers in the profession remind us, we have been reconsidering Congress again and again and again. In fact, however, if you'll forgive our immodesty, a major reason why we devote a significant part of our time to the book—one year out of every four—is that its users have come to expect a new edition.

The prospect of producing a new edition is always attractive to us because of the wonderful people we are fortunate to work with at CQ Press. Their professionalism, their tolerance of and compensation for our shortcomings, their capacity to deal with a book that relies on so many cooks, and their patience—despite the seemingly unreasonable deadline of getting the book to the printer so that it will be available less than two months after elections—are unsurpassed. For the eighth edition, we were lucky to again work with old friends Brenda Carter, Charisse Kiino, and Gwenda Larsen, as well as to interact regularly with Colleen Ganey and Nancy Geltman for the first time. It's great fun to work with such skilled people.

Of course, throughout our careers we have been aware of how important the APSA Congressional Fellowship has been to our professional development. Dodd split his year between the Office of the Majority Whip and Rep. Bob Eckhardt,

D-Texas, and Oppenheimer spent the entire year with Rep. Gillis Long, D-La. These experiences proved invaluable in fostering our research interests at the time, in improving our repertoires as teachers, in providing us with a better understanding of how Congress works and what motivates member behavior, and in stimulating more research questions than we will be able to address in our careers. From our perspective, the APSA Congressional Fellowship program has been the prime ingredient in the continued vibrancy of the legislative research community for more than half a century.

As in the past, the majority of the chapters in this edition of *Congress Reconsidered* are new. Revisions have been made to several previous essays that readers find of special and continuing value. The new and revised chapters are both based on cutting-edge research, innovative theoretical analysis, and timely scholarly assessments of Congress. Moreover, to make the volume as current as possible, the prologue analyzes the 2004 presidential election and evaluates the House and Senate outcomes, assessing their probable effects in Congress. All of the chapters, together with the prologue, have been prepared specifically for this volume; there are no reprints from other sources.

The overall organization of the book has changed with this eighth edition. Because of the growing primacy of party government in Congress, the discussion of committee politics is now nested within the broader section on parties. The result is a book divided into five parts that represent substantive divisions in current research and organized the way one might logically teach the contemporary Congress. Part I, "Patterns and Dynamics of Congressional Change," includes two overview chapters. One, by Barbara Sinclair, traces the rise of individualism and partisanship in the contemporary Senate. The other, which we have written, looks at the effects of ten years of Republican control on policymaking and governing strategies in the House. In the third chapter, John Hibbing and Christopher Larimer add to the overviews of the two chambers with a broad portrait of changing citizen assessments of Congress as a whole.

Part II deals with congressional elections and representation. It consists of Robert Erikson and Gerald Wright's analysis of the linkages between voters' opinions and candidates' issue positions in congressional elections; Paul Herrnson's close look at the McCain-Feingold reforms of campaign finance and their implications for congressional elections; and Oppenheimer's examination of the causes and consequences for the House of declining partisan competitiveness in congressional districts. The section concludes with an essay by Morris Fiorina in which he revisits his classic argument of incumbency advantage from *Congress—Keystone of the Washington Establishment,* first published in 1977, and assesses new developments in American politics that are shaping congressional elections in the twenty-first century.

Part III turns to the inner workings of Congress, with five chapters focusing on the rise of party government and the impact of this trend on committee politics. It opens with Steven Smith and Gerald Gamm's discussion of the historical conditions giving rise to party government in the modern era and how analyses must be sensitive to differences between the House and the Senate. Eric Schickler and Kathryn Pearson's essay on partisan warfare in the House and Lawrence Evans and Daniel Lipinski's discussion of obstructionism in the Senate amplify the distinctions between House and Senate partisanship. The chapter by John Aldrich and David Rohde examines how partisan patterns are reshaping committee politics in the two chambers, with extended attention to the House and to contrasting patterns in the Senate. Joshua Gordon's chapter concludes the section by concentrating on the impact that partisanship has had on the House Appropriations Committee; he considers the extent to which it is unraveling the bipartisan comity and internal cohesiveness that Richard Fenno has argued is so central to the successful exercise of the power of the purse by the Appropriations Committee and Congress.

Attention is paid in Part IV to the role of Congress in controversial areas of contemporary policymaking: Sarah Binder and Forrest Maltzman look at the politics of judicial appointments, Catherine Rudder analyzes the politics of taxing and spending, and Donald Wolfensberger focuses on the policy response to the 9/11 tragedy and terrorist threats.

Part V addresses the forces of change that are operating on Congress and their implications for that institution's future direction. This final section opens with a seminal essay by Joseph Cooper that seeks to inform our understanding of the modern Congress by contrasting it with the Congress of the late nineteenth century, concentrating on electoral politics, institutional politics, and legislative-administrative relations. The next chapter, by Kerry Haynie, examines the impact of the politics of inclusion by focusing on the growing African American presence in Congress and that group's influence on organizational politics and policy outcomes. Dodd's final chapter seeks to explain the rise and growing solidification of Republican control of Congress and to identify factors likely to shape and constrain the party's long-term consolidation of power over the national government.

As in the past seven editions, the contributors to this volume deserve the credit for its success. Once again they have delivered first-rate chapters that will inform and stimulate a readership with a shared interest in Congress as an institution but with varied levels of knowledge and methodological sophistication.

In addition, we appreciate the support we have received from our academic institutions and our departmental colleagues and students. Dodd would also like to express his appreciation to the Woodrow Wilson International Center for Scholars for funding a research leave during which portions of the planning and preparation of this book were done. Oppenheimer wishes to thank three exceptional former colleagues from Vanderbilt for their professional and personal support: John Vasquez, Donna Bahry, and Geoff Layman, all of whom have now moved to greener pastures.

Through thirty years of working together on this project, we have remained the best of friends, tolerating each other's shortcomings, sharing the joy in our successes, and empathizing when there have been disappointments. We cannot recall ever having tried to measure our individual contributions to this collective effort. The fact that we have many personal and professional differences has never bothered us much. Dodd long ago accepted that the chances of Oppenheimer becoming a country music fan were about as good as those of Oppenheimer believing that Dodd would have a late growth spurt so that they could really see eye to eye. The irony, of course, is that Oppenheimer resides in the "home of country music," and Dodd was raised among long, tall Texans. Sometimes nurture simply cannot overcome nature.

Finally, we would like to thank our respective family members, who tolerate our inattentiveness when we are working on a new edition. Leslie, Susan, and Anne must all think we are incapable of hearing. Larry also extends special appreciation for his first and only grandchild, Andrew Wotman, for the special joy he has brought to his life.

Prologue: Perspectives on the 2004 Congressional Elections

Lawrence C. Dodd and Bruce I. Oppenheimer

The 2004 congressional elections continued the trends that began a decade earlier, and the results make it likely that those trends will persist into the foreseeable future. Republican control of the House and the Senate was further cemented. For the sixth consecutive election, Republicans won the right to organize both chambers. Democratic hopes for winning back either chamber, which may have been realistic following the 2000 elections, and still were a possibility in the Senate going into the 2004 elections, are now quite bleak. Even though the numerical sizes of the Republican House and Senate majorities are relatively small historically, structural features make it increasingly difficult for Democrats to challenge for either chamber.

In consolidating Republican control of Congress, the 2004 elections did more than sustain the already high levels of partisan polarization; they actually increased them. In both chambers, the Republicans will be a more uniformly conservative party and the Democrats a more uniformly liberal one. Conservative Democrats are about to join liberal Republicans as an extinct species in Congress, and moderates in both parties are endangered but unprotected.

The cementing of Republican control, combined with the reelection of George W. Bush, will have noticeable effects on the workings of the 109th Congress. Not only will Republicans interpret the 2004 election as giving them a clearer mandate to pursue a conservative policy agenda, but the Democrats are in a far weaker position to thwart their efforts or to push competing policies. Republicans will no longer have to rely on the remaining party moderates to get legislation through the Senate, and Democrats will find it more difficult to produce the forty-one votes necessary to defeat cloture resolutions. Instead, the minority will have to be more selective in choosing the opportunities "to go to the mat." No longer concerned with reelection, the president can pursue his policy preferences more aggressively. In this prologue we will examine these three trends—the cementing of Republican control, the increase in polarization, and the ability of Republicans to pursue and accomplish a conservative legislative policy agenda—in detail.

The 2004 Congressional Elections

The House and Senate elections continued Republican control, with minimal gains in the House and more sizable ones in the Senate, as Republicans won all but one close Senate contest. In both institutions, the elections gave a greater sense of permanence to Republican control than has existed since the party won its majorities in the 1994 election.

In the Senate, Republicans returned to the fifty-five-seat level that the party enjoyed in the 105th and 106th Congresses. Of the nine races that were thought to be close in the final weeks of the campaign, Republicans won eight. All were in states that Bush carried, and among such states, only in Colorado, the state of the lone Democratic victory, and in Florida did Bush receive less than 55 percent of the vote. Even as formidable a politician as Senate minority leader Tom Daschle could not overcome the electoral tide that gave Bush 60 percent of the South Dakota vote.

The other main feature of the Republican Senate gains is Republican domination of Senate seats in southern states. As can be seen in Table P-1, by winning open-seat contests in Florida, Georgia, Louisiana, North Carolina, Oklahoma, and South Carolina, five seats of which were previously held by Democratic incumbents, Republicans increased their advantage in the South to 22–4. The South is the only region in which the Republicans have gained Senate seats since 1994. Democratic gains in the East have not been large enough to offset what has become Republican dominance of southern Senate contests, while the Midwest and West have remained fairly constant in the party split of their Senate seats.

One other feature of recent Senates has been the large number of states that elect same-party senators. Thirty-eight states (if one includes Vermont) have both senators who organize with the same party in the 109th Congress. That's up from thirty-one in the 104th Congress. Following the 1980 election, half the states had one senator from each party. The concept of red states and blue states is surely overstated, but there are fewer states in which a candidate of either party can easily win in statewide elections.

For the Democrats, it is the structural feature of the Senate representational scheme that makes recapturing a majority now appear so difficult. Republicans have a partisan edge in more states. Bush carried thirty states in 2000 and thirty-one in 2004. In a period when party attachments are stronger, voters are less likely to vote for a presidential candidate of one party and a senator of another.

It will not be easy for Democrats to narrow the Republican Senate advantage in 2006. As in 2004, Democrats will have more seats to defend than Republicans will. Fortunately for the Democrats, few of the seats are in the South, but unfortunately, there are few obviously vulnerable Republican incumbents to target. In addition, there are two Democratic incumbents in Nebraska and North Dakota, small states that Bush won easily. Emboldened by their ability to unseat Daschle in a similar context, Republicans may well target those two seats. Democrats' best targets may be among eastern Republican incumbents. Interestingly, many of the potential targets in both parties are Senate moderates, about which we will have more to say later in this prologue.

The 2004 House elections produced a result of unparalleled stability, especially when one excludes redistricted seats in Texas. Of the remaining 403 House seats (including two Louisiana races undecided at press time), only six changed party hands.[1] Only three incumbents (less than 1 percent) outside of Texas were defeated, and in 90 percent of the open seats outside of Texas, the winner was of

Table P-1 Distribution of Senate Seats, 1994–2004, and Seats to Be Contested in 2006 (by Party and Region)

Congress		East	Midwest	South	West	Total
104th[a]	Democrats	14	13	10	10	47
	Republicans	10	11	16	16	53
105th	Democrats	14	13	8	10	45
	Republicans	10	11	18	16	55
106th	Democrats	15	12	8	10	45
	Republicans	9	12	18	16	55
107th[b]	Democrats	16	15	9	10	50
	Republicans	7	9	17	16	49
	Independents	1				1
108th	Democrats	16	13	9	10	48
	Republicans	7	11	17	16	51
	Independents	1				1
109th	Democrats	16	13	4	11	44
	Republicans	7	11	22	15	55
	Independents	1				1
110th	Democrats	7	5	1	4	17
	Republicans	3	3	4	5	15
	Independents	1				1

Notes: **East** = Conn., Del., Maine, Mass., Md., N.H., N.J., N.Y., Pa., R.I., Vt., W.Va.; **Midwest** = Ill., Ind., Iowa, Kan., Mich., Minn., Mo., Neb., N.D., Ohio, S.Dak., Wis.; **South** = Ala., Ark., Fla., Ga., Ky., La., Miss., N.C., Okla., S.C., Tenn., Texas, Va.; **West** = Alaska, Ariz., Calif., Colo., Hawaii, Idaho, Mont., Nev., N.M., Ore., Utah, Wash., Wyo.

[a]For the purpose of this table Richard Shelby, Ala., is counted as a Republican and Ben Nighthorse Campbell is counted as a Democrat at the start of the 104th Congress. Both switched to the Republican Party, but Shelby switched shortly after the election, whereas Campbell switched after Congress convened.

[b]Jim Jeffords is listed as an independent although he did not leave the Republican Party until several months into the 107th Congress. We do this because, upon his switch, the Democrats controlled the Senate.

the same party as the incumbent. In Texas, the Republican-orchestrated redistricting resulted in one Democrat's retiring, because his district was divided up, and in the defeat of four of the five Democrats that the Republican redistricting plan had targeted. Even including the four Texas incumbents who were defeated in November, more than 98 percent of incumbents were general election victors. Overall, the Republicans made a net gain of three House seats. (Excluding Texas, Democrats actually gained two seats.)

One of the reasons for the constancy in House results is that so many districts now have a clear underlying partisan advantage. As Oppenheimer demonstrates in Chapter 6, compared with the three previous decades, incumbent success since the 1990s has been relatively more dependent on the partisan composition of the district and less dependent on any personal advantage that individual incumbents build up. One result is that open seats are less competitive than in the past.

The partisan stability of House seats creates problems for the majority and the minority parties. For the Republicans, it makes it difficult to expand the size of their majority. Republicans, thanks to Texas, only barely exceeded the 230-seat level that they achieved in 1994. For the Democrats, the seat stability of the House is more problematic. It severely limits their opportunity to become the majority party. By looking at the small number of House contests in 2004 that were close, we get a clearer understanding of the problem the Democrats face. Based on unofficial results of House elections, in only twenty contests did the winner receive 55 percent of the two-party vote or less.[2] Democrats won eight of those races, and Republicans won twelve. Assuming that the Democrats had won 5 percent more of the vote in all House contests and garnered all of the close races, the Republicans still would have won 220 seats and maintained control of the House.

As they do in the Senate, Republicans in the House have a structural advantage. In 2000, despite Democratic candidate Al Gore's winning the popular vote, Bush carried more House districts, 228–207. Redistricting in 2002 further increased the Republican advantage in terms of the number of districts Bush carried, 238–197.[3]

Table P-2 shows another similarity with respect to the basis of Republican control of the House and Senate. Since 1994, House Republicans have continued to make seat gains in the South. Although Democrats continue to hold a far higher percentage of southern seats in the House (36 percent) than they do in the Senate (15 percent), the Republican margin in southern House seats has grown from nine following the 1994 elections to forty following the 2004 elections. The biggest regional Democratic House gains have come in the West, primarily in California, which has 54 percent of the West's House seats but only 7.6 percent of its Senate seats.

In addition to changes in the partisan composition of the 109th Congress, there were also some modest changes in the gender and racial composition of the House and the Senate. The House in the 109th Congress will have sixty-five women as voting members, an increase of five, nearly twice as many of them Democrats (42) as Republicans (23). In the Senate, the number of women remains the same as in the 108th Congress, as all five incumbent female senators running for reelection retained their seats, leaving the chamber with nine Democratic women and five Republicans. Five nonincumbent women, all Democrats, ran unsuccessfully as major-party general election candidates (three for open seats and two as challengers). Whatever change may have occurred in the gender gap in the presidential election, there is no indication that it is closing in the composition of Congress. After significant growth in the number of women in Congress following the 1992 election, change, especially in the House, has been incremental. There are only seventeen more women in the House in 2005 than there were in 1993.

Table P-2 Distribution of House Seats, 1994–2004 (by Party and Region)

Congress		East	Midwest	South	West	Total
104th	Democrats	54	46	64	40	204
	Republicans	45	59	73	53	230
	Other	1				1
105th	Democrats	60	50	55	43	208
	Republicans	39	55	82	50	226
	Other	1				1
106th	Democrats	61	51	55	44	211
	Republicans	38	54	82	49	223
	Other	1				1
107th	Democrats	59	48	55	50	212
	Republicans	40	57	81	43	221
	Other	1		1		2
108th	Democrats	57	39	57	52	205
	Republicans	37	61	85	46	229
	Other	1				1
109th[a]	Democrats	58	40	51	53	202
	Republicans	36	60	91	45	232
	Other	1				1

Notes: **East** = Conn., Del., Maine, Mass., Md., N.H., N.J., N.Y., Pa., R.I., Vt., W.Va.; **Midwest** = Ill., Ind., Iowa, Kan., Mich., Minn., Mo., Neb., N.D., Ohio, S.Dak., Wis.; **South** = Ala., Ark., Fla., Ga., Ky., La., Miss., N.C., Okla., S.C., Tenn., Texas, Va.; **West** = Alaska, Ariz., Calif., Colo., Hawaii, Idaho, Mont., Nev., N.M., Ore., Utah, Wash., Wyo.

[a]At the time this table was constructed the outcomes of two House races in Louisiana awaited a run-off election. For this table we are assigning one of those seats to each party.

In the Senate, the first two Hispanic members, Ken Salazar, D-Colo., and Mel Martinez, R-Fla., and only the third directly elected African American senator, Barack Obama, D-Ill., provide the Senate a tinge more diversity. In the House, the 2004 elections increased the number of black and Hispanic members, building on a good-sized base. The number of African American representatives increased by three, to forty-two, and the number of Hispanics grew by two, to twenty-three. All of the African American representatives and nineteen of the Hispanics are Democrats. The Republican Party lags badly in recruiting minority candidates even more so than it does in electing women. It is difficult for the Republican Party to appeal to minority voters when it cannot demonstrate diversity among its House members.

A Yet More Polarized Congress

Partisan polarization has been a growing characteristic of the House and Senate for the past two decades or more, and the 2004 congressional elections give little indication that the trend has peaked. Moderates will be scarcer in the 109th Congress. The Senate's reputation as the less-partisan body, in which a core of moderate members in each party hold the decision-making balance on many issues, will surely be in need of reevaluation given the membership changes. Only because the House took yet another step in the direction of partisan-based ideological polarization will the Senate preserve its relative position as the less partisan of the two bodies.

The retirements of three moderate Democratic senators—Ernest Hollings of South Carolina, John Breaux of Louisiana, and Bob Graham of Florida—and their replacement, respectively, with two extremely conservative Republicans—Jim DeMint and David Vitter—and one conservative Republican—Mel Martinez—will have the effect of making the Senate Democrats a more uniformly liberal aggregation and the Republicans an even more conservative party in the Senate.[4] The replacement of the independent, if unpredictable, Republican senator Peter Fitzgerald of Illinois with liberal Barack Obama adds to the two parties' ideological homogeneity. Three other Republican newcomers—Richard Burr of North Carolina, Tom Coburn of Oklahoma, and John Thune of South Dakota—have close ties to religious conservatives. As one journalist commented on the Senate, "Many centrists are leaving Congress; unvarnished conservatives are arriving in their place." [5] Senate moderate Olympia Snowe, R-Maine, described the election as "a sea change in terms of losing the political center." [6]

With few incumbents defeated or open seats switching parties and the House already so polarized, one might assume that the elections would have had little effect on institutional partisanship, but they did. As in the Senate, in the House, seat changes further polarized the parties. The Texas redistricting led to the forced retirement of one member of the conservative "Blue Dog" Democrats and the defeat of two others. Two of the departing Texans were among the three co-chairs of the Blue Dogs. The third co-chair, Baron Hill of Indiana, was the incumbent Democrat outside of Texas defeated for reelection. Ken Lucas of Kentucky, a Blue Dog who retired at the end of the 108th Congress, represented the only Democratic open seat that Republicans won. Two other Blue Dogs, Ralph Hall of Texas and Rodney Alexander of Louisiana, switched parties. Nearly 20 percent of the Blue Dog membership in the 108th Congress is gone.[7]

Thus, the 2004 elections resulted in an increase in intraparty homogeneity and interparty polarization in both the House and the Senate. It is likely that those changes will affect the internal workings of the House and Senate and the legislative policies they produce.

Governing in the 109th Congress

Against this backdrop, Republicans approach the 109th Congress with high hopes and expanded expectations. The scope of the Republicans' election victories creates opportunities and expectations for enactment of the party's conservative domestic agenda. Simultaneously the party will need to address continuing issues associated with the war on terrorism, and Congress will need to oversee and continue funding the Iraq war. Yet all such actions will go forward amid mounting deficits that could greatly restrict Republicans' capacity to enact additional spending legislation. They also may find an already polarized environment greatly complicated should openings in the Supreme Court or the president's cabinet occur that generate fights over controversial nominees early in Bush's second term.

As Congress prepares to address such issues, increased majorities, especially in the Senate, allow Republicans to expand their numerical control of congressional committees. Such expanded control aids the ability of party leaders to use committees to achieve the party's legislative goals along the lines that Aldrich and Rohde discuss in Chapter 11. The increased margins also give Republican leaders room to maneuver in crafting majorities that can pass party legislation through each chamber. They may be forced to do so, however, without the support of Democrats, who enter the new Congress chastened but largely unrepentant in their unified opposition to the conservative Republican agenda.[8] In addition, the Bush administration and the Republican congressional leadership must confront differences between the two houses. Both chambers are more ideologically polarized than in the 108th Congress, but what this means in the context of each chamber is somewhat different, with potential consequences for legislation.

The Senate

During Bush's first term, the Senate was the moderating force within the Republican national government, owing to close margins between parties and the leverage this gave to its moderate members. Now Senate Republicans will have a larger seat margin, with new members generally expected to be more conservative.[9] They will join a Senate caucus with experienced and conservative leadership, headed by Bill Frist of Tennessee as majority leader and Mitch McConnell of Kentucky as majority whip. These leaders will be pushed to the right by the new tilt of the party and by their own ideological leanings. However, there still will be constraints operating on them that could somewhat mitigate this tilt.

Given the rules of the Senate, Republican leaders must worry about generating sixty-vote victories on controversial legislation to overcome filibusters by Democrats. In addition, strong conservative rule is complicated by an increased ethos of individualism in the Senate, as Sinclair discusses in Chapter 1, and by permissive rules that allow individual members to obstruct Senate action, as Evans and Lipinski discuss in Chapter 10. These factors mean that Republican moderates must be assuaged to some extent by party leaders, yet such efforts could be greatly complicated by conservatives' sense that they have a strong mandate for action on their agenda. Just how difficult the situation could become was demonstrated forcefully the week after the election, when conservative groups nationwide demanded that Sen. Arlen Specter of Pennsylvania be deprived of the chairmanship of the Senate Judiciary Committee in the new Congress.[10] Their concern was that he could use the position to block nominees to the Supreme Court who oppose abortion. As an indication of how sensitive the situation was, almost two weeks into the controversy Majority Leader Frist continued to distance himself from Specter.[11]

Underlying tension between conservative and moderate Republicans pales, moreover, in comparison to the likely conflict between Senate Republicans and the Democratic minority. Not only are the two parties more polarized ideologically, but Democrats enter the 109th Congress stung by the role that Majority Leader Frist played in campaigning for the defeat of their leader, Tom Daschle. The damage to bipartisan relations generated by Frist's behavior could be somewhat offset by the selection of Harry Reid of Nevada as Democratic leader, because Reid is a Democratic moderate who as minority whip gained a reputation of working successfully with Republicans in speeding the passage of legislation.[12] On the other hand, he is a superb party tactician who has the capacity to unite his Democratic colleagues when an emerging consensus within the party appears possible.

Facing potential difficulties within his party and between the two parties, Frist and others have threatened rules changes that could give him and his party greater leverage in pushing legislation and judicial nominations through the Senate. Within the party, the Republican Conference could ignore seniority in doling out committee positions, thereby creating greater incentives for Republican senators to toe the party line in critical Senate votes.[13] With respect to the conflict between the parties, Frist has shown particular concern about the influence that the Senate filibuster gives to the minority party over judicial nominations, so he has proposed that judicial nominations be made immune from filibusters.

In light of the fissures within the Senate, expectations are that the Senate Republican leadership has a window of six months to a year during which to pass major policy initiatives. In this period, members' deference to the newly reelected president, combined with pressures toward Republican party loyalty and Democrats' desire not to be labeled obstructionist, could defuse conflict.

This window of opportunity for Senate action dictates that Bush and his Senate supporters move swiftly and skillfully on their legislative agenda. The administration enjoys a reputation for political savvy and advance preparation, so it may be well positioned to take advantage of its opportunity, as illustrated by the rapid move on tax cuts at the beginning of Bush's first term. Yet there also are early indications that the administration is less clear about how best to address major policy concerns, such as Social Security or tax code reform, in the second term than it was about tax reductions four years earlier.[14] Such indecisiveness could slow the momentum toward early legislative action, while fights over judicial or cabinet nominations could generate renewed partisan and ideological polarization that would likewise complicate legislative action in the Senate. Such complications could then be reinforced by the action-oriented dynamics likely to characterize the new House.

The House

With the increase in the size of their House majority and the emergence of an even more polarized membership, there appear to be few obstacles to the movement of the Republican agenda through the lower chamber. Moreover, an experienced, conservative Republican leadership returns in the 109th Congress, headed by Speaker J. Dennis Hastert of Illinois but led in all practical regards by the most skillful, even ruthless, majority leader of modern times, Tom DeLay of Texas. Moreover, the 2004 elections greatly strengthened DeLay's hold on the party.[15]

It was DeLay who devised the strategy of re-redistricting Texas congressional seats as a way to ensure Republican control of the House. DeLay paid a price for his innovative tactic, with some of his related actions leading to admonishments from the House Ethics Committee. His efforts, however, paid off for his party, cementing its House majority and strengthening the control of conservatives within it. The election successes fortified DeLay's support within the House party.[16] He is now expected to use that support in forceful pursuit of a conservative Republican agenda.

In contrast to the self-confident stance that DeLay brings to the House Republicans, the Democrats approach the 109th Congress somewhat embarrassed and disoriented.[17] Minority Leader Nancy Pelosi of California had insistently predicted that Democrats would win a majority of House seats, unrealistically hoping that a strong Kerry victory would push House Democrats to majority status. Despite the Democrats' inability to live up to these lofty predictions, no changes are expected in their House leadership. Thus Pelosi should remain as leader through the 109th Congress, pushing House Democrats to continue their strong opposition to DeLay and the Republican agenda. However, there are signs of concern within the party that could complicate her survival beyond 2006, particularly a sense that having a liberal leader from California may not be the best way to reach out to the moderate and rural voters who would seem essential to Democratic resurgence in the House.[18]

The politics of the House in the 109th Congress thus is likely to be at least as polarized as in the 108th and as conservative in its orientation. Although the three-seat increase in Republican control may help ensure that the House will not have the cliff-hanger votes of the 108th Congress, such as the three-hour battle to pass the prescription drug bill, which Schickler and Pearson discuss in Chapter 9, an aggressive, "take no prisoners" approach by Republicans probably will continue. Indeed, House Republicans are likely to push forward in unrelenting fashion on a conservative agenda in order to have a strong record of action going into the 2006 elections, perhaps even driving the president as well as the Senate, rather than following.[19]

Should House Republicans push forward forcefully, they may greatly complicate matters for Senate Republicans, stimulating rifts between conservative and moderate factions. They could also undercut the ability of the president to craft a domestic program of social reform that could pass both chambers and produce an enduring legacy. Alternatively, close cooperation between House and Senate leaders—and between them and the president—could yield historic legislative enactments that ensure his legacy and theirs.

Notes

1. Technically, the Louisiana Fifth Congressional District also changed. In that case, however, the Democratic incumbent, Rodney Alexander, filed for reelection as a Republican just prior to the filing deadline and has switched parties.
2. We exclude the Vermont House seat, which was won handily by independent candidate Bernard Sanders.
3. Gary C. Jacobson, *The Politics of Congressional Elections,* 6th ed. (New York: Longman, 2004), 9.
4. We do not see the replacement of Zell Miller in Georgia with Republican Johnny Isakson as being as significant. Although Miller was certainly the most conservative Senate Democrat, he worked and voted so closely with Senate Republicans that his influence within Democratic Party ranks was minimal.
5. Janet Hook, "Losing Its Middlemen, Senate Shifts to Right," *Los Angeles Times,* latimes.com, November 14, 2004.
6. Ibid.
7. Three other Blue Dog Democrats retired; Democrats have won two of those open seats, and one seat is still undecided. For the purpose of calculating the decline in Blue Dog membership, we assumed that the replacements would become Blue Dogs.
8. Charles Babington and Dan Balz, "Democrats Vow to Hold Bush Accountable," *Washington Post,* November 10, 2004, A7.
9. Kirk Victor and Marilyn Werber Serafini, "A Tighter Grip," *National Journal* 45 (November 6, 2004): 3405.
10. John Cochran, "Common Ground or Continental Divide?" *CQ Weekly* 43 (November 6, 2004): 2599.
11. Helen Dewar, "For Specter, a Showdown over Judiciary Chairmanship," *Washington Post,* November 15, 2004, A3.
12. Andrew Taylor, "Taciturn Reid Steps in to Lead a Leaner Democratic Caucus," *CQ Weekly* 43 (November 6, 2004): 2600.
13. Allison Stevens, "More Power to the Leader?" *CQ Weekly* 43 (November 6, 2004): 2607.
14. David Nather, "Social Conservatives Propel Bush, Republicans to Victory," *CQ Weekly* 43 (November 6, 2004): 2589.
15. Susan Crabtree and Jonathan Allen, "GOP Gains Strengthen Hand of DeLay, House Leadership," *CQ Weekly* 43 (November 6, 2004): 2618–2620.
16. Richard E. Cohen and David Baumann, "A Fortified House," *National Journal* 45 (November 6, 2004): 3407–3411.
17. Crabtree and Allen, "GOP Gains," 2619; Cohen and Baumann, "A Fortified House," 3409–3411.
18. Babington and Balz, "Democrats Vow," A7.
19. Crabtree and Allen, "GOP Gains," 2619.

CONGRESS RECONSIDERED

Part I
Patterns and Dynamics of Congressional Change

1. The New World of U.S. Senators

Barbara Sinclair

- A courtly older gentleman—probably a conservative southern Democrat, perhaps even white haired and clad in a white linen suit—working in committee behind closed doors
- A policy entrepreneur—Democrat or Republican, liberal or conservative—pursuing his cause singly or with a few allies on the Senate floor, aggressively using nongermane amendments and extended debate as his weapons
- A partisan warrior, acting as a member of a party team, dueling with his opposing party counterparts in the public arena and on the floor, using all the procedural and PR tools available

These three images capture the differences among the Senates of the 1950s, the 1970s, and the 1990s and beyond. To be sure, they are simplifications, and some elements of the 1950s Senate and many of the 1970s Senate still persist. Yet the Senate of the early twenty-first century is very different from the 1950s Senate, which fictional and some journalistic accounts still often depict as current, and appreciably different from the 1970s Senate.

The U.S. Senate has the most permissive rules of any legislature in the world.[1] Extended debate allows senators to hold the floor as long as they wish unless cloture is invoked, which requires a supermajority of sixty votes. The Senate's amending rules enable senators to offer any and as many amendments as they please to almost any bill, and those amendments need not even be germane. The extent to which senators make full use of their prerogatives under the rules has varied over time. The Senate as it enters the twenty-first century is characterized by fairly cohesive party contingents that aggressively exploit Senate rules to pursue partisan advantage, but also by the persistence of the Senate individualism that developed in the 1960s and 1970s.

In this chapter, I briefly examine how and why the Senate changed from the 1950s to the present. I then analyze the impact of individualism and intensified partisanship on how the contemporary Senate functions and on legislative outcomes.

Development of the Individualist, Partisan Senate

The Senate of the 1950s was a clubby, inward-looking body governed by constraining norms; influence was relatively unequally distributed and centered in strong committees and their senior leaders, who were most often conservatives, frequently southern Democrats.[2] The typical senator of the 1950s was a specialist who concentrated on the issues that came before his committees. His legislative activities were largely confined to the committee room; he was seldom active on the Senate floor, was highly restrained in his exercise of the prerogatives the Senate rules gave him, and made little use of the media.

The Senate's institutional structure and the political environment rewarded such behavior.[3] The lack of staff made it hard for new senators to participate intelligently right away, so serving an apprenticeship helped prevent a new member from making a fool of himself early in his career. Meager staff resources also made specialization the only really feasible course for attaining influence. Restraint in exploiting extended debate was encouraged by the lack of time pressure, which would later make extended debate such a formidable weapon; when floor time is plentiful, the leverage senators derive from extended debate is much less.[4] Furthermore the dominant southern Democrats had a strong, constituency-based interest in restricting and thus protecting the filibuster for their one big issue—opposition to civil rights.

The majority of senators, especially the southern Democrats, faced no imminent reelection peril so long as they were free to reflect their constituents' views in their votes and capable of providing the projects their constituents desired. The system of reciprocity, which dictated that senators do constituency-related favors for one another whenever possible, served them well. The seniority system, bolstered by norms of apprenticeship, specialization, and intercommittee reciprocity, assured members of considerable independent influence in their area of jurisdiction if they stayed in the Senate long enough and did not make that influence dependent on their voting behavior. For the moderate-to-conservative Senate membership, the parochial and limited legislation such a system produced was quite satisfactory. The Senate of the 1950s was an institution well designed for its generally conservative and electorally secure members to further their goals.

Membership turnover and a transformation of the political environment altered the costs and benefits of such behavior and induced members to change the institution; over time, norms, practices, and rules were altered.[5] The 1958 elections brought into the Senate a big class of new senators with different policy goals and reelection needs. Mostly northern Democrats, they were activist liberals, and most had been elected in highly competitive contests, in many cases having defeated incumbents. Both their policy goals and their reelection needs dictated a more activist style; these senators simply could not afford to wait to make their mark. Subsequent elections brought in more and more such members.

In the 1960s, the political environment began a transformation. A host of new issues rose to prominence—first civil rights, then environmental issues and consumer rights, the war in Vietnam and the questions about American foreign and defense policy that it raised, women's rights and women's liberation, the rights of other ethnic groups, especially Latinos and Native Americans, of the poor, of the disabled, and by the early 1970s, gay rights. These were issues that engaged, often intensely, many ordinary citizens, and politics became more highly charged. The interest group community exploded in size and became more diverse; many of the social movements of the 1960s already had or spawned interest groups. So a hoard of environmental groups, consumer groups, women's groups, and other liberal social welfare and civil rights groups joined the Washington political community and made it more diverse. Then, in response to some of these groups' policy successes—for example, on environmental legislation—the business community mobilized; in the 1970s, many more businesses established a permanent presence in Washington and specialized trade associations proliferated. The media—especially television—became a much bigger player in politics.

This new environment offered tempting new opportunities to senators.[6] The myriad interest groups needed champions and spokespersons, and the media needed credible sources to represent issue positions and for commentary. Because of the small size and prestige of the Senate, senators fit the bill. The opportunity for senators to become significant players on a broader stage, with possible policy, power, reelection, or higher-office payoffs, was there, but to take advantage of the opportunity senators needed to change their behavior and their institution.

From the mid-1960s through the mid-1970s, senators did just that. They increased the number of positions on good committees and the number of subcommittee leadership positions and distributed them much more broadly. Staff too was greatly expanded and made available to junior as well as senior senators. Senators were consequently able to involve themselves in a much broader range of issues, and they did so. Senators also became much more active on the Senate floor, offering more amendments and to a wider range of bills. Senators exploited extended debate to a much greater extent and the frequency of filibusters shot up.[7] The media became an increasingly important arena for participation and a significant resource for senators in the pursuit of their policy, power, and reelection goals.

By the mid-1970s the individualist Senate had emerged. The Senate had become a body in which every member, regardless of seniority, considered himself entitled to participate on any issue that interested him for either constituency or policy reasons. Senators took for granted that they—and their colleagues—would regularly exploit the powers the Senate rules gave them. Senators became increasingly outward directed, focusing on their links with interest groups, policy communities, and the media more than on their ties to one another.

The 1980 elections made Ronald Reagan president and, to almost everyone's surprise, brought a Republican majority to the Senate. As president,

Reagan was more conservative and confrontational than his Republican predecessors of the post–World War II era, and his election signaled an intensification of ideological conflict that increasingly fell along partisan lines.

Realignment in the South, the Proposition 13 tax-cutting fever, the rise of the Christian Right, and the development of the property rights movement were changing the political parties. In 1961 not a single senator from the eleven states of the old Confederacy was a Republican; by 1973, seven were, and by 1980 that number had risen to ten. In 2004 the number stood at thirteen, or 59 percent of the senators from the once solidly Democratic old South. As conservative southern Democrats were replaced by even more conservative southern Republicans, the congressional Democratic Party became more homogeneously liberal and the Republican Party more conservative. Outside the South as well, Republican candidates and activists were becoming more ideologically conservative.

Voting on the Senate floor became increasingly partisan. In the late 1960s and early 1970s, a majority of Democrats opposed a majority of Republicans on only about a third of Senate roll call votes. By the 1990s, from half to two-thirds of roll calls were such party votes, and that continues today. The frequency with which senators voted with their partisan colleagues on party votes increased significantly as well. By the 1990s a typical party vote saw well over 80 percent of Democrats voting together on one side and well over 80 percent of Republicans on the other. In the 107th Congress (2001–2002), 89 percent of Democrats opposed 88 percent of Republicans on a typical party vote.

Partisan polarization has made participation through their parties more attractive to senators than it was when the parties were more heterogeneous and the ideological distance between them was less. Recent Senate party leaders have sought to provide more channels for members to participate in and through the party.[8] Increasingly, senators of the same party are acting as a party team and are exploiting Senate prerogatives to gain partisan advantage.

Over this same time period, the Senate membership has become more diverse. Although most senators are still white men, the 108th Congress (2003–2004) did include fourteen women—an all-time high—one Japanese American, one of Hawaiian and Chinese descent, and one Native American. By contrast, in the 85th Congress (1957–1958), every senator was white and only one was female. This greater diversity influences how the Senate operates, but its impact cannot compete with that of individualism and intense partisanship.

The Legislative Process in the Contemporary Senate

What effect has the combination of individualism and partisanship had on the legislative process in the Senate? Individualism changed how Senate committees work and altered even more floor-related legislative routines, complicating the Senate majority leader's job of floor scheduling and coordination. Intensified partisanship exacerbated the problems the majority leader faces in keeping the Senate functioning as a legislative body.

Senate Committees

Senators hold multiple committee assignments and usually at least one (often more) subcommittee leadership position. In the 108th Congress, senators averaged 3.9 committee assignments and 8.1 subcommittee assignments each; majority party members averaged 1.7 chairmanships.[9] Thus senators are stretched very thin; they treat their committees not as work groups in which to participate on a continuous basis but as arenas in which they pick and choose whether to participate depending upon their interest in the issues being considered. Senators rely heavily on staff for committee work. Committee decisions on many issues are made by the "interesteds," who make up considerably less than the full committee membership.[10] A major tax bill will elicit active participation from all the members of the relevant committee; a rewrite of copyright law, important but narrower and more technical legislation, may be left to a handful of senators.

Because of senators' workloads and the large number of subcommittees, subcommittees are usually "starring" vehicles for their chairs. The chairs can use their subcommittees to publicize problems and policy solutions, to cater to allied interest groups, to promote themselves, or to do all three. Under most circumstances, other senators, even the committee chair, are too busy to interfere.

The marking up of bills, however, most frequently takes place in full committee.[11] Paradoxically, Senate committees remain more centralized than House committees in this respect. However, the reason most Senate committees actually write legislation in full committee rather than marking it up in subcommittee first is not deference to full committee leaders but, again, the enormous workload of senators and the expectation of all committee members to have the opportunity to participate in decision making should they so desire. Those senators on the subcommittee do not have time to go through two mark-ups, and they know that any interested committee member not on the subcommittee would insist on having a say at the full committee level.

Committee decision making must be sensitive to the policy preferences of interested senators who are not members of the committee. Because any senator can cause problems for a piece of legislation on the floor, and may in fact be able to block it from getting to the floor, committee proponents of the legislation have considerable incentive to try to anticipate other senators' views and to bargain with those with intense preferences before the committee reports the bill. Senate committees are perforce highly permeable.

With the heightening of partisanship, majority party committee contingents have also become increasingly responsive to their party leader and their party colleagues. Majority leaders now often involve themselves in the substance of legislation in committee, as well as after a bill has been reported. Then majority leader Tom Daschle, D-S.D., with the full cooperation of the committee chair, even took the energy bill away from the committee and had it redrafted to make sure it reflected Democratic priorities.

Table 1-1 The Increase in Filibusters and Cloture Votes, 1951–2002

Years	Congresses	Filibusters (per Congress)	Cloture Votes (per Congress)	Successful Cloture Votes (per Congress)
1951–1960	82nd–86th	1.0	0.4	0.0
1961–1970	87th–91st	4.6	5.2	0.8
1971–1980	92nd–96th	11.2	22.4	8.6
1981–1986	97th–99th	16.7	23.0	10.0
1987–1992	100th–102nd	26.7	39.0	15.3
1993–1998	103rd–105th	28.0	48.3	13.7
1999–2002	106th–107th	32.0	59.0	30.5

Sources: Data for 82nd–102nd Congresses: column 3, Congressional Research Service, comp., "A Look at the Senate Filibuster," in *Democratic Studies Group Special Report,* June 13, 1994, app. B; columns 4–5, Norman Ornstein, Thomas Mann, and Michael Malbin, *Vital Statistics on Congress 1993–1994* (Washington, D.C.: CQ Press, 1994), 162. Data for 103rd Congress: Richard S. Beth, "Cloture in the Senate, 103rd Congress," memorandum, Congressional Research Service, June 23, 1995. Data for 104th–107th Congresses: *Congressional Quarterly Almanac* for the years 1995–2002 (Washington, D.C.: Congressional Quarterly).

Majority Leadership and the Senate Floor

In the contemporary Senate, floor scheduling is of necessity an exercise in broad and bipartisan accommodation.[12] Although he is not the Senate's presiding officer and lacks many of the powers the House Speaker commands, the Senate majority leader is as close to a central leader as the chamber has, and he is charged with scheduling legislation for floor consideration. To bring legislation to the floor, the majority leader uses his right of first recognition, a prerogative he has had under Senate precedents since the 1930s. The majority leader can move that a bill be taken off the calendar and considered, but the motion to proceed is a debatable—and thus filibusterable—motion. Or he can ask unanimous consent that the bill be taken off the calendar and considered, a request that can be blocked by any senator's objection. Clearly, any senator can cause problems for the majority leader.

How Senators Cause Trouble: The Strategic Use of Senate Rules. Understanding the problems of legislative scheduling in the Senate and the routines that have developed requires a look at the strategic use of Senate rules by the individualistic and now also increasingly partisan Senate membership.

The filibuster, the use of extended debate to prevent a vote on a motion or measure unless a supermajority can be mustered, is certainly the best-known strategic use of Senate rules. With the development of the individualist Senate, the use of extended debate and of cloture to try to cut it off increased enormously (see Table 1-1). To be sure, the data must be regarded with some caution.[13] When lengthy debate becomes a filibuster is, in part, a matter of judgment. Furthermore, as I show below, filibusters have changed their form in recent years, and threats to filibuster have become much more frequent than actual talkathons on the floor. As a consequence, cloture is sometimes sought before any overt evidence of a filibuster manifests itself on the floor. Nevertheless, experts and participants agree that the frequency of obstructionism has increased. In the 1950s filibusters were rare; they increased during the 1960s and again during the 1970s. By the late 1980s and the 1990s they had become routine, occurring at a rate of more than one a month—considerably more, if only the time the Senate is in session is counted. Cloture votes have increased in tandem, and more than one cloture vote per issue is now the norm. Cloture votes were, however, decreasingly likely to be successful through the late 1990s; in the early to middle 1980s, 43 percent got the requisite sixty votes to cut off debate; in the late 1980s and early 1990s, 39 percent did; in the period 1993–1998, only 28 percent did. In 1999–2002, the likelihood of a cloture vote being successful increased again to a bit more than half but only because more were taken after an agreement had been reached. Almost all of the winning cloture votes were very one-sided. When the parties split on a cloture vote, cloture was very unlikely to be imposed. The rate of successful cloture votes plunged to an all time low in 2003, when only one of twenty-three was successful.

As filibusters became more frequent, the character of the filibusterers and of the targeted legislation broadened. By the 1970s liberals as well as conservatives frequently used this weapon, and senators used it on all sorts of legislation, parochial as well as momentous. For example, as Congress was rushing to adjourn in October 1992, Sen. Alfonse D'Amato, R-N.Y., held the floor for fifteen hours and fifteen minutes to protest the removal from an urban-aid tax bill of a provision he said could have restored jobs at a New York typewriter plant.[14]

Senators use actual or threatened filibusters for a variety of purposes. Their aim may be to kill legislation, but it may also be to extract substantive concessions on a bill. Sometimes senators' use of extended debate is a form of position taking; the senator may know he cannot kill or weaken the legislation but wants to make a strong statement about his position and its intensity. Targeting one measure in order to extract concessions on another, sometimes known as hostage taking, has become an increasingly frequent use of extended debate. In a particularly elaborate instance, in 1995 Jesse Helms, R-N.C., then chairman of the Senate Foreign Relations Committee, sponsored a State Department reorganization bill that the Clinton administration and many Democrats opposed. Helms brought the legislation to the floor, but after two attempts at imposing cloture failed, Majority Leader Robert Dole, R-Kan., stopped floor consideration. Frustrated, Helms began bottling up ambassador nominations, the START II treaty, and the Chemical Weapons Convention. Democrats responded by blocking action on a flag desecration constitutional amendment and a Cuba sanctions bill, both priorities of Helms. Negotiations and concessions eventually unstuck the impasse, although only the Cuba sanctions bill actually became law.

Nominations as well as legislation can be filibustered. Senators use their powers to block nominations they oppose, even if a Senate majority clearly supports the nomination. Cloture votes showed a sizable majority for the confirmation of Henry Foster as surgeon general during the Clinton administration, but lacking the sixty votes to cut off debate, the nomination died. Democrats blocked a number of President George W. Bush's judicial nominations. Republicans failed to get the requisite sixty votes to cut off debate and bring to a vote the nomination of Miguel Estrada to the U.S. Court of Appeals for the District of Columbia; after the seventh unsuccessful cloture vote, Estrada withdrew.

Senators now often block nominees they do not oppose in order to gain a bargaining chip for use with the administration. The nomination of William Holbrook as ambassador to the United Nations in 1999 was held up for months over matters having nothing to do with him. Sen. Charles Grassley, R-Iowa, wanted the administration to respond to his concerns about the treatment of a State Department whistleblower; Sens. Mitch McConnell, R-Ky., and Trent Lott, R-Miss., hoped to extract from the president a promise to appoint their candidate to the Federal Elections Commission. In 2003, Sen. Larry Craig, R-Idaho, placed holds on all Air Force promotions—which, of course, are normally approved routinely. Senator Craig had no objections to any of the Air Force personnel up for promotion; he wanted to force the Air Force to deliver on a promise he claimed it had made to station several planes at a base in Idaho.

The offering of large numbers of not necessarily germane amendments on the floor is a signature characteristic of the individualist Senate. When major bills are considered, dozens of amendments are routinely offered. Budget resolutions frequently see more than forty amendments offered and pushed to a recorded vote. On S.1, the Medicare prescription drug bill in 2003, 150 amendments were submitted and twenty-seven went to a roll call vote. Most amendments are germane, and the sponsor's aim is to influence the substance of the bill. Individual senators do use nongermane amendments to pursue their personal agendas and to bring to the floor issues the leadership might like to avoid. Thus during his long career (1973–2002), former Senator Helms forced innumerable votes in every Congress on hot-button issues such as abortion, pornography, and school prayer.

With the growth of partisan polarization, the minorities making use of Senate prerogatives are more often organized, partisan ones. In the 103rd Congress the minority Republicans used actual and threatened filibusters to deprive President Bill Clinton and the majority Democrats of numerous policy successes. Clinton's economic stimulus package, campaign finance and lobbying reform bills, and bills revamping the Superfund program, revising clean drinking water regulations, overhauling outdated telecommunications law, and applying federal labor laws to Congress were among the casualties. In the 104th and 105th Congresses, minority Democrats used extended debate to kill many Republican priorities, including ambitious regulatory overhaul legislation and far-reaching property rights bills. In the 103rd Congress, Republicans extracted concessions on many major Democratic bills—voter registration legislation ("motor voter") and the national service program, for example. Then, in the 104th Congress, Democrats used the same strategy to force concessions on product liability legislation, the Freedom to Farm bill, and telecommunications legislation, among others. In 2002 Republicans, then in the minority in the Senate, refused to allow a vote before the elections on the Democrats' version of the bill setting up the new Homeland Security Department; Democrats had the votes to pass a bill Bush disliked, and Republicans wanted to use a bill's not having passed as a campaign issue. At the end of the first session of the 108th Congress in 2003, minority Democrats refused Republicans an up-or-down vote on the conference report for the massive energy bill that Bush and most Republicans very much wanted to enact and many Democrats strongly opposed.

In the 1990s exploiting Senate prerogatives to attempt to seize agenda control from the majority party became a key minority party strategy. The lack of a germaneness requirement for amendments to most bills severely weakens the majority party's ability to control the floor agenda. If the majority leader refuses to bring a bill to the floor, its supporters can offer it as an amendment to most legislation the leader does bring to the floor. The majority leader can make a motion to table the amendment, which is nondebatable. That does, however, require his members to vote on the issue, albeit in a procedural guise, and the leader may want to avoid that. Furthermore, even after the minority's amendment has been tabled, the minority can continue to offer other amendments, including even individual parts of the original amendment, and can block a vote on the underlying bill the majority party wants to pass. The leader can, of course, file a cloture petition and try to shut off debate, but he needs sixty votes to do so. The minority party can use this strategy to bring its agenda to the floor and, if accompanied by a sophisticated public relations campaign (which the Senate parties are increasingly capable of orchestrating), can gain favorable publicity and sometimes pressure enough majority party members into supporting the bill to pass it. In 1996, Senate Democrats used this strategy to enact a minimum wage increase, and since then, they have forced highly visible floor debates on tobacco regulation, campaign finance reform, gun control, and managed care reform, all issues the majority party would have preferred to avoid. In 2001, campaign finance legislation passed the Senate before the Democrats took control of the chamber. John McCain, R-Ariz., and the Democrats had threatened to use the add-it-as-an-amendment-to-everything strategy, which would have wreaked havoc with the consideration of President Bush's program. Furthermore, Republicans knew that the cost of trying to stop campaign finance from being considered would be terrible publicity. So the Senate Republican leadership capitulated and agreed to bring it to the floor.

Getting Legislation to the Senate Floor. Given the extent to which senators as individuals and as party teams now exploit their prerogatives, how does the Senate manage to legislate at all? As shown in Table 1-2, major legislation is now

Table 1-2 The Increasing Frequency of Extended-Debate–Related Problems

Congress	Years	Measures Affected (in percentages)[a]
91st	1969–1970	10
95th	1977–1978	24
97th	1981–1982	22
101st	1989–1990	30
103rd	1993–1994	51
104th	1995–1996	50
105th	1997–1998	55
107th	2001–2002	55

Source: Author's calculations.

[a]Figures represent percentage of "filibusterable" major measures that were subject to extended-debate–related problems.

very frequently subject to some sort of extended-debate–related problem discernible from the public record.[15] In the 103rd, 104th, and 105th Congresses (1993–1998), about half of the major legislation that was vulnerable to a filibuster actually encountered some sort of filibuster-related problem, and the rate was about the same in the 107th, the Bush administration's first Congress. If measures protected by rules from filibusters (budget resolution and reconciliation bills) are included, the proportion decreases only marginally.

The Senate has long done most of its work through unanimous consent agreements (UCAs). By unanimous consent, senators agree to bring a bill to the floor, perhaps to place some limits on the amendments that may be offered or on the length of debate on specific amendments, and then maybe to set a time for the final vote. Some UCAs are highly elaborate and govern the entire floor consideration of a bill, but a series of partial agreements is more frequent than one comprehensive agreement.[16] As a highly knowledgeable participant explained: "Usually you have a UCA only to bring something to the floor, and then maybe you have another one that will deal with a couple of important amendments, and then perhaps a little later, one that will start limiting amendments to some extent, and then perhaps one that specifies when a vote will take place. So it's done through a series of steps, each of which sort of leaves less and less leeway."

Ordinarily, Senate floor consideration of legislation begins with the majority leader asking and receiving unanimous consent to take a bill off the calendar and proceed to consider it. This seemingly simple and easy process for getting legislation to the floor has been preceded by an elaborate consultation process to ensure that unanimous consent is forthcoming. The party leaders oversee the negotiation of unanimous consent agreements and are deeply involved in the more contentious cases. The majority and the minority party secretaries of the

Senate now are the most important staffers involved; they serve as clearinghouses and as points of continuous contact between the parties and often do much of the negotiating. When the majority leader, after consultation with the relevant committee chairman, decides he wants to schedule a bill, he may leave the negotiation of the agreement to the committee chairman or he may take the lead role himself. The more complex the political situation and the more important to the party the legislation at issue is, the more likely the majority leader is to take the lead. In either case the majority party secretary will be involved; he or she keeps the list of those senators who have requested that they be consulted before the bill is scheduled. If a fellow party member has expressed opposition to the bill being brought to the floor, negotiations may be necessary to take care of his or her concerns. When the majority has an agreement it can support, the majority party's secretary will convey it to the minority party's secretary in writing, who will give it to the minority leader and the relevant ranking minority member. The minority secretary will also call any senators on the minority side who have asked to be notified and find out their concerns. Eventually, the minority will respond with a written counteroffer and convey it to the majority through the secretaries. This process may go through several rounds. If and when the leaders reach a tentative agreement, both parties put out a recorded message on their "hotline" to all Senate offices. The message lays out the terms of the agreement and asks senators who have objections to call their leader within a specified period of time. If there are objections, they have to be taken care of. When every senator is prepared to assent to the unanimous consent agreement, the majority leader takes it to the floor and makes the request.

When a senator informs his leader directly or through the party secretary that he wishes to be consulted before a measure is scheduled, the senator may just want to be sure he is not otherwise committed, that he is prepared for floor debate or ready to offer an amendment. Often, however, such a notification is a *hold.* "A hold," as a knowledgeable participant explained, "is a letter to your leader telling him which of the many powers that you have as a senator you intend to use on a given issue." A typical such letter, addressed to then Majority Leader Trent Lott and copied to the majority secretary, reads, "Dear Trent: I will object to any time agreement or unanimous consent request with respect to consideration of any legislation or amendment that involves———, as I wish to be accorded my full rights as a Member of the Senate to offer amendments, debate and consider such legislation or amendment. Many thanks and kindest personal regards." Most holds, then, are threats to object to a unanimous consent agreement, and in a body that conducts most of its business through UCAs that is, in effect, as a leadership staffer said, "a threat to filibuster."

The party secretaries confer every morning and tell each other what new holds there are on legislation or nominations. They do not reveal the names of their members who have placed the holds, so holds can be secret.

Thus, visible filibusters are now just the tip of the iceberg. The Senate's permissive rules have much more effect on the legislative process through filibuster threats than through actual filibusters. (See Table 1-2; remember that holds and filibuster threats as well as actual filibusters are reflected in those figures.) "Classic" filibusters with the Senate in session all night, senators sleeping on cots off the Senate floor, and filibusterers making interminable speeches on the floor no longer occur. Occasionally the majority leader will force senators opposing a matter to take to the floor and sometimes those senators want to. The judicial nomination of Miguel Estrada was debated for almost one hundred hours over the course of a month before the majority leader filed a cloture petition, and during that period the Senate did little else.[17] Even then, only two late-night and no all-night sessions were held; the President's Day recess was not canceled as the majority leader had at one point threatened; and, once the first cloture vote failed, Majority Leader Bill Frist, R-Tenn., went on to other business (though there were more cloture votes). Holds are the "lazy man's filibuster," a staffer complained. Sometimes placed by staff on their own initiative, sometimes at the instigation of lobbyists, holds require little effort on the part of senators, the staffer continued, and yet they enormously complicate the legislative process and not infrequently kill or severely weaken worthy legislation. Many other participants and observers make similar complaints.

Since holds are nowhere specified in Senate rules, why do Senate leaders condone and, in fact, maintain the hold system? "It's to the majority leader's advantage to have holds because it gives him information," a knowledgeable observer explained. "He's always trying to negotiate unanimous consent agreements, and he needs to know if there are pockets of problems, and holds do that." An expert concluded succinctly, "The only way you could get rid of holds would be to change the rules of the Senate drastically."

Critics often argue that leaders should be tougher and call the bluff of members more often. The threat to filibuster supposedly inherent in holds would, in many cases, prove to be empty rhetoric if put to the test, such critics claim. In fact, holds are not automatic vetoes. A hold cannot kill *must-pass* legislation such as appropriations bills, and in deciding how seriously to take a hold on less vital legislation, the leader weighs the reputation of the senator placing the hold; "some people are taken more seriously because it's just assumed they're willing to back it up," a leadership aide explained.

Although holds are certainly not absolute, the time pressure under which the Senate operates gives them considerable bite. Frist could let the Estrada nomination dominate floor business in February 2003 because it was early in the first year of a Congress and not much legislation was ready for floor consideration. By March, that situation had changed; if Republicans had forced Democrats to continue, it would have been at the expense of President Bush's initiatives. As a staffer explained, "Holds are effective because the majority leader has a finite amount of time. If there are going to be cloture votes and the like, it can take days to ram something through this place. You can't do it on every bill. You can only do it on a selected few bills." Senators, most of whom have legislation they want considered on the floor, as well as many other demands on their time, want floor time used productively, and the majority leader needs to use the time efficiently if he is to pass as much of the party agenda as possible. In making a choice of which bills to bring to the floor, the majority leader must consider how much time the bill will take and what the likelihood of successful passage is. As a result, senators who want their bills to receive floor consideration are under tremendous pressure to negotiate with those who have holds on them. "Things that aren't a top priority for the majority leader, he wants you to work it out," a senior staffer explained. "If you go to him and say you want something brought to the floor, he'll say, 'You work it out. You find out who has holds on it. You work out whatever problems they have, and I'll schedule it when you've worked it out.' " Thus, often simply to get to the floor, a measure must command a substantial majority. When time is especially tight—before a recess and at the end of a session—a single objection can kill legislation.

Majority and Minority, Cooperation and Conflict

Keeping the Senate functioning as a legislature requires broad accommodation; it dictates satisfying every senator to some extent. A reasonably cohesive majority party can run the House without consulting the minority. The Senate only runs smoothly when the majority leader and the minority leader cooperate and not always then. The party leaders consult on a daily basis. "The two leaders talk extensively to each other during the day," a knowledgeable participant explained. "You see it during votes. We'll have two or three votes a day at least, usually, and that's one of the times when they confer. But they have to talk to each other; if they don't, that's when things break down." A telephone hotline connects the leaders' offices directly to facilitate quick communication.[18] The leaders often work together to get unanimous consent agreements and to get essential legislative business done.

Yet the Senate leaders are party leaders, elected by their party members in the chamber, and are expected by those members to pursue partisan advantage. With the increase in partisan polarization, the narrow margins, and the shifts in partisan control of the chamber, senators' expectations that their leader promote their collective partisan interests have intensified. With the change in the character of politics and the role of the media in political life, those expectations have also changed in form. Over the second half of the twentieth century, the role of the media in American politics increased enormously; national politics have come to be played out much more on the public stage than they used to be, often with audience reactions determining who wins and who loses. In the 1990s, policy battles increasingly came to be fought out in public through public relations, or PR, wars.[19] Whether in the majority or in the minority, senators now expect their party leader to promote their collective partisan interests through message strategies directed at the public as well as through internal procedural and legislative strategies. When Republicans chose a new leader in 2003, Bill Frist's presumed media skills were a major consideration. And early criticism of his performance focused on his not being a sufficiently aggressive spokesman. "What we're looking for in the majority leader's position is a Republican Tom Daschle," a Republican explained, "someone who will steer the debate in the direction we want it to go."[20]

These expectations create a dilemma for the leaders, especially for the majority leader. Majority party senators expect their leader to promote the party agenda by passing legislation and publicizing party positions and successes; they also expect their leader to keep off the floor the other party's agenda, which often consists of issues on which the minority party and the public agree and thus puts the majority party in a tough position. And all senators expect their leaders to keep the Senate functioning. Yet, in the Senate, unlike the House, a majority is not sufficient to act; to keep the Senate functioning requires supermajorities, and this almost always requires that the majority leader accommodate the minority to some extent.

With the narrow margins and frequent switches in control of recent years, both Republican and Democratic leaders have faced the conundrum of leading a nonmajoritarian chamber in a partisan age. As majority leader in the late 1990s, Lott often responded with hardball procedural tactics. He filed for cloture on a bill immediately, then pulled the bill from the floor until the cloture vote was due. If cloture succeeded, he had barred all nongermane amendments, since Senate rules require that all amendments be germane after cloture is invoked. If cloture failed, he did not bring up the bill. He sometimes used the tactic of "filling the amendment tree," that is, he used the majority leader's prerogative of first recognition to offer amendments in all the parliamentarily permissible slots, thus preventing Democrats from offering their amendments. Outraged Democrats reacted by maintaining high cohesion on cloture votes, thus denying the majority the sixty votes needed to make the tactic work. Consequently, when the majority employed these tactics, the result was most often gridlock, with no legislative work accomplished on the Senate floor until an accommodation was reached. As the Republican Policy Committee chairman explained, "Inevitably, anybody who wants to get a vote on the floor of the United States Senate will get it if they're persistent."[21] After Bush became president, Lott had to change his approach so as to avoid gridlock on Bush's program. Thus, he did not even attempt to keep campaign finance reform legislation off the floor, a decision that made many of his Republican colleagues extremely unhappy. When Sen. Jim Jeffords, R-Vt., left the Republican party and thereby turned control of the Senate over to the Democrats, Lott was criticized by fellow Republicans for letting it happen, just as he had been criticized earlier for being too accommodating to moderate Republicans and Democrats.

Tom Daschle and Bill Frist, the succeeding majority leaders, faced the same dilemma. Both kept the Senate floor process open, allowing full and unfettered debate. With Daschle as majority leader, Democrats passed some of their top priorities in the Senate—a patients' bill of rights, for example; they tempered or blocked a number of Bush initiatives with which they disagreed—energy legislation for instance. Yet, facing a partisan Republican House of Representatives and a determined conservative president, Senate Democrats could seldom enact legislation in a form they favored. And even when Republican filibusters prevented action, as on the Homeland Security Department bill, Democrats collectively and Daschle specifically were excoriated for blocking legislation. Daschle's decision to hang tough on the Homeland Security Department bill may have cost Democrats their majority in the 2002 elections; yet many of his fellow Democrats would have been extremely upset had he been willing to give in to Bush.

Bill Frist became majority leader in 2003 in a more favorable political climate; his party had won a considerable victory in the 2002 elections, controlled the House, and had a popular and politically formidable president. Frist did lead Senate Republicans to some major policy successes, most notably enactment of the Medicare prescription drug bill. Yet at the end of his first year as leader, the energy bill conference report, a number of less visible bills that Republicans very strongly desired, such as legislation tightening rules on class action law suits, and six prominent Bush judicial nominations were stalled because they lacked the sixty votes necessary for cloture. The Senate had been unable to pass a number of the thirteen appropriations bills funding the government and had rolled them into a massive omnibus appropriations bill, and the conference report on that was also stuck and under a Democratic filibuster threat.

The pressure to pursue partisan advantage and avoid policy compromise is particularly great on contemporary Republican Senate leaders. A considerable part of the Republican Senate membership consists of junior conservatives, many of whom were schooled in the highly partisan House of Newt Gingrich and Tom DeLay. Leaders are frequently pressed to accede to the more conservative House position in conference committee, but then the resulting conference report can be hard to pass in the Senate. This happened with the energy bill in 2003.

Senate Republicans' "reverse" filibuster on judicial nominations in fall 2003 illustrates the strains of a highly partisan and ideological majority operating in a nonmajoritarian chamber, as well as the contemporary congressional parties' penchant for "going public." Frustrated by the Democrats' successful filibuster of several conservative Bush judicial nominees and by criticism from conservative groups of their own lack of a sufficiently strident countercampaign, Senate Republicans mounted a thirty-nine hour, three-day-and-two-night talkathon to excoriate Democrats for blocking the nominees. Instigated by junior conservatives, the effort eventually included most Republican senators and became a major PR production. Amid a media throng, Frist led the phalanx of Republican senators from his office to the floor at 6 p.m., the hour appointed for the debate to begin. A news conference cum rally was held throughout the first night in a room right off the Senate floor; conservative broadcasters were housed in "Talk Show Alley" in one of the Senate office buildings. Democrats countered with their own PR effort, debating Republicans on the floor, holding a rally for activists, and appealing to the media. The campaign changed no votes and none of the nominees won approval.[22]

At the same time that Senate leaders have to deal with sometimes unmeetable expectations from their members for the aggressive pursuit of partisan advantage, they also must handle the individualism within their own party that can derail partisan and bipartisan strategies alike. Sen. Ted Kennedy, D-Mass., usually a party stalwart, decided on his own and against the wishes of Democratic leaders to work with Bush and Republicans on the Medicare prescription drug bill in 2003. Frist's first major embarrassment as majority leader came when several moderate Republicans held out against Bush's tax cut; to pass it, Frist and Finance Committee Chairman Charles Grassley, R-Iowa, were forced to agree to a decrease much larger than what they had promised House Republican leaders to deliver. Sen. John McCain made his name by bucking the Republican Party establishment on tobacco taxes and campaign finance reform, among other issues.

Individualism, Partisanship, and Legislative Outcomes

How does the combination of individualism and intense partisanship that characterizes the contemporary Senate affect legislative outcomes? As shown in Table 1-3, the likelihood of a major measure becoming law is less in recent Congresses than in earlier ones. In the three 1990s Congresses and the first of the twenty-first century, all of which saw at least half of the major measures subject to some sort of filibuster problem, 42 percent of the major measures failed enactment. By contrast, in three earlier Congresses, characterized by lower filibuster activity, 27 percent of the major measures failed. Of course there are many steps in the legislative process, and these figures by themselves do not prove that the Senate is responsible for the increase in legislative failures. However, as also shown in Table 1-3, for the latter four Congresses, legislation was much more likely to pass the House but fail in the Senate than the reverse; in the earlier Congresses, the difference was not very great.

Does the increasing frequency with which measures encounter extended-debate–related problems in the Senate explain this pattern? Filibuster problems do, in fact, depress a measure's chances of surviving the legislative process. Of those measures that did not encounter such a problem, either because senators chose not to use their prerogatives or because the measure enjoyed statutory protection, 74 percent were enacted; only 54 percent of those that did experience a filibuster problem became law.[23] Since filibusters and filibuster threats are by no means always intended to kill legislation, those figures suggest a considerable effect. Filibuster problems are more likely to occur on partisan legislation, and when a measure is partisan at the committee level and also encounters a filibuster problem, its chances of enactment are significantly decreased. Less than half (46 percent) of such measures were successfully enacted, in contrast to 80 percent of the measures that were not partisan and did not experience an extended-

Table 1-3 Where Major Measures Failed

What Happened?	Number of Failed Measures: 91st, 95th, and 97th Congresses	Number of Failed Measures: 103rd, 104th, 105th, and 107th Congresses
Passed by neither House nor Senate	16	22
Passed by House but not by Senate	12	33
Passed by Senate but not by House	8	3
Passed by House and Senate	6	22
Total number of failed measures	42 (of 156 measures)	80 (of 192 measures)
Percentage of total measures that failed	27%	42%

Source: Author's calculations.

debate–related problem, and 57 percent that had one but not both of these characteristics.

Thus, the combination of individualism and intense partisanship that characterizes the contemporary Senate does depress the likelihood of legislation successfully surviving the legislative process. Yet given the character of Senate rules and the ways in which senators currently exploit them, it is perhaps more surprising that the Senate manages to legislate at all. The Senate does pass a lot of legislation, both must-pass measures such as appropriations bills and other major bills. To be sure, some measures—budget resolutions and reconciliation bills, most importantly—are protected from filibusters and nongermane amendments by law, and that has been vital to the passage of some of the most important legislation of the last decade.[24] But much legislation without such protection gets through the Senate as well.

Dodging Legislative Breakdown

Clearly, the Senate could not function if senators maximally exploited their prerogatives—if, for example, every senator objected to every unanimous consent agreement on any matter he or she did not completely support. What, then, keeps senators as individuals and as party teams from pushing their prerogatives over the limit and miring the Senate in gridlock?

Asked that question, senators, staff, and informed observers uniformly responded that almost all senators want to "get something done" and that they are aware that many senators' exploiting their prerogatives to the limit would make that impossible. As one knowledgeable insider phrased it, "I like to think of the Senate as a bunch of armed nuclear nations. Each senator knows he can blow the place up, but most of them came here to do something, and if he does blow things up, if he does use his powers that way, then he won't be able to do anything." Using one's prerogatives aggressively entails concrete short-run costs, most also argued. "If you do object [to a unanimous consent request], it's going to hurt someone and maybe more than one person," a senior staffer explained, "so the next time you want something, it may very well happen to you." In the Senate, individuals can exact retribution swiftly and often quite easily on those they believe have harmed them. Because of that, a junior senator and former House member reported, "In the Senate, you don't go out of your way to hack people off." In the House there is less such concern, he explained. The likelihood that some retaliation will be forthcoming forces the wise senator to be selective in the employment of his prerogatives.

The importance of guarding their reputations also constrains senators. Placing a hold or objecting to a unanimous consent request costs little senator or staff time; following through and actually employing delaying tactics on the floor costs a great deal of time. "Threats are taken seriously in the Senate," a senior staff aide said, "but they depend on a perception that you'll carry out your threat, so you need to do it selectively." A senator's reputation influences the leadership's reaction to a senator's threat. As a leadership aide explained, "When you get a letter [putting on a hold], you ask what is his track record in order to judge how seriously you need to take it."

Similar considerations restrain senators as party teams and especially their leaders. The leaders are very much aware that as much as senators want to gain partisan advantage on the big issues, they also want, for both reelection and policy reasons, to pass bills. As the earlier discussion of the interactions between the party leaders indicated, the leaders are instrumental in maintaining the cooperation necessary to keep the Senate functioning. They do so by working together closely, by adeptly employing both procedural and peer pressure to encourage the recalcitrant to deal, and by accommodating to some extent all senators with problems.[25] Although the procedural resources and the favors the leaders command are fairly meager, they do have one persuasive argument for inducing cooperation. As a knowledgeable insider put it, "[Senators] can use the powers they have to create chaos and confusion on the floor, in which case senators don't have a life. . . . where the floor debate goes on to all hours without any knowledge of when anything will happen, or they can defer to their leaders to create a structure with some predictability, and then they do have a life. And that's the bargain they have made."

Leaders also need to concern themselves with guarding the party's reputation within the chamber and with the public. The minority party's influence within the chamber depends upon its being able to block cloture when a party effort is made to do so, and that depends on using obstructionism selectively. The reputation with the public of both parties, but especially that of the majority party, suffers if the Senate seems incapable of legislating. The minority has to avoid being perceived as obstructionist, especially on issues the public cares about. Minority Leader Tom Daschle's decision not to support a filibuster against the final version of the Medicare prescription drug bill most likely rested on the calculation that, if Democrats blocked the bill, the public would blame them, whereas if a bad bill became law, Republicans would get the blame.

In its everyday functioning, the contemporary Senate exhibits a peculiar combination of conflict and cooperation, of aggressive exploitation of rules and accommodation. The hottest partisan legislative battles are studded with unanimous consent agreements. And the more intense the partisan fight, the more frequently the majority and minority leaders confer. On bills not at the center of partisan conflict, senators routinely cooperate across the partisan divide. As a senior aide expressed the consensus, "If you really want to move stuff, if it's not a big partisan matter, a big ideological issue, and you really want to move it, then you really have to be bipartisan. You've got to work out the difficulties, and you've got to work across the aisle." Bipartisanship is especially important on legislation of secondary importance because the majority leader requires that the problems be resolved before he attempts to bring such bills to the floor. Senators as individuals do put holds on each other's bills, but they also often attempt to accommodate each other on an individual basis in ways that extend far beyond what occurs in the House. A senior aide to a Democratic senator who had previously served in the House illustrated this point:

> [The senator] was a senior member of the [House] Energy and Commerce Committee, and we would call [committee chairman John] Dingell's [D-Mich.] staff director and say *X* or *Y* is *really, really* important to [us]. And . . . the staff director would say no, we can't do that and sort of explain why, and then we'd spend three weeks trying to figure out a way of getting him to change his mind. And this, remember, is a senior member of the chairman's party. Here, in the Senate, I call a Republican staffer on a committee that [the senator] doesn't serve on and explain the same sort of thing—that we've got a problem, and 60, 70, 80 percent of the time it will get done. It will get taken care of.

The staffer explained such responsiveness not by norms of civility and reciprocity but by the facts of life in the contemporary Senate. It is "because they need to accommodate you to move something," the aide continued. "They want to get something done. They want to get legislation, and to do that you have to take care of people's problems."

Thus senators' acute awareness of the weapons all senators command can work to produce cooperation and some restraint. Everyone knows that legislative breakdown is a very real possibility, and this seems to have a sobering effect. Yet, in an era of intensified partisanship combined with the continuing individualism that has characterized the Senate since the 1970s, the Senate legislative process is fragile. Senate party leaders are under considerable pressure from their members to pursue partisan advantage aggressively, and partisan battles aimed at electoral gain are zero-sum. The rewards of Senate individualism can be great, as John McCain's presidential candidacy demonstrated. Most of the time, the Senate manages to maintain the minimum restraint and cooperation necessary to avoid total gridlock, yet the chamber regularly seems to teeter on the precipice of legislative breakdown.

A Less Effective Senate?

Have individualism and partisanship and their impact on the legislative process made the Senate of today less effective than the Senate of the 1950s? Does the Senate play a less important role in our political life than it used to?

The contemporary Senate performs certain important functions well. It provides senators with an excellent forum for agenda setting, debate framing, and policy incubation.[26] Using their prerogatives under Senate rules and their access to the media, senators as individuals, and now as party teams, publicize problems, promote solutions, speak for a wide variety of claimant groups, and provide a visible and legitimate opposition view—and increasingly an alternative agenda—to the president's. Even were the Senate to have less impact on the details of legislation, so long as it significantly influenced the national agenda, one would have to conclude that it continues to play an important role in national politics.

Furthermore, some scholars and journalists argue that Senate rules and the ways they are currently used actually give the Senate a bargaining advantage over other political actors. In particular, when the Senate and House meet in conference committee to resolve their differences over a bill, Senate conferees can, and sometimes do, use the fact that Senate approval effectively requires a supermajority to their advantage; if the conferees move the bill too far from the Senate version, a filibuster will block the bill in the Senate, they argue. Certainly, House members complain bitterly about such Senate "blackmail."

Finally, the enactment into law of nonincremental policy change seems considerably more a function of the external political environment than of the institutional structure within the legislative chambers.[27] For example, in 1995–1996, Democrats and some moderate Republicans, using Senate rules, blocked much of Newt Gingrich's Contract with America that the House had passed. On the one hand, Senate rules were instrumental, but on the other, it is most unlikely that, had there been strong public support for the bills in question, senators would have been willing to incur the public's wrath and kill the legislation.

So the question, Is the Senate of today a less effective legislative body? has no simple answer. The Senate's nonmajoritarian rules as currently used greatly exacerbate the problems of building winning coalitions, and so the contemporary Senate is always at risk of legislative breakdown. If a legislature cannot respond to the problems that concern the people it represents, it loses legitimacy. That has not happened to the Senate yet, but the possibility is not farfetched.

Notes

The definitive work on the Senate in the 1950s is Donald Matthews's *U.S. Senators and Their World* (New York: Vintage Books, 1960). The title of this chapter is intended as a tribute to Don and his classic, but should he consider an apology more appropriate, I offer that too. All unattributed quotations in the main text of this chapter are from interviews conducted by the author.

1. Barbara Sinclair, *Unorthodox Lawmaking,* 2nd ed. (Washington, D.C.: CQ Press, 2000); Sarah Binder and Steven S. Smith, *Politics or Principle? Filibustering in the United States Senate* (Washington, D.C.: Brookings Institution Press, 1997).
2. Matthews, *U.S. Senators and Their World.*
3. Barbara Sinclair, *The Transformation of the U.S. Senate* (Baltimore: Johns Hopkins University Press, 1989); Ralph Huitt, "The Internal Distribution of Influence: The Senate," in *The Congress and America's Future,* ed. David Truman (New York: Prentice Hall, 1965).
4. Bruce Oppenheimer, "Changing Time Constraints on Congress: Historical Perspectives on the Use of Cloture," in *Congress Reconsidered,* 3rd ed., ed. Lawrence C. Dodd and Bruce I. Oppenheimer (Washington, D.C.: CQ Press, 1985).
5. Sinclair, *The Transformation of the U.S. Senate;* Michael Foley, *The New Senate* (New Haven: Yale University Press, 1980); David Rohde, Norman Ornstein, and Robert Peabody, "Political Change and Legislative Norms in the U.S. Senate, 1957–1974," in *Studies of Congress,* ed. Glenn R. Parker (Washington, D.C.: Congressional Quarterly, 1985).
6. See also Burdett Loomis, *The New American Politician* (New York: Basic Books, 1988).
7. Binder and Smith, *Politics or Principle?*
8. Patrick J. Sellers, "Winning Media Coverage in the U.S. Congress," in *U.S. Senate Exceptionalism,* ed. Bruce Oppenheimer (Columbus: The Ohio State University Press, 2002); Donald Baumer, "Senate Democratic Leadership in the 100th Congress," in *The Atomistic Congress,* ed. Ronald Peters and Allen Hertzke (Armonk, N.Y.: M. E. Sharpe, 1992); Steven S. Smith, "Forces of Change in Senate Party Leadership and Organization," in *Congress Reconsidered,* 5th ed., ed. Lawrence C. Dodd and Bruce I. Oppenheimer, (Washington, D.C.: CQ Press, 1993); Mary Jacoby, "Waiting in Wings, a Kinder, Gentler Lott?" *Roll Call,* March 9, 1995, 22.
9. *CQ Weekly,* April 12, 2003, C2–C17.
10. Richard L. Hall, *Participation in Congress* (New Haven: Yale University Press, 1996).
11. Christopher J. Deering and Steven S. Smith, *Committees in Congress* (CQ Press, 1997).
12. Roger H. Davidson, "Senate Leaders: Janitors for an Untidy Chamber?" in *Congress Reconsidered,* 3rd ed., ed. Lawrence C. Dodd and Bruce I. Oppenheimer, (Washington, D.C.: CQ Press, 1985); Sinclair, *The Transformation of the U.S. Senate;* Smith, "Forces of Change in Senate Party Leadership and Organization."
13. See Richard Beth, "What We Don't Know about Filibusters" (paper presented at the annual meeting of the Western Political Science Association, Portland, Ore., March 15–18, 1995); also Barbara Sinclair, *Unorthodox Lawmaking* (Washington, D.C.: CQ press, 1997), 47–49. Sources for the data are given in the note to Table 1-1. The House Democratic Study Group publication relies on data supplied by Congressional Research Service experts; these experts' judgments about what constitutes a filibuster are not limited to instances in which cloture was sought. For the 103rd through the 107th Congresses, instances in which cloture was sought are used as the basis of the "filibuster" estimate. One can argue that this overestimates because in some cases cloture was sought for reasons other than a fear of extended debate (a test vote or to impose germaneness); however, one can also argue that it underestimates because those cases in

which cloture was not sought—perhaps because it was known to be out of reach—are not counted. For an estimate based on a different methodology, see Table 1-2.

14. Phil Kuntz, "Drawn-Out Denouement Mirrors Character of 102nd Congress," *Congressional Quarterly Weekly Report,* October 10, 1992, 3128.
15. Holds and threats to filibuster, as well as actual extended-debate–related delay on the floor, were coded as filibuster problems (see note 23 below). The definition of major legislation used here—those measures in lists of major legislation published in CQ almanacs and the *CQ Weekly* plus those measures on which key votes occurred, again according to Congressional Quarterly—yields forty to sixty measures per Congress. Thus, although truly minor legislation is excluded, the listing is not restricted to only the most contentious and highly salient issues.
16. C. Lawrence Evans and Walter Oleszek, "The Procedural Context of Senate Deliberation," in *Esteemed Colleagues: Civility and Deliberation in the U.S. Senate,* ed. Burdett Loomis (Washington, D.C.: Brookings Institution Press, 2000).
17. *Congressional Record,* March 6, 2003, S3216.
18. Tom Daschle, *Like No Other Time* (New York: Crown, 2003).
19. See Sellers, "Winning Media Coverage"; Barbara Sinclair, "The Plot Thickens: Congress and the President," in *Great Theatre: The American Congress in Action,* ed. Herbert Weisberg and Samuel Patterson (Cambridge: Cambridge University Press, 1998); C. Lawrence Evans and Walter Oleszek, "Message Politics and Agenda Control in the U.S. Senate," in *The Contentious Senate,* ed. Colton C. Campbell and Nicol C. Rae (Lanham, Md.: Rowman and Littlefield, 2001).
20. *CQ Weekly,* August 30, 2003, 2066.
21. *Roll Call,* July 5, 1999.
22. *CQ Weekly,* November 15, 2003, 2817–2821.
23. Based on 91st, 94th, 97th, 101st, 103rd and 105th Congresses. Measures that did not get far enough to encounter the prospect of a filibuster problem are coded as missing data on the filibuster variable.
24. See the case studies of the 1993, 1995, and 1997 reconciliation (that is, budget) bills in Sinclair, *Unorthodox Lawmaking,* 2nd ed.
25. Barbara Sinclair, "The Senate Leadership Dilemma: Passing Bills and Pursuing Partisan Advantage in a Non-Majoritarian Chamber," in *The Contentious Senate.*
26. Nelson Polsby, "Good-bye to the Senate's Inner Club," in *Congress in Change,* ed. Norman Ornstein (New York: Praeger, 1975).
27. David Mayhew, *Divided We Govern* (New Haven: Yale University Press, 1991); Barbara Sinclair, *Congressional Realignment* (Austin: University of Texas Press, 1982).

2. A Decade of Republican Control: The House of Representatives, 1995–2005

Lawrence C. Dodd and Bruce I. Oppenheimer

It seems not all that long ago that the Republicans defied expectations and won control of the House for the first time in forty years. Yet with the start of the 109th Congress, what was once viewed as the "permanent minority" in the House will begin its second decade as the majority party. Throughout this period Republicans have walked a tightrope because they have never been able to expand their control beyond a narrow margin and have continuously dealt with uncertainty about what the next election would bring. Lacking an overwhelming mandate from the electorate, a party might opt for a coalitional style of legislating in an effort to expand its majority. Most of the time, however, House Republicans and their leaders have rejected that approach and have risked pursuing their conservative policy agenda. Although the party's majority has remained tenuous, a decade of control has allowed the Republicans to achieve many of their policy goals.

Our purpose in this chapter is to analyze the context in which Republicans won control of the House and how they have used that control to alter the distribution of power within the institution and to pursue their electoral goals and policy preferences. To begin, however, we must first examine the changes that occurred while the Democrats controlled the House, in which parties and party leaders eventually displaced committee government as the source of power and influence in the House, and how those changes laid the foundation for the way the Republicans have chosen to operate since 1994.

The Era of Democratic Control

Long-term Democratic control of the House began with the Great Depression and the election of a Democratic majority to the seventy-second Congress, which took office in 1931.[1] With the subsequent election of President Franklin D. Roosevelt and a Democratic Senate in 1932, the party unified control of government and enacted the New Deal legislation that laid the foundations of the modern social service state. The Democratic activists' response to the Great Depression created broad popular support that sustained the party's dominance in the House for sixty of sixty-four years.

When the Democrats came to power in 1931, they inherited an organizational structure based on committee government.[2] In the late nineteenth and early twentieth centuries, both parties solidified control of the House under strong Speakers such as Thomas B. Reed, Charles F. Crisp, and Joseph G. "Uncle Joe" Cannon. Such Speakers appointed committee members and committee chairs, dominated the Rules Committee, and exercised extensive authority over floor proceedings. That ended in 1910, when deep disagreements over policy and the distribution of power within the Republican Party led GOP progressives to turn against "Czar Cannon" and his conservative allies and unite with House Democrats, stripping the speakership of its prerogatives and shifting power to committees. Thereafter, committees became the central policymaking entities in Congress, with committee chairs selected increasingly on the basis of committee seniority within the majority party, thereby creating a complex and decentralized structure of House policymaking. This structure fostered policy expertise and stabilized policymaking processes, but the majority party found itself stymied in pursuing coordinated policy activism.

Democratic control of the House from the 1930s until the 1970s was a continuing effort to use the policymaking expertise of the standing committees while overcoming the obstacles to party government that seniority and committee government created. During the first four years of Franklin Roosevelt's presidency, the House Democratic leadership used the extensive public support for the New Deal, enormous House majorities, and the resources of the presidency to generate committee and floor support among Democratic members. But in the late 1930s, as public support for the New Deal ebbed, conservative Democrats, particularly southern Democrats, united with Republicans to oppose New Deal legislation in committees and on the House floor.

When allied with Republicans in the so-called conservative coalition, southern Democrats were a substantial force in the House from the late 1930s into the 1960s. Their power flowed not just from the fact that the conservative coalition constituted a House majority, but also from the fact that southern Democrats represented safe seats and easily accrued seniority. Accordingly, they dominated committee chairmanships. These southern committee chairs blocked liberal Democratic legislation and pushed conservative policies to passage by the House. As a result, one cannot equate Democratic control of the House from the late 1930s to the 1960s with liberal Democratic Party dominance of congressional policymaking. Those years, rather, were characterized by strong committee government, coalitional politics, and conservative policies.

Only with the liberal successes in the 1958 elections and the election of President John Kennedy in 1960 did the House Democrats begin a sixteen-year reform process that would constrain the conservative coalition. Not until the 1970s, however, was moderate-to-liberal control of the House Democratic Party solidified with reforms that restricted the power of seniority, weakened committee government, and brought greater authority to party leaders. The passage of these reforms particularly benefited from the presence in the ninety-fourth Congress (1975–1977) of a large number of reform-minded Democratic freshmen, who were elected in the Watergate elections of November 1974.

The conservative coalition declined as a voting bloc throughout the 1970s and 1980s.[3] The changes occurred in part because the internal reforms undercut the procedural basis of its power, in part because of the growing numbers of moderate-to-liberal northern legislators in the Democratic Party, and in part because of the changes in southern Democratic representation in Congress resulting from the 1965 Voting Rights Act. With the registration of large numbers of black voters, southern Democratic members became more moderate. As a consequence, the Republican Party attracted conservative southern white voters and became more competitive in many southern districts. The distinction between southern and northern congressional Democrats waned, and interparty differences increased. In the short run these shifts increased the unhappiness among Republicans over their isolation in the House and their lack of a strong institutional role. Only episodically could they exercise considerable "hidden" power in the House through the conservative coalition. Over the long run the changes laid the foundation for growing Republican representation in the South.

The Republican Challenge

Republican frustration increased when the Reagan landslides of 1980 and 1984 failed to produce Republican control of the House, even though Republicans won some conservative southern House districts previously controlled by Democrats and even held a Senate majority from 1981 to 1987. House Republicans began a more aggressive assault on Democratic dominance. The impetus for this attack came from the younger and more conservative Republicans and was led by Newt Gingrich of Georgia. Their goal was to end Democratic control of the House and to institute Republican rule. Their strategy was to combine the growing number of southern Republicans with the preexisting group of House Republicans and replace the conservative coalition with a conservative Republican governing party in control of the House.

Laying the Foundations

In the ninety-eighth Congress (1983–1985), Gingrich and other junior Republicans organized the Conservative Opportunity Society and challenged the House Democrats on procedural, policy, and political grounds.[4] They pushed issues such as the balanced budget amendment, reform of House rules, the line-item veto, and social concerns. Many of their proposals would form the basis of the Contract with America a decade later. They also mounted sustained assaults on the ethics of House Democrats, leading among other things to the resignation of Speaker Jim Wright, D-Texas, under an ethics investigation of his conduct, and continuously called for rules reform and reorganization of the House. In addition, when the term limits movement began to gain momentum in the late 1980s and early 1990s, many House Republicans embraced it as a vehicle to undermine Democratic dominance of Congress.

Gingrich increasingly became a force in the House Republican Conference. In 1988 he became head of GOPAC, a Republican political action committee, and used it to recruit conservative Republicans to run for state and local office. In March 1989, House Republicans narrowly elected Gingrich as their minority whip over a more moderate candidate, positioning him to succeed their long-term minority leader, Bob Michel of Illinois, who would retire at the end of the 103rd Congress. As minority whip and prospective party leader, Gingrich pushed Republicans closer to confrontation with majority party Democrats, pointing to the 1994 elections.

Gingrich and the House Republicans built their 1994 campaign around a common national agenda, the Contract with America, which constituted a direct attack on the "liberal" agenda and long-term Democratic control. The Contract was dedicated to extensive reform of the House and the implementation of conservative policies. Republicans relied on a mix of strong, experienced candidates and antigovernment amateurs and on extensive campaign funding strategies that the party had built over the previous decade. They focused on winning many open seats, on defeating freshmen Democrats elected in 1992, and on challenging a few key Democratic leaders, such as Speaker Tom Foley.

The result was the first election of a Republican majority in the House since 1952. In winning control of the House, the Republicans made a net gain of 52 seats, the largest partisan swing since 1948. They defeated 34 Democratic incumbents, including Speaker Foley, and picked up 18 seats in open-seat contests. The party proved particularly successful in the South, turning a 54–83 southern deficit into a 73–64 advantage. Republicans emerged with a 230–204 House majority.

The "Republican revolution," as the election outcome was dubbed in the press, was a testament to the hard work that Gingrich and others had done over the previous decade to prepare the groundwork for a serious challenge to Democratic dominance. The pressing political concern was whether the Republicans could consolidate a new period of long-term Republican rule in Congress.

Asserting Control of the House

Following the 1994 elections and through much of the 104th Congress (1995–1997), it appeared that czar leadership, akin to that of the 1889–1910 era, had returned to the House. In keeping with Reed, Crisp, and Cannon, Speaker Gingrich sought a level of control of the House and its committees that had not been seen since the revolt against Cannon.[5] Ironically, over the previous two decades Democrats had done much to strengthen the speakership. Appreciative of his role in leading them to majority party status, House Republicans allowed Gingrich to assume powers that had been stripped from the speakership in 1910.[6] Gingrich's personal choices were appointed to chair committees, even when it meant bypassing more senior members. Republican committee chairs were limited to three terms as head of a specific committee, depriving them of the ability to establish independent, long-term bases of power from which to challenge the power of the Speaker. The new Speaker assumed considerable influence in the appointment of members to key committee slots, thereby increasing his power within the committee system. And although Gingrich did not assume the chairmanship of the Rules Committee, as Cannon had, he was allied with Republican members of the committee, who provided control over the agenda and the scheduling of House legislation. Gingrich himself was subjected to a new restraint that previous Speakers had not faced, when Republicans imposed a four-term limit on their Speakers. Nevertheless, Gingrich's overall authority looked unassailable as the 104th Congress began.

Relying on a kind of Speaker's cabinet to set the policy direction, and using Majority Leader Dick Armey and Majority Whip Tom DeLay in running the House and whipping party members into line, Gingrich presented the House Republicans as an aggressive, cohesive, and irresistible force that could not fail to create a new Republican era in Congress. He then used party leadership resources to ensure cooperation from the standing committees, often having committees do little more than rubber-stamp legislation the party leadership had drafted. And once legislation came to the floor he was prepared to push for united Republican support.

The high point of Gingrich's effectiveness came during the first hundred days of the 104th Congress, when House Republicans acted on the major promises of the Contract with America. This success then encouraged Gingrich to seek a level of legislative control and policy impact beyond anything envisioned by previous Speakers and to put his speakership at risk in a high-stakes confrontation with President Bill Clinton. That confrontation came in late 1995 and early 1996, in a conflict between the president and Congress over the national budget that produced the low point of Gingrich's speakership during the 104th Congress.

Gingrich and House Republicans saw the budget struggle as an opportunity to gain political dominance over a sitting Democratic president. Clinton's refusal to accept the Republicans' budget, which they presented to him weeks after the end of the fiscal year because of their slowness in passing appropriations legislation, left the national government with no budget at all and produced two government shutdowns. The public largely blamed the shutdowns on the Republicans, which undermined rather than strengthened their political situation. Further, the events exposed the limitations of congressional policy leadership and Gingrich's shortcomings within the House. The party never fully recovered its momentum after the budget "train wreck," with other House Republicans blaming Gingrich and his leadership team for the debacle.

The Democrats made small seat gains in the 1996 election, but Republicans succeeded in maintaining control of the House for two consecutive elections. Nevertheless, their narrowed majority limited their opportunity for major legislative accomplishments and cast doubt whether the party would consolidate long-term dominance of the House. Unhappiness with Gingrich then continued into the 105th Congress, coming to a head midway though 1997 when a group of House Republicans plotted unsuccessfully to oust Gingrich from the speakership.[7]

Lacking a policy agenda that could unite the House Republicans now that the Contract with America had passed the House, Gingrich came to rely on the impeachment of President Clinton over the Monica Lewinsky scandal as a way to unite House Republicans and lead them to success in the 1998 elections.[8] But the public again stood with Clinton rather than Gingrich and the Republicans in the 1998 elections, disapproving of the president's behavior but hostile to the impeachment efforts against him. The Republicans maintained control of the House for a third straight election but with another reduction in their seat margin. The election thus was interpreted as a major defeat for House Republicans, beyond what the small seat loss would suggest. For the first time since 1934 the president's party actually gained House seats in a midterm election. Faced with political calamity, and informed by friend and foe alike of his collapsing support among House Republicans, Gingrich stepped down as Speaker and resigned from the House.

By the time of Gingrich's departure, any lingering thoughts of a czar-like speakership had been abandoned. After some initial confusion, Republicans turned to Dennis Hastert of Illinois as Speaker. Hastert served as deputy whip to the Republican Whip, Tom DeLay, and was considered a loyalist to the powerful but abrasive DeLay. Although well respected for his hard work among House Republicans, Hastert lacked the public visibility of Gingrich. Rather than being a czar in the 106th Congress, Hastert was expected to proceed in a more collegial manner, helping the House Republicans regroup, find their legislative bearings, and compete for reelection in a more effective manner in 2000, while also being committed to the party's conservative agenda.

Preparing for the 2000 Elections

As the 106th Congress opened in January 1999, House members, both seasoned veterans and first termers, were virtually in shock. In the previous two months they had witnessed the resignation of the Speaker of the House, and then they proceeded to vote two impeachment charges against the president of the United States, despite public opinion polls showing popular support for the president. As they grappled with these extraordinary developments and prepared for the new legislative year, members confronted a more evenly divided House than any since the 72nd Congress (1931–1933).

The overriding goal for Speaker Hastert was to position the House Republicans to maintain and expand their majority in the 2000 elections.[9] Seeking to stabilize and unify the House Republicans, Hastert kept in place the Gingrich leadership team of Majority Leader Dick Armey and Majority Whip Tom DeLay. He then proceeded to emphasize a "mainstream" Republican agenda focused particularly on a huge, across-the-board tax cut, which most House Democrats opposed. With a narrow majority and a largely unified opposition party, the Republicans failed to generate truly visible new laws in 1999. Their problems were aggravated by polls demonstrating strong public support for various health and education issues that House Democrats were pushing.

Hastert and fellow Republicans switched strategies early in 2000 and began to focus on ways to build a legislative record by working with Clinton and elements of the House Democratic Party.[10] Rather than focus on Republican party dominance of the policy process, they shifted toward a form of "constructive partisanship" designed to build a record of legislative accomplishment that would demonstrate their capacity to govern effectively.[11] In doing so, they gave up on across-the-board tax cuts and focused instead on targeted tax cuts (to revoke the marriage penalty, for example), on popular social programs dealing with health and education that had Democratic support, and on an alliance with Clinton to pass legislation normalizing trade relations with China.

The expanded activism of House Republicans in 2000 generated legislative accomplishments sufficiently visible to offset a do-nothing image. The great success of Republicans in the 106th Congress thus lay in Hastert's ability to move his party beyond the calamity of the 1998 elections and accomplish enough so that Clinton and the Democrats could not easily campaign against the "do-nothing Congress." In the auspicious phrase of Richard Cohen and Eliza Carney, the 106th was more nearly a "do-little Congress."[12] But that proved to be just enough.

Although Republicans lost seats in 2000 for a third straight election, they held onto a slim majority in the House despite an aggressive campaign by House Democrats. Simultaneously, George W. Bush eked out a razor-thin electoral college majority in the presidential race, and Senate Republicans gained control of the evenly divided Senate based on the tie-breaking vote of Vice President Dick Cheney. Suddenly, the Republican Party had united control of government for the first time since the presidency of Dwight D. Eisenhower and the opportunity to work toward consolidation of a Republican era in American national politics.

The Elusiveness of United Party Control: The 107th Congress (2001–2003)

The 107th Congress was not simply the first time since Eisenhower—generally considered a relatively moderate president—that Republicans had held united control of government; it was the first time conservatives had held united power since Herbert Hoover.[13] The narrowness of Republican control appeared to dictate a cautious approach to governing. But the party's long-pent-up desire for conservative government, which had led the vast majority of congressional Republicans to Washington, combined with the substantial policy distance between them and congressional Democrats to create a push toward conservative activism.

Reflecting the party's eagerness to assert itself, and seeing assertive action as the key to long-term Republican control of government, George W. Bush made it clear from the start of his presidency that "he would ask as much from Congress as he would if he had won a landslide victory."[14] His opening agenda included the massive tax cuts that conservative Republicans had been seeking since the Republican takeover of Congress but that Clinton, congressional Democrats, and moderate Republicans had previously forestalled. It also included education reforms, a voucher program and "faith-based initiatives" that made it easier for religious charities to qualify for federal social service funds. Bush's overall plans were based on his administration's estimate of a ten-year, $5.6 trillion surplus, $2.6 trillion of which was in the Social Security trust fund. Against the backdrop of this emerging policy agenda, House Republicans returned to Washington in early January 2001 to organize for the new Congress and carve out the role they would play in supporting their president and consolidating united Republican control of government.

The First Session: Pre-9/11/2001

Backed by the vote-gathering skills of Whip DeLay, Speaker Hastert and his leadership team moved in the early months of the new session to pass the president's proposed tax cuts. Hastert resisted Bush's insistence that the tax cuts be considered in one package and instead took a piecemeal approach to them. Nevertheless, over a three-month period the House passed a series of bills that together embodied the president's overall tax cut proposal, doing so "with only slight tinkering by GOP leaders and new Ways and Means Committee Chairman Bill Thomas" of California.[15] House Republicans voted in near-unity for the tax cut bills, as did a small number of "Blue Dog" conservative Democrats. House conservatives also supported a budget resolution that embraced the president's tax and spending proposals.[16]

Republican unity in support of his tax cuts was a vital contribution to George W. Bush's early policy success as president, but it masked deeper divisions within the House conference.[17] It ensured that a conservative bill would reach conference with the Senate, giving the president's desired massive tax cuts a chance to emerge from a House-Senate conference despite the likelihood that a more moderate tax cut would pass the Senate. Yet unity on the House bill was not a true reflection of the policy position of House Republicans. Conservative House Republicans wanted even larger tax cuts, and moderates in the party favored smaller ones, leaving revenues available for funding other programs, such as education. The ability of the House leadership to keep these members in line owed partly to the members' desire to be part of the Republican team but also to the expectation by House moderates that the Senate would adjust the size of the tax cuts downward in response to the greater power of moderates and Democrats in the Senate.

In May, five months into Bush's presidency, the Republican Congress passed a $1.35 trillion tax cut package. After negotiations with the Senate, the amount was less than the House had supported, as Republican moderates had anticipated, but it was still the largest reduction since the Reagan presidency.

With the enactment of the tax cuts and the emergence of Democratic control of the Senate (after James Jeffords left the Republican Party), the House moved into a summer of adjustment.[18] The House leadership embraced more fully the passage of highly conservative bills—as on the president's faith-based initiative, omnibus energy legislation, and the overhaul of managed care—that would force the Democratic Senate conferees to compromise on terms more acceptable to the president and his party.[19] House Republicans thus became even more central to the enactment of Bush's conservative agenda, but in ways that frustrated Republican moderates and generated occasional rebellions that the leadership had to address.[20] The appropriations process in the House moved forward slowly in the face of conflicts between those supporting social spending and supporters of more defense spending, so that just five of the thirteen regular fiscal 2002 bills were ready for conference when members began their month-long August recess.[21] Simultaneously, nervousness began to rise among House Republicans over the nation's deteriorating economy, with the country moving deep into a recession just as the tax cuts began to enter into revenue projections.[22]

As members returned from the recess in the first week of September, gloom was descending on House Republicans as they contemplated the economic figures.[23] Revised assessments of the nation's surplus showed that the tax cuts, combined with the deteriorating economy, were generating a dramatic decline in the surplus inherited from the Clinton administration, with the surplus essentially disappearing unless Social Security funds were included in it. This meant that the work of Congress over the coming months, in passing appropriations bills and responding to defense and social needs, would be far more onerous than had appeared to be the case when the tax cuts were enacted in May. Adding to the Republicans' concern were the president's falling poll numbers and declining public confidence in the job he was doing in managing the economy. All such concerns pointed to an early end to Republican control of the House and a larger margin of Democratic control of the Senate. Writing on September 8 of "storm clouds on the horizon" that could descend on Bush, his party, and the country, James Barnes of the *National Journal* concentrated on the economy, as were all commentators of the time, little expecting what was coming next.[24]

The First Session: 9/11 and Its Aftermath

The events of September 11 affected the U.S. Congress more deeply than all but a few institutions.[25] Terror spread throughout Capitol Hill with news of the attack on the World Trade Center and the Pentagon. Fearing another attack directly on Congress, police emptied the Capitol and congressional office buildings, sending members and staffs "into streets already filled with running crowds and snarled traffic, and lined with heavily armed police."[26] Speaker Hastert, next in the line of presidential succession after Vice President Cheney, was moved to a military bunker in rural Virginia, to be joined later by the other congressional leaders. The next morning members returned to begin crafting the nation's legislative response. Within five weeks they found themselves again closed out of their offices owing to an anthrax attack focused directly on them.

Both houses of Congress and both parties rallied behind President Bush.[27] Over the coming weeks the president called for a world war against terrorism, initiated a ground war in Afghanistan to root out the leaders of the al Qaeda terrorist network that appeared responsible for 9/11, and proposed a series of legislative actions to secure the homeland and sustain foreign war.[28] In less than a week following the attack, the members of both parties and both chambers voted to authorize the use of force against terrorists and to provide the president with $40 billion in emergency spending authority to begin the national recovery and pursue the war on terrorism. A stronger resolution, giving the president even more sweeping discretionary war power, was opposed on Capitol Hill, as members "compared it with the 1964 Gulf of Tonkin resolution" that Lyndon Johnson had used to justify the Vietnam War.[29] Similarly, initial proposals to give the president a "blank check" for spending on the war and homeland security faced opposition within both parties on Capitol Hill. Following the early actions in support of the war effort, Congress provided $15 billion to aid airline recovery, gave the attorney general extraordinary new authority to pursue suspected terrorists on the home front, and passed legislation to strengthen airport security.[30] Again, these actions were taken with strong bipartisan support, but also with congressional scrutiny that provided a degree of restraint on executive action.

As Congress acted in response to 9/11, it returned to its domestic agenda but did so within a transformed political landscape. Ignoring the president's uneven early response to the crisis, the public had rapidly sent his approval scores soaring.[31] Gone were the August doubts about his stewardship of the nation and the dark clouds hanging over the congressional Republicans. Amid the calls for national unity, Bush emerged as the most widely supported president in the history of national opinion surveys, with a 90 percent approval rating in late September.[32] Less than three weeks following 9/11, it already seemed clear to astute congressional observers, such as Charlie Cook, that the political fallout of the terrorist attack would aid the Republicans in Congress.[33] The Republican advantage, moreover, lay not just with the "rally round the flag" component of the public's response, which gave the president and his party a natural boost.[34] The coming of war also gave the president and congressional Republicans a way to explain sustained fiscal crisis and to justify fiscal and domestic policies that otherwise would have seemed imprudent or politically untenable.

As the new partisan reality became clear and the immediacy of 9/11 receded, bipartisanship lessened on Capitol Hill and partisan maneuvers increased.[35] In the House, Ways and Means chair Bill Thomas, pushed a capital gains tax cut a few days following 9/11, justifying it as a way to boost the sagging wartime economy. He thereby raised one of the most partisan tax issues possible and did so in a way that appeared to be using the crisis for partisan ends. His timing found critics even among House Republican leaders.

Thomas proceeded in the week of October 8 to push through his committee an economic stimulus plan composed of more tax cuts and legislation extending presidential trade negotiating authority, thereby igniting divisive partisan debates on the House floor. In doing so, "he soured relations within Ways and Means, and he dealt a serious blow to high-level House-Senate efforts at bipartisanship."[36] Nevertheless, Thomas and the House Republican leadership continued the push in November and December, so that the House passed stimulus legislation and the fast-track trade legislation based on partisan majorities, only to have the Senate refuse to act for the remainder of the session.[37] Partisanship likewise returned to infuse other areas of domestic policymaking in the House, and in House-Senate negotiations. The exception was education reform, where the final bill passed with overwhelming support in both chambers, reflecting a true bipartisan process that started with the drafting of the initial legislation and continued thereafter.[38]

Along with the rebound in partisanship, the closing months of the 2001 session also witnessed emerging shifts in the long-term leadership structure of both parties in the House. On the Republican side, Majority Leader Dick Armey of Texas announced his retirement in mid-December, effective at the end of the 107th Congress,[39] thereby opening the path for Whip DeLay to replace him as the party's leader and heir apparent to the speakership should Hastert step down.[40] For their part, the Democrats experienced a dramatic leadership shift in October, as Minority Whip David E. Bonior of Michigan announced his intent to resign in January 2002 to run for governor.[41]

Following a hard-fought campaign, Nancy Pelosi of California won the Democratic whip position, defeating Steny Hoyer of Maryland by a secret ballot vote of 118–95.[42] Pelosi became the first woman to serve in such a high-ranking House post, in line to become the first woman to lead a congressional party should Rep. Dick Gephardt, Mo., resign as leader at the end of the Congress to run for president. It also opened the possibility that she could be the first woman to serve as Speaker should Democrats reclaim the House, becoming second in line of succession to the presidency.

As the first session ended, the House thus moved beyond the immediate crisis and returned to politics as usual, but a substantial long-term legacy of the terrorist attacks also seemed to be emerging: The shift toward wartime standing was raising issues of the relevancy of the House in national policymaking.[43] Issues of foreign policy are the natural province of the Senate, with its special role in approving treaties and ambassadorial nominations. The great power of the House, as Josh Gordon discusses in Chapter 12, lies in its power over appropriations. Yet insofar as the Republican House was becoming handmaiden to the Republican president in the pursuit of his wartime agenda, it risked losing autonomous leverage over appropriations, with the Democratic Senate becoming the primary counterbalance to executive policy.

The Second Session: 2002

The quest for united Republican control of government had proved elusive during the first session of the 107th Congress, with the loss of the Senate. Accordingly, the struggle took on greater urgency as the 2002 elections loomed over the horizon. Although the economy was still struggling, in ways that might hurt Republicans at the polls, the 2002 House elections would be fought according to new apportionment figures and district lines that could help them in light of the movement of the national population to the south and southwest. And the party was basking in Bush's extraordinary approval scores, giving him a chance to frame public debate and the election dynamics.

The president focused his January 29 State of the Union speech squarely on the war on terrorism and did so in an expansive manner.[44] He broadened the war to look beyond al Qaeda and Afghanistan and focus on regimes that sponsor terrorism, particularly the "axis of evil" composed of Iraq, Iran, and North Korea. And he called for attention to programs that would secure the homeland. Over the coming months, other concerns would momentarily attract public attention and focus, including corporate scandals, symbolized by the collapse of Enron Corporation, and the nation's deteriorating economy. In response to these varied concerns, the second session would pass a tough corporate accountability bill and overhaul the nation's campaign finance laws. And despite the president's early objections, Congress would create an independent commission to investigate the 9/11 disaster and reforms that might help avoid a repeat. In addition, by year's end the House would pass a variety of bills—on such issues as prescription drugs, medical malpractice, and additional tax cuts—that "it knew had no chance in the closely divided Senate but that promised political benefit to House Republicans."[45] Yet throughout this period Congress focused primarily on issues of homeland security and on Iraq.

Initial movement on homeland security came from the Democratic Senate, whose Governmental Affairs Committee approved a bill creating a department of homeland security, despite the apparent opposition of the president, who had appeared tepid to the reorganization of government that such a bill envisioned. Then in June, the administration "did an about face and puts its own stamp on the idea," with the president making a prime time television address in support of a substantially different proposal. Most controversially, it gave to the president broad flexibility to hire, fire, promote and set salaries for the 170,000 workers in the new department, "seeming thereby to deny union representation to government workers."[46]

Once the president's support for a department of homeland security was clear, the House moved forward on the issue. Speaker Hastert and Minority Leader Gephardt united to create a Select Committee on Homeland Security and produced a bill reconciling various proposals. With Gephardt encouraging Democratic cooperation despite the personnel issue, a substantial majority of the House voted for it in late July. Homeland security legislation then stalled in the Senate, with key members of both Senate parties hesitant to give the administration the powers over department personnel that it sought. Acrimonious conflict emerged between Bush and the Senate during September, with the president blaming its Democratic leadership for the failure to enact the bill. This accusation then became a centerpiece of the November 2002 elections.

September also saw the administration reverse course with respect to Iraq in ways that likewise trapped the Democrats in a last-minute political conundrum.

At issue was whether the nation should engage in unilateral, preemptive strikes against another nation, reversing a long-standing commitment to international coalition building when the United States contemplated military action. Again, senators from both parties had doubts about the policy shift, and great concern existed that in any case Congress should be involved in such a decision, insofar as it entailed the potential of war against a sovereign nation such as Iraq. After steadfastly resisting calls for a congressional vote before launching an Iraqi war, Bush announced on September 4 that he would seek such a vote, but that for national security reasons it had to come as soon as possible and prior to the November elections. The prospect of a war against Iraq, together with issues of homeland security, then came to dominate the election season, overshadowing the economy.

Despite the normal preeminence of the Senate in foreign policy, the House took on a special role in the crafting of a resolution in support of the president's authority to wage war in Iraq. The Democratic Senate, led by Majority Leader Tom Daschle, S.D., preferred substantial limits on presidential authority, whereas House Minority Leader Gephardt again supported working more closely with the administration, helping to craft language that gave Bush broad war-making authority. The House passed the resolution on October 10, less than a month before the election, with most House Democrats breaking with Gephardt and opposing it. Thereafter, boxed in by the House action and the upcoming election, Daschle and most other Senate Democrats joined Republican colleagues and voted for of the resolution. Winning the day was Gephardt's strong argument that Democrats could not remain complacent in the face of the president's concern about Iraq's weapons of mass destruction.[47]

Thereafter Congress broke for the last weeks of the 2002 election campaign, and members returned to their home constituencies. President Bush likewise took to the campaign trail, calling for a return of united party government that would give him more loyal support for his agenda. In particular, he called for a Republican Senate and for firmer party control of the House. By the barest of margins, Republicans increased their seat margin in the House and won control of the Senate, once again attaining united party control. Sensing a moment of opportunity, given the acclaim he was receiving for engineering the election results, Bush asked for and received action on the homeland security bill and related items during the subsequent, lame-duck session of Congress.

Following the Democratic losses in the congressional elections, House Minority Leader Gephardt resigned from the leadership, accepting responsibility for the outcome.[48] His rapid decision to step down came amid a sense widely shared among Democrats that his move toward bipartisan cooperation with the president on homeland security and the war resolution had undermined party unity and demoralized its base supporters, only to be rewarded by the president's aggressive, last-minute campaign against congressional Democrats. With his resignation, Gephardt turned attention to a race for the Democratic presidential nomination in 2004, and his House colleagues elected Whip Nancy Pelosi the first woman minority leader in either chamber, choosing Steny Hoyer as the new whip.

There was a changing of the guard among Republicans in the House. As expected, the conference selected Whip Tom DeLay to replace retiring Majority Leader Dick Armey and then strengthened DeLay's perceived dominance in the party by selecting his protégé, Roy Blunt of Missouri, as whip. Simultaneously, the party retained Hastert in the speakership and repealed the four-Congress term limit for the Speaker. With the selection of Blunt and new Senate Majority Leader Bill Frist, R-Tenn., the congressional leadership cemented even closer ties to the Bush administration.

Congressional Republicans hoped that close ties with Bush would allow Republican congressional candidates to ride on the coattails of a popular president in the 2004 elections and sweep the party to an expanded majority and long-term dominance in Congress. This hope was based on the belief that Bush had made the critical difference in the 2002 elections, returning the party to united control. Yet there were concerns among political analysts as to what the election results of 2002, and those of 2000, actually meant, and thus doubts about the likely success of this strategy. To address these concerns with respect to the House of Representatives, we turn first to a closer look at 2000 and 2002 elections and what they tell us about overall political environment as the 108th Congress opened.

The 2000 and 2002 Elections

Prior to the 2002 elections, the Republican House majority had eroded slightly in each of the three elections following its becoming the majority party in 1994. Although offsetting some Democratic general election inroads with net gains from House members who switched parties and in special elections, Republicans entered the midterm elections holding only a nine-seat edge. The Democrats had even gained seats in 1998, the first time since 1934 that a party holding the presidency did not suffer a midterm seat loss. Republicans thus faced the 2002 elections in a precarious situation, holding a thin majority entering a midterm with a Republican president.

Again in 2002, however, the party in the White House gained seats in a midterm election, with the Republicans winning 229 seats, only one fewer than after the 1994 election. This did not, however, appear to be the start of a new trend toward the Republicans. As Gary Jacobson has observed, the Republican seat gain "was more a consequence of redistricting than of any national shift in public sentiment toward the Republican Party."[49] In addition, the consequences of the 9/11 attack may have had a positive impact on Republican fortunes in 2002. Not only did the attack greatly improve President Bush's approval ratings, but it may have insulated his administration and Republican House members from vulnerability on domestic issues. Available data also suggest that the president's high approval ratings discouraged quality Democratic candidates from challenging Republican incumbents in 2002.[50] And as previously discussed, the president effectively used issues of homeland security and the war against terrorism against Democratic candidates in 2002 congressional races.

More important, the 2002 House elections continued the trend, established in the three previous House elections, of very little change in the House seat balance after Republicans won the House majority in 1994. None of those elections had given the Republicans more than 230 seats or fewer than 221 (or the Democrats more than 212 or fewer than 204).[51]

Not only did the net seat balance maintain Republican control and keep the party split within a very narrow range, but in gross terms there was very little partisan shifting of seats. Overall turnover of the House membership remained extremely low, especially in the three elections since 1996. In 1998 and 2000 only seventeen and eighteen seats respectively shifted between the two parties.[52] And combined, those two general elections resulted in the defeats of only twelve members, with 98 percent of incumbents seeking reelection being successful. With few voluntary retirements and an even smaller number of electoral defeats, a fraction over 90 percent of the membership of the preceding House returned to office following each of those elections.

Even in 2002, with reapportionment and redistricting in place, there was amazingly little turnover in the House. Of the 435 members of the House in the 107th Congress, 396 sought reelection to the 108th. Only eight of them lost in primaries and another eight in the 2002 general election. Moreover, of those sixteen losses, half were in contests that pitted two incumbents against each other in the aftermath of reapportionment and redistricting.

Compared to the elections following the three previous redistrictings (1972, 1982, and 1992), House turnover through retirements and defeats in 2002 was the lowest. In those earlier elections following redistrictings, 369, 354, and 323 members, respectively, were reelected to the succeeding Congress; in 2002, 380 (87.4 percent) were returned to the House. The redistricting that took place in 2002 did not endanger as many incumbents as those earlier ones. In some states, such as California, redistricting made incumbents even safer. Using the 2000 presidential vote as a measure of underlying partisanship in the districts that were created in 2002, we find an even further reduction in the partisan competitiveness of House districts. (In Chapter 6, Oppenheimer analyzes the reasons for this decline in competitiveness.)

Another indication of the electoral safety of the House districts as they exist after the 2002 redistricting is the further decline in the number of split-results congressional districts—ones that voted for a presidential candidate of one party and a House candidate of another. That number, which had declined markedly in the 1990s from levels in the 1960s through the 1980s, dropped to eighty-six (19.8 percent) in 2000, the lowest level since 1952. But if we look at the party of the House members holding the districts just prior to the 2004 elections and the presidential choice among voters in those districts in 2000, we find that there remained only sixty-one split districts.[53] Absent a landslide in the 2004 presidential election, that number is likely to drop even lower. Not only are fewer members in party competitive districts, but those representing districts that were won by the other party's presidential candidate will continue to decrease. Incumbent safety, which from the mid-1960s through the 1980s had largely been built on the personal skills, resources, and attention that many House members invested in their constituents, has since the 1990s become increasingly the result of the underlying partisan composition of House districts.

The House's new electoral context has a number of important effects on both the internal workings of the institution and what the two parties are now doing externally. First, it means that it is unlikely that there will be a sizable partisan seat shift in the House. Few seats are competitive between the two parties. In its June 19, 2004, preview of the upcoming House elections, *CQ Weekly* rated only thirty seats as highly competitive (only four of those were rated as having "no clear favorite").[54]

Second, with the party division of the House so close and with few seats in play, every seat becomes critical. The attention that the national parties and their leaders gave to elections to fill vacant seats in Kentucky and North Dakota during the first half of 2004 was indicative. Of great significance was the unusual effort of House Majority Leader Tom DeLay to foster the Texas legislature's redistricting of the state's congressional seats for the 2004 election. The result has led one Democratic incumbent to switch parties, another to retire, two to be defeated in primaries in redrawn districts (although both seats will be retained by the Democrats), and five other incumbents to face tough reelection fights in less-favorable districts. (A similar effort to improve the partisan composition of the Colorado seventh district for its Republican incumbent failed when challenged in the courts.)

Normally, states only redraw district lines following the decennial Census to adjust for seat gains or losses due to reapportionment and to redistrict to adjust for population changes. Those district lines then remain in place until the next Census. For a state to redraw it congressional districts a second time following a Census is unusual. When that has occurred previously, it has normally been the result of court challenges to the initial redistricting. Such was the case during the 1990s when courts overturned district plans in a number of southern states, where there were challenges to racial gerrymandering intended to ensure the election of African American and Latino candidates. In the Texas case, however, the impetus came from a party that saw it as a vehicle for winning additional seats. Only in the context of a closely divided House, in which few seats are competitive, would party leaders view the potential benefits of engaging in this undertaking as justifying the costs. For Republicans the potential seat gains in Texas are an insurance policy for maintaining majority control of the House in the 109th Congress and beyond. (Five of the thirty seats that *CQ Weekly* listed as in play in 2004 are ones involved in the Texas redistricting.)

Third, after relatively high membership turnover in the 1992, 1994, and to a lesser degree the 1996 elections, the House has entered a period of low turnover. And that condition is likely to continue for the foreseeable future. The

Figure 2-1 Ebb and Flow Patterns in House Membership, 83rd–108th Congresses (1953–2003)

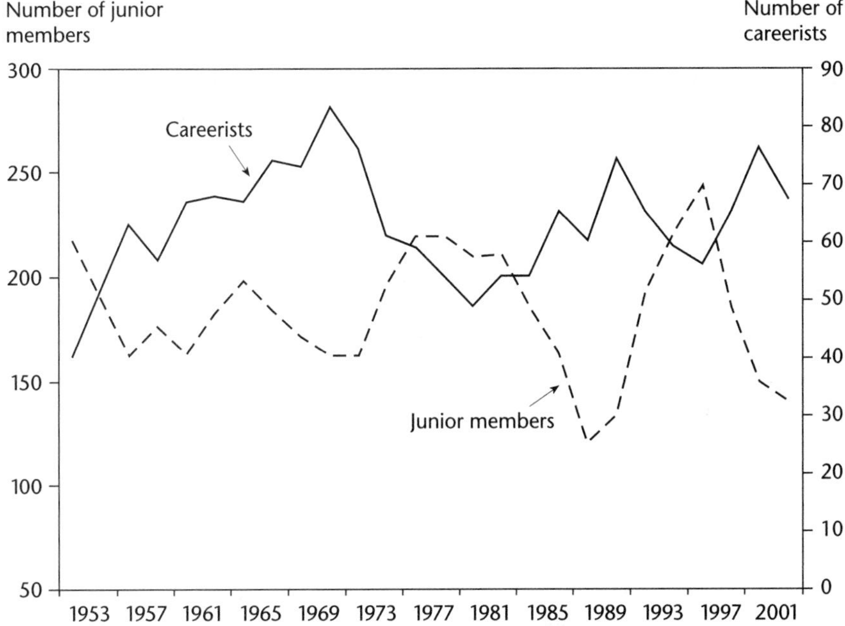

Source: Data through 2000 from Norman J. Ornstein, Thomas E. Mann, and Michael J. Malbin, *Vital Statistics on Congress, 2001–2002* (Washington, D.C.: American Enterprise Institute Press, 2002), 40–41.

percentages of returning members at the start of the 106th and 107th Congresses have only been exceeded one time since 1946. And as previously mentioned, the turnover in 2002 was exceptionally low for an election following reapportionment and redistricting. To some degree, this is just part of a natural cycle. The ebbs and flows in the influx of new members and the opposed changes in the number of very senior House members are not a new phenomenon. As shown in Figure 2-1, the recent decline in junior members (those serving in three or fewer terms) and the increase in careerists (those serving in their tenth or greater term) have occurred in a fairly patterned fashion. Thus, although the large number of new members who entered the House in the early 1990s may have been viewed as unusual, it actually was not. During the late 1940s and early 1950s, the number of new members grew, but then membership turnover dropped and careerism increased. At the start of the 83rd Congress in 1953, there were 218 (50 percent) junior House members and only 40 (9 percent) careerists. Despite some fluctuation along the way, by 1971 the number of junior members had declined to 162 (37 percent) and careerists had increased to 83 (19 percent). A new wave of membership turnover in the 1970s brought junior member numbers above 200 for four consecutive Congresses (95th–98th), and the number of careerists reached a low of 49 (11 percent) at the start of the 97th Congress in 1981. This was followed by another cycle of low turnover. With few members retiring or being defeated from 1984 to 1990, the House was again ripe for turnover in the early 1990s. And we are now once again in that part of the cycle in which membership turnover is extremely low and careerism is on the rise. As we will explain shortly, the current period of low turnover may persist somewhat longer than usual.

The regular waves of House turnover over the past half-century or more are not typical of all of congressional history. In much of the nineteenth century, turnover was consistently high. Contextual conditions of the post–World War II era have resulted in this fairly regularized pattern. For most of the period, continuing membership was rewarded. Rewards diminished only slightly during the early years of subcommittee government in the mid-1970s, and to an even lesser degree during the period of Republican control, when the majority party has bypassed some more senior members in selecting committee chairs and limited chairs to three terms. Most members have recognized that the institution extends power and perks to those who stay. Further, with a large number of safe House seats, there are few incentives to leave the institution, except for those members who are using it as a stepping-stone to higher office.

But rewarding seniority and safe seats are ingredients that would suggest a steady level of junior members and careerists in the House. Instead we find that members have tended to enter and leave the House in waves. Some of this results from elections that produce large partisan swings, such as those of 1948, 1964, 1974, 1980, and 1994. And often the losing party recoups a sizable number of seats two years later. In addition, the cycles of reapportionment and redistricting, mentioned previously, usually result in spurts of voluntary and involuntary departures from the House. Prior to 2002, the five previous elections immediately following reapportionment and redistricting produced a third more new members, on average, than did all the other Congresses in that time period. When states gain districts, that obviously results in new members' being elected. And the redrawing of district lines may make some previously safe incumbents more vulnerable, leading to higher-than-normal numbers of retirements and defeats. Finally, many of those entering the House will be between forty and fifty years of age. Having come in waves, those who stay will tend to reach careerist status in clusters and may also exit in clusters.

Taken together, these factors have led to ebbs and flows in the seniority mix in the House. The elections of 1992–1996 brought large numbers of new members to the House, after four consecutive elections in which turnover averaged less than 10 percent. Having emptied the House of members prone to retirement and also weeded out some vulnerable freshmen, those election periods created a set of incumbents prepared to run effectively from 1996 to 2000, limiting the capacity of either party to make significant seat gains. What is different, however, is that

2002 did not produce the normal level of turnover for an election following reapportionment and redistricting. And all evidence is that we will see a longer-than-normal period of low House turnover.

We may have to reexamine the notion of ebbs and flows in House turnover that we have come to expect since the end of World War II as the American electoral context changes. There will be cycles in voluntary retirements, with series of Congresses when few members are so advanced in their House careers or in age that they choose to leave, being followed by a series of elections in which growing numbers of members retire. But with fewer districts that are competitive in partisan terms, the fraction of members who choose to retire because of reluctance to face tough campaigns will diminish. Moreover, given the partisan safety of so many House districts, turnover due to general election defeats will get even smaller.[55] Two of the ingredients that in the past few decades have been essential to one party or the other's increasing its House membership by a significant number, a large number of open seats due to retirements in the opposing party and a large number of freshman legislators of the opposing party running for reelection after winning such opens seats, will not be present as often or will be of smaller magnitude.

The opportunities that the Republicans had in the early 1990s, and specifically the ones that they exploited in the 1994 elections, will become less frequent. Democratic retirements in 1994 created a large number of open seats, and first-term Democratic incumbents elected in marginal seats with Bill Clinton's victory in 1992 were potentially vulnerable. (Many of these districts, especially in the South, had been voting for Republicans in presidential elections but had continued to reelect Democratic representatives. Previously, many of these seats had become open when the partisan forces favored the Democrats—1974, 1976, and 1982—allowing a new generation of Democrats to replace an old one.) For the first time since the 1980 election the short-term forces in 1994 favored the Republicans at a time when the Democrats were forced to defend a large number of open and insecure seats. In 1994 Gingrich and his allies targeted such seats, recruited effective challengers, and concentrated resources on the most promising contests.

The landscape of congressional districts a decade later, however, is different. There is little prospect for a large number of open seats or a sizable number of first-term members. And even if there were, few would be in districts that are competitive in partisan terms. Thus, even if the short-term partisan winds strongly favored one party or the other, the seat shift would be modest.

The electoral landscape critically conditions the way the House operates. With a close party seat balance and with so many members representing partisan-safe districts, the Republican House leadership has selected a highly partisan operating strategy with which to pursue its legislative goals. And that strategy is congruent with the increasing ideological polarization and cohesiveness of both parties in the House. If one uses as a rule-of-thumb the definition of "liberal Republicans" and "conservative Democrats" as House members who vote at least half the time with a majority of the other party on party votes, then the former are extinct and the latter are about to become so. Since the Republican takeover of the House following the 1994 elections, only one of their House members even reached the 50 percent threshold in a single Congress, Connie Morella of Maryland, and she was defeated for reelection in 2002. During the first session of the 108th Congress in 2003, House Republicans averaged a party unity score of 91 percent, tying the level they reached in 1995 and 2001. In fact, only five Republican House members had scores below 80 percent. Although there were a handful of House Democrats who voted with the Republicans at least as often as with their own party, that number has been declining. In 2003 only one member, Ralph Hall of Texas, voted with the Republicans more than 40 percent of the time, and he decided to switch parties after the Republican redistricting of Texas. Twenty-seven Democrats had party unity scores below 80. Still the House Democrats recorded a mean party unity score of 87. But even before the 2004 elections, we know that there will be substantial attrition among the ranks of Democratic House members who vote most frequently with the Republicans. Of the thirteen House Democrats whom *CQ Weekly* lists as the "leading scorers," in terms of opposing their party on party unity votes during 2003, two have become Republicans, four are not seeking reelection to the House, and two others face difficult reelection battles.[56] Not only are conservative House Democrats about to join liberal House Republicans among the extinct species, but the number of moderates in both House parties is on the decline as well.

It is clear that the party polarization in the House is substantially attributable to the changing electoral bases of the two parties nationally. But we also need to recognize how much the work of parties and party leaders, who now have the capacity to mobilize their members in a more unified manner, has contributed to the polarization in the House and in the electorate. And it is important to note that much of the ideological polarization in Congress preceded the polarization that has occurred in the electorate. The two, however, reinforce each other.

The Republican Campaign for National Dominance: The 108th Congress (2003–2005)

As Republicans took control of the House for the fifth consecutive Congress, they were basking in the glow of election success and looking forward toward the new Congress and the 2004 elections with great anticipation.[57] With united government again in place, Republicans now had greater opportunity to deliver on the president's full agenda and in doing so to control their own destiny. With this opportunity came the prospect that the 2004 elections could finally provide the great breakthrough moment when the party gained dominant control of Congress and the presidency.

House Republicans believed that they had played a critical role in creating this opportunity. By uniting behind the president on critical issues in the 107th Congress, despite the momentary frustration of seeming to be irrelevant to the policymaking process, they had provided him with the passage through the House of legislation that he could then use to highlight the obstructionist role that he attributed to the Democratic Senate during the 2002 campaign. With a larger seat margin in the 108th Congress, the conservatives who dominated the House Republican conference now believed they could pass more of the president's agenda through the House. In league with a Republican Senate, they could lay the foundations for long-term and conservative Republican control of government. Moreover, this possibility was reinforced by disarray among House Democrats in the wake of the election loss, Gephardt's resignation, and uncertainty within the party over how best to proceed.[58]

Yet uncertainty also confronted House Republicans and their national party, as well.[59] The focus on terrorism, homeland security, and the move toward war with Iraq had diverted public attention from the poor economy and to some extent had served to explain it away. But it was doubtful that the public would continue to give Republicans a pass on the economy four years into a Bush presidency, when his tax cut stimuli should finally be working and the war on terrorism firmly in hand. Thus much depended on how the economy fared. In addition, the country was moving inexorably toward war in Iraq, with the president leading the way and the nation deferring to his judgment.

The party's momentum toward majority party consolidation appeared to depend on Bush's success in conducting the war and winning the peace. Moreover, while winning the war and overseeing economic recovery, Republicans needed to demonstrate that they could govern effectively by addressing the nation's social ills and providing a compelling vision of how domestic life and international politics would proceed beyond the current period of war and economic recovery. These latter concerns put great responsibility on the first session of the 108th Congress to move forward on unfinished legislative business while also addressing the president's emerging agenda.

The First Session: 2003

The most immediate unfinished business facing the House was to complete the 2003 appropriations bills. The 107th Congress had finished only two of the thirteen bills before adjourning, a sign of continuing disarray in the appropriations process and the inability of House appropriators to assert their authority over the spending legislation as in past decades. It was not until late February that the House and Senate agreed on an omnibus appropriations package that largely deferred to the spending parameters the president set. Thereafter, Congress turned to address the concerns that Bush outlined in his State of the Union address. Major proposals included his call for a new round of tax cuts to stimulate the ailing economy, his proposal to set aside $400 billion to add a prescription drug benefit to Medicare, and a proposal that Congress limit its increase in discretionary spending to 4 percent in 2004. Bush also made clear his commitment to the removal of Saddam Hussein but left unaddressed whether or when the nation would go to war in Iraq and the price tag for doing so. Less than three weeks later, on March 19, Bush announced the incursion into Iraq, reshuffling both domestic and international politics and reshaping the congressional debate over his proposed policy agenda.

The Iraq war greatly complicated passage of the president's request for additional tax cuts, estimated at $726 billion over eleven years. The House passed a budget resolution on March 21 that included a commitment to the tax cuts, but it did so only under great pressure from Republican Party leaders and the administration and in the face of opposition from Republican moderates. Four days later, the president submitted a request for a $74.7 billion supplemental appropriation for the war, and rebellion against his tax cut proposal then broke loose in the Senate. Senate moderates forced Republican leaders to hold to a $350 billion tax cut, despite negotiations with the House that had appeared to commit the Senate to a $550 billion cut. The president accepted the Senate proposal and signed the final bill in late May. The reduction of the tax cuts to less than half of the level presented in the original House budget resolution highlighted the continuing difficulty that the House was having in maintaining its historic control over fiscal policy and left House Republican leaders embarrassed by a Republican Senate and their own president. They went along with the final bill to ensure that the party would have in place an additional tax cut victory, and any economic stimulus it might generate, as the party prepared for the 2004 elections.

Much of the first session of the 108th Congress was preoccupied by the need to craft and enact supplemental spending legislation for the war. Given the apparent success of the war in April 2003, members of both the House and Senate were prepared to provide the president with all the money he requested. Yet there were reservations about how much discretionary control over military spending to provide the administration. Again, the two chambers divided, with the House closely adhering to the White House's request, the Senate placing greater restraints on discretionary spending, and the president compromising largely on the Senate's terms, signing the bill on April 16. Thereafter, American troops completed their takeover of Iraq, only to find that occupation and stabilization of the country were much harder, more dangerous, and ultimately more expensive than was the initial invasion.

By September, Bush was forced to return to Congress for an additional supplemental spending bill to cover the war, doing so as it became increasingly evident that the weapons of mass destruction that had been the most persuasive justification for the war were nowhere to be found. The debate over the second supplemental thus became much more heated, with much of the controversy centering on whether oil-rich Iraq should cover the $20 billion set aside in the supplemental for the country's reconstruction. Again, Republican leaders in the House succeeded in holding the line for the president's initial request, with the major difficulties coming in the Senate. Bush's success in passing the second supplemental, despite deteriorating conditions in postwar Iraq, owed in part to the staunch support of the House Republican leadership and in part to the effectiveness of his lobbying efforts. The same factors also helped ensure what was probably his greatest and most improbable success of the 108th Congress, the enactment of a prescription drug provision as part of the Medicare program that Democrats had originally created during the presidency of Lyndon Johnson in the 1960s.

The president sought the enactment of a prescription drug program as a way to reach out to senior citizens and win their allegiance for the Republican Party, seeing this as a step towards consolidation of long-term Republican rule. This was a daring move in that it challenged the Democrats on their own policy turf. Yet it was also a strategy that many Republicans questioned on policy grounds. The party had historically seen such entitlement programs as irresponsible use of tax funds and a major factor in the growth of a social service state. Moreover, passing it seemed particularly questionable during a period of tax cuts, war, and rising deficits. Nevertheless, the president and Republican supporters persevered, maintaining that enactment of a prescription drug provision prior to the 2004 elections was essential. In addition, key Republicans also saw it as a vehicle through which to transform Medicare by incorporating into the new law substantial incentives for privatization and competitive delivery of benefits.

House Ways and Means Committee chairman Bill Thomas became the driving force behind a highly partisan prescription drug program that incorporated competition between Medicare and private plans. His bill passed the House by a single vote on June 27, setting the stage for tough negotiations with the Senate, which had passed a more moderate plan that drew conservative Democratic support. House Republicans shut out all Democrats from the conference committee negotiations, which included only two Senate Democrats, so that the final bill was largely designed to attract Republican support and thus maintained substantial elements of Thomas's bill. The House Republican leadership then engaged in one of the most controversial roll call votes of modern times, holding the vote open for three hours, well beyond the fifteen-minute norm, as they maneuvered to produce a majority in support of the bill. With Democrats showing virtual unanimity in opposing it because of fears it would undercut Medicare over the long run, it took the Republican leadership the full three hours to induce support from wavering Republicans.

The House Republican leadership pushed the final prescription drug bill to passage despite opposition from Republican conservatives who opposed the creation of new entitlement programs, party moderates who thought the bill was too restrictive in its benefits, and deficit hawks who were concerned about the $400 billion price tag. The Senate then passed the bill and the president signed it, with Speaker Hastert and other Republican leaders asserting that the legislation ensured long-term Republican control of Congress by cracking the Democrats' core support base. Almost immediately, however, the law was criticized as being too confusing for seniors to understand and too oriented towards the interests of pharmaceutical and insurance companies.[60] There was also great concern as to whether the cost of the bill could actually be held within the president's target figure. Nevertheless, its passage provided the president and his party a victory that they could stress in 2004 to convince voters of their compassion toward disadvantaged citizens.

As with prescription drugs, the House Republicans supported the president's agenda across an array of other policy areas during 2003, though with mixed results and occasional flare-ups among moderates. Thus, successful House action came on an omnibus energy bill, on the restructuring of Head Start preschool programs, and on imposition of stricter work requirements for the nation's welfare program. In each of these cases, the Republican Senate produced a more moderate version of the legislation, and final decision was postponed. Other bills faced momentary difficulties within the House itself, as Republican moderates occasionally asserted concerns. The House and the Senate were able to agree on a law outlawing "partial-birth abortions," which the president signed in November, giving social conservatives their most important legislative victory of his presidency. Yet appropriators continued to face great difficulty in completing the spending legislation that funds the government.

The Second Session: 2004

In the second session, the House proved to be considerably less active, if not less partisan, than in the first. The House Republican leadership believed that it now had put in place the major legislation that would be the hallmark of the 108th Congress and that would lead to electoral success in 2004. The task in the second session thus was "to do no harm," so that the leaders sought to keep the legislators out of Washington as much as possible. They even planned no action on the recommendations of the 9/11 Commission, expected to arrive in July, as the president hoped to downplay the commission in an effort to deflect any political fallout over the terrorist attacks' occurring under his watch. Without major legislative initiatives, the second session became preoccupied by hearings into the adequacy of government intelligence, the scandalous behavior of some troops at Abu Ghraib prison in Iraq, and domestic social concerns. One such hearing, by the Ways and Means Committee, produced the disconcerting news that the Bush administration or officials within it may have purposefully withheld from the Congress the actual projected cost of the new drug provision attached to Medicare, underestimating the cost by $150 billion. Additionally, the House found itself struggling to produce a budget resolution that could reconcile the revenue and spending commitments of the administration, so that House appropriators were forced to proceed during the summer to craft spending bills without guidance from a budget resolution.

In July, as the second session prepared to recess for six weeks for the two political parties' national conventions, House Republicans prepared a "recess kit" to aid members in presenting constituents with a common message in support of the party.[61] As a guide to the accomplishments of the second session, and the governing strategy of the House leadership, it was quite instructive. It included "virtually nothing about recent legislative successes," because the Republicans had enacted "no significant bills" during the session and were resting on their laurels from the passage of Medicare prescription drug and tax cut legislation the previous year. Rather, in a sign that the House leaders were tying their fate even more closely to that of the president, the kit proposed that House Republicans stress the president's successes in Iraq and the improvements in the economy. Clearly, House leaders believed that they had done all that they could the previous year to prepare the party for the elections, particularly in light of the growing divisions among House Republicans over how to handle budgetary and fiscal problems created by the war, the prescription drug benefits, and the tax cuts. In the face of such divisions, a long August recess and a short, pro forma September session seemed the best strategy, relying on the president's political skills to see the party through to victory.

Considerable pressure from Democrats and national commentators, and a change of heart by the president, led Republican leaders to authorize serious consideration of the reform recommendations of the 9/11 Commission when the House returned in early September. They did so as it became clear that acting on some or all of the recommendations, or at least making a strong effort at doing so, could defuse a potent issue Democrats might use to highlight the "do-nothing" character of the second session and thereby put responsibility on congressional Republicans for leaving the nation unnecessarily vulnerable to terrorism as citizens went to the polls on election day. During September, House Republicans also succeeded in passing a five-year extension of three middle-class tax cuts, including tax relief for married couples. Later passed by the Senate as well, the legislation gave Bush his fourth major tax victory in four years. These actions then set the stage for the final month of campaigning and the 2004 elections. At issue was whether Republicans could build on their legislative victories of the 108th Congress and overcome difficulties with the Iraqi war and the economy, not only to sustain united government but to increase Republican margins in the Congress and consolidate long-term control. Also at issue was the altered nature of House governance in an era of partisanship and conservative rule.

Emerging Patterns of Republican House Governance and Policymaking

Aside from an external strategy that has resulted in between-Censuses redistricting struggles to solidify existing seats or gain new ones, the Republican House leadership has had to develop strategies to achieve its legislative goals in a closely divided House composed overwhelmingly of members representing safe districts. Since taking control in the 104th Congress, this strategy has largely been geared to producing legislative outcomes by holding together the party's small majority, rather than developing bipartisan or cross-partisan coalitions. What Rohde and Aldrich label "conditional party government," in which the legislative parties are cohesive and polarized and in which the majority party membership provides its leadership with the resources to pursue median party positions on legislation, accurately describes how Republicans have operated much of the time over the past decade. But achieving legislative success has not always been easy. The Republican leadership has had to develop strategies to deal with a number of ongoing problems.

One difficulty they faced was the narrowing of the party's majority in three consecutive elections (1996, 1998, and 2000). Although few seats were lost in each of these elections, a shrinking majority gave the leaders less leeway. In the simplest terms, it meant that they could not afford as many defections on key roll call votes. Governing the House with 229 Republican members in the 108th Congress provided a more comfortable cushion. Second, with a small majority, the role of the twenty or thirty Republican House moderates was potentially crucial. If unified, they could threaten to join with House Democrats and defeat or amend legislation, unless the leadership was willing to move to more centrist policy positions. And this meant that there was also a need to counteract Democratic efforts to attract the support of the moderate Republicans. Third, the leaders had to concern themselves with the electoral consequences of pursuing median party positions. In particular, requiring moderate Republicans to vote for conservative policy options had the potential to make those members more vulnerable electorally and thus to threaten the party's majority status. Finally, they were faced with problems of bargaining with a more moderate Senate. Passing legislation narrowly, with almost no Democratic support, did not place the Republican House leaders in a strong position in negotiations with the Senate. This was clearly most difficult during the 107th Congress, after Senator Jeffords left the Republican Party and Democrats obtained party control of the Senate. But it continued in the 108th Congress when the party leaders of the two chambers could not work out legislative compromises.

For House Republican leaders, coping with a narrow majority and with moderates who often hold the balance are largely two sides of the same coin. Were the party to have a sizable majority, neither threats of moderates to desert the party on key votes nor the need to maintain high levels of party cohesion would be a major problem. Without the luxury of such a majority, the Republican leadership has perfected a series of tactics to produce House majorities nevertheless. First, they have made it clear continuously over their decade of control that party loyalty is essential for reaping rewards. The most visible, but far from the only, examples of this have come in the selection of committee chairs. In nearly every instance of a committee chair contest, the party leaders have selected the more reliable, and normally the more conservative, candidate. Interviews with the selection committee also are a vehicle for gaining commitments to the party legislative agenda from chair candidates. If a Republican House member is interested in advancing to a position of influence, the message is quite clear.

To hold their members together the House Republican leadership has been willing to go beyond what had previously been considered acceptable tactics. In several instances they have held roll call votes open for inordinately long periods, until they were able to switch a sufficient number of votes of party defectors. In

2004 a vote on a Democratic-sponsored budget resolution proposal was held open an extra twenty-three minutes, until the measure could be defeated on a tie vote. Of course, this paled compared to the three-hour extension a few months before on the conference report on the Medicare prescription drug bill. Reports of unsuccessful efforts to coerce Rep. Nick Smith, R-Mich., into voting for the conference report, based on threats to give or withhold commitments to his son's campaign to succeed him, resulted in a House ethics committee investigation and an eventual formal ethics rebuke of Majority Leader DeLay.[62]

Second, Republican leaders have tried to limit roll call votes on issues that divide the party or to frame legislative votes in a way that is conducive to retaining the support of party members. These tactics include using the Rules Committee to limit the time available for debate and voting on amendments, as well as limiting the amendments that may be offered. In addition, holding particularly tough votes at a very late hour minimizes the amount of immediate media attention they receive, giving some insulation to members who cast votes that might be unpopular in their constituencies. In other instances, the leadership has simply kept certain issues off the House floor or has only been willing to schedule legislation that is in line with party goals. Even when the House Republican leaders have suffered floor defeats, however, they have named conferees who favor the party position. A classic example of this came in House passage of patients' bill of rights legislation that would have allowed patients to sue HMOs. The leadership simply did not appoint Republicans who supported that provision to the conference committee.

Third, the Republicans have perfected a strategy of limiting Democratic participation until their party members are fairly united. Committee markup sessions at times have taken on a pro forma appearance, as differences among Republicans have already been resolved in committee caucus sessions or in informal negotiations with the leadership. Democratic efforts to modify bills at the committee level are often acts of frustration. Little debate occurs, and votes are predictably party line. This same method has been used in conference committees as well, as in the previously mentioned conference on the Medicare prescription drug bill, when no House Democrats were allowed to participate in the negotiations.

As might be expected, locking out the Democrats has led to high levels of distrust between members and leaders of the two parties in the House. Longtime observers note that as recently as the early 1990s, Speaker Foley and Minority Leader Michel regularly talked several times a week, conversations that "were essential to the smooth running of the House." In contrast, Speaker Hastert and Minority Leader Pelosi had no regular conversations during the 108th Congress, nor much of a relationship. In explaining the lack of contact, Pelosi has said she "sees no use in trying to confer regularly . . . when . . . the Republican majority has made very clear its intention to trample on the rights of the Democratic minority."[63] Other signs of incivility and distrust include a committee meeting characterized by such conflict that Capitol Police were called, the pressure exerted on Nick Smith, and the filing of ethics charges by a Democratic member against

Majority Leader DeLay over his actions in support of state legislative races and congressional redistricting in Texas.

Fourth, the Republican leadership has been more successful in dealing with the moderates than one might have anticipated. Over the decade that Republicans have controlled the House, the number of moderates seemingly has declined. In this regard the fact that fifty-three House members of the 108th Congress belonged to the Republican Main Street Partnership, a group perceived as moderate, is misleading because they include many members whose voting records indicate that they rarely stray from their party. More important, the moderates are rarely united. In explaining why only three other moderates supported Mark Foley, R-Fla., in his efforts to change faith-based initiatives legislation in 2001 to require religious groups to comply with state antidiscrimination laws, Mark Kirk, R-Ill., explained, "Moderates are a different group of people depending on the issue. I'm a moderate on civil rights, but I'm an ardent free-trader. It's a different group of members each time."[64] The lack of unity among Republican moderates also serves the goals of both the moderates and the party leaders. Moderates have opportunities to vote against their party and demonstrate their independence to constituents in the fairly competitive districts that many of them represent without its resulting in defeats for their party on floor votes. Democratic leaders did largely the same thing when their party was in the majority. On any close roll call, there was always a pool of moderate Democrats willing to vote with the leadership if their votes were needed. For the past two Congresses, Republicans have also had the resources of the Bush administration to assist their efforts to rein in potential mavericks.

Despite the overall success of their strategy, Republican House leaders have not been universally successful in managing their legislative agenda. Certain wedge issues, such as campaign finance reform and a patients' bill of rights, have garnered sufficient support from Republicans that party positions have been impossible to sustain. And during the 108th Congress the leadership had to deal with threats of defection from conservatives, not just from moderates, on prescription drug legislation and on budget deficit issues. Issues related to the intelligence community's shortcomings and the conduct of the Iraq war also have the potential to undermine Republican unity in the House. The biggest source of frustration, however, has been the more moderate and tenuous Republican majority in the Senate. Major conflict over an energy bill, extending the Bush tax cuts, appropriations bills with substantive riders attached to them, and even a budget resolution have tested inter-chamber cooperation among Republican party and committee leaders.

Overall, however, the House Republicans have been amazingly successful over the past decade in achieving their policy goals, especially given the narrowness of their majority. Normally, one would expect that with such a small and tenuous majority a party would have taken a more incremental approach to policy change. Even with Bush's election in 2000, there was little evidence of anything approaching a popular mandate for the party's policy agenda. Yet this has not deterred Republican House leaders from pushing many of the items on their agenda or led them to seek bipartisan compromises with House Democrats. Nowhere is the impact more marked than on issues of taxing and spending, discussed in depth in Chapter 14 by Catherine Rudder. The long-term effects of extending the Bush tax cuts and financing the wars on terrorism and in Iraq are to minimize revenues available for a range of current domestic programs, for the creation of new ones, and for maintaining the solvency of major entitlement programs without major eligibility, contribution, or benefit changes. What was labeled the "starve the beast" strategy has been largely put in place.

Conclusion

One is always reluctant when speculating about the future in politics. A decade ago few predicted lasting Republican control of the House. Compared with the presidency and the Senate, it appeared to be the institution in which the Democrats had the strongest competitive advantage. But now it is the House where Republican control, although narrow, appears to be the firmest. With good reason, few political observers gave the Democrats much chance of recapturing the House in the 2004 elections, but the presidency, and to a lesser degree the Senate, are viewed as in play. Should Democrats win the presidency and/or the Senate in 2004, it is likely that House Republicans will again face many of the frustrations they did during the Clinton presidency and for that part of the 107th Congress following the Jeffords switch. Should President Bush be reelected in 2004 and Republicans maintain or even marginally increase the size of their House and Senate majorities, House Republicans will be in a far stronger position to push a conservative policy agenda. With a president who no longer faces the moderating influence of reelection concerns and with a few additional Republican senators, an increasingly uniform, conservative Republican House majority with an empowered party leadership will not simply be able to pass its policy preferences through the House. It will also no longer see many of its efforts stymied elsewhere. Under those circumstances we may witness a Republican revolution that, unlike the one of 1994, is more substantive than symbolic. Ironically, the capacity to advance its legislative agenda beyond the support levels that exist in the public is perhaps the biggest potential threat to extending the era of Republican House control.

Notes

1. For a more extensive discussion of the era of Democratic dominance, and the subsequent takeover by Republicans in the 104th Congress, see Lawrence C. Dodd and Bruce I. Oppenheimer, "Revolution in the House: Testing the Limits of Party Government," in *Congress Reconsidered,* 6th ed., Lawrence C. Dodd and Bruce I. Oppenheimer, (Washington, D.C.: CQ Press, 1997). See also David W. Rohde, *Parties and Leaders in the Postreform House* (Chicago: University of Chicago Press, 1991); Gary W.

Cox and Mathew D. McCubbins, *Legislative Leviathan: Party Government in the House* (Berkeley: University of California Press, 1993); Barbara Sinclair, *Legislators, Leaders, and Lawmaking: The U.S. House of Representatives in the Postreform Era* (Baltimore: Johns Hopkins University Press, 1995).

2. For a helpful discussion of the development of the committee system and its contemporary role, see Christopher J. Deering and Steven S. Smith, *Committees in Congress,* 3rd ed. (Washington, D.C.: CQ Press, 1997).
3. See "Influential Since the 1940s, the Conservative Coalition Slips into History in 1998," *1998 CQ Almanac* (Washington, DC.: CQ Press, 1999), section B, 9. Congressional Quarterly designated a vote as signaling the appearance of the conservative coalition when a majority of southern Democrats and Republicans voted against a majority of northern Democrats.
4. Douglas L. Koopman, *Hostile Takeover: The House Republican Party, 1980–1995* (Lanham, Md.: Rowman and Littlefield, 1996); William F. Connelly Jr. and John J. Pitney Jr., *Congress' Permanent Minority? Republicans in the U. S. House* (Lanham, Md.: Rowman and Littlefield, 1994).
5. An excellent discussion of the development of the speakership is Ronald M. Peters Jr., *The American Speakership* (Baltimore: Johns Hopkins University Press, 1990). For a helpful analysis of the Gingrich speakership, see Peters's essay "The Republican Speakership" (paper presented at the annual meeting of the American Political Science Association, San Francisco, August 29–September 1, 1996).
6. C. Lawrence Evans and Walter J. Oleszek, *Congress under Fire: Reform Politics and the Republican Majority* (Boston: Houghton Mifflin, 1997).
7. On the coup effort, see Jackie Koszczuk, "Coup Attempt Throws GOP off Legislative Track," *Congressional Quarterly Weekly Report,* July 19, 1997, 1671–1674.
8. Richard E. Cohen, "The Rise and Fall of Newt," *National Journal* 31 (March 6, 1999): 598.
9. Richard E. Cohen, "It's Campaign 2000, Stupid," *National Journal* 31 (September 25, 1999): 2714.
10. David Baumann, "A Republican Resurgence," *National Journal* 32 (May 6, 2000): 1414
11. On the strategy of constructive partisanship and its potential advantages to House Republicans, see Lawrence C. Dodd and Bruce I. Oppenheimer, "Congress and the Emerging Order: Conditional Party Government or Constructive Partisanship?" in *Congress Reconsidered,* 6th ed., ed. Dodd and Oppenheimer, 410–412.
12. Richard E. Cohen and Eliza Newlin Carney, "A Do-Little Congress?" *National Journal* 31 (February 13, 1999): 394.
13. On Eisenhower's moderate domestic stance and the limits of his early presidency as a period of conservative policy initiatives, see Richard E. Cohen, "When Foreign Policy Was the Focus," *National Journal* 33 (January 13, 2001): 124.
14. "A Tumultuous Year in Congress," *CQ 2001 Almanac Plus, 107th Congress, 1st Session,* Vol. 57 (Washington, DC.: Congressional Quarterly, 2003), section 1, 4.
15. Richard E. Cohen and David Baumann, "The GOP's Drive to Deliver," *National Journal* 33 (May 12, 2001): 1402.
16. Richard E. Cohen, "Incivility Reigns," *National Journal* 33 (March 10, 2001): 707–708; Alexis Simendinger and Richard E. Cohen, "The Comeback Challenge," *National Journal* 33 (May 12, 2001): 1386.
17. Cohen and Baumann, "The GOP's Drive to Deliver," 1402–1403.
18. David Baumann, "Senate's Earthquake Shakes Up the House," *National Journal* 33 (May 26, 2001): 1577.
19. Richard E. Cohen and David Baumann, "The Burden of the House, *National Journal* 33 (July 21, 2001): 2325–2326.

20. Karen Foerstel with Lori Nitschke, "Revolt of the Moderates Tests House Leadership," *National Journal* 33 (July 21, 2001): 1744–1745.
21. "A Tumultuous Year in Congress," section 1, 8.
22. Cohen and Baumann, "The Burden of the House."
23. David Baumann and Richard E. Cohen, "As the Surplus Drops, So Do Expectations," *National Journal* 33 (September 1, 2001): 2672.
24. James A. Barnes, "The Economic Blame Game," *National Journal* 33 (September 8, 2001): 5770.
25. The characterization of the congressional response on 9/11 is based on a fuller summary in "A Tumultuous Year in Congress," 9, 12.
26. Ibid., 9.
27. Burt Solomon, "All Leadership, All the Time," *National Journal* 33 (December 1, 2002): 3663.
28. Our overview discussion of the president's initiatives and the congressional response relies in substantial part on "A Tumultuous Year in Congress," 9–11.
29. Ibid., 10.
30. Ibid., 10–11.
31. Solomon, "All Leadership, All the Time."
32. William Schneider, " 'Daddy Issues' Grab Center Stage," *National Journal* 34 (January 26, 2002): 278.
33. Charlie Cook, "Crisis Dims Democrats' Recruiting Prospects," *National Journal* 33 (September 29, 2001): 3022.
34. William Schneider, "Nation's New Attitudes Boost GOP," *National Journal* 33 (October 20, 2001): 3298; David Baumann, "Time for Domestic Tranquility," *National Journal* 33 (September 15, 2001): 2845–2846.
35. "A Tumultuous Year in Congress," 11.
36. Richard E. Cohen, "The Mean Season at Ways and Means," *National Journal* 33 (October 20, 2001): 3260.
37. William Schneider, "Domestic Issues Making a Comeback," *National Journal* 33 (December 15, 2001): 3890.
38. "A Tumultuous Year in Congress," section 1, 12.
39. David Nather, "Years of Power and Penance: His Standing Restored, Armey Bows Out," *CQ Weekly Report* (December 15, 2001): 2967.
40. Karen Foerstel, " 'The Hammer' Becomes the Heir Apparent," *CQ Weekly Report* (December 15, 2001): 2963.
41. Charlie Cook, "Whip's Race Is Personal for House Democrats," *National Journal* 33(October 6, 2001): 3112–3113.
42. "A Tumultuous Year in Congress," section 1, 11.
43. Richard E. Cohen, "The Struggle for Relevancy," *National Journal* 33 (November 17, 2001): 3599.
44. Our discussion of the 2002 session relies in particular on the more extensive analysis in "Politics, Security Shape Agenda," *CQ 2002 Almanac Plus, 107th Congress, 2nd Session,* Vol. 58. (Washington, D.C.: Congressional Quarterly, 2003), section 1, 3–15.
45. Ibid., section 1, 7.
46. "Politics, Security Shape Agenda," section 1, 7
47. James Kitfield, "Deferring to the President," *National Journal* 34 (October 19, 2002): 3054; "Politics, Security Shape Agenda," section 1, 8.
48. James A. Barnes, "Stumbling Toward 2004," *National Journal* 34 (November 9, 2002): 3340–3341.
49. Gary C. Jacobson, *The Politics of Congressional Elections,* 6th ed. (New York: Pearson Longman, 2004), 194–195.
50. Ibid., 196.

51. With five party switchers and a seat gain in a special election, the Republican total during the 104th Congress did reach 236 seats.
52. Norman J. Ornstein, Thomas E. Mann, and Michael J. Malbin, *Vital Statistics on Congress, 2001–2002* (Washington, D.C.: AEI Press, 2002), 67.
53. This counts Louisiana's Democratic congressman Rodney Alexander as a Republican because he announced that he would seek reelection as a Republican.
54. Peter E. Harrell, "Counting on a National Surge," *CQ Weekly,* June 19, 2004, 1464–1465.
55. The underlying partisan safety of so many House districts may also reduce the attractiveness of leaving the House to run for other offices.
56. "Leading Scorers: Party Unity," *CQ Weekly,* January 3, 2004, 16.
57. Richard E. Cohen and Marilyn Werbert Serafini, "A House Less Divided," *National Journal* 34 (November 9, 2002): 3280–3283; Carl M. Cannon and Richard E. Cohen, "The Politics of Promise," *National Journal* 34 (November 16, 2002): 3382–3386.
58. Gebe Martinez, "Despite Post-Election Opportunities, Democrats Struggle to Find One Voice," *CQ Weekly,* December 14, 2002, 3258–3260; Charlie Cook and Amy Walter, "House Democrats Face Long Odds in 2004," *National Journal* 34 (November 23, 2002): 3508–3509.
59. Clive Crook, "What If This Is as Good as It Gets," *National Journal* 34 (November 16, 2002): 3380–3381; Alexis Simendinger and Kirk Victor, "Dangerous Curves Ahead," *National Journal* 34 (November 16, 2002): 3387–3391.
60. Jonathan E. Kaplan, "Selling Medicare Reform," *The Hill,* February 24, 2004; Ralph Z. Hallow, *Washington Times,* February 18, 2004.
61. Richard E. Cohen, "A Message that Might Need Messaging?" *National Journal* 36 (July 3, 2004): 2099. The quotes in this paragraph are from Cohen's analysis in this article.
62. John Cochran, "Disorder in the House—And No End in Sight," *CQ Weekly,* April 3, 2004, 790.
63. Ibid.
64. Karen Foerstel with Lori Nitschke, "Revolt of the Moderates Tests House Leadership," *CQ Weekly,* July 21, 2001, 1744.

3. What the American Public Wants Congress to Be

John R. Hibbing and Christopher W. Larimer

Congress is designed to be a permeable institution. If it is doing its job, public opinion should be able to enter and affect the policy actions that Congress takes. This reflection of public views in congressional policy decisions is called "representation," and Congress is specially designed to facilitate it. Large collections of formally equal officials, who are subject to frequent elections and remarkably open operating procedures, and who are all directly responsible for acting in the interests of specific groups of constituents, should generate policy representation, if any institutional structure can. Indeed, if Congress were not representative, why would we have it? A smaller, more hierarchical body is far better at getting things done, but "getting things done" is not the only goal of government. After all, the cry of the American Revolution was not "No taxation unless it is enacted by an efficient, hierarchical body"; it was "No taxation without representation."

The question of whether or not Congress is successful in fulfilling its constitutional mission to provide policy representation is one that has occupied observers for quite some time. Although liberals tend to think Congress is too conservative, and conservatives tend to think it is too liberal, for the most part the people prefer centrist policies and believe Congress provides centrist policies. Certainly, on some issues policy can be out of step with majority public sentiment, but occasional policy inconsistencies seem to be more the exception than the rule. In general, Congress addresses the issues the public believes to be important and acts on those issues in the moderate ways the public prefers.

But public opinion can also affect Congress in a manner quite different from its influence on specific policy decisions. The public's opinion of Congress itself can serve as an important institutional constraint on it. If the public strongly disapproves of Congress, sitting members may decide against seeking reelection and prospective candidates may decide against running for a seat in the first place. If members are traumatized by negative public opinion of them and of Congress, they may be reluctant to address new policy initiatives, especially any that are controversial. And solid evidence even suggests that negative views of Congress render people less likely to comply with the laws it passes.[1]

Given these important consequences of public attitudes toward Congress, it is imperative that we understand the factors that lead the public to regard the institution favorably or unfavorably. In this chapter we employ data and arguments from a variety of sources to explicate the reasons people feel as they do toward the American Congress. Our presentation is divided into five main parts. In the first, we look at variations in the public's opinion of Congress since the mid-1970s, asking why attitudes seem to be more favorable at some times than others. In the second, we briefly compare attitudes toward Congress with attitudes toward other institutions, especially political institutions. In the third, we look at public opinion of the many different parts of Congress. In the fourth, we determine the kinds of people who seem most willing to proffer negative evaluations of Congress. These sections are tied together by the hope that determining the situations under which a favorable (or unfavorable) judgment of Congress is returned will permit a clearer view of the reasons the public feels as it does. We then conclude with a summary of our theory of public support for the political system, for political institutions, and especially for the Congress.

Why People Like Congress More at Certain Times

Maybe the public simply detests Congress, and that is all that needs to be said on the matter. Perhaps it is erroneous to think that Congress, under any circumstances, could be even remotely popular. As tempting as it may be to jump to this conclusion and as much as popular press coverage encourages such inclinations, the situation is actually much more complex. Survey data from across the decades reveal a surprising amount of variation, as is apparent in Figure 3-1, which presents the percentage of people approving of Congress from 1974 through 2003, according to various Gallup polls.

The last quarter of the twentieth century began with Congress (and the rest of the political system) struggling to pull itself out of a trying period. In fact, although soundings were taken much less frequently prior to 1975, the data that are available demonstrate that the mid-to-late 1960s was a period of relative popularity for Congress and for all of government. But starting about 1968 and continuing into the first half of the 1970s, the public's approval of political institutions and, indeed, societal institutions generally declined precipitously.[2] Thus the opening data points in the figure, coming on the heels of the Watergate scandal and other societal frustrations, reflect a disillusioned people, and barely one out of four American adults approved of Congress.

After these initial low ratings, the rest of the figure suggests three phases of congressional approval: high, low, and high again. By 1985 Watergate and perhaps the economic difficulties of the late 1970s and early 1980s were distant memories, and the Reagan "feel-good" period had arrived. Well over half of the American public approved of the job Congress was doing in the latter 1980s. But by 1992 approval levels had reverted to 1970s levels or worse, with sometimes just one in five adults approving of Congress. Just before the 1994 midterm elections, Congress's popularity bottomed out with a whopping 75 percent of the population *disapproving* of the job Congress was doing.

This high level of dissatisfaction with Congress continued well into the mid-1990s even though by then the economy had long been booming. In fact, it was not until very late 1997 that approval levels turned around. By January 1998 more people approved of Congress than disapproved, a situation that had not been seen since the late 1980s. Approval levels then stayed high until

Figure 3-1 Approval of Congress, 1974–2003

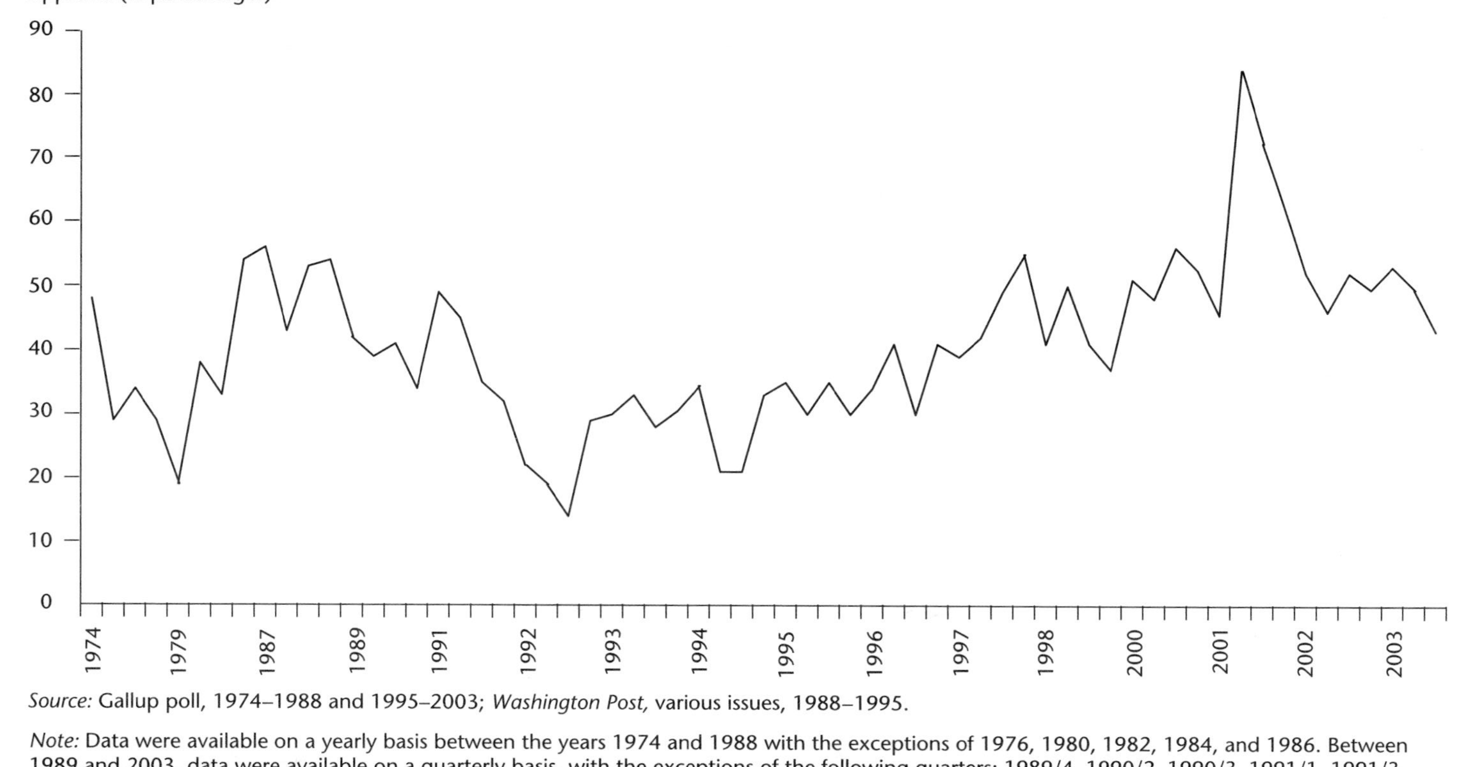

Source: Gallup poll, 1974–1988 and 1995–2003; *Washington Post,* various issues, 1988–1995.

Note: Data were available on a yearly basis between the years 1974 and 1988 with the exceptions of 1976, 1980, 1982, 1984, and 1986. Between 1989 and 2003, data were available on a quarterly basis, with the exceptions of the following quarters: 1989/4, 1990/2, 1990/3, 1991/1, 1991/3, 1992/3, 1992/4, 1994/2, 1995/2, 1996/4, 1999/4, 2000/2, and 2002/2.

impeachment proceedings were commenced in the House against President Bill Clinton. In August 1998 Congress was enjoying 55 percent public approval, but as soon as impeachment of the president became the dominant congressional issue these marks began to drop, although perhaps not as much as might have been expected. By early 1999 approval was down more than 10 points to 44 percent. And then, as the painful national episode faded, approval of Congress improved slightly, to the upper 40s by the end of 1999. The divisive period reduced public approval of Congress but never threatened to return approval to the low levels of the late 1970s or early 1990s.

In fact, congressional approval remained high from George W. Bush's election in 2000 until September 11, 2001, the day of the tragic terrorist attacks on New York and Washington. For a period of time after the attacks, the American public responded favorably to any symbol of the country, including Congress. Approval of Congress spiked to 84 percent, an unprecedented level. During this time, people did not feel comfortable criticizing a pillar of American government such as Congress, and they were pleased that members of Congress were united on the tasks of repairing the damage, punishing the perpetrators, and preventing future attacks. People are much more favorable toward politics when politicians are not disagreeing among themselves.

Predictably, however, support levels as high as those in late 2001 proved ephemeral. Members of Congress began to debate specifics, unity evaporated, partisanship re-emerged, and more typical congressional approval levels quickly returned. By early 2002, not even six months after 9/11, congressional approval had returned to its pre–9/11 level (but bear in mind that pre–9/11 approval levels were high by historical standards, between 40 and 50 percent). Even setting aside the post–9/11 spike, congressional approval from 1998 to early 2004 looks much more like the high levels of the mid and late 1980s than the low levels of the 1970s and the early 1990s.

Taken as a whole, the pattern is not an easy one to explain. Societal conditions seem to affect the public's approval of Congress, but the relationship is not as powerful as is usually anticipated. The effects of 9/11 were brief, and economic conditions are sometimes strong when approval of Congress is weak (the mid-1990s, for example) and sometimes weak when approval is strong (2000–2002). The authors of the most systematic effort to account for the ups and downs of public approval discovered that economic conditions have far less impact on congressional than on presidential approval.[3] A broader analysis of attitudes toward various parts of government, including Congress, found that "it is by no means clear that economic performance has actually played a decisive role in generating [the] decline in trust."[4]

If societal conditions such as the health of the economy and international incidents explain only a portion of changes in the public's attitudes toward Congress (and the entire polity), then what accounts for the rest? One obvious possibility is that people are more influenced by congressional actions than by societal conditions and events. Rather than holding Congress accountable for society generally, approval of the job Congress is doing may actually depend, sensibly enough, on perceptions of the job Congress is doing. Evidence presented in previous research supports this possibility, but the particular congressional actions that warm the hearts of most Americans are not the actions that one might expect. The substance of legislation that Congress passes rarely affects the institution's popularity, but its mode of operation does. In fact, when Congress is engaged in debate, when it is busy passing legislation (any legislation) and checking presidential power, people are more likely to be dissatisfied.[5] One writer correctly observes that "the less people hear from Congress, the higher Congress' ratings soar."[6]

This surprising finding suggests that conflict in the political arena is not something the American public likes to see, largely because the public commonly believes that consensus is wide in the United States, and so conflict in the political arena is unnecessary. Many people may prefer divided government, but that does not mean they like to see open conflict between Congress and the president and between the parties in Congress.[7] The more that parties and institutions are at odds, the more the people believe the interests of ordinary Americans are being neglected. For most people, the model for how government should work is the response to 9/11 or the passage of the balanced budget agreement in late 1997. Here were instances in which the major institutions of government, as well as politicians of all parties, quietly cooperated in addressing problems the public felt to be the most pressing facing the country at the time. People were spared the partisan hyperbole and gamesmanship they so dislike. It is probably not a coincidence that approval of Congress went up shortly after each of these events.

People do not want an activist, contentious, marketplace-of-ideas Congress, and they are unable to fathom why earnest problem solving cannot be the norm rather than the exception. Citizens are more likely to approve of Congress when it is being still and not rocking the boat, even though, somewhat contradictorily, they like having Congress check presidential power in the abstract. For much of the public, conflict is a sign that elected officials are out of touch with ordinary, centrist Americans and that they are too much "in touch" with nefarious special interests. The leaders of Congress have recognized the public's inclinations and have been known to trim the sails of the legislative agenda when they are concerned about public perceptions of the institution. Thus, Congress may go into "hibernation" when an election is approaching and approval ratings are high.[8]

Why People Like Other Components of the Political System More Than Congress

So, public approval of Congress varies and does so in predictable, if in some respects counterintuitive, ways. If conditions (especially economic ones) are

Figure 3-2 Approval of the Federal Government and Its Parts, 1998

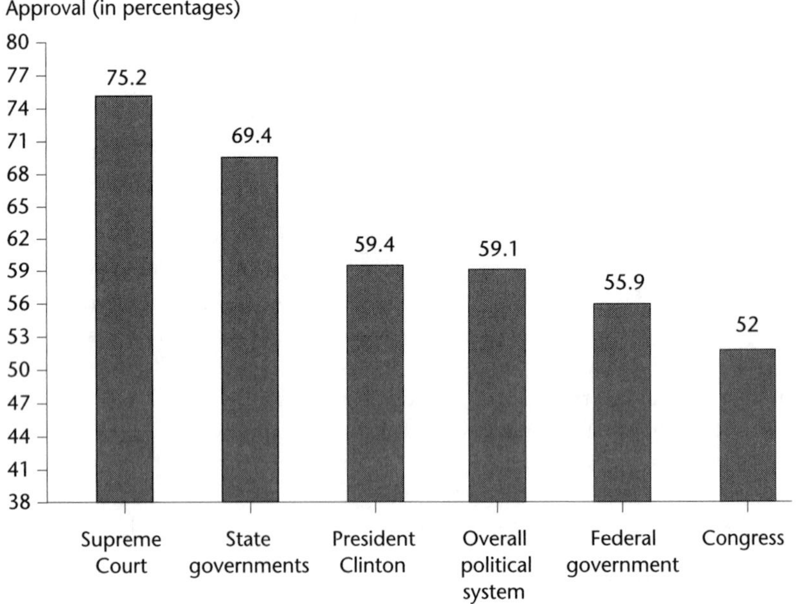

Source: 1998 Gallup Survey on Preferences for Government Processes; see John R. Hibbing and Elizabeth Theiss-Morse, *Stealth Democracy: Americans' Beliefs about How Government Should Work* (New York: Cambridge University Press, 2002).

favorable and Congress is not caught in the unforgivable acts of openly debating tough policy issues, representing diverse views, and pursuing activist legislative agendas, Congress is likely to be approved of by more than half of the American public. Still, it is unlikely that even under these conditions Congress will be nearly as popular as just about any other feature of government in the United States. Despite ups and downs over time, relative to other institutions and levels of government, Congress is consistently liked the least. This conclusion is apparent in Figure 3-2.

These results come from a Gallup survey administered in early 1998 to a random sample of 1,266 adults in the United States.[9] Respondents were asked whether or not they approved of six different aspects of government, including the "overall political system." As may be recalled from Figure 3-1, this particular (pre-impeachment) time period was one in which Congress was relatively popular, so we see that a respectable 52 percent of the respondents approved of Congress. Compared with other components of the political system, however, approval of Congress fares much worse. Specifically, Congress is the least liked part of the political system. Even the federal government as a whole is more popular (56 percent approval). The overall political system (including state governments) is at 59 percent approval, which is about the same approval level accorded President Clinton at that time (it may be recalled that a few months later, with impeachment proceedings in full swing, his popularity, unlike Congress's, went up several percentage points). Levels of approval for state government are quite a bit higher than for the federal government (69 to 56 percent), and the Supreme Court is easily the most popular political body, with better than three out of four Americans approving of it.

Lest it be thought that the spring of 1998 was unusual, we present Figure 3-3. According to those data (taken from the Harris poll's annual "confidence" battery), the Supreme Court is almost always the most popular institution and Congress is almost always the least popular. If anything, the gap between congressional approval and approval of both the Supreme Court and the president has grown in the last fifteen to twenty years, but the gap has always been there. Even through the Watergate scandal, the public expressed more confidence in the presidency than in Congress, although confidence in Jimmy Carter late in his term did momentarily dip below confidence in Congress. Thus, the rank order of the popularity of governmental institutions is quite consistent over time, and the distance separating the institutions appears to have grown.

The variations in approval displayed in Figure 3-2 are not easy to explain. The two most popular referents are two of the most different. State government, we might speculate, is relatively popular because it is perceived to be close to the people. But if that is what people like, why is the Supreme Court even more popular than state government? Of all the elements of government, the Supreme Court is undoubtedly the most detached from the people: just nine justices, all with life terms and no real representational role, and who seem to delight in being distant and insular. What is it about the Supreme Court that makes it so much more popular than Congress?

The answer offered in the previous section—that people are put off by political conflict—fits equally well with the results in this section. Compared with Congress, the Supreme Court has developed an amazing capacity to cloak its conflict. If open warfare occurs among the justices, it is hidden behind curtains and a vow of secrecy; and if conflict occurs between the Court and another political institution, it is not typically the stuff of front-page news stories. Thus, the Supreme Court is popular for all the reasons Congress is not, particularly its ability to keep the people from seeing what is going on inside. Contrary to common interpretations, political popularity is not enhanced by openness, by democratic accountability, or by representation of diverse popular views. Rather, it is often enhanced by processes that move to some kind of resolution without a lot of fuss and blather, even if some measure of accountability is sacrificed in the process. Congress is relatively unpopular with the public precisely because it is so public.

Figure 3-3 Confidence in Political Institutions, 1972–2003

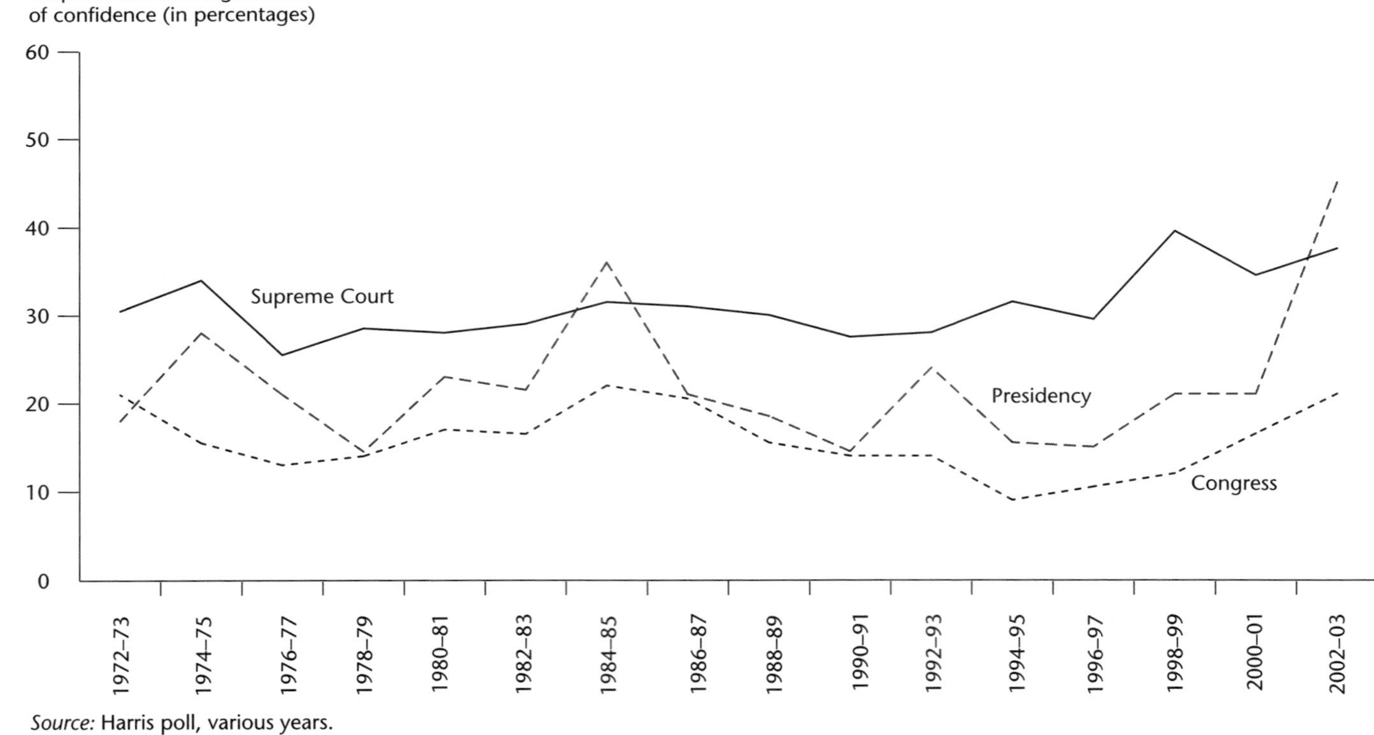

Source: Harris poll, various years.

Note: Data for Congress for the years 1973 and 1991 and for the presidency for 1972 were unavailable.

Why People Like Certain Parts of Congress More Than Others

Further information on the reasons people feel as they do about Congress can be obtained by paying careful attention to the aspects of Congress they do and do not like. Congress, of course, is an amazingly multifaceted institution. It is not just organized into many different parts, but it is organized along many different lines: Parties, committees, caucuses, delegations, leadership structures, staffs, and two separate houses all play important roles in congressional organization, and it is quite likely that, just as the people like some components of the political system more than others, they also like some components of Congress more than others.

Love Our Member but Hate Our Congress?

One of the most oft-repeated points about congressional popularity is that people "hate Congress but love their own member of Congress."[10] Survey research consistently provides support for this observation. According to polling conducted by the National Election Studies at the University of Michigan in 1980, 88 percent of the people approved of their own member of the House, but only 41 percent approved of Congress itself. In recent years this gap diminished a little but remained quite large. People clearly distinguish between their own member and a generic "Congress."

This conclusion may be only part of the story, however. When people are asked to evaluate "Congress," what comes to their mind? Most of them probably envision a tumultuous collection of 535 members, and they often do not approve of this image. But when the public actually thinks of Congress less as a collection of inevitably flawed human beings and more as an important institutional component of the nation's governance, reactions are likely to change noticeably. This speculation is supported by the results obtained from a 1992 survey that are presented in Figure 3-4.

In the battery of questions used to compile this figure, respondents were asked whether or not they approved of four different congressional referents. The first was "all members of Congress." The second was "the leaders of Congress." The third was "their own member of Congress." And the fourth was "Congress as an institution of government, no matter who is in office."[11] The different reactions evoked by these various referents are noteworthy. Dissatisfaction is certainly generated by mention of "all members" and of "congressional leaders." Only one in four Americans approved of these groups at the time the survey was taken. Approval levels of the respondent's "own member" were, as previous research has consistently demonstrated, much higher, with two of three responding favorably. But people were even more approving of Congress "as an institution," with a remarkable 88 percent approving. Although it is not tremendously surprising that people would respond positively to a question that weeds human foibles out

Figure 3-4 Evaluations of Congressional Referents, 1992

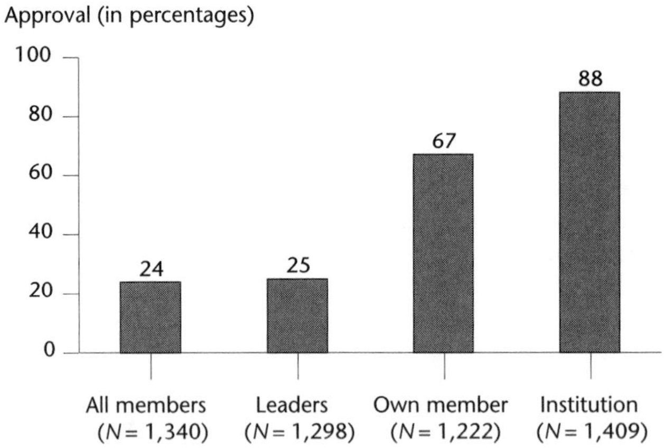

Approval (in percentages)

	All members (N= 1,340)	Leaders (N= 1,298)	Own member (N= 1,222)	Institution (N= 1,409)
Approval	24	25	67	88

Source: Perceptions of Congress Survey, 1992, conducted by the Bureau of Sociological Research at the University of Nebraska; see John R. Hibbing and Elizabeth Theiss-Morse, *Congress as Public Enemy* (New York: Cambridge University Press, 1995).

of the mix, it is still worth noting that people do not really disapprove of Congress; rather, they disapprove of the membership of Congress, their own member excepted of course.

Political Parties in Congress

In light of the fact that people are put off by conflict in the governmental process, it will come as no surprise that they view the political parties with disfavor. People believe that parties argue for selfish reasons rather than out of a desire to better the entire country. Parties are believed to be a central reason there is so much conflict and ineffectiveness in government. The following exchange occurred in a focus group session conducted in 1992 and is indicative of the public's stance:

> **Bob:** I think that there has to be major communication between . . . the Democrats and Republicans and the Senate and the House, you know, everybody. Just have to say, "There's a problem. We won't leave this room until it's fixed."
>
> **Lisa:** They never could do that.
>
> **Barb:** Take them all to Camp David.
>
> **Lisa:** No, they don't deserve anything that good. They need to be put in small spaces in the summertime that is not air conditioned, and say, "Get on the ball and do something!" And they'd do it.[12]

Although people do not think highly of parties in Congress generally, perhaps they are more favorable to their own party and any dissatisfaction stems from reaction to the other party. For the most part, this expectation is unfounded. Certainly, Democrats tend to be more pleased with Congress when there is a Democratic majority (as was the case for most of the second half of the twentieth century) and Republicans are more pleased when there is a Republican majority (as has been the case since 1994), but for many people party control is either unknown or irrelevant. Approval of Congress is influenced by partisanship, but not heavily.

After the Republican takeover of Congress in late 1994, many polling organizations began posing new questions. Rather than just asking people to evaluate the job of Congress (see Figure 3-1), they asked people to evaluate the job "the Republicans in Congress are doing" and, separately, the job "the Democrats in Congress are doing." By asking distinct questions about the two major parties, it has become possible to determine if evaluations of them move together or move in more of a zero-sum fashion. In turn, it has become possible to draw inferences about the manner in which people view the parties' role in Congress. If one party's demise in the eyes of the public is accompanied by the other party's rise, it would suggest that people credit (and blame) just one party, with the other party becoming an automatic counterbalance to the touchstone party (presumably the majority party). But if evaluations of the two parties in Congress move together—that is, if high approval of the Democratic Party in Congress is typically accompanied by relatively high approval of the Republican Party—it suggests a more institutionalized Congress in which the two parties, however much they seem to disagree with each other, share a common fate.

The data used to create Figure 3-5 come from various issues of the Harris polls and therefore follow the Harris practice of not just asking respondents if they approve or disapprove but asking them to evaluate performance as *excellent, pretty good, only fair,* or *poor. Excellent* and *pretty good* responses are then collapsed into positive verdicts, whereas *only fair* and *poor* responses are collapsed into negative verdicts. The figure plots positive reactions from December 1994 until the end of 2003, and there is less support for the "teeter-totter" than the "joined at the hip" view.[13]

We start our discussion of Figure 3-5 by noting the relative evaluation of the two parties in Congress. Setting aside the brief honeymoon period experienced by Republicans in Congress immediately after their ascension to majority status in late 1994, the figure breaks clearly into two periods demarcated by September 11, 2001. Prior to that date, Democrats in Congress (the minority party) were consistently more popular than Republicans in Congress (the majority party), a situation that, when more data are available, may well prove to be the norm. With power come expectations. But after 9/11 the pattern has been different, with Republicans, the majority party, being more popular. Our suspicion is that this change is due in part to the public's desire for a unified response in the wake of a threat to the nation and the associated popularity of providing

Figure 3-5 Evaluations of Parties in Congress, 1994–2003

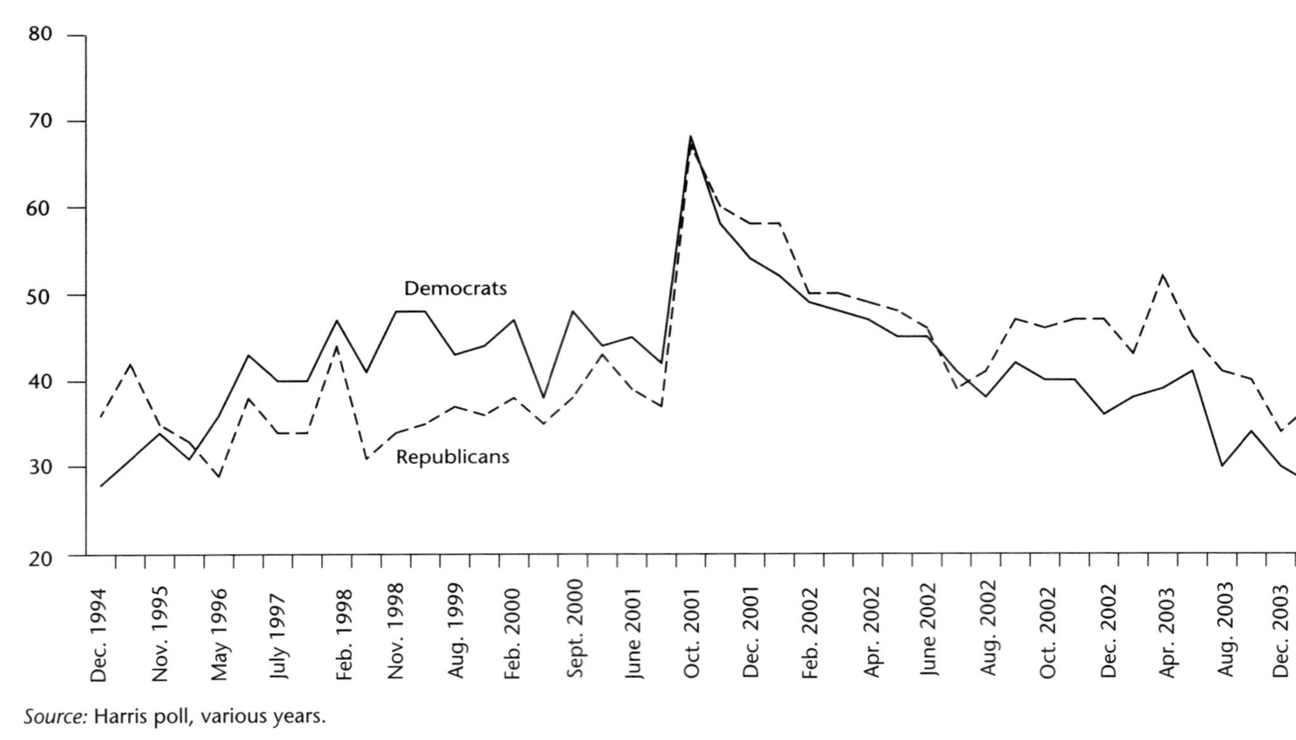

Source: Harris poll, various years.

Note: Questions were posed in uneven intervals, only during the months listed on the horizontal axis.

support for President Bush. It may be that with time the pattern will revert to one in which the majority party in Congress is usually marginally less popular than the minority.

Still, in overall terms it is clear that the congressional parties generally move up and down together. When support for one goes up, support for the other does too, though sometimes by slightly different amounts. As to level, take away the surge in approval after 9/11 and the message is one of stability. Approval levels have not changed much in the ten years these data have been collected, generally hovering in the 30 percent to 40 percent range. Some hint is present that support at the very beginning and the very end of the period is lower than it is during the other years.

Interest Groups

Political parties may not be viewed very favorably by the American public but they are not viewed nearly as unfavorably as interest groups or, as they are usually called by the people, "special interests." Whereas parties have an institutionalized place in the organization of Congress, it may seem that interest groups are not actually a part of Congress and thus not appropriate for this section. Although this is technically true, the American public sees an intimate and unseemly connection between Congress and special interest groups. In the 1998 Gallup survey mentioned earlier, respondents were asked whether they agreed or disagreed with the following statement: "Interest groups should be banned from contacting members of Congress." This proposal clearly violates the First Amendment right to "petition" the Congress, but an amazing 45 percent of all respondents agreed with it, suggesting the extent to which interest groups are viewed with suspicion. In another item from the same survey, 69 percent of all respondents felt special interests had "too much power," far higher than any other aspect of the political system.

Focus group comments concerning interest groups and their allegedly undeserved influence are equally unfavorable:

> **Maria:** They [politicians] think about who's in power, who's the dominant group. And they do the laws according to who's going to benefit from it. And they forget about the people down here, you know. . . . It doesn't work for the benefit of all the people, which it should.
>
> **Robert:** I think interest groups have too much control of what our elected officials say in our government. And Congresspeople are basically just like, well this guy gave me ten million dollars so no matter what I think, I've got to vote this way. They're bought, you know, bought by the interest group.
>
> **Sally:** I don't like the way they [members of Congress] seem so easily influenced by lobbyists. I don't . . . there should be a better way that money and influential groups that have a lot of money shouldn't be, shouldn't be able to influence the decisions . . . so easily.

The basis for this intense suspicion toward interest groups is easier to understand if we recall earlier references to the tendency of people to believe that real Americans are generally in agreement and thus to believe that noisy special interests must be a part of something else and must want to benefit only themselves and not the country as a whole. If this is people's perception, it is not surprising that they would see interest groups and the connection they have with members of Congress as the root of all that is evil in the political system.

Staffs and Other Features of the Institutionalized Congress

Because people tend to think members of Congress are acting to benefit themselves rather than ordinary Americans, they tend to be skeptical of the perquisites associated with the office, and there is an accompanying public desire to reduce the level of those perquisites. Thus, proposals to reduce the salary of members of Congress, to reduce the staff assistance of members of Congress, and to shorten the length of stay permitted members of Congress (term limits) are wildly popular with the American public. Typically, about 75 percent of the adult population wants to lower congressional salaries and limit terms of service. Questions measuring public support for congressional staff reductions are asked less frequently but, when they are, receive endorsement from almost as many people as term limits and salary cuts.

Lest it be thought that people's enthusiasm for these reforms is driven by an overestimation of the actual salary, staff support, and mean length of service in Congress, results obtained from a survey in late 1992 found that people do misperceive the salary and staff available to members of Congress, but they tend to underestimate, not overestimate, these benefits. On average, respondents guessed that members of Congress had 7.5 personal staffers, when at the time of the survey representatives averaged 17.4, and they underestimated the congressional salary by about $30,000. Finally, respondents also underestimated the typical length of career in Congress, guessing (on average) eight years when the real answer was eleven. Thus, providing the public with accurate information on salary, staff, and service would not put out the flames of public unrest with Congress but would actually fan those flames.[14]

It is difficult, but not impossible, to find aspects of Congress the public likes. Most people view the institution of Congress and their own member in favorable terms, but offsetting these positive feelings are strong negative feelings toward political parties, special interests, and the membership of Congress.[15] Moreover, the public does not seem to like the activities in which Congress is typically engaged. Fifty-six percent of respondents in the 1998 Gallup survey said they believed that compromise was just "selling out on principles." Eighty-four percent agreed that "elected officials would help more if they stopped talking and took action." And 69 percent expressed the belief that "the current system does not represent the interests of all Americans." If debate and compromise are viewed negatively, and if it is believed that Congress is not representing the interests of the people, it is no wonder that the overall reactions to the body are often negative.

Why Do Some People Like Congress More Than Others?

It is easy to lose sight of the fact that many people do approve of Congress—around 50 percent, in fact, since 1998. Just as Congress is more popular at some times than at others, so, too, is Congress looked upon more favorably by some people than by others. Identification of the kinds of individuals most likely to either approve or disapprove of Congress should allow us to say more about why Congress generates the kind of public reaction that it does. Thus, first, we compute the mean score of various demographic groups on our standard question regarding approval of Congress. Respondents were asked if they strongly approved, approved, disapproved, or strongly disapproved of "the way Congress has been handling its job lately."[16] *Strongly approve* responses were coded 4; *approve*, 3; *disapprove*, 2; and *strongly disapprove*, 1. A mean score of 2.5 would indicate that approving and disapproving answers were perfectly balanced among people falling in that category. The larger the number, the more approving the group. We computed mean approval scores for several demographic groups and report them in Table 3-1.

For example, there has been much talk lately about "angry, white males." Is it the case, then, that males and whites are less approving of Congress? Table 3-1 suggests there is little difference between males and females and between whites and nonwhites in attitudes toward Congress. The anticipated patterns are in evidence, but barely. Males are a little less approving of Congress than females (2.42 to 2.50) and whites are a little less approving than nonwhites (2.45 to 2.50), but differences of 0.08 and 0.05 on a 4-point scale are quite modest. The findings for most of the other demographic variables are similar. More education, perhaps surprisingly, does not bring much improvement in attitudes toward Congress. The pattern across income levels is not consistent. The youngest age bracket (eighteen to twenty-five) is the most approving of Congress, but after that there is no apparent pattern. And those who scored well on a four-question political knowledge test were not any more approving of Congress than their less-informed compatriots.[17]

Once we move to the area of simple political attitudes and identifications, relationships are only marginally more visible. With regard to party identification, even though Republicans controlled both houses of Congress at the time the survey was administered (1998), respondents identifying with the Democratic Party were more approving (but only slightly) than Republicans (2.57 to 2.53). The only real difference is produced by "independents." They are more negative toward Congress than either Democrats or Republicans (2.32) and, in fact, are the most negative of virtually any group. With regard to political ideol-

Table 3-1 Approval of Congress by Various Demographic Groups, 1998

	Mean Approval (1–4)	*N*
Gender		
Male	2.42	590
Female	2.50	620
Race		
White	2.45	1,008
Other	2.50	203
Age		
Less than 26	2.57	196
26–39	2.47	362
40–54	2.40	325
55–69	2.41	204
More than 70	2.49	123
Education		
Less than high school	2.43	144
High school	2.44	465
More than high school	2.47	312
4-year college	2.51	165
More than college degree	2.50	92
Income		
Less than $10,000	2.60	70
$10,000–$20,000	2.50	115
$20,000–$30,000	2.36	147
$30,000–$40,000	2.49	199
$40,000–$50,000	2.43	226
$50,000–$100,000	2.53	167
More than $100,000	2.31	63
Political knowledge (answers correct)		
0	2.40	90
1	2.55	270
2	2.45	485
3	2.42	349
4	2.46	18
Party identification		
Democrat	2.57	377
Independent	2.32	327
Republican	2.53	298
Ideology		
Liberal	2.35	275
Moderate	2.54	342
Conservative	2.47	569

Source: Computed by the authors from a 1998 Gallup Survey; see John R. Hibbing and Elizabeth Theiss-Morse, *Stealth Democracy: Americans' Beliefs about How Government Should Work* (New York: Cambridge University Press, 2002).

ogy, the pattern is the opposite of the one that might have been expected on the basis of party identification. Whereas partisan independents are the least supportive of Congress, ideological moderates are the most supportive (2.54), and whereas Democrats are the most supportive of Congress, ideological liberals are the least (2.35). Conservatives, like their closest partisan equivalent, Republicans, are in the middle (2.47). Independents may dislike Congress, but this should not be taken to mean that moderates do.

But the more important point is that the differences across all these standard demographic groups are surprisingly modest. If one attempts to describe the type of individual who is most likely to disapprove of Congress, it is clear that basing a description on people's age, gender, skin color, income, education, political knowledge, or even party identification and ideology will not be particularly helpful. To the extent that there are predictable patterns in who likes and dislikes Congress, we must look beyond demographics toward more specific political attitudes and preferences.

One reasonable expectation is that those who are satisfied with the policies government produces, other things being equal, will be more likely to approve of one of the most important shapers of those policies, the United States Congress.[18] The specific survey item we employ asked if respondents strongly agreed, agreed, disagreed, or strongly disagreed with the statement that they were "generally satisfied with the public policies the government has produced lately." But one of the themes that has surfaced throughout this chapter is that people's attitudes toward Congress are influenced by more than just the policies produced; they also seem to be influenced by people's attitudes toward certain processes of making policy.

For example, as alluded to earlier, two central activities in Congress are debate and compromise. Congress is designed to give voice to a wide variety of opinions from across the country and then to negotiate some type of brokered solution from this welter of preferences, so debate and compromise occupy much of the time of members of Congress. But, as indicated by the survey results referred to above, some ordinary people are not particularly tolerant of debate and compromise. In light of this fact, one obvious expectation is that those people who are less persuaded of the importance of debate and the necessity of compromise will also be disapproving of an institution as heavily invested in debate and compromise as Congress. The item we selected to measure people's perception of the necessity of compromise reads as follows: "The American people disagree with each other so much that politicians need to compromise in order to get anything done." The hypothesis is that the more strongly people agree with this statement, the more likely they will be to approve of Congress. To measure people's attitudes toward debate, we used this item: "Elected officials would help the country more if they would stop talking and just take action on important problems." We expect that the more strongly people agree with this statement, the less likely they will be to approve of Congress.

To test these hypotheses, we use regression analysis. Although the numbers generated by this technique seem confusing at first glance, a major advantage of

Table 3-2 Causes of Approval of Congress, 1998

Independent Variable	Regression Coefficient	Standard Error	Significance Level
Age	−0.01	0.02	.63
Gender	0.05	0.04	.24
Nonwhite	0.01	0.06	.87
Education	0.01	0.01	.16
Income	0.00	0.01	.47
Party identification	0.01	0.01	.38
Political knowledge	−0.08	0.03	.00[a]
Ideology	0.08	0.03	.00[a]
Like recent policies	0.34	0.04	.00[a]
See little value in debate	−0.10	0.03	.00[a]
See little need for compromise	−0.11	0.03	.00[a]
Constant	2.16	0.20	.00[a]

Source: Computed by the authors from a 1998 Gallup Survey; see John R. Hibbing and Elizabeth Theiss-Morse, *Stealth Democracy: Americans' Beliefs about How Government Should Work* (New York: Cambridge University Press, 2002).

$R^2 = .15$

Adj. $R^2 = .14$

$F = 12.63$ ($p < .00$)

$N = 795$

[a] = significant at (.01)

regression is that it is possible to control for the other variables included. If we relied only on results such as those presented in Table 3-1, we would not know, say, if young people (eighteen to twenty-five years old) were more favorable toward Congress because they tend to be ideological moderates or if ideological moderates tend to be more favorable toward Congress because many young people tend to be in the ideological middle. Thus, in Table 3-2 we present the results obtained when approval of Congress is regressed on all the variables in Table 3-1 plus the one policy and two procedural variables just described.

The top portion of the table indicates that most of the conclusions implied in Table 3-1 hold up in a more complete, multivariate specification. Age, gender, race, education, income, and party identification exert minimal or no effect on approval of Congress.[19] This leaves only two variables from Table 3-1 with significant coefficients. Other things being equal, conservatives are more likely to approve of Congress (which had a Republican majority at the time of the survey) than are liberals, and more surprisingly, the more political knowledge a person possesses the *less* likely that person is to approve of Congress. Although observers might have expected that political knowledge would lead to an understanding of the challenges of governing and, therefore, a more approving attitude toward institutions such as Congress, this is not the case. In fact, more knowledge seems to lead to higher expectations of government and, inevitably, disappointment with the actual performance of government. Knowledge of government does not equal an appreciation of the difficulties of arriving at a decision in the face of tremendously divided public opinion on most issues. This seems to be why variables tapping education and political knowledge tend to be either insignificant or in the unexpected direction. This is true of the findings we report here as well as the findings reported in much previous work.[20]

Certainly, people are more likely to approve of an institution if they are pleased with the policies it helps to produce. This is apparent to some extent in the results for ideology and even more directly in the coefficient for "like recent policies." In fact, this is the most powerful variable in the equation. People who like recent governmental policies are substantially more likely to approve of Congress, although with a question such as this there is always the danger that many people who approve of Congress are merely projecting desirable traits (such as agreeable policy choices) onto it. In any event, approval is undeniably connected to policy satisfaction.

What may be more surprising for some readers (but perfectly consistent with our expectations) is that even when controlling for the influence of policy satisfaction, people's attitudes toward the desirability of debate and the need for compromise are important predictors of attitudes toward Congress. These general attitudes toward abstract activities are unlikely to be the product of the kind of reverse causation described in the previous paragraph. Although a favorable attitude toward Congress may lead people to like recent policies, it is less likely to lead them to have positive attitudes toward compromise and debate. But these attitudes toward compromise and debate certainly are related to approval of Congress. The more that people believe "the country would be helped if elected officials would stop talking," the less likely they are to approve of Congress. And the more that people believe "compromise is unnecessary because of Americans' level of agreement with each other," the less likely they are to approve of Congress. These two relationships are strong and statistically significant.

This means that if more people realized the extent of policy disagreement in American society and the resultant need to discuss our differences and reach accord by being willing to compromise with those holding divergent views, Congress would then be a more popular institution. But when people view debate as bickering and see compromise as selling out, they naturally are less likely to approve of an institution that spends much of its time bickering and selling out. Even if people were given the exact policies they want, the results in Table 3-2 suggest that some of them would still be unhappy with Congress, assuming Congress continued to rely, as any representative institution in a divided society must, on open presentation of diverse opinions, discussion of those opinions, and brokered solutions.

Summary

When is Congress unpopular? Not surprisingly, it is unpopular when negative economic and other societal conditions exist, but also when Congress is particularly active and newsworthy in proposing and debating important legislative matters and balancing presidential power. Why is Congress less popular than other parts of government? The reason is that, more than those other parts, Congress is charged with giving voice to tremendously varied interests from across the country and then, in full public view, coming to a single policy decision in the face of that diversity. Which parts of Congress are particularly unpopular? Any part that can be seen as serving an interest narrower than the entire country, whether that interest belongs to a political party intent on winning an election, a special interest intent on securing a benefit for that particular group, or members of Congress (other than one's own member) intent on getting reelected so they can continue to lead the high life at the expense of hardworking American taxpayers. What kind of person is most likely to disapprove of Congress? Not surprisingly, it is someone who dislikes recent policy actions, but also someone who dislikes debate and who believes there is little need for politicians to compromise.

Taken together, these findings make it difficult to deny that the processes by which decisions are made matter. People are not consumed solely by the desire to obtain a certain policy outcome. Indeed, on an amazing number of issues, most people have weak or, more likely, nonexistent policy preferences. But even when people do not have a pre-existing preference on a policy issue, government action can still affect attitudes. In fact, it is precisely when people see governing officials spending copious amounts of time arguing about what the people regard to be trifling issues that they become most disgusted with government. Moreover, whether or not people have a pre-existing stake in a particular policy outcome, they have a standing preference that all policies result from a process designed to benefit the general welfare of all Americans rather than the specific welfare of fractious, overly influential, individual interests. The public unquestionably errs by assuming there is a reasonably consensual general will in as heterogeneous a country as the United States, but the fact remains that congressional popularity is damaged when the institution is perceived to act on the basis of narrow, selfish interests. And because virtually every congressional action is perceived by the people in precisely these terms, a popular Congress is usually an inert Congress.

Notes

The authors gratefully acknowledge the assistance of Elizabeth Theiss-Morse. Some of the data for this chapter were gathered thanks to a grant from the National Science Foundation (SES 97-09934).

1. On choosing to retire, see Sean Theriault, "Moving Up or Moving Out: Career Ceilings and Congressional Retirement," *Legislative Studies Quarterly* 23 (August 1998): 419–434; on deciding against running for Congress in the first place, see Linda L.

Fowler and Robert D. McClure, *Political Ambition: Who Decides to Run for Congress* (New Haven: Yale University Press, 1989); on avoiding controversial issues, see David Hess, "Congress Hibernating till Fall," *Houston Chronicle,* March 19, 1998, A8; and on not complying with the law, see Tom Tyler, *Why People Obey the Law* (New Haven: Yale University Press, 1990).

2. See Seymour Martin Lipset and William Schneider, *The Confidence Gap* (Baltimore: Johns Hopkins University Press, 1987).
3. Robert H. Durr, John B. Gilmour, and Christina Wolbrecht, "Explaining Congressional Approval," *American Journal of Political Science* 41 (January 1997): 195.
4. See Robert Z. Lawrence, "Is It Really the Economy, Stupid?" in *Why People Don't Trust Government,* ed. Joseph S. Nye Jr., Philip D. Zelikow, and David C. King (Cambridge: Harvard University Press, 1997), 111.
5. See John R. Hibbing and Elizabeth Theiss-Morse, *Congress as Public Enemy* (Cambridge: Cambridge University Press, 1995); Durr, Gilmour, and Wolbrecht, "Explaining Congressional Approval."
6. Hess, "Congress Hibernating till Fall."
7. On the public's preference for divided government, see Morris Fiorina, *Divided Government,* 2nd ed. (Boston: Allyn and Bacon, 1996).
8. Hess, "Congress Hibernating till Fall."
9. For more details, see John R. Hibbing and Elizabeth Theiss-Morse, *Stealth Democracy: Americans' Beliefs about How Government Should Work* (Cambridge: Cambridge University Press, 2002).
10. Richard F. Fenno Jr., "If, As Ralph Nader Says, Congress Is 'the Broken Branch,' How Come We Love Our Congressmen So Much?" in *Congress in Change: Evolution and Reform,* ed. Norman J. Ornstein (New York: Praeger, 1975).
11. For more information, see Hibbing and Theiss-Morse, *Congress as Public Enemy,* 42–46.
12. Ibid., 97.
13. It would be instructive to have this information extending back before the 1994 elections and the resulting switch in majority party, but these questions were not asked before December 1994.
14. Hibbing and Theiss-Morse, *Congress as Public Enemy,* 72–74. The national survey was commissioned by John Hibbing and Elizabeth Theiss-Morse and funded by the National Science Foundation. It was conducted by the Bureau of Sociological Research at the University of Nebraska.
15. We wish we had questions on committees, but the only one available comes from the 1998 Gallup survey and merely asks whether or not respondents agree that "Congress needs to have committees to get its work done." Better than 70 percent agreed that it did.
16. This national survey was commissioned by John Hibbing and Elizabeth Theiss-Morse and was funded by the National Science Foundation. It was conducted in 1998 by Gallup.
17. Only the bivariate relationships for age and gender are significant at the 0.05 level.
18. In fact, respondents view Congress as a more important shaper of policy than the president. See Hibbing and Theiss-Morse, *Congress as Public Enemy,* 51–53.
19. A separate code for "independent" would have shown a small but statistically significant negative effect.
20. See Roger H. Davidson, David M. Kovenock, and Michael K. O'Leary, *Congress in Crisis: Politics and Congressional Reform* (Belmont, Calif.: Wadsworth, 1968). For an extended discussion of the relationship between high expectations of Congress and subsequent evaluations, see Samuel C. Patterson and David C. Kimball, "Living up to Expectations: Public Attitudes toward Congress," *Journal of Politics* 59 (August 1997): 701–728.

Part II
Elections and Constituencies

4. Voters, Candidates, and Issues in Congressional Elections

Robert S. Erikson and Gerald C. Wright

Elections for the U.S. House of Representatives fascinate observers of American politics almost as much as presidential elections do. Unlike Senate elections, which come at staggered six-year intervals, House elections provide a regular biennial measure of the national electoral pulse. Interest in House elections centers on the partisan balance of seats and the electorate's collective motivations that underlie this verdict.

Another source of fascination with House elections is their large number. Every two years the composition of the new U.S. House is the result of 435 separate contests for 435 separate seats. In part, these outcomes are determined by national electoral forces. But also, to a large extent, they are determined by the candidates in the contests and the conduct of their individual campaigns.

In this chapter, we first examine the national forces in House elections and their influence on the partisan division of votes and seats. Next, we look at the role of candidates in individual House contests. Finally, we compare elections for the House with elections for the Senate.

The National Verdict in House Elections

The Founders designed the House of Representatives to be the popular branch of government. They expected elections for the House to reflect the ebb and flow of public preferences. And even though the Senate has also become responsive to public opinion, analysts and journalists continue to watch House elections for what they say about what the public wants and the future directions of U.S. public policy.

Until recently, the question of the partisan makeup of the House of Representatives would be framed as interest in the precise size of the Democrats' majority. For forty years—from the elections of 1954 to 1994—the Democrats controlled the House. Then, remarkably, in 1994 the electorate gave the Republicans the majority, surprising virtually all observers. Since the watershed 1994 election, the national campaign for the House of Representatives has transformed from a

Figure 4-1 Democratic House Seats and Vote Share, 1946–2002

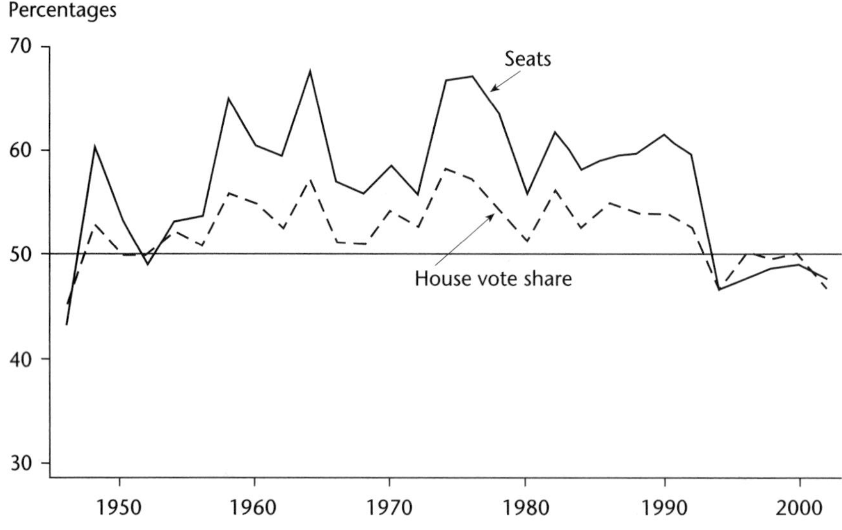

Source: Compiled by the authors.

tug-of-war over the majority Democrats' seat margin to a high-stakes battle for control of the institution itself. In the four elections from 1996 through 2002, the Republicans retained their newly won control, albeit by narrow margins. For the foreseeable future, House elections will be a battleground, with party control of the institution a matter of contention and doubt from one election to the next.

Over the second half of the twentieth century, the party division of House seats varied from 67 percent Democratic and 33 percent Republican (after the 1964 election), to 53 percent Republican and 47 percent Democratic after the historic 1994 contest. In terms of numbers, this is a range of ninety-one seats, out of 435, between each party's high-water and low-water marks. As Figure 4-1 shows, the partisan seat division follows closely (but imprecisely) from the national vote division. On average, the party that gains seats gains seven new seats (about 1.5 percent of the total) for each added percentage of the major-party vote. This ratio of seat percentage gained or lost per vote percentage gained or lost (1.5) is called the swing ratio.

The exact swing ratio varies from one election to the next, depending on several factors, such as where the votes are won and lost, as well as the competitiveness of the seats. For example, if one party gains most of its votes where the other party previously won by a large margin, then its added votes may not result in additional seats. If the party gains the same number of votes where the opposition party barely squeaked by in the last election, it gains more seats for the same number of votes.[1]

The Democratic run of party control that lasted for forty years was based on a stable but small Democratic majority of the congressional vote. In the twenty

House elections between 1954 and 1992, the national division of the major-party vote varied only within the narrow range of from 51 percent to 59 percent Democratic. Thus, a swing of only eight votes in a hundred separated the most Republican electoral tide from the most Democratic tide. Even when the electoral landscape changed dramatically in the Republicans' favor with the 1994 Republican landslide, the swing was due to a small minority of voters. Between 1992 and 1994, the national major-party vote shifted only six percentage points.

To summarize, changes in the party composition of congressional seats typically are a function of a small fraction of the electorate switching from one party to the other with its congressional vote. What causes these small changes in the partisan tide? Relevant explanatory variables include the electorate's party identification, the electorate's ideological mood, and reactions to the current presidential administration's performance.

The Partisan Base of the Congressional Vote

Most voters in the United States identify with one of the two dominant political parties—the Republicans or the Democrats. This identification provides voters with a standing decision to vote for their favored party—unless information from the current campaign gives them reason to temporarily defect with their vote. Most votes are partisan votes, and voters rarely change their partisanship. This provides a certain stability to the national congressional vote over time. The national division of party identification—sometimes called "macropartisanship"—is not a constant, however; small changes in macropartisanship imply small changes in the electorate's collective standing decision, and these carry electoral consequences. Macro-level changes in partisanship typically represent shifting evaluations of the parties' relative competence in governing, including the country's economic performance.

The national verdict in House elections closely follows the national division of party identification. Most Democrats vote Democratic; most Republicans vote Republican; and Independents usually split about fifty-fifty. The outcome of this process is the "normal vote." [2] Figure 4-2 illustrates macropartisanship and the House seat division over time.[3]

Now we gain some understanding of how the Democrats were able to control the House of Representatives for forty years. The Democrats were the dominant party in terms of party identification; thus more people voted Democratic than Republican. The Democrats' loss of their competitive advantage in partisanship in the late 1980s and early 1990s eventually caught up to them in 1994, with the Republicans' takeover.

Policy Mood

Partisanship is not the only force that shapes long-term voting patterns. In addition, the national verdict depends on the nation's collective preference for

Figure 4-2 Partisanship and House Seat Shares, 1946–2002

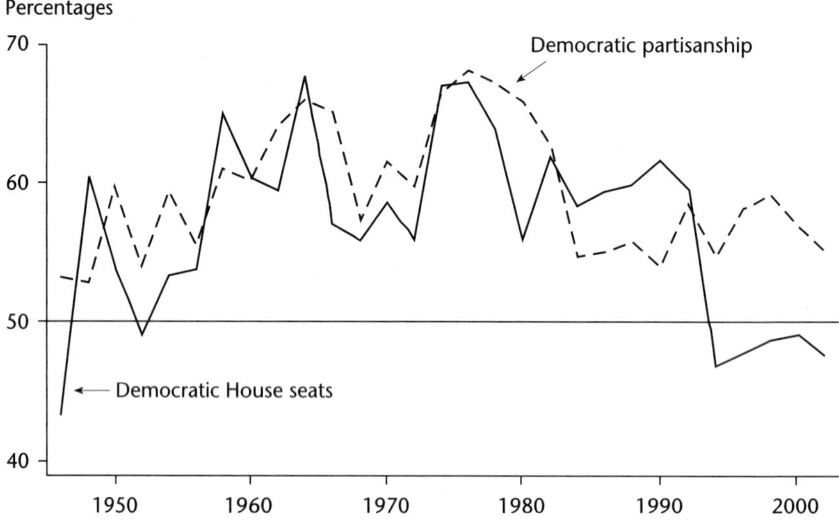

Source: Compiled by the authors.

Note: Partisanship is the average percentage of respondents identifying themselves as Democratic in third quarter Gallup national polls (the quarter just before the election).

more liberalism or more conservatism in its national policies—the nation's policy or ideological "mood." James Stimson has measured the nation's policy mood annually as a sophisticated composite of available public opinion polls.[4] The national electoral verdict for the House—as with elections for the presidency and for the Senate—is significantly related to the nation's ideological mood. When the public is in the mood for more government activism from Congress, it votes more Democratic. The most liberal mood, according to Stimson's index, was in the early 1960s, which was also a time of Democratic congressional dominance. The most conservative times were around 1952, at the start of Stimson's series, and around 1980, when Reagan was elected president with the help of considerable Republican strength in Congress.[5]

Presidential Election Years

In presidential years, the short-term forces of the presidential election and the House elections run in the same partisan direction, so that the party that performs better than the normal vote for president will also perform better than normal for Congress. Whether this happens because the House vote and the presidential vote are independently influenced by the same national issues or because some people decide their congressional vote based on their presidential vote is not clear. Whatever the cause, the phenomenon is known as the coattail effect, as if an extraordinary number of candidates of the winning presidential party are swept into office on the president's coattails.

Democratic coattails were at their strongest in 1964, when Lyndon Johnson's landslide victory created an overwhelming 295–140 Democratic majority. Republican coattails were particularly strong in 1980, when Ronald Reagan won the presidency. In some elections, presidential coattails appear to be virtually nonexistent. For instance, Clinton's reelection in 1996 carried so few Democratic House candidates to victory that the Democrats were unable to regain control of Congress.

The size of the coattail effect is decidedly irregular. One statistical estimate for post–World War II elections puts it at +.31 congressional votes nationally for every percent of the vote gained by the party at the presidential level.[6] Put another way, every added percentage point of the vote gained by a presidential candidate also adds almost one-third of a percentage point to the totals of the presidential candidate's congressional running mates. Before World War II, presidential coattails appeared stronger than they are today. The national presidential vote and the national congressional vote moved more in lockstep. One consequence of the weakening of the coattail effect is the increase in divided control of government, with one party controlling the presidency and the other party controlling at least one house of Congress.

Midterm Years

If one regularity has governed House elections throughout history it is the phenomenon of midterm loss—that the party controlling the presidency suffers a net loss of congressional seats in the election following the presidential contest. Through 1994, only once in the twentieth century, in 1934, did the presidential party gain seats at midterm.

In 1998 the midterm rule broke down, as the Democrats gained congressional seats while in control of the presidency, even as President Clinton was undergoing an impeachment investigation over the Lewinsky scandal. It happened again in 2002 when the Republicans gained seats as the presidential party, with President Bush still enjoying the fruits of his post-9/11 popularity. Although some congressional observers now see the rule of midterm loss as nothing more than an obsolete statistical oddity, that is a mistake. The string of sixteen consecutive midterm elections (1938–1994) in which the presidential party lost congressional seats is a regularity too strong to dismiss. It requires explanation.

The two leading explanations for midterm loss are "withdrawn coattails" and "ideological balancing." The former explanation ties the presidential party's midterm loss to the loss of presidential coattails. The latter ties it to an electoral tendency toward ideological balancing of the presidency and Congress.

The "withdrawn coattails" argument goes as follows: in presidential years the congressional vote for the president's party is inflated by presidential coattails. At the next midterm the congressional vote reverts to its "normal vote" outcome. The result is an electoral decline for the president's party.

This "withdrawn coattail" thesis has its plausibility.[7] Larger winning margins in the presidential elections usually lead to greater seat losses in the next midterm. Over the fourteen midterms from 1946 through 1998, on average the presidential party suffered a decline of 1 percent of the seats for every additional percentage of the vote in its win over the opposition in the prior presidential election. In other words, the larger the coattails that are withdrawn, the greater is the decline in seats. The "withdrawn coattails" thesis has a special appeal to explain the violation of the midterm loss rule in 1998. Clinton had virtually no coattails in 1996; therefore, with no coattails to withdraw in 1998, the Democratic congressional vote did not decline.

While the "withdrawn coattails" argument explains midterm loss in terms of the circumstances in the prior election, the "ideological balancing" thesis explains the loss in terms of the circumstances at midterm itself. By this theory, the electorate votes against the president's party at midterm as an ideological hedge. Moderate voters, seeing themselves ideologically between the Democratic and Republican positions, have some incentive to balance the president's ideology with a congressional vote for the "out" party. The process encourages divided government, with one party controlling the presidency and the other at least one house of Congress.[8]

Like "withdrawn coattails," the "balancing" thesis has its plausibility. On average over the fourteen midterm elections from 1946 to 1998 (equally divided between Republican and Democratic presidencies), each party has enjoyed about thirty-five more House seats when it did not control the presidency. In other words, the way for a party to achieve the highest level of success at midterm is to lose the prior presidential election. "Balancing" theory has its special appeal in that it would explain the violation of the midterm loss rule in 1998. In 1996, with party control of the House at stake, a potent partisan argument of the congressional campaign was that moderate voters should vote Republican for Congress to block Clinton, who everybody knew was about to be reelected. The 1996 result was no coattails and balancing in anticipation of Clinton's reelection. With balancing in advance (and no coattails to withdraw), the 1998 election became the exception to the rule of midterm loss for the presidential party.[9]

Neither coattails nor balancing, of course, can explain the Republican gains of 2002. The 2002 exception may have been due to the huge boost in Bush's popularity following the attacks of 9/11, as well as the Democrats' inability to mount an effective campaign.[10] Moreover, Republicans gained from redistricting following the 2000 Census.[11]

Electoral Change as a Search for Policy Direction

Every two years the electorate collectively chooses a new Congress, with a new partisan makeup. Does Congress's party composition reflect the electorate's policy preferences? The popular view, often propounded by pundits at election time, is that partisan tides reflect the electorate's changing ideological mood, as if Democratic gains signify a demand for more liberalism and Republican gains a demand for more conservatism. For example, the major Democratic gains associated with Johnson's landslide victory in 1964 were interpreted at the time as a mandate for a new liberal policy agenda. A conservative mood switch is identified with Reagan's surprise win in 1980 and the accompanying Republican gains in Congress. More recently, the Republican takeover of Congress in 1994 was widely proclaimed by the victors and the media to indicate a sharp rejection of the liberalism of President Clinton and the Democratic Party. In each case, Congress responded with legislation that matched the purported public cries for change.

It would be dangerous, however, to read every turn in partisan electoral fortunes as a demand for a change in policy direction. Many variables affect the national verdict apart from ideological demands, from the personal appeal of the presidential candidates, to the degree of national prosperity at the moment, to variables that are beyond our ability to measure. Still, among the conflicting signals from congressional election outcomes, the electorate's collective preference for more liberalism or more conservatism is an important part of the mix. Actually, the electorate was relatively liberal at the time of the Great Society and conservative when the Reagan revolution began; similarly, it was liberal when it elected Clinton and a Democratic Congress in 1992 but conservative in 1994. The electorate chooses the partisan makeup of the Congress (House and Senate) based in part on its preferred degree of policy liberalism, adjusting also for the expected ideological pressure from the occupant of the White House.

The Policy Consequences of Electoral Change

Election outcomes matter because the candidates who run under different party banners generally stand for very different policy agendas. We begin by showing how the parties differ on some representative issues, drawing on a survey of candidates in the 2002 elections conducted by Project Vote Smart (PVS).[12] Among other questions, PVS asked House candidates whether they wanted changes in a number of spending programs. In Figure 4-3 we plot the average responses of Democratic and Republican candidates to a set of questions asking them about what changes they would like to see in different policy programs. Here are the options they were given for each (along with the scores we used to construct the figure): *greatly increase* (+2), *slightly increase* (+1), *maintain status* (0), *slightly decrease* (−1), *greatly decrease* (−2), or *eliminate* (−3). The length of the bars in the figure indicates the averages (means) of how much party members wanted to increase or decrease each of the programs, and the direction of the bar indicates whether they wanted an increase or decrease: A bar to the left of the vertical line indicates more party members wanted to decrease than to increase the program; a bar extending to the right indicates an overall preference for increases in spending.

Figure 4-3 Spending Preferences of Republican and Democratic Congressional Candidates, 2002

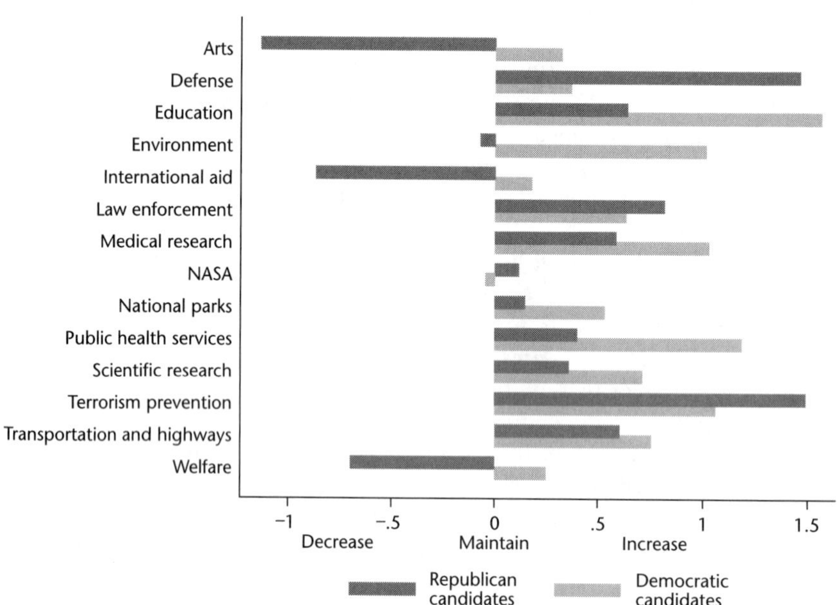

Source: Compiled by the authors from the 2002 Project Vote Smart Congressional National Political Awareness Test survey.

Note: Candidates were asked their preferences for spending for each program—decrease, maintain, or increase. The bars represent the average response for each party's candidate.

We see at the top of the figure that Republican candidates were strongly opposed to funding for the arts, while their Democratic counterparts held a slight preference for increases in spending. There are also some other areas in which the directions of preferences for changes in spending are quite clear: Republicans would cut funding for international aid and welfare, whereas Democrats prefer slightly more spending for those programs. By contrast, for several other programs the parties agree about the direction of spending changes but differ in how much. For example, Republican candidates, on balance, tend to favor modest increases in spending on education and on public health services, while Democrats are overwhelmingly in favor of increases in these policy areas. Republicans would provide the largest increases in funding to fight terrorism; Democrats agreed on the direction of funding but not on as high a level. All of these substantial differences align nicely with the programs identified with the two parties. Some policy areas are less partisan. Notice the small differences in spending preferences for NASA (the National Aeronautical Space Administration) and for transportation and highway infrastructure. In the overall pattern, we see that

Figure 4-4 Party Differences among House Candidates on Selected Issues, 2002

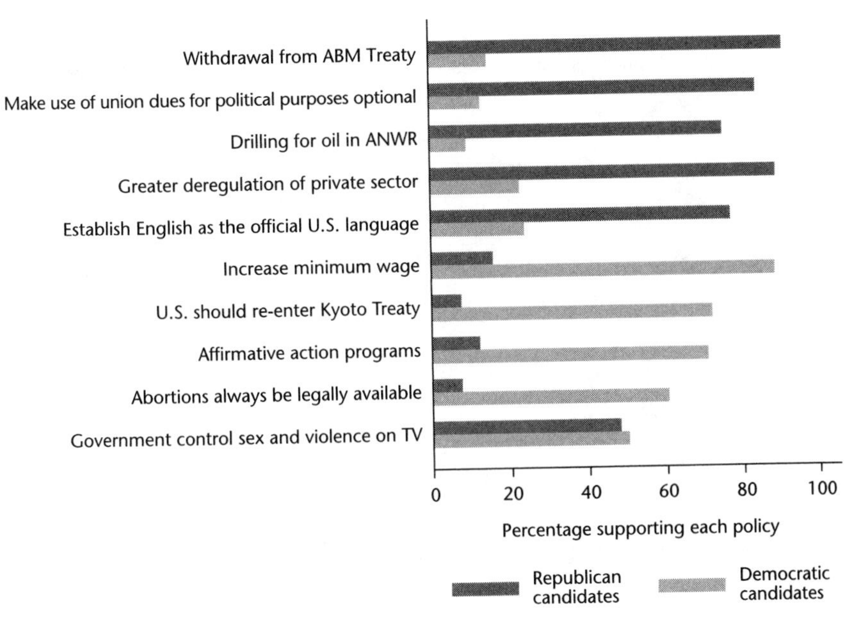

Source: Data are from the 2002 Project Vote Smart Congressional National Political Awareness Test survey sent to all congressional candidates.

Note: The ABM Treaty is the Anti-Ballistic Missile Treaty; ANWR is the Arctic National Wildlife Refuge.

Democrats are generally more favorable than Republicans to government spending, with the exception of the areas that involve protecting citizens, whether from external or internal agents; for defense, law enforcement, and fighting terrorism Republican candidates favored higher levels of spending than Democrats did.

Party differences also extend to issues beyond spending. Figure 4-4 displays differences in party responses to ten different policy proposals. Candidates were given lists of policy proposals and could check all those that they would support. The bars indicating the percentages of Republican and Democratic candidates supporting each policy show the two parties differing greatly on many of them. Republicans showed high levels of support for Bush's withdrawal of the United States from the 1972 Anti-Ballistic Missile (ABM) treaty, for drilling for oil in the Arctic National Wildlife Refuge (ANWR), for federal laws to give union members the option of not having their union dues used for political activities, and for making English the country's official language. Democrats, in contrast, showed at best quite modest support for those proposals but embraced increasing the federal minimum wage, continuing federal affirmative action programs,

Figure 4-5 Distribution of Candidate Ideology by Party, 2002

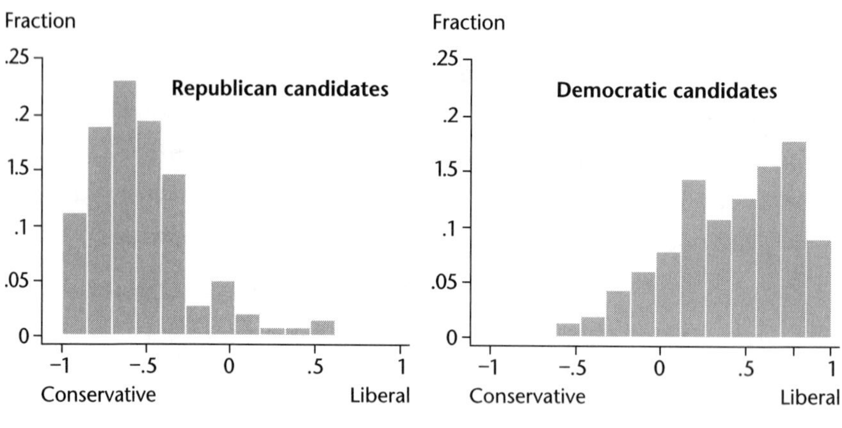

Source: Compiled by the authors.

Note: The scores are our candidate ideology index, derived from the 2002 Project Vote Smart Congressional National Political Awareness Test survey, www.vote-smart.org.

and keeping abortions legally available. On all of these issues, the parties' candidates took distinct stands. Some issues, however, have not made their way onto the agendas of the parties. For example, there is concern from many quarters about the amount of sex and violence on television. About half of all the candidates supported government action on that, but these preferences were largely unrelated to party.

The accumulated Democratic and Republican differences over specific issues can be seen in their overall ideological tendencies. To examine these differences we developed an index of candidate ideology, which measures the general policy liberalism or conservatism of House candidates, based on their responses to the Project Vote Smart survey. The index includes responses on a wide array of policy areas, from taxing and spending to affirmative action and foreign policy (see the appendix to this chapter). The index ranges from approximately −1 to +1, with higher scores indicating greater liberalism.

Figure 4-5 shows the distribution of the two parties' candidates for the House in the 2002 campaign. Republicans cluster on the conservative side; Democrats are grouped on the liberal side. Although the parties have become more polarized in recent years—largely as a result of dwindling numbers of conservative southern Democrats—we do see variation within each of the parties, so that some candidates clearly represent ideas that are some distance from their party's norm. As we discuss in the next section, these exceptions play a significant role in the dynamics of congressional representation.

The Role of Candidates in House Contests

Voters in congressional elections vote not only on the basis of national issues and the parties' policy positions but also on the basis of what they learn about their local candidates. At first glance, it would seem that voters generally have insufficient information about the candidates to vote on anything more than a partisan basis. Consider some evidence from surveys: Only about one-half of voters can name their U.S. representative, and slightly fewer claim to have "read or heard" something about him or her. The content of this information is generally vague ("He is a good man"; "She knows the job"), and it rarely touches on policy issues or roll call voting. Only on the generous test of recognition of the representative's name does the electorate score well. More than 90 percent claim to recognize their representative's name when supplied with it. Candidates for open seats are even less visible than incumbent candidates, and challengers trying to defeat incumbent representatives are the least visible of all. Typically only about 20 percent of the voting electorate can recall the challenger's name or anything else about that person. Only about half will claim to recognize the challenger's name when supplied with it.[13]

Although voters generally are not well informed about their local House candidates, it does not follow that the candidates have little impact on election outcomes. Movement by relatively few voters in a constituency can create a major surge for or against a candidate. This movement, the "personal" vote, results from the constituency's reaction to the specific candidate, as opposed to the "partisan" vote, which results from the constituency's partisanship. The personal vote is about as important as the partisan vote in deciding elections.

The Success of House Incumbents

One prominent fact about House elections is the success rate of incumbents. Averaged over many election years, over 95 percent of incumbent candidates have been reelected. In 2002, only four incumbents lost to an out-party challenger. (Four more lost when forced to face a rival incumbent following redistricting.) Even in 1994, the year of the "Republican revolution," 93 percent of incumbent candidates returned to Congress.[14] Why do incumbents do so well at the ballot box? Several factors contribute to their electoral success.

To guide our discussion of incumbency, Figure 4-6 graphs the relationship between the House district vote in 2002, as percentage Democratic (on the vertical axis), and the 2000 presidential vote, as the percentage for Gore (on the horizontal axis).[15] The district-level Gore vote is a useful indicator of underlying district partisanship and ideology. Figure 4-6 is divided among three panels on the basis of incumbency. The middle panel presents the data for the baseline of 2002 open seats (with no incumbent running). Without an incumbent in the race, the vote followed closely from district partisanship, as reflected in the Gore vote. The top and bottom panels show the data for districts where Democratic and

Figure 4-6 The Incumbency Advantage in the House, 2002

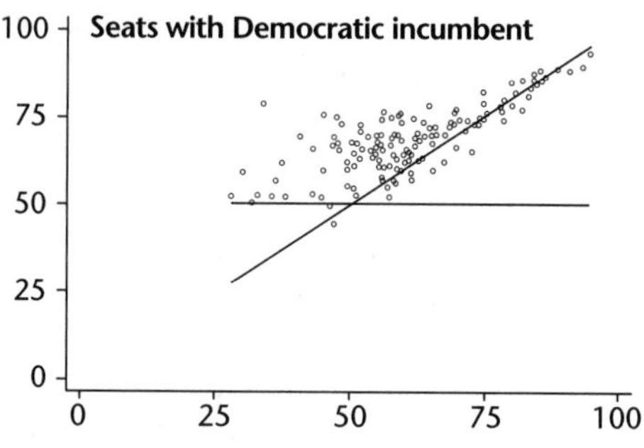

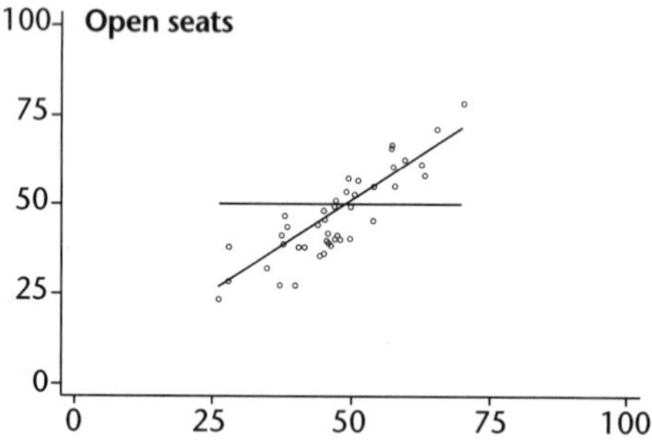

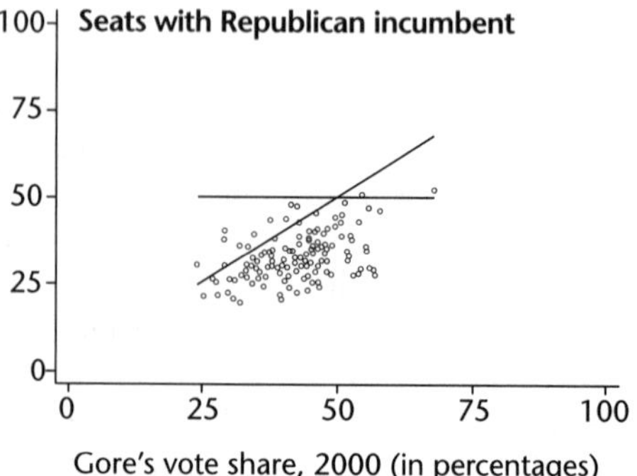

Source: Compiled by the authors.

Note: Dots above the diagonal line indicate that the district House vote for the Democratic candidate in 2002 exceeded the vote for Gore in that district in 2000. Dots below the diagonal line indicate that the Democratic House candidate in 2002 ran behind Gore's percentage in 2000. Dots above the horizontal line at 50 percent indicate a Democratic victory; dots below this line a Republican victory. (The 2000 district presidential vote is calculated using the district lines in 2002 rather than 2000.)

Republican incumbents, respectively, were seeking reelection. Inspection of Figure 4-6 shows most incumbents winning sufficient votes for reelection, often running ahead of their (2000) presidential ticket.

District Partisanship. When we ask why incumbents generally win reelection, the most obvious explanation is district partisanship. Most districts are either one-party Republican or one-party Democratic (as measured in Figure 4-6 by the presidential vote). Most House seats, therefore, are nearly guaranteed for the candidate of the locally favored party.

We see the importance of district partisanship from the following statistics. The close 2000 presidential election provides a benchmark for partisan competitiveness. We can set a strict definition of a very competitive district (in terms of underlying partisanship) as one in which neither presidential candidate received more than 53 percent of the major-party vote in 2000. Of the 435 districts in place for the 2002 election, only 60 (or 14 percent) had met this standard of closeness in their 2000 presidential voting. Not surprisingly, the two parties divided these districts evenly in the 2000 congressional election. In the other 84 percent of districts, the Bush-Gore vote diverged by at least three percentage points from fifty-fifty and therefore could be considered at least reasonably safe for the dominant party. Ninety-two percent of these seats were won by the dominant party in 2002.

Electoral Selection. One simple but sometimes overlooked reason why incumbents win is that in competitive districts incumbency status must be earned at the ballot box. Apart from district partisanship and partisan trends, elections are won on the basis of which party can field the stronger candidate. Strong candidates tend to win and to retain their strength in subsequent contests as incumbents. They survive until they falter or lose to even stronger candidates. Retirement of a successful incumbent starts the process again.

Weak Challengers. Incumbents augment their electoral success from their ability to draw weak challengers. Candidates and their supporters behave strategically, so they are reluctant to expend funds and political reputations against formidable foes.[16] Strong challengers conserve their political resources and tend to run when they can win, whether because the incumbent is vulnerable, the national short-term forces favor the party, or they have a shot at an open seat.

The tendency for potential challengers to behave strategically can be seen in the pattern of challenger quality in safe and competitive districts. In 2002 (as in other years), incumbents with safe margins were the least likely to face experienced challengers (see Table 4-1). Experienced and otherwise attractive candidates are scared off by strong incumbents. In their place, we find weak challengers who hand even larger victories to the incumbent.

Strategic Retirements. One reason why incumbents rarely lose is the process of "strategic retirements." When incumbents are threatened by an imminent loss

Table 4-1 Incumbents Facing Quality Challengers in the 2002 House Elections

2002 Election Margin	Democratic Incumbents	Republican Incumbents
Safe: won by 60% or more	15% (123)	9% (131)
Competitive: received less than 60%	30% (27)	25% (19)

Source: Data on candidate experience (quality) supplied by David Rohde.

Note: Figures represent the percentages of incumbents running for reelection who faced experienced challengers. The numbers of incumbents are in parentheses. Experienced challengers are defined as those who have previously held elective office. The challenger is more likely to be experienced when the election is competitive.

they generally announce their retirement rather than face the verdict from the voters. On average, incumbents retire with about the same frequency as their objective probability of defeat. For instance, House members facing a 60 percent chance of losing retire about 60 percent of the time. Strategic retirement is one reason why more incumbents were not defeated in 1992, following the House check-bouncing scandal. Rather than face risky reelection battles, about one-third of the House members with overdrafts at the House bank chose to quit.[17]

The Incumbency Advantage. Finally, there is the incumbency advantage—the electoral benefits that accrue to the incumbent by virtue of being the incumbent. More precisely, incumbents have opportunities to strengthen their electoral position that come from serving in the House. Most members exploit these resources, some more energetically than others.

Several means can be used to measure the incumbency advantage. Arguably the best is the "sophomore surge," or the percentage of the vote that candidates gain between their first election (as a nonincumbent) and their first reelection attempt (as an incumbent). Averaged across elections and adjusted for the national partisan trend, the sophomore surge is a simple and accurate way to measure the typical vote share gained from incumbency. The value of incumbency has increased substantially. The sophomore surge ran only about two percentage points in the 1950s, when partisanship was the dominant consideration in congressional elections. By the 1970s, the sophomore surge had reached about seven percentage points, where it remains today.[18]

This increase in the incumbency advantage coincides with two important trends. One is the loosening of voters' party ties. Weaker party identification and more independent voters mean that other forces can have more sway. The other trend is that members of Congress have increasingly turned their offices into reelection machines.[19] In the mid-1960s, Congress changed its rules to bestow on its members several increases in the resources of office, or "perks." These perks included free mailing privileges (the frank), increased travel allowances to visit their districts and build district favor, and increased staff to handle constituents' growing concerns with the federal bureaucracy.[20] The result is that incumbents are well thought of by their constituents, often for reasons that have nothing at all to do with policymaking considerations.

It may seem surprising that a seven-point incumbency advantage is sufficient to ensure success for most incumbents. The explanation is that the incumbency advantage is not a simple seven points across the board for all incumbents under all circumstances, but instead an average. Some incumbents work harder than others to please their constituents. Members trying to stay in office in districts with adverse partisanship have the greatest incentive to expand their incumbency advantage. Meanwhile, members from very safe districts have little incentive to attract additional voters: As long as the district votes close to its partisan predisposition, the member should be fine. In this instance we expect the incumbent to earn little or no incumbency advantage at all.

Referring back to Figure 4-6, one can see this logic at work. Incumbents in 2002 from very safe seats earned about the same vote margin as their party's presidential ticket, no more and no less. Meanwhile incumbents in districts in the competitive range received far more votes than their presidential ticket. Many of these would lose their reelection bids without this incumbency advantage. If they could earn no more votes than their party's presidential ticket, virtually all the Democratic incumbents running in districts where Gore lost to Bush (those to the left of 50 on the horizontal axis) would be out of office. Similarly, those Republican incumbents from districts where Gore beat Bush (to the right of 50 in the bottom graph of Figure 4-6) would also have lost without the incumbent advantage

The Incumbency Advantage as an Investment. Because incumbents almost always win, it might seem that incumbents can ignore constituency concerns, but this impression would be quite mistaken. A central source of the incumbency advantage is the careful reading of district interests. Incumbents like to stay elected and they know that providing constituents with what they want is the way to do so. Incumbents are well aware that their long-term electoral security depends on satisfying their constituencies. Even though House members know that they are unlikely to lose the next election, they also understand that the chances are roughly one in three that they will eventually lose. After all, roughly one in three got to Congress in the first place by defeating a sitting incumbent.[21]

If House members were to ignore their districts, we would see no incumbency advantage but instead rapid turnover. House members, we have argued, do not get their incumbency advantage automatically; they must earn it by hard work. Part of the work is constituency service and bringing home the pork in the form of government construction projects, local government contracts, and the like. But there is also an important policy component to the incumbent's investment. One way House members earn the incumbency advantage is by representing their districts' policy interests. Often those interests can be expressed as a summary ideological preference. As we shall see in the next section, House members add to their vote margins by representing the policy interests of their constituencies.[22]

Candidates, Issues, and the Vote

In this section, we explore how House members hold onto their seats by offering their constituents ideological representation. As we have seen, the typical constituency will be given a choice between a relatively conservative Republican and a relatively liberal Democrat. The process works as follows: Voters select in part based on which candidate is closest to their own views, and this gives the candidates incentive to move to the constituency's center—toward the position of the district's median voter.[23] The strength of this incentive is proportional to the attentiveness of the electorate and the extent to which the contest is close as a result of nonideological factors.

If ideological proximity were all the voters cared about, candidates would always converge toward the center, because to do otherwise would be to lose. But in reality, voters are only partially attentive and responsive to ideological appeals, limiting candidates' electoral gains from moderation. Moving to the center gains the support of some, but not all, voters who are ideologically closer to them than to their opponent. As a result, candidates do not converge at the center. Instead they strike a balance between the electoral security gained from adopting the position of the constituency's median voter, on the one hand, and the ideological satisfaction and support that come from adopting their own "extreme" ideological position and that of their activist supporters, on the other.[24]

Figure 4-7 shows candidate ideological positions as a function of both party and district partisanship. We measure candidate ideology using the PVS data, as described earlier. For open seats, we include only cases where PVS successfully surveyed both major-party candidates. For incumbent races, we omit cases where the challenger failed to respond to the PVS questionnaire. When the challenger responded but the incumbent did not, we estimated the incumbent's ideology by projecting from observed roll calls using Poole and Rosenthal's D-NOMINATE scores.[25] Ideology scores are scaled so that high scores are liberal and low scores are conservative. Throughout this section, all demonstrations are based solely on the districts where ideological positions can be scored for both the Republican and the Democratic candidate.

Although some Republican candidates in the nation are to the political left of some Democrats, it is rare to find a Republican candidate on the left of the Democratic opponent within the same district. Indeed, among the 165 districts for which we have ideology scores for both candidates, the Republican was the more conservative in all but one contest. The candidate's party affiliation clearly provides voters the basis of ideological choice.

Figure 4-7 also shows that the ideological variation within parties is a function of constituency. The more liberal and Democratic the district (as measured by the 2000 Gore vote), the more liberal are the two parties' candidates. This

Figure 4-7 Republican and Democratic Candidate Ideology, 2002 (by District Presidential Vote in 2000)

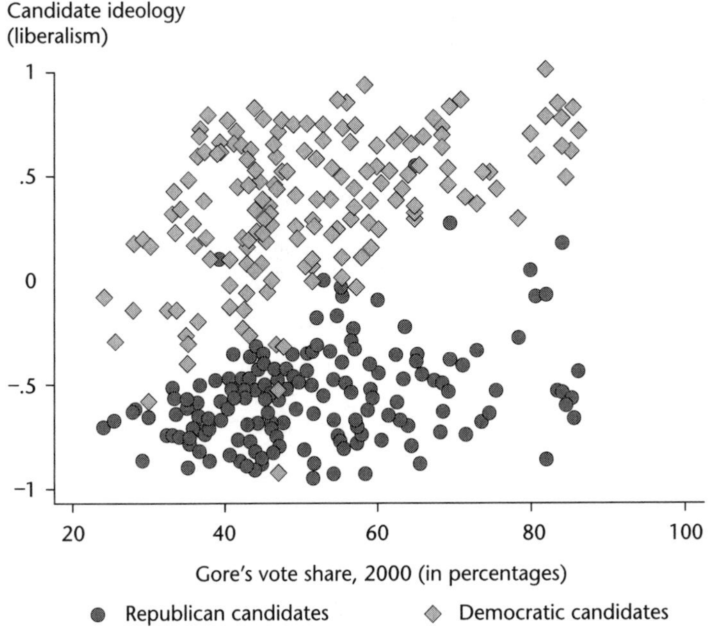

Source: Candidate ideology is measured using the 2002 Project Vote Smart Congressional National Political Awareness Test survey.

Note: High scores are liberal, and low scores are conservative.

congressional responsiveness to constituency preferences indicates that candidates believe that constituencies vote on the basis of ideological proximity to the candidates. Next, we examine the evidence as to whether this belief is correct.

We examine the effect of candidate ideology on the vote, while controlling for district presidential voting and the candidates' relative spending. We present regression equations for incumbent candidates in 2002 separately for Democratic-held and Republican-held seats. We ignore open seats because of a dearth of cases. Since our hypothesis is that moderation (conservatism) wins votes for Democrats and moderation (liberalism) wins votes for Republicans, we expect the signs of the ideology variables to be negative.

The equations are shown in Table 4-2. In a pattern consistent with other election years, we see that incumbent ideology is a significant predictor of the vote for both Democrats and Republicans and that challenger ideology shows only a small effect, significant for Democratic challengers but not Republican challengers.[26] Candidate ideology evidently matters once a House member achieves office, although the exact position of House challengers is not discernibly relevant. This is consistent with evidence from voter surveys, which consistently show that challengers are considerably less visible to voters than are incumbents.

Table 4-2 Regression of 2002 Democratic Vote on 2002 Candidate Ideology, 2000 District Presidential Vote, and 2002 Candidate Spending, for Incumbent Races

Independent Variable	Regression Coefficient	*t*-ratio	Beta
Republican incumbents			
Incumbent ideology (liberalism)	−7.02	−3.09[a]	−0.29
Challenger ideology (liberalism)	−2.67	−2.17[a]	−0.18
% Gore, 2000 presidential vote	0.31	4.11[a]	0.40
Log Democratic spending minus log Republican spending	1.99	7.23[a]	0.58
Constant	21.87	5.18[a]	
Adjusted $R^2 = .495$; $N = 81$			
Democratic incumbents			
Incumbent ideology (liberalism)	−4.95	−2.03[a]	−0.18
Challenger ideology (liberalism)	−1.15	−0.56	−0.04
% Gore, 2000 presidential vote	0.50	7.84[a]	0.79
Log Democratic spending minus log Republican spending	1.52	3.81[a]	0.28
Constant	35.24	10.05	
Adjusted $R^2 = .671$; $N = 78$			

Source: Compiled by authors.

Note: Candidate ideology scores are based on Project Vote Smart data (Dimension 1) or (if the Project Vote Smart data are missing) equivalently scaled incumbent DW-NOMINATE scores. The presidential vote is the 2000 Democratic percentage of the two-party vote in the 2002 district. Candidate spending is measured in units of thousands of dollars.

[a] Significant at .05 or higher.

We can visualize the estimated effects of incumbent ideology the following way. The coefficients are −4.95 for Democrats and −7.02 for Republicans, for an average of about −6. One unit of ideology on our PVS scale equals about half the total range of our scale from the most conservative Republican to the most liberal Democrat. Thus, shifting from a party's extreme to about the midpoint should yield about a six percentage point gain in the vote. If a member did an extreme swing and moved 1.5 units, which is roughly the maximum range of ideological distance within each party, the vote gain could be even larger. This shift would yield about a nine percentage point difference in the vote (1.5 units times 6 percentage points/unit = 9). This means, for instance, that the most conservative Republican member could gain about nine points by adopting the position of the least conservative Republican member. Similarly, the most liberal Democratic member could gain about nine points by adopting the same position as the least liberal Democratic member.[27]

We show the process visually in Figure 4-8, which displays the relationship between the 2002 congressional vote and 2000 presidential voting (the marker for district partisanship) for incumbents with distinctive ideological positions. Within each party, we separate out the most moderate from the most extreme.

For Democrats, we separate out the most liberal incumbents, at least one standard deviation more liberal than the party mean (Ls in the top panel), and the moderates at least one standard deviation more conservative than the party mean (Ms in the top panel). Two things should be noted: First, while the liberals represent safe seats, the moderates represent competitive seats, where the Gore vote was about fifty-fifty. This is evidence that politicians moderate according to electoral need. Second, while the liberals ran about even with Gore in their districts, the moderates all led the 2000 Gore vote by a considerable amount. One can readily project from this figure that the moderate Democrats depicted would have been in considerable electoral trouble had they pursued liberal ideological postures in their more moderate and competitive districts.

For Republicans, we find a mirror image pattern, although not quite as distinct. We separate out the most conservative incumbents, at least one standard deviation to the right of the party mean (Cs in the bottom panel), and the moderates at least one standard deviation to the left of the party mean (the Ms in the bottom panel). We observe that the conservatives tend to represent the more anti-Gore districts. And, while most Republicans of all ideological stripes did better than the benchmark of the 2000 presidential election (that is, most led Bush), the moderates led by more. One could readily project that if the moderates from competitive districts had run as extreme conservatives, many would have lost in 2000.[28]

Congressional Elections and Representation

The political parties and the candidates provide the mechanism by which constituencies can electorally determine the policy positions of their representatives in Congress. First, consider the role of political parties. Democratic and Republican candidates for Congress are sufficiently divergent from one another on the liberal-conservative spectrum to provide their constituencies with a clear choice. Liberal districts generally vote Democratic and elect liberals, and conservative districts generally vote Republican and elect conservatives.

Second, not only the parties' general reputations but also the precise ideological positions of the candidates matter. Candidates for Congress often deviate from their party's ideological orthodoxy. By moving toward a more moderate position, one that is closer to a constituency's prevailing views, the candidate enhances his or her electoral chances and by doing so enhances the representation of constituency views.

As Figure 4-9 shows, the net result is a clear pattern wherein the most liberal districts elect the most liberal members and the most conservative districts elect the most conservative members. Here we plot the member's ideology on the

Figure 4-8 Ideology and the House Vote, 2002

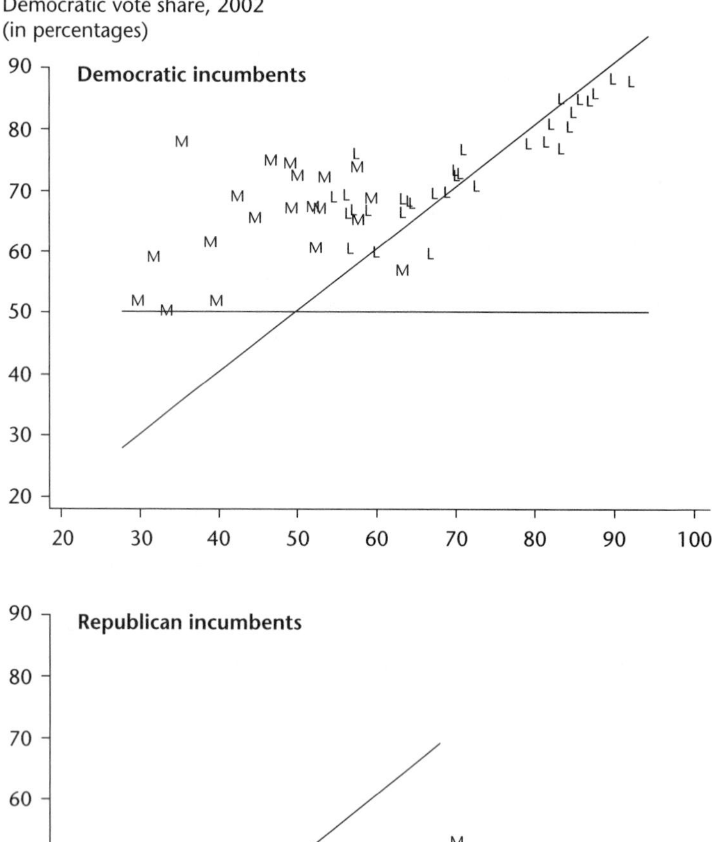

Source: Compiled by the authors.

Notes: C denotes conservative Republicans, M denotes both moderate Democrats and moderate Republicans, and L denotes liberal Democrats. The diagonal line indicates where equal vote percentages for the Democratic House candidate in 2002 and Gore in 2000 would be plotted. The horizontal line indicates 50 percent of the House vote. Districts above the horizontal line were won by the Democratic candidate, and those below it were won by the Republican.

Figure 4-9 Winner's Ideology by District Presidential Vote

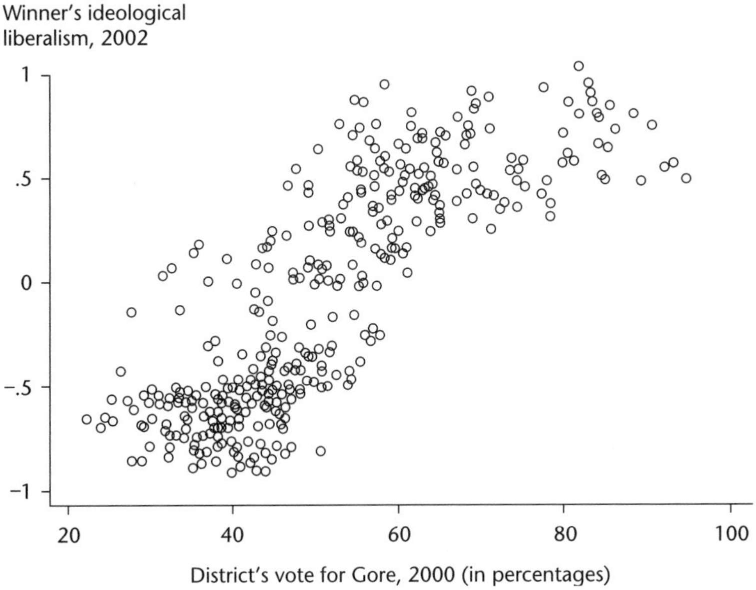

Source: Winner's ideology is calculated from the Project Vote Smart Congressional National Political Awareness Test survey and roll call data.

Note: Higher scores for the winner's ideology indicate greater liberalism, and higher vote percentages for Gore indicate greater constituency liberalism.

vertical axis; the horizontal axis represents constituency liberalism, as measured by presidential voting in the district. Representatives' ideological positions and constituency opinion (proxied by the presidential vote) correlate at a substantial +.82. Very liberal districts almost always elect Democrats; very conservative districts almost always elect Republicans. In the battleground districts in the middle, candidate ideology can be the decisive factor. Although we find no evidence that nonincumbent candidates' ideologies matter, once they become incumbents their electoral survival often depends on satisfying their constituencies ideologically.

Interestingly, although we observe evidence of considerable representation, we cannot be sure about the prevalence of a residual ideological bias. We compare ideology scores of congressional candidates, on the one hand, with the presidential voting of constituencies on the other. While both may reflect ideological positioning, they are not calibrated on a common scale. It could be the case, for instance, that members of Congress are systematically more liberal (or systematically more conservative) than their constituencies, despite the evidence of district-level representation.

Similarly, we can ask whether the House as a whole is too liberal, too conservative, or just right in terms of the net taste of the American electorate. A

Table 4-3 Voters' Perceptions of the Ideology of Their House Representatives

Percentage who see their representative as	1978	1980	1982	1986	1990	1994	1998	2002
More conservative than themselves	27	33	31	37	37	34	36	39
Similar to themselves	26	26	27	24	21	26	20	16
More liberal than themselves	47	41	42	40	42	41	43	45

Congress that is off-center from the people ideologically would be a Congress out of equilibrium. To restore equilibrium, either Congress would realize its mistake and change its policymaking, or the populace would realize its mistake and vote in a more ideologically compatible Congress. Another possibility would be a system in equilibrium because of forces beyond public opinion. For instance, the persistent influence of money on politics could permanently skew congressional policymaking away from the trajectory preferred by public opinion.

One way to estimate the ideological match between Congress and the public is to compare voters' ideological ratings of their recently elected representative with their personal ideological preferences. Relevant data from several elections, available from the National Election Studies, are displayed in Table 4-3. For several Congresses, approximately the same percentage of voters see themselves as more liberal than the member they just elected as see themselves as more conservative. This balance indicates that, at least perceptually, Congress has not been too liberal or conservative for the electorate. Actually, in most years when the public has been surveyed, slightly more see their member as too liberal than as too conservative. Offsetting this, however, is that the people who have the greatest difficulty sorting out the parties in abstract ideological terms tend to be less educated and to vote Democratic. Even though they tend to be silent on the exact ideological position of their representative, we can presume that they still know their political interests.

House-Senate Differences in Representation

The Framers of the Constitution intended the Senate to be an elite chamber, isolated from the popular demands on the House. Regardless of how well or poorly this intention has been realized, there are fundamental constitutional differences between the two chambers. The most remarkable difference has been eliminated. Before ratification of the Seventeenth Amendment in 1913, state legislatures selected their state's senators. Today, voters elect their senators directly. Because senators have six-year terms, they are relatively free from the never-ending campaigns carried on by representatives. And, for the most part, the constituencies that senators represent are larger and much more diverse than those of representatives.

Election Results and the Senate

In terms of national election results, the party composition of the Senate reflects the same forces that determine the party composition of the House. The division between Democrats and Republicans in the Senate is influenced by presidential coattails in presidential years and by the bounce to the out party at midterm. The Senate's partisan division responds more sluggishly to national trends, however, because only one-third of the senators are up for reelection in any election year.

As a general rule, Senate elections are more competitive than House elections. Senate races with no incumbent are almost always sharply contested by both parties, and an incumbent senator who seeks reelection has a considerably greater chance of defeat than does an incumbent House member who seeks reelection. Incumbent senators are reelected at a rate of about 78 percent, in comparison to 95 percent for House incumbents. One reason that Senate races are more closely contested is that the statewide Senate constituencies are rarely dominated by one political party, as the smaller House districts are. Another major factor is that Senate races attract strong challengers. A senator is far more likely than a House member to face a politically seasoned and well-financed opponent. Finally, senators seem unable to obtain the strong incumbency advantage that House members enjoy, attaining no better than a few percentage points as their average sophomore surge. (Evidently, senatorial challengers find it easier to generate visibility for their campaigns than do challengers to House incumbents.) Senators perform well electorally, compared with nonincumbent candidates of their party, partly because they had to be good candidates to be elected the first time.

Although reelection to the Senate is more difficult than reelection to the House, senators need to run only once every six years. The appropriate comparison of electoral security is a comparison of survival rates over the same period of time. Measured over six years, House members seeking reelection have a survival rate of approximately 78 percent—about the same as the reelection rate for senators.[29] Therefore, the six-year term for senators almost exactly offsets the greater incumbency advantage of the House. Senators run less often but at higher risk. The long-run survival rates for the two houses appear to be roughly equal.

Is the Senate any less responsive to popular opinion than the House? Six-year terms would seem to provide senators with ample freedom from electoral concerns, except for the final run-up to election. Moreover, when senators decide to be attentive to their electorates, their diverse constituencies make full representation difficult.

As are House members, senators are sensitive to constituency opinion, with each party's most conservative senators found in conservative states and most liberal members found in liberal states. In terms of partisan politics, the states are competitive enough that each party has a chance at a Senate seat. As a result, many states send both a Republican and a Democrat to the Senate, a pattern that baffles some observers. In a pattern similar to that of the House, senators from states in which the other party dominates often are ideologically atypical for their party.[30]

State Populations and the Senate

Although states vary considerably in population, each has two senators. California's 34 million people get the same number of senators as Alaska's 600,000. To some extent, this constitutionally designed "malapportionment" favors political conservatism. Indeed, state population correlates rather strongly (+.34) with our measure of citizen liberalism, based on pooled CBS News/*New York Times* surveys.[31] Small, politically conservative states enjoy an extra margin of representation in the Senate.

During the Reagan years, when the Republicans enjoyed a six-year Senate majority, the Senate was the more conservative chamber. One is tempted to attribute this senatorial conservatism to the Senate's overrepresentation of small states. However, in the immediate aftermath of the Republican takeover of both houses of Congress in 1994, the Senate was the more moderate of the two chambers. The greater responsiveness of the House to national forces in that year brought in a crew of conservative freshmen legislators who, with vigorous conservative leadership, put the House distinctly in the lead of the Republican revolution that the 1994 election launched. A decade later the Republicans in the House remain distinctly more conservative than their Senate counterparts.

The Six-Year Term

Because the next election for representatives is never more than two years away, electoral considerations are always important for members of the House. For senators, the six-year term can provide some leeway. Voters—so it sometimes seems—are electorally myopic, forgetting what senators do early in their terms and remembering only what they do close to the election.

Whether or not such a view of the electorate is valid, there is a good deal of evidence that senatorial roll call voting responds to the six-year cycle.[32] In the year or two before they must run again, incumbents move away from their party's extreme. Democrats inch in a conservative direction and Republicans edge over to the left. The purpose in each instance is to appeal to moderate voters.

Because senators moderate their ideological positions as reelection approaches, they presumably have good reason to do so: Senators must believe that moderation enhances their chances of electoral success. Earlier we saw evidence that House members with moderate ideological positions are more likely to be reelected. Is the same true for senators?

Candidates' policy positions affect their election chances. For the Senate, candidates do better if they avoid their party's ideological extremes. Gerald

Wright and Michael Berkman estimated the effect of candidates' issue positions by comparing different pairings of ideological positions, while statistically controlling for the effects of several constituency characteristics and attitudes.[33] They estimated that whether a Senate candidate represents the party's moderate wing or more extremist wing creates a difference ranging from five to eight percentage points. This effect is similar to that observed for House elections. The evidence suggests that the same electoral connection leading to representation exists in the Senate as in the House, with the added twists of the larger, more heterogeneous constituencies and the latitude of the six-year Senate term.

Conclusion

Along with presidential elections, congressional elections provide citizens with their main opportunity to influence the direction of national policy. When elections bring about significant changes in the party composition of Congress, we can be fairly confident of two things: The first is that the new Congress will have a different ideological cast. Democratic and Republican candidates for the House and Senate stand for quite different things. Therefore, electing more Democrats or more Republicans increases the likelihood of policy movement in the ideological direction of the advantaged party. Ironically, the second is that such changes do not always stem from the electorate's desire for new policy directions. The Republican takeover in 1994 did coincide with an increase in conservative Republican sentiments in the mass electorate. Other, less-substantial changes, however, have stemmed from factors such as presidential coattails or the usual slump that the presidential party experiences at midterm.

We see the electorate's influence on policy direction most clearly in the relationship between constituencies and their elected representatives. In their ideological direction, individual House and Senate members respond to their constituencies. In turn, ideological direction matters when constituencies decide which candidates they will elect and which they will not.

The average voter knows little about his or her representative and only a bit more about his or her senators. House challengers are almost invisible, and only a portion of the electorate has even a modest amount of information about senatorial challengers. Nevertheless, the electorates that candidates and parties face are smart and discerning, and they reward faithful representation. Candidates, generally desirous of attaining and staying in office, heed their electorate's wishes and work to give them what they want. Elections bring about much higher levels of policy representation than most observers would expect based on the low levels of citizen awareness.

Appendix: The Project Vote Smart Ideology Scores

Project Vote Smart attempts to provide American voters objective and useful information about candidates for public office. One of its main activities is the administration of the National Political Awareness Tests (NPATs), which are comprehensive questionnaires in which all candidates for the presidency, Congress, and state legislatures are asked to indicate the policy positions that they support. The congressional NPATs provided the basis for our scoring of candidates' ideologies for the 2002 election. These questionnaires asked candidates almost two hundred questions on their issue positions in a wide range of policy areas. The questions were grouped into twenty-one policy areas and subareas and included batteries of items on abortion, spending and taxation, campaign finance, crime, education, the environment, health, gun control, immigration, welfare, foreign policy, and national security. The format for most of the congressional NPAT is to ask candidates whether they support a particular policy option. Not checking an item does not necessarily mean opposition to the policy.

All items were converted to simple dummy (1, 0, or missing) variables. Where candidates checked none of the options for an entire policy area they were given missing values for all items in that section of the NPAT. We then used the NOMINATE program to reduce the patterns of answers to a small number of dimensions.[34]

In this analysis we used the first NOMINATE dimension, which is clearly liberalism-conservatism. We see this in correlating the winning candidates' scores from the NPAT with a simple index created from the 2003 ratings by the liberal Americans for Democratic Action and the conservative American Conservative Union. The correlation is a robust .940. We also scored the NPATs using factor analysis to see if our ideology scores are sensitive to the measurement approach used. For this alternative measure we factor analyzed each of the twenty-one issue areas separately, extracting the first principal component from each. We then used Stata's best-fitting regression approach to impute the missing data on each factor, using the candidates' factor scores in other issue areas as well as party affiliation and region. In the last step we extracted a single factor from a principal components analysis of the candidates' scores across the twenty-one issue areas. The ideology scores from our factor analysis approach correlate very highly with our NOMINATE-generated scores, r = .986. It is comforting to know that we obtain virtually identical results from applying two quite different measurement techniques to the NPAT data.

Finally, for the incumbents who answered the NPAT, we correlated their NPAT ideology scores with their roll call NOMINATE scores from the 107th Congress (2001–2002).[35] The correlation here is a strong .938. For the incumbents who did not respond to the NPAT, we imputed their ideology scores based on their roll call voting (NOMINATE scores) in the 107th Congress. Similar estimates of congressional candidate ideology based on Project Vote Smart NPATs have been developed by Ansolabehere, Snyder, and Stewart; however they use the Heckman-Snyder factor analysis approach, which yields scores almost identical to those obtained from the NOMINATE procedure.[36]

Notes

The authors would like to thank Gary Jacobson, David Rohde, and Project Vote Smart for sharing data they collected and Jon Winburn and Jennifer Clark for their assistance. Of course we are solely responsible for the analysis and interpretation offered in this chapter.

1. The swing ratio is inversely related to the size of the incumbency advantage, discussed below. The more incumbents can protect themselves with a strong incumbency advantage, the less the seat swing depends on the national division of the vote. The classic discussion of this point is David Mayhew, "Congressional Elections: The Case of the Vanishing Marginals," *Polity* 6 (spring 1973): 295–318.
2. At one time, the "normal vote" was thought of as an essentially constant 53–47 or 54–46 Democratic advantage. On the origin of the "normal vote" concept, see Philip E. Converse, "The Concept of the Normal Vote," in *Elections and the Political Order,* ed. Angus Campbell, Philip E. Converse, Warren E. Miller, and Donald E. Stokes (New York: Wiley, 1966), 9–39.
3. Macropartisanship is measured here as the Democratic percentage of Republican and Democratic identifiers in the third quarter of the election year. The correlation between macropartisanship and the vote is +.56.
4. James A. Stimson, *Public Opinion in America,* 2nd ed. (Boulder: Westview, 1999).
5. See Stimson, *Public Opinion in America*; Robert S. Erikson, Michael B. MacKuen, and James A. Stimson, *The Macro Polity* (New York: Cambridge University Press, 2002). The electorate's mood is not the same as its macropartisanship and the two should not be confused with each other. In fact, if anything the sign of the over-time correlation between mood and macropartisanship is negative rather than positive. (When Democratic identification is high, policy preferences tend conservative.) In part, mood is driven by the nation's economy—inflation worries trigger desires for conservatism or less government; unemployment worries stimulate demand for liberalism or more government. Mood is also a function of past policies. For instance, when a pent-up demand for more liberalism goes unmet, the electorate becomes even more liberal; as the government produces the more liberal policies in response, the demand eases and the public becomes more conservative.
6. John A. Ferejohn and Randall L. Calvert, "Presidential Coattails in Historical Perspective," *American Journal of Political Science* 28 (February 1984): 127–146.
7. Angus Campbell, "Surge and Decline: A Study of Electoral Change," in *Elections and the Political Order,* ed. Campbell et al., 40–62. See also James A. Campbell, "The Presidential Surge and its Midterm Decline in Congressional Elections," *Journal of Politics* 53 (1991): 477–487.
8. Alberto Alesina and Howard Rosenthal, *Partisan Politics, Divided Government, and the Economy* (New York: Cambridge University Press, 1995); Morris Fiorina, *Divided Government* (New York: Allyn and Bacon, 1995).
9. Congressional balancing can occur in presidential election years as well as midterms—when the outcome is a landslide that is anticipated in advance. An argument can be made that in the landslides of 1956, 1972, 1984, and 1996, presidential coattails appeared weak because they were offset by ideological balancing against the presidential party. Balancing may have been the cause of the largest congressional surge of a presidential party in the twentieth century. In 1948, President Truman's Democratic Party gained over eighty seats in the House, in part perhaps because people were voting Democratic to defeat "President" Dewey. (Almost all observers in 1948 anticipated that Dewey would defeat Truman.) Truman's campaign against the "do nothing" Republican Congress was surprisingly effective. Note, however, that the emphasis of his message was "vote for me to stop the congressional Republicans," not "vote Democratic for Congress." The 1948 example suggests that votes for president can be

affected by the anticipated party control of Congress as well as the reverse. For more on balancing in a larger context, including Senate elections, see Robert S. Erikson, "Explaining National Party Tides in Senate Elections: Macropartisanship, Policy Mood, and Ideological Balancing," in *U.S. Senate Exceptionalism,* ed. Bruce I. Oppenheimer (Columbus: Ohio State University Press, 2002).

10. In the past, almost all presidents have had lower job approval ratings at midterm than at the time of their election, when they typically enjoy a "honeymoon" in the 70 percent range. See Robert S. Erikson and Kent L. Tedin, *American Public Opinion,* 7th ed. (New York: Longman, 2004), 110. Bush's initial approval ratings were only 57 percent—perhaps due to the extended controversy that decided the outcome of the 2000 presidential election—but his ratings at the midterm election were at 68 percent. Thus, to the extent that changes in presidential popularity affect the midterm voter, Bush's unusual trajectory would have worked against the usual midterm loss of seats for the presidential party. (Approval statistics are from the Gallup poll archive.)
11. In terms of the two-party vote, the 2002 Republican gain was 2.6 percentage points, which is sizable as congressional vote shifts go. Some of this gain, however, was due to the Democrats' contesting fewer seats than usual. With the shifting district lines, one can measure the 2000–2002 shift as the change in the mean deviation of the House vote in contested seats, relative to the 2000 presidential vote in the new (2002–2010) and old (1992–2000) districts. By this measure, the Republicans gained only about 1 percent of the vote. The Republicans gained more seats than usual from a one percentage point vote gain. This was partially due to population movement, so that Republican states gained more seats with the 2000 Census. Republicans also controlled more state legislatures than the Democrats did, giving them a political advantage when carving out the new congressional districts. On the partisan impact of congressional redistricting, see Gary W. Cox and Jonathan N. Katz, *Elbridge Gerry's Salamander: The Electoral Consequences of the Reapportionment Revolution* (Cambridge, UK: Cambridge University Press, 2002).
12. Project Vote Smart is a national nonpartisan organization focused on providing citizens with information about the political system, issues, candidates, and elected officials. One of the organization's main activities is making available candidates' answers to their National Political Awareness Test (NPAT), which asks candidates where they stand on a wide variety of issues. Information about Project Vote Smart and access to NPAT answers, as well as a host of other data about candidates running for office, can be found on the Web at www.vote-smart.org.
13. The limits to the public's knowledge of congressional candidates have been known for some time. See Donald E. Stokes and Warren E. Miller, "Party Government and the Salience of Congress," in *Elections and the Political Order,* ed. Campbell et al.; and Thomas E. Mann, *Unsafe at Any Margin: Interpreting Congressional Elections* (Washington, D.C.: American Enterprise Institute, 1978). For a discussion incorporating recent data on voter information, see Michael X. Delli Carpini and Scott Keeter, *What Americans Know about Politics and Why It Matters* (New Haven: Yale University Press, 1996).
14. The balance of incumbents' success in 1994 decidedly favored the Republicans, who reelected all their incumbent candidates, compared to the Democrats who, while losing their majority status, still managed to reelect 84 percent of their incumbents.
15. The Gore vote is Gore's percentage of the major-party vote in the districts redrawn for the 2002 election. Throughout the vote analysis of this chapter, all vote totals for Congress or president are the percentage of the major-party vote. Third parties and independent candidates are ignored
16. Gary C. Jacobson and Samuel Kernell, *Strategy and Choice in Congressional Elections,* 2nd ed. (New Haven: Yale University Press, 1983).

17. Susan A. Banducci and Jeffrey A. Karp, "Electoral Consequences of Scandal and Reapportionment in the 1992 House Elections," *American Politics Quarterly* 23 (January 1994): 3–26; Gary C. Jacobson and Michael A. Dimock, "Checking Out: The Effects of Bank Overdrafts on the 1992 House Elections," *Journal of Politics* 57 (November 1995): 1143–1159; Timothy Groseclose and Keith Krehbiel, "Golden Parachutes, Rubber Checks, and Strategic Retirements from the 102nd House," *American Journal of Political Science* 38 (February 1994): 75–99.
18. Robert S. Erikson, "Estimating the Incumbency Advantage in Congressional Elections" (paper presented at the annual meeting of the Political Methodology Society, St. Louis, July 1990); Andrew Gelman and Gary King, "Measuring the Incumbency Advantage without Bias," *American Journal of Political Science* 34 (1990): 1142–1164. For earlier estimates, see Robert S. Erikson, "Malapportionment, Gerrymandering, and Party Fortunes in Congressional Elections," *American Political Science Review* 66 (December 1972): 1234–1245; and David Mayhew, "Congressional Elections: The Case of the Vanishing Marginals," 295–318.
19. David Mayhew, *Congress: The Electoral Connection* (New Haven: Yale University Press, 1974).
20. Morris Fiorina, *Congress: Keystone of the Washington Establishment* 2nd ed. (New Haven: Yale University Press, 1989).
21. Robert S. Erikson, "Is There Such a Thing as a Safe Seat?" *Polity* 9 (1976): 623–632.
22. Because of the incumbency advantage, the winning party in a "landslide" election can protect its lead over subsequent elections. Democratic surges sent waves of freshman Democrats to Congress in 1964 and 1974 (among other years), who were then able to stay in office after the initial Democratic tide receded, thanks to the incumbency advantage. The Republican surge of 1994 had the same effect, as their newfound incumbency advantage insulated new Republican House members from defeat in subsequent elections. For more on incumbency, the swing ratios, and party strength in Congress, see Cox and Katz, *Elbridge Gerry's Salamander.*
23. Anthony Downs, *An Economic Theory of Democracy* (New York: Harper and Row, 1957); Chapter 8 is the classic source on ideological moderation.
24. Gerald C. Wright, "Policy Voting in the U.S. Senate: Who Is Represented?" *Legislative Studies Quarterly* 14 (November 1989): 465–486.
25. Keith T. Poole and Howard Rosenthal, *Congress: A Political-Economic History of Roll Call Voting* (New York: Oxford University Press, 1997).
26. See our analyses of the 1974, 1978, 1982, 1990, 1994, and 1998 congressional elections in the 4th, 5th, 6th, and 7th editions of *Congress Reconsidered,* ed. Lawrence C. Dodd and Bruce I. Oppenheimer (Washington, D.C.: CQ Press, 1989, 1993, 1997, 2001).
27. These results are comparable with our findings in other elections. In addition to the items cited in the previous footnote, see Robert S. Erikson, "The Electoral Impact of Congressional Roll Call Voting," *American Political Science Review* 65 (December 1971): 1018–1032; Gerald C. Wright, "Candidates' Policy Positions and Voting in U.S. House Elections," *Legislative Studies Quarterly* 3 (August 1978): 445–464; Robert S. Erikson and Gerald C. Wright, "Policy Representation of Constituency Interests," *Political Behavior* 1 (summer 1980): 91–106; Robert S. Erikson and Gerald C. Wright, "Representation of Constituency Ideology in Congress," Chap. 8 in *Continuity and Change in Congressional Elections,* ed. David Brady and John Cogan (Stanford: Stanford University Press, 2000). See also Stephen Ansolabehere, James M. Snyder Jr., and Charles Stewart II, "Candidate Positioning in U.S. House Elections," *American Journal of Political Science* 45 (January 2001): 136–159; and Brandice Canes-Wrone, David W. Brady, and John F. Cogan, "Out of Step, Out of Office: Electoral Accountability and House Members' Voting," *American Political Science Review* 96 (March 2002): 127–140.

28. To see the electoral advantage from moderation, consider the following: Although the 2000 presidential vote was more Republican in the districts held by our "conservative" Republican incumbents than in those held by our "moderates" (by eleven percentage points), the mean vote margins for the conservative and moderate Republican representatives were virtually identical in 2002. Moderation led to seats that were safer than those held by conservative Republicans from more Republican districts.
29. Amihai Glazer and Bernard Grofman, "Two Plus Two Plus Two Equals Six: Tenure of Office of Senators and Representatives, 1953–1983," *Legislative Studies Quarterly* 12 (November 1987): 555–563.
30. Robert S. Erikson, "Roll Calls, Reputations, and Representation in the U.S. Senate," *Legislative Studies Quarterly* 15 (November 1990): 623–642.
31. Robert S. Erikson, Gerald C. Wright, and John P. McIver, *Statehouse Democracy* (New York: Cambridge University Press, 1993), Chap. 2. For a detailed examination of asymmetries of state size and senatorial representation, see Frances E. Lee and Bruce I. Oppenheimer, *Sizing Up the Senate: The Unequal Consequences of Equal Representation* (Chicago: University of Chicago Press, 1999).
32. Richard F. Fenno Jr., *The United States Senate: A Bicameral Perspective* (Washington, D.C.: American Enterprise Institute, 1982); Martin Thomas, "Electoral Proximity and Senatorial Roll Call Voting," *American Journal of Political Science* 29 (February 1984): 96–111; Gerald C. Wright, "Representation and the Electoral Cycle in the U.S. Senate" (paper delivered at the annual meeting of the Midwest Political Science Association, Chicago, April 15–17, 1993).
33. Gerald C. Wright and Michael B. Berkman, "Candidates and Policy in U.S. Senatorial Elections," *American Political Science Review* 80 (June 1986): 576–590.
34. Poole and Rosenthal, *Congress: A Political-Economic History of Roll Call Voting.*
35. The roll call NOMINATE scores for the 107th Congress were obtained from Professor Keith Poole's Web site, http://voteview.uh.edu/dwnl.htm.
36. Stephen Ansolabehere, James M. Snyder Jr., and Charles Stewart, "The Effects of Party and Preferences on Congressional Roll-Call Voting," *Legislative Studies Quarterly* 26 (2001): 533–572; Ansolabehere, Snyder, and Stewart, "Candidate Positioning in U.S. House Elections."

5. The Bipartisan Campaign Reform Act and Congressional Elections

Paul S. Herrnson

The Bipartisan Campaign Reform Act (BCRA) of 2002, sometimes referred to as the McCain-Feingold Act, for its Senate sponsors, or the Shays-Meehan Act, for its sponsors in the House, was the first major piece of campaign finance reform legislation to become law in more than two decades. The politics of its passage by Congress and its implementation involves many of the recurring themes in American politics: a clash of deep-seated values, a system of regulations desperately in need of an overhaul, a legislative journey marked by high levels of partisanship and hyperactive interest group activity, one or more scandals to serve as catalysts, and reliance on the Supreme Court to act as the ultimate arbiter of the law. In this chapter I analyze these aspects of the BCRA and speculate about the law's impact on the conduct of congressional elections, primarily elections for the House.

A Clash of Values

Elections are the hallmark of a democracy. The principle of one person, one vote, suggests that citizens should have equal opportunity to influence government. The tenet that elections must involve a free exchange of opinions implies that individuals should be able to discuss candidates, political parties, and issues. Few scholars or citizens would quibble with these statements. Where individuals disagree is about the role of money in elections.

Underlying arguments about the proper role of money in politics are two fundamental values that are often in tension: liberty and equality. Those who emphasize equality typically prefer to limit the role of campaign contributions and spending in elections, maintaining that the private financing of elections gives individuals and groups that commit large sums to electoral politics disproportionate influence over election outcomes. These donors also enjoy greater political access than do other citizens, which helps them gain influence in the policymaking process.[1] Some critics believe that large contributions create relationships that give the appearance of corruption, border on bribery, and may on occasion involve both.

Those who emphasize liberty generally argue that individuals and groups that contribute or spend money in elections are simply using those funds to give voice to their opinions and the interests they represent. They consider the flow of campaign money to be part of a larger marketplace of ideas and believe that inequalities in campaign resources among candidates, parties, and other groups are a reflection of the intensity of their political support. Advocates of private financing also point out that the money for campaigning must come from somewhere, and making contributions is part of a broader pattern of civic involvement.

The BCRA's Predecessors

A host of laws governed federal elections before passage of the BCRA.[2] The earliest laws focused on eliminating the extortion of contributions from those employed by, or holding contracts with, the federal government; severing the links between campaign contributions and government regulations and contracts; limiting the influence of money in elections generally; and opening political campaign financing to public scrutiny. Nevertheless, the laws were laced with loopholes that allowed for easy evasion by candidates, parties, individuals, and interest groups. Moreover, because those charged with enforcing them had neither the political motivation nor the resources to do so, some politicians and donors felt free to commit brazen violations.

Despite some attention-grabbing examples of corruption reported by the press, only limited progress was made toward controlling the flow of campaign money during most of the twentieth century. Commissions were formed, bills introduced, and proclamations made. However, ideological disagreements over the proper role of money in politics, political leaders' desire to gain partisan advantage, and the self-interest of individual members of the House and Senate and the party committees and interest groups that supported them made it difficult for significant campaign finance reform to survive the legislative process.

The Federal Election Campaign Act of 1974

The passage of the Federal Election Campaign Act (FECA) of 1974 followed the public furor that arose as a result of the Watergate scandal.[3] The investigation following the break-in at Democratic Party headquarters in Washington's Watergate Hotel revealed that President Nixon's Committee to Re-elect the President accepted illegal contributions, gave ambassadorships and other political appointments to large donors, granted favors to businesses that made large campaign contributions, and used a slush fund to finance the break-in itself and other illegal activities.

The 1974 reform had several objectives, including reducing candidates' and parties' dependence on large contributions; increasing candidates' and parties' incentives to raise large sums in small donations; diminishing the political influence of businesses, unions, and other interest groups; decreasing the costs of running for federal office; bringing transparency to the financing of elections; and eliminating corruption. It created contribution limits for candidates, individuals, parties, and interest groups, and it prohibited contributions from the treasuries of corporations, unions, trade associations, and other groups. The resultant campaign finance system was funded solely with money that originated as limited contributions from individual donors. The new law instituted spending limits for all federal campaigns and created opportunities for candidates for president to fund their primary campaigns with a mix of private and federal funds and their general election campaigns entirely with public money. The law included rigorous reporting requirements for all federal campaign finance activity and created the independent Federal Election Commission (FEC) to administer its provisions.

Shortly after the FECA went into effect it was challenged in court. In January 1976 the Supreme Court ruled in *Buckley v. Valeo* that the provisions of the law limiting candidates' contributions to their own campaigns, limiting spending by candidates' campaign committees, and prohibiting others from spending independently of a campaign were in violation of constitutionally protected free speech rights. The Court also ruled that the method used to appoint members to the FEC was unconstitutional. Congress responded by amending the FECA in 1976, eliminating those aspects of the law that were found to violate the Constitution.[4]

An important aspect of the Court's ruling, found in a footnote to the opinion, narrowed the regulation of political expenditures in federal elections to only those activities that "expressly advocate" the election or defeat of a candidate. This later resulted in what came to be known as the "magic words" test, which limited the regulation of campaign spending to communications that included words such as "vote for," "elect," or "defeat." It laid the foundation for the parties and interest groups to sponsor non–federally funded, election-related communications, often referred to as "issue advocacy advertising."

A third set of amendments to the FECA, passed in 1979, simplified reporting requirements and made it possible for state and local parties to spend unlimited amounts on grassroots campaign activities without its counting toward the federal limits. Around the same time that Congress was enacting these amendments, the FEC issued regulatory decisions allowing parties to raise unregulated, nonfederal funds (often referred to as "soft money") and use the money to pay for a portion of their administrative costs and voter identification and mobilization efforts. The FECA of 1974, its amendments, and associated Court rulings and regulatory decisions were extremely successful for the first twenty years of their existence.

Adaptation to the FECA

After the FECA was enacted, political parties, interest groups, individual donors, and congressional candidates learned to operate within its confines. National party organizations improved their operations, raising large sums of money in small and medium-sized contributions, redistributing some funds to federal candidates, and helping state party committees improve their organizational structures, fund-raising activities, and campaign assistance programs.[5] The Republicans responded particularly well, raising more money, and providing more campaign support to candidates than did the Democrats.[6] The parties' congressional and senatorial campaign committees—the Democratic Congressional

Campaign Committee (DCCC), the Democratic Senatorial Campaign Committee (DSCC), the National Republican Congressional Committee (NRCC), and the National Republican Senatorial Campaign Committee (NRSC)—became expert in identifying the close races that would benefit most from party contributions and services. They disseminated information designed to encourage political action committees, or PACs, and individual donors to support the candidates in those races.[7] These organizations encouraged members of Congress and congressional retirees to redistribute funds they raised to help those same candidates. The Democratic National Committee (DNC) and Republican National Committee (RNC) also aired campaign ads designed to set a national political agenda. Party organizations located in Washington, D.C., and in many states helped organize voter identification and mobilization efforts, often referred to as "coordinated campaigns," to help candidates and party committees. Although party organizations accounted for only a small amount of the financial resources of candidates in major-party contested races—approximately $10.4 million for those competing for the House and $14.25 million for Senate candidates, or 2 percent of the respective totals, during the 2002 elections—the parties' influence on congressional elections extends well beyond their monetary contributions.[8]

Early adaptations to the law by interest groups involved the formation of PACs, which raise money from individuals and contribute the funds to candidates, party committees, and other groups. PACs became the major electoral arm of most interest groups. By 1988 their number had reached 4,832. Then, their ranks dipped slightly and stabilized. PACs contributed approximately $164.2 million to House candidates and $53.3 million to Senate candidates in major-party contested elections in 2002, accounting for roughly 34 percent and 18 percent of these candidates' total resources. A few PACs provided political expertise in the form of in-kind contributions of polls, media, or other campaign services to candidates, giving the PACs a measure of influence over the conduct of a candidate's campaign.

A small number of PACs made independent expenditures designed to directly inject information into the campaign agenda that could help or harm one of the candidates. A handful of so-called "lead PACs" distributed information about candidates, their issue stances, and the competitiveness of their races for the purpose of influencing the decisions of the leaders of like-minded PACs. Others, most notably EMILY's List, championing pro-choice Democratic women candidates, practiced "bundling," or collecting checks made out to designated candidates from the PAC's members and then packaging (in a bundle) and delivering them to each candidate. All of these activities fell within the guidelines established by the FECA.[9] Other interest group activities involved providing candidates with endorsements, advocating that organization members support specific candidates, conducting and publicizing research on individual candidates, and organizing campaign volunteers and other grassroots activities to help candidates.

Limited by the FECA in the amounts they could directly contribute, some individuals sought to increase their influence by forming PACs, hosting fund-raising events, bundling contributions, and adopting some of the other techniques that political organizations used. Some also made contributions in the names of family members, including children not yet old enough to vote. During the 2002 elections, individuals accounted for $237.1 million, or 48 percent, of the resources collected by candidates in major-party contested House races and $174.9 million, or 60 percent, of the resources collected by their counterparts in Senate elections.

Candidates also learned how to operate within the confines of the FECA's regulatory regime. Those who adapted best understood that to win an election they needed to wage a campaign for resources that focused on raising small and moderate-sized contributions from many donors. They assembled campaign organizations comprising professional fund-raising consultants and other political operatives whose reputations assured potential donors that the candidate was running a serious campaign. This was especially important to challengers, who because of their long odds of success need to make the case that their candidacies were viable, and to candidates for open seats, who generally need to raise large sums because their races tend to be among the most competitive.[10]

The Demise of the FECA

Many donors and recipients of political contributions also sought ways to influence federal elections outside of the FECA. Some continued to challenge aspects of the law to test their constitutionality and to see whether the FEC or the Department of Justice would prosecute violators. These efforts are consistent with those of other individuals and groups whose activities are subject to government regulation. They weakened the regulatory regime the FECA had established, and in the minds of many they created a need for further reform.[11]

Political parties were among the most aggressive organizations in finding ways to spend money outside the confines of the law. Following the FEC's decision allowing party committees to raise and spend soft money to finance administrative and electioneering activities, party organizations in Washington began to step up their soft money–raising efforts, often funneling what they raised to states where there were competitive contests and that could legally accept the funds. By the 1996 elections, party soft money fund raising had begun to skyrocket. New spending opportunities were the primary impetus for the change. Several courts had ruled that political communications that did not expressly advocate the election or defeat of individual federal candidates were not subject to the FECA. The rulings opened a major breach in the regulatory system, freeing political parties and interest groups to spend virtually unlimited amounts of soft money on issue advocacy advertising to influence federal elections.

The parties' response was to raise record amounts of soft, or unregulated, money and blanket the airwaves. The parties' soft money receipts roughly tripled between the 1992 and 1996 elections, and they almost doubled between 1996 and 2000.[12] The Democrats were particularly aggressive in taking advantage of the soft money option, using these funds to substantially reduce the Republicans' fund-raising advantage. The increases in spending in midterm elections were not quite as large as those in presidential election years, but they also were impressive.

Most soft money was raised by party organizations in Washington and distributed to the states, where state party leaders were instructed, sometimes in great detail, how to spend it. This enabled the national parties to capitalize on the fund-raising ability of the president, cabinet officials, congressional leaders, and other powerful individuals and to impose a national strategy on state party committees. The parties spent soft money on highly organized "independent," "parallel," and "coordinated" campaigns designed to set a national campaign agenda or to influence agendas, issues, and candidate images in individual House, Senate, and presidential campaigns. These campaigns involved teams of pollsters, issue researchers, media consultants, grassroots organizers, and direct-mail and telemarketing experts hired to carry out party-sponsored activity to influence specific contests.[13]

The independent campaigns involved what the FEC categorizes as "independent expenditures," including radio, television, and direct-mail communications that expressly call for the election or defeat of a federal candidate. Because these expenditures must be made with hard money and without a candidate's prior knowledge or approval, they became less popular following the introduction of issue advocacy advertisements. The parties spent a mere $3.6 million on these in the 2002 election.[14]

Parallel campaigns are similar to independent campaigns in that they are designed to influence competitive contests, require substantial organization and planning, and involve communications that flow directly from party committees to voters. However, they were partially financed with soft money, did not expressly advocate a candidate's election or defeat, and were not fully subject to federal reporting requirements, making it impossible to determine exactly how much the parties spent in connection with individual congressional races. It is estimated that parties spent $101 million on the television advertising component of their parallel campaigns in 2002.[15]

Coordinated campaigns involve traditional grassroots campaigning enhanced by innovations in voter targeting, communications, and mobilization. Party committees used a combination of hard and soft money to register voters, print and distribute leaflets, and organize door-to-door visits and other grassroots activities. During the 2002 elections some party committees used the Internet as an organizing and fund-raising tool for their coordinated campaigns. Although it is difficult to estimate the amounts party committees spent on coordinated campaigns in 2002, the national-to-state-party financial transfers suggest a figure of about $95 million.[16]

Interest groups also learned to navigate outside the FECA. Some called on prominent politicians to help them raise funds that they used to carry out their own independent, parallel, and coordinated campaigns. Several created so-called 527 committees, tax exempt organizations (in some cases merely separate bank accounts) named after the portion of the Internal Revenue Code that defines them. These organizations consisted of teams of interest group leaders and consultants who raised and spent nonfederal funds on candidate-centered campaign communications consisting of nonexpress advocacy. A small number of interest groups coalesced behind new groups to which they gave innocuous names. This enabled the groups to spend large amounts of money to influence the outcomes of individual elections without revealing to voters the actual sources of that money. For example, during the 2002 elections many of the nation's major pharmaceutical companies joined behind the name "United Seniors Association" to spend $8.7 million on nonexpress television advertising in support of Republican candidates who favored the companies' interests. The name "United Seniors" gave the ads more credibility and influence than they would have received had they been attributed to a list of large drug companies.[17]

In addition to helping party committees and allied interest groups raise money for their independent, parallel, and coordinated campaigns, current and retired members of Congress formed their own 527 committees and used them to carry out similar campaigns. In 2002, the top 125 such organizations spent more than $73.5 million on various political activities.[18] Prior to the commencement of the 2002 elections, and certainly by the elections' end, it was apparent to most political observers that the FECA's regulatory system had become as much loophole as law.

The Enactment of the BCRA

The enactment of the BCRA bore similarities to the histories of other pieces of campaign finance reform legislation in that public perception of corruption was necessary but not sufficient for its passage. For members of Congress to pass campaign finance legislation that has the potential to affect their political careers and livelihoods, the public must be galvanized and clamoring for reform. Scandal is often needed for that to happen. In addition, legislators often must take extraordinary measures to build the broad-based coalitions required to overcome the obstacles that other members of the House and Senate routinely erect to prevent reform proposals from becoming law. They also need to craft a bill that the president will be willing to sign.[19] These political ingredients aligned in just the right way to make the enactment of the BCRA possible.

Public Perceptions of Corruption

Just as media reports had raised misgivings about the role of money in politics in the past, they raised them prior to the enactment of the BCRA. Public opinion research revealed that substantial majorities considered large political contributions and political fund raising a major source of corruption. The public was particularly troubled by large, soft money donations and believed that restrictions should be placed on the amounts that corporations and unions may contribute to political campaigns.[20] Considerable numbers of Americans also were found to believe that members of Congress sometimes cast their votes based on what big contributors to their party want and that the will of big contributors takes precedence over the views of constituents.[21] Further research indicated that sizable percentages of the public considered campaign finance reform a high-priority issue.[22]

Political candidates and congressional donors were just as critical of the campaign finance system as the public. When asked what they thought about the campaign finance system, 82 percent of the public agreed that it was broken and needed to be replaced or that it had some problems and needed to be changed. Almost 80 percent of individuals who made significant contributions ($200 or more) to congressional candidates agreed with this position, as did a similar number of Democratic and Republican candidates who ran for Congress in 2000. Minuscule numbers of citizens, donors, and candidates believed that the law was fine and should not be changed.[23]

Insurmountable Obstacles?

Despite public sentiment in favor, passing campaign finance reform legislation is always a major challenge because the members of Congress whose votes are necessary to enact it will be regulated by it. These legislators consider themselves experts on electoral politics, and each possesses a keen understanding of the provisions of the election system that work to his or her individual advantage or disadvantage. Party and interest group leaders also know which aspects of the system benefit their organizations. All of these stakeholders are predisposed to speculate on how different reform packages could affect their ability to participate in elections and influence the policymaking process.

Given the nature of public opinion on the subject, members of Congress, congressional candidates, and party leaders routinely portray themselves as reformers while advocating changes that reflect their own self-interest. Most incumbents are preoccupied with protecting elements of the system that benefit them, and most challengers are just as vocal about reforming away those advantages. Most Republicans prefer high contribution limits or none at all because such would enable them to take advantage of their superior fund-raising prowess and larger donor base. Democrats are typically more favorably disposed toward public funding for campaigns and free media time and postage, which would reduce the impact of the Republicans' financial advantages. More Democrats than Republicans have been inclined toward eliminating nonfederal money and party and interest group issue advocacy ads, despite the fact Democrats, not Republicans, have relied more heavily on those resources.[24]

Members of Congress's two chambers also have differing points of view, reflecting differences between running in a House district and in a statewide Senate campaign. Variations in legislators' opinions about reform also derive from the demands that fund raising makes on different types of candidates. Women, African Americans, ethnic minorities, and members of other traditionally underrepresented groups, who depend on national donor networks, have preferences that differ from those of most white male candidates. Candidates' opinions about campaign reform further vary according to the nature of their constituencies. Candidates from wealthy, urban seats tend to have fund-raising opportunities, spending needs, and views on reform that are different from those of candidates from poor, rural states or districts. Of course, not all differences are grounded in personal or partisan advantage. Philosophical principles are also important. As noted earlier, Republicans tend to favor marketplace approaches, and Democrats generally prefer regulatory measures accompanied by public subsidies.

Finally, many legislators, and others, are skeptical about the government's ability to regulate the flow of political money. Some believe in what has been referred to as the "hydraulic theory," which maintains that money, like water, will flow through other channels or find new ones if an existing route is closed. They believe that any campaign finance reform will have only a limited effect at best. Others have embraced what might be called the "principle of inadequate results." They contend that a reform law that fails to accomplish all of its supporters' goals is not worth enacting. Still others base their skepticism on the well-established "law of unintended consequences," which holds that once a reform is passed, the unexpected is bound to happen.

Skepticism, difference of opinion, and the complexity of the issue have historically made it difficult for legislators to find the common ground needed to pass meaningful campaign reform. The sometimes-inflammatory rhetoric of reform groups occasionally widens the gaps between members of Congress. Nevertheless, between 1979 and 2002 House members and senators of both parties introduced an estimated nine hundred campaign finance bills.[25] Some of these were sincere attempts to improve the campaign finance system. Others were less sincere: Legislators who knew their bills would never be adopted introduced them to provide political cover for themselves rather than to actually enact reform.

Some progress was made prior to the enactment of BCRA. In 1992, Congress actually succeeded in passing a reform measure whose major feature was its potential to even the playing field among congressional candidates. The bill used a combination of public matching funds and other incentives to encourage candidates to abide by voluntary spending limits, including voluntary limits on funds raised from PACs. However, despite the bill's success in Congress, it was vetoed by President George H. W. Bush and died when the Senate was unable to muster the two-thirds majority needed to override the veto.[26]

Undeterred by the failure of the 1992 bill, reformers continued to press their case. A number of developments strengthened their position. Growing soft money expenditures and issue advocacy advertising increased concern about the role of money in politics among the public, political contributors, reform groups, legislators, and politicians. Media coverage of White House sleepovers; weekend getaways for wealthy donors and federal politicians; and private policy briefings for donors featuring high-ranking administration officials and congressional leaders added a whiff of scandal to a system that the public already believed favored special interests over ordinary citizens.

Leading reformers also made a tactical decision to scale back their goals. Previous reform efforts, such as the one in 1992, focused on the introduction of public funding, communications subsidies, or other measures designed to restructure the financing of federal elections. Sens. John McCain, R-Ariz., and Russell Feingold, D-Wis., and Reps. Christopher Shays, R-Conn., and Martin Meehan, D-Mass., sought instead to restore those FECA regulations that had been overwhelmed by loopholes. Led by these champions, reformers both in and out of Congress became more skillful at bipartisan coalition building and the use of unorthodox approaches to lawmaking.[27] A combination of resourceful insider lobbying, grassroots mobilization, and sympathetic media coverage enabled the sponsors of the BCRA to achieve a modicum of success in advancing their goal in the 105th and 106th Congresses.[28] During both, the bill's House sponsors were able to pass precursors to the BCRA over the opposition of the Republican leaders who controlled the House. The bill's Senate sponsors were less successful, as the bill twice fell victim to filibusters.

The Politics of Passage

The dynamics of the 107th Congress were different in some important respects from those of the two that preceded it. First, although the Republicans maintained procedural control over the House and won the White House, the Democrats gained control over the Senate when Sen. Jim Jeffords of Vermont quit the Republican Party to become an independent. Second, the turnover associated with the 2000 elections led to a small but important increase in the number of pro-reform members of Congress. Third, McCain's unexpected success in raising the profile of campaign finance reform in the Republican presidential nominating contest emboldened reformers. Fourth, the Enron scandal put names and faces to questions about the influence of corporate contributions on government regulatory decisions. It led some legislators to conclude that a vote for the BCRA was a good vehicle for showing their willingness to take action against corporate abuses.[29]

The sequencing of events was one of the most important differences between reform efforts in the 107th and preceding Congresses. In both the 105th and 106th Congresses the House passed a reform package first, with a significant number of those voting yea anticipating that the Senate would later vote it down. In the 107th Congress the order was reversed. Once the Senate had passed the BCRA it was up to the House to determine the bill's fate because President George W. Bush had previously announced that if given the opportunity to do so, he would sign a campaign finance reform bill into law. This left representatives who had previously voted for reform, but did not actually want it to go into effect, in an awkward position. They could cast their votes consistently in support of the bill and live with the consequences of the new law, or they could reverse their position, deny the bill passage, and look like hypocrites. Legislators undoubtedly felt considerable constituent pressure to support the BCRA. Those who had previously voted for it probably felt the most pressure, because reversing positions would give a challenger the opportunity to hold them politically accountable for flip-flopping on a highly salient vote.

Partisan pressure also was high. Most Republicans, led by the GOP House leadership, opposed the legislation, and the leadership would not have brought it to a vote if the bill's supporters had not garnered sufficient backing for a discharge petition to force it to the floor. House Democrats and their leaders generally supported reform. The positions taken by each party's legislative majority in the House, as well as the Senate, are somewhat ironic. The Republican Party organizations' prowess in fund raising gave them a tremendous advantage in collecting hard money, and the BCRA's ban on soft money and restrictions on interest group issue advocacy have the potential to be more harmful to the Democrats and their allies. Indeed, the Democratic Party organizations' failure to build a broad individual donor base meant that the only place in which they had competed with the GOP in fund raising was in the realm of soft money. However, as noted above, both ideology and pragmatism often influence how members of Congress vote. In the case of the BCRA, members of both parties seemed predisposed to vote in accordance with their philosophical beliefs. Some Democratic lawmakers also probably voted for the reform to please some of their core voters, whereas some Republicans perceived opposing the bill as a way to shore up their electoral base.

Congressional debate over the bill was heated. Backers of the BCRA argued that it would help improve the legitimacy of the federal government. Meehan argued, "Ending the soft money system will go a long way towards restoring public confidence in the decisions our government makes . . . . it will cut the ties between million dollar contributions and the legislators who write the laws that govern our nation." [30] Shays agreed, maintaining, "Our legislation bans soft money, insists that sham 'issue ads' are covered under campaign law, and gives the FEC the teeth necessary to enforce that law." [31]

Many of the BCRA's opponents argued that the bill threatened to trample on free speech rights. In the words of then House majority whip Tom DeLay, R-Texas, "The central issues in this debate are the preservation of a vibrant freedom of speech and full political participation. I am fighting . . . to defend these core constitutional freedoms." [32] Speaker Dennis Hastert, R-Ill., declared the clash over the BCRA "Armageddon." [33]

Ultimately, Republican congressional leaders lost the battle over the BCRA. The House voted to pass a slightly different version of the bill than the Senate had passed. Senate sponsors McCain and Feingold successfully pressed their colleagues to accept the House version as a substitute for the version the Senate had previously adopted. On March 27, 2002, President George W. Bush signed the BCRA into law.

Major Provisions of the BCRA

The reform bill that the second President Bush signed was far more modest in its goals than the one that the first President Bush vetoed. The BCRA mainly sought to close some of the loopholes that had undermined portions of the FECA, rather than to revamp the campaign finance system. Most of the law seeks to prevent political parties and interest groups from circumventing federal contribution and expenditure limits and avoiding federal disclosure requirements. It also aims to reduce corruption and the appearance of corruption associated with federal candidates' raising huge unregulated donations from wealthy interests for political parties.

The act has three major components: a ban on soft money, increased contribution limits, and restrictions on issue advocacy advertising.[34] The provisions prohibit national party organizations, such as the DNC, DCCC, DSCC, RNC, NRCC, and NRSC, or any entity they establish or control from raising, spending, or transferring funds that are not subject to federal regulation. Similar provisions apply to federal officeholders and their agents. The law requires national, state, and local parties to use only federal funds for all electioneering communications featuring a federal candidate. The act's definition of such communications is more inclusive than the "magic words" test that was previously used. Under the BCRA any broadcast, cable, or satellite television or broadcast radio ad that mentions a federal candidate, is targeted at their voting electorate, and is aired within thirty days of a primary or sixty days of the general election is considered an electioneering communication. The BCRA also requires that all voter registration drives conducted during the last 120 days of a federal election that mention a federal candidate be financed with federal funds.

The law's increased hard money contribution limits were designed to partially compensate for the loss of party soft money. Among other things, the law raises from $1,000 to $2,000 the amount an individual can contribute to a congressional candidate in each phase of the election (primary, general, and runoff; see Table 5-1). It raises from $50,000 to $95,000 the ceiling for aggregate biennial contributions to federal candidates, party committees, and political action committees and sets some constraints on how those funds can be allocated. Other aspects of the law concern coordinated expenditures on behalf of candidates, over which candidates have significant influence, and other expenditures, which are made with less or no candidate involvement (see Table 5-2).

The BCRA's provisions for issue advocacy advertising are designed to bring under federal regulation broadcast communications intended to affect the outcomes of congressional or presidential elections. The act's limits on broadcast electioneering communications create a "federal spending period" in which only regulated, hard money can be used to finance campaign ads designed to expressly influence federal elections. Issue advocacy broadcasts made prior to this federal spending period could still be financed with unregulated, outside money during the 2004 elections.

Table 5-1 Federal Contribution Limits to Congressional Candidates and Political Parties

Donors or Spenders	House Candidates	Senate Candidates	National Party Committees	State Party Committees' Federal Accounts	Federal PACs
Individuals	$2,000	$2,000	$25,000 per year	$10,000 per year	$5,000 per year
National party committees	$15,000	$35,000	Unlimited transfers to other party committees	Unlimited transfers to other party committees	$5,000 per year
State party committees' federal accounts	$5,000	$5,000	Unlimited transfers to other party committees	Unlimited transfers to other party committees	$5,000 per year
Federal PACs	$5,000	$5,000 per year	$15,000 per year	$5,000 per year	$5,000 per year
Corporations and unions	Prohibited	Prohibited	Prohibited	Prohibited	Prohibited
Section 527 committees	Prohibited	Prohibited	Prohibited	Prohibited	Prohibited
501 (c)(4s) and 501 (c)(6s) and nonprofit social welfare organizations	Prohibited	Prohibited	Prohibited	Prohibited	Prohibited

Source: Adapted from Federal Election Commission, "Contribution Limits" (www.fec.gov/pages/brochures/contrib.htm) and Campaign Legal Center, "The Campaign Finance Guide" (Washington, D.C., 2004).

Notes: Individuals may give a contribution of $2,000 in each phase of the election (primary, general, and runoff). They are limited to a biennial contribution of $95,000 ($37,500 to all federal candidates and $57,500 to all party committees and PACs). The limits for individual contributions to candidates, national party committees, the biennial individual limit, and the national party committee limit for contributions to Senate candidates are indexed for inflation. In the event the millionaire's amendment is triggered, the limits for individual contributions increase. The parties' national, congressional, and senatorial campaign committees are considered separate committees when making contributions to House candidates, so they can contribute up to $5,000 each, for a total of $15,000.

Table 5-2 Federal Spending Limits in Congressional Elections

	Coordinated Expenditures on Behalf of Candidates		Other Expenditures		
	House Candidates	Senate Candidates	Independent Expenditures	Electioneering Communications	"Levin" Accounts
Individuals	Considered a contribution	Considered a contribution	Unlimited	Unlimited	Whatever state law permits, up to $10,000
National party committees	$10,000	$20,000 or $.02 times a state's voting age population, whichever is greater	Unlimited	Unlimited	Prohibited
State party committees' federal accounts	$10,000	$20,000 or $.02 times a state's voting age population, whichever is greater	Unlimited	Unlimited	Prohibited
Fderal PACs	Considered a contribution	Considered a contribution	Unlimited	Unlimited	Whatever state law permits, up to $10,000
Corporations and unions	Prohibited	Prohibited	Prohibited	Prohibited	Whatever state law permits, up to $10,000
Section 527 committees	Prohibited	Prohibited	Prohibited if committee is incorporated	Prohibited if committee is incorporated. If not incorporated, unlimited	Whatever state law permits, up to $10,000
501 (c)(4s), 501 (c)(6s), and nonprofit social welfare organizations	Prohibited	Prohibited	Prohibited except for qualifying 501(c)(4) and nonprofit social welfare organizations	Prohibited except for qualifying 501(c)(4) and nonprofit social welfare organizations	$10,000 if permitted by state law

Source: Adapted from Federal Election Commission, "Contribution Limits" (www.fec.gov/pages/brochures/contrib.htm) and Campaign Legal Center, "The Campaign Finance Guide" (Washington, D.C., 2004).

Notes: The limits for coordinated expenditures in House and Senate elections are indexed for inflation. The limit for House elections in 2004 was $37,310 each for all national party committees and for state party committees, except for states with only one representative, in which case the limit was $74,620. The limit for Senate elections in 2004 ranged from $74,620 for all national party committees and for state party committees for the smallest states to $1,994,846 for all national party committees and for state party committees in California. In the event the millionaire's provision is triggered, the limits for coordinated expenditures in both House and Senate elections increase.

Additional parts of the law were intended to allow party committees to make either limited coordinated expenditures on behalf of federal candidates or unlimited independent expenditures, but not both. The so-called millionaire's provision of the law uses a complicated formula to raise the limits for individual contributions and for party coordinated expenditures when a self-funded House candidate contributes more than $350,000 to his or her own campaign, or a self-funded Senate candidate contributes $150,000 plus an amount equal to four cents times the state's eligible voting population. Another provision bars minors aged seventeen and younger, who cannot legally vote, from making contributions. A final aspect of the law, the so-called "stand by your ad" provision, requires candidates to state in their television and radio ads that they approve the message.

The Supreme Court Rules on the BCRA

Just as the FECA of 1974 faced stiff legal challenges, so did the BCRA. Indeed, reform opponents began preparing to mount such challenges while the bill was still being debated in the Senate. Leading the charge was Sen. Mitch McConnell, R-Ky., who while still filibustering against the reform, pledged that if the bill became law he would be the lead plaintiff.[35] Among the dozens of others who joined the cause to overturn the law were the RNC, House Speaker Hastert, the California Democratic and Republican Parties, the Cato Institute, the American Civil Liberties Union (ACLU), the AFL-CIO, the National Rifle Association, and eight state attorneys general. These plaintiffs maintain that the law's ban on issue advocacy advertising and restrictions on party financial activity are unconstitutional violations of free speech rights. The National Voting Rights Institute, the U.S. Public Interest Research Group (associated with consumer advocate and presidential candidate Ralph Nader), and some other voter groups joined the suit for a different reason, claiming its increased contribution limits were unconstitutional because they favor the wealthy. Writing in defense of the law were the Committee on Economic Development (comprising many of the nation's business leaders), almost every living former member of the ACLU leadership, and twenty-one state attorneys general.[36] Numerous political scientists and other academics also played roles in the suit, providing testimony and advice to plaintiffs on both sides.[37]

In addition to the legal wrangling that was destined to find its way to the U.S. Supreme Court, the BCRA encountered another set of challenges when the FEC began drafting the regulations for administering the law. The BCRA was not warmly received by some members of the commission. This was not surprising, given that two commissioners—Bradley Smith and Chairman David Mason—made speeches and released statements challenging the bill during the congressional debate.[38] Some of the FEC's rules weakened provisions of the law designed to prevent soft money from influencing federal campaigns. McCain, Feingold, Shays, and Meehan considered the rule allowing federal candidates to be involved in state party soft money fund-raising events particularly troubling. They responded to it by filing a legal challenge and drafting a congressional resolution to overturn the regulations under the Congressional Review Act.[39]

On May 2, 2003, a special three-judge panel of the U.S. District Court for the District of Columbia handed down a 1,638-page verdict in *McConnell v. FEC.*[40] The judges were sharply divided on many issues. The verdict upheld most of the BCRA's main provisions, but the parties to the suit and most others viewed it as little more than a fact-finding mission because of their belief that the Supreme Court would chart its own route on this important case. Perhaps in recognition of this the lower court judges issued a stay of their own ruling, leaving the provisions of the original BCRA in effect pending review by the Supreme Court.

The Supreme Court's ruling on the BCRA was no less divided than that of the special three-judge panel. On December 10, 2003, the Court handed down a five-to-four decision upholding most of the BCRA's major provisions. Perhaps the most noteworthy provision of the law overturned was one that required the parties to choose at the time of the nomination whether to make coordinated expenditures or unlimited independent expenditures. An important aspect of this provision is that once the decision was made it would bind an entire party organization, including national, state, and local committees. Hence, it would prohibit a party's national committee from making coordinated expenditures on behalf of a federal candidate if a state party committee made an independent expenditure on behalf of that same candidate (and vice versa). The Court ruled the provision unconstitutional, indicating that party committees could make both coordinated and independent expenditures in one election. The Supreme Court also overturned the prohibition against contributions by minors. It declined to rule on challenges to the millionaire's provision, the increased limits for hard money, and the regulations governing coordination among different political committees, stating that the plaintiffs lacked standing on most of these issues because no party had yet suffered injury.

Speculations about the BCRA's Impact

Speculation about the impact of any new law is difficult. Speculations about the impact of the new campaign finance law are particularly challenging because these laws are being probed for weaknesses by some of the nation's best political and legal talent. Moreover, one should expect the act's short-term effects to differ from its medium-range effects because it will take time for candidates and individuals and groups that raise, contribute, and spend campaign money to adapt to the new regulations. History also suggests the act's long-range effects will differ from its short- and medium-range effects. Decisions by FEC commissioners and federal judges will probably reshape the BCRA just as they reshaped the FECA and the campaign finance statutes that preceded it. Nevertheless, some informed speculation about the act's immediate impact is possible, even before the FEC has released complete figures for the financing of the 2004 elections.

Congressional Candidates

One of the immediate effects of the BCRA was to inspire a major jump in the fund-raising activity of congressional candidates. It is doubtful that this was one of the reformers' goals, but it is not surprising given that most politicians tend to be cautious and like to protect themselves from the impact of change. House general election candidates raised 16 percent more money in the 2004 election cycle than they did in the 2002 cycle.[41] Senate general election candidates increased their take by 27 percent, but that jump can be attributed in part to the fact that some of the largest states, including New York and California, did not have Senate elections in 2002 but had them in 2004.[42]

Altering the balance of fund-raising power among congressional incumbents, challengers, and open-seat candidates also was not one of the reformers' goals. Yet many opponents of the act argued that raising the ceilings for individual contributions could work to the advantage of incumbents. They predicted that incumbents would use their positions in Congress to leverage contributions of $4,000 (for both their primary and general election campaigns) instead of $2,000 from donors seeking access to the legislative process. Many proponents of the law argued that by enabling challengers and open-seat candidates to raise larger contributions from their intense followers the act would work to the nonincumbents' advantage. Figures from the 2004 elections suggest that the act's opponents were correct: House incumbents raised more than 66 percent of all of the funds contributed in those elections, as compared to the approximately 60 percent or less they had raised in the last six elections (see Figure 5-1). Differences in the sizes, populations, and traditions of the fifty states and the fact that only a third of all Senate seats are up for election in a given year make trends related to Senate elections more difficult to interpret. Nevertheless, the 2004 Senate elections also support the contention that the BCRA worked to the advantage of incumbents, who raised roughly 36 percent of the money raised by candidates for the upper chamber, a substantially greater proportion than incumbents had raised in recent previous elections and considerably more than the 15 percent raised by their challenger opponents.[43]

Republican House candidates appear to be faring somewhat better under the BCRA than the Democrats. During the 2004 elections the Republicans raised 57 percent of the total campaign funds raised by major-party candidates; Democrats raised 43 percent (see Figure 5-2). It is more challenging to assess the impact of the BCRA on the fund raising of Democratic and Republican Senate candidates. Among the incumbent senators running for reelection in 2004 were Barbara Boxer, D-Calif., Charles Schumer, D-N.Y., and Democratic leader Tom Daschle, D-S.D. Their prodigious fund-raising skills contributed to a 51 percent to 49 percent Democratic fund-raising advantage during the first twenty-two months of the 2004 election season. Blair Hull, a candidate for the Democratic nomination to the Senate from Illinois, also significantly contributed to the Democrats' advantage in receipts by self-financing his campaign to the tune of

Figure 5-1 The Impact of BCRA on House Incumbent, Challenger, and Open-Seat Candidates' Receipts

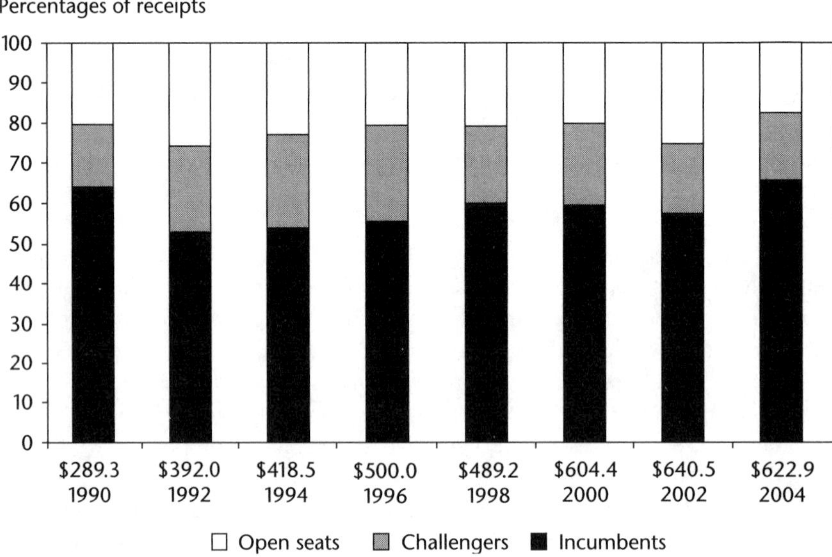

Source: Compiled from Federal Election Commission data.

Notes: Figures are in millions of dollars. Figures for the 2004 cycle are preliminary and only include contributions made from January 1, 2003, through October 13, 2004.

almost $29 million. Given that the mix of Senate seats up for election will not be the same in 2006 and that the Republicans will enjoy an enlarged majority prior to that race, Senate Democrats may lose the razor-thin advantage they enjoyed in early 2004.

The BCRA also appears to have accelerated a trend toward greater reliance on large contributions from individuals. Contributions of between $750 and $1,000 accounted for less than 30 percent of all donations made by individuals in 1990 (see Figure 5-3). Then they increased steadily, until they amounted to almost half in 2002. The figures for the 2004 elections suggest that such contributions will comprise a considerably larger portion of all individual contributions in the future. Roughly 27 percent of all individual contributions were in the $750–$1,000 range, and another 29 percent were between $1,001 and $2,000. Not surprisingly, a pattern of increasing reliance on large contributions also was present for the Senate. Preliminary (and somewhat incomplete) figures indicate that Senate candidates raised approximately 28 percent of their individual contributions in amounts of $750 to $1,000 and another 38 percent in amounts of more than $1,000.[44] The fact that some House and Senate candidates contributed enough to their own campaigns to trigger the millionaire's provision

Figure 5-2 The Impact of BCRA on House Democratic and Republican Candidates' Receipts

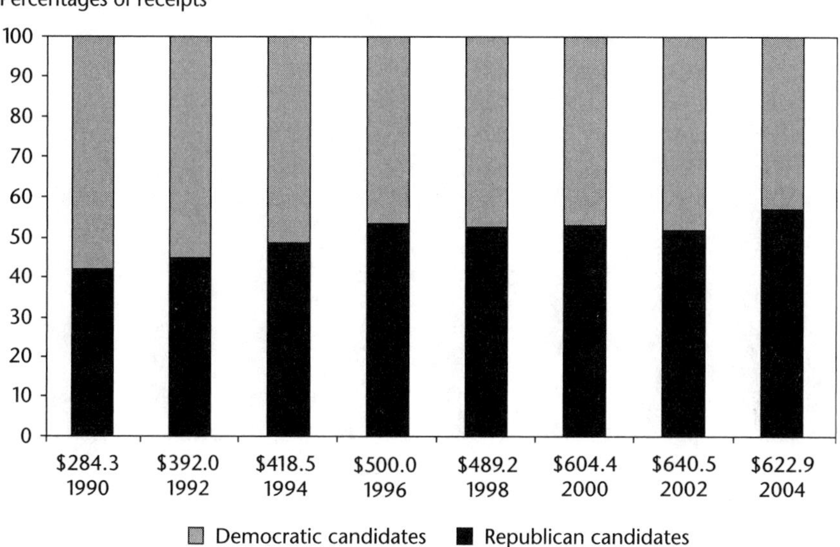

Source: Compiled from Federal Election Commission data.

Notes: Figures are in millions of dollars. Figures for the 2004 cycle are preliminary and only include contributions made from January 1, 2003, through October 13, 2004.

enabled their opponents to collect contributions of more than $4,000 from some individual donors.

The early evidence suggests only small differences in the partisan distribution of individual contributions to congressional candidates. Republican candidates for the House raised almost 28 percent of their individual contributions in amounts of $750–$1,000 and another 30 percent in sums greater than $1,000. House Democrats were only slightly less dependent on large individual contributions, raising roughly 26 percent in amounts of $750–$1,000 and another 28 percent in amounts of $1,000 or more. Preliminary figures indicate that there were no substantial differences in the amounts Republican and Democratic Senate candidates raised in large individual contributions in 2004.[45]

Party Organizations

Following the BCRA's enactment numerous party leaders complained that it would virtually eliminate the parties' roles in congressional elections. The act's ban on soft money clearly has reduced the parties' influence in elections, but the claim that it would leave the parties irrelevant is hyperbole. Although congressional

Figure 5-3 The Impact of BCRA on Individual Contributions to House Candidates

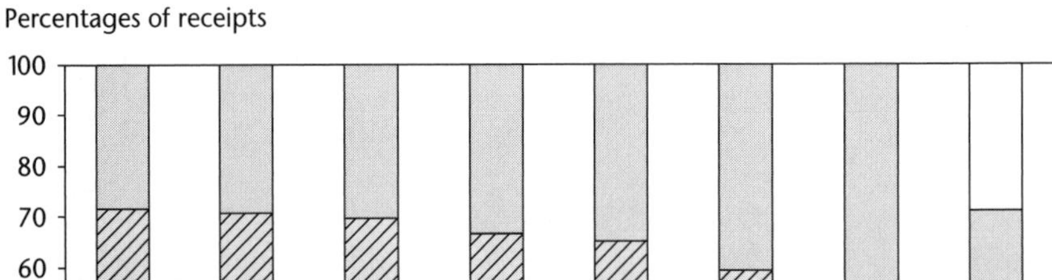

Source: Compiled from Federal Election Commission data.

Notes: Figures are in millions of dollars and do not include third-party candidates. Figures for the 2004 cycle are preliminary and only include contributions made from January 1, 2003, through October 13, 2004.

elections will probably become somewhat more candidate centered as a result of the act, the parties undoubtedly will find ways to play influential roles.

In fact, formal party organizations began preparing to adapt to the BCRA as soon as it was enacted. They entered a new phase of party building that centers on expanding their donor networks to include more individuals who give small and medium-sized contributions; on advising candidates about how to participate in the new campaign finance system; and on instructing state and local party leaders how to further develop their organizations' institutional capacities, fund raising, and campaign service programs without violating the law. These developments parallel those that took place shortly after passage of the FECA.[46]

As noted earlier, during the elections leading up to the BCRA most party soft money was raised by party organizations located in the nation's capital and transferred to, and spent by, state and local party committees. That national party money often came with strings that reduced the autonomy of state party organizations. In many cases the national parties gave state party committees detailed directives on the services they were to use the money to purchase, the vendors they were to purchase from, and the congressional candidates who were to benefit. The new prohibitions against national party soft money fund raising, soft money transfers to state parties, and soft money fund-raising assistance for state parties can be expected to weaken the national parties' abilities to impose a strategy on their state affiliates. As a result, state parties should become somewhat more financially independent and autonomous and perhaps less involved in congressional election campaigns.

This does not mean that party organizations will lose their roles in congressional elections. The Democratic and Republican congressional and senatorial campaign committees, for example, have continued to carry out tasks that are important to congressional campaigns. They remain important sources of campaign contributions, coordinated expenditures, and independent expenditures. They also recruit candidates and provide them with assistance in campaign management, fund raising, and the other aspects of campaigning that require technical expertise, in-depth research, and connections with the political consultants who possess the knowledge and skills needed to run a contemporary congressional campaign. The congressional and senatorial campaign committees also continue to have a hand in coordinating the contributions and campaign efforts of wealthy interest groups and individuals.[47]

The prohibitions against party soft money and issue advocacy advertising can be expected to alter parties' campaign communications in close elections. They can be expected to substitute coordinated and independent expenditures for issue ads in competitive House and Senate races, particularly those races where a self-funded candidate triggers the BCRA's millionaire's provision. Preliminary figures for 2004 indicate that the parties spent about $100 million, roughly thirty-one times more than was spent in the previous election.[48] Both parties expended substantial sums on television, radio, direct mail, and other forms of advertising expressly calling for the election or defeat of selected House and Senate candidates.

Political commentators voiced somewhat divergent expectations about which party committees would benefit most from the soft money ban. A few argued that the fact that the Democrats provided the vast majority of congressional votes cast in support of the BCRA suggested the reform would work to that party's advantage. However, most predicted that the Republicans' long-established hard-money fund-raising advantage would combine with the Democrats' traditional dependence on soft money to work to the GOP's advantage.

The evidence provided by the last seven election cycles is not so clear cut. During the 1990 election season, before national party organizations began raising substantial sums of soft money, Republican party committees raised 72 percent of all party money reported to the FEC (see Figure 5-4). During the 1990s the amount of soft money the parties raised and spent continued to grow. By relying heavily on those funds the Democrats were able to make significant steps toward reducing the gap between themselves and the Republicans.

Figure 5-4 The Impact of BCRA on Party Fund Raising

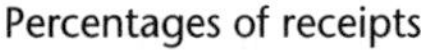

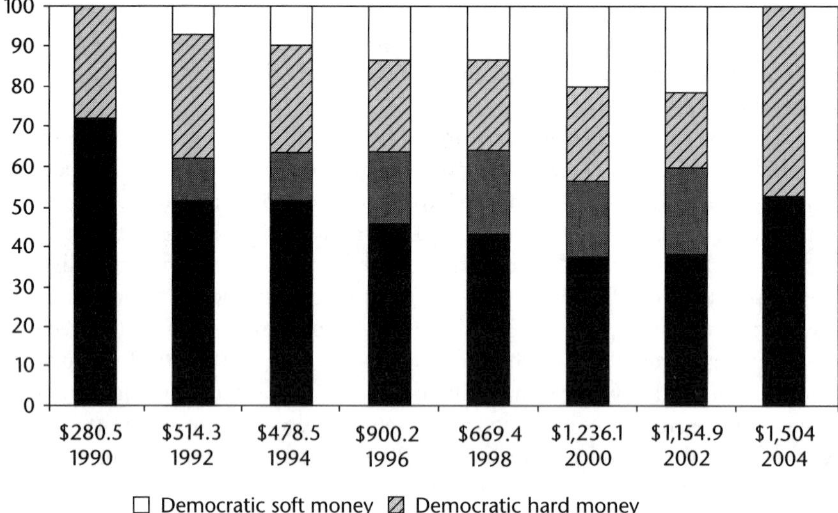

Source: Compiled from Federal Election Commission data.

Notes: Figures are in millions of dollars and represent the combination of federal and nonfederal receipts. The FEC did not start keeping records of nonfederal receipts until the 1992 election. The 1990 and 2004 figures are for federal money only. The 2004 figures only include receipts from January 1, 2003, through November 22, 2004.

The figures for the 2004 elections suggest that the BCRA's ban on national party soft money fund raising and strict limitations on state and local party soft money fund raising did not undermine the parties, as they both raised record funds. The Democratic Party committees raised approximately 47 percent of both parties' total dollars, which is a slightly larger proportion of the total party funding than they had collected in either 2000 and 2002. The figures for 2004 demonstrate that the Democrats' much-touted push to improve their direct-mail, telemarketing, and Internet fund raising has helped them substitute hard dollars for soft dollars and move closer to parity with the Republicans, at least in the short term. That Democratic Party committees will be able to reach full parity with their Republican counterparts remains unlikely, given the Republicans' ability to re-elect President Bush to the White House and increase their congressional majorities in 2004.

Another party activity that may increase in importance as a result of the BCRA is party-connected campaigning, which includes fund raising and spending by partisan individuals and groups that often act in concert with the formal party apparatus and work to advance some of its goals. Contributions from the leadership PACs and the campaign accounts of members of Congress and congressional retirees constitute an important set of party-connected activities. During the first eighteen months of the 2004 elections these sources accounted for $26.1 million in contributions to congressional candidates.[49] This figure constitutes a significant sum, and it was important because the vast majority of this money was spent in competitive House and Senate contests where it had the potential to have the greatest impact on the outcomes.

Some party-connected campaign activities involve outside groups. As noted above, members of Congress and congressional retirees used a variety of organizations, including 527 and 501(c) committees, to spend tens of millions of dollars to influence the 2002 congressional elections. The BCRA prohibits such activities, but its prohibitions against soft money fund raising and spending do not apply to party allies that are neither running for federal office nor working for a formal party organization. Several such allies have formed groups to spend nonfederal money to influence congressional elections. One pro-Republican group is the Leadership Forum. Run by former House member Bill Paxon, R-N.Y., and Susan Hirschmann, former chief of staff to House Majority Leader Tom DeLay, this group's goal is to raise contributions of $25,000 or more from an advisory board of donor–fund raisers and spend the money to help GOP candidates.[50] Another is the National Committee for a Responsible Senate (NCRS), which has strong connections to the NRSC and is incorporated as a 501(c)(6) organization, the tax designation used by most trade associations.[51] Among the Democratic-leaning groups is the Democratic Senate Majority Political Action Committee, headed by Monica Dixon, a former aide to Al Gore and a former executive director of the House Democratic Caucus. This organization has a federal PAC to make contributions to congressional candidates and uses a separate account to finance political advertisements, presumably during the nonfederal spending period.[52] Another Democratic-leaning group, America Votes, is a 527 committee directed by Cecile Richards, a former aide to Democratic House leader Nancy Pelosi. This organization sought to raise $3 million in 2004 to coordinate various outside groups allied with the Democratic Party.[53] Numerous other organizations were more focused on the 2004 presidential election, but the efforts of the Democratic-leaning Media Fund, run by Harold Ickes, President Clinton's former deputy chief of staff, and the Republican-oriented Progress for America, run by Chris LaCivita, a former NRSC political director, will be felt in congressional and other elections.[54] The FEC's rule-making activities have the potential to limit these organizations' activities, but the groups' arrival on the political scene demonstrates that party allies already have begun to explore ways to raise and spend nonfederal money to influence congressional elections.

Interest Groups

One of the major targets of the BCRA's sponsors was interest groups. One of the key rationales for banning party soft money was to shut down an avenue that some groups used to gain access to public officials and some public officials used to pressure groups for large contributions. The prohibitions against using unregulated funds to finance issue advocacy ads during the preprimary and pre–general election federal spending periods also were intended to decrease the influence of interest groups. A chief goal of the BCRA was to direct more interest group activity through federally regulated PACs. The act provides incentives for those groups that already have PACs to strengthen them and for others to create new ones. It also encourages PAC managers to expand their PACs' donor bases; to collect, bundle, and deliver checks from their donors to specific candidates; to televise independent expenditure ads during the federal spending period; and to contribute hard money to party committees. There is systematic evidence indicating that PACs are increasing their fund-raising efforts and receipts: Early figures suggest that PAC fund raising was up by about one-fourth during the 2004 election cycle. Anecdotal evidence suggests that some PACs and other organizations are preparing to devote greater attention to bundling campaign contributions and to making increased independent expenditures.[55] Preliminary figures demonstrate that by mid-October 2004, PACs made at least $8.8 million in independent expenditures in connection with congressional elections. Most of these expenditures were made by nonconnected, trade, and labor PACs. Such expenditures are consistent with these organizations' strategies that aim to influence the composition of Congress and in some cases also to secure access to powerful members. Corporate PACs rarely make independent expenditures because such expenditures can be counterproductive when the goal is to enable an organization's lobbyists to gain access in order to influence policy. Independent expenditures can backfire, provoking the anger of members of Congress.[56]

Some interest groups have responded to the BCRA by using existing organizations or forming new ones to raise and spend unregulated campaign funds. Among those that are working to help Democrats are America Coming Together, a 527 committee headed by Ellen Malcom, president of EMILY's List, and Steven Rosenthal, former political director of the AFL-CIO. The group intended to spend $94 million in 2004 for voter education and get-out-the-vote drives in competitive states.[57] Among those seeking to help Republicans is the Club for Growth, a 527 committee that spends money in congressional primaries and general elections to support pro–free market Republicans.[58]

Finally, the BCRA has the potential to influence the balance of power within the interest group community. Because business PACs, including those sponsored by corporations, trade associations, and cooperatives, raise substantially more money than labor PACs—about $442 million compared with $168 million in 2004—business interests will probably continue to hold a significant edge in contributions to congressional candidates. Moreover, business interests are in a better position than organized labor to increase their influence through bundling.

Business PACs outnumbered labor PACs by 2,563 to 303 in 2004. Business PAC contributions are collected through personal solicitations, direct mail, and many other approaches that rely on deliberate decisions on the part of donors, whereas labor PAC contributions are collected using automatic payroll deductions from which members must take deliberate steps to withdraw their contributions. Business PACs also have wealthier donors who are used to supporting a variety of organizations and groups. These contrasts suggest that business PACs would be in a better position to ask their donors to write checks to specific candidates than would labor PACs. However, labor organizations and progressive groups have formed more 527 committees and raised more money with them than have business groups. Depending on the regulations written by the FEC, labor-backed organizations will probably spend more unregulated money than business groups. Labor also will probably be able to continue to outpace business interests in the provision of campaign volunteers.

Individual Donors

Few members of the public contribute to political campaigns. Roughly 7 percent of all voters claim to have made a contribution to any candidate for public office, and only 0.2 percent donated $200 or more to a congressional candidate.[59] The average individual contribution is less than $75, and the top 1 percent of all individual donors account for roughly 10 percent of all individual donations.[60] BCRA-inspired efforts by candidates, parties, and PACs to raise more individual contributions may broaden the base of congressional donors, but the law's increased contribution limits probably will have a greater impact on individuals who are in a position to make large contributions. As a result, one can anticipate that the law will result in fewer donors accounting for a larger share of all individual contributions.

Conclusion

The Bipartisan Campaign Reform Act is one of many reforms enacted over the course of United States history to address concerns about the role of money in the political process. Despite the fact that the law's goals were modest, it sparked intense debate in Congress and among the general public. Proponents of reform raised issues concerned with the corrupting effects of money in politics and notions of equality. Opponents charged that the law's prohibitions against large soft money expenditures and issue advocacy ads would deprive individuals of some of their liberties and violate free speech rights. Pragmatic concerns about the impact the law would have on individual politicians and their party's election prospects also influenced the votes of members of Congress. Despite the difficulties that reform bills encounter in the legislative process and in the judiciary, the BCRA was finally enacted in 2002 and survived a Supreme Court challenge almost completely intact.

The act's major provisions ban party soft money, raise contribution limits, and place new restrictions on the airing of issue advocacy advertisements.

Whether these and the act's other provisions succeed in reducing corruption, real and perceived, is an open question. However, the early evidence suggests that the BCRA has had an immediate impact on various aspects of the financing of congressional elections. The law has encouraged congressional candidates to rely more on large individual contributions than they had previously. It has reduced the opportunities political parties have to spend money to influence congressional races. Moreover, it has stimulated partisan interest group leaders to raise and spend more non–federally regulated political funds through 527 committees and other organizations.

It also is important to recognize the things that the BCRA probably will not accomplish either in the short term or the long run. The act will probably not do away with the tremendous fund-raising and reelection advantages that congressional incumbents enjoy. It will not prevent the wealthiest and best organized segments of society from having more influence in elections and greater access to officeholders than ordinary citizens. It is too much to expect the BCRA or any other law to eradicate Americans' overall distrust of the role of money in politics and their ambivalence about politics more generally. Any groundswell of support for the political system or massive increase in voter turnout or any other form of citizen participation also is beyond the scope of the new law. Further changes in the campaign finance system, the redistricting process, the laws governing voting and voter registration, and other aspects of the larger political, economic, and sociological environment in which elections are conducted would be needed to bring about those changes. Nevertheless, the enactment of the BCRA was a positive step in addressing some of the shortcomings in congressional elections.

Notes

I wish to thank Robert Biersack and Sheila Krumholz for providing campaign finance data and Robert Biersack and Anthony Corrado for their helpful comments and suggestions. Nathan Bigelow, Peter Francia, and Juliana Horwitz-Menasce provided able research assistance.

1. Laura Langbein, "Money and Access: Some Empirical Evidence," *Journal of Politics* 48 (1986): 1052–1062; Richard Hall and Frank Wayman, "Buying Time: Moneyed Interests and the Mobilization of Bias in Congressional Committees," *American Political Science Review* 84 (1990): 797–820.
2. See Herbert E. Alexander, *Financing Politics* (Washington, D.C.: CQ Press, 1984), 23–31. Much of this section is drawn from Paul S. Herrnson, "The Money Maze: Financing Congressional Elections," in *Congress Reconsidered,* 7th ed., ed. Lawrence C. Dodd and Bruce I. Oppenheimer (Washington, D.C.: CQ Press, 2001), 97–123.
3. An earlier reform, the FECA of 1971 made some modest changes in the law, but it had little impact on the financing of congressional elections.
4. *Buckley v. Valeo,* 424 U.S. 1 (1976).
5. Cornelius P. Cotter and John F. Bibby, "Institutional Development of Parties and the Thesis of Party Decline," *Political Science Quarterly* 95 (1980): 1–27.
6. Paul S. Herrnson, *Party Campaigning in the 1980s* (Cambridge: Harvard University Press, 1988).

7. Ibid.; and Paul Herrnson, *Congressional Elections: Campaigning at Home and in Washington,* 4th ed. (Washington, D.C.: CQ Press, 2004), 90–128.
8. These figures include party contributions to and coordinated expenditures on behalf of candidates. Herrnson, *Congressional Elections,* 103–105, 115–121.
9. Ibid., 129–152.
10. Ibid., 176, 183; and Paul Herrnson, "Campaign Professionalism and Fundraising in Congressional Elections," *Journal of Politics* 54 (1992): 859–870.
11. Frank J. Sorauf, *Inside Campaign Finance* (New Haven: Yale University Press), 27–28.
12. Federal Election Commission, press release, May 15, 2001.
13. Herrnson, *Congressional Elections,* 115–121.
14. Federal Election Commission, press release, March 20, 2003.
15. Ken Goldstein and Joel Rivlin, "Political Advertising in the 2002 Elections," unpublished manuscript.
16. Herrnson, *Congressional Elections,* 119–121.
17. David B. Magleby and J. Quinn Monson, *Campaign 2002: The Perfect Storm* (Provo, Utah: Center for the Study of Elections and Democracy, 2003).
18. Herrnson, *Congressional Elections,* 121–122.
19. It is a major challenge to assemble a large enough legislative coalition to pass a campaign finance reform bill over a presidential veto.
20. Robert Y. Shapiro, "Public Attitudes toward Campaign Finance Practice and Reform," in *Inside the Campaign Finance Battle,* ed. Anthony Corrado, Thomas E. Mann, and Trevor Potter (Washington, D.C.: Brookings Institution Press, 2003), 259–265.
21. Mark Mellman and Richard Wirthlin, "Public Views of Party Soft Money," in *Inside the Campaign Finance Battle,* 266–267.
22. Shapiro, "Public Attitudes toward Campaign Finance Practice and Reform."
23. Herrnson, *Congressional Elections,* 285.
24. Ibid., 282–283.
25. Colton Campbell, Congressional Research Service, personal communication, February 29, 2004.
26. Helen Dewar, "Campaign Overhaul Bill Passed," *Washington Post,* May 1, 1992, A1; Tim Curran, "Dead Again: Senate Fails to Override Bush Veto of Campaign Finance Bill," *Washington Post,* May 14, 1992.
27. On these approaches, see Barbara Sinclair, *Unorthodox Lawmaking: New Legislative Procedures in the U.S. Congress,* 2nd ed. (Washington: D.C.: CQ Press, 2000).
28. On the passage of the Bipartisan Reform Act in the House, see Diana Dwyre and Victoria A. Farrar-Myers, *Legislative Labyrinth: Congress and Campaign Finance Reform* (Washington, D.C.: CQ Press, 2001); on unorthodox lawmaking, see Barbara Sinclair, *Unorthodox Lawmaking.*
29. Anthony Corrado, "Money and Politics," in *The New Campaign Finance Sourcebook,* ed. Anthony Corrado, Thomas Mann, Daniel Ortiz, and Trevor Potter (Washington, D.C.: Brookings Institution Press, 2003).
30. Rep. Martin Meehan, "Time to Kick the Soft Money Habit," February 28, 2002, www.house.gov/apps/list/press/ma05_meehan/NRCFROpEd022802.html.
31. Rep. Christopher Shays, "Shays' Statement on the Successful Discharge Petition for the Bipartisan Campaign Reform Act," press release, January 24, 2002, www.house.gov/shays/news/2002/january/jan24.htm.
32. Majority Whip Tom DeLay, "Bill Jeopardizes Freedom," Tuesday, April 3, 2001, www.majoritywhip.gov/News.asp?FormMode=SingleOpEds.
33. Dana Milbank, "Tactics and Theatrics Color Decision Day," *Washington Post,* February 14, 2002.
34. For a more detailed review of the BCRA, see Corrado et al., *The New Campaign Finance Sourcebook.*

35. Adam Clymer, "Foes of Campaign Finance Bill Plot Legal Attack," *New York Times,* February 17, 2002.
36. Helen Dewar, "Lawsuits Challenge New Campaign Law," *Washington Post,* May 8, 2003.
37. Corrado et al., *Inside the Campaign Finance Battle.*
38. Amy Keller, "Debate Rocks FEC," *Roll Call,* March 4, 2002; Helen Dewar, "FEC Rules on 'Soft Money' Challenged," *Washington Post,* October 9, 2002.
39. Dewar, "FEC Rules"; quotation is from Thomas B. Edsall, "FEC to Allow 'Soft Money' Exceptions," *Washington Post,* June 21, 2002.
40. For some useful commentaries on the ruling, see Thomas E. Mann, "A District Court Panel Rules on Campaign Finance," May 5, 2003; Roger Witten, Seth Waxman, Randolph Moss, and Fred Wertheimer, "Summary of *McConnell v. FEC* Decision"; and the other summaries available at www.campaignlegalcenter.org.
41. Unless otherwise indicated figures for 2004 are for data collected between January 1, 2003 and October 13, 2004.
42. These figures are for receipts collected between January 1, 2003 and September 30, 2004.
43. These figures are for receipts collected between January 1, 2003 and September 30, 2004.
44. These figures are for receipts collected between January 1, 2003 and June 30, 2004.
45. These figures are for receipts collected between January 1, 2003 and June 30, 2004.
46. See, for example, Herrnson, *Party Campaigning.*
47. For more information on these activities, see Herrnson, *Congressional Elections,* 90–128.
48. Spending figures for party coordinated expenditures were not available at press time.
49. Figures provided by the Center for Responsive Politics.
50. Eliza Newlin Carney, Peter H. Stone, and James A. Barnes, "New Rules of the Game," *National Journal,* December 20, 2003, 3800; Paul H. Stone, "A Catalog of Key Groups," *National Journal,* December 20, 2003, 3803.
51. Paul Kane, "NRSC or NCRS," *Roll Call,* November 25, 2002.
52. Ibid.
53. Carney, Stone, and Barnes, "New Rules of the Game"; Stone, "A Catalog of Key Groups."
54. Ibid.
55. Ibid.
56. The figures are for independent expenditures made between January 1, 2003, and October 13, 2004.
57. Carney, Stone, and Barnes, "New Rules of the Game." See also Stone, "A Catalog of Key Groups."
58. See www.clubforgrowth.org/.
59. The 7 percent figure is from the *2002 National Election Study* (Ann Arbor: University of Michigan, Center for Political Studies, 2002); the other figure is from the Center for Responsive Politics, www.opensecrets.org.
60. Peter L. Francia, John C. Green, Paul S. Herrnson, Lynda W. Powell, and Clyde Wilcox, *The Financiers of Congressional Elections: Investors, Ideologues, and Intimates* (New York: Columbia University Press, 2003).

6. Deep Red and Blue Congressional Districts: The Causes and Consequences of Declining Party Competitiveness

Bruce I. Oppenheimer

After more than three decades of scholarly research and writing, the existence of incumbency advantage in House elections has achieved the electoral equivalent of death and taxes. The conventional wisdom would have us believe that incumbency advantage is inescapable and ubiquitous. Since the mid-1960s, all House incumbents have had the means and motivation to earn it, and there was little reason that it would not continue to exist at the high levels it reached in the 1970s. Although congressional scholars have offered competing explanations for incumbency advantage—use of office resources, name identification, constituency service, incumbency as a voting cue, institutionally designed facilitation, weak challengers, campaign financing disparities—they have, with a couple of notable exceptions, viewed it as an important given in any discussion of House elections.[1] And in the rare instances when incumbency has been a political liability in House elections, there have not been challengers sufficiently strong to take advantage of the situation.[2]

To paraphrase the late Rep. Mo Udall, however, when you find something in politics about which everyone is agreed, it's bound to be wrong. In this chapter I will explore some of the shortcomings in viewing House incumbency advantage as a constant in American political life of the past forty years. Through the analysis presented here, we will find, first, that not all House members receive (or earn) incumbency advantage. It accrues the most to those who need it most to win reelection. Second, it has not become constant. In fact, it declined markedly during the 1990s, to levels not seen in forty years, and should remain at lower levels for the foreseeable future. And third, these two findings are linked. It is precisely because fewer members need incumbency advantage that incumbency advantage in House elections has declined. The reason that fewer members need incumbency advantage is that the underlying partisan competitiveness of congressional districts has declined markedly. As we shall see, more congressional districts today are overwhelmingly safe Democratic or safe Republican districts than at any point since 1960, at least.

It will be insufficient to end this inquiry with the finding that incumbency advantage has declined because the underlying partisan competitiveness of congressional districts has declined. Instead this finding stimulates two additional questions that this chapter will address: (1) Why has there been a decline in the underlying partisan competitiveness of congressional districts? and (2) Does this change in the basis of electoral safety for House members, from safety built on incumbency advantage to safety built on partisan noncompetitiveness of districts, affect the way House members behave and the workings of the institution?

I will present three different explanations to answer the former question. The first argues that the decline in competitiveness is the result of the improved data and computer technology available to those doing the redistricting and the incentives they have to create noncompetitive districts. The second, also a redistricting explanation, sees declining partisan competitiveness resulting from the creation of an increasing number of majority-minority districts. And the last suggests that the increasing ability of Americans to select where they reside, and their tendency to do so on bases that are strongly correlated with political party preferences, is the underlying cause for the decline in partisan competitiveness. Preliminary tests of the first two of these will raise significant doubts about their ability to account for the decline in competitiveness, and I will argue that much of the decline is due instead to the collective effects of the behaviors of individual citizens. In sum, Americans today live in uncompetitive congressional districts because they choose residential patterns that make it easy for them to be placed in overwhelmingly Democratic and overwhelmingly Republican districts.

The final section of this chapter will address the institutional effects of having a large number of House members elected from districts lacking party competitiveness. In that section I will link the composition of the districts to the increased polarization of the two congressional parties. Before moving ahead to the analysis of the change in incumbency advantage and its effects, however, we first need a good understanding of what is and is not incumbency advantage.

Measuring Incumbency Advantage

Much of the early work on incumbency advantage dealt largely with the period since the early 1950s and attempted to explain the increase that occurred beginning in the 1960s. Subsequent research extended the findings into the 1980s and questioned whether increased margins of victory necessarily meant greater electoral safety for incumbents.[3] Another challenge to this work came in the research of James Garand and Donald Gross, who studied the competitiveness of House elections from 1824 to 1982 and found that incumbents have always had an advantage. They concluded that there were even times when the advantage exceeded that of the 1960s and 1970s.[4] In an effort to deal with the seemingly contradictory findings, John Alford and David Brady argued that one has to differentiate between sources of incumbency advantage.[5] Reliance solely on measures of marginality, such as the share of the vote incumbents received, the percentage of incumbents in close elections, or the reelection rates of incumbents, does not allow one to distinguish between incumbency advantage that resulted from the underlying partisanship of the district and that which resulted from the activities that incumbents engage in to increase their vote share. Alford and Brady called the former of these "partisan incumbency" advantage and the latter "personal incumbency" advantage. In operational terms they conceived of personal incumbency advantage as "the difference between a party's vote share in an open-seat contest . . . and the vote margin of an incumbent of that party in an immediately adjacent election."[6] They rely on two measures of this conceptualization—sophomore surge and retirement slump—to demonstrate the ebbs and flows in personal incumbency advantage from 1846 to 1990. Alford and Brady's findings show that personal incumbency advantage was nearly nonexistent until the post–World War II period and that it largely explains the sizable increase in overall incumbency advantage that appears in House election data since the mid-1960s.

In the 1993 revision of their article, Alford and Brady reported that there appeared to be a slight decline in sophomore surge in 1990 but not a corresponding decline in retirement slump.[7] They suggest that the cause was the anti-incumbent mood of the 1990 election and not a more systematic change. Nevertheless, this serves as a warning that contextual factors could affect the size of personal incumbency advantage.

One thing that even Alford and Brady did not do, however, was examine the fluctuations in partisan incumbency advantage. If personal incumbency advantage did not exist prior to the 1950s, then the fluctuations in the marginality of incumbents that Garand and Gross uncovered must have been due to changes in partisan incumbency advantage. As we shall see in the following sections, in the apportionment decade from 1992 to 2000, personal incumbency advantage declined and partisan incumbency advantage increased. Moreover, as I will attempt to demonstrate, the increase in one has led to the decline in the other.

Before moving ahead, however, it is important to recognize that the term "partisan incumbency advantage," although providing a useful distinction for Alford and Brady, is really a misnomer. The underlying partisan advantage of a congressional district exists for a nonincumbent of the favored party, as well as for the incumbent. Accordingly, from this point on I shall use the term "underlying partisan advantage" instead of "partisan incumbency advantage."

Sophomore Surge and Retirement Slump, 1992–2000

On the surface little seemed to change in success rates of House incumbents seeking reelection from 1992 to 2000, compared with the previous three decades. Although in 1992 redistricting and the residue of the House bank scandal trimmed the success rates of incumbents, the other four elections produced incumbent reelection in excess of 90 percent. Even when Republicans took control of the House in 1994, 90.2 percent of incumbents won reelection. And the 1998 and 2000 elections tied 1986 and 1988 for the fewest incumbents defeated in a House election in the post–World War II era.[8] As the data in Table 6-1 show, incumbents in the 1992–2000 apportionment decade suffered a total of 91 general-election losses, only 13 more than in 1982–1990, and 25 and 38 fewer than in the 1972–1980 and 1962–1970 decades, respectively. In addition, although the percentage of incumbents winning with over 60 percent of the vote in the 1992–2000 period did not reach the levels of 1982–1990, it was slightly

Table 6-1 Number of House Incumbent General-Election Defeats, by Apportionment Decade, 1962–2000

Years	Incumbents Defeated in General Elections
1962–1970	129
1972–1980	116
1982–1990	78
1992–2000	91

higher than in 1972–1980. Overall, incumbency success during the 1990s apportionment decade was consistent with the levels that have been reached since the mid-1960s.

Another indicator of the stability of incumbent success is the ability of incumbent House members to run ahead of their party's presidential candidate. In Table 6-2 are data on the percentage of incumbents in major party contested races who received a higher percentage of the two-party vote than their party's presidential candidate in 1960, 1976, and 2000. There is almost no difference between 1976 and 2000. What is somewhat surprising is that in 1960, when incumbency advantage was not as great, the percentage of incumbent House members running ahead of their party's presidential candidate was nearly as high as it was in 1976 and 2000, especially in districts held by Democrats. Overall, the data in Table 6-2 support the conclusion that incumbent success remains strong for House members.

In keeping with the findings of Alford and Brady, it is appropriate to examine the separate contributions of personal incumbency advantage and underlying partisan advantage before drawing any conclusions about the changes in incumbency advantage over time. To do so I have calculated both the sophomore surge and retirement slump (as well as the "slurge," which is an average of the absolute values of the two) for each election from 1994 to 2000.[9] Sophomore surge measures the change in the percentage of the vote received when a House member first runs for reelection, compared with the percentage of the vote that individual received in winning the seat originally. Retirement slump is the difference in the percentage of the vote received when a House member is elected to a last term (prior to voluntary retirement, death, or primary election defeat) and the percentage that the new candidate of the incumbent's party receives in the following, regularly scheduled general election. These data for 1994–2000 appear in Table 6-3, along with data from Alford and Brady for earlier periods.[10] I have calculated the measures for the 1994–2000 elections in a manner entirely consistent with the method that Brady and Alford used. I have included only those cases where candidates ran with major party opposition, and the percentages are based only on the two-party vote. To compute the sophomore surge and retirement

Table 6-2 Incumbents Who Ran Ahead of Their Party's Presidential Candidate in Their Districts, 1960, 1976, and 2000 (in percentages)

Year	Democrats	Republicans	All
1960	89.4	78.0	84.7
1976	91.4	86.7	89.7
2000	92.8	88.5	90.7

Note: Only districts where the incumbent House member had a major party opponent are included.

slump values for each year, I first calculated the mean for each party separately and then averaged the two party means. This removes the bias of the partisan swing of a given election and avoids the problems associated with computing the partisan swing for each election. In this way the partisan swing in 1994, for example, which increased the mean sophomore surge for Republicans running for reelection for the first time, is offset by its negative impact on the sophomore surge of Democrats running for reelection for the first time. Finally, I have treated members first elected in by-elections using the same set of assumptions as Alford and Brady. In sum, the data for 1992–2000 should be fully comparable with those from earlier years in terms of the method of calculation.

Looking first at the sophomore surge data in Table 6-3, one sees a marked decline in the period 1994–2000, compared with both the 1972–1980 and 1982–1990 apportionment decades. Elections in both of those decades produced sophomore surges averaging slightly over 7 percent, compared with 4.5 percent in the most recent decade. In fact, sophomore surge for each of the four elections in the 1994–2000 period is weaker than for any of the elections in the preceding two decades (Table 6-3 does not show data for individual years for 1974–1980). What is more remarkable is that sophomore surge in the most recent period is even lower than that for 1964–1970. True, sophomore surge from 1994 to 2000 is not as low as it was in the 1950s, but it markedly eroded from the levels that were common from the mid-1960s.

Although the data on retirement slump display the same tendency seen in the sophomore surge figures, the magnitude is more modest, and the mean for 1994–2000 is not lower than that of 1964–1970. I believe the change in retirement slump is smaller because retirement slump may lag behind sophomore surge in showing changes that are occurring in personal incumbency advantages. Many of those retiring in the 1990s were members who were first elected in the 1970s and early 1980s, when there were strong incentives for incumbents to devote resources to establishing personal incumbency advantage. They were the ones with large sophomore surges. And these members may have retained that personal incumbency advantage throughout their careers in the House. Thus, even though personal incumbency advantage is declining for members elected more recently, and that shows up immediately in the lower sophomore surge figures, one might reasonably expect a lag in the retirement slump data.

Table 6-3 Sophomore Surge and Retirement Slump in the House of Representatives, 1950s–2000

Year	Sophomore Surge	Retirement Slump	Slurge
Mean 1954–1960	2.0	−4.0	3.0
Mean 1964–1970	5.5	−5.4	5.5
Mean 1974–1980	7.2	−9.2	8.2
1984	8.8	−11.4	10.1
1986	6.4	−9.3	7.8
1988	6.6	−11.0	8.8
1990	6.5	−11.0	8.8
Mean 1984–1990	7.1	−10.7	8.9
1994	3.7	−9.3	6.5
1996	2.8	−5.9	4.4
1998	6.0	−5.0	5.5
2000	5.4	−8.4	6.9
Mean 1994–2000	4.5	−7.2	5.9

Source: John Alford supplied the data for 1954–1990. They correspond to those appearing in John Alford and David Brady, "Personal and Partisan Advantage in U.S. Congressional Elections," in *Congress Reconsidered,* 5th ed., 1993, 149.

Further, I place less emphasis on retirement slump as an indicator of personal incumbency advantage because of issues of challenger quality. Although I do not have the data to support this contention, it seems reasonable that members running for reelection for the first time are likely to attract stronger challengers than incumbents do very late in their careers. If that contention is correct, then retirement slump is more contaminated by low challenger quality than is sophomore surge. Although I will not pursue this proposition here, it is a testable hypothesis.

The data in Table 6-3, however, run contrary to those presented in Table 6-2, which show relative stability in the capacity of House incumbents to run ahead of their party's presidential candidate. After all, the vote for president (as I shall employ it later in this chapter) is often used as a measure of underlying congressional district partisanship. And running ahead of the underlying partisanship of one's district is, in fact, an indicator of personal incumbency advantage. The data in Table 6-4 help resolve the inconsistency. Instead of only looking at the percentage of House incumbents running ahead of their party's presidential candidate, the data in Table 6-4 show how much better, on average, House incumbents run. Much as with sophomore surge, the mean differences between the vote percentages of House incumbents and those of their party's presidential candidate increase between 1960 and 1976 and then drop between 1976 and 2000 (for Democratic incumbents and for all incumbents).[11]

The overall conclusion one can draw from Tables 6-3 and 6-4 is that personal incumbency advantage has declined in the 1992–2000 apportionment decade from its previous levels. Before investigating why this decline has

Table 6-4 Mean Difference between Percentage of Vote for House Incumbents and Percentage for the Presidential Candidate of the Incumbent's Party, 1960, 1976, and 2000

Year	Democratic Incumbents	Republican Incumbents	All Incumbents
1960	8.04 (190)	3.97 (132)	6.37 (322)
1976	12.44 (211)	8.81 (121)	11.08 (332)
2000	9.25 (169)	8.82 (166)	9.03 (335)

Notes: Numbers in parentheses indicate the number of observations for each cell. Only districts where the incumbent had no major party opposition are excluded. The percentages are based on the percentage of the two-party vote for both the incumbent House member and the presidential candidate of the incumbent's party.

occurred, it will make sense first to examine changes in underlying partisan advantage. As we shall see later, a fuller understanding of the decline in personal incumbency advantage is directly linked to the increase that has occurred in underlying partisan advantage.

Partisan Composition of House Districts

Rather than assume that underlying partisan advantage has increased because overall incumbency success has been relatively unchanged and personal incumbency advantage has declined, it makes sense to document the change in the underlying partisanship of House districts. To do this I have chosen to use the presidential vote by congressional district as a surrogate for the underlying district partisanship. The presidential vote is not without problems as an indicator of partisanship, however. The short-term forces of a given election may make the overall electorate appear more Democratic or more Republican than it actually is. When there are major third party candidacies, as has been the case in four of the past ten presidential elections, using the two party vote for president may produce a misleading indicator of underlying district partisanship. It would be a mistake, for example, to assume that in 1992 Perot took voters equally from Bush and Clinton. Moreover, the mere presence of those third party candidates may affect the entire nature of the campaign, as well as voters' choices.

To minimize the problems associated with using presidential vote as a measure of partisanship at the congressional district level, I selected the presidential elections of 1960, 1976, and 2000 for this analysis. All three were unusually close contests between centrist candidates of the two parties. Despite the effect that the Nader candidacy in 2000 may have had on the final outcome, none of the three elections featured a third party candidate whose fraction of the popular vote will substantially distort this analysis.[12] In each of the elections there was no elected incumbent president running, so that any skewing of the results through presidential incumbency advantage is minimized. Finally, the three elections are con-

Figure 6-1 Republican Presidential Vote by Congressional District, 1960, 1976, and 2000

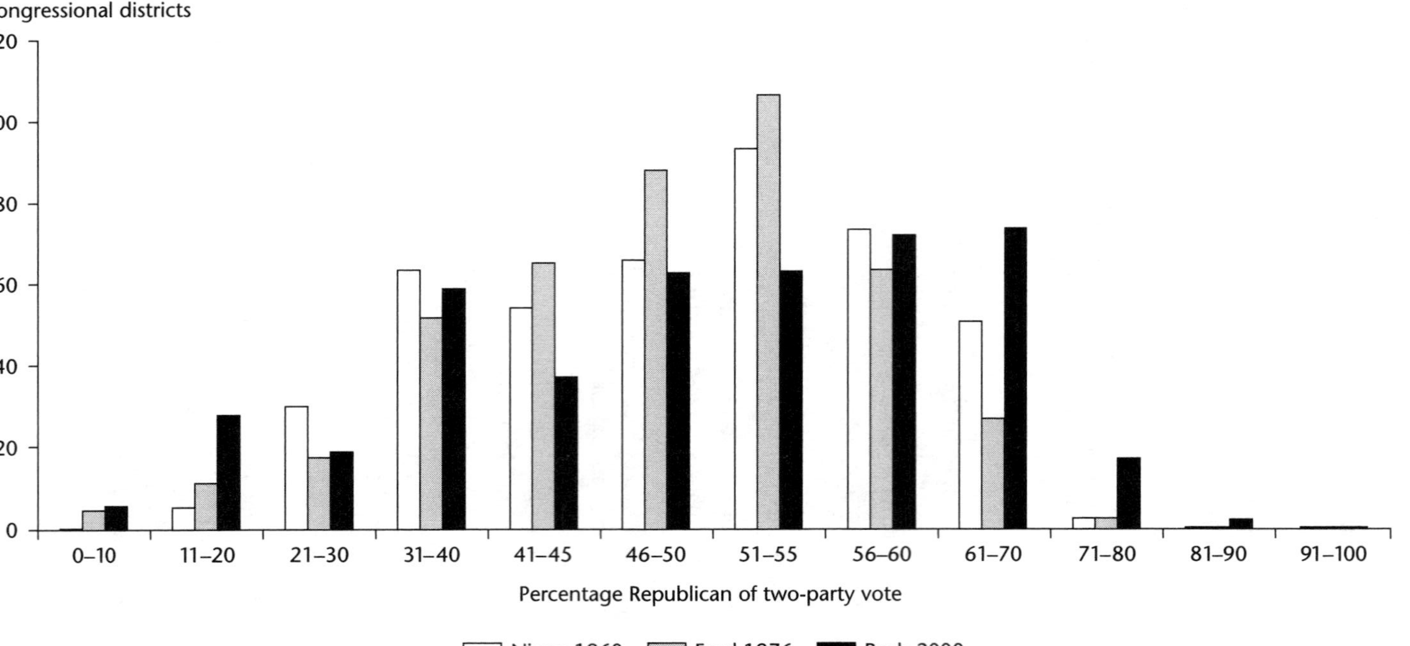

veniently spaced in terms of the level of personal incumbency advantage that existed for House members: One occurred at a time when it was relatively low, one at a point when it had reached high levels, and the last when personal incumbency advantage had seemingly declined.

Figure 6-1 presents the distribution of the presidential vote by congressional district, showing the percentage of the vote the Republican candidate received in 1960, 1976, and 2000. We should recall that in 1960 there existed a substantial number of largely one-party areas in both the South and the North and that, prior to Supreme Court decisions in apportionment cases, districts in some states were still unequal in population. Accordingly, it is not surprising that there were a large number of districts in which the Kennedy-Nixon contest was not close. In fact, there are only 159 districts (36.5 percent) in which the vote was between the 55–45 percent range and 288 districts (66.2 percent) in which it was in the 60–40 percent range. By 1976, as the figure shows, the number of congressional districts where the presidential race was close had grown. There are 197 districts (45.2 percent) in the 55–45 range, and 325 (74.7 percent) within the 60–40. Not only did the number of districts where the presidential vote was highly competitive increase, but, correspondingly, the number in which it was not competitive (outside the 60–40 range) declined from one-third to a quarter of all districts.

By 2000 the trend had reversed. Only 123 districts (28.2 percent) fell in the 55–45 percent range, and 234 (53.7 percent) were in the 60–40 range. It is also worth noting at the tails of the distribution in Figure 6-1 the marked increase by 2000 in the number of districts in which the Republican or the Democratic candidate for president received more than 70 percent of the vote.

The decline in party competitiveness at the congressional district level is reflected in the House races as well as in the presidential vote. Figure 6-2 depicts the percentage of the vote that the Republican candidate received in all House districts for 1960, 1976, and 2000. Note that as with the presidential vote, the 2000 election had the fewest competitive races. Only 42 contests fell in the 55–45 range, as opposed to 65 in 1976 and 85 in 1960. And after a decline, from 77 in 1960 to 51 in 1976, in the number of House districts in which a candidate ran without opposition from the other party, that number was back up to 64 in 2000.[13]

Remembering how competitive the 2000 election was at the national level, and even within several states, it is a stark contrast to see how relatively uncompetitive it was at the congressional district level. (Ironically, the 1976 election, which was the least competitive of the three in terms of the national popular vote, was the most competitive at the congressional district level.) Using the presidential vote as a measure of underlying partisanship, the data in Figure 6-1 show that party competitiveness was markedly less at the congressional district level in 2000 than it had been in 1976.

This finding helps us understand why incumbents were reelected at such high rates and by such large margins in the 1992–2000 election decade, despite the decline in personal incumbency advantage. With congressional districts that

Figure 6-2 House Seats by Percentage Vote Republican, 1960, 1976, and 2000

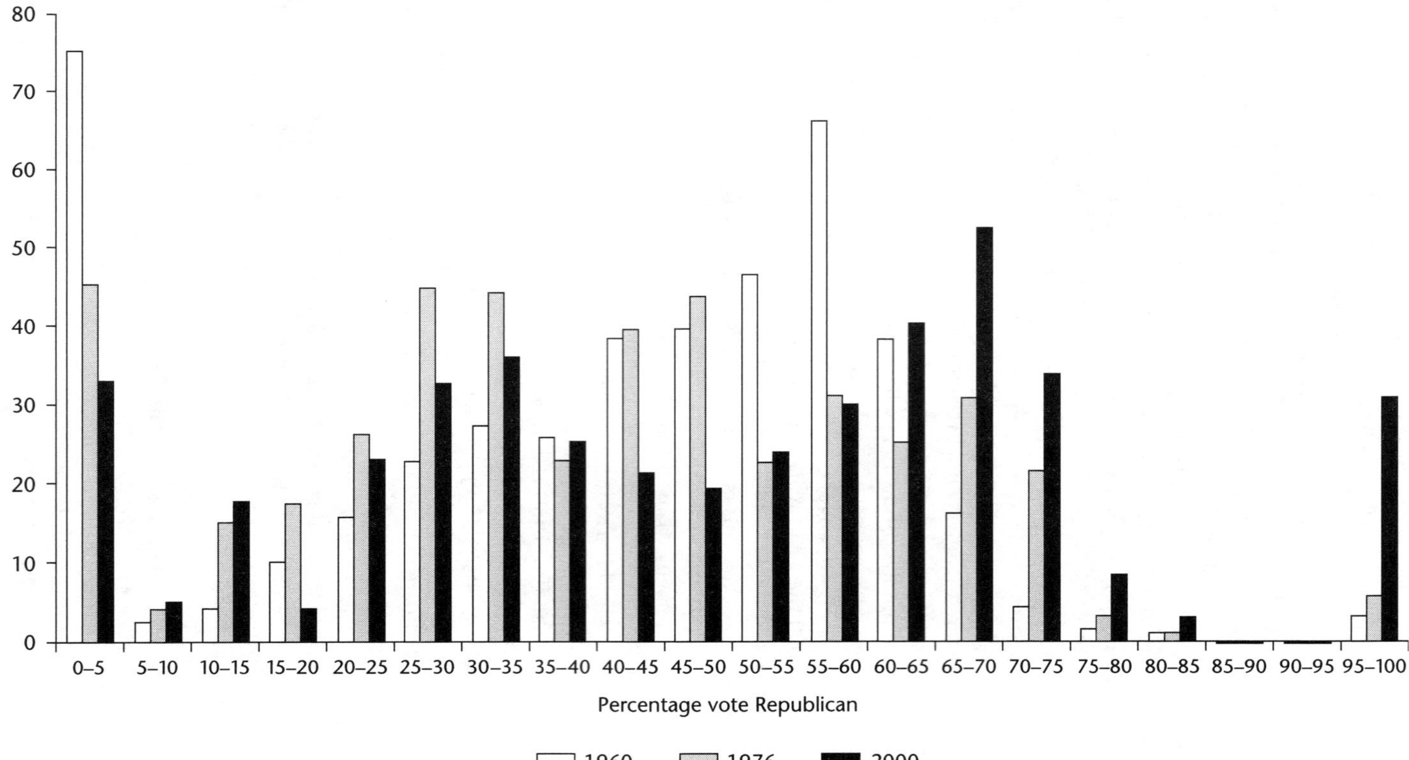

were less competitive in partisan terms, incumbent success levels remained for all practical purposes unchanged. What did change were the components of electoral success.

In the period since the mid-1960s, when incumbents have seemingly honed the techniques that are necessary to establish personal incumbency advantage—servicing constituent needs, traveling home to their districts with great frequency, using their staff resources and media to reach constituents, raising campaign funds, and so forth (and also indirectly discouraging potentially strong challengers)—it is puzzling to see personal incumbency advantage decline as it did during the 1992–2000 apportionment decade. In searching for possible explanations, I speculated that the decline in personal incumbency advantage could be linked to the increase in underlying partisan advantage. Some indication that this may be the case is alluded to in the work of Erikson and Wright.[14]

Erikson and Wright include in their article a scatter plot for incumbent House members who ran for reelection in 1990, based on the percentage of the two-party vote that each received versus the percentage of the vote that Dukakis won in the incumbent's district in 1988. They place a par line on the scatter plot that is based on the best-fitting regression line that "represents the expected Democratic vote, given the district's partisanship (1988 presidential vote) and assuming an open seat."[15] Among other things, Erikson and Wright found that in 1990 incumbents from the safest districts did no better than par, but those from competitive districts exceeded par by large margins in a direction favorable to them. They demonstrate that not all incumbents earn the same level of personal incumbency advantage and conclude that it is incumbents who need "an exceptional vote appeal" to win reelection who "are able to earn it."[16]

Assuming that what Erikson and Wright found was not peculiar to the data for the 1990 House elections, it offers a means for understanding the linkage between the growth in underlying partisan advantage during the 1992–2000 apportionment decade and the decline in personal incumbency advantage. Accordingly, I have applied their approach to examining the degree to which incumbents seeking reelection exceeded par expectations in 1960, 1976, and 2000. The scatter plots for these years are presented in Figure 6-3.

In each of the three scatter plots the par line is the product of the regression line drawn from predicting the House vote from the presidential vote in the open-seat districts for the respective election year. Note first that in each of the scatter plots, incumbents in overwhelmingly strong Democratic districts, those where the presidential vote for the Democratic candidate is 65 percent or greater, and those in the overwhelmingly Republican districts, those in which the Democratic presidential candidate receives 35 percent or less of the vote, the points fall very close to the par line. As the districts become more competitive in terms of the presidential vote, the points are scattered farther away from the par line. This is fully in keeping with the Erikson and Wright finding.

Second, it is worth observing that in 1960 many incumbents in party-competitive districts remain relatively close to the par line. This election occurred

Figure 6-3 Incumbency Advantage in the House, 1960, 1976, and 2000

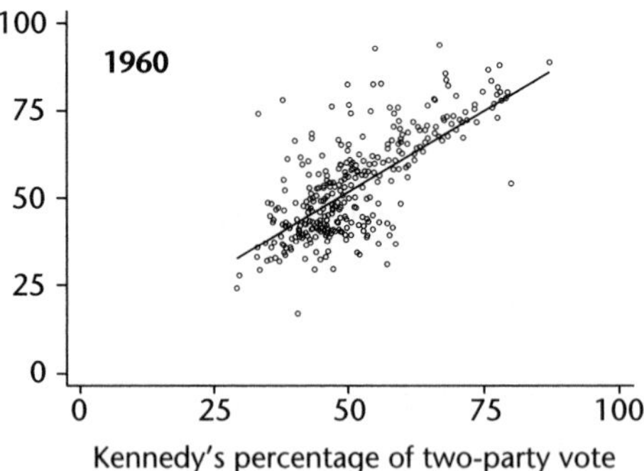

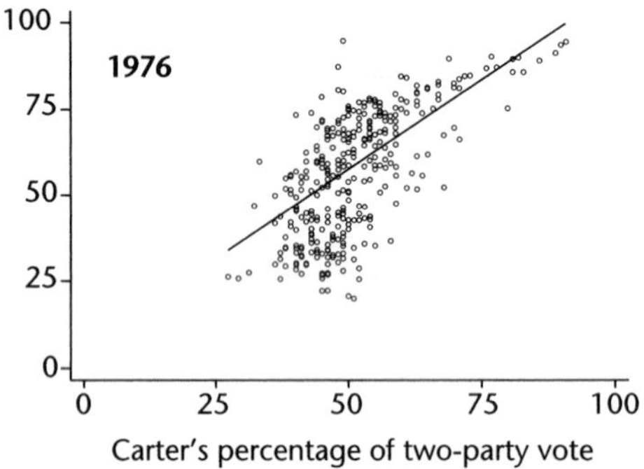

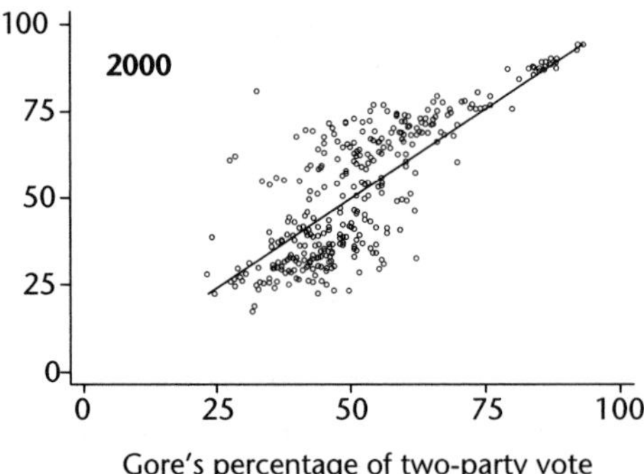

before many incumbents had fully developed the resources that became the foundation of personal incumbency advantage, and accordingly even those in competitive districts fit close to the line for predicting House vote from presidential vote for open seats. In 1976 and in 2000, however, the spread away from the par line in party-competitive districts is far greater. (Recall that few incumbents are losing, so that those above 50 percent on the *y* axis are overwhelmingly Democratic incumbents, and those below it are overwhelmingly Republican incumbents.) This is evidence of personal incumbency advantage being achieved by incumbents in districts that are party-competitive, and it is especially evident in those districts where the presidential candidate of the incumbent's party does not carry the district. And the spread of observations in the party-competitive districts in 1976 and 2000 appears very similar.

Third, and most important, what is different between the 1976 and 2000 scatter plots is the distribution of the observations along the *x* axis. There are more districts in 2000 than in 1976 in which the presidential vote was either heavily Democratic or heavily Republican. Recall—as Erikson and Wright found among House incumbents in the 1990 election and as these scatter plots confirm—that incumbents from safe partisan districts do not get much, if any, personal incumbency advantage. So as the number of these heavily Democratic and heavily Republican districts increases, there is a resulting decline in the average personal incumbency advantage. In sum, there is a connection between the increase in partisan incumbency advantage and the decline in personal incumbency advantage that occurred in the 1992–2000 apportionment decade.

Because it was not the focus of their article, Erikson and Wright did not fully address the question of why incumbents from safe partisan districts did not exceed the par prediction but those from competitive districts did, beyond the fact that personal incumbency advantage is earned by incumbents who need it but not by incumbents who don't need it. Given my comparable findings for 1976 and 2000, that question deserves some exploration. Assuming that House incumbents are strategic about how they use their limited resources (time, money, staff), I suggest two related explanations: First, incumbents in safe partisan districts have little incentive to expend scarce resources to enlarge their electoral support, whereas those from competitive districts have a big incentive to do so. For the latter it may make the difference between winning and losing, while for the former it does not. Surely the payoff of getting 52 percent of the vote instead of 48 percent is huge, but the payoff for getting 72 percent instead of 68 percent is minimal. It may make sense, however, for a risk-averse House incumbent from a district that has a partisan leaning, or is even modestly safe (perhaps up to 60 percent or more voting for the presidential candidate of the incumbent's party), to invest in activities that will produce some personal incumbency advantage. After all, elections by their nature involve imperfect information for candidates, and incumbents would like some insulation from negative, short-term forces of a given election. Moreover, incumbents may realize some benefit from winning by a comfortable margin rather than winning narrowly. A safer margin may allow incumbents to discourage future challengers, for example, or to make a claim for an assignment to an exclusive committee or a leadership position in the House.

Examined from the Washington perspective, members from party-safe districts may find that the demands of service in Washington limit their ability to cater to their constituencies. These members may, for example, have assignments on the control committees (Rules, Ways and Means, or Appropriations) that require more time in Washington, and party leaders may expect them to be able to make tough decisions.[17] In fact, coming from a safe district may be a prerequisite for serving on these committees. These incumbents, therefore, may choose not to go home as often or not to allot as much of their staff to constituency matters, and they may be expected to handle increased Washington responsibilities that limit their capacity to provide additional constituency tending, even if they would prefer to do so. Thus, in Fenno's conceptualization, some members will make the strategic choice of an expansionist home style, while others will select a protectionist one.[18]

Second, the actual payoff in terms of electoral support gained from investing resources in activities designed to increase personal incumbency advantage will be less for those from very party-safe districts. If one goal of such activities is to attract the support of opposite-party partisans, then the safer the district, the fewer the number of opposite-party partisans there are to attract. In a district where the opposition is 50 percent of the electorate, an incumbent capable of using resources to attract 20 percent of those voters would increase his vote share by ten percentage points. But in a district where opposite-party partisans are only 30 percent of the electorate, winning 20 percent of them would only increase the incumbent's vote share by six percentage points. Moreover, it might be claimed that the cost of obtaining an increased vote share rises as the percentage of the vote share one already has increases.

Taken together, these two arguments mean that in a party-safe district the benefits to an incumbent from investing resources in increasing vote share beyond the partisan base are small, and the costs of doing so are relatively high. Accordingly, the incentives for doing so are normally few. By contrast, the incumbent with a district in which the partisan base is competitive can derive much greater benefits and at relatively lower costs. The result of these different incentive structures is precisely what Erikson and Wright found and what the analysis in this research supports: Personal incumbency advantage is reaped by those who need it but not by those who do not. With fewer members needing personal incumbency advantage in the 1990s, it has declined.

Explaining the Increase in Underlying Partisan Advantage

Having found that the decline in personal incumbency advantage in House elections in the 1992–2000 apportionment decade is tied to the increase in the number of districts that are overwhelmingly safe in partisan terms (underlying partisan advantage), one must still try to understand why partisan competitiveness declined at the congressional district level. In this section I will explore three explanations that might be offered to explain the change and present some preliminary arguments and testing. The explanations are not necessarily competing ones, although they do emphasize different root causes for the decline in competitiveness. All three are based on apportionment explanations. The first two, however, are linked to the changing goals of, and resources available to, those with the authority to draw congressional district lines, whereas the third is based on the change in the way the American population distributes itself.

District Packing versus Seat Maximizing

The first theory simply argues that over time, the mix of preferences among those trying to influence congressional redistricting and the information available to those doing the districting have changed. In the nineteenth century, when House turnover was high and relatively few incumbents desired to make House service a career, there was little pressure on those with redistricting responsibilities to make incumbents safer when district lines were redrawn. Under those circumstances party officials, whose goal was to maximize the seats the party won, would hold sway over the redistricting process. Because the data they had available were inexact, they did have to provide for some margin of error. Nevertheless, the process produced a large number of highly competitive districts. As careerism in the House grew during the twentieth century, especially in its second half, incumbents increasingly tried to influence the redistricting process. Unlike party officials, incumbents desired districts drawn that increased their partisan safety or, among those already in safe districts, minimized the alteration to the district that they were representing. These desires conflicted with the seat maximization goal and decreased the partisan competitiveness of districts. Especially in states where no single party controlled the redistricting process, compromises that protected incumbents of both parties provided a vehicle to resolve redistricting conflicts. In their book *Elbridge Gerry's Salamander,* Gary Cox and Jonathan Katz contend that in the aftermath of Supreme Court reapportionment decisions in the 1960s, those in control of redistricting, even in states where a single party dominated the process, designed districts that contributed substantially to the growth in the electoral success of incumbents.[19]

Although this theory helps explain why there may have been a general move toward the creation of more party-safe districts in the last third of the twentieth century, it does not explain why there was a marked increase in the 1992–2000 apportionment decade. With improved census and political data available and the development of appropriate computer software, however, new redistricting strategies are increasingly being employed that allow party officials to meet simultaneously the conflicting goals of maximizing seats and further protecting incumbents of their own party. The strategy involves packing as many identifiers of the opposite party as possible into a relatively small number of districts, making those districts overwhelming safe for the other party. Because this removes so many of the opposite-party identifiers from the remaining districts, it leaves those districts comfortably, but not overwhelmingly, safe for the candidate of the party controlling the redistricting. By creating more overwhelmingly safe districts for candidates of the opposite party, this packing strategy has also produced more highly safe partisan districts for incumbents, in which the incentives to pursue personal incumbency advantage are few.

The distribution of U.S. congressional districts across states provides a natural control group that allows us to test whether the decline in the underlying partisan competitiveness of congressional districts is the result of the efforts of those doing the redistricting. There are seven states that have only a single congressional district, and in them, of course, no redistricting has occurred. If redistricting is primarily responsible for the decline in the underlying partisan competitiveness of congressional districts, then we would expect the change to be far less noticeable in those states that have not been redistricted. To test this hypothesis, I created a hypothetical state comprising the seven congressional districts in the single-district states and compared the underlying partisan competitiveness of that hypothetical state with other states of similar size (those having between five and ten congressional districts at some point between 1960 and 2000).[20] The results appear in Table 6-5, in which the states are listed by the number of congressional districts that each had in 2000. The table lists the mean margin above 50 percent of the two-party presidential vote for the congressional districts within each state that the presidential candidate carrying the district received. (Thus, for example, in West Virginia, in the 2000 presidential election, the mean percentage of the two-party vote of the presidential candidate carrying the district was 54.3 percent.)

There are several things that one can observe from the data in Table 6-5. In only five of the twenty-seven states (including our hypothetical state) did the underlying partisan competitiveness of the congressional districts increase. And three of those five states were in the South, which was still largely one-party Democratic in 1960. This is certainly in keeping with the redistricting argument. Note, however, that it is our hypothetical state, the one in which no redistricting occurred, that had the biggest decline in partisan competitiveness between 1960 and 2000. And in only four states was the mean of partisan competitiveness of the congressional districts lower. These data raise doubts about the ability of redistricting schemes to explain the decline in the underlying party competitiveness of congressional districts. Why does competitiveness decline to a similar extent where no redistricting has occurred? One could speculate that different forces were at work in states that did not redistrict that resulted in the declining competitiveness of their congressional districts, while redistricting explains what has happened in states where congressional redistricting occurred. Exactly what that might be, however, is not immediately clear.[21] But the finding does lead one to consider competing explanations for the decline in underlying partisan competitiveness.

Table 6-5 Mean Margin above 50 Percent of the Presidential Vote, by Congressional District, for States with Five to Ten Districts at Some Point

State (# Cong. Dists. in 2000)	2000	1976	1960	Change 1960–2000
West Virginia (3)	4.3	8.3	5.4	−1.1
Kansas (4)	11.4	3.8	11.0	0.4
Arkansas (4)	3.8	15.8	7.7	−3.9
Iowa (5)	3.4	1.8	7.0	−3.6
Mississippi (5)	12.1	4.8	11.7	0.4
Oregon (5)	7.4	4.8	2.5	4.9
Arizona (6)	6.4	8.8	5.3	1.1
Colorado (6)	9.5	4.0	4.9	4.6
Connecticut (6)	9.2	3.7	5.3	3.9
Kentucky (6)	8.6	7.9	5.5	3.1
Oklahoma (6)	11.0	7.8	8.7	2.3
South Carolina (6)	11.9	6.7	10.5	1.4
Alabama (7)	13.7	8.7	10.3	3.4
Louisiana (7)	11.4	5.6	17.6	−6.2
Hypothetical State (7)	**12.9**	**6.0**	**3.1**	**9.8**
Maryland (8)	16.1	6.6	7.9	8.2
Minnesota (8)	6.6	7.1	4.7	1.9
Missouri (9)	10.6	5.5	6.5	4.1
Tennessee (9)	8.8	8.0	8.5	0.3
Washington (9)	7.7	2.9	3.0	4.7
Wisconsin (9)	6.6	4.8	5.9	0.7
Indiana (10)	11.4	6.0	8.0	3.4
Massachusetts (10)	15.4	8.3	11.7	3.7
Georgia (11)	13.2	17.1	14.9	−1.7
Virginia (11)	8.0	3.4	5.8	2.2
North Carolina (12)	9.7	6.1	9.2	0.5
Florida (23)	10.2	5.1	9.0	1.2

Majority-Minority Districts

A second explanation for the decline in the partisan competitiveness of congressional districts is related to the first in that it also involves district packing. In this case, however, the packing results from efforts to create districts that are favorable to the election of minority members, in particular African Americans and Latinos. Although this occurred to some degree previously, the creation of majority-minority districts was an important priority of many states following the 1990 census (and Voting Rights Act revisions). In some states this involved drawing gerrymandered districts that cut across existing jurisdictions in an effort to include minority populations and exclude majority white populations. Because the minority voters are overwhelming Democratic, one effect was to create heav-

Table 6-6 Percentage of Partisan Competitive Districts in States with and without Majority-Minority Districts, 1976 and 2000

Range of Percentage Vote Split in Two-Party Presidential Vote	Districts in States with Majority-Minority Districts in 2000	Districts in States without Majority-Minority Districts in 2000
55–45	1976: 47.2 2000: 28.0 Difference: 19.2	1976: 52.2 2000: 29.9 Difference: 22.3
60–40	1976: 73.9 2000: 53.3 Difference: 20.6	1976: 81.6 2000: 55.1 Difference: 26.5

ily Democratic, majority-minority districts and deplete Democratic voters from surrounding districts, thus making them more favorable for Republican candidates. Court decisions and the resulting redrawing of district lines in a number of states (North Carolina, Georgia, Texas, and Louisiana, most notably) did ease some of the packing. Nevertheless, much of the effect of packing remained in place. And there is some evidence to support this explanation. In the bottom (year 2000) panel of Figure 6-3, for example, all of the observations in the far upper right of the figure are majority-minority districts.

To provide a more systematic test of whether the creation of more racially gerrymandered districts has affected the overall partisan competitiveness of House districts, I compared the competitiveness of districts in states with and without majority-minority districts in 2000, using the percentage of the two-party presidential vote.[22] I also calculated how much the competitiveness of districts in those two groups of states has changed since 1976. The results appear in Table 6-6. They show very little difference (less than 2 percent) in the percentage of party-competitive districts in 2000 in states with majority-minority districts and in states without them, using both ranges to define competitiveness. The differences between the states with and without majority-minority districts (as determined in 2000) were greater in 1976, before such districts were established in many of the states. In addition, the decline in the percentage of competitive districts between 1976 and 2000 was greater in the states without majority-minority districts.

Of course, one might wish to control for some other variables that might affect the level of partisan competitiveness. This first test, however, suggests that the establishment of majority-minority districts is not responsible for the level of, or overall decline in, partisan competitiveness of congressional districts.

Residential Self-Selection

A final theory that I offer to explain the decline in partisan competitiveness at the congressional district level rests on the increased mobility of Americans and the corresponding growth in the freedom to select where they will reside. A century ago, or even a decade or two ago, Americans were likely to spend their entire lives close to the place they were born. As the economy has become more diverse, however, and as the ease and speed of transportation have increased, people have more options of where to live.[23] This has been true not just of professional and white collar workers, but of blue collar workers as well. (Automobile assembly lines, for example, exist in various parts of the country and are no longer concentrated in Michigan.) In addition, retirees increasingly leave the place where they resided during their working years for communities in other parts of the country. Even college students are less frequently limited to attending universities within a few hours' drive of their parents' home, and major universities now recruit nationally to ensure highly competitive applicant pools and entering classes.

All of this would be without partisan consequences if residential choices were not correlated with partisanship. I argue, however, that although partisanship is not necessarily a conscious consideration when people select a place to live, the criteria on which they make those decisions are linked to partisanship. Thus, I would contend that new college graduates seeking employment who decide to look in Boston, New York, and San Francisco are quite different politically from those preferring Atlanta, Dallas, and Salt Lake City. Similarly, retirees who move to the southeast coast of Florida or to retirement communities near major universities may have a mix of party loyalties quite the opposite of those who settle in Hilton Head, Scottsdale, or Pensacola.

Once people select a general locale in which to reside, they also make choices about where to live within that locale—in the central city, in the first tier of suburbs, or in the second tier. And again, they may base those choices on factors that correlate with partisan preference. One result, for example, is the disappearance of Republican congressional districts in and immediately around major northern cities. This is not to say that there was no residential self-selection in the past. It's simply that it was not as extensive, and the choices were more limited.

If the above theorizing is correct, then Americans now tend to live in more party-homogeneous locales.[24] One analysis concluded that the level of political segregation in U.S. counties increased 47 percent between 1976 and 2000.[25] As a consequence, "voters on average are less likely today to live in a community that has an even mix of Republican and Democratic voters than at any time since World War II. They are less likely to live near someone with a different political point of view and are more likely to live in a political atmosphere either overwhelmingly Republican or Democratic."[26]

When it comes to drawing congressional district lines, this residential selection into more politically homogeneous patterns has made it easier for those doing the redistricting to pack voters into heavily one-party districts or for packing to occur without intent. And if the goal were instead to create more party-competitive districts, that may have become far more difficult to do than in the past.

In a hypothetical state with an equal number of Democrats and Republicans, and with Democrats and Republicans distributed like the red and black squares on a checkerboard, it would be impossible to pack districts. Of course, actual distributions of voters do not approach that hypothetical pattern; that makes packing possible. But populations can be arrayed so that they make partisan district packing more or less difficult, even with advanced technology and data.

Impact on the House and Its Members

What differences does it make for the workings of the House of Representatives and the behavior of its members that personal incumbency advantage has declined because of an increase in underlying partisan advantage in House districts? After all, incumbents are still being reelected at historically high rates, and the margins of victory are largely unchanged from those of the 1970s and 1980s. With few incumbents holding competitive seats, the parties have a limited number of races to target. The news remains discouraging for potential challengers. Those investing dollars in House campaigns will still give the overwhelming percentage of their contributions to incumbents. Despite these continuities, I would argue that this shift in the basis of incumbency success has significant implications. Let me discuss a couple of the effects.

First, the opportunity for a sizable seat shift between the two parties has declined. Not only do incumbents remain difficult to defeat, but open-seat contests are likely to be less competitive. More seats are safe for one of the two parties, because of the increase in underlying partisan advantage, than was previously the case. Parties once saw open seats as presenting great opportunities for seat gains because of the loss of personal incumbency advantage that occurred when members retired or died (retirement slump), but they now find that fewer open seats are competitive. Since Republicans won control of the House in 1994, the seat shifts in the four subsequent elections have moved the party balance within an extremely narrow range. From the 104th Congress to the 108th, there is only a nine-seat difference between the low and high for each party.

Second, the growth in underlying partisan advantage in congressional districts may help explain the increasing partisanship in the House and the growing polarization of the parties. To win reelection in districts that are safer in terms of the partisan composition of the constituents, members do not have to concern themselves as much with appealing to independents or opposite-party adherents. Accordingly, fewer members need to moderate their policy positions for electoral purposes. In many cases they now may have more to fear from a challenge in their own party's primary than from a candidate of the other party in the general election. And appearing to be a moderate in a party primary may be a liability. The strategic argument that the moderates stand a better chance in the general election because they can appeal to independents and members of the opposite party carries less weight in districts where one party holds a comfortable majority.

Perhaps no vote in the House better illustrates the impact of this change in the basis of incumbent reelection success than the votes on the impeachment of President Clinton. Although national polls showed around 60 percent of the electorate opposed to impeachment, nearly all House Republicans could vote for it without fear of electoral repercussions because they came from districts with Republican majorities that tended to favor impeachment. And party leaders reminded several moderate Republican House members who were reluctant to vote for impeachment about the effects that failure to vote with the party would have on campaign contributions and the likelihood of strong primary opposition.

Although one may argue over whether increased polarization in the House has led to a more polarized electorate, or a more polarized electorate has chosen an increasingly polarized House membership, one effect is clear. With a more polarized electorate, segmented into increasingly safe partisan districts, House members face few electoral consequences from sticking with party positions. In his chapter in this book, Morris Fiorina acknowledges this change in noting that the basis of incumbency success has changed as elections became more national and less based on attentiveness to constituents (see Chapter 7).

Partisan Safety into the Future

The trend toward incumbent success increasingly based on the underlying partisanship of districts as opposed to personal incumbency advantage seems likely to continue. If anything, the House districts drawn for 2002 incrementally continue the decline in underlying partisan competitiveness. Allocating the 2000 presidential vote across the reapportioned 2002 districts led to nine fewer districts in which the Bush–Gore vote split was 55–45 or closer.

Another indication of the continuation of the underlying partisan safety of House districts came in the results of the 2002 elections. Typically, an election following a decennial redistricting results in a larger number of strategic retirements and general-election defeats for incumbents, as redistricting often undermines their electoral security. For members who relied on constituency tending to build personal incumbency advantage and ensure reelection, the ten-year altering of district lines created considerable uncertainty. Thus it was traditionally a time when incumbents were more likely to retire than to try to win over new constituents or when challengers would think incumbents might be more vulnerable. But this was not the case in 2002. Compared with the 1972, 1982, and 1992 elections, more incumbents sought reelection in 2002, and fewer lost in general elections than in any of those three previous election years that followed redistricting.

At least for the foreseeable future, the reelection success of most House incumbents will continue to rest on the underlying partisan advantage they have in the districts they represent rather than on the development of personal incumbency advantage. Many congressional districts have taken on far more intense red or blue tones than the noncompetitive states on a presidential election map. And their House members can behave with the understanding that they are not in play.

Notes

1. Robert S. Erikson, "The Advantage of Incumbency in Congressional Elections." *Polity* 3 (1971): 395–405; David R. Mayhew, *Congress: The Electoral Connection* (New Haven: Yale University Press, 1974); Albert D. Cover and David R. Mayhew, "Congressional Dynamics and the Decline of Competitive Congressional Elections," in *Congress Reconsidered,* 2nd ed., ed. Lawrence C. Dodd and Bruce I. Oppenheimer (Washington, D.C.: CQ Press, 1981), 62–82; Morris Fiorina, *Congress: Keystone of the Washington Establishment* (New Haven: Yale University Press, 1978); Gary C. Jacobson, *The Politics of Congressional Elections,* 4th ed. (New York: Longman, 1997); Paul S. Herrnson, *Congressional Elections: Campaigning at Home and in Washington,* 4th ed. (Washington, D.C.: CQ Press, 2004); Alan I. Abramowitz, "Incumbency, Campaign Spending, and the Decline of Competition in U.S. House Elections," *Journal of Politics* 53 (February 1991): 34–56.
2. For the case of incumbency not always being an advantage see Thomas E. Mann, *Unsafe at Any Margin: Interpreting Congressional Elections* (Washington, D.C.: American Enterprise Institute, 1978). Gary Jacobson, however, argues that sufficiently strong, well-financed challengers are often not available to take advantage of incumbent liabilities. Gary C. Jacobson, "The Misallocation of Resources in House Campaigns," in *Congress Reconsidered,* 5th ed., ed. Lawrence C. Dodd and Bruce I. Oppenheimer (Washington, D.C.: CQ Press, 1993), 115–140.
3. Gary C. Jacobson, "The Marginals Never Vanished: Incumbency and Competition in Elections to the U.S. House of Representatives, 1952–1982," *American Journal of Political Science* 31(1): 126–141.
4. James C. Garand and Donald A. Gross, "Change in the Vote Margins for Congressional Elections: A Specification of Historical Trends," *American Political Science Review* 78(1): 17–30.
5. John R. Alford and David W. Brady, "Personal and Partisan Advantage in U.S. Congressional Elections, 1846–1986," in *Congress Reconsidered,* 4th ed., ed. Lawrence C. Dodd and Bruce I. Oppenheimer (Washington, D.C.: CQ Press, 1989), 153–169.
6. John R. Alford and David W. Brady, "Personal and Partisan Advantage in U.S. Congressional Elections, 1846–1990," in *Congress Reconsidered,* 5th ed., ed. Lawrence C. Dodd and Bruce I. Oppenheimer (Washington, D.C.: CQ Press, 1993), 147.
7. Alford and Brady, "Personal and Partisan Advantage in U.S. Congressional Elections, 1846–1990," 154–155.
8. Norman J. Ornstein, Thomas E. Mann, and Michael J. Malbin, *Vital Statistics on Congress, 2001–2002* (Washington, D.C.: AEI Press, 2002).
9. The first year of every apportionment decade is excluded because changes in district boundaries make the results from the preceding election, which are needed in calculating sophomore surge and retirement slump, not comparable.
10. I would like to thank John Alford for supplying the data that he and David Brady used to construct the figures on sophomore surge and retirement slump in their article.
11. I speculate that the reason there is no drop for Republican incumbents between 1976 and 2000 is that the Republican incumbents in 1976 were ones who survived the Democratic landslide of 1974. Accordingly, they may have represented districts that were among the safest Republican districts in the country. As such, and consistent with arguments that I will substantiate later in this chapter, they are members who do not have incentives to invest resources in building large personal incumbency advantages. If this is correct, it means that the 1976 figure is lower than it might otherwise be.
12. In 1960 Kennedy and Nixon combined for 99.2 percent of the popular vote. Carter and Ford got 98.1 percent, and Bush and Gore got 96.3 percent. Regardless of the assumptions one might want to use for deciding what choices Nader voters would

have made had he not been on the ballot, they would only affect calculations of the underlying partisanship of the House districts at the margins.

13. Because Figure 6-2 includes both open seats and seats in which incumbents ran for reelection, it should not be used to conclude anything about whether the decline in the number of competitive races indicates that incumbency advantage had actually increased. In fact, much of the difference between the number of competitive races in 1976 and the number in 2000 reflects the fact that open-seat contests had become less competitive in 2000 because of the decline in underlying partisan competitiveness of the congressional districts.
14. Robert S. Erikson and Gerald C. Wright, "Voters, Candidates and Issues in Congressional Elections," in *Congress Reconsidered,* 5th ed., ed. Lawrence C. Dodd and Bruce I. Oppenheimer (Washington, D.C.: CQ Press, 1993), 91–114.
15. Ibid., 101.
16. Ibid.
17. These are members who according to Mayhew (1974) keep the House functioning on important legislative matters while most of the other members pursue activities designed to enhance reelection.
18. Richard F. Fenno Jr., *Home Style: House Members in Their Districts* (Boston: Little, Brown, 1978).
19. Gary W. Cox and Jonathan N. Katz, *Elbridge Gerry's Salamander: The Electoral Consequences of the Reapportionment Revolution* (Cambridge: Cambridge University Press, 2002).
20. One would be correct in noting that some of the states with a single district in the 2000 election (Montana and both Dakotas) had two districts for some period after 1960. But in these cases the reduction from two to a single district provided no room for those doing redistricting to make the remaining single district less competitive.
21. This test is a preliminary one. A multivariate analysis that takes into account other factors that might affect partisan competitiveness is an appropriate next step.
22. In almost every instance, I have included only those states in which at least one congressional district had a combined African American and Latino population over 50 percent. The only exception is New Mexico, where no district reached that level.
23. For example, the 2000 U.S. Census found that those working in the Washington, D.C., area are more likely to commute to jobs in other jurisdictions than was the case a decade earlier. D'Vera Cohn, "Commuters Crossing Lines: Census Finds Majority Employed Far from Home," www.washingtonpost.com, March 6, 2003, B01.
24. A number of journalists and scholars have been writing about the creation of this homogeneity in residential patterns and its consequences for American politics. See, for example, David Brooks, "People Like Us," *The Atlantic,* September 2003; Timothy Noah, "Mister Landslide's Neighborhood," Slate.com, April 7, 2004; Bill Bishop, "The Schism in U.S. Politics Begins at Home," *Austin American Statesman.com,* April 4, 2004; Richard Florida, "The Rise of the Creative Class: Why Cities without Gays and Rock Bands Are Losing the Economic Development Race," *Washington Monthly Online,* May 2002; and Peter H. Schuck, "Bringing Diversity to the Suburbs," www.nytimes.com, August 8, 2002.
25. Bishop, "The Schism in U.S. Politics Begins at Home."
26. Ibid.

7. *Keystone* Reconsidered

Morris P. Fiorina

At a recent meeting of the Midwest Political Science Association a panel of congressional scholars conducted a retrospective on my book *Congress—Keystone of the Washington Establishment,* first published in 1977.[1] This chapter is an expansion and updating of my remarks at that panel. Compared with the congressional literature of the time, *Keystone* was distinctive in two respects. First, it applied a rational actor analysis to Congress, an institution studied mostly in institutional or behavioral terms up to that time. Second, in contrast to much of the scholarly literature on Congress, *Keystone* was critical, arguing that the unbridled pursuit of constituency benefits had made members of Congress more electorally secure but at the cost of efficient and effective policies as well as the faithful representation of national preferences.

I begin with some personal remarks about the social and intellectual context that generated such a book. These serve to emphasize that the research agenda is a collective enterprise. I then consider the changes in congressional elections in the intervening years and the relationship of those changes to the research agenda today.[2] I conclude with some general thoughts about Congress and American democracy as we begin a new century.

The Context

It was my good fortune to enter the profession at the young end of a cohort of terrific scholars of congressional elections and representation: Herbert Asher, David Brady, Charles Bullock, Lawrence Dodd, Robert Erikson, John Ferejohn, John Jackson, Gary Jacobson, Samuel Kernell, Warren Kostroski, Thomas Mann, Bruce Oppenheimer, Norman Ornstein, Glenn Parker, David Rohde, Jim Stimson, Herbert Weisberg, Gerald Wright, and others. Although we hailed from different graduate programs and our research emphases varied, we were not purely political behavior scholars in the Michigan mold, nor were we purely "Congress jocks" in the mold of the scholars who participated in the American Political Science Association's Study of Congress project in the 1950s and 1960s. We were deeply interested in broader questions of representation, and our interest in elections and Congress reflected that larger concern. Most of us also had an interest in the internal operations of Congress, but we believed that elections and their anticipation significantly shaped those operations.

That group of scholars had something else in common: skepticism that the existing empirical depiction of Congress's electoral environment was accurate. The literature told us that most members had safe seats and had little to fear from unaware constituents and overrated interest groups.[3] Supposedly, members were free agents whose behavior was shaped more by internal expectations and norms than by electoral or interest group pressures.[4] Looking back, I am not sure just why so many of us found this picture unsatisfying, but we did. Probably our dissatisfaction reflected the divisions evident in Congress in the late 1960s, divisions that seemed clearly related to the demands of aroused constituents and groups. At any rate, that cohort of scholars formed a self-conscious research community in the best sense. We regularly engaged each other at meetings and conventions, and although many political science departments rationed long-distance phone privileges and first-class postage in those days, we managed to circulate and critique our work widely and quickly in the B.E. (before e-mail) era.

Junior scholars live in fear of being "scooped," a fear generally discounted by their senior colleagues. In 1974 I was a junior member of the community, eagerly awaiting publication of my first book to put me on the scholarly map. *Representatives, Roll Calls, and Constituencies* would be the first sustained effort to apply rational choice analysis to legislative behavior. Tenure—if not fame—would be assured. Unfortunately for me, David Mayhew had the same general idea at the same time, but he executed it much more ambitiously, not to mention far more readably. When my book was published it was largely overlooked amid the buzz over the slightly earlier publication of Mayhew's pathbreaking work. I considered applying to law school, but my wife nixed that suggestion. So, I decided to start my academic career over with another idea I'd been pondering since graduate school—retrospective voting.

It was not to be. Early in 1975 my colleague at Caltech, John Ferejohn, asked whether I'd seen Mayhew's latest article. "No," I replied. "What's he writing on now—retrospective voting?"[5] Ferejohn proceeded to describe Mayhew's vanishing marginals analysis, taking care to point out that it undermined another of the intended contributions of *Representatives, Roll Calls, and Constituencies.*[6] In that book I had grounded electoral competition in the demographic homogeneity or heterogeneity of legislative districts. Since the demographic composition of districts was unlikely to change significantly in the short term, if electoral competition had dramatically lessened during the 1960s, my argument was wrong.

Redistricting was the obvious suspect. There had been a great deal of it in the aftermath of *Wesberry v. Sanders* (1964), which extended "one person, one vote" to congressional districts. Conceivably, congressional districts had become significantly more homogeneous as a result. I waited with anticipation as Ferejohn studied the effect of redistricting on the vanishing marginals, only to be disappointed by his negative conclusions.[7] In the ensuing months I kibitzed his investigation of other possibilities. Ultimately he concluded that voters had changed—they were cuing less on party and more on incumbency. By this point I was thoroughly intrigued by the phenomenon and dissatisfied with the preliminary answers, so I put retrospective voting on the shelf and decided to do what Richard Fenno had been urging his students to do for years—go out into the field and "soak and poke." I did so in the summer of 1975, and the result was *Keystone* two years later.

For this retrospective I listened to the ten hours of tape recordings I made following the interviews in Districts A and B.[8] Listening reminded me that I was frustrated for most of the first week in District A. There, local observers informed me that the new representative had made this previously marginal district safe. Although time might prove them right, the question was, why? No one could tell me, or at least tell me in terms that made sense. They only offered general comments to the effect that he was being a "better congressman." That might be true for this particular district, of course, but from a social science standpoint it was an explanation without "legs," unlikely to provide a general explanation of the vanishing marginals across the country. Why would a plethora of "better congressmen" suddenly have appeared on the scene in the late 1960s? It was not until the last interview in District A that earlier comments clicked into place. Implicitly, I had been searching for some sort of policy-based reason for the change. But a young Democratic state representative doing quite nicely in a Republican area set me straight with this argument, quoted in the book:

> You've got to understand. The little guy just can't get through the bureaucracy. He can't get anything done. They ——— him over all the time. What a state representative can do is to protect the little guy and help the little guy. That's what you do to get reelected. That's the job of the elected official today.

Policy-shmalicy—it's all about license plates! I realized that I had been hearing comments like this all week. A number of interviewees on the Republican side reported that the district's agricultural sector was under siege by fanatical inspectors from the Occupational Safety and Health Administration (OSHA), and the member was defending his constituents against these misguided OSHA efforts. Others observed that having come out of the educational establishment, the new member was working closely with Parent-Teacher Associations (PTAs) and schools to take advantage of opportunities that federal programs provided. Constituents viewed him as a "better congressman" because he and his (greatly enlarged) staff were working closely with them on problems that touched their everyday lives. It's not about policy, stupid; it's about implementation.

Interviews in District B the next week confirmed what I'd learned in District A. The representative from District B simply had found the winning formula some years earlier. Satisfied that I understood at least part of the cause of the vanishing marginals, I headed home, drafted a brief article for the *American Political Science Review,* then tried to go back to retrospective voting.

Again, it was not to be. I taught both undergraduate and graduate seminars on Congress during the academic year 1975–1976, while the presidential campaign was heating up. During the spring primaries Americans were warned repeatedly about a Washington Establishment. Jimmy Carter was not a member, to be sure, in contrast to all those Democratic senators he was running against, but even career congressman and accidental president Gerald Ford denied membership.[9] The bureaucrats were out of control, it was said, and the judiciary had become a law unto itself. The Washington Establishment was running the government, not the people's representatives. I told my students this was at best half the story—members of Congress rarely were named in these indictments, but it was *their* agencies that were trying to implement *their* statutes. Moreover, judges were trying to interpret and oversee the processes Congress had structured. In a sense Congress was getting away with a great frame-up—everyone else was taking the blame for its transgressions. Colleagues encouraged me to make this bolder argument in print.

Originally I titled the manuscript, *Is There a Washington Establishment?* arguing that yes, there was, but it's not who you might think. Being a financially strapped junior professor, I first sent the manuscript off to a large number of trade publishers, all of whom rejected it. Thankfully, Marian Ash at Yale University Press felt differently, although she vetoed the wishy-washy title, and so the manuscript became *Congress—Keystone of the Washington Establishment.* There were a few stinging reviews, and I had to spend quite a bit of time and energy defending the argument, but twenty-seven years and 70,000 copies later, I can say that the pain was worth it.

The Hunt for the Incumbency Advantage

The research community went after the incumbency advantage like hounds after prey. Several of our number described and dissected the vote advantage itself. When exactly had it occurred? Did it increase linearly with seniority or happen all at once as a "sophomore surge"? Knowing more about its specifics, we then tried to evaluate the hypothesized causal mechanisms. Was it something incumbents had done, or were the changes rooted in challengers and their behavior, or neither? As systematic campaign finance data became available, some of us began to pursue that subject. In the midst of this exploding interest in congressional elections a newly reconstituted American National Election Studies (NES) decided to bring these elections under its aegis, and in the next decade newly available NES data enabled scholars to paint a far richer and more nuanced portrait of voting in congressional elections than had existed in the 1960s.

The outpouring of work led some journal editors to complain about the number of submissions dealing with incumbency in one way or another, and a few scholars suggested that the subfield had overinvested in studying the subject.[10] But editors and referees have it in their power to push resources in other directions, and so I doubt that any harm was done. On the contrary, although the jumping-off point was a relatively narrow question (What underlies the incumbency advantage, and why did it increase?), the literature pursued larger questions as scholars examined the implications of the incumbency advantage for swing ratios, presidential coattails, midterm seat swings, party strength in the legislature, the separation of the presidential and congressional electoral arenas, and other important questions of representation and governance. We became increasingly aware of the incentives created by electoral institutions, comparing behavior in the United States with that in other single member, simple plurality systems.[11] Before this literature developed, Americanists tended to take our electoral system for granted. Now we understand that it is an important variable.

The Era of Incumbency and Insulation

By the late 1980s the research community had painted a detailed portrait of what I have called "the era of incumbency and insulation." [12] After World War II an array of social, economic, and technological changes began to undermine the state and local party organizations. And in the 1960s new issues and an assortment of crises buffeted citizen allegiances to the political parties. The result was the growth of candidate-centered politics, wherein candidates personalized campaigns and elections, running not as members of long-lived teams but as individuals who would behave independently in office. Members of Congress were particularly adept at developing electoral techniques that enabled them to personalize their supporting coalitions. Increasingly, they were able to avoid association with their party's presidents and presidential candidates, their national party's image, and larger questions of national policy. Instead, they were able to win on the basis of their personal characteristics, their personal policy positions, their record of service to the district, and their great resource advantages that enabled them to discourage strong challengers and beat those whom they could not discourage. Defeat was a rarity, a result of scandal, political miscalculation, or just plain laziness. Some particulars of this portrait did not rest on as solid empirical ground as others, and we continued to argue over details, but few of us doubted that we had a good general picture. In 1984 Ronald Reagan won the presidency in a landslide, but his coattails were of little help to congressional Republicans. The midterm swing in 1986 was trivial, incumbent reelection rates reached a record high, and the Gelman-King unbiased estimate soared to a record 13 percent.[13] The 1986 reelection record fell in 1988 when 98 percent of all incumbents who ran, won. Seemingly the era of incumbency and insulation was at its apogee.

Increasingly I have come to believe that professional consensus on a subject means that it is about to change—or it already has done so but the change has gone unnoticed. Here was another example. Notification that things had changed came with thunderous force in 1994.

All Politics Is Not as Local as Before

"All politics is local," the famous aphorism of Speaker of the House Tip O'Neill, was the mantra of our generation of congressional scholars. Everyone recognized that it was overstated, of course, but it was a pretty good way of summing up the main features of the era of incumbency and insulation. Little did we know that the fit of the aphorism to empirical reality was growing worse even at the apparent height of the power of incumbency. In 1994 the Republicans gained fifty-three seats in the House and eight in the Senate to take control of Congress for the first time since the elections of 1952. The House swing was the largest since 1948, an election well before the era of incumbency, which arrived in the late 1960s, and forecasting models developed during the 1970s and 1980s were far off the mark. To my knowledge no one in the research community saw the upheaval coming (at least they didn't rush to publish their prediction). In the weeks before the elections most of us confidently told journalists that Newt Gingrich was just blowing smoke—Republicans had talked about nationalizing the elections before, but no one knew how to do it with incumbency so strong. We had discounted similar pronouncements for nearly two decades and had been right; this time we were wrong.

After the elections the Hoover Institution held a conference attended by many of those who had painted the 1970s and 1980s portrait of congressional elections, joined by a younger generation that included many of their students. Several of the conference papers reported that indications of increased nationalization of the congressional electoral arena were clearly evident in the record but simply had not been appreciated until 1994. In Figures 7-1 and 7-2 I have graphed coefficients from regressing the current district House vote on the past House and presidential vote in the district.[14] The past presidential vote is treated as an indicator of national forces, and the past House vote as an indicator of local forces—crude, but temporally comparable measures often used in this literature. The picture is similar whether one looks at on-year or off-year elections, whether one includes uncontested elections or excludes them, and whether the South is included or omitted.

Consistent with the portrait in the literature, the presidential and House arenas separated in the late 1950s and maintained a good deal of separation until the mid-1970s, a development that probably encouraged candidate-centered politics and reinforced it as well.[15] But—importantly—the national component of the vote began to recover after the traumas of the 1960s, whereas the local component began to drop back from its high. By the midpoint of Reagan's first term the two components had reached statistical parity. Thus, at the time the incumbency literature was in full flower, the phenomena that had generated it were in decline! Probably the principal reason the research community did not notice these developments is that the elections of the late 1980s arrested these trends, showing significant drops in the national component and seemingly validating the prevailing picture. In retrospect, however, they were the last hurrahs of the old era—the national coefficient for 1994 actually is lower than a simple extrapolation of the trend from 1966 to 1982.

Gary Jacobson also reported indications of increased nationalization of House elections.[16] For one thing, Republican seat gains in the 1990s came disproportionately in districts where Republican presidential candidates ran well—in the South of course, but outside the South, too. For another thing, the standard deviation of the vote swing fell, indicating that House returns in the 1990s

Figure 7-1 Decomposition of Midterm House Elections (Contested and Uncontested Seats), 1954–1998

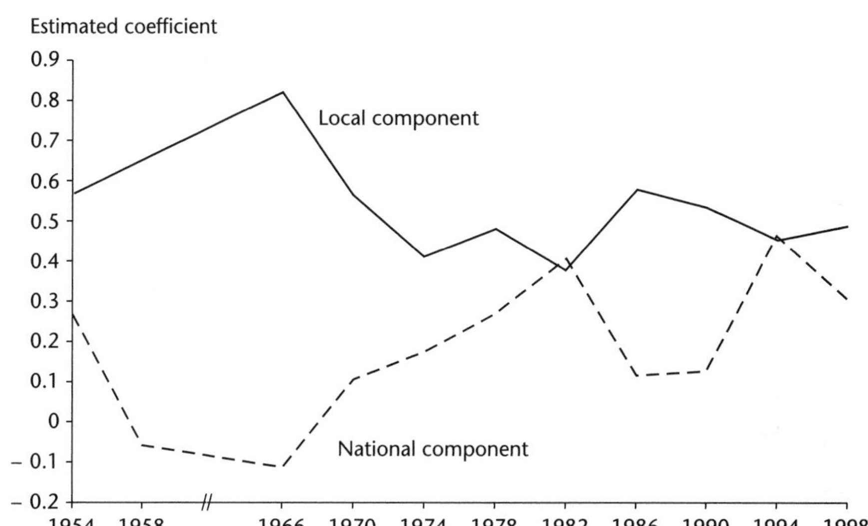

Source: David Brady, John Cogan, and Morris Fiorina, *Continuity and Change in House Elections* (Stanford: Stanford University Press, 2000).

Note: No calculation for 1962 is possible because the past presidential vote in the newly redrawn congressional districts is unavailable. (Congressional Quarterly provided estimates for 1982.)

were moving together to a greater extent than in earlier postwar elections. Other researchers have noted that levels of House-president ticket splitting have dropped in recent elections, both measured at the individual level and in the aggregate.

Of course, the important changes evident in the 1994 returns should not lead us to overlook the continuities that are equally evident. Most obviously, in a terrible year for incumbents 90 percent of those who ran, won. To be sure, there was a major partisan asymmetry, as all thirty-three of the losing incumbents were Democrats. But even for Democrats the Gelman-King measure registered a larger advantage than in 1990, when no one had any inkling that important changes were in progress. The advantages of incumbency were overcome in many cases, but by no means did they disappear.

Nor did the standard techniques by which incumbents in previous decades had built their advantage. After winning control, congressional Republicans acted more or less in the manner of a responsible party for the better part of 1995, leading some to wonder whether the entire literature on Congress needed revision. But after the politically disastrous government shutdowns in the winter of

Figure 7-2 Decomposition of Presidential-Year House Elections (Contested and Uncontested Seats), 1956–1996

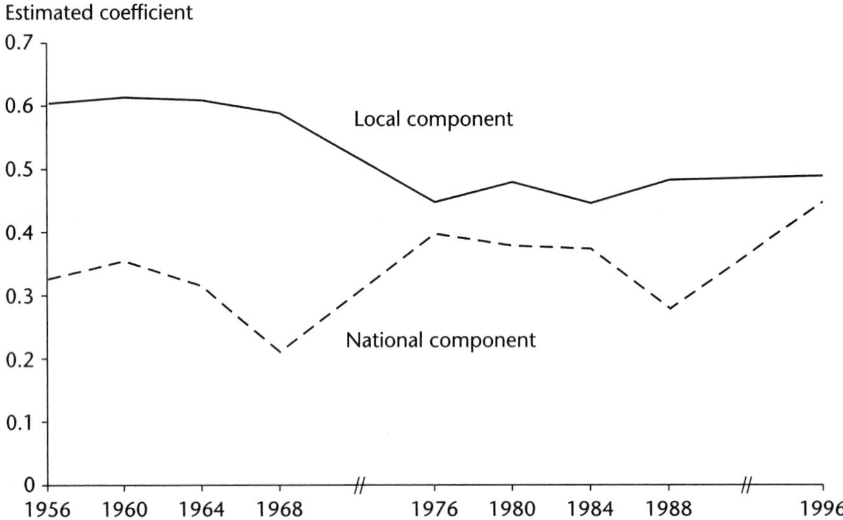

Source: David Brady, John Cogan, and Morris Fiorina, *Continuity and Change in House Elections* (Stanford: Stanford University Press, 2000).

Note: No calculations for 1972 and 1992 are possible because the past presidential vote in the newly redrawn congressional districts in unavailable.

1995–1996 electorally apprehensive Republicans rediscovered tried-and-true formulas, such as putting daylight between themselves and Speaker Gingrich and emphasizing the services rendered for their districts.

After the Republican majority survived the 1996 elections, Transportation Committee chair Bud Shuster, R-Pa., demonstrated the continued strong appeal of pork barrel politics as he rolled the Republican leadership. And at the end of the session the leadership itself capitulated in the face of electoral realities and negotiated an omnibus appropriations bill that at the time was called the largest pork barrel bill in history. In the wake of this return to more traditional congressional politics, the 1998 election outcomes were something of a throwback to 1986 and 1988. Of 401 incumbents who sought reelection, only five lost, for a new success record of 98.5 percent. Incumbents registered 8.0 on the Gelman-King scale.

Still, the changes of the 1990s are consequential. Even in 1998 there were continued indications of increased nationalization. The standard deviation of the vote swing dropped to an even lower level than it had in 1994. And a recent extension of the analysis reported in Figure 7-1 results in a smaller national coefficient in the 1998 regression than in the 1994 regression, but one larger than that for any other midterm since 1954, although the 2000 presidential coefficient dropped back to its 1988 level. In sum, the 1994–1996 elections may have been a high-water mark for nationalization, but indisputably, congressional elections today are more nationalized than they have been since the 1960s. The old equilibrium of incumbency and insulation clearly has been disrupted. But the important consequences for national politics have followed from relatively small changes in the electoral arena, not the first time we have seen the consequences of small electoral changes magnified in congressional process and output.[17]

Finally, it is worth pointing out that not all the contributors to the incumbency literature would have been surprised by the electoral transformation in the 1990s. Indeed, taking a more national and party-centered orientation, one of the editors of this book foreshadowed the Republican revolution, arguing that the electoral entrenchment of the majority party would lead to policy failure, if not crisis, and eventual electoral retribution.[18] Although he didn't predict when the revolution would occur, on the morning after the 1994 elections one could understand Larry Dodd feeling quite satisfied with the outcome (professionally, at least!). Other scholars had not been sufficiently bold to predict an eventual reaction, but at least they had noted that the individual responsiveness of incumbents went along with the lack of institutional responsiveness and accountability that was politically damaging to the collective Congress.[19]

Why the Change?

Why has the personal electoral insulation that characterized the preceding era of congressional elections eroded? I think that there are at least three reasons, although these thoughts are more impressionistic than I would like.

The first reason is that the activities that produced the earlier insulation became routinized and in consequence probably less worthy of voter appreciation, or even notice. In the late 1960s a member of Congress who established multiple district offices and came home every two weeks stood out from the crowd. By the late 1980s such a member was just doing what everyone else did, maybe even a little less. There have been numerous attempts, using various techniques, to measure the magnitude of the incumbency advantage over time. All tend to show a similar pattern—a sudden surge in the incumbency advantage in the elections of the late 1960s from the level typical of the early postwar period. Fluctuation or more gradual increase characterizes the elections of 1972–1988; then the magnitude of the estimate recedes.[20] The period of greatest change occurred at the same time as the greatest change in member resources and behavior.

Several analysts have attempted to determine what factors produced the growth in the incumbency advantage. The major candidates are incumbent resources and behavior, campaign funds, and the ability to scare off strong challengers, although these factors are surely somewhat related. Moreover, my suspicion is that attempts to answer this question are hindered by the fact that the nature of the incumbency advantage may have shifted over time. From approxi-

Figure 7-3 Personal Staffs of Representatives and Senators, 1957–1997

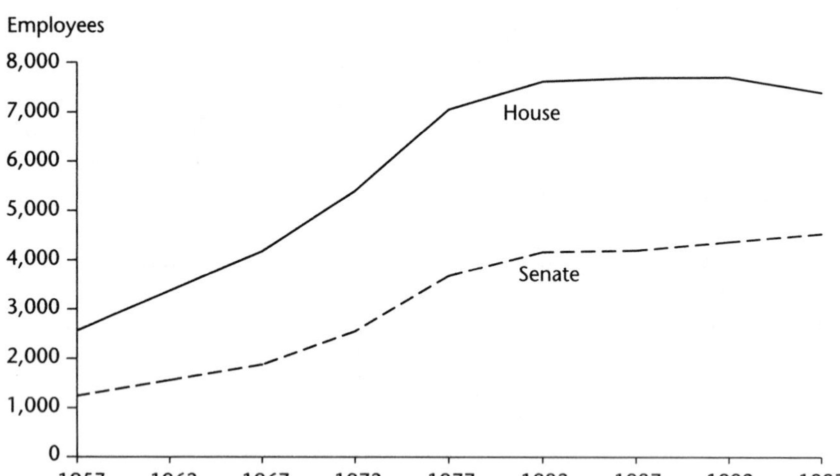

Source: Norman J. Ornstein, Thomas E. Mann, and Michael J. Malbin, eds., *Vital Statistics on Congress, 1999–2000* (Washington, D.C.: American Enterprise Institute, 2000), 131.

mately the mid-1960s through the 1970s, I believe, it was based primarily on member resources and activities. But as increases in member resources leveled off (Figures 7-3 and 7-4) and a high level of constituency attentiveness became a universal expectation, they declined in importance. During the 1980s elections became much more expensive, incumbents were able to raise far more money than challengers, and the nature of the incumbency advantage increasingly came to reflect those facts. Then, as alternative means of recruiting and financing challengers developed in the 1990s, elections became more national and the incumbency advantage declined.

That brings us to the second reason for the electoral changes evident in the 1990s. Incumbents were able to maintain a huge advantage in campaign fund raising in the 1980s and consequently deter strong challengers and defeat weaker ones (see Figure 7-5). That advantage eroded in the 1980s. Why? An anecdote from the *Keystone* interviews suggests an answer.

In listening to the tapes I was struck by the fact that in ten hours of recordings there is only one reference to money in a campaign context.[21] And that lone reference is extremely revealing. In District A, I spent an enjoyable evening with a defeated Democratic candidate and his campaign manager. The candidate had run relatively poorly for a challenger in this marginal district, although he still managed a bit more than 45 percent of the vote. As we spoke it became apparent that the man, a lawyer, was a complete amateur, politically speaking, and so I naturally asked how he had become the Democratic candidate. He told me that he had become increasingly outraged over American involvement in Vietnam, and

Figure 7-4 Mail Franked by Representatives and Senators, 1955–1993

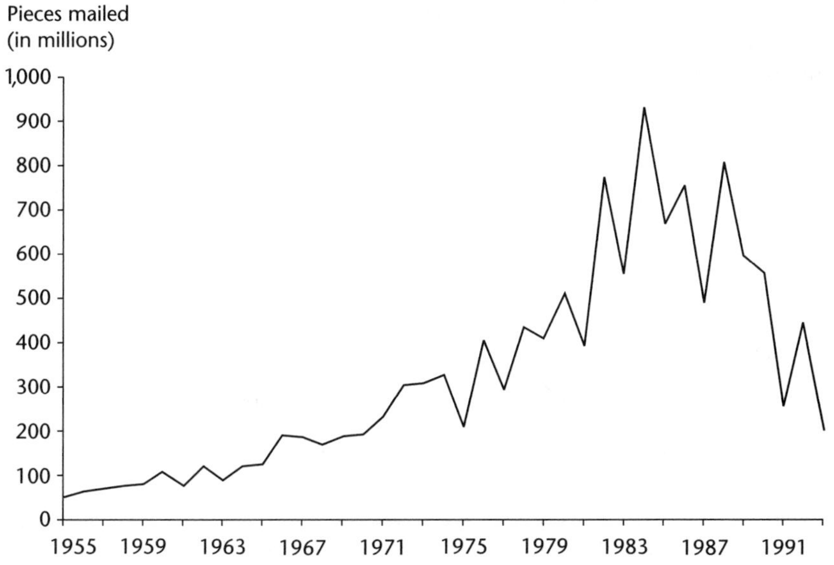

Pieces mailed
(in millions)

1,000
900
800
700
600
500
400
300
200
100
0

1955 1959 1963 1967 1971 1975 1979 1983 1987 1991

Source: Norman J. Ornstein, Thomas E. Mann, and Michael J. Malbin, eds., *Vital Statistics on Congress, 1999–2000* (Washington, D.C.: American Enterprise Institute, 2000), 165.

finally, he felt compelled to try to do something about it. A practical man, he had pondered the alternatives and decided that running for Congress seemed like a reasonable place to start.

The prospective candidate learned that the local Democratic organization—the most important in the district—was headed by a "boss," who called the shots. "So I called him up, and he took the call while he was shaving," the candidate recalled. "I introduced myself and told him that I wanted to run for Congress on the Democratic ticket, and he asked, 'Just why in the hell should we give you the nomination?'" And the prospective candidate replied, "I'll put $15,000 of my own money into the race." According to the candidate, the "boss" suddenly became very supportive of his candidacy.

Now, even allowing for some exaggeration, and the fact that his personal contribution was nearly $50,000 in current dollars, can anyone imagine the Democratic Congressional Campaign Committee today standing by while an amateur walks away with the nomination in a marginal district? Can anyone imagine one of today's major cause groups standing by while a candidate motivated by their cause fights alone for a winnable district? For that matter, can anyone imagine making a serious run for the House today on a $50,000 budget? I think that what did not happen in this marginal district in the 1970s that would surely happen now is an important part of the explanation for the increased nationalization of elections in the 1990s.

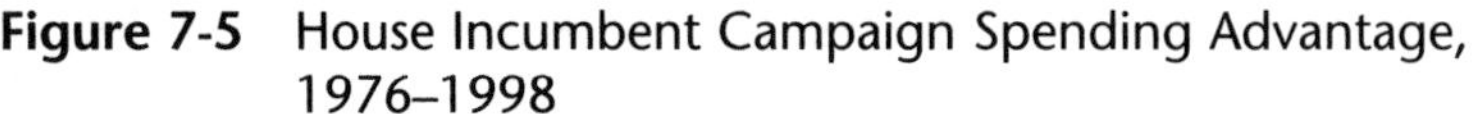
Figure 7-5 House Incumbent Campaign Spending Advantage, 1976–1998

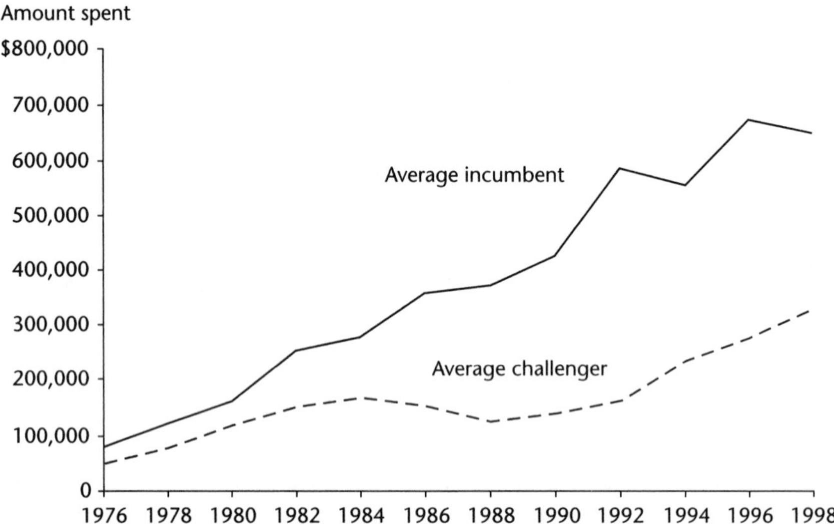

Source: Norman J. Ornstein, Thomas E. Mann, and Michael J. Malbin, eds., *Vital Statistics on Congress, 1999–2000* (Washington, D.C.: American Enterprise Institute, 2000), 81.

Beginning in the late 1970s the national party organizations began a resurgence, first on the Republican side and then later on the Democratic side. To be sure, today's parties are different from those of yesteryear. Rather than patronage-based local organizations headed by "bosses," they are national campaign organizations, with a heavier dose of ideological motivation than previously. These parties became increasingly active at the local level, first identifying and encouraging strong candidates, then training them and supporting them. With this increasing involvement (some called it "interference" when it first began) came an increasing orientation toward the national parties by the candidates they recruited and supported.

The rise of issue advocacy by the parties reinforces these developments. One of the standard contemporary techniques is to associate your candidate with a popular party leader or party issue and link the other candidate to an unpopular party leader or issue (morphing advertisements are a familiar example). The very concept of a popular or unpopular party leader other than the president also is a recent notion. Morphing House candidates into the visages of Gerald Ford, John McCormack, Hugh Scott, and Mike Mansfield would not have struck 1970 campaign professionals as a particularly effective campaign technique. But when party leaders are Dick Gephardt and Nancy Pelosi, Newt Gingrich and Tom DeLay, the technique makes a lot more sense.[22] The implications of such developments for nationalization could hardly be more transparent. Incumbents today do not find it as easy to separate themselves from party leaders, party images, and party performance as did incumbents of twenty years ago.

Along the same lines, I noted in the second edition of *Keystone* that interest groups and political action committees (PACs) that collected and disbursed money nationally could strengthen the hand of interests not tied to specific districts. In retrospect, that was an understatement. So long as interest group spending consisted largely of hard money contributions to individual campaigns, the existing equilibrium was not seriously threatened. But with the rise of independent expenditure campaigns the picture shifts. As abortion, environmental, health care, and other groups increasingly engage in independent issue advocacy, candidates lose control of the agenda. Twenty years ago most of us agreed with congressional scholar Glenn Parker's pithy observation that "the information people have about House incumbents comes from House incumbents." Today, that is less true, as incumbents see an assortment of advertisements about themselves, produced by the opposing party and hostile groups, running on TV screens in their districts. Even if *both* candidates would prefer that an issue not arise in their contest, they may have little say in the matter.

The third reason I think that congressional elections have changed is even more impressionistic than the preceding two. Put quite simply, I believe that today's candidates have deeper policy commitments than their counterparts of a generation ago. In the pre-incumbency days of party-dominated elections, the professional literature told us that the parties were approximately Downsian, motivated to win elections because of the value their members attached to jobs, contracts, and other tangible benefits of office holding. The parties chose candidates on the basis of qualities such as electability, and if that was not an issue, on the basis of such qualities as loyalty to the organization, length of service, local or ethnic claims, and so forth.

That does not seem to be the case today. A comment by a recent chair of the California Republican Party illustrates the difference: When asked about his priorities he replied that "killing our babies is the issue of the century. . . . cutting taxes or any other issue pales in comparison."[23] Fifty years ago the reply likely would have been more along the lines of "to elect as many Republicans as possible."

As traditional, patronage-based organizations withered, a wide variety of groups stepped into the space left unoccupied. Increasingly such groups generate candidates and take an important role in organizing and funding campaigns. But the reason for belonging to such groups is commitment to group goals, and that is also a prerequisite for gaining group support. James Sundquist remarked on the increased policy commitment of new members as early as the 1970s, and Burdett Loomis provided a more comprehensive discussion in the 1980s.[24] It seems likely that members increasingly motivated by policy goals would be more likely to establish records rich in policy content, to emphasize issues as part of their personal political image, and to attract the notice of groups and individuals with similar policy commitments. If all politics still were local, they would not find the job nearly as interesting.

In sum, the rising nationalization of congressional elections probably has a number of different sources, including diminishing returns from established election strategies, the innovative and increasingly aggressive behavior of reconstituted parties and a host of new interest groups, and the changing motivations and behavior of members themselves. These broad claims are only hypotheses, of course, although there is impressionistic evidence consistent with each.

A New Party Era?

Shortly before the publication of *Keystone,* David Mayhew wrote, "The fact is that no theoretical treatment of the United States Congress that posits parties as analytic units will go very far."[25] Here we see once again an instance of a firm political science conclusion serving as a leading indicator of change. Mayhew was not alone in his thinking. Parties played no role in the arguments presented in *Keystone,* not even in the second edition, in which I was admittedly a little slow to pick up on developments in that arena. At the retrospective panel, David Rohde, a leading scholar of party behavior in Congress, asked what I would say about parties now if there were to be a third edition.

Part of the answer lies in the preceding hypothesis that active party committees and visible party leaders are part of the explanation of the increased nationalization of congressional elections. Although I have written in broad outline, I will say no more on that subject here. Instead, I will shift direction somewhat and offer some observations about the current research agenda, one that is dominated by discussions of and arguments about the extent and nature of party influence in Congress today.

Soon after scholars began to write about the resurgence of the congressional parties, Keith Krehbiel stimulated an important and productive debate in the congressional subfield with a series of contrarian articles. He first pointed out that commonly used indicators of party influence, such as measures of cohesion and unity, are highly ambiguous; they can just as easily reflect similarity of legislator preferences as party discipline. Krehbiel then argued that there are conceptual ambiguities in discussions of party strength, party influence, and so forth. Most recently he has contended that, empirically, congressional data are more consistent with preference-based models than with party discipline models.[26] Given the widespread belief in the resurgence of congressional parties during the 1980s and 1990s, Krehbiel's arguments have provoked equally widespread reaction from scholars such as Rohde, John Aldrich, Gary Cox, Mat McCubbins, and Barbara Sinclair. How one conceptualizes and measures party influence is among the leading questions on the congressional research agenda today. Krehbiel's critique has stimulated researchers to innovate in order to find new ways of demonstrating party effects on roll call voting. Recent examples include articles by James Snyder and Tim Groseclose, Gregory Hager and Jeffery Talbert, and David Brady, Judith Goldstein, and Daniel Kessler.[27] Thus, the near-universal belief that "parties matter" now rests on a firmer footing than a decade ago, although there is plenty of room for further work on the subject.

In the contemporary debate the principal poles are party and preference, but I think it would be valuable to bring constituency back into the picture. The notion of preference that advocates of preference-based theories hold is that of "induced preference," also called "revealed" or "public" preference. We measure such preferences by observing member votes and then conduct analyses to see whether party membership exerts any independent effect over and above preferences. The problem is that induced preferences are themselves an amalgam of personal ideology, constituency preferences, interest group pressures, and party pressures, an obvious point whose implications are not yet fully appreciated even after nearly three decades of argument.[28]

If observed behavior, such as roll call voting, shows a strong relationship with the party affiliation of the representative, at least three possible mechanisms may underlie the correlation. The first is pure selection. For example, if all candidates belonged to one of two types—liberals, who join the Democratic Party, or conservatives, who join the Republicans—then there would be a strong relationship between voting and party, but it would be epiphenomenal: party labels simply would be shorthand for the personal ideologies of the members. Some have interpreted this as Krehbiel's null hypothesis, although in fact his null hypothesis is agnostic about the source of the revealed preferences. This case also illustrates one of Krehbiel's "paradoxes," that parties appear strongest when there is the least need for strong parties—there would be perfect party unity even in the absence of any kind of party influence. It is likely that many of what we casually refer to as "party effects" are of this kind. Rohde and others of the party resurgence school, for example, see increasing homogenization of intraparty preferences as a precondition for increasing party strength.[29]

A second mechanism underlying a strong relationship between party and legislative behavior is party influence in the strict sense that the term *pressure* connotes. Party leaders in Congress, the caucus, or perhaps the administration overtly attempt to influence members either by promising carrots, such as committee assignments, district projects, support for pet bills, and consideration of specific amendments, or by threatening sticks, such as withholding the same sorts of prizes, or some mixture of the two. The literature contains examples of such behavior, to be sure, but there are also examples that suggest its limitations. For example, at the height of Newt Gingrich's power in the 104th Congress, dissident junior Republicans on the Agriculture Committee torpedoed "Freedom to Farm," an important piece of party legislation. Gingrich threatened sanctions, but after an outcry he was forced to back down.[30] Party *influence* in this strong sense means the ability of party leaders to persuade or coerce members into behaving differently from the way they would behave in the absence of party pressure. Clearly there is a huge inferential leap from a correlation between party and behavior to the conclusion that active (or anticipated) party influence in this strong sense is the underlying cause. More detailed analyses that document the actions and effects of party leaders are necessary. An exemplar of such research is a recent article by Aldrich and Rohde in which—among other things—they explicitly link the activities of party leaders to changes in member behavior and the achievement of nonmedian outcomes in the House.[31]

There is yet a third path for parties to exert influence that has been largely ignored in the current discussion. That path lies in the electoral arena rather than in the institution. It has become increasingly clear that the classic median voter model of party competition is a poor description of the realities of congressional elections. At least since the work of Fenno we have understood that a congressional district—a legal entity—is seldom the undifferentiated mass that the spatial models assume. Rather, a district contains numerous constituencies, and Democrats and Republicans will build on different ones to form winning coalitions. Moreover, incumbents of different parties can be drawn even farther from the median by distinct primary constituencies. Numerous models rationalize the taking of such noncentrist positions by candidates.[32]

Thus, when moderate House Republicans announced that they would vote to impeach President Clinton in the winter of 1998, it was widely interpreted as party pressure, since most such members had indicated that they personally favored censure rather than impeachment. The media clearly favored this interpretation, and certainly there was enough bluster within Congress to suggest that pressure was operating. But it is also very plausible, and consistent with my observations of a few of those members, that they were making a calculation of the following sort: "If I do not vote for impeachment, I will antagonize the hard-core partisans in my district. That certainly may hurt me in the primary, and even if I get by that, it will hurt me in the general election." If this sort of thinking is at work, the induced preference of the member can be a reflection of party-in-the-electorate.

Note that this third path is partly consistent with the arguments of the party skeptics on the one hand and the party resurgence theorists on the other, but it also is partly inconsistent with both sets of arguments. Krehbiel may be correct in doubting that party discipline is being exerted within the institution and believing that, instead, members are voting their induced preferences. But if those preferences are induced by party in the district, then that is a kind of party effect, although not the one he has argued against. Similarly, Aldrich, Rohde, Sinclair, and others may be quite correct that parties matter, and matter more than they used to, but the way in which they matter may not be as much through the institutional paths that their arguments often presume. Instead, the paths that produce party differences may lie primarily in the way candidates are recruited and elected in their districts.[33]

The truth, of course, is probably somewhere in between, and that is a question that future research will resolve. My point is simply that this lively and important discussion of the role of the congressional parties could benefit from more explicit consideration of the concerns that animated the literature of the 1970s and 1980s—electoral concerns. I think it would be a valuable contribution if the party skeptics were to develop models that are more explicitly grounded in the electoral arena; beginning the exercise with induced preferences abstracts away too much that is of interest and importance. For their part, party resurgence theorists would do well to think harder about different paths of party influence and to evaluate the state of the evidence consistent with each.

Congress at the Beginning of the Twenty-first Century

In the early 1970s the attitude of congressional scholars toward Congress was generally positive. My recollection is that those positive scholarly attitudes reflected an appreciation for the values that the legislative branch exemplified, particularly representation and responsiveness. Critics—and there were many outside the fraternity of congressional scholars—who valued efficiency and programmatic coherence more highly were viewed with some suspicion as narrow policy wonks or presidential loyalists who failed to appreciate the complexities of the democratic process in a large, heterogeneous country. When it was really necessary, Congress would behave responsibly and coherently. It was Congress, after all, that stepped in and stopped the abuses summarized by "Watergate" that were the inevitable accompaniment of the development of the imperial presidency.

To a younger generation coming along, however, there was somewhat less to admire. New problems, such as rampant inflation and the energy crisis, illustrated all too well the shortcomings of the weak and outmoded organization of Congress, as well as the deeper problem—that unconstrained representation of the parts of this country left the whole of the nation inadequately represented. *Keystone* reflected my belief that distributive politics was out of hand, with consequences not sufficiently understood or appreciated.

Today I am much less concerned about distributive politics and its consequences. For one thing, distributive politics has declined in importance. The subgovernments that fostered distributive politics were overrun and dismantled by scores of new interest groups opposed to their activities, not to mention journalists hungry for critical stories. In addition, the hostility of the administrations of Ronald Reagan and George H. W. Bush to traditional grant programs and to government regulation (along with twenty years of budget deficits that squeezed their funding) slowed the growth of government in these areas. Deficit politics brought its own set of problems, of course, but by their very nature these called for a more coordinated response by the national parties and national institutions. Compared with the Congresses of the prereform era, the Congresses of the postreform era are more efficiently organized, and along with the nationalization of elections discussed earlier in this chapter, they have constrained distributive tendencies and increased the amount of collective responsibility that exists.[34]

My concern today is less with a Washington Establishment dominated by Congress than with a political class that is out of touch with, and out of step with, the mass of Americans. Many members of Congress are part of this class, but in the era of the permanent campaign they are joined by others—interest groups, activists, contributors—whom we used to lump together under the rubric of the congressional "environment." Today, the Congress is far less insulated, and the boundary between the environment and the institution has grown very fuzzy. Indeed, members today spend more time in and with the environment than they do in and with the institution.

The Washington Establishment of the 1970s permitted national problems to fester because of unwillingness to harm constituency interests, and indeed used such problems to advance constituency interests. The political class today allows national problems to fester because its members insist on having the entire loaf, not just a portion, and/or because they would rather have an election issue than have incremental progress. Moreover, today's parties have only shallow roots in the population at large; they are increasingly dependent on specific constituencies whose interests are not shared by the general population. These are serious charges that I have developed more fully elsewhere.[35] For now, two related examples will suffice to illustrate the argument.

First, consider the abortion issue. In the 2000 primaries Bill Bradley charged Al Gore with being insufficiently pro-life because years earlier, as a Tennessee congressman, Gore had expressed the personal belief that a fetus was not merely a clump of tissue. On the Republican side, John McCain was attacked as pro-choice because he would permit abortion in the cases of rape, incest, and birth defects. Analysts of public opinion are well aware that about 80 percent of the population share the conditional views expressed by McCain and a younger Gore rather than the unconditional views of the "wing-nuts" of the two parties. Americans believe that this is a difficult issue, that rights collide, and that trade-offs are inevitable. Consequently, polls show that clear majorities are willing to live with various restrictions such as those permitted by the *Casey* decision in 1992.

The politics of the issue are another matter. The 20 percent who hold more extreme views than the mass of Americans dominate the debate within the parties. The volunteers and resources that the pro-choice and pro-life activists provide are especially important in the primaries, and their high activity levels make them important components of each party's base. But because both are decidedly minority viewpoints, we have had thirty years of contentious politics, even though most Americans could agree to compromise and move on, and thirty years of policy stalemate in which courts determine policies when the elected branches cannot act. Too much of contemporary politics is like this—defined by groups whose preferences and goals do not reflect those of the citizenry in general.

Second, consider some of the constituency groups with which the parties are most closely associated, the so-called party bases such as the teachers' unions and trial lawyers for the Democrats and the religious right for the Republicans. As the parties have ceased to represent broad societal interests such as "the working man," and "the middle class," they have become increasingly dependent on smaller, intensely self-interested or self-righteous groups that many Americans view as detracting from the good of the nation. The state of the educational system in urban areas threatens to destroy the traditional American ideal of success in life through merit and hard work, but today's Democratic Party is nearly helpless to propose anything that might seriously disrupt union control of public education. And, as mentioned above, its constituency groups make it difficult for today's Republican Party to strike reasonable compromises on contentious social issues, thus contributing to the harsh tone of contemporary politics and the public disaffection with it.

Examples of these problems abound in Congress, but Congress did not create them. It is the processes of political participation and nonparticipation, recruitment, fund raising, and campaigning that created them. Today, as it always has, Congress reflects what is going on in the larger electoral environment. Those concerned with the operation of Congress today and its contribution to American democracy in the twenty-first century should pay close attention to that environment.

Notes

1. Originally scheduled for the 1997 meeting of the Southern Political Science Association, the twenty-year retrospective panel was canceled when fog grounded the flights of several participants. Rescheduled for the 1999 meeting of the Midwest Political Science Association, the panel was organized and chaired by Lawrence Dodd and included David Brady, John Hibbing, and David Rohde. David Mayhew and Timothy Prinz also prepared comments for the canceled 1997 panel. I am grateful to these scholars for their comments, many of which have informed this chapter. The editors of the present volume—coincidentally first published in the same year as *Keystone*—graciously invited me to expand on my remarks for this new edition. Thanks also to Sam Abrams for excellent research assistance.
2. This chapter does not revisit topics and questions treated in the second (1989) edition. Written in the aftermath of two incumbency-dominated elections (1986, 1988), that discussion was more one of additions and refinements, which I will allow to stand as written. Changes that became evident in the 1990s are more consequential for the original argument and the literature in which it is embedded.
3. Donald Stokes and Warren Miller, "Party Government and the Saliency of Congress," *Public Opinion Quarterly* 26 (1962): 531–546; Raymond Bauer, Ithiel de Sola Pool, and Lewis Dexter, *American Business and Public Policy* (New York: Atherton, 1968).
4. As in such classic works as Donald Matthews, *U.S. Senators and Their World* (Chapel Hill: University of North Carolina Press, 1960), and Richard Fenno, "The House Appropriations Committee as a Political System: The Problem of Integration, *American Political Science Review* 56 (1962): 310–324.
5. In 1989 or 1990 I circulated an e-mail to Harvard University graduate students indicating my intention to offer a seminar on divided government. One e-mailed back asking whether we'd be reading Mayhew's new manuscript. It was déjà vu all over again!
6. "Congressional Elections: The Case of the Vanishing Marginals," *Polity* 3 (1974): 295–317.
7. The most recent analysis concludes that Ferejohn may have dismissed the importance of redistricting a bit too quickly. See Gary Cox and Jonathan Katz, *Elbridge Gerry's Salamander* (Cambridge: Cambridge University Press, 2002).
8. Nowadays many scholars tape interviews verbatim. Way back then, Fenno still advocated recording or transcribing one's recollection of the interview after conducting it.

Being a novice at this sort of research I followed his advice, putting everything on tape that I could remember after the interview.

9. Recall that Sens. Birch Bayh, Fred Harris, Hubert Humphrey, and Henry Jackson, along with Rep. Morris Udall, all sought the presidency in 1976.
10. R. Douglas Arnold, "Overtilled and Undertilled Fields in American Politics," *Political Science Quarterly* 97 (1982): 91–103.
11. Bruce Cain, John Ferejohn, and Morris Fiorina, *The Personal Vote* (Cambridge: Harvard University Press, 1987).
12. "Epilogue: The Era of Incumbency and Insulation," in *Continuity and Change in House Elections,* ed. David Brady, John Cogan, and Morris Fiorina (Stanford: Stanford University Press, 2000).
13. Andrew Gelman and Gary King, "Estimating Incumbency Advantage without Bias," *American Journal of Political Science* 34 (1990): 1142–1164.
14. The equations control for incumbency and national tides. Essentially, they are Gelman-King equations augmented with the previous presidential vote in the district. The desirable qualities of the equations are unaffected by addition of this variable. For details see David Brady, Robert D'Onofrio, and Morris P. Fiorina, "The Nationalization of Electoral Forces Revisited," in Brady, Cogan, and Fiorina, *Continuity and Change in House Elections.*
15. One naturally wonders what these coefficients might have looked like before the arenas separated in the Eisenhower administration. Although we presume that the elections from the mid-1950s to 1970 are the exception, not the norm, that may not necessarily be the case. We are currently compiling the presidential vote by district for whole-county congressional districts for the entire twentieth century, which should enable us to provide an approximate answer to the question.
16. Gary Jacobson, "Reversal of Fortune: The Transformation of U.S. House Elections in the 1990s," in Brady, Cogan, and Fiorina, *Continuity and Change in House Elections.*
17. David Brady, *Critical Elections and Congressional Policy-Making* (Stanford: Stanford University Press, 1988).
18. Lawrence C. Dodd, "The Cycles of Legislative Change: Building a Dynamic Theory," in *Political Science: The Science of Politics,* ed. Herbert Weisberg (New York: Agathon Press, 1986), 82–104.
19. I was something of a broken record on this point. See, among other essays, Morris Fiorina, "The Decline of Collective Responsibility in American Politics," *Daedalus* 109 (1980): 25–45. Gary Jacobson also made this argument regularly in the concluding chapter of the successive editions of his textbook. See, for example, *The Politics of Congressional Elections* (New York: HarperCollins, 1992).
20. Gelman and King, "Estimating Incumbency Advantage without Bias," Fig. 3; Steven Levitt and Catherine Wolfram, "Decomposing the Sources of Incumbency Advantage in the U.S. House," *Legislative Studies Quarterly* 22 (1997): Fig. 1; John Alford and David Brady, "Personal and Partisan Advantage in U.S. Congressional Elections, 1846–1986," in *Congress Reconsidered,* 4th ed., ed. Lawrence C. Dodd and Bruce I. Oppenheimer (Washington, D.C.: CQ Press, 1989), Fig. 6-3.
21. There are various references to money in the context of political corruption and local payoffs. One of those interviewed in District B began serving a prison sentence a few months after we spoke.
22. My recollection is that Tip O'Neill was the first congressional leader to be the subject of an attack ad, by the Reagan campaign in 1984.
23. Quoted in Carla Marinucci, "GOP to Play Musical Chairs over Abortion," *San Francisco Chronicle,* May 15, 2000, A1.
24. James Sundquist, *The Decline and Resurgence of Congress* (Washington, D.C.: Brookings Institution Press, 1981), 371; Burdett Loomis, *The New American Politician* (New York: Basic Books, 1988).

25. David Mayhew, *Congress: The Electoral Connection* (New Haven: Yale University Press, 1974), 27.
26. Keith Krehbiel, "Where's the Party?" *British Journal of Political Science* 23 (1993): 235–266; Keith Krehbiel, "Paradoxes of Parties in Congress," *Legislative Studies Quarterly* 24 (1999): 31–64; Keith Krehbiel, "Party Discipline and Measures of Partisanship," *American Journal of Political Science* 44 (2000): 212–227.
27. James Snyder and Tim Groseclose, "Estimating Party Influence in Congressional Roll-Call Voting," *American Journal of Political Science* 44 (2000): 193–211; Gregory Hager and Jeffery Talbert, "Look for the Party Label: Party Influences on Voting in the U.S. House," *Legislative Studies Quarterly* 25 (2000): 75–99; David Brady, Judith Goldstein, and Daniel Kessler, "Does Party Matter in Senators' Voting Behavior: An Historical Test Using Tariff Votes," *Journal of Law, Economics, and Organization* 18 (2002): 140–154.
28. The most complete statement of the argument is by John Jackson and John Kingdon, "Ideology, Interest Groups Scores, and Legislative Votes, *American Journal of Political Science* 36 (1992): 805–823.
29. David Rohde, *Parties and Leaders in the Post-Reform House* (Chicago: University of Chicago Press), esp. Chap. 3.
30. David Hosansky, "House Torn on Agriculture: Senate Makes Progress," *Congressional Quarterly Weekly Report,* September 30, 1995, 2980–2984.
31. John Aldrich and David Rohde, "The Consequences of Party Organization in the House: The Role of the Majority and Minority Parties in Conditional Party Government," in *Polarized Politics,* ed. Jon Bond and Richard Fleisher (Washington, D.C.: CQ Press, 2000), 31–72.
32. Morris P. Fiorina, "Whatever Happened to the Median Voter?" (paper presented at the annual meeting of the Midwest Political Science Association, Chicago, April 1999).
33. In their masterly study *Legislative Leviathan* (Berkeley: University of California Press, 1993) Gary Cox and Mathew McCubbins recognize a variety of forms of party effect, but they do not integrate them into one model.
34. Scholars aware of the explosion of earmarks since Republicans took control of Congress may question whether distributive politics has been constrained, but I only mean relative to what distributive politics otherwise might have been in Congresses organized as in the prereform era.
35. Morris P. Fiorina with Samuel J. Abrams and Jeremy C. Pope, *Culture War? The Myth of a Polarized America* (New York: Longman, 2005).

Part III
Parties and Committees

8. The Dynamics of Party Government in Congress

Steven S. Smith and Gerald Gamm

On rare occasions, events in American politics conspire to reveal the fundamentals of congressional politics. One such occasion was the aftermath of the 1998 elections, when a remarkable transfer of power took place in the House of Representatives. Newt Gingrich, R-Ga., who had been touted in 1995 as the most powerful Speaker in almost a century, stepped down from the speakership and resigned his seat in the House. The Republicans had just lost five seats in the midterm elections of an opposition president's second term, a nearly unprecedented event. In less than four years Gingrich had fallen from grace with his Republican colleagues. For many of them, the 1998 elections were the last straw. Republican members of the House voted first to replace Gingrich with Rep. Robert L. Livingston, R-La.—but Livingston himself resigned within a matter of weeks, before ever formally assuming the office of Speaker. In December 1998, in the aftermath of these two startling resignations, Republicans chose Rep. Dennis Hastert, R-Ill., someone who was virtually unknown to the public and the media, to be the next Speaker. Hastert instantly proved to be a reserved leader who gladly shared power with other party leaders and committee chairs.

While House Republicans were changing leaders and shifting gears, Senate Republicans made no changes. Senate Majority Leader Trent Lott, R-Miss., had assumed his leadership post in the summer of 1996, when Sen. Robert Dole, R-Kan., relinquished the position to run full-time for president. No discussion of replacing Lott took place in late 1998; in fact, little blame was placed on Lott for the poor showing of congressional Republicans in the November elections. Those elections generated no net change in the size of either of the two Senate parties, which certainly was a disappointment for the Republicans. As in the preceding Congress, the new Senate was made up of fifty-five Republicans and forty-five Democrats. In advance of the elections, many Republicans had hoped for a "filibuster-proof" majority of sixty-plus senators in the 1998 elections, one that could force a vote on legislation that the Democratic minority filibustered. But Lott was seldom mentioned in the postmortem media coverage of the elections. If anything, Lott was placed in a favorable light: he would fill the void created by the change from Gingrich to Hastert as the chief spokesperson of the party. Although Lott would step down as Republican leader four years later, after making comments praising Strom Thurmond's presidential candidacy, he suffered nothing in 1998.

The events of late 1998 represent a puzzle for political scientists who attempt to analyze the nature of party leadership in Congress. The purpose of this chapter is to outline the standard view of party leadership, to evaluate its strengths and weaknesses, and to suggest some new perspectives on congressional leadership. We draw two conclusions. First, the 1998 developments reflected long-standing differences between the House and Senate in the nature of party leadership that are too often ignored. Second, those developments highlight the importance of distinguishing between the policy and electoral goals of congressional parties, a distinction that is avoided in the standard account.

The Ebb and Flow of Leadership Power

Observers of Congress describe the policymaking process in terms of the degree to which it is centralized or decentralized. When a party leader (of the majority party) controls the agenda and influences how other legislators vote on the legislation considered, power is considered to be *centralized.* At the extreme, the central leader dictates outcomes. An alternative is to have agenda control and influence placed in the hands of the many standing committees, or their chairs, so that power appears *decentralized.* In the decentralized pattern, the central party leader defers to committee chairs, performs the ministerial duty of scheduling, and, as circumstances require, bargains with influential members. Power in Congress often is characterized as shifting back and forth along the centralized-decentralized continuum.

There is a third alternative. Power may remain in the hands of the full chamber. In principle, legislative initiatives can originate on the floor, and all members can exercise their votes there. In practice, of course, certain responsibilities are delegated to leaders and committees, but the full membership need not defer to leaders and committees. Thus, a more *collegial* pattern is possible. Indeed, the Senate has retained a more collegial pattern, whereas the larger House delegates more responsibility to leaders and committees.

The most influential account of the ebb and flow of party leadership power is an essay written by the political scientists Joseph Cooper and David Brady.[1] In Figure 8-1 we outline their argument. The root source of leaders' assertiveness is election results. The degree of polarization in electoral coalitions of the two congressional parties determines the strength and policy polarization of the congressional parties themselves. For example, if Democrats are elected from uniformly liberal districts and Republicans from uniformly conservative districts, the elected Democratic representatives are likely to be cohesive and quite different from the cohesive elected Republicans. In this view, aggressive party leaders are the product of a polarized electorate and the polarized congressional parties it elects to office. If partisan differences weaken in the electorate and in Congress, the formal

Figure 8-1 The Conditional Party Government Thesis

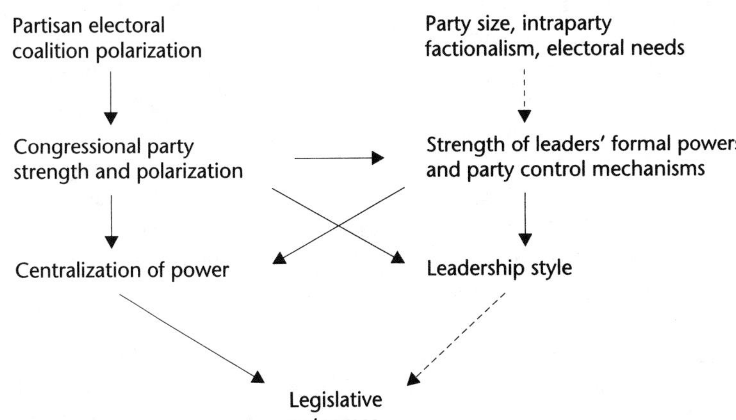

Notes: The Cooper-Brady thesis is depicted with solid lines. The conditional party government thesis is depicted with dashed lines.

powers of party leaders will be pared back and policymaking will be more decentralized.

Equally important in the Cooper-Brady argument is what is *not* deemed central to an explanation of centralization: leaders' styles and personalities. Leadership style—assertiveness—is a by-product of party strength and formal powers, but it does not make a strong independent contribution to legislative outcomes. Personality may affect leadership style, but it is less important than party cohesiveness that flows from who is elected to Congress. Thus the personal qualities that are so often emphasized in accounts of congressional leadership are of relatively little significance in the Cooper-Brady explanation of shifts in the degree of centralization or decentralization in the decision-making process of the House.

Sophisticated observers of recent Congresses agree with the Cooper-Brady thesis. David W. Rohde has applied the term *conditional party government* to capture the idea that assertive majority party leadership occurs only when the parties are polarized—that is, when intraparty cohesiveness is high and interparty differences are great.[2] These observers emphasize how party polarization since the 1980s provided a foundation for aggressive strategies by House Speakers, particularly Jim Wright, D-Texas, who was Speaker from 1987 to 1989, and Newt Gingrich, who was Speaker from 1995 to 1998.

The conditional party government thesis differs from the Cooper-Brady argument in one critical respect: it asserts that strong party leadership makes a difference. A legislative party benefits from assertive leaders who aggressively employ the resources and procedural tools given to them by their party colleagues. Rohde, for example, concludes that "parties are consequential in shaping members' preferences, the character of the issues on the agenda, the nature of legislative alternatives, and ultimate political outcomes, and they will remain important as long as the underlying forces that created this partisan resurgence persist."[3] Rather than being mere instruments of party members, as the Cooper-Brady argument suggests, these leaders (with the help of rules strengthening their formal authority) play an independent role in shaping party behavior. That is, leaders act to further reinforce party discipline and further enhance the prospects of the achievement of collective policy goals. In this view, the lower dashed arrow in Figure 8-1 represents a significant political influence.

The Cooper-Brady argument and the conditional party government thesis implicitly differ in the assumptions made about legislators' motivations. The Cooper-Brady argument assumes that legislators only seek to enact the policy goals of their electorates. Legislators do not grant their leaders any power beyond what is required to serve those policy interests. For legislators to be persuaded that they should grant additional power to their leaders, they must see some additional value in allowing leaders to influence them to support policies that they otherwise would not support, at least occasionally. A likely reason for granting such power is that legislators believe that effective leaders will help the party create a favorable image for the party and, in doing so, enhance their own electoral prospects. In fact, in this view, leaders must sometimes pursue strategies that represent trade-offs between the policy and electoral goals of party members.[4] These strategic choices are represented by the upper dashed arrow in Figure 8-1. This distinction between the electoral and policy interests of congressional parties will prove critical to explaining the election of Hastert as House Speaker.

In this chapter we examine whether the Cooper-Brady polarization argument or the polarization-plus-leadership variation can account for leadership behavior and party effects. We make two arguments. First, the thesis does not fit the Senate as well as it fits the House. The ability of a Senate minority to obstruct the chamber's business affects the extent to which power can ever be effectively centralized in the Senate, even when the electoral coalitions and congressional parties are polarized. The absence of a powerful presiding officer further limits the centralization of power in the Senate. Second, we argue, in contrast to Cooper and Brady but consistent with more recent scholarship, that policy and electoral objectives are not always fully compatible, at least in the short term. Consequently, at any given time the acquired institutional context is partly inherited, partly shaped by electoral challenges, and only partly shaped by short-term policy objectives.

We examine House and Senate party leadership in two eras—the years just before and after 1900, and the years just before 2000. These were eras of high party polarization. In the earlier period, it is often claimed, the Senate's majority leadership looked similar to the House leadership in its ability to control the chamber. Looks prove deceiving. The "centralized" power of Senate leaders a century ago was grounded in few formal institutions; it could not be transferred, and it could not be reliably employed even by its most powerful practitioners. We argue, in fact, that the century-long effort to equate the Senate's "Aldrichism" with "czar rule" in the House reflects a misunderstanding of Senate leadership in this era. In the 1990s strong majority party leadership did not emerge at all in the Senate. Meanwhile, in the House, both parties allowed strong central leaders to emerge. But in both eras these strong House leaders were followed by weaker leaders, reflecting the countervailing electoral interests of individual legislators and the party rather than the reintroduction of heterogeneous constituencies and congressional parties.

1890 to 1910

The period from 1890 to 1910 generated the strongest party leaders in the history of the House. A comparable group existed in the Senate in that era, although it lacked the tools necessary to exercise firm control. In both cases scholars have argued that sharp party polarization, rooted in a polarization in electoral constituencies, created centralized policymaking processes. For the House the argument is strongly supported by the evidence, but for the Senate the story is more complicated.

The House of Speakers Thomas Brackett Reed and Joseph Cannon

House Republicans enjoyed the leadership of two aggressive Speakers—Thomas Bracket Reed and Joseph Cannon—when they found themselves in the majority during most of the 1890–1910 period.[5] Speakers appointed all members to standing committees and chairmanships. They chaired the Committee on Rules, which wrote the resolutions that brought major legislation to the floor. During floor sessions, they exercised discretion over the recognition of members to make motions, including motions to bring up legislation. And the Republicans gave their leader a special tool—a vote of the party caucus would bind all party members to support the party's policy position. These tools gave the Speaker important formal controls over the flow of legislation and a set of rewards and sanctions with which to influence the behavior of legislators. Reed and Cannon were known as "czars" of the House.

The conditional party government thesis associates the power of these Republican Speakers with a polarization of the parties. Figure 8-2 characterizes one component of polarization—interparty difference—in the roll call voting record of the House. The figure is based on statistical estimates of the liberal-conservative positions of legislators.[6] In the figure, we indicate the difference between the two parties' median scores. As shown in the figure, the period of strong Speakers in this period corresponds closely to a wide separation of the two parties.

The second component of polarization—intraparty cohesiveness—does not show the same strong relationship to party centralization. This can be shown by using a measure of dispersion (the standard deviation) for the liberal-conservative positions within each party. As Figure 8-3 indicates, both parties in the House demonstrated considerable cohesiveness throughout the late nineteenth

Figure 8-2 Differences between the Parties in Median Liberal-Conservative Scores in the House, 1857–1998

Differences between the parties

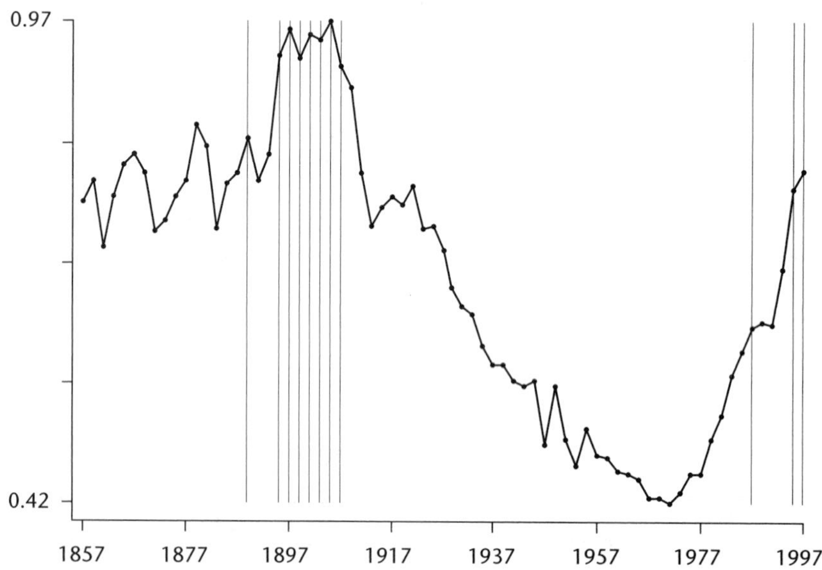

Source: DW-NOMINATE scores are available at http://voteview.uh.edu/dwnomin.htm. See Keith Poole and Howard Rosenthal, *Congress: A Political-Economic History of Roll Call Voting* (New York: Oxford University Press, 1997).

Notes: Each entry represents the absolute difference between the parties in median DW-NOMINATE scores. DW-NOMINATE scores represent legislators' placement on a liberal-conservative scale, based on their roll-call voting record. High values indicate a large degree of difference between the parties. Scores for an entire session of Congress are assigned to the first year the Congress met. Vertical rules indicate Congresses led by a strong Speaker.

century. They showed no greater cohesiveness under the strong Republican Speakers than during other periods. In general, Republicans were somewhat more cohesive than the Democrats, who had long suffered differences between conservative Democrats, who favored the gold standard, and those sympathetic to populism and free silver. The 1890s polarization of the parties, then, appears to have been driven more by their widening differences than from any changes in their internal cohesiveness.

So far the evidence is generally consistent with the conditional party government thesis. But as the political scientist Eric Schickler observes, a qualification of the thesis is required—the thesis does not explain the adoption of the Reed rules in 1890.[7] Speaker Reed and his fellow Republicans put in place landmark rules in 1890 that undercut minority party obstructionism. The parties had

Figure 8-3 Dispersions in the Parties' Liberal-Conservative Scores in the House, 1857–1998

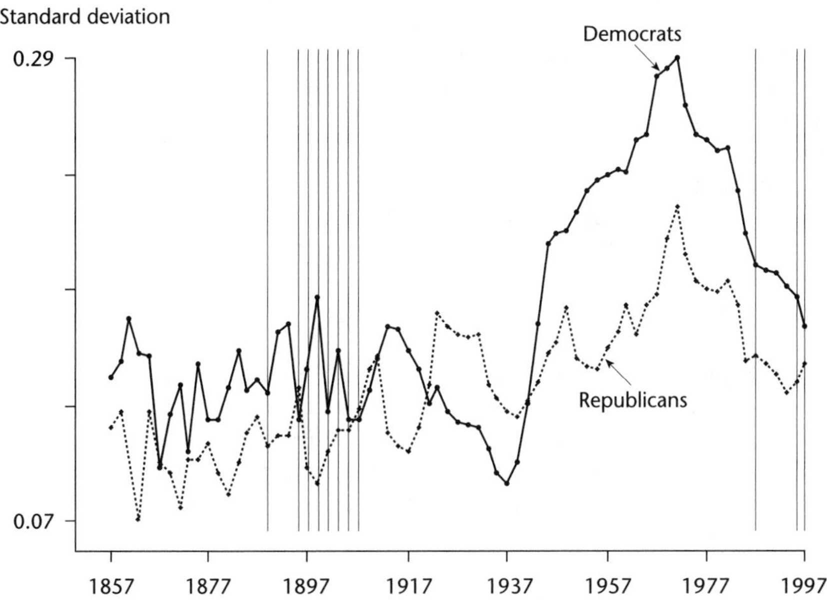

Source: DW-NOMINATE scores are available at http://voteview.uh.edu/dwnomin.htm. See Keith Poole and Howard Rosenthal, *Congress: A Political-Economic History of Roll Call Voting* (New York: Oxford University Press, 1997).

Notes: Each entry represents the standard deviation DW-NOMINATE score for the party. High values indicate a large dispersion within the party. Scores for an entire session of Congress are assigned to the first year the Congress met. Vertical rules indicate Congresses led by a strong Speaker.

distinct policy preferences but were not yet as polarized as they were soon to become (see Figure 8-2).[8] Even Republicans had noteworthy internal divisions on important issues, such as currency and tariffs.

A reasonable hypothesis is that the relative sizes of the two parties played a critical role in the adoption of the Reed rules in 1890. The House parties were nearly equal in size in 1890—156 Democrats and 173 Republicans—and party margins had been narrow for some time. This meant that a few absent majority party members would be a serious problem for their party. By refusing to answer quorum calls and offering repetitive dilatory motions, a minority party could prevent the House from conducting business. The "Reed rules," as they came to be known, gave the Speaker the power to count members as present if they were in the chamber but not answering to a roll call, reduced the quorum in the Committee of the Whole from a majority of the House to just 100 members, and allowed the Speaker to ignore dilatory motions. Speaker Reed skillfully exploited a partisan debate over contested elections to increase his party's marginal control over the House. He did so not by proposing rules changes in the usual way—offering a resolution at the start of a new Congress—but by making rulings from the chair at opportune moments and asking his fellow Republicans to back him up.

Oddly, immediately after the Democrats gained a majority in the 1890 elections, they dropped the Reed rules.[9] In spite of their interest in preventing minority obstruction, they felt obliged to follow through on campaign promises to restore "democratic" procedures to the House. To be sure, the Democrats were not a unified party and so may not have tolerated a powerful Speaker, as the conditional party thesis suggests, but it does appear that electoral motivations rather than policy considerations led to this precipitous action. Over the next few years, as the Republicans proved obstructionist, the Democrats reestablished some of the Reed rules, often with prodding from Reed himself and other minority Republicans.

Thus, when the Republicans regained a House majority in 1895, their Speaker enjoyed procedural advantages that were not the product of a newly cohesive majority in a polarized House. Rather, they were inherited from previous majority parties that were concerned about election outcomes and party reputations—and perhaps concerns about the functionality of the House by members on both sides of the aisle. It is fair to say that Speaker Cannon soon came to use the procedural tools on behalf of a cohesive party in a polarized House, but the tools were the product of a mix of political considerations.

The era of the czars came to an end when divisions within the House Republican Party led to a revolt against Speaker Cannon in 1909–1910. The increasing dispersion that Figure 8-3 depicts during the late 1890s and 1900s gives a hint of what took place. Progressive Republicans from the Midwest and West became unhappy with the policy direction of the eastern establishment of their party, and they resented the strong-arm tactics that Cannon used to try to keep them in line. Moreover, the addition of Progressives to the House Democratic caucus began to reduce the distance between the parties.

Progressive Republicans eventually joined with Democrats to impose new rules that reduced the Speaker's control over the flow of legislation to the floor. In 1909 the consent calendar was created and a procedure allowing committees to call up bills every Wednesday was established. More important, in 1910 the coalition pushed through rules that prevented the Speaker from sitting on the Rules Committee and provided for its election by the House. When the Democrats took over majority control in 1911, they amended the House rules to provide for election of all standing committees.

During most of the rest of the twentieth century, the Speaker was less powerful, and bargaining became the modus operandi of the majority party leadership. In fact, during the middle decades of the century, a conservative coalition of minority party Republicans and southern Democrats held sway on many issues. As shown in Figures 8-2 and 8-3, party polarization declined; the parties became less distant, and intraparty cohesiveness declined. Legislative initiative slipped from central party leaders and shifted to committees and their chairs. Many bills were passed with cross-party coalitions, often with little trace of party leader influence.

The Senate of Nelson W. Aldrich and William Boyd Allison

During the 1890–1910 era, Republican leadership in the Senate was centered in a handful of men: Nelson Aldrich, R-R.I., William Allison, R-Iowa, Orville Platt, R-Conn., and John Spooner, R-Wis. A few others—such as Eugene Hale, R-Maine, Henry Cabot Lodge, R-Mass., and James McMillan, R-Mich.—were considered to be insiders, too. The group functioned as an interlocking directorate of Republican committee and party leaders. With no powerful presiding officer, the Senate parties looked to other means to facilitate collective action.[10] In the 1890s, Aldrich and his comrades assumed personal responsibility for leading the Republican cause. Aldrich, in part because of his leading role on the Finance Committee and in part because of his personality and political connections, helped lead the group. Allison chaired the Appropriations Committee and, beginning in 1897, the Republican caucus. From 1892–1893 onward, the group dominated the Committee on Committees, which made committee assignments for the party, and the Steering Committee, which set a legislative agenda for the party.

The Senate's "Aldrichism" was often equated with the House's "Cannonism" by Progressive politicians and journalists in those years—and by scholars in the century since then. On the surface, the Aldrich-Allison team appears to be the Senate counterpart of the House czars, and the conditional party government thesis may fit the Senate equally well. But does it? Our answer has two parts. First, the relation between polarization and centralization is weaker in the Senate than in the House, which is evidenced by the timing of the emergence of a centralized leadership team for Senate Republicans. Second, Aldrichism represented much less centralization and control than Cannonism. Unlike Reed and Cannon, Aldrich possessed no special procedural tools or party office. His leadership was exercised jointly with other senators and, given their positions as committee chairs, reflected the decentralized nature of the Senate chamber. On his own, and even in cooperation with the others, Aldrich showed considerably less ability than the House Speakers of the period to push party legislation through the chamber.

Polarization and Centralization in the Senate. Strong partisanship in the Senate predates the surge in House partisanship in the mid-1890s. In fact, the Senate was remarkably partisan from the end of Reconstruction in the 1870s until the 1910s. In Figure 8-4 we show that the interparty difference on the liberal-conservative scale was large throughout that period. And in Figure 8-5 we show that both Senate parties were internally cohesive during most of the same period.[11] Consequently, it is not possible to associate the period of strong Republican leadership in the Senate with a surge in party polarization. Instead, the

Figure 8-4 Differences between the Parties in Median Liberal-Conservative Scores in the Senate, 1857–1998

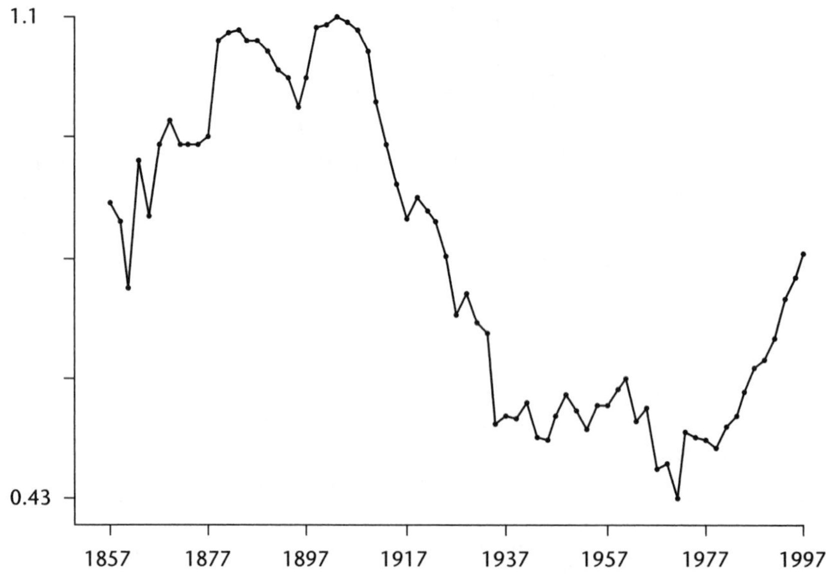

Source: DW-NOMINATE scores are available at http://voteview.uh.edu/dwnomin.htm. See Keith Poole and Howard Rosenthal, *Congress: A Political-Economic History of Roll Call Voting* (New York: Oxford University Press, 1997).

Notes: Each entry represents the absolute difference between the parties in median DW-NOMINATE scores. High values represent a large difference between the parties. Scores for an entire session of Congress are assigned to the first year the Congress met.

Aldrich-Allison leadership emerged long after partisan polarization surfaced in the 1870s, when Democrats regained southern seats in the aftermath of Reconstruction.[12] Thus, the nearly one-to-one correspondence between polarization and centralization that Cooper and Brady, and others, emphasized does not appear to fit the Senate.

Why is correspondence between polarization and centralization far less perfect in the Senate than in the House? The primary reason appears to be the inherited institutional context of the post–Civil War Senate. The essential features of that context were the absence of a presiding officer empowered to act in the interest of the majority party and the absence of a limit on debate and amendments.

Unlike the House, the majority parties in the Senate did not empower the presiding officer of the Senate. The Constitution provides that the vice president serve as president of the Senate, and nineteenth-century vice presidents generally served faithfully. But vice presidents need not be of the same party as the Senate

Figure 8-5 Dispersions in the Parties' Liberal-Conservative Scores in the Senate, 1857–1998

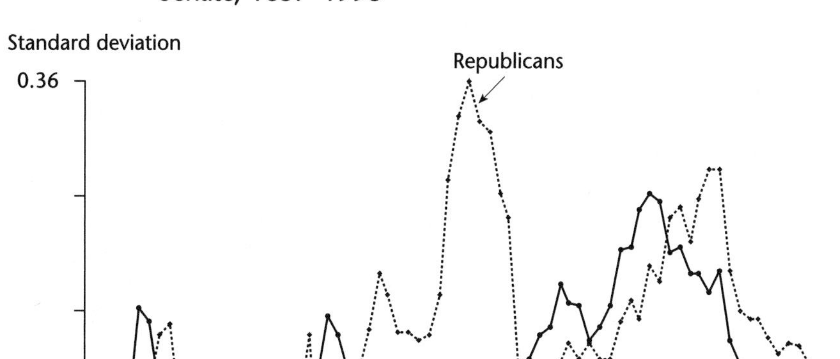

Source: DW-NOMINATE scores are available at http://voteview.uh.edu/dwnomin.htm. See Keith Poole and Howard Rosenthal, *Congress: A Political-Economic History of Roll Call Voting* (New York: Oxford University Press, 1997).

Notes: Each entry represents the standard deviation DW-NOMINATE score for the party. High values indicate a large dispersion within the party. Scores for an entire session of Congress are assigned to the first year the Congress met.

majority and, even when they were, were not beholden to senators. Senate presidents pro tempore, who were elected in the absence of the vice president, also proved feeble vessels for majority leadership; nineteenth-century senators believed that the term of a president pro tempore ended abruptly upon the return of the vice president, and they also believed that the Senate lacked the constitutional authority to remove a president pro tempore from office under any other circumstance, including a shift in majority control. Although the Senate experimented occasionally with the assignment of some powers to its presiding officer, the Senate emerged from the nineteenth century with a presiding officer with very little authority, even over routine floor proceedings.[13] The Senate, therefore, lacked a formal leader who could combine the powers of the presiding officer with the influence of a party leader, as did the Speaker of the House.

Furthermore, unlike the House, where cohesive majorities could impose rules changes, the Senate majority confronted a filibuster of any change in rules that might put a minority at a disadvantage. Until 1917 the Senate had no way to limit debate as long as senators sought recognition to speak. Consequently, in spite of repeated appeals by Senate majority parties for some limit on debate, minority party members regularly killed any hope of such a change.[14] The immediate consequence of this was that Senate majority parties that might have wanted to enhance the formal power of its leadership did not have the ability to do so. Any enhancement of the influence of majority party leadership in the Senate would be limited to innovations within the parties' internal caucuses—proceedings invisible in the official Senate record. The Senate floor, unlike the House floor, was an inhospitable place for establishing majority party prerogatives.

Still, even informal leaders did not emerge until relatively late in the period of partisan polarization in the Senate. The most important innovation—the emergence of an elected majority leader—did not occur until after Aldrich, Allison, and their allies had all died or retired. Yet Aldrich clearly stood at the center of a powerful group of senators. Their leadership was grounded, first, in their control of Senate committees and, second, in the establishment of a regular steering committee in 1892–1893.

Accumulated seniority allowed members of the Aldrich-Allison faction to gain positions of potential influence just as they gained an increment of additional cohesiveness.[15] In 1893, Allison was named chairman of both the Republican Committee on Committees and the newly strengthened Republican Steering Committee, and both were peopled by his allies. By virtue of his seniority, Allison became caucus chairman in 1897 and retained the chairmanship of the Republican Steering Committee, the party's agenda-setting group. Aldrich and Hale, both named to the Republican Steering Committee in 1893, kept this assignment continuously until they left the Senate in 1911—and Allison chaired the Steering Committee until his death in 1908. To the chairmanship of the Committee on Committees, Allison appointed McMillan in 1897, Aldrich in 1899, Platt in 1901, and Hale in 1903, 1905, and 1907. Meanwhile, Allison continued to chair the Appropriations Committee, as he had done for many years when the Republicans were in the majority. Aldrich chaired the Rules Committee in 1897, then became Finance Committee chairman two years later. No new rules facilitated this accumulation of power in a few senators' hands. The seniority rule, which governed committee chairmanships as well as the caucus chairmanship, enabled Allison and Aldrich to coordinate in this fashion.

The only significant structural change in this era was the establishment of a permanent Republican Steering Committee (and, simultaneously, the Democratic Steering Committee) in the winter of 1892–1893. Members of the caucus created the steering committee to pursue policy as well as electoral goals, but it was an election crisis that was the immediate cause of this institutional innovation. Republicans, who had controlled the Senate for a decade, realized in November 1892 that their majority was in serious jeopardy. State elections throughout the country portended an imminent transfer of control to the Democrats. Rather than acquiesce in the result, the Republican caucus established a steering committee, charging it to seek ways to influence the votes being cast for United States senators in state legislatures where the outcome was in doubt.

Once established, these steering committees proved to be durable institutions for both Senate parties. Through the 1890s and the first decade of the new century, the steering committees set policy agendas and shaped legislation. Although the Senate party caucuses had often formed committees in the past, the earlier committees had been ad hoc, single-purpose creations, which reported quickly and then dissolved. The new steering committees assumed permanence, and Allison and Aldrich understood the importance of these institutions in coordinating decision making in the Senate.

The Nature of Aldrichism. There is considerable testimony that Aldrich had become the dominant force in the Senate by the time Cannon became Speaker of the House in 1903. Was Aldrich, perhaps with Allison, comparable to Cannon? At a minimum, a heavy qualification must be placed on the claim. Long before the winter of 1892–1893, party caucuses had become actively engaged in debating legislation, developing and often negotiating policy positions, and fashioning legislative strategies.[16] Polarization of the parties in the 1870s and 1880s was associated with intensified activity in the party caucuses but without clear leadership on either side of the aisle. In both parties, of course, some senators were more central to party deliberations than others. The Aldrich-Allison team asserted itself at a time when intraparty decision making was shifting decisively from the caucus to the steering committee. But the creation of the steering committee had little to do with the centralization of power in the hands of Aldrich and Allison and much more to do with the intense partisan competition for control of the Senate.[17]

Control over the machinery of the Senate majority party did not translate into control over the chamber as directly or fully for party leaders as it did for the Speaker of the House. In part, this was due to the pivotal place of Populists in the Senate in the 1897–1900 period. But the Republican establishment did not demonstrate the degree of control over committees and policy outcomes that the Speaker of the House did. On an important tariff bill in 1897, at the height of Aldrich's and Allison's power, Republican committee members refused to support the party line and forced significant policy concessions before the bill could be reported from Aldrich's committee. In 1905 another Republican president's top priority, railroad regulation, was derailed by Republican committee members until Democrats provided the votes required to report the bill to the floor. And then a Democrat had to be called upon to manage the bill.[18]

Moreover, majority party leaders' control over the Senate floor agenda was far less perfect than the Speaker's control of the House agenda. In early 1900, for example, Republicans committed themselves to the passage of a gold standard bill. On this issue, Aldrich was the bill manager, and he committed himself fully to the effort. In a story entitled "Mr. Aldrich's Clever Move," the *Washington Post* reported how Aldrich took advantage of a nearly empty Senate chamber to secure unanimous consent to have the bill considered to the exclusion of all other business until it came to a vote eight days later. "The agreement was secured by Senator Aldrich yesterday afternoon," the *Post* stated, "when there were only eighteen Senators in the chamber, and when Senator Chandler, who is in charge of the Quay case; Senator Pettigrew, who is a persistent opponent of the administration's policy in the Philippines; and Senator Jones, the Democratic leader, were all absent."[19]

When the Senate entered the final days of consideration of the gold standard bill, the *Post* reported that the chamber's remaining order of business remained unsettled. "After that measure is disposed of there will be a contest for precedence in the interest of several measures. These include the bills for providing forms of government for Hawaii and Puerto Rico, the Nicaragua canal bill, and the resolution for the seating of Senator [Matthew] Quay," according to the *Post*. "Which of these will take precedence remains to be determined. Just now there is some sharp sparring for first place."[20] In 1899–1900 the sparring took place directly among majority party bill managers. The *Post*, which thoroughly covered Aldrich's management of the gold standard bill, makes it clear that no individual senator coordinated the chamber's agenda. The paper described the chaos, noting that "as soon as the Senate had disposed of the financial bill yesterday, Senator [Shelby] Cullom and Senator [William] Chandler sought recognition, the former to press the Hawaiian bill and the latter to suggest consideration of the Quay case."[21] We have found the same general pattern in a review of typical weeks of Senate floor action reported in the *Congressional Record*.

Additional examples illustrate the limitations of Aldrichism. In 1903 a statehood bill and a banking bill, the latter sponsored by Aldrich, died under filibuster and threatened filibuster, respectively. In 1907 a filibuster killed a bill long championed by the Republicans to increase subsidies for American merchant shipping. Democrats, who viewed subsidies for shipping as a gift to the steel industry, easily prevented a vote on the measure. In both years a determined minority was able to thwart the legislative plans of the Aldrich-Allison team and a Republican president.[22]

Even successful attacks on the institutional bases of power of the Aldrich-Allison group were possible. In 1899, junior and western senators combined to force the adoption of a rule that gave seven committees authority to report appropriations (spending) bills for programs under their jurisdiction. The new rule substantially reduced the jurisdictional reach of Allison's Committee on Appropriations. Both Aldrich and Allison opposed the new rule (as did Democratic leader Arthur Pue Gorman of Maryland), yet many members of the majority party supported the effort to decentralize control over the initiation of spending bills.[23]

Thus the control of the chamber's proceedings by the Aldrich-Allison team was measurably weaker than the control over the proceedings of the House by the Speaker, even when bills of great importance to the faction were involved. In the Senate, control over the party's own committee contingents was weaker. Stealth was sometimes required to get a major bill to the floor. Disputes over the floor agenda among the majority party's bill managers often were not resolved by party leaders. Aldrichism was not Cannonism.[24]

Less complete centralization of leadership functions within the majority party is part of the reason for differences between the two houses at the turn of the twentieth century, but so is the fact that intraparty centralization did not extend to chamber centralization in the case of the Senate. No Senate presiding officer was empowered to enforce an agenda set by party leaders. Floor debate and amendments could not be limited, a situation that continued to generate bargaining power for committee members. And single senators could object to requests for unanimous consent to consider legislation or limit debate, even then important to the majority party, which continued to give every senator a source of leverage. In such a setting, alienating a colleague by imposing penalties on him for noncompliant behavior entailed risks of its own.

In 1913, two years after Aldrich retired, the Democrats gained a Senate majority for the first time since 1895. Having regarded their caucus chairman as their floor leader since the 1890s, the Senate Democrats established the position of majority leader when they elected John Kern, D-Ind., as their new caucus chairman in 1913. They used their caucus to impose discipline on votes important to the new Democratic president, Woodrow Wilson. But they discontinued the practice after a few years. When the Republicans regained a Senate majority in 1919, the party represented great regional diversity and lacked a strongly motivated caucus chair and floor leader. But, like the Democrats before then, the Republican Senate caucus now relied on an elected leader to help keep order on the floor and manage the caucus's affairs. Senate leaders, however, generally deferred to committee chairs on policy matters.

From 1990 to 2000

The party polarization of the late 1990s was similar to the polarization of the late 1890s. In both the House and the Senate, the central tendencies of the two parties diverged, reaching a peak in the 1995–1998 period after years of widening party differences. Moreover, unlike what happened in the 1890s, when intraparty cohesiveness remained at already high levels, both parties of the 1990s became more cohesive (see Figures 8-3 and 8-5), generating conditions conducive to centralization of policymaking within each house.

The late 1890s and late 1990s exhibit one critical difference. The 1896 elections created unified party control of the House, Senate, and presidency—with Republicans gaining control of the presidency that year, two years after they regained control of the House and Senate—whereas the 1994 elections created divided party control of Congress and the presidency. A reasonable speculation is that this difference would affect which party is credited for good times or blamed for hard times, influence public perceptions of the legislative program of the congressional majority party, affect who wins and who loses in legislative battles, shape the relation between the policy and electoral interests of the congressional majority party, and condition the value of centralization for the congressional majority party. If these assumptions are sound, the conditional party government thesis requires some elaboration.

The House of Speakers Newt Gingrich and Dennis Hastert

When the House Republicans gained a majority of seats in the 1994 elections, they inherited a decision-making process that already was more centralized than the committee-centered process of the middle decades of the twentieth century. Since the 1970s, the Democratic majority had steadily centralized more agenda-setting responsibility in the speakership. Speakers Thomas P. "Tip" O'Neill, D-Mass. (1977–1987), Jim Wright, D-Texas (1987–1989), and Thomas S. Foley, D-Wash. (1989–1995), possessed stronger formal powers than their immediate predecessors. These powers gave the Democratic Speakers greater influence over committee assignments, bill referral, and the Rules Committee. Speaker Wright used these powers to push a legislative agenda more vigorously than any Speaker had done in many decades, at a time when an opposition party president was in the White House. His effort was brought to an end when he resigned from the House after the House Committee on Standards of Official Conduct charged him with several violations of ethics rules.

Oddly, from the point of view of the conditional party government thesis, House majority party Democrats enhanced the formal powers of their central party leader at the lowest point in party polarization in the history of the two parties—in the early 1970s (see Figure 8-2). Sharp intraparty factionalism, more than interparty differences, stimulated liberals to strengthen their central party leader and weaken the powers of full committee chairs, many of whom were conservatives. The Speaker at the time, Carl Albert, D-Okla., neither sought nor fully exploited these powers. Only later did Democratic Speakers begin to draw on these new powers, particularly control of the Rules Committee, and interparty competition clearly stimulated this new aggressiveness. These developments led observers to refer to the "postreform House" of the 1970s, 1980s, and 1990s, which was much more centralized and party oriented than the House of the mid-twentieth century.[25]

The postreform Democratic House set a standard for centralization that the Republican House would rapidly exceed. With his assumption of the Speaker's chair in January 1995, Newt Gingrich quickly, and deservedly, became known as the most assertive Speaker since Cannon. Gingrich had taken the lead in recruiting Republican candidates, in fundraising for Republicans, and in developing the Contract with America, the Republicans' ten-point policy platform for the 1994 campaign. When the Republicans won a majority of House seats, surprising nearly everyone, Gingrich was given much of the credit. He used his standing with his party colleagues to assert centralized direction over the House, going well beyond the standard set by Wright. He handpicked full committee chairs, who were later endorsed by the party conference, and picked several subcommittee chairs, who were then appointed by committee chairs. He exercised great influence over all important committee assignments and even reviewed the appointments of top committee staff. He directed the content and timing of committee actions on legislation to implement the Contract with America. He limited conference committee delegations to a few top committee leaders and was proactive in conference negotiations. And he pursued an aggressive strategy to force President Bill Clinton to accept the Republican budget. Standing at the head of a unified party in a polarized House, Gingrich, by his behavior, seemed to confirm the conditional party government thesis.[26]

Gingrich's speakership ended in political disaster. The seeds of this disaster were planted early, when in 1995 Gingrich led House Republicans as they held spending bills hostage in order to get President Clinton's approval of their budget plan. Clinton won the showdown, persuading a majority of Americans that congressional Republicans were responsible for shutting down many federal agencies when spending authority expired. Republicans eventually agreed to accept the president's compromise legislation and suffered badly in public opinion polls. In the aftermath of this crisis, Gingrich became less aggressive and reduced his public visibility, a strategy that led to criticism from his colleagues. Adding to his troubles was an ethics investigation into the financing of a college course he taught and the campaign fundraising conducted by organizations he created. By the summer of 1997 he was considered to be so ineffective that several Republican leaders considered a scheme to depose him as Speaker. The plan was spoiled when newspaper accounts disclosed it and Gingrich challenged his detractors, but Gingrich never regained his aggressiveness in confronting a now very popular Democratic president.

The last straw came at the end of 1998 when Republicans lost seats in the House. In modern American history, no party had lost seats in the midterm elections of an opposition president's second term in office. Gingrich's greatest strength, election strategy, seemed to have faded. Gingrich was immediately challenged by Bob Livingston, who complained that Gingrich had failed to give voters a reason to vote Republican. Other Republicans seemed to agree; Gingrich announced his retirement and Livingston quickly gained enough support to become his party's nominee for Speaker. Livingston promised to be a more effective manager than Gingrich had become, but he also promised to give committees greater independence and to be more inclusive in the party's legislative efforts. Livingston went so far as to say that he hoped to model himself after Speaker Tip O'Neill, who managed to combine partisanship, an inclusive strategy of building support within his party, and occasional efforts to attract support from the other party.[27]

Livingston's emergence as a replacement for Gingrich was not inconsistent with the conditional party government thesis. He promised to be a strong Speaker, although not as domineering as Gingrich in 1995. Moreover, the timing of Livingston's challenge and the rationale he offered showed the interdependency of the policy and electoral goals of congressional parties. But there is little evidence that any Republican shifted support away from Gingrich because of legislative battles that he lost or because Gingrich's policy views had somehow fallen out of step with his party. Instead, Gingrich failed to fashion a legislative program that would be attractive to the electorate. Electoral failure, not a change in the policy alignments within the House, was the immediate cause of his downfall.[28]

Livingston did not last long. Soon after Republicans made him their candidate for Speaker, Larry Flynt, publisher of *Hustler* magazine, disclosed that Livingston had had extramarital affairs years earlier. This was a particularly embarrassing disclosure because the House was about to impeach President Clinton for behavior related to his affair with White House intern Monica Lewinsky. Livingston, in fact, announced his retirement from the House during the December 19, 1998, debate on the articles of impeachment. Suddenly, just as Republicans were adopting articles of impeachment that were unpopular with a majority of Americans and just a month before a new Congress, the Republicans were without a leader.

Emerging from the rubble was Dennis Hastert, a virtual unknown, even to many Washingtonians, who had not been mentioned at all as a possible replacement for Gingrich just a few weeks earlier. No leader is selected for a single reason and it would be unrealistic to attribute Hastert's election as Speaker to just one trait. Hastert was a close ally of Tom DeLay, R-Texas, the Republican whip, and was just as conservative as other Republican leaders. But Hastert promised to be even better suited than Livingston to resolving intraparty disputes and reducing partisan tensions. He seemed to have a spotless background and he didn't have any enemies within the party.

Hastert proved to be a Speaker very different from Gingrich—and, it seems reasonable to speculate, very different from the one Livingston would have been. Not only did he follow through on his promises to allow committee chairs more independence and to act with the advice of a much wider range of Republicans, he proved to be nearly invisible in the media. The Republicans' agenda was very small in 1999, because Speaker Hastert preferred to slow action on taxes and other legislation to avoid conflict with an opposition-party president whose poll ratings remained very high.

The shifting of gears in House Republican leadership occurred without a measurable change in party polarization. The policy differences between the two parties did not change greatly with the 1998 elections. The Republicans had experienced an uptick in intraparty diversity in the previous two Congresses (Figure 8-3), but by any historical comparison, the House remained highly polarized. The composition of the House had changed only marginally in the 1996 and 1998 elections.

Explaining the new direction of House Republican leadership requires moving beyond policy—and party polarization—to electoral concerns. The strength of public support for the Republican policy program of tax and spending cuts had waned considerably by 1998, and public impatience with the Republican-led impeachment proceedings was growing. Furthermore, public views on a few issues, such as education spending, environmental protection, and health care, appeared to be shifting in the Democrats' direction. Electoral conditions had changed, which generated disagreements among Republicans about how to respond to them. Livingston and, even more, Hastert promised to work with all Republicans to address their concerns and to reduce the partisanship that the public seemed to blame more on the Republicans than the Democrats. Hastert followed through with this approach in 2000 when he produced a ten-point list of "items of agreement between Republicans and Clinton" that he hoped would receive legislative action.[29] The Republicans' legislative strategy was adjusted to their electoral needs.

Moreover, the 1998 elections left Republicans with only a six-vote margin. The slim margin of control meant that the leaders of the still-cohesive party had to worry more about the behavior of a few party members. The balance of policy preferences among Republicans had not changed markedly, but the bargaining power of moderate Republicans had been enhanced by the election outcome. Leaders' legislative sights had to be readjusted accordingly.

The conditional party government thesis has little to say about Hastert's selection and behavior. Without a significant change in the polarization of House parties, but with a substantial change in the electoral circumstances of their party, House Republicans chose a less assertive leader, one who openly adopted a collegial, bargaining style within his party, who resisted the temptation to endorse candidates for committee chairmanships, and who promoted a more committee-centered decision-making process. The emphasis changed from cracking the whip to emphasizing team spirit in the Speaker's approach to garnering support from fellow partisans.

Nevertheless, consistent with the conditional party government thesis, Hastert and his second in command, Majority Leader Tom DeLay remained far more involved in shaping legislative strategy, influencing the timing of committee action, and overseeing conference committee proceedings than House leaders of the mid-twentieth century. Hastert became more assertive after the election of a new Republican president in 2000. He set strategy on measures important to the new administration and insisted on timely committee action.

The Senate of Senators Bob Dole, Trent Lott, and Bill Frist

Centralization is not a term that any senator would apply to Senate decision-making processes in the late 1990s, in spite of the intensified partisanship of the period. Party activity increased and party leaders were somewhat more fully engaged in policymaking, but bargaining, not command, remained the modus operandi of both parties' floor leaders. The contrast with Gingrich's House could not be sharper.

By 1985, when Bob Dole, R-Kan., became Senate majority leader, both parties had rejuvenated their party conferences and created leadership offices, party committees, and task forces that performed a variety of functions. These forms of party activity and organization had atrophied by the middle of the century. Republicans started regular luncheon meetings in the late 1950s. Democrats did not do so until 1987, after they regained a majority, and even then Democratic

Majority Leader Robert Byrd, D-W.Va., did so only under pressure from colleagues. Beginning in the 1980s, each party's leader occasionally appointed task forces to help formulate a party strategy on an important issue. In 1989 Democratic Majority Leader George Mitchell, D-Maine, reinvigorated the party's Policy Committee, which, for the first time had a co-chair who controlled a sizable staff. The policy committee, led by Sen. Tom Daschle, D-S.D., developed and approved an annual legislative agenda. Still, only in exceptional cases did party leaders assume primary responsibility for developing and promoting specific legislation. Thus, by the mid-1990s, and in a manner consistent with the conditional party government thesis, party activity had increased, but the decision-making process remained less-centralized than in the House.[30]

Little changed in intraparty decision-making processes after the Republicans gained a majority in the 1994 elections. The new majority Republicans had been led by Bob Dole for ten years by that time. Dole continued his reliance on weekly meetings, sessions with committee chairs, and occasional task forces. Trent Lott, who took over for Dole when Dole began to run full-time for president in 1996, took the approach a step farther. In what one Republican senator called "participatory management," Lott appointed a diverse set of senators to serve in leadership posts and participate in weekly leadership meetings. He also appointed task forces in major policy areas, which would help set the party's agenda but would leave the writing of legislation to committees, several of which were chaired by party moderates. The facilitation of intraparty communication, bargaining, and consensus building—not centralization of power—was the purpose.[31]

Intraparty centralization would have served little purpose for Dole and Lott. Even a cohesive, centrally directed majority party could not force Senate action on legislation if the minority party was reasonably cohesive and chose to filibuster or could credibly threaten to filibuster. Moreover, without invoking cloture, the majority leader has difficulty limiting amendments from determined minority party members. On most legislation, in the absence of cloture, unanimous consent is required to limit debate and amendments.

If Senate partisanship does not produce centralized decision making, it does breed obstructionism. In the 1993–1998 period about half of all major legislation was subject to filibusters or threatened filibusters, many times the rate that was typical of previous decades.[32] Many bills on a wide range of subjects—taxes, health care, labor relations, lobbying, and campaign reform, to name a few—were killed by filibuster. For many more, concessions to the minority were required to overcome or avoid a filibuster. Majority party leadership, even House leadership, has been forced to adjust its strategy to the Senate filibuster. In 2000, for example, House Republican leaders agreed to split up a major tax proposal into separate bills in order to avoid a successful Senate filibuster of the entire package, as had happened the previous year.[33]

Senate minorities realize that the filibuster is an all-purpose hostage-taking device. By threatening to block action on bills, the minority can sometimes force the majority to schedule a debate and a vote on other legislation. The strategy is particularly effective if the minority position on the issue is popular with the electorate. Democrats successfully used this strategy to gain action on measures providing for increases in the minimum wage, gun control, and a patients' bill of rights.

The Senate majority's bills also are subject to nongermane amendments. Thus, however centralized the majority party might be, it cannot prevent a determined minority from gaining floor consideration of its proposals. A majority party can filibuster the minority's proposals, but that only prevents action on other legislation that the majority has responsibility for processing. The majority party can try to invoke cloture, which, if accomplished, bars nongermane amendments. And the majority leader, who has the right of first recognition on the Senate floor, can offer amendments of his own, filling the "amendment tree" and preventing other amendments from being offered until his amendments receive action. The minority, of course, can deny cloture. And filling the amendment tree is only a temporary solution; the minority can wait for an opportunity to offer an amendment to that bill or some other bill.[34]

The result is a procedural arms race—one parliamentary maneuver stimulates a countermove and then other moves. The process seems to intensify partisanship as party members support their leaders' responses to the "unfair" tactics of the other side. As long as the minority party is reasonably cohesive, as it is in a highly polarized Senate, the majority party cannot readily translate its own cohesiveness into significant policy accomplishments. That is precisely what Senate Republicans experienced in the late 1990s and into the next decade.

In late 2002, a videotape of Trent Lott saying that "we wouldn't have had all these problems over all these years" if Strom Thurmond's segregationist bid for the presidency in 1948 had been successful was shown in the national media. Lott apologized, but the media soon disclosed that he had made similar remarks earlier in his career. Only a few colleagues rallied to his defense. Some observers noted that Lott lacked warm relations with many of his colleagues, even those who appreciated his service as floor leader. But the embarrassment to the party led many Senate Republicans to conclude that Lott could no longer serve as their leading spokesman. In spite of his best efforts, Lott failed to persuade his colleagues to give him a second chance. After Lott bowed out, Sen. Bill Frist, R-Tenn., who is far more soft-spoken than Lott, but perhaps a more effective spokesman, was elected to replace him. The party image, more than its legislative agenda, appeared to propel Frist to the top post.

Conclusion

The comparison of patterns of party leadership in the late nineteenth and late twentieth centuries confirms three related propositions about the sources of centralization in Congress:

- Institutional context influences the degree to which party polarization is translated into the centralization of power within the House and Senate.
- Party polarization appears to be a necessary, but not a sufficient, condition for centralization.
- Other factors, particularly a party's electoral circumstances and size, influence the creation of leadership powers. These powers are sometimes used later by assertive leaders.

In the House, where inherited rules allow a determined majority to gain action on its policy agenda, party polarization appears to stimulate the centralization of majority party leadership. Polarization was intense in the late nineteenth and late twentieth centuries, and in both cases House Republicans allowed a strong central leader to emerge and direct the decision-making process. However, even in the House, evolving electoral circumstances in the 1990s led to a change in leadership and a significant diminution in the centralization of the decision-making process.

The fairly tight correspondence between polarization and centralization of the House was not duplicated in the Senate. The Senate majority party centralization in the late nineteenth century was delayed and not as complete, and centralization did not appear in the late-twentieth-century Senate. Ironically, truly polarized Senate parties—including a cohesive minority party—may be less conducive to majority party centralization and success than somewhat less polarized parties that make the support of some minority party members for the majority's program feasible. Cross-party coalitions are more important to the Senate than the House for shepherding legislation through a thicket of potential filibusters, nongermane amendments, and other parliamentary maneuvers.

The conditional party government thesis, then, which relies on the observed correlation between party polarization and centralization, can be elaborated to recognize that institutional context and the forces that shape it are not entirely a product of the ebb and flow of party polarization. Our hunch is that centralization occurs when the parties are polarized, electoral conditions are favorable to the majority party, *and* the institutional context permits control of legislative outcomes by a centralized majority party. Even in the House, electoral circumstances are not always conducive to centralization when intraparty cohesiveness is strong. In certain circumstances, as when its policy program is not popular, a cohesive majority party may de-emphasize the policy goals shared by its members and so be in little need of centralized leadership. And in the Senate, inherited rules limit the degree to which the chamber's decision-making process can ever be centralized in the majority party leadership.

Notes

1. Joseph Cooper and David W. Brady, "Institutional Context and Leadership Style: The House from Cannon to Rayburn," *American Political Science Review* 75 (1981): 411–425. The thesis has been extended to the Senate; see David W. Brady, Richard

Brody, and David Epstein, "Heterogeneous Parties and Political Organization: The U.S. Senate, 1880–1920," *Legislative Studies Quarterly* 14 (1989): 205–223; David W. Brady and David Epstein, "Intraparty Preferences, Heterogeneity, and the Origins of the Modern Congress: Progressive Reformers in the House and Senate, 1890–1920," *Journal of Law, Economics, and Organization* 13 (1997): 26–49.

2. David W. Rohde, *Parties and Leaders in the Postreform House* (Chicago: University of Chicago Press, 1991).
3. Ibid., 192.
4. See Barbara Sinclair, *Majority Leadership in the U.S. House* (Baltimore: Johns Hopkins University Press, 1983); Barbara Sinclair, *Legislators, Leaders, and Lawmaking: The U.S. House of Representatives in the Postreform Era* (Baltimore: Johns Hopkins University Press, 1995); and Barbara Sinclair, *Unorthodox Lawmaking: New Legislative Processes in the U.S. Congress* (Washington, D.C.: CQ Press, 1997). Others make the same point. See John Aldrich and David W. Rohde, "The Consequences of Party Organization in the House: The Role of the Majority and Minority Parties in Conditional Party Government," in *Polarized Politics: The President and the Congress in a Partisan Era,* ed. Jon Bond and Richard Fleisher (Washington, D.C.: CQ Press, 2000); Stanley Bach and Steven S. Smith, *Managing Uncertainty in the U.S. House of Representatives* (Washington, D.C.: Brookings Institution Press, 1988); and Steven S. Smith, *Call to Order: Floor Politics in the House and Senate* (Washington, D.C.: Brookings Institution Press, 1989). For an electoral account of party leadership, see Gary Cox and Mathew McCubbins, *Legislative Leviathan: Party Government in the House* (Berkeley: University of California Press, 1993).
5. On the Speakers of this era, see David W. Brady, *Congressional Voting in a Partisan Era: A Study of the McKinley Houses* (Lawrence: University of Kansas Press, 1973); David W. Brady, Joseph Cooper, and Patricia Hurley, "The Decline of Party in the U.S. House of Representatives, 1887–1968," *Legislative Studies Quarterly* 4 (1979): 381–407; George Brown, *The Leadership of Congress* (Indianapolis: Bobbs-Merrill, 1922); Chang-Wei Chiu, *The Speaker of the House of Representatives Since 1896* (New York: Columbia University Press, 1928); Paul DeWitt Hasbrouk, *Party Government in the House of Representatives* (New York: Macmillan, 1927); Cooper and Brady, "Institutional Context and Leadership Style."
6. DW-NOMINATE scores, a measure of legislators' placement on the liberal-conservative scale, are used. The authors thank Keith Poole for their use. For an excellent discussion of party polarization, see Keith Poole and Howard Rosenthal, *Congress: A Political-Economic History of Roll Call Voting* (New York: Oxford University Press, 1997), 80–85.
7. See Eric Schickler, *Disjointed Pluralism: Institutional Innovation and the Development of the U.S. Congress* (Princeton: Princeton University Press, 2001), Chap. 2. Sundquist emphasizes the factionalism within the Republican Party prior to the realignment of 1896. See James L. Sundquist, *Dynamics of the Party System: Alignment and Realignment of Political Parties in the United States* (Washington, D.C.: Brookings Institution Press, 1983).
8. For a different perspective and different account of party polarization in the House of the 51st Congress (1889–1891), see Cooper and Brady, "Institutional Context and Leadership Style."
9. Schickler, *Disjointed Pluralism.*
10. See Gerald Gamm and Steven S. Smith, "Last among Equals: The Presiding Officer and the Struggle for Order in the 19th Century Senate" (paper presented at the Robert J. Dole Institute's Conference on Civility and Deliberation in the U.S. Senate, Washington, D.C., July 16, 1999).
11. These observations comport with historian David Rothman's more detailed account of developments in the Senate, in which cohesive parties date back to the late 1880s.

See David J. Rothman, *Politics and Power: The United States Senate, 1869–1901* (Cambridge: Harvard University Press, 1966), 90–108.

12. See Poole and Rosenthal, *Congress: A Political-Economic History of Roll Call Voting,* 82.
13. Gerald Gamm and Steven S. Smith, "Senate Party Leadership in the 1890s" (paper presented at the annual meeting of the Midwest Political Science Association, Chicago, April 2000).
14. On the history of filibusters and filibuster reform, see Franklin Burdette, *Filibustering in the Senate* (Princeton: Princeton University Press, 1940), and Sarah Binder and Steven S. Smith, *Politics or Principle? Filibustering in the United States Senate* (Washington, D.C.: Brookings Institution Press, 1997).
15. Our emphasis is different from that of Brady, Brody, and Epstein, "Heterogeneous Parties and Political Organization," 211–213, who emphasize the committee seniority of northeastern Republicans. What seems more critical is that members of the Aldrich-Allison faction enjoyed such seniority that they held both top party and top committee posts.
16. Rothman, *Politics and Power,* 90–108.
17. Gamm and Smith, "Senate Party Leadership in the 1890s."
18. See Brown, *The Leadership of Congress,* 102, 134–135; and DeAlva Stanwood Alexander, *History and Procedure of the House of Representatives* (Boston: Houghton Mifflin, 1916), 6–7.
19. "Mr. Aldrich's Clever Move," *Washington Post,* February 7, 1900, 4.
20. "Vote on Finance Bill," *Washington Post,* February 12, 1900, 3.
21. "Hawaiian Bill Taken Up," *Washington Post,* February 16, 1900.
22. Burdette, *Filibustering in the Senate,* 69–80.
23. Eric Schickler and John Sides, "Intergenerational Warfare: The Senate Decentralizes Appropriations," *Legislative Studies Quarterly* 25 (2000): 551–575.
24. Thus, we would qualify the assertion of Brady, Brody, and Epstein in "Heterogeneous Parties and Political Organization," 209, that "in 1900, the U.S. Senate was, in fact, hierarchical, centralized, and heavily partisan. The top leadership controlled committee assignments, set the agenda, and had sanctions to help them enforce party discipline on the floor."
25. Roger Davidson, *The Postreform Congress* (New York: St. Martin's, 1992).
26. John Aldrich and David W. Rohde, "The Transition to Republican Rule in the House: Implications for Theories of Congressional Politics," *Political Science Quarterly* 112 (1997–1998): 541–567; Barbara Sinclair, *Unorthodox Lawmaking,* 175–216.
27. Bruce Alpert, "Grab for Top House Job Comes after Plan to Quit," *Times-Picayune,* November 15, 1998, sec. A, p. 18.
28. On the expectations for Livingston, see Richard E. Cohen and David Baumann, "After the Riot," *National Journal,* November 14, 1998, 2700.
29. Many journalistic accounts support this interpretation. See Mary Agnes Carey, "New Strategy, Old Disputes," *CQ Weekly,* January 22, 1999, and Karen Foerstel, "Parties Set Ambitious Agendas in the Shadow of Old Grudges," *CQ Weekly,* January 2, 1999. On the ten-point plan, see Andrew Taylor, "Issues Held Hostage in War between Action, Gridlock," *CQ Weekly,* February 26, 2000, 394–399.
30. On Senate party activity, see Donald Baumer, "Senate Democratic Leadership in the 101st Congress" (paper presented at the annual meeting of the American Political Science Association, San Francisco, September 1990); Samuel Patterson and Thomas Little, "The Organizational Life of Congressional Parties" (paper presented at the annual meeting of the Midwest Political Science Association, Chicago, April 1992); and Steven S. Smith, "Forces of Change in Senate Party Leadership and Organization," in *Congress Reconsidered,* 5th ed., ed. Lawrence C. Dodd and Bruce I. Oppenheimer (Washington, D.C.: CQ Press, 1993), 259–290.

31. Donna Cassata, "Lott's Task: Balance the Demands of His Chamber and His Party," *Congressional Quarterly Weekly Report,* March 8, 1997.
32. Barbara Sinclair, "Hostile Partners: The President, Congress, and Lawmaking in the Partisan 1990s," in *Polarized Politics,* 145.
33. Lori Nitschke, "GOP Plans an Election Year Push for Tax Cuts Rejected in 1999, *CQ Weekly,* January 8, 2000.
34. Andrew Taylor, "Senate Leaders' Parliamentary Ploys," *CQ Weekly,* February 26, 2000, 399.

9. The House Leadership in an Era of Partisan Warfare

Eric Schickler and Kathryn Pearson

The start of the twenty-first century has been a time of much hand-wringing about the state of Congress. After decades of calling for more distinct, "responsible" parties, political observers have decried the intense partisan acrimony that has shaped the debate over a wide array of issues in both chambers.[1] The House, in particular, is sharply divided into competing camps that have considerable contempt for one another. Democrats view Republican leaders as tyrants bent on abusing the legislative process to achieve their narrow aims. Republicans have come to view Democrats as an obstructive minority concerned only with disrupting business and blocking policy for political advantage. Incivility and acrimony reached a new peak during the 108th Congress (2003–2004), as Republicans enjoyed unified control of government and could often afford to cut House Democrats entirely out of the deal-making process. Democrats claimed that this led to policies out of step with a nation essentially divided evenly between the parties; Republicans, however, believed it imperative to adopt an ambitious program in order to persuade voters to grant them a longer hold on power.

One irony of the intense partisan atmosphere is that many observers had expected a shift to "regular order" and a degree of comity with the replacement of the fiery Georgia Republican Newt Gingrich by the milder Dennis Hastert, R-Ill., as Speaker following the 1998 elections. Although Hastert has largely remained out of the public spotlight, many of the centralizing moves made by Gingrich—along with his Democratic predecessors, particularly Speaker Jim Wright, D-Texas—have been extended under his leadership. This essay assesses the Republican leadership system in the House. We consider its continuities with past practices and the ways in which Republicans have pushed their prerogatives even further in adapting to unified party control of government. We also assess Democrats' response to the GOP's innovations and ask to what extent a new, highly partisan order is becoming institutionalized in the House.

The "Revolution" of 1995 and Its Aftermath

After forty years in the minority, Republicans picked up fifty-two seats in the 1994 elections to gain control of the House of Representatives. The new Republican majority, which included seventy-three freshmen, proclaimed that their election provided a mandate for their "Contract with America," a party manifesto that GOP candidates had pledged to support. The Contract called for dramatic reductions in the size of government and in taxes; it also pledged to reform welfare programs for the poor, toughen penalties on crime, and uphold "family values." The GOP election victory catapulted Gingrich, the party's whip in the preceding Congress and one of the lead authors of the Contract, to newfound prominence as Speaker of the House and as the Republicans' most visible national leader.

The Republicans adopted an array of reforms intended to transform the legislative process and centralize party control. Perhaps most important, Speaker Gingrich seized a more active role in determining committee assignments and in selecting committee chairmen. In the past, committee chairmanships were largely governed by the seniority system, in which the majority party member with the longest tenure on a committee would be its chairman, subject to a vote of the Democratic Caucus. This system had limited the Democrats' ability to control committee politics, which often were dominated by cooperative relationships between senior members of both parties. But Gingrich bypassed the seniority system in appointing more junior conservative loyalists to chair three key committees, including the Appropriations Committee, which handles the spending bills considered by Congress. These appointments sent the clear message that this would be an activist, assertive leadership. Gingrich even required incoming Appropriations Committee members to sign a pledge of support for the Contract at the beginning of the 104th Congress.[2] When committees drafted legislation that did not satisfy party leaders, Gingrich circumvented them by appointing special party task forces to craft legislation for the floor instead. New rules setting a six-year term limit for both committee and subcommittee chairs further eroded committee leaders' power. The GOP reforms also set an eight-year term limit for the Speaker, but this change was repealed in January 2003.

Although this system was credited with noteworthy successes, particularly the swift passage of most of the Contract items by the House, it soon came under challenge. Beyond his role internally in organizing the House, Gingrich took on a highly public role as the party's spokesman and principal strategist. Most notably, Gingrich became the party's chief negotiator in battles with President Clinton. This forced the Speaker into the untenable position of either making compromises that alienated the party's conservative base, particularly the freshmen members unconcerned about institutional maintenance, or standing firm in showdowns with the increasingly popular president. The extended battle over the budget and government shutdowns in 1995–1996 tarnished Gingrich's reputation and enabled Clinton and his allies to depict the Speaker as an extremist. The Speaker's own penchant for highly charged public rhetoric made the Democrats' task much easier. Democratic congressional candidates across the country nationalized their elections by running against Newt Gingrich in their home districts. As a result, many Republicans blamed Gingrich's poor public image when the party lost seats in the 1996 and 1998 congressional elections. A coup proposed in July 1997 by disgruntled conservatives to dislodge Gingrich had disintegrated before it could be executed, but disappointment after Republicans lost five seats in the 1998 elections led to his withdrawal as a candidate for reelection as Speaker and his resignation from the House.

The selection of Dennis Hastert to replace Gingrich appeared to portend the return to a less aggressive speakership. Hastert had never served as an elected leader: DeLay had appointed him chief deputy whip. The new Speaker was known for his legislative skill as the leader of two task forces appointed by Gingrich. Commenting on Hastert's selection as Speaker, Congressional Quarterly observed that "in rallying behind him, Republicans signaled their interest in a new type of leader who would not follow the bomb-throwing style of Gingrich, but instead focus on the behind-the-scenes consensus building."[3]

Indeed, Hastert has adopted a much lower public profile than Gingrich. The role of the Speaker as the public face of his party had begun to take shape in the 1980s under the leadership of Tip O'Neill, who became the Democrats' symbolic leader in battles with Ronald Reagan.[4] Speaker Jim Wright accentuated the public role of the Speaker, pursuing a partisan policy agenda in a highly visible way during his brief tenure (1987–1989), and it peaked under Gingrich, who envisioned becoming something of a prime minister, directing the government as a whole against a president struggling to remain relevant. Hastert has greatly scaled back the Speaker's public role, preferring to allow a broader range of Republicans to speak for the party. Thus, a search of major papers in *Lexis/Nexis* shows that Hastert's name appeared in the headline or lead paragraph of 483 stories in all of 2003, whereas Gingrich was similarly featured 2,373 times in the *first three months* of 1997. The result is that there is no plausible way for Democrats to campaign for Congress by running against Hastert in the way that they targeted Gingrich.

The Hastert speakership, however, has by no means resulted in a retreat from the strong, centralized approach under Gingrich. In fact, under Hastert's leadership, Republicans have extended many of Gingrich's innovations. Working with his close ally Majority Leader Tom DeLay, R-Texas, and Whip Roy Blunt, R-Mo., Hastert has continued to push an ambitious party agenda, while marginalizing Democrats' role in the process. Observers anticipated that Republican committee chairs would gradually emerge as a decentralizing force as they became more experienced and entrenched.[5] However, the GOP's implementation of term limits for the chairmen—combined with the repeal of the term limit for the Speaker—has mitigated the tendency for committees to emerge as independent power bases. The process of interviewing prospective chairs by the leadership-dominated Steering Committee—on which the Speaker and the majority leader control seven of the twenty-eight votes—highlights the chairmen's dependence on the leadership and encourages loyalty to the party program. In November 2002 the Republican Conference passed a rule subjecting Appropriations subcommittee chairs to the same interview process. In 2003, party leaders installed loyal party members in two of the four vacant committee chairmanships—the Government Reform Committee and the Resources Committee—skipping over much more senior members. Given committee chairs' incentives to be highly responsive to the leadership, along with leaders' close oversight of their legislation, committees have not returned to their historical central place in the legislative process. As the *National Journal* concluded, with only modest exaggeration, "more and more bills have been written by majority-party leaders, or by small numbers of committee members closely aligned with the leaders. Committee markups these days are often for show."[6]

Although Hastert, DeLay, and Blunt lead in setting GOP strategy, they are part of a broader team of loyal and generally conservative Republicans who serve in the inner leadership circle. The Republican Conference, comprising all Republican members of Congress, nominates the Speaker and elects the majority leader, majority whip, Conference chair, National Republican Congressional Committee chair, and House Policy Committee chair. Republican leaders attain and maintain their positions through their loyalty, expressed in their voting records, legislative activities, and electoral teamwork. In 2003, every leader voted with their party more often than the average, rank-and-file Republican did (91 percent of the time). Party leaders actively campaign for their colleagues, frequently attending their fundraisers and raising money to distribute. With the exception of Policy Committee Chairman Christopher Cox, leaders contributed between $340,000 and $952,000 to Republican House candidates from their own leadership PACs in 2002.

The whip appoints a chief deputy majority whip, who is now also considered a member of the elected leadership, and several deputy whips. Deputy whips are charged with helping the majority whip find the votes necessary to pass partisan legislation, using their regional or committee connections to reach out to recalcitrant members. The majority whip's office does not disclose the names of the deputy whips, though the deputies are free to self-identify. For example, Todd Tiahrt, R-Kan., a member of the House Appropriations Committee, is a deputy whip who serves as the liaison between the committee and the Republican whip team.

The GOP whip system has had a series of noteworthy successes on the House floor, often characterized by one-vote margins and the leadership's willingness to push its prerogatives to the limit. While the overwhelming majority of Republican members readily support their party's legislative agenda, most major issues have given at least a few GOP members pause, whether for ideological or constituency reasons. With only a handful of votes to spare, a small number of defections can sink legislation in the face of near-unified Democratic opposition.

GOP leaders proved effective in persuading wavering members to switch their votes when necessary in 2003. On June 27, a tearful Jo Ann Emerson, R-Mo., switched her vote on H.R. 1, the House version of the Medicare prescription drug bill, after the leadership promised to bring a separate drug importation bill to the floor.[7] The importation bill passed, despite DeLay's active opposition, but was excluded from the final conference report. Two weeks later, Republican leaders exerted pressure on wavering Republicans to narrowly fend off a Democratic amendment to the 2004 Labor–Health and Human Services–Education appropriations bill that would have barred the implementation of a Bush administration regulation changing overtime pay rules. Leaders held the vote open for several minutes while they found a few extra votes to defeat the amendment by a vote of 210–213. On September 5, Republican leaders narrowly passed an amendment to the District of Columbia appropriations bill authorizing vouchers for low-income students to attend private schools. The measure had appeared headed for defeat, but in the closing minutes of the vote, a Republican switch secured a 205–203 victory.[8]

The high-water mark of the leadership's willingness to push its prerogatives on the House floor occurred on November 22, 2003. Beginning at 3 a.m., Republican leaders held open the vote on the Medicare prescription drug bill for nearly three hours until the vote totals shifted from a 215–219 defeat to a 220–215 passage.[9] Republican leaders refused to bring down the gavel—even though the nay vote had surpassed the critical 218 mark—until they had persuaded enough Republicans to switch their votes. Democrats expressed outrage, though Republicans were quick to remind them that Speaker Jim Wright had held open a vote long enough to convince fellow Texas Democrat Jim Chapman to change his vote to pass a budget reconciliation bill in 1987.[10] Fueling the acrimony over the Medicare vote were reports from retiring Republican Nick Smith, Mich., who ultimately voted against the bill, that unnamed members had offered $100,000 in donations to his son's congressional campaign if he would change his vote. Smith later issued a statement saying that he had been "technically incorrect," though Democrats pressed successfully for an investigation, breaking an Ethics Committee "détente."[11]

Acting as an arm of the Republican leadership, the House Committee on Rules routinely crafts restrictive rules that limit or deny Democrats' opportunities to offer amendments during debate on the House floor. Republicans had sharply criticized the Democratic majority for such practices during the late 1980s and early 1990s, and indeed, according to the *National Journal,* by 1993–1994, Democratic leaders employed restrictive rules 70 percent of the time.[12] In their first years in the majority, 1995–1996, Republican leaders relied on restrictive rules only 56 percent of the time. However, they have increasingly denied Democrats the opportunity to offer floor amendments, and by 2003, 76 percent of all rules governing debate on the House floor were restrictive.[13]

Republican leaders push their prerogatives at virtually every stage in the legislative process. Democrats charge that majority party leaders exclude them from participating in House-Senate conference committee deliberations. Most of the Medicare prescription drug bill conference committee meetings were open only to the ten Republicans and two moderate Senate Democrats who supported the bill, while the remaining five Democratic conferees were not permitted to participate. Similar complaints arose from Democratic conferees on the energy bill and the Federal Aviation Administration reauthorization bill. The degree to which Republicans exclude Democrats from conference deliberations is unprecedented in the modern era, though Democrats at times sidelined Republicans during key points of the negotiations when they were in the majority. Under Democratic control, leaders often made conference committees so large that most of the decisions were negotiated by a few key leaders, mainly Democrats. However, unlike current majority party practices, Democrats held public conference committee meetings with all of the conferees, providing Republicans a forum to highlight their positions to Democrats and the public. Democratic conferees then at least gave the appearance of working with their minority party counterparts, which does not occur today on some controversial bills, according to a longtime Democratic leadership staffer.[14]

Republicans' aggressive use of the Appropriations Committee for partisan advantage, particularly recently, marks a shift in the committee's traditionally collegial operations. Since 1995, Republican leaders have attached policy riders to many of the thirteen annual spending bills, infusing partisanship into a budgeting process that had generally featured considerable bipartisan cooperation. When it came to earmarks allocating funds to members' districts—committee members' districts in particular—a bipartisan spirit in which the appropriators' requests would be funded had generally prevailed. In October 2003, however, Labor–HHS–Education Subcommittee Chairman Ralph Regula, R-Ohio, sent a letter to ranking member David Obey, D-Wis., informing him that any member who did not support the Labor–HHS–Education appropriations bill on the House floor, which included all Democrats and nine Republicans, would not get any earmarks in the House-Senate conference committee.[15] Democratic appropriators charged that Regula was responding to demands from his party's top leadership and pointed out that the chairman's letter followed Republican rules changes in the selection of appropriations subcommittee chairmen, whereby they are subject to approval by the leadership-influenced Steering Committee.[16]

At times, Republicans have exerted their power in ways that have gotten them in trouble. During the consideration of a pension reform bill in the Ways and Means Committee in July 2003, ranking member Charles Rangel, D-N.Y., complained that Democrats had not had time to review the final bill, as Republicans had distributed it around midnight the night before. Democrats thus required a full reading of the bill, a process normally waived, and then moved to the committee library in protest. Ways and Means Committee Chairman Bill Thomas, R-Calif., called in the Capitol Police to remove the Democrats from the committee's library. After Democrats expressed outrage, Thomas issued a contrite, tearful apology on the House floor the following day. Such episodes sparked a fresh round of news reports about the decline in comity on Capitol Hill. According to the *Christian Science Monitor*, "By any measure, last Friday's meeting of the Ways and Means Committee—and its subsequent rehash on the floor of the House—sank comity in the people's house to a new low."[17] A key question for Democrats became whether they could use such moments to dramatize their complaints about Republicans' tight control of the legislative process.

The Democratic Response

Although Republicans have clearly been driving the changes in congressional politics since their 1995 takeover of the House, the Democratic response to these GOP innovations has reinforced the underlying dynamic. The Democratic Caucus has long been renowned for its internal fractiousness, yet the GOP's aggressive pursuit of a sharply conservative agenda, combined with the defeat and retirement of many conservative, southern Democratic members, has helped transform the Democrats into a well-organized and relatively coherent opposition. Minority Leader Nancy Pelosi, D-Calif., frequently blasts Republican leaders for their tactics. In early 2004 she lamented that "there is a very, very heavy hand of partisanship prevailing."[18] Democratic leaders, however, have responded with their own heavy dose of partisanship and by pushing their own, albeit more limited, prerogatives.

The transition from Minority Leader Richard Gephardt, D-Mo., to Pelosi in the 108th Congress energized the Democratic Caucus. Gephardt had served as majority leader from 1989 to 1994 under Speaker Thomas Foley, D-Wash., and when Republicans took control of Congress, Democrats elected Gephardt as their leader. Gephardt headed a party struggling to adapt to life in the minority. Taking back majority control was the top priority. With every election cycle, however, Democrats' hopes of regaining their majority were dashed, and Republicans picked up seats in 2002. In the wake of that election, Gephardt resigned to devote himself to running for president.

The Democratic Caucus had become increasingly unified during Gephardt's tenure. In 2002, however, Gephardt had divided the caucus over his support of the resolution authorizing the Iraq war, which three-fifths of House Democrats voted against. Pelosi, by contrast, unabashedly represents the liberal wing of the Democratic Caucus and voted against the resolution to go to war. To win back the House, she focuses not just on raising money for Democratic House candidates (which she does with enormous success) but also on highlighting differences between the two parties to an even greater extent than Gephardt did. Pelosi had only been Democratic whip for one year when Gephardt stepped down after the 2002 elections, but she easily defeated Harold Ford Jr., Tenn., to win the position by a vote of 177–29. In the years immediately preceding, as well as in her year as whip, Pelosi proved her political skills, contributing well over $1 million to Democratic House candidates in 2002 from her leadership PACs alone. Some moderate Democrats, however, expressed concern about her liberal views, and four Democrats abstained from voting for her for Speaker on the House floor. The crucial challenge for Pelosi as leader has been to bridge the gap separating the party's dominant liberal wing and its faction of moderates and conservatives, such as the thirty-seven "Blue Dog" Democrats. Holding onto the support of the moderates is crucial both in policy terms—to make it more difficult for Republicans to pass their agenda—and politically, in persuading voters that GOP legislative triumphs reflect partisan brute force rather than bipartisan cooperation.

The selection of Pelosi made clear that Democrats wanted a leader who would be more aggressive in battling the Republicans and would emphasize party unity. This marks, to some extent, a resolution—at least for now—of internal debates among the Democratic Caucus. In previous years, some Democrats favored working with President George W. Bush to try to influence legislation, even just at the margins, and thus share in the credit. The midterm election, however, ended most calls for cooperation, as Bush went after even cooperative Democrats, particularly in highly visible Senate races, and because the Democrats were seen as a party lacking a message in the wake of the Iraq resolution. Furthermore, Republican leaders have a clear strategy of attaining 218 votes from the Republican Conference. According to a longtime Democratic leadership staffer, "Our people who would normally deal with Republicans are rebuffed."[19] These debates culminated in Pelosi's resounding victory.

The changing tactics of the Blue Dogs illustrates the shift in the overall Democratic response. Blue Dog Democrats organized in 1995 to craft policy alternatives and publicly assert their moderate-to-conservative ideological identity within the context of their Democratic partisan identity. The average Blue Dog Democrat voted with their party 78.7 percent of the time in 2003, nearly ten percentage points below the average Democrat but noticeably more often than when the group initially organized.[20] The Blue Dogs are well organized and active, staking out positions on many policy issues, particularly fiscal policy. Each year they draft their own version of a centrist budget resolution that attracts many other Democrats but only a handful of Republicans. Notwithstanding their legislative outreach, there is less bipartisan cooperation among Blue Dogs and moderate Republicans than in past years and less than one might predict given their ideological overlap. As one aide to a Blue Dog Democrat lamented, "The GOP leadership has adopted a Republicans-only approach to passing all bills; they have the strategy of getting 218 votes with Republican votes. We have no opportunity for input; it's a Republicans-only process."[21] Republican leaders have chosen to move policy as much to the right as possible to keep their conservative members on board rather than seek more moderate compromises to attract the Blue Dogs. Republican leaders reject overtures from the Blue Dogs, and Democratic leaders increasingly stress party unity. Thus despite some disagreements, Blue Dogs generally operate as team players within the Democratic Caucus.

House Democrats had more demographic, racial, and gender diversity in their leadership organization than Republicans in the 108th Congress, as is typically the case. Elected leaders include Minority Whip Steny Hoyer, Md., Caucus Chairman Robert Menendez, N.J., and Vice Chairman James Clyburn, S.C., an African American representing a rural district, all of whom vote with their party more often than the average Democrat. In her leadership appointments, Pelosi's choices have been largely party loyalists and her own loyalists, though she has also tried to enhance cooperation with moderates and conservatives. Pelosi appointed longtime friend and fellow Californian Robert Matsui to chair the Democratic Congressional Campaign Committee. In an effort to appease moderates, Pelosi tapped John Spratt, S.C., the ranking member of the Budget Committee, as assistant to the Democratic leader. Pelosi selected liberal allies Rosa DeLauro, Conn., and George Miller, Calif., as Democratic Steering Committee co-chairs.

The Democratic whip organization parallels the Republicans' in that it includes a broad range of members appointed to many positions—only the more senior of whom are made public—to maximize leaders' efforts to persuade members using regional, ethnic, racial, and ideological connections. Democrats have eight chief deputy whips, led by Senior Chief Deputy Whip John Lewis, Ga., an African American known for his leadership in the civil rights movement. In 2003, Hoyer restructured the whip organization, also selecting senior whips, assistant whips, regional whips, and at-large whips. According to his staff, Hoyer "is careful to ensure that the whip organization is inclusive and diverse and that there are representatives of all the various groups within the caucus, such as Blue Dogs, Progressives, Congressional Black Caucus and Congressional Hispanic Caucus members and that the whip operation is geographically diverse."[22]

The task facing the whips is facilitated by the Democratic Caucus's increased ideological homogeneity. The defeat and retirement of numerous conservative Democrats, particularly southerners, during the last decade means that the Democratic Caucus has lost most of its routine dissenters. Ralph Hall, Texas, the Democrat who had voted most frequently with Republicans in 2003 (49 percent), switched parties at the end of the year.[23] Furthermore, the GOP's ideologically charged agenda has made it easier for Democrats to vote together on most issues. As a result, Democratic party unity reached its highest point yet in 2003: the average Democrat voted with their party on the House floor 87 percent of the time.[24] This increase—reflecting greater party-line voting than occurred during Democratic control of Congress—reflects the increasing homogeneity of the Democratic Caucus but also increased emphasis on party loyalty.

With the slim margins between the parties, Democratic leaders emphasize the importance of presenting unified opposition to Republicans' major legislative priorities. By providing Republicans with no support for their proposals, Democratic leaders hope to force conflicted Republicans to cast votes that are tough to defend in their districts, or better yet, cause Republican leaders to suffer the embarrassment of losing on the House floor or pulling a bill from consideration. Although they still lost nearly every vote, the Democratic whip team had considerable success in achieving and highlighting their near-unified opposition to Republican plans under Pelosi's leadership.

The leadership's response in the aftermath of the first House vote on the Medicare prescription drug package alerted Democrats that defections from the party's position were being noted. Frustrated by Republicans' one-vote margin of victory on the House version of the bill, Democratic leaders rebuked the nine Democrats who supported it, particularly those from safe districts. In the Democratic Caucus meeting following the vote, Pelosi threatened, "I don't want that to happen again. This can never happen again."[25] When the House considered the conference report, a somewhat more moderate version of the plan, sixteen Democrats voted yes, although a few waited to support the bill until it was clear that it would pass anyway. In defending his own tactics on the passage of the conference report, Speaker Hastert charged that Pelosi put great pressure on Democrats to oppose the bill. "Without those threats, I think we would have had a lot more," Hastert said, adding of the unusual tactics, "we had to do it."[26] In any case, it is striking that all but 16 of the 205 House Democrats casting votes (7.8 percent) opposed a bill that created the largest new entitlement program in decades. By contrast, 11 of the 46 Democratic senators voting supported the final drug bill.

A rare success for the Democrats came in June 2003, when Republican leaders scheduled a floor vote on legislation to allow companies to give employees "comp time" instead of overtime pay. Labor unions strongly opposed the legislation, but in the past Republican leaders had managed to attract enough Democratic supporters to pass legislation that labor opposed, despite pro-labor Republican defections. This time, GOP leaders found that they were unable to pick up significant Democratic votes. According to Congressional Quarterly's analysis, Republicans could not garner the votes "in large part because of a renewed, effective drive led by Minority Whip Steny Hoyer."[27] The bill was pulled, embarrassing Republican leaders.

More generally, Democratic leaders take advantage of their limited minority rights to showcase their opposition to Republican legislation and tactics. According to a longtime Democratic leadership staffer, both the Democratic leadership and members are more aggressive than they have been in previous years, taking greater advantage of their opportunities to obstruct the process and highlight their differences.[28] Democrats' tactics include filing discharge petitions, appealing rulings by the chair, and offering motions to instruct. For example, in July 2003, spurred by a recent Democratic victory on a nonbinding motion to accept the Senate position on the child care tax credit issue, Pelosi employed a strategy of slowing House business, and drawing attention to the issue, by offering daily motions to instruct. "House Democrats will use every procedural weapon at our disposal," she said.[29]

Democratic leaders also see partisan gain in politicizing the substantive differences between the parties. In many respects, Pelosi's vocal criticism of Republican legislation on the House floor and in press conferences, coupled with her willingness to obstruct legislative business, mirrors the tactics of the Gingrich-led "bomb-throwers" during the 1980s and early 1990s. The critical difference is that Pelosi heads the minority party, whereas Gingrich's group generally worked outside of it. Gingrich's success as a "bomb-thrower" was due in part to the ethics charges he leveled against Speaker Wright and Majority Whip Tony Coelho in 1989, leading to their resignations and a major shake-up of the Democratic leadership. In 1997, Gingrich himself was the subject of ethics charges. By all accounts, the ethics investigations had exacerbated the partisanship in the House. After the investigation of Gingrich, a détente began whereby the Ethics Committee, not members, has initiated all formal ethics investigations. In the wake of the three-hour Medicare prescription drug vote, and especially the reports alleging efforts to bribe Rep. Nick Smith, Pelosi threatened to end the détente on December 8, 2003, when she came to the House floor with a privileged resolution denouncing the extended Medicare vote and the alleged "bribery of public officials." A party-line vote of 207–182 tabled the resolution, but the attendant publicity kept the issue alive. A letter from Minority Whip Hoyer to Speaker

Hastert the following month demanded that he seek an investigation. Democratic leaders have revived Gingrich's tactic of tarring the institution's leadership with accusations of scandal in hopes of scoring political points.

Republicans' aggressive use of their prerogatives and the Democratic response in kind—interacting with narrow margins and uncertainty going into every election—have exacerbated what many have termed the civility breakdown in Congress. According to a Democratic leadership staffer, "the process has become highly partisan and polarizing, getting worse and worse over the last year. It has reached the point where there is little cooperation between the two sides."[30] Indeed, the number of party unity votes tallied by Congressional Quarterly, on which one or both parties voted unanimously, has skyrocketed since the late 1990s. As Figure 9-1 shows, Democratic unanimity reach an all-time high in 2003; Democrats voted unanimously on 94 of the 349 roll call votes (27 percent) in which the two parties opposed one another in 2003. Republicans voted unanimously on 109 of the party unity votes (31 percent), a continuation of their increased unanimity under Speaker Hastert. In the 1970s and 1980s, the number of unanimous votes achieved by either party typically ranged between ten and twenty and rarely exceeded 10 percent of all party unity votes. The number of unanimous votes increased dramatically for Republicans in the 1990s, while Democrats began to achieve perfect unity with greater frequency only in 2002–2003. Although unanimous votes are partly a reflection of the increased ideological divergence between the parties, they also reflect and reinforce the sense that the House now comprises two unified teams who view themselves as engaged in an intense, no-holds-barred battle.

The New System in Historical Context

A crucial question in evaluating the Republican leadership system and the attendant Democratic response is whether current partisan warfare on Capitol Hill is an aberration or instead reflects a return to prior historical precedents. In many ways, the GOP organization bears a resemblance to that in the legendary era of so-called czar rule, when powerful Republican Speakers Thomas Reed (1889–1891, 1895–1899) and Joseph Cannon (1903–1911) dominated the House. Speakers Reed and Cannon used control of committee assignments and of the Rules Committee to shape legislation in the House. The few dissenters from the GOP program were marginalized in the early twentieth century, just as the handful of moderate Republicans in the House today face intense pressure to toe the party line. Cannon's leadership was dramatically weakened in 1910 when a coalition of insurgent Republicans and Democrats voted to remove the Speaker from the Rules Committee and to expand the committee and make it subject to election by the House. Following the 1910 revolt, committee leaders gradually gained the security provided by the seniority system, and party leaders largely became brokers among contending ideological and committee-based factions.

Figure 9-1 Unanimous House Votes, 1954–2003

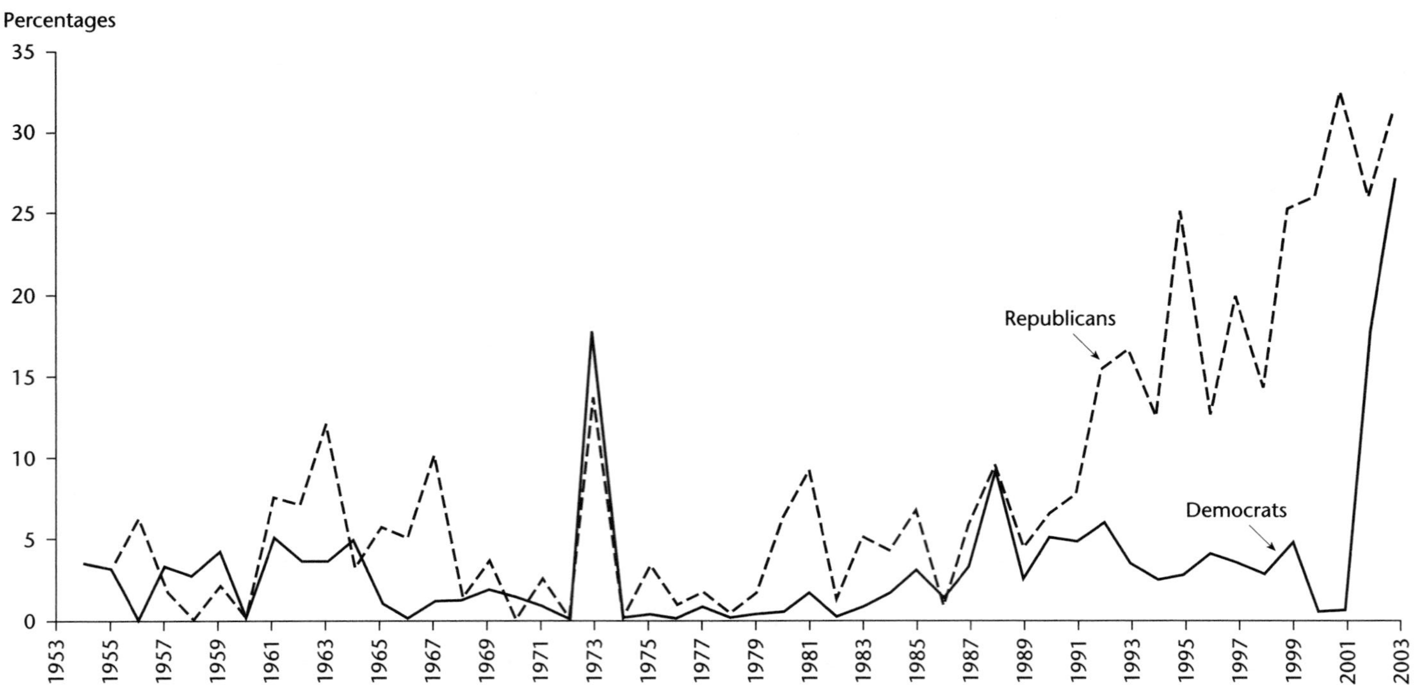

In the decades that followed, even the most prominent Speaker, Democrat Sam Rayburn of Texas (1940–1961), lacked the influence over his caucus that Reed and Cannon once wielded over theirs. Instead, Rayburn was constantly pleading with chairs to report bills favored by most Democrats and generally lacked the power to bypass the powerful, often conservative committee leaders. It was not until the 1970s, when liberals gained an overwhelming majority in the Democratic Caucus, that party leadership began to revive. A series of reforms adopted from 1971 to 1975 enhanced the Speaker's influence over committee assignments, bill referrals, and the Rules Committee, while undercutting the position of the chairmen by chipping away at the seniority system.

Although the first postreform Speaker, Tip O'Neill, generally refrained from using his prerogatives aggressively (1977–1986), his successor, Jim Wright, took full advantage of the Speaker's enhanced resources and public visibility. Wright did not hesitate to intervene in committee deliberations or to use restrictive rules, committee assignment decisions, and threats of retribution to promote his ambitious policy agenda.[31] Wright's tactics generated intense resentment among Republicans and considerable restiveness among Democrats. This left the Speaker vulnerable to Gingrich's ethics onslaught, which led to Wright's resignation in 1989 and the subsequent election of Speaker Thomas Foley. Members initially viewed Foley's reserved style and bipartisan overtures as an antidote to Wright's partisan combativeness. Foley had access to far more tools than Sam Rayburn or other prereform speakers, but in the view of many Democrats he did not use them effectively to promote a partisan agenda. Foley's tenure was characterized by legislative failures in the domestic policy arena and disunity among the Democratic Caucus, particularly during the two years of unified Democratic control of government (1993–1994). The 1994 election debacle was attributed at least in part to Democrats' failure to act effectively as a team during Clinton's first two years in office.[32]

What are the prospects for the new Republican leadership system to become institutionalized in the House? The sources of Joe Cannon's downfall in 1910–1911 provide a framework for evaluating the prospects for Republicans to sustain their current experiment in reinvigorating party government. Three forces combined to foster the success of the revolt against Cannon. First, starting in 1905, a progressive faction gained strength within the GOP, as President Theodore Roosevelt began to give voice to demands for major policy change. Although progressive Republicans only numbered approximately two dozen or so members by 1910—a figure comparable to the number of Republican moderates today—Roosevelt's public support, combined with the popularity of progressivism in their home districts, made them far more confrontational and aggressive than the contemporary moderates. Thus, ideological divisions within the GOP became more pronounced than is currently the case. With both parties using redistricting to foster increasingly safe seats, it seems unlikely that the GOP will experience this sort of intense factional strife in the foreseeable future. Indeed, the main organization of moderate Republicans—the "Tuesday Group," which formed in 1995—is dwindling in numbers, and its members rarely defect on major votes even when the leadership does not respond to their efforts to modify legislation. Unlike the influence that some Democratic member organizations wield in the Democratic Caucus, for example, the Congressional Black Caucus and the Blue Dogs, the Tuesday Group carries little clout within the Republican Conference and does not even publicize its members' names. A more powerful—and larger—internal faction is the "Conservative Action Team" (CATs), a group of conservative Republicans that also organized in 1995. At critical points, some of its members have been willing to vote against the leadership, yet since their general ideological orientation is consonant with that of the leadership and most fellow Republicans, it is unlikely that conservative discontent will undermine the current GOP system.

A second force exacerbating dissatisfaction with Cannon was the perception that his tight personal control deprived individual members of opportunities to exert influence. A major difference today is that Hastert's leadership of the Republican Conference is more collegial than Cannon's was: Where Cannon worked with a small circle of personal intimates in attempting to run the House, Hastert's team is far more extensive, drawing upon several deputy whips to reach out to rank-and-file members based on regional and even ideological interests. In the current organization, Republicans who demonstrate party loyalty through their voting record and fund-raising efforts have considerable opportunities to advance within the power structure of the House. Although committees are no longer outlets for extensive autonomous action, the party itself provides opportunities for individual member involvement through the whip system. Party leaders also contribute generously to members' campaigns, particularly the campaigns of those who need help. Parties also recognize, to some extent, individual legislative leadership. As long as the member supports the party position, leaders are happy to cede leadership on particular issues to knowledgeable members on the House floor, particularly when it comes to determining whose amendments are in order.[33] Again, this mitigates the resistance to vigorous party leadership without sacrificing the GOP's ability to close off opportunities for Democrats to undermine the party's priorities.

A third source of Cannon's downfall was the minority party's reaction. Democrats responded to being shut out of the policy process by attacking the House as an institution and making Cannon the symbol of an undemocratic and unresponsive legislative branch. Democrats' dissatisfaction with current arrangements mirrors the minority's dissatisfaction during the Cannon era. The recent maneuvers by Pelosi and other Democrats to highlight the Republicans' alleged excesses—including the renewed effort to use ethics investigations as a political tool—suggest that this is one component of the Cannon revolt that is likely to reappear in full force. However, Hastert's low public profile may make the strategy less successful than when Cannon—or Newt Gingrich—occupied the chair. It is more difficult to dramatize leadership abuses when the public face of the leadership is a genial former high school wrestling coach who seeks to stay out of the public eye. Were the combative Tom DeLay, often referred to as "the Hammer," much to his delight, to replace Hastert as Speaker following the Illinois Republican's planned retirement in 2006, Democrats' prospects for personalizing majority party excesses might improve.

Still, on the whole, the sources of the Cannon revolt do not appear likely to recur anytime soon. The prospects for institutionalizing the GOP system are also reinforced by turnover patterns. A mere 175 members running for reelection in 2004 had served in the House prior to Gingrich's election as Speaker in 1995. Therefore, less than half of the current members have direct experience with an era prior to the intense partisan warfare of recent years. The era in which the Speaker and minority leader played golf and poker together is beyond the memory of all but the most senior members. Even if Democrats were to recapture the House in the next few years, it is likely that most party members would expect their leaders to emulate the Republicans' aggressive use of the rules.

Unified Party Government

One additional factor that will influence the prospects for institutionalizing the Republicans' highly partisan system is unified party control of Congress and the White House. With a Republican president, GOP leaders have many incentives to pass their party leader's priorities and little incentive to attract Democratic votes in the House, unlike the case during the Clinton years. Victorious GOP bill signings at the White House compel Republicans to do everything possible to pass legislation with Republican votes, whereas President Clinton's veto threats gave Republicans the alternatives of attracting Democrats or blaming the ensuing gridlock on the Democratic president.

Traditionally, strong congressional parties have been identified with movements to defend congressional power against executive branch encroachments.[34] But since the arrival of a Republican president in January 2001, strong House leadership has coincided with close working relations with the White House to attain common legislative goals. Indeed, the cooperative relationship between Republican leaders and the Bush administration contrasts sharply with the unruly interactions between the Clinton White House and Democratic leaders in 1993–1994. The Bush administration worked with GOP leaders to develop legislation that could pass with wide Republican support, such as the tax cuts of 2001 and 2003, the No Child Left Behind Act, the resolution authorizing the war with Iraq, Iraq reconstruction, and a ban on certain types of late-term abortions. At times, President Bush worked with Republican leaders to "capture" popular Democratic legislation that he initially opposed and transform it into Republican legislation, for example, HMO reform and legislation to establish the Department of Homeland Security. Some of Bush's House victories included bills that would go nowhere in the Senate but nonetheless allowed for good press, including legislation to limit class action lawsuits. In 2003, Bush threatened vetoes over issues of privatization of the federal workforce, Cuba sanctions, media ownership, and Iraq reconstruction aid, but he never needed to wield his veto pen.

Republicans' widely shared conservatism facilitates cooperation. Equally important, congressional Republicans have viewed Bush's success as essential to their own ability to maintain majority status. Bush's "compassionate conservatism" succeeded in the 2000 election in allowing Republicans to neutralize traditionally Democratic advantages on issues such as education and helped the party develop a more moderate image.[35] Two years later, Bush's personal popularity and strength on national security issues in the wake of September 11 were widely credited with the GOP's gains in the 2002 midterm elections.[36] Looking toward the 2004 congressional and presidential elections, Speaker Hastert explained to the *National Journal* that the White House and congressional Republicans would run as a united party with a common record: "The president is going to be fighting with us."[37]

Since Republicans view their success as intertwined with the president's, GOP leaders have been able to push through legislation that many Republicans likely would have opposed if not for pressure from the White House. The most noteworthy example was the Medicare prescription drug benefit bill. The $395 billion program—which was revealed to be a $534 billion program a few weeks after passage—was unpopular with many conservatives who loathed the idea of creating a new, expensive entitlement. But the White House and GOP leaders argued that passing such a bill would be essential to the president's reelection campaign and would solidify their party's popular standing. The leadership used all of its tools to push for passage in spite of the internal dissension. Congressional Quarterly observed that "a few GOP members who were opposed to the bill on principle felt sufficient party loyalty to promise Hastert they would change their no votes to yes if they absolutely had to."[38] In the end, although twenty-five Republicans voted nay, four others switched their votes to save the bill. One of the final switchers was conservative Ernest Istook, R-Okla., an Appropriations Committee subcommittee chairman who depends on the leadership-controlled GOP Steering Committee to approve his reappointment every two years.[39] One Republican who voted against the conference report lamented the pressure tactics, saying, "It was an outrage. It was profoundly ugly and beneath the dignity of Congress."[40] But in an era of narrow majorities, intense partisan warfare, and unified party government, many Republicans have been willing to go along with policies that they personally oppose because of the shared sense that the fate of the party demands that it avoid the perception of gridlock. Again, the failures of the first two years of the Clinton administration no doubt provide a useful counterpoint for the Republicans.

Critics argue that Republicans' close cooperation with the White House has come at the expense of congressional autonomy in the domains of both legislation and oversight. Republican Senator Chuck Hagel, Neb., commented that "Congress has abdicated much of its responsibility. . . . It could become an adjunct to the executive branch."[41] The Republican-controlled House Government Reform Committee issued no subpoenas to the Bush administration in its first three years in office, as compared to the 1,050 subpoenas that the committee issued from 1995 to 2001. To be sure, the same committee did not issue any subpoenas to the Clinton administration in the two years of Democratic control (1993–1994). But the lack of investigations under unified party control in recent years is a departure from the dominant pattern starting in the late 1930s, in which prominent investigations of the executive branch characterized both unified and divided government.[42] As long as House Republicans view their fate as inextricably linked to the president's political standing, it is reasonable to expect continued strong resistance to aggressive oversight. Concerns about congressional power have been exacerbated by President Bush's dominant role in setting the legislative agenda. Most major legislative initiatives emerge from the White House, not Capitol Hill, although they are amended by Republicans and Democrats alike as they progress through both chambers. Therefore, as long as the Republicans are unified in their belief that President Bush's success is essential for their continued majority party control, centralization on Capitol Hill is unlikely to coincide with a reassertion of congressional prerogatives vis à vis the White House.

Perhaps the main intraparty strain challenging this unity is the rising discontent among some congressional Republicans, particularly fiscal conservatives, over mounting budget deficits. The strains were obvious in the Medicare prescription drug vote and the budget resolution vote for Fiscal Year 2005 and are likely to become more acute over the next several years as Republicans attempt to reconcile demands to make Bush's tax cuts permanent with pressure to raise defense spending and with resistance to cutting popular domestic programs.

The growth in spending and deficits, combined with the expanded federal role brought about by the No Child Left Behind Act, the creation of the Department of Homeland Security, and the Medicare prescription drug bill, suggests the need to reconsider the legacy of the 1994 Republican revolution. Republicans took over Congress with the ambition of dramatically scaling back the role of the national government. The House passed legislation to eliminate entire cabinet departments, ban unfunded mandates placed on the states, balance the budget, cut taxes, and scale back the size of Medicare, Medicaid, and other entitlements. Only a fraction of these initiatives were enacted. Excepting the dedication to lower taxes, the imperative of working with the White House and appealing to moderate voters in order to maintain their majority has led House Republicans to temper, and at times even surrender, these programmatic goals. The antigovernment zeal has all but disappeared, but the internal institutions Republicans established in 1995 to accomplish their legislative goals have been extended. The current politics surrounding a balanced budget amendment are illustrative. A centerpiece of the Contract with America was a constitutional amendment requiring a balanced budget, which passed the House but failed in the Senate by a single vote in 1995. In 2003, Representative Istook introduced the identical amendment, H.J.Res. 22. Although it was considered by the Judiciary Committee in September 2004, it did not reach the House floor for consideration during the 108th Congress. The Democrats had filed a discharge petition to bring it to the floor, H.Res. 275, in June 2003, but no Republicans signed on (including the constitutional amendment's lead sponsor, Ernest Istook), as discharge petitions are considered an affront to congressional leaders' power.[43] There is no clearer indicator of the potential institutionalization of the new GOP system than its persistence even in the face of the significant shifts in the programmatic aspirations of the party and its leaders.

Notes

1. See David Rapp, "Editor's Notebook: Politics of Last Resort," *CQ Weekly,* November 8, 2003, 2742; and Richard E. Cohen, Kirk Victor, and David Baumann, "The State of Congress," *National Journal,* January 10, 2004.
2. Jeff Shear, "Budget—Pain's the Game," *National Journal,* January 14, 1995.
3. Dan Carney, Karen Foerstel, and Andrew Taylor, "A New Start for the House," *CQ Weekly,* December 19, 1998, 3333.
4. Ronald M. Peters, Jr., *The American Speakership: The Office in Historical Perspective* (Baltimore: Johns Hopkins University Press, 1990; 1997).
5. See Andrew Taylor, "Is Livingston the Manager the House Needs?" *CQ Weekly,* November 14, 1998, 3050; Jeffrey L. Katz, "House Opens a New Session with a Coach and a Prayer, *CQ Weekly,* January 9, 1999, 57.
6. Cohen, Victor, and Baumann, "The State of Congress."
7. John Cranford, "2003 'Key Votes' Highly Partisan," *CQ Weekly,* January 3, 2004, 24.
8. Ibid.
9. Gebe Martinez, "Long Back-and-Forth House Vote Ran Afoul of Democrats, Not Rules," *CQ Weekly,* November 29, 2003, 2962.
10. Juliana Gruenwald, "Retirement: Chapman to Leave House, May Challenge Gramm," *Congressional Quarterly Weekly Report,* September 30, 1995, 3027.
11. Susan Ferrechio, "Democrats Clamor for Probe as House Ethics Committee Weighs Smith Bribery Charge," *CQ Weekly,* February 7, 2004, 382.
12. Cohen, Victor, and Baumann, "The State of Congress."
13. Ibid.
14. Interview with longtime Democratic leadership staffer.
15. Bill Swindell, "Regula to Labor–HHS Naysayers: Don't Tug on Superman's Cape," *CQ Weekly,* November 15, 2003, 2838.
16. Ibid.
17. Gail Russell Chaddock, "Democrats See Ruckus in the House as a Rallying Call," *Christian Science Monitor,* July 21, 2003, USA2.
18. Cohen, Victor, and Baumann, "The State of Congress."
19. Interview with Democratic leadership staffer.
20. The mean party loyalty score rose 13.5 points from 1995 to 2003 for those Blue Dogs who were members of the House in both years.
21. Interview with an aide to a Blue Dog Democrat.
22. This quote is from an e-mail from Hoyer's press secretary.
23. Although the proposed Texas redistricting plan actually made his GOP-leaning district a little less Republican, Hall is still expected to win reelection.
24. This is more than any year since 1960, when Congressional Quarterly began tallying party unity scores.
25. Mark Wegner, "House Leadership—Dem Leaders Upbraid Members for Supporting GOP Drug Bill," *National Journal's CongressDaily AM,* online version, July 10, 2003.

26. Mark Wegner, "Health—Night of House Drama Yields a Narrow Medicare Victory," *National Journal's CongressDaily AM,* online version, November 24, 2003.
27. Bill Swindell, " 'Family Friendly' Bill to Foster Comp Time Flexibility Gets Laid Off House Schedule," *CQ Weekly,* June 7, 2003, 1388.
28. Interview with longtime Democratic leadership staffer.
29. Mark Wegner, "House Leadership—GOP Members Asked Not to Support Dem Motion to Instruct Conferees," *National Journal's CongressDaily,* online version, July 16, 2003.
30. Interview with longtime Democratic leadership staffer.
31. John M. Barry, *The Ambition and the Power: The Fall of Jim Wright* (New York: Viking, 1989); Peters, *The American Speakership.*
32. Strategic choices made by the White House clearly exacerbated this problem.
33. Kathryn Pearson, "Party Discipline in the Contemporary Congress: Rewarding Loyalty in Theory and in Practice," Ph.D. diss., University of California, Berkeley, 2004.
34. James L. Sundquist, *Decline and Resurgence of Congress* (Washington, D.C.: Brookings Institution Press, 1981); and Lawrence C. Dodd, "Congress and the Quest for Power," in *Congress Reconsidered,* 1st ed., ed. Lawrence C. Dodd and Bruce I. Oppenheimer (New York: Praeger, 1977).
35. James A. Barnes, "Political Analysis: The GOP's Shifting Terrain," *National Journal,* November 11, 2000.
36. William Schneider, "A Popularity Contest," *National Journal,* November 16, 2002.
37. Mark Wegner, "House Leadership—Hastert: GOP to Take Political Offensive," *National Journal's CongressDaily AM,* online version, March 15, 2004.
38. Jackie Koszczuk and Jonathan Allen, "Late-Night Medicare Vote Drama Triggers Some Unexpected Alliances," *CQ Weekly,* November 29, 2003, 2958.
39. Ibid.
40. Wegner, "Health—Night of House Drama Yields a Narrow Medicare Victory."
41. Quoted in Robert G. Kaiser, "Congress-s-s-s: That Giant Hissing Sound You Hear Is Capitol Hill Giving Up Its Clout," *Washington Post,* March 14, 2004, B1.
42. See David R. Mayhew, *Divided We Govern: Party Control, Lawmaking, and Investigations, 1946–1990* (New Haven: Yale University Press, 1991); and Eric Schickler, *Disjointed Pluralism: Institutional Innovation and the Development of the U.S. Congress* (Princeton: Princeton University Press, 2001), Chap. 4.
43. As of August 2004, the only two Republicans to sign the petition were Ralph Hall of Texas and Rodney Alexander of Louisiana. Both were Democrats when they signed but subsequently switched parties.

10. Obstruction and Leadership in the U.S. Senate

C. Lawrence Evans and Daniel Lipinski

In April 2004, the U.S. Senate was mired in conflict over must-pass legislation to temporarily extend the federal highway program. The political stakes were high. Unless the measure was signed by President George W. Bush by midnight on April 30, the highway and traffic safety agencies of the federal government would be shut down, triggering thousands of layoffs across the country. One observer likened the scene to "a spaghetti Western–style standoff, with a damsel in distress—surface transportation programs at the Department of Transportation—tied to the tracks."[1]

Why were Senators at loggerheads over the highway program, which deals with issues that usually are characterized by bipartisan accommodation and pork? The impasse came to a head on April 29, when Sen. Christopher Bond, R-Mo., requested unanimous consent for the chamber to appoint conferees to bargain with the House over a comprehensive, six-year reauthorization of the nation's mass transit programs. Unanimous consent agreements are used in the Senate to set the terms of debate for most chamber business and are only binding if no member objects. On the highway reauthorization, Democratic leaders believed that the conference committee, if appointed, would capitulate to White House demands for spending cuts. As a result, Minority Whip Harry Reid, D-Nev., objected to Bond's request. He asked for unanimous consent that the chamber instead take up a temporary measure that would have kept federal highway programs running until a deal could be cut on the broader reauthorization. In anticipation of Reid's move, however, Bond earlier had placed a "hold" on the temporary extension bill. The hold is an informal practice through which individual senators can signal party leaders that they will attempt to block floor action on a matter pending before the Senate. Indeed, Bond followed up on his hold by objecting on the floor to Reid's request for unanimous consent, bringing chamber action on the temporary extension bill to a halt. Bond's gambit? Agree to the appointment of conferees on the highway reauthorization, he demanded, or he would block a short-term extension of the program.

Majority Leader Bill Frist, R-Tenn., however, preferred a less-confrontational approach to bargaining with the Democrats over the highway reauthorization. Later that day, Frist was able to convince Bond to withdraw his objection to the temporary extension in exchange for a pledge that Republican leaders would schedule a cloture vote the following week to publicize Democratic intransigence on the broader bill. The "damsel in distress" was released from the tracks. But the procedural wrangling over the matter illustrates the central role that obstructionist tactics play in the modern Senate. During the 108th Congress (2003–2004), Democratic leaders regularly blocked floor action on major legislation until Majority Leader Frist allowed them to offer nongermane amendments of importance to key party constituencies, such as organized labor. Members of the minority party routinely stymied the confirmation of the Bush administration's judicial and executive branch nominees. Indeed, Minority Leader Thomas Daschle, D-S.D., temporarily put a freeze on all judicial nominees in spring 2004. As the fall 2004 elections approached, obstructionism within the Senate extended to traditionally noncontroversial matters. Senate Democrats believed that they had been shut out of negotiations the previous year over a landmark Medicare bill and a major rewrite of the nation's energy laws. As a result, Daschle began blocking the creation of conference committees to bargain with the House over the final versions of legislation unless guarantees were made that Democratic views would be fully considered. That was the reason why Reid objected to the unanimous consent request on the highway reauthorization. And much of the obstructionism that occurred during the 108th Congress did not relate to party strategizing and received almost no publicity. Working independently of their leaders, individual lawmakers from both sides of the partisan aisle used holds and other dilatory tactics on hundreds of items to promote their personal policy goals and the parochial interests of their constituents.

In the modern Senate, the job of party leader can only be understood from the perspective of the rampant obstructionism that characterizes—some would say defines—the consideration of chamber business. As a senior aide to Majority Leader Frist put it, "Obstructionism is woven into the fabric of things. The leadership deals with it on a day-to-day, even a minute-to-minute basis. The new style is mostly old tactics used more often and in a more sophisticated and refined way. But you can't overestimate the importance of it. There are offshoots of obstructionism every day."[2] What precisely is this new style of Senate obstructionism, why did it emerge, and what are the consequences for leadership and deliberation? The main procedural ingredients—the filibuster, unanimous consent agreements, cloture motions, and the hold—are closely related and evolved over time as institutional adaptations to a unique feature of the chamber's standing rules: the lack of a motion on the previous question. Indeed, the practice of the hold, which often is vilified by politicians and pundits as an instrument of delay, is best viewed as an informational device that helps chamber leaders deal with the pervasiveness of dilatory behavior. Among other effects, the primacy of obstructionism in the Senate conditions the way that leaders bargain, and it increases the incidence of policy parochialism and partisan position taking in the chamber, potentially undermining the quality of deliberation.

The Filibuster and Its Offshoots

Party leaders in the Senate fulfill a number of important tasks. They coordinate the flow of legislation within the chamber; manage the internal partisan bureaucracy; bargain with House leaders and executive branch officials; and increasingly take the lead in formulating and publicizing their party's legislative program.[3] In performing these duties, the Senate majority leader lacks most of the procedural advantages afforded to the Speaker of the House. The central prerogatives of leadership in Congress relate to the floor agenda. The Speaker has effective control over the House Rules Committee and through it can set the terms of debate on the floor. House Rule 16 stipulates that amendments must be germane to the underlying measure, adding an important dose of predictability to chamber business. In contrast, the agenda-setting powers of the Senate majority leader are severely constrained. By chamber precedent, the majority leader receives priority recognition on the floor. But unless there are sixty votes to invoke cloture, the right to filibuster a bill or nomination into oblivion gives rank-and-file senators (especially members of the minority party) enormous leverage. Most business in the Senate is conducted by unanimous consent, which greatly empowers individual members. And there is no general germaneness requirement in Senate rules, further limiting the ability of majority party leaders to manage legislative action on the floor. Little wonder, then, that Senate leaders have been described as "janitors for an untidy chamber."[4]

Many aspects of Senate procedure give an advantage to political minorities, but the ability to filibuster bills and nominations is the central minority prerogative. Interestingly, the filibuster (often referred to as "extended debate") was almost certainly an unintended consequence of an early effort to streamline chamber rules and make the Senate a more efficient legislative body. Extended debate is feasible in the Senate because the chamber, unlike the House, lacks a "motion on the previous question"—the parliamentary device that representative assemblies generally use to proceed to a decision on the underlying matter. The rules of the early Senate included a previous question motion, but it was dropped in 1806 at the suggestion of Vice President Aaron Burr, largely because members believed that the motion was superfluous.[5] Perhaps the most important rule change in congressional history, then, was made without any significant understanding of the long-term repercussions. The result? For most legislation and all nominations considered by the Senate, any debatable motion can be filibustered.[6] Indeed, the tactic can be used at six principal junctures in the life of a single bill—the motion to bring legislation to the floor, during the amendment process, on the bill itself, and on three motions relating to the creation of a conference committee.[7]

Although the abolition of the motion on the previous question created the possibility of extended debate as a consequential tactic, filibustering did not become a prominent part of the Senate legislative process until shortly after the Civil War, when the workload and policymaking role of the chamber grew dramatically. By the end of the nineteenth century, the tactic was employed on some of the most important legislation before Congress. The first notable filibuster concerned an 1841 initiative by President Andrew Jackson to establish a national bank. Other significant filibusters from the era dealt with statehood for Kansas (1856), the "Force Act" mandating the federal supervision of elections (1890–1891), and efforts to repeal the "Silver Act" (1893). Between 1879 and the adoption of the cloture procedure in 1917, thirty filibusters occurred and over half of them resulted in the defeat of the targeted measure.[8]

The mounting importance of the filibuster coincided with the early institutionalization of the central mechanism for coordination in the Senate—the unanimous consent agreement (UCA). UCAs, often called "time agreements," are a device by which senators unanimously waive the standing rules of their chamber and instead opt for specific limitations for considering a pending matter. On major bills, Senate action may be structured by dozens or even hundreds of separate UCAs, including agreements about when to bring legislation to the floor, which amendments will be permissible, the order for considering amendments, when votes on amendments will occur, and the day and time for a decision on final passage. While the simpler UCAs (perhaps dealing with a single amendment or granting time for members to speak) are informally devised by rank-and-file senators and often emerge spontaneously on the floor, the more complex agreements are carefully negotiated by party leaders and key members of the committee of jurisdiction. Although an objection from just one senator can block a UCA, these procedural pacts should not be viewed primarily as yet another mechanism through which individual members can exercise their remarkable prerogatives on the floor. Instead, UCAs emerged as a *leadership tool* in the 1880s after a succession of attempts to curtail obstructionism via formal rule changes met with failure. By contemporary standards, the early UCAs were relatively informal, and there was no means for enforcement beyond the desire of individual senators to maintain their reputations for reciprocal cooperation.[9]

Further expansions in the Senate workload and continued use of the filibuster set the stage for two critical rule changes during the administration of President Woodrow Wilson. In 1913, UCAs were made binding orders of the Senate, providing an institutionalized mechanism for enforcement and significantly increasing their value as a leadership tool. Then, in 1917, the Senate adopted Rule 22, which enables a supermajority of senators to invoke cloture and end a filibuster. The rules changes were sparked by two different policy disputes on the Senate floor, but the temporal proximity of their adoption reflects the close relationship that exists between the filibuster and the process of unanimous consent. Indeed, the two aspects of Senate decision making are best viewed as flip sides of the same coin. Senate leaders have come to rely on UCAs rather than majority rule, or some other mechanism, to structure floor action precisely because the filibuster gives individual senators the power (potentially) to bring chamber business to a halt.

Since 1917 the number of votes necessary to invoke cloture has been altered from two-thirds of those present and voting (the 1917 level) to two-thirds of the full membership (in 1949), back to two-thirds of senators present and voting (in 1959), and then to the current level of sixty votes (in 1975).[10] From 1917 to the early 1970s, filibusters were used fairly sporadically. Both chambers of Congress were dominated by a conservative coalition of Republicans and southern Democrats, and with the important exception of civil rights measures there was little need for the opponents of policy change to resort to extended debate. During this period, Senate leaders also stepped up their reliance on UCAs as a management tool. Between February 1927 and August 1947, for instance, at least 120 motions were made on the Senate floor to limit or close debate, with over three-quarters coming from the majority leader.[11] In a July 1952 floor speech, Wayne Morse, R-Ore., one of the great mavericks of Senate history, underscored the chamber's growing reliance on UCAs: "In my judgment," Morse complained, "the growing tendency in the Senate of the United States almost to insist upon the transaction of business by unanimous consent agreements is doing great injury to the procedures of the Senate. . . .under the modern, postwar practice, unanimous-consent agreements are made to close debate on almost every major bill."[12]

In the 1960s, a significant transformation of the broader political environment helped produce a sharp increase in the use of dilatory tactics in the Senate, and chamber leaders responded with further innovations in the agenda-setting process.[13] The enfranchisement of black voters altered the face of southern politics, breaking up the conservative coalition in Congress. The scope of federal policy increased markedly with the passage of Lyndon Johnson's "Great Society" program and several important statutes enacted during the first term of Richard Nixon. These new programs were the impetus behind the creation of a large number of advocacy coalitions, dramatically increasing the array of interest group pressures confronting the Senate.[14] During this period, both political parties also shifted to mass participation primaries for selecting candidates for the national legislature, spurring individual lawmakers to create their own campaign organizations and to be less reliant on party officials at home and in Washington. One consequence of these changes in the political environment was an explosion of obstructionism in the Senate. By the mid-1970s, most members of the Senate were making regular use of dilatory tactics, and few aspects of the chamber agenda were left untouched.

Once again, changes in the use of the filibuster led to compensatory alterations in the process of unanimous consent. Here the key innovator was Robert C. Byrd, D-W.Va., who served as majority whip from 1971 to 1976 and majority leader from 1977 to 1981. Faced with mounting obstructionism from both sides of the partisan aisle, Byrd began crafting highly complex UCAs that dealt with a host of tactical exigencies.[15] In the early 1970s, Byrd also introduced the "track system" to the Senate.[16] If one measure is derailed by obstructionist tactics, the chamber can shift to an alternative "track" and proceed with a different item. And early in the decade, Democratic and Republican leaders implemented a systematic process for communicating and monitoring possible objections to UCAs—the Senate hold. The hold process begins when a senator (either directly or through staff) informs the majority or minority leader (depending on the senator's party affiliation) that he or she intends to object to a UCA. Staff to that leader mark down the objection on a master copy of the Senate Calendar, which lists all items that are pending for floor consideration. As demonstrated by Senator Bond's hold on the highway extension measure, party leaders have come to take holds very seriously, and some observers have even labeled the practice "the silent filibuster."[17] The impact of a hold, however, can vary significantly, depending on the nature of the objection, the credibility of the threat, and the importance of the targeted item to the leadership.

As early as the mid-1970s, then, the main procedural components of the rampant obstructionism that we now observe in the Senate were already in place. The remaining ingredient—intense party polarization—began to emerge during the Reagan administration and became a central feature of congressional policymaking during the 1990s. Although individual lawmakers continue to use obstructionist tactics to promote their personal agendas, Senate leaders now routinely employ filibusters and cloture motions for explicitly partisan purposes. Party-line votes on cloture motions, for instance, have become the norm. In 1981–1982, nineteen attempts at cloture reached the roll call stage, and of these, eleven (57.9 percent) were successful. In contrast, from January 2003 through mid-May 2004, there were thirty votes on cloture in the Senate, of which just eight (20.8 percent) received the sixty votes necessary to bring debate to a close. Almost all of the failed cloture attempts in 2003–2004 were party-line votes, with a cohesive Democratic minority blocking Republican attempts to pass bills and nominations on the floor.

Over time, there also has been an increase in member frustrations with the hold. In 1982, Majority Leader Howard Baker, R-Tenn., warned his colleagues that the practice was complicating the timely consideration of legislation and pledged that holds would no longer be treated as de facto vetoes. By most accounts, however, the practice changed little in the years that followed.[18] During the Reagan administration, Democrat Howard Metzenbaum, Ohio, implemented a formal clearance process that was rooted in the hold. Unless an item was cleared by Metzenbaum or his staff, he would object to all related UCA requests on the floor.[19] In the 1990s, Senate leaders repeatedly attempted to clamp down on anonymous holds, in which the names of the potential objectors are kept secret by the relevant party leadership. But these secret holds continued to be an important part of the process. According to Ron Wyden, D-Ore., a leader in the effort to abolish anonymous holds, "One of the Senate's most popular procedures cannot be found anywhere in the United States Constitution or in the Senate rules. It is one of the most powerful weapons that any Senator can wield in this body. And it is even more potent when it is invisible. The procedure is popularly known as the 'hold.'"[20] Or as Senator Daschle once put it: "There are holds on holds on holds. There are so many holds, it looks like a mud wresting match. I think we're stuck in the mud."[21]

Senate Obstructionism: A Look behind the Curtain

Although filibusters are common in the contemporary Senate, the actual incidence of extended debate constitutes only the tip of the obstructionist iceberg. The *threat* of obstruction can have a significant effect on chamber business even in situations when no filibuster actually occurs. To understand the strategic use of obstruction as a bargaining tactic, then, we need to systematically examine the practice of the hold. Unfortunately, very little is known about the practice because holds are treated as confidential by Senate leaders. As Wyden's comments indicate, the chief sponsors of a bill may not know who has placed a hold on their handiwork. However, we were able to gather from the personal papers of former Republican leader Howard Baker information pertaining to almost one thousand holds that were placed by GOP senators during the 95th (1977–1978) and 97th (1981–1982) Congresses.[22] These records are the only systematic evidence available about the hold. The Baker data can shed valuable light on the practice during the period when it was first implemented. And the timing of these records enables us to draw some tentative distinctions about the use of holds by majority and minority party members. During 1977–1978, Republicans were the minority party in the Senate, and Baker was minority leader. In 1981–1982, the GOP controlled the chamber, and Baker was majority leader.

What do these data reveal about use of the hold as a bargaining tactic? For one thing, it is apparent that the practice encompasses a wide range of requests to the leadership, reflecting different gradations of potential obstruction. Among other requests, the hundreds of hold letters sent by Republicans to Baker in 1981–1982 include the following:

- Explicit requests for a hold, but with no additional information
- Requests that no UCAs be entered into or that a bill not be brought up
- Requests that a bill not be taken up until a certain date
- Requests that a bill not be taken up until some action occurred
- Requests for notification about negotiations for a UCA or the scheduling of a bill
- Statements reserving the right to offer amendments or object to UCAs
- Requests to be consulted on any motions
- Requests that earlier holds or requests for information be disregarded

Although hold requests clearly come in a variety of forms, they can be usefully collapsed into a threefold categorization scheme: (1) requests for an unrestricted hold; (2) requests for a temporary hold of some kind; and (3) requests for notification or consultation. On Capitol Hill, all three categories are commonly referred to as "holds," but they clearly differ from one another, and, not surprisingly, the leadership interprets them differently.[23] Unrestricted and temporary holds are explicit threats to block a bill or nomination. In contrast, requests for notification—occasionally called "Mae West" holds ("Come up and see me sometime")—are usually requests by a member to be kept in the decision-making loop.[24]

The frequency of the different kinds of requests for the two Baker Congresses is summarized in Table 10-1. Notice that the total number decreased from 1977–1978 to 1981–1982. The reduction probably occurred because of the shift in 1981 to a Republican majority and a floor agenda more congenial to GOP interests. The more striking change observable in Table 10-1, however, is the

Table 10-1 Frequency of Different Forms of the Hold, Senate Republicans, 1977–1978 and 1981–1982

Type of Hold	1977–1978	1981–1982
Unrestricted hold	367 (68.5%)	216 (45.1%)
Temporary hold	33 (6.2%)	26 (5.4%)
Request for notification	136 (25.4%)	237 (49.5%)
Total	536	479

Source: Compiled from data in the Howard H. Baker Jr., Collection, Special Collections Library, James D. Hoskins Library, University of Tennessee, Knoxville.

marked decrease in the percentage of requests that were unrestricted holds, as opposed to requests for notification. This difference almost certainly derives from the 1981 shift to majority status. With a GOP majority, it was only natural that fewer measures on the agenda would diverge from mainstream Republican preferences, reducing the need to place holds. The Baker data also demonstrate that as early as the mid-1970s most senators were making use of unrestricted holds. In 1977–1978, the typical Republican senator placed 9.7 holds, and only three senators did not use the tactic at all. Still, there was considerable variation among members. James McClure, R-Idaho, for instance, was an extreme outlier, accounting for ninety holds. At the time, McClure was chair of the Senate Steering Committee, an informal caucus of conservative Republicans that served (and continues to serve) as a clearinghouse of sorts for GOP holds. In 1981–1982, the average number of unrestricted holds per Republican senator fell to 4.1, reflecting the shift to Republican control. But the vast majority of Republicans (all but nine) still placed holds on legislation.

Beyond majority or minority status, what other factors influence how often senators place holds? To explore this question, we conducted a multivariate analysis of hold use during the two Congresses for which systematic records are available. Of particular interest are five factors: ideology, membership on the Senate Steering Committee, seniority, the proximity of reelection, and electoral vulnerability.[25] As indicated in Figure 10-1, there is a strong relationship between ideology and hold usage, with the nature of the relationship varying in important ways across 1977–1978 and 1981–1982. The measure of ideology is the DW-NOMINATE value, which places individual legislators on a liberal-to-conservative scale depending on the roll call votes they cast in a given Congress. The scale ranges from −1, *very liberal,* to +1, *very conservative,* and is the most widely used indicator of the ideological preferences of legislators.[26] Figure 10-1 portrays the number of unrestricted holds that we would expect from GOP senators at each point along the ideological scale, based on the results of the multivariate analysis and controlling for other factors. For 1977–1978, the number of holds increases the more conservative the senator. During that Congress, Majority Leader Byrd and his Democratic colleagues sought to advance an ambitious legislative agenda

Figure 10-1 Relationship between the Number of Holds and Member Ideology, Senate Republicans, 1977–1978 and 1981–1982

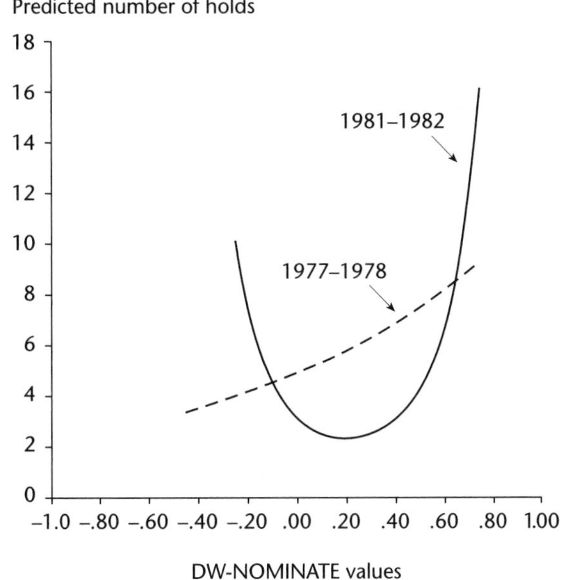

that featured such Carter administration priorities as a labor law revision and a sweeping energy reform bill. For the most part, the Democratic majority wanted to move public policy in a liberal direction, and the level of opposition among Republican senators increased the further a member's preferences were from the liberal end of the ideological spectrum. Not surprisingly, it was the more conservative legislators who disproportionately used the hold.

In 1981–1982, Ronald Reagan was in the White House and Republicans had assumed majority status in the Senate. The Senate floor agenda moved sharply to the right. As the new majority leader, Howard Baker largely functioned as Reagan's legislative field marshal within the chamber. Notice that the relationship between ideology and hold usage for this Congress was U-shaped. Holds were disproportionately placed by the most liberal and the most conservative wings of the Republican Conference. Baker was attempting to advance legislation that reflected his party's ideological mainstream. Members near the party's ideological center were least likely to be confronted by measures they opposed and had little need for the hold. Liberal Republicans, such as Robert Packwood, Ore., and Lowell Weicker, Conn., perceived that the legislative agenda was moving excessively to the right, and they used the hold in opposition to certain conservative initiatives. The far right wing of the party also made regular use of the hold. Conservatives, such as Jesse Helms, N.C., and Don Nickles, Okla., employed the tactic to block initiatives that appealed to Senate moderates, as well as on parochial measures that they viewed as wasteful. A decade or more before the 1990s rise in party polarization, then, there was a strong partisan and ideological cast to obstructionism in the Senate. And the nature of the challenge that obstructionism created for Senate leaders differed dramatically depending on whether the party was in the majority or the minority.

The partisan-ideological basis of Senate obstructionism also is apparent in the role of the Steering Committee, an organized faction within the Republican Conference.[27] Our multivariate analysis indicates that members of the group were disproportionately likely to place holds, especially during 1977–1978.[28] The Steering Committee helped pioneer use of the hold and other obstructionist tactics as a minority party strategy for impeding the majority party agenda. Majority Leader Byrd remarked at the time that 1978 was a pivotal year for the use of the filibuster and related tactics: "It used to be that [the filibuster] was resorted to infrequently and on the grave national issues, mostly on civil rights [but] now it's just resorted to promiscuously, I think."[29] In 1977–1978, the Democrats had the sixty-vote supermajority necessary to invoke cloture without GOP support, but the presence of the policy divisions that characterize most partisan majorities often provided Republicans with the leverage necessary to impede legislation. As chair of the Steering Committee during the late 1970s, James McClure served as the primary vehicle for much of this obstructionism. During the 95th Congress, he placed holds on ninety different pieces of legislation—far more than any other Republican member. In part, the GOP reliance on obstructionist tactics reflected the small size and relative weakness of the Republican Conference following Watergate and the 1976 elections. As McClure observed, "The more threatened we are, the more militant we must become to protect ourselves."[30] McClure's tactics also were a response to efforts by Majority Leader Byrd to be more aggressive in bringing Democratic measures to the floor. McClure summed up the GOP strategy on obstructionism: "We can make life unpleasant enough for other people that they'll wish they'd been more accommodating."[31]

Along with partisan and ideological imperatives, our multivariate analysis indicates that certain other factors also can have an impact on hold use. In 1977–1978, there was no statistically discernible relationship between seniority and holds. But during 1981–1982, more-senior members were disproportionately likely to place unrestricted holds on legislation and much less likely to submit requests for notification.[32] The higher percentage of unrestricted holds from senior members may indicate that there is a learning curve to obstructionism: Experience in the chamber may make members more effective at using their procedural prerogatives. Requests for notification, in contrast, are primarily informational. Senior members may be less reliant on such requests to ensure that their interests are considered in the negotiations that occur between chamber leaders. The multivariate analysis also provides some evidence that senators are more likely to use holds the nearer they are to a reelection campaign and that members who are electorally endangered are particularly likely to place holds.[33] Senators apparently believe that the hold can be used as a bargaining chip to help pass items important to their constituents.

Do holds routinely kill legislation, and is the impact of a hold particularly devastating toward the end of a Congress? Here the results are striking. During 1977–1978, 73.8 percent of the holds placed on legislation (and here we are referring solely to unrestricted holds, not temporary holds or requests for notification) targeted measures that eventually were passed by the chamber in some form. For 1981–1982, the "kill ratio" was much higher: Only 27.7 percent of the holds targeted items that eventually passed the chamber.[34] Holds from majority party members, it appears, are substantially more consequential than are holds from the minority party. During 1977–1978, Majority Leader Byrd routinely brought up legislation on the floor in the presence of Republican holds, and he was usually successful in securing passage. As majority leader, Howard Baker was far more deferential to Republican holds. It is noteworthy, however, that even in 1981–1982 over one-quarter of the measures targeted with unrestricted holds still passed the Senate. Either the members placing these holds were accommodated in some way prior to floor action, or the underlying matter was of sufficient importance to the majority party that Baker brought it up anyway, and the "holders" were unwilling or unable to block final passage. Based on when the hold letters were sent to the leadership and when holds were initially placed on the marked calendars, there also appears to be an increase in hold use as scheduling deadlines loom. In both Congresses for which records are available, there was a steep rise in holds in the months preceding the end of the Congress. From August to October 1978, Republican members placed almost one hundred holds, and more than 40 percent of the affected measures did not pass the chamber. During August to October 1982, there were forty-five new Republicans holds, and about 70 percent of the targeted bills died on the floor.[35]

Interviews that we have conducted with floor staff of current Senate leaders reveal that the hold process has not changed fundamentally since Baker's time in the leadership. A longtime aide to the Republican Conference summed up current practices:

> We still keep track of holds with marked Senate calendars. . . . The quantity of holds hasn't changed all that much since the 1980s, although the letters are more carefully worded now; fewer use the word "hold" because it has become controversial. The big difference is whether you are in the majority or the minority. There are more holds from the minority. The number isn't twice as much but there are a lot more. . . . Holds help the leadership by providing information. Opponents are less able to hide in the weeds. If a bill is a priority for Frist or the conference, it will get scheduled with or without holds. The impact of a hold is up to the leadership.

Even unrestricted holds are no more—and no less—than a threat to object to a UCA. If a bill is not a majority party priority, or if there are many holds and time on the floor is scarce, the majority leader may choose not to bring up the targeted measure. On the other hand, if Senate passage of a bill or nomination is important to the majority party, then the presence of a few holds probably will not keep the leadership from scheduling the matter for floor consideration. The majority leader will bring the matter to the floor and deal with potential objections as they arise. Senate leaders may also respond to a hold by encouraging the chief sponsors and opponents of the targeted bill to work out their differences, and then, once an agreement is achieved, proceed with floor action. The impact of threatened obstruction, in other words, depends on the bargaining context and the strategic response of the leadership.

Implications for Bargaining

How does the primacy of obstructionism in the modern Senate influence the process of bargaining? First, the strategic use of filibusters, cloture motions, and holds significantly *delays* decision making in the Senate. House leaders, for example, were able to process the highway reauthorization in a relatively expeditious fashion during the 108th Congress. The measure was reported to the floor by the Transportation and Infrastructure Committee on March 24, 2004. On April 1, the Rules Committee reported the special rule for the legislation, which delineated all of the permissible floor amendments, the order for considering the amendments, and the time allocated for debating each (just ten minutes for all but two of them). Floor action began later that day, and the bill passed the chamber on April 2. Speaker Dennis Hastert, R-Ill., had considerable discretion about when to proceed to conference committee negotiations with the other body. In the Senate, legislation to reauthorize the highway program was reported from committee in January 2004. Initial floor action began on February 3 and continued for over a week. Dozens of UCAs and two separate cloture motions were necessary to bring the matter to a vote. Following initial passage, Democratic leaders blocked the appointment of conferees for over three months. Relative to the House, then, bargaining in the Senate is especially prone to delay because of the ability of individual members to engage in obstructionism. Delay in turn can result in fewer initiatives' passing.

Second, because of the minority's ability to block UCAs and credibly threaten to filibuster, *bipartisan leadership bargaining* is the normal order of business in the chamber. For over two decades, the Senate majority party has lacked the sixty votes necessary to invoke cloture without some support from the minority. In the House, it is not unusual for many months to pass without any direct communication between the Speaker and the minority leader. In the Senate, the majority and minority leaders and their staffs have to interact meaningfully almost on a daily basis. Top aides to Frist and Daschle meet early each week when the Senate is in session to discuss which bills can be easily brought to the floor by unanimous consent and which matters will require more extensive negotiations. On significant or controversial issues, the leaders themselves are often the key bargainers, along with the chair and ranking minority member of the relevant committee or subcommittee. Frist and Daschle played critical roles, for instance, in crafting the agreement that broke the logjam on the highway reauthorization. Such leader-to-leader bargaining is commonplace in the Senate but relatively rare in the House, largely because of the procedural differences between the two chambers.

In recent years, much of the leadership bargaining over procedure has concerned efforts by the two parties to promote their respective message agendas, which touch on the "issues, themes, and policy symbols that legislators believe will generate a positive response to their party among voters."[36] In the House, the Speaker's control over the Rules Committee makes the floor an effective arena for publicizing the message priorities of the majority party. The ability that all senators have to engage in obstructionism and to offer nongermane amendments makes the Senate floor the ideal forum for message politics by the minority. Often, the procedural wrangling that occurs over message is driven by minority party attempts to secure floor consideration of measures important to that party's core constituencies, with majority party leaders attempting to minimize such opportunities and keep the floor agenda focused squarely on the policy priorities of the majority. In February 2004, for example, Republican leaders sought floor action on legislation that would bar lawsuits against firearms manufacturers by victims of gun violence. The measure appealed strongly to the GOP base. Democrats refused to allow floor action to begin on the gun bill until they were guaranteed the right to offer an amendment extending emergency unemployment benefits to laid-off workers, a proposal that was important to core Democratic constituencies.

Third, the primacy of obstructionism creates incentives for *preconsensus,* that is, for Senate leaders to work out key differences about procedure and substance prior to floor action. The Senate floor traditionally has been less scripted and more deliberative than the House, with policy agreements sometimes emerging spontaneously during the course of debate. The post-1970 explosion in obstructionism, however, has heightened the importance of crafting deals on procedure and substance prior to formal action. Often this preconsensus concerns the parameters for bargaining rather than the details of legislation. The main policy disputes on the highway reauthorization, for instance, were about funding levels. Senate Democrats believed that their Republican colleagues would not fight for the $318 billion authorization in the Senate-passed measure and would instead acquiesce to White House demands that spending not exceed $256 billion.[37] As a result, they refused to allow the conference to proceed without what Daschle termed "an agreement through conference." He wanted a public pledge from Frist that all of the provisions in the Senate-passed measure that had received bipartisan backing would be included in any deal cut with the House or the Bush administration. After months of partisan posturing, Frist and Daschle agreed on guidelines for bargaining over the highway bill. Frist described the arrangement in a May 2004 colloquy on the Senate floor:

> The transportation bill we passed this year was a model of bipartisan cooperation that was marked by good faith on both sides. . . . I have spoken to Senator Inhofe, who will chair the conference. He has agreed that he will not pursue a conclusion to the conference, nor sign any conference report that would alter the text of [the Senate-passed bill] in a way that undermines the bipartisan working relationship that has existed in the Senate.[38]

In response, Daschle noted, "Our side understands that changes will have to be made, and we are not entering this process demanding a specific outcome on any provision. Instead we are asking [that] any changes [to the bill] be the result of the mutual agreement of the lead Senate conferees acting in good faith."[39] It is difficult to imagine Speaker Hastert and Minority Leader Nancy Pelosi, D-Calif., striking an analogous "good faith" agreement on the House side.

Fourth, in recent Congresses the high incidence of obstructionism in the Senate, especially by the minority party on party message issues, has resulted in a more *tactical use of cloture* by majority party leaders. Occasionally, the majority leader will file a cloture motion prior to the commencement of floor action to test whether the votes are there (if necessary) to end debate. Rule 22 also stipulates that all amendments considered after cloture is invoked must be germane to the underlying measure. By invoking cloture early on a bill, the majority leader can thwart attempts by the minority to "change the subject" by offering floor amendments that highlight the minority's issue priorities. In 2004, for example, Senate Republicans were able to invoke cloture on an Internet tax bill earlier than Democratic leaders preferred, precluding action on certain minority party priorities during the floor amendment process.[40] And if Frist had been able to invoke cloture on the motion to proceed to the gun liability measure, the Democrats would have been unable under the rules to offer their unemployment compensation amendment. By filing for cloture and bringing the motion to a vote, the majority leader also can force minority party members to take a public position on an issue that otherwise might not come to a roll call because of minority obstructionism. Many of the cloture motions voted on during 2003–2004 had little chance of adoption but instead were aimed at publicizing what Republicans viewed as dilatory behavior by Senate Democrats. Repeated cloture votes were conducted on high-profile judicial nominees (seven on the circuit court nomination of Miguel Estrada) and on selected GOP message priorities (three on the energy bill).

Fifth, the incidence of obstruction fundamentally alters *endgame politics* in the Senate. As the end of a Congress nears on the House side, the majority leadership usually implements so-called martial law procedures that streamline the legislative process on the floor. For instance, when the leadership wants to pass a special rule (to govern floor action on a particular measure) on the same day that the procedure is reported by the Rules Committee, House rules require a two-thirds supermajority for the special rule to be binding. The two-thirds requirement generally is waived, however, during the closing days of a Congress, facilitating leadership efforts to expedite the flow of legislation. Endgame bargaining is very different in the Senate. If anything, the procedural prerogatives of individual senators are more effective for killing legislation in the closing days or weeks of a Congress. As we have seen, the number of holds rises during the endgame, and the presence of one or two holds may be enough to convince the leadership that a measure does not warrant the time necessary to counter obstructionism on the floor. The time constraints of the endgame also create incentives for the proponents of a targeted bill to compromise with the holders—otherwise, their handiwork may not see the light of day. The relative effectiveness of obstructionism during the endgame also induces congressional leaders to make greater use of omnibus bills (mega bills that are aggregations of many freestanding measures). By placing a targeted item in a larger package, the leadership can reduce the likelihood that the item will be singled out for obstruction.

Sixth, the primacy of obstructionism in the Senate alters the nature of *bicameral and interbranch bargaining.* Senate conferees, for example, can credibly claim that the rules of their chamber enable a minority of members to block a conference report when the report is brought up for a final vote on the floor. The conferees from the House may want to include a provision in a conference report that already has been targeted by a hold in the Senate. The presence of the hold can provide Senate conferees with the leverage necessary to keep such items out of the conference report, thereby augmenting the chamber's bargaining power relative to the House. Senate obstructionism also can alter bargaining dynamics with the executive branch. The agreement between Frist and Daschle for handling final negotiations over the highway bill is an example. Their accord reduced the probability that the bargaining outcome would diverge from the Senate-passed legislation toward language preferred by the Bush administration.

Seventh, much of the obstructionism that occurs in the Senate is really a form of *hostage taking.* A large proportion of the holds placed on bills and nominations are so-called hostage or retaliatory holds in which a senator will threaten to block an item unless he or she is accommodated in some way on a different matter. In 1998, the late Sen. Paul Wellstone, D-Minn., learned that a hold had been placed on legislation he supported to name the U.S. post office building in St. Paul after one of his political heroes, former senator Eugene McCarthy. Who would oppose the naming of an obscure federal building after a long-retired former senator? By most accounts, Kay Bailey Hutchison, R-Texas, had placed the hold in retaliation for Wellstone's opposition to a Hutchison-backed initiative to create a three-state nuclear waste compact important to her constituents. Wellstone's response? He placed his own holds on thirteen other measures that would have renamed post offices after prominent people in other states. As he put it, "Everyone knows that I've got holds on the other bills. I don't intend to back down. That is what you do when you're faced with this kind of situation. All of these bills are going to pass or none of them are."[41] Obstructionist tactics, then, can be used to leverage concessions on unrelated matters, further complicating the coalition-building efforts of chamber leaders.

Eighth, the most significant and pervasive effect of obstructionism within the Senate is to make the floor legislative process highly *unpredictable.* In the House, the majority leadership is seldom caught by surprise by developments on the floor. The special rules that the Rules Committee crafts essentially determine the course of floor action on most major bills. Occasionally, the leadership will lose control over the floor agenda because of the emergence of a cross-partisan coalition of minority party members and moderate elements of the majority party, but such occurrences are exceedingly rare (managed care reform in 1999 and campaign finance reform in 2002 are recent examples). On the Senate side, the minority party has ample opportunity to catch the majority leader by surprise. Indeed, the majority leader can be blindsided by members of his own party. The UCAs that structure legislative action are usually devised in a piecemeal and ad hoc manner. It is not always clear when opponents of a measure will follow up on a filibuster threat. Nongermane amendments can be used to alter the terms of debate in significant and unexpected ways. The tactical challenges that regularly confront the Senate majority leader, in short, are far more daunting than are those that confront majority party leaders in the House.

Conclusion

The procedural privileges extended to individual senators undercut the central prerogative of leadership in a representative assembly—control over the chamber agenda. As a result, majority party leaders have developed strategies and tools to help them maintain a semblance of control. The unanimous consent process and the hold both emerged as devices by which Senate leaders can cope with obstructionism. UCAs first came into regular use in the late 1800s, as filibustering became an accepted floor tactic. The incidence of filibusters and threatened filibusters increased dramatically during the 1970s. In response, Senate leaders developed the hold process and the track system and for a time made use of more elaborate UCAs. Holds, as we have seen, serve as an early warning system by which the leadership monitors potential obstructionism on the floor. From the 1980s onward, the Senate grew increasingly polarized along partisan lines. Not surprisingly, the use of filibusters, cloture motions, and holds took on an increasingly partisan cast, which in turn affected the bargaining tactics of chamber leaders in important ways.

One result, many observers claim, has been a decline in the quality of deliberation in the Senate. In a May 2004 floor statement, Robert C. Byrd, a forty-year veteran of the Senate, asserted, "This great deliberative body . . . has become a factory that manufactures sound-bite votes that make great fodder for 30-second political ads but which do very little to address the many challenges facing this country."[42] Byrd particularly emphasized the strategic use of cloture by Republican leaders to restrict amending opportunities on the floor and to publicly "bash Democratic Senators as obstructionists."[43] Republicans usually respond that the real cause for the decline of deliberation is excessive obstructionism by members of the minority party. Mitch McConnell, R-Ky., answered Democratic complaints about the decline of deliberation by telling Byrd and his colleagues, "You have met the enemy, and it is you."[44]

What have been the consequences of rampant obstructionism for the Senate's deliberative capacity? For one, the primacy of obstructionism makes the policymaking process more parochial. It enhances the promotion of narrow over general interests. Legislative politics in the United States tends toward parochialism, anyway, because of the geographic basis of member constituencies and the significant role that organized interest groups play at all levels of government.[45] But the procedural prerogatives of individual senators add yet another dose of parochialism to the legislative process. Senators can place holds, object to requests for UCAs, or engage in filibusters with an eye toward making legislation more responsive to the needs of their constituents. The parochial use of obstructionism is particularly common on second-tier bills and nominations. In June 2003, for example, Larry Craig, R-Idaho, placed a hold on the promotions of 212 air force officers (military promotions require formal Senate approval) as leverage to convince the Pentagon to locate four C-130 transport planes at a National Guard base in his home state.[46] There are incentives for Senate leaders to promote the parochial concerns of their fellow partisans, thereby aiding their reelection efforts and the party's prospects overall. But Senate leaders also seek to pass legislation and unify their caucuses internally, and that may require that they promote the collective interests of their party and sometimes of the chamber as a whole.[47] By empowering individual lawmakers to pursue parochial goals, the primacy of obstructionism undermines such efforts at collective responsibility.

The most common criticism of the filibuster is that the tactic routinely blocks passage of major legislation that otherwise would be enacted. It is difficult to gauge what would have happened to a measure absent the filibuster and its offshoots. The number of votes cast in favor of cloture provides a clue, but cloture motions are at best a rough indicator of support for the underlying measure. Also, extended debate on one bill might be responsible for the demise of many other items that are left waiting in the wings. And some measures with broad support might not be placed on the agenda to begin with because proponents anticipate dilatory tactics somewhere down the line. The best scholarly compilation of significant legislation that died because of the filibuster is provided by Binder and Smith.[48] According to their research, we can be confident that at least thirty-one major bills (clearly backed by the president and a majority of both chambers of Congress) were stymied solely because of the filibuster between 1789 and 1994. Included are a number of civil rights initiatives during the period 1920–1950 and items such as striker replacement and lobby disclosure reform during the early 1990s. More recently, Mitch McConnell used extended debate to derail the McCain-Feingold campaign finance reform bill for several Congresses, and more of President George W. Bush's judicial nominees probably would have been confirmed if Senate rules included a motion on the previous question. Recall that our analysis of GOP holds during the Baker years revealed that 26.2 percent of the bills targeted with holds during 1977–1978 and 72.3 percent targeted during 1981–1982 did not pass the Senate. The best evidence, in short, suggests that Senate obstructionism does kill some legislation that otherwise would have been enacted.

These procedural barriers, we believe, create additional incentives for chamber leaders to engage in message politics, that is, to use the legislative and confirmation processes for the purposes of party campaigning. In the presence of consequential obstructionism, the alternative to striking bargains and passing legislation is to schedule "show" votes and focus on partisan position taking. There are certain benefits to message politics. The need to foster a favorable party name brand among voters helps produce party discipline among legislators from disparate constituencies.[49] When party elites take clear positions on significant policy issues and there are discernible differences between the party programs, ordinary citizens are better able to form their own opinions about the major issues of the day, and that can improve the overall quality of political discourse.[50] The benefits of message politics, however, also come at a cost. In itself, partisan position taking is not a form of deliberation. Members invest little effort to weigh policy alternatives or to learn from the arguments of their colleagues. With message politics, the legislative process instead takes on the zero-sum cast of the political campaign: One side wins and the other side loses. To the extent that the primacy of obstructionism promotes message politics in the Senate, it also impedes the constructive exchange of legislative ideas across the partisan aisle.

In recent years there have been regular calls for institutional reform to curb obstructionism in the Senate. Charles Grassley, R-Iowa, and Ron Wyden, D-Ore., for instance, have proposed that Senate rules be amended to clamp down on anonymous holds.[51] No holds should be honored by chamber leaders, they maintain, unless the name of the objector is printed in the *Congressional Record.* Others have suggested that extended debate not be permitted on the motion to proceed to floor action or on motions that relate to the establishment of conference committees.[52] Majority Leader Frist and Sen. Zell Miller, Ga., a conservative Democrat, have introduced a resolution providing for "cascading" cloture procedures in which, for judicial nominees, the number of votes necessary to end debate would be reduced from 60 to 57 to 54 to 51 on successive cloture motions.[53] In 1995, Tom Harkin, D-Iowa, and Joseph Lieberman, D-Conn., proposed similar changes to Rule 22 that would have covered legislation, as well as nominations.[54] And in the 108th Congress, Republican leaders periodically mentioned the so-called nuclear option for curbing obstruction. Under it, Republican senators would use certain obscure chamber precedents to abolish the filibuster by a simple majority vote.[55]

Are we likely to witness anytime soon institutional changes that significantly reduce obstructionism in the Senate? The Grassley-Wyden proposal to abolish anonymous holds is an attempt to regulate what is essentially an informal bargaining tactic via a formal rules change, and it is unlikely to be effective.[56] Even if dilatory tactics are ruled out on motions to take up legislation or proceed to conference, senators still could filibuster individual bills at multiple junctures and continue to obstruct nominations. Such incremental rules changes are unlikely to make much of a difference. To obviate obstructionism in the Senate and end its primacy, reformers will have to fundamentally change the nature of the chamber and provide leaders with an institutional mechanism for ending debate by a majority vote. Some form of cascading cloture probably would do the trick. But Rule 22 stipulates that changes to the cloture process must be supported by a two-thirds supermajority, which is not achievable in a Senate polarized along partisan lines. The nuclear option has generated much entertaining speculation among Senate observers, but actually implementing the tactic would destroy the essential working relationships that exist among Republicans and Democrats on Capitol Hill. In addition, many Republican senators are wary of potential Democratic majorities of the future, and they do not want to disarm themselves by seriously restricting the right to extended debate. The bottom line? The primacy of obstructionism will almost certainly confound majority leadership in the Senate for the foreseeable future.

Notes

1. Isaiah J. Poole, "Senate Clears 60-Day Extension of Surface Transportation Bill, but Partisan Standoff Simmers," *CQ Weekly,* May 1, 2004, 1026.
2. All unattributed quotations are from personal interviews conducted by the authors with Senate leadership staff during spring 2004.
3. Steven S. Smith, "Forces for Change in Senate Party Leadership and Organization," in *Congress Reconsidered,* 5th ed., ed. Lawrence C. Dodd and Bruce I. Oppenheimer (Washington, D.C.: CQ Press, 1993). See also Barbara Sinclair, *The Transformation of the U.S. Senate* (Baltimore: Johns Hopkins University Press, 1989).
4. Roger Davidson, "Senate Leaders: Janitors for an Untidy Chamber?" in *Congress Reconsidered,* 3rd ed., ed. Lawrence C. Dodd and Bruce I. Oppenheimer (Washington, D.C.: CQ Press, 1985).
5. Sarah A. Binder and Steven S. Smith, *Politics or Principle? Filibustering in the United States Senate* (Washington, D.C.: Brookings Institution Press, 1997).
6. There are statutory limits on debate for budget resolutions, budget reconciliation bills, many trade items, and certain other matters, restricting somewhat the use of obstructionism in the Senate.
7. By "during the amendment process," we are referring to adoption of the committee substitute if there is one. Notice that we also refer to six "principal" junctures in the life of a bill. There may be many other opportunities to engage in extended debate depending on the legislative context. Motions to instruct conferees are debatable, for instance, as are some motions to appeal the ruling of the chair. Such motions can be filibustered because they are open to debate. Moreover, senators can filibuster conference reports once they are brought back to the chamber for a final up or down vote.
8. Binder and Smith, *Politics or Principle?,* 60.
9. C. Lawrence Evans and Walter J. Oleszek, "The Procedural Context of Senate Deliberation," in *Esteemed Colleagues: Civility and Deliberation in the U.S. Senate,* ed. Burdett A. Loomis (Washington, D.C.: Brookings Institution Press, 2000), 105–136.

10. Rule 22 also was amended in 1979 and 1986 to restrict the ability of members to engage in dilatory tactics after cloture is invoked. Currently, all postcloture debate is limited to no more than thirty hours.
11. *Congressional Record,* July 2, 1952, 8828.
12. Ibid., 8827–8828.
13. Sinclair, *The Transformation of the U.S. Senate.*
14. Jack L. Walker, "The Origin and Maintenance of Interest Groups in America," *American Political Science Review* 77 (June 1983): 390–406.
15. Steven S. Smith and Marcus Flathman, "Managing the Senate Floor: Complex Unanimous Consent Agreements since the 1950s," *Legislative Studies Quarterly* 14 (1989): 349–373.
16. The track system was first implemented during Mike Mansfield's (D-Mont.) tenure as majority leader. But on matters of floor scheduling Mansfield generally deferred to his majority whip, Robert Byrd, and the West Virginian was primarily responsible for devising the innovation.
17. Walter J. Oleszek, *Congressional Procedures and the Policy Process,* 6th ed. (Washington, D.C.: CQ Press, 2004).
18. Steven S. Smith, *Call to Order* (Washington, D.C.: Brookings Institution Press, 1989), 111.
19. C. Lawrence Evans, *Leadership in Committee: A Comparative Analysis of Leadership Behavior in the U.S. Senate* (Ann Arbor: University of Michigan Press, 1991), 117–121.
20. *Congressional Record,* April 17, 2002, S2850.
21. *Congress Daily P.M.,* October 2, 1996, 6.
22. For 1977–1978, we were able to find the "marked Senate calendars" upon which hold requests typically are initialed. For 1981–1982, Baker's papers include the letters written by GOP senators to the leadership requesting a hold. Such requests are then marked on the aforementioned calendars. Although our focus here is on legislation, we also gathered hold letters for 1981–1982 that relate to judicial and executive branch nominations. These data will be analyzed in other research.
23. Some of the hold letters sent to Baker were signed by multiple individuals. For the purposes of analysis, we treat each individual as having placed a separate hold on the matter. Some hold letters are authored by individual senators but refer to multiple bills. In such cases, we coded a separate hold or request for notification for the senator on each measure. A small number of the requests were difficult to interpret and have been dropped from the analysis. In addition, for some holds on the marked calendars, it is not possible to discern the identity of the holder, and for some of the letters the specific matter targeted by a request is likewise unclear. As a result, the number of observations that we use in different parts of the analysis varies somewhat, depending on the question or topic that is being addressed.
24. Toby McIntosh, "Senate 'Holds' System Developing as Sophisticated Tactic for Leverage, Delay," *Daily Report for Executives* (No. 165), Bureau of National Affairs, August 26, 1991, C1–C5.
25. The dependent variable in the multivariate analysis was an event count—the number of times an individual placed a hold during a particular Congress. As a result, we employed a negative binomial regression model (there was significant evidence of overdispersion). The independent variables included ideology, membership on the Senate Steering Committee, seniority, proximity of reelection, a measure of electoral insecurity, and state size (as a proxy for constituency heterogeneity). Squared terms also were included for ideology and seniority to test for the existence of quadratic relationships. Full results for the statistical analysis can be obtained from the authors.
26. Keith Poole and Howard Rosenthal, *Congress: A Political-Economic History of Roll Call Voting* (New York: Oxford University Press, 1997). In this chapter, we use the first dimension DW-NOMINATE values.

27. The only Democrat to ever be a member was James Allen, Ala., pioneer of the post-cloture filibuster and the preeminent Senate obstructionist of the period. For a more detailed discussion of the Senate Steering Committee, see C. Lawrence Evans, Daniel Lipinski, and Keith J. Larsen, "The Senate Hold: Preliminary Evidence from the Baker Years" (paper delivered at the annual meeting of the Midwest Political Science Association, Chicago, April 2003).
28. There also was a positive relationship between Steering Committee membership and hold usage in 1981–1982, but the size of the effect was much smaller and not statistically significant.
29. Ann Cooper, "The Senate and the Filibuster: War of Nerves—and Hardball," *CQ Weekly,* September 2, 1978, 2307.
30. Ibid., 2307.
31. Ibid., 2310.
32. For 1977–1978, there is a negative relationship between member seniority and hold usage, but the parameter estimate is not statistically significant.
33. The population of a senator's state was also included as an explanatory variable to test whether members representing more heterogeneous constituencies make greater use of the hold. There was no discernible relationship for the two Congresses.
34. For a small number of the holds, we were unable to discern the legislative fate of the targeted item. Those observations have been dropped from this part of the analysis.
35. The "kill rate" does not appear to spike during fall 1982, probably because it already was fairly high throughout that Congress.
36. C. Lawrence Evans, "Committees, Leaders, and Message Politics," in *Congress Reconsidered,* 7th ed., ed. Lawrence C. Dodd and Bruce I. Oppenheimer (Washington, D.C.: CQ Press, 2001); Daniel Lipinski, "The Outside Game: Communication as a Party Strategy in Congress," in *Communication and U.S. Elections: New Agendas,* ed. Roderick Hart and Daron Shaw (Lanham, Md.: Rowman and Littlefield, 2001); Patrick J. Sellers, "Winning Media Coverage in the U.S. Congress," in *U.S. Senate Exceptionalism,* ed. Bruce I. Oppenheimer (Columbus: Ohio State University Press, 2002), 132–156.
37. Isaiah J. Poole, "Highway Bill Conferees' Quest: A Rewrite Bush Will Buy," *CQ Weekly,* April 3, 2004, 802–804.
38. *Congressional Record,* May 19, 2004, S5358.
39. Ibid.
40. The Republicans were able to invoke cloture earlier than Democratic leaders preferred by drawing support from rank-and-file Democrats, typically by first allowing wavering members of the minority party to offer the amendments that they wanted considered, and then invoking cloture and cutting off further nongermane proposals from the minority side of the aisle. According to Senate leadership staff, this essentially was the bargaining dynamic on the "FSC/ETI" (export subsidy repeal) legislation in spring 2004.
41. Albert Eisele and JoAnn Kelly, "Texas-Minnesota Senate Feud Blocks Measure Honoring LBJ Foe Former Sen. McCarthy," *The Hill,* October 7, 1998, 6.
42. *Congressional Record,* April 28, 2004, S4474.
43. Ibid., S4474.
44. Ibid., S3434.
45. Frances E. Lee, "Interests, Constituencies, and Policymaking," unpublished manuscript, Case-Western Reserve University, 2004.
46. "Craig Releases Batch of Holds," *National Journal's CongressDaily,* June 17, 2003.
47. Barbara Sinclair, *Majority Leadership in the U.S. House* (Baltimore: Johns Hopkins University Press, 1983).
48. Binder and Smith, *Politics or Principle?* 127–160.

49. Gary Cox and Mathew McCubbins, *Legislative Leviathan: Party Government in the House* (Berkeley: University of California Press, 1993).
50. Edward Carmines and James Stimson, *Issue Evolution: Race and the Transformation of American Politics* (Princeton: Princeton University Press, 1989); John R. Zaller, *The Nature and Origins of Mass Opinion* (New York: Cambridge University Press, 1992).
51. See S. Res. 151, 108th Congress.
52. Over the years, many members and Senate observers have proposed that the number of motions subject to extended debate be reduced. Consult, for example, *Background Materials: Supplemental Information provided to Members of the Joint Committee on the Organization of Congress,* 103rd Cong., 1st sess., S. Prt. 103-55, 1024–1032. According to knowledgeable staff, Senate Republican leaders seriously considered recommending such changes during 2004.
53. See S. Res. 138, 108th Congress.
54. See S. Res. 85, 104th Congress.
55. Alexander Bolton, "Frist Finger on 'Nuclear' Button," *The Hill,* May 13, 2004.
56. For multiple explanations for why the Grassley-Wyden proposal would be ineffective, consult the prepared statements of witnesses at a hearing on the matter before the Committee on Senate Rules and Administration, U.S. Senate, June 17, 2003.

11. Congressional Committees in a Partisan Era

John H. Aldrich and David W. Rohde

The two principal organizing structures of Congress are the parties and the committee system. During the history of the institution the relative influence of these two structures has shifted back and forth. From 1890 to 1910, the majority party dominated the House of Representatives, with the Speaker empowered to appoint committees and their chairs and to control the legislative agenda. After the revolt against Speaker Joe Cannon in 1910, power shifted to committees, whose leaders were selected based on seniority. From the 1920s through the 1970s, party influence was relatively weak, and that period became known as the era of committee government. Then, beginning with the reform period in the 1970s, institutional changes were adopted that strengthened parties and weakened the sway of committees and their chairs. Moreover, the extent and intensity of partisan conflict in Congress increased.

In this chapter we discuss the transformation of the party-committee balance from the 1970s to the present, focusing mainly on the House but also considering the Senate. We begin by considering the Democratic Party reforms of the 1970s that launched the transformation and how the Democrats applied the party leadership's new powers. Then we focus in more detail on the further developments after the Republicans won control of both houses in the 1994 elections. We include discussion of additional institutional changes passed by the GOP and of the ways in which the Republican Party leadership has interacted with the committee system to achieve its legislative goals. The next section will demonstrate that although increased party influence is important, a large share of committee activity does not involve partisan issues. We will briefly discuss Senate committees and then offer some conclusions.

The Committee System and the Era of Committee Government

The most important thing to recognize about the House and Senate committee systems is that they are designed institutions. That is, they are created by the membership to serve the interests of the chamber and its members. Committees, through division of labor, permit the chamber to stretch its capabilities by having only a subset of members consider each issue and piece of legislation in detail. Furthermore, committees encourage the development of expertise through members' specialization in the issue areas covered by their committees' jurisdictions.[1] In addition to these benefits to the chamber, committees also provide benefits to individual members. Richard Fenno has argued that members of Congress pursue one or more of three goals: reelection, power within the chamber, and good public policy.[2] The achievement of each of these goals is potentially influenced by committee membership. Members can use committee service to identify themselves with issues that are important to constituents and to secure benefits for their districts, thus enhancing their chances for reelection.[3] Committee and subcommittee chairmanships also provide members with positions of power in the chamber. Thirdly, committee members are in the best positions to influence the course of public policy within their committees' jurisdictions.[4]

Committees were used to conduct congressional business from the beginning of the institution, although it took most of a century for the system to develop into the form we know today.[5] Standing committees (that is, permanent committees with recognized substantive jurisdictions) were widely used by the 1820s. They included members from both the majority and minority parties, and as committees developed expertise their parent chambers began to defer to their judgments on legislative policy. Throughout the 1800s, the influence of the majority party leadership over committees grew. Speakers had the right to appoint committee members and chairs. The Speaker also chaired the Rules Committee, which set the terms of debate for bills on the House floor. The Speaker lost these powers in the revolt against Speaker Cannon in 1910. He could no longer appoint committees, and each party developed its own procedures for that purpose. Seniority in committee service became the almost inviolable basis for choosing committee chairs. Moreover, the Rules Committee was made independent and the Speaker barred from serving on it.

As a result of these developments, committees became largely independent from party influence. Because committee chairs were chosen by seniority, and maintained their positions because of it, they had no particular incentive to be responsive to the wishes of their party or its leaders in producing legislation. The chairs shaped their committees' agendas, appointed subcommittees (and usually chose their chairs), and decided when hearings would be held and how bills would be handled. These developments might have been less consequential if the committee leaders were ideologically representative of their party, but that was not the case. From 1930 on, the Democrats were usually in the majority, and because southern Democrats were more likely to accumulate seniority than their northern counterparts, they were disproportionately represented among committee leaders. Conservative southerners often allied with Republicans to block or alter Democratic legislation, a situation that greatly frustrated northerners.

Of particular consequence was the independence of the Rules Committee, the "traffic cop" of the House floor agenda. Most major bills needed a special resolution from the committee to go to the floor for a vote. If Rules granted a resolution, it also specified the procedures for debate—how much time, which amendments would be permitted, and so on. Under committee government, the "conservative coalition" of southern Democrats and Republicans on Rules often refused to permit liberal Democratic legislation to reach the House floor. In other instances the procedures they adopted disadvantaged the liberal Democrats' preferred alternatives. Therefore, liberal Democrats sought ways to alter institutional arrangements to remove what they perceived to be an unfair bias against their priorities.

Party Reform: Gateway to the Partisan Era

Initial attempts at reform of committee government included a successful effort in 1961 to expand the Rules Committee to reduce the influence of southern conservatives on the panel. Then in 1970 Congress passed the Legislative Reorganization Act. It contained a number of important features, such as the requirement that committees make public roll call votes; it encouraged committees to permit the public to attend their meetings. The act also made it much easier to obtain recorded votes on amendments on the House floor and set the stage for electronic voting, which markedly sped up floor voting. These changes started to shift the locus of legislative decision making from the committees to the floor. The act, however, took no action to revise the seniority system or to reduce the powers of committee chairs.[6] The conservative coalition was able to block any such actions that would have undermined their institutional position.

However, the makeup of the House membership (and the Senate's, too) was changing. The Voting Rights Act of 1965 had enfranchised black voters in the South, and their strong tilt to the Democratic Party was liberalizing the party's voter base there. Reinforcing that effect was the gradual departure from the party of conservative voters who no longer saw the Democrats as standing for their interests. As a consequence of these developments, new southern Democrats were becoming more like their northern colleagues, and the Democratic congressional delegation was becoming less divided and more homogeneous.[7] This set the stage for efforts to strengthen the majority party leadership relative to the committee system. Since the revolt against Cannon, the diverse memberships of the congressional parties had been reluctant to enhance party power because that very diversity meant that there would be great uncertainty about the ends for which that power would be used. That is, members could not be sure what policies leaders would seek, and so individual members had to worry that powerful leaders would seek policies far different from their own preferred outcome. If, on the other hand, the preferences of party members were to become more similar, members would not have to be as concerned that leaders with preferences different from theirs would be chosen, and it would be safer to grant leaders stronger powers.

This relationship is the essence of the theoretical perspective that we have labeled *conditional party government*, or CPG for short.[8] If the legislators in a party have very heterogeneous policy preferences, they will not be likely to grant strong powers to their leadership. As policy preferences become more homogeneous, members will be progressively more likely to empower their party leaders because they will have less reason to fear the use of those powers. This tendency will be further reinforced as the positions of the two parties become more different, because the consequences to members of each party of the other party's being successful in the competition to control policy outcomes will become more and more negative.

By the early 1970s, liberal Democrats were a clear majority of the House Democratic Caucus, but not of the entire House membership. Because they could not win a majority on the floor for the kinds of reforms they favored, the liberals targeted the rules of the Democratic Caucus instead. Only Democrats could vote on these efforts, which combined strategies dealing both with committees and with the party and its leadership. First they sought to undermine the independence and power of committee leaders, so that the remaining conservatives would be less able to impede passage of their desired legislation. This strategy followed two tracks. First, the liberals wanted to end the automatic nature of the seniority system. To this end the caucus adopted rules providing for an automatic, secret ballot vote on all committee chairmen at the beginning of every Congress. If the prospective chair (usually still the most senior Democrat on the committee) was voted down, there would be a competitive election of the chair in the caucus. This change was shown to have real consequences when in 1975 three southern Democrats were removed from committee chairmanships and replaced by more loyal northerners. Chairs were put on notice that they could not buck their party's policy wishes with impunity.

The second track of this strategy involved adopting rules that restricted the powers of those chosen as chairs. The principal vehicle was a set of rules known as the Subcommittee Bill of Rights, which required that committee members bid for subcommittee chairs in order of seniority, ending the ability of full committee chairs simply to appoint those positions. Subcommittees had to receive specific jurisdictions, and committee legislation had to be referred to subcommittees accordingly. In addition, subcommittee chairs would control their own budgets and staffs, rather than the full committee chair.

The other strategy of the reformers was to give more powers to the party leadership. The Speaker received the right to appoint the chair and Democratic members of the Rules Committee. That meant that the leadership could again control the flow of legislation and strategically shape the terms of floor consideration. In addition, the power to assign Democrats to other committees was vested in a new Steering and Policy Committee, most of whose members were party leaders or appointed by the Speaker. The reformers wanted the leadership to have more influence over the allocation of prized assignments, to make members more responsive to them. Finally, the Speaker was given the authority to refer bills to more than one committee and to set deadlines for reporting, further reducing the ability of committees to act as roadblocks.

Partisanship Takes Hold: 1983–1994

The reforms were adopted by the mid-1970s, and some of their consequences were quickly apparent, but divisions remained in the Democratic Caucus, preventing the full effects of the changes from being visible. Indeed, many observers complained that the reforms had merely made Congress less efficient and productive by further decentralizing power to subcommittees. This viewpoint was reinforced by Ronald Reagan's success in 1981 at splitting off southern

Democrats to support his budget and tax proposals. Then came the recession of 1982, which helped the Democrats make significant House gains in that year's elections. Fifty-seven freshman Democrats came to the House in 1983, including many moderate-to-liberal southerners. Consequently the conservative coalition was no longer a majority of the House. The newcomers made up over one-fifth of the Democratic Caucus, and they provided support for stronger use of the leadership's powers to advance the party agenda and to compete with the priorities of the Reagan administration.

As we noted earlier, one reform strategy sought to induce committee chairs to refrain from blocking party bills and to support the Democratic Party's legislative program. After the removal of the three southern chairs in 1975, committee chairs recognized that their continued hold on their positions depended to a degree on their party support, and their behavior changed accordingly. Research shows that members who occupied, or were close in seniority to, committee chairs dramatically increased their levels of party support between 1971 and 1982.[9] For example, in 1973–1974 the party unity score of Rep. Jamie Whitten, D-Miss., was thirty-eight points below the party average and eighteen points below the average for southern Democrats. Anticipating a liberal challenge when the chairmanship of the Appropriations Committee (where he ranked second) became vacant, Whitten began to change his behavior. By 1988, Whitten's party unity score was not only higher than the average southern Democrat's, it was two points higher than the average Democrat's.[10] Moreover, the Democratic Caucus continued to use the mechanism for voting on chair candidates to pressure or remove committee leaders whose performance was deemed unsatisfactory.

The other reform strategy was to strengthen the party leadership, and it had a substantial impact on the relationship between the leadership and committees. As Barbara Sinclair has said, "Party and committee leaders must work together . . . since both are agents of and ultimately responsible to the Democratic Caucus."[11] In the context of the changed environment, committee leaders came to think of themselves as part of a team with the majority leadership. Committee chairs realized that they could not act independently of party priorities in drafting legislation. In turn, they expected party leaders to provide adequate staff support and assistance in moving bills to passage on the floor.[12]

One of the most important tools available to the party leadership was control of the Rules Committee. During the 1980s, the Democrats increasingly used the resolutions (called "special rules") that set the terms for floor consideration of legislation to structure the agenda to the advantage of the party.[13] For example, special rules could bar amendments completely, giving members a take-it-or-leave-it choice between the bill the leadership favored and nothing. Alternatively, the rule could permit just those amendments that the leadership wanted to consider, barring others that the Republican minority wanted but that would have caused policy or electoral difficulties for some Democrats. Moreover, if the reporting committee had not adequately taken the majority party's wishes into account, special rules could be used to alter the bill as reported to bring the policy closer to the preference of the majority. This was done multiple times on defense authorization bills from the Armed Services Committee.

Not surprisingly, the majority party's use of its powers provoked anger and frustration among Republicans. One response from the GOP was to change its party rules to mimic those of the Democrats, so as to make its own leadership more able to compete. For example, the Republicans gave the minority leader the right to make Republican appointments to the Rules Committee and created a new committee assignment system in which the leadership had more voting power. The party leader was also empowered to designate "leadership issues," and on those bills all members of the party leadership were obliged to support the positions of the Republican Conference.

The Republicans also adopted progressively more confrontational tactics to protest their treatment and to undermine the Democratic majority. Some complaints came from GOP leaders and mainline conservatives, but most active were members of a group of populist conservatives known as the Conservative Opportunity Society (COS), led by Newt Gingrich of Georgia, then a backbencher. Gingrich and COS believed that the Republicans would be a perpetual minority unless they stopped going along with the Democrats as a means of attempting to have some influence on legislation. Instead, they argued that the GOP had to draw contrasts with the Democrats and let the public make a choice. The COS organized protests against the Democrats' management of the chamber and fought against the use of special rules to control the agenda and limit Republican influence. The culmination of these efforts occurred in late 1988, when Gingrich filed a formal complaint with the House Ethics Committee against Speaker Jim Wright. The ensuing investigation led to Wright's resignation from the House.

Republican Rule and Its Consequences: 1994–2000

Republican confrontations with the Democratic majority continued into the 1990s, and especially after President Clinton was elected in 1992, restoring unified government. The GOP was able to take advantage of the political context in 1994, successfully exploiting negative public feelings against government performance, the condition of the nation, and Clinton personally.[14] As a result, the Republicans won majority control of both houses of Congress for the first time since the election of 1952. The new majority in the House chose Newt Gingrich as their speaker, and the party set out to transform the operation of the chamber in order to set the stage for major changes in government policy.

Republican Procedural Changes

Gingrich's transforming efforts commenced almost immediately.[15] Little more than a week after Election Day he made clear his intent to depart from the seniority system for the selection of committee chairs to a greater extent than the Democrats ever did. At a press conference, Gingrich announced that he was choosing Bob Livingston of Louisiana as the new chair of the Appropriations Committee. Livingston ranked fifth in committee seniority but was considered more ideologically dependable and more effective than the more senior committee members. A few days later, it was also announced that the most senior member would also be bypassed on two other committees: Judiciary and Commerce. The reasons were similar: the new GOP leadership wanted more committed and dependable leaders for the committees that were to be important for enacting the Contract with America and other major party initiatives.

It is important to note that unlike the Democrats' removal of chairmen in 1975, the Republicans' actions were not the result of pressure from the large new class of House members. Indeed, virtually none of the new members were yet in Washington, and they had no advance notice of what would occur. Gingrich simply asserted the right to name the new chairs, and the Republican Conference members tacitly ratified his decisions by their acquiescence.

The powers of committees and their chairs were also changed significantly. Three committees were abolished outright, and most remaining committees were limited to five subcommittees. These actions eliminated twenty-five subcommittees and 12 percent of full committee slots. Staff allocations for committees were reduced by one-third. Supporters of these innovations made it clear that their intent was to reduce the ability of the committee system to act as an independent locus of power. As one COS member said, "Our system will prevent members from getting locked into the status quo."[16]

Other rules changes directly affected committee chairs, to whom the Republican leadership gave the right to appoint subcommittee chairs (rather than following seniority as the Democrats had) and control of all committee staff. This reflected Gingrich's view that chairmen should control their committees, but he also believed that the party should control the chairmen. He required committee chairmen to consult with him before choosing subcommittee chairs, and he pressured one chair to name two freshman representatives to head subcommittees. Gingrich also required each member of the Appropriations Committee to sign a "letter of fidelity," pledging to cut the budget as much as the Speaker wanted. To further undermine the capacity of committee leaders to build an independent power base, the Republicans adopted a six-year term limit for all committee and subcommittee chairmen.

In addition to limiting committee and subcommittee power, the new majority further strengthened their leadership. One change was the adoption of a new committee assignment system, designed by Gingrich, announced by him only eight days after the election, and adopted by the Republican Conference in December. There were a total of thirty votes on the committee on committees, and five of these were given to Gingrich (plus two to the majority leader). No one else had more than one vote. The party also confirmed their leader's right to appoint the members and chair of the Rules Committee, ensuring his ability to structure the floor agenda. Thus, overall, under the new GOP majority, committees had less independent power and the party leadership had more.

It is worth noting one thing that the GOP did not do. It didn't adopt a wholesale realignment of committee jurisdictions, as some reformers had wanted. The last complete restructuring of committee jurisdictions had occurred in the Legislative Reorganization Act of 1946. In the intervening half century, the agenda of the committee system had changed substantially and new issues had arisen. Much overlap in committee jurisdictions had developed, and reformers repeatedly tried, and repeatedly failed, to rationalize and clarify these arrangements.[17] The existing pattern of jurisdictions had too many implications for the reelection, policy, and power goals of members, and most of them were unwilling to accept the risks involved in major change.[18] When the GOP took over the majority, Gingrich authorized Rep. David Dreier of California (vice chair of a joint committee on congressional reform in the previous Congress) to draft four plans of varying comprehensiveness for revamping the committee system. The most ambitious plan (and the one Dreier favored) called for abolition of five committees and major redistribution of jurisdictions. After it became apparent that there would be significant resistance from the chairs and members of affected committees, Gingrich opted for a version of the least extensive plan. Thus we see that although Republican members were willing to support strengthening their leadership's influence over committees, they were not willing to sacrifice their other interests that were served by the committee system.

Party Leaders and Committees

The rules changes that the new Republican majority adopted thus set the stage for greater influence by party leaders over the activities and legislative products of committees. We now discuss the GOP leadership's use of these tools to shape the initial actions of committees, to bypass them when desirable, and to reshape the content of legislation after committees acted. Because of limited space we can only present a few examples, mostly drawn from the 104th Congress (1995–1997), but we will discuss more recent events in the concluding section below.

Influencing Bill Creation in Committees. Majority leadership involvement in the crafting of bills in committee did not originate with the 104th Congress. As Sinclair shows,[19] such activity had become more frequent as committee autonomy decreased in the postreform era. It was, however, still infrequent in the Democrat-controlled Congresses, as most leader activity involved stages of the process after initial drafting. The 104th marked a major increase in this role for majority leadership.

The most extensive instance of leadership influence on bill creation was the drafting and revision of the legislation designed to implement the Contract with

America.[20] Although there was substantial initial consultation on general matters during the crafting of the Contract, the drafting of bills was left to sitting GOP representatives, and to a relatively small subset of them. Moreover, the top GOP leaders determined the set of issues to be included and many of the particulars. This maximized the opportunity for those choices to be made on strategic grounds, on behalf of the general party's political interests, rather than simply on the basis of ideology. For example, it was Gingrich who decided that school prayer would not be included. This context also ensured that although party moderates would have input, the actual decisions on the content of the Contract rested almost entirely with conservatives. Committee consideration of these predrafted bills was largely pro forma, a necessary consequence of the leadership's pledge to pass them in the Congress's first hundred days.

The Contract was of central importance, but the leadership's involvement in committees' initial consideration of bills was not limited to that legislation. We will examine leadership influence over the Appropriations Committee below. Another example involves the major reform of agriculture subsidy policy that became known as the Freedom to Farm Act. In September 1995, the GOP leadership sent a letter to the Agriculture Committee chair, Pat Roberts of Kansas. They wrote, "We give the committee leave" to write major budget-cutting farm legislation. They indicated that they hoped the committee would support Roberts's bill, but if not "we will feel compelled" to bring the bill to the floor allowing unlimited amendments, or to replace the committee's bill with true reforms."[21] Moreover, during the consideration of the bill in committee, John Boehner of Ohio (a member, who was also GOP Conference chair) went so far as to say, "If this committee can't do it [make $13 billion in cuts called for in the budget plan], the future of this committee is seriously in doubt."[22] Rarely in congressional history has the majority leadership sought to dictate to and threaten a committee in so direct a fashion.

Dealing with Committees and Chairs. The efforts by the majority leadership to influence bill content and committee action extended beyond initial bill construction. Consider the major telecommunications bill (H.R. 1555) produced by the Commerce Committee in 1995. It was intended to increase competition and reduce regulation in the industry, and one point at issue was the competing interests of long-distance phone companies and the regional Bell companies. The chairman of the committee, Thomas Bliley of Virginia (another chair personally picked by Gingrich in violation of seniority), pushed the interests of the long-distance companies and produced a bill that the committee reported by a 38–5 vote. However, the Bells approached the GOP leadership and organized support among others in the Republican Conference, complaining that the committee bill was too regulatory. The GOP leadership met with Bliley and—in the words of Gingrich's press secretary—advised him on "the party's judgment on where the party ought to be on this bill."[23] Shortly thereafter, Bliley held a briefing for executives of the long-distance companies, at which he indicated that changes the Bell companies desired would be made in the bill. According to one participant, "He said he did so [changed the bill] because he was under instructions by the House leadership and was facing a mini-revolt within his committee."[24]

Bypassing Committees and Postcommittee Adjustments. In some instances, the Republican leadership simply bypassed committees to achieve its policy and political goals. A number of such cases involved the Judiciary Committee. It was one of the committees for which Gingrich had personally picked the chair, the independent-minded Henry Hyde of Illinois. Hyde was suitably responsive to the leadership and the Republican Conference during the speedy processing of a large number of bills from the Contract with America. Even there, though, he exercised independent judgment. For example, he reported the term limits constitutional amendment even though he opposed it (and later led the fight for its defeat on the House floor), but while doing so he engineered changes in it during the committee markup that displeased its supporters and the leadership. In another example, the bill to repeal the 1994 ban on assault weapons, which Hyde also opposed, went to the floor without committee consideration. When asked why Judiciary was not given the opportunity to consider the bill, the chairman said: "We have a reputation of being deliberative."[25]

Another device for bypassing committees was the use of leader-appointed party task forces.[26] Often, but not always, task forces were created with the assent of committees (or at least their leaders), and they usually contained some members of the appropriate committees. A key difference, however, was that they contained only Republicans, and at times they were used to secure a different policy outcome than the committee of jurisdiction preferred. For example, in 1995 the Government Reform and Oversight Committee approved a bill to abolish the Commerce Department that was insufficiently radical to satisfy many of the GOP freshmen. The dissenters expressed their displeasure, and in response the leadership chose a different, more radical bill to accomplish the goal. The source of the bill was a GOP task force set up by Gingrich and chaired by a freshman. The bill had no hearings and no committee markup.[27]

The leadership could also use its control over the Rules Committee to make adjustments in the content of legislation after the committees had made their decisions. Barbara Sinclair's research shows that under the Republicans this kind of action was most frequent in the "revolutionary" 104th Congress (occurring in the cases of nearly half the major bills). But postcommittee adjustments continued to occur in later Congresses, for example, on more than one-third of the major bills in the 105th Congress.[28] One instance was the 1997 budget resolution, when Gingrich supervised adjustments to placate dissident Republicans and the White House. Another occurred in 1999, when moderate Republicans threatened to oppose the GOP tax bill because it was not sufficiently concerned with deficit reduction. Speaker Hastert brokered a change that made the tax rate cut dependent on a declining national debt.[29]

Special Rules and Control of the Floor. As we noted earlier, leaders of the majority can use their powers to support and defend the decisions of committees or to undermine them if the committees have not produced a result the party wanted. One way is through their general control of the floor agenda. That is, the majority leadership determines which bills will be taken up and when. Favored bills are advantaged and will be pressed to passage; lesser priorities may fall to the wayside under the press of time. In addition, the leadership can use the Rules Committee to craft special rules that will improve the chances of party priorities and frustrate the minority's efforts to secure an alternative policy.

We saw that when they were in the minority, GOP members frequently attacked the Democrats for writing rules that barred them from offering amendments. As the majority in the 104th, however, they demonstrated that they were quite prepared to do the same thing when they needed to in order to accomplish their objectives. In one instance, on the recissions bill (legislation to make cuts in previously appropriated funds) taken up in March 1995, the Rules Committee wrote a rule that required proposals for spending increases to be offset by cuts elsewhere but prohibited the cuts from being taken from a different section of the bill. This blocked, for example, cutting defense to increase social spending. The rule prompted strong objections from a number of GOP moderates.[30]

Another somewhat ironic example occurred on the bill to revise the Medicare program. The GOP had long contended that the Democrats had restricted amendments because they were afraid to let their own moderate-to-conservative members offer alternatives to liberal, party-approved policies. Indeed, a Republican member of Rules made this claim before the 104th Congress convened, contending that conservative Democrats would often side with the GOP on the floor because "their agenda is similar to ours."[31] When the Medicare reform bill came up, however, and a group of conservative Democrats wanted to offer a substitute amendment for the Republican plan, the Rules Committee barred their amendment. Gene Taylor, D-Miss., said, "I am furious. . . . The Republicans came to power promising change, open rules." He charged, "They are no more fair than the Democrats."[32] As we will see in the next section, the use of this strategy also persisted beyond the 104th Congress.

Republican Leadership and the Appropriations Committee

Nothing better illustrates the changed relationship between the majority leadership and House committees than the case of the Appropriations Committee. Research on the Appropriations Committee before the Republican majority had shown it to be a relatively nonpartisan and collegial committee, with largely autonomous subcommittees.[33] It strived for bipartisan support for its legislation within the committee and on the floor. After the 1994 elections, however, Appropriations was central to the GOP agenda, both because the Republicans wanted to cut federal spending (which the committee oversees) and for more unconventional purposes.[34] As we saw above, Gingrich handpicked the chair of the committee (Bob Livingston, La.), and he required Republican committee members to pledge to support his efforts to cut the budget. The Speaker worked closely with Livingston and the subcommittee chairs, and his staff monitored their actions. Some of the budget cutting was difficult for some GOP members, but they generally stuck together and accomplished their assignment.

More difficult was the unconventional part of their task: Gingrich wanted appropriations bills to be the vehicles for substantial legislative change as well. What was remarkable about this is that House rules prohibit legislative language in appropriations bills. Other committees decide what policies they will follow, but Appropriations is only supposed to set spending levels. While committee bills had included legislation (called "riders") in the past, nothing like the magnitude and scope of the GOP efforts had ever been seen before. For example, on the Labor–HHS (Health and Human Services) bill, Republicans (with leadership support) added amendments to reduce the enforcement powers of the Occupational Safety and Health Administration and to restrict Medicaid funding of abortions. Chairman Livingston was worried that these efforts would undermine passage of his bill, and he complained to Gingrich. The Speaker indicated that he wanted the controversial provisions to remain, and more. Livingston came back to the committee for consideration of another rider, saying that it "had been a leadership decision to move ahead with this initiative."[35] These efforts sharply increased partisan conflict within the Appropriations Committee. In the entire previous Congress there had only been fourteen partisan roll call votes in the committee; in 1995 alone there were 133.

Because House rules barred riders, leadership control of the Rules Committee was essential for the Republican strategy. Special rules could grant exceptions to the House rules. The Veterans–HUD bill, for example, included thirty pages of legislative language, more than one-third of the bill. But even better for Republican purposes, this strategy made it virtually impossible for the Democrats to offer amendments. The special rules protected GOP-supported legislative provisions, but unless the rules also protected Democrat-proposed alternatives (and they did not), the latter could be barred by a point of order.

Disagreements over riders were at the heart of presidential-congressional conflict that led to the government shutdowns in 1995–1996. As a result, Gingrich substantially reduced use of this strategy in 1996 and 1997, but in 1998 employment of riders increased again. For example, the District of Columbia bill included four controversial riders that appealed to social conservatives, including funding for school vouchers, and the Veterans–HUD bill included a provision for a major revamping of federal housing programs. Thus we see that Republican leadership used its powers to dominate the policymaking of a major House committee to advance the party's agenda and change government policy. Moreover, this was often done over the objections of the committee's leaders.

As we said, in addition to their efforts to use appropriations bills to carry out legislative change, the GOP wanted to influence the allocation of federal spending. We will conclude this section with some information about that effort.

The Appropriations Committee in the Appropriations Process

At the same time that Democrats were adopting reforms to strengthen their party, the House began to reform the appropriations process itself. The House passed the Congressional Budget and Impoundment Control Act of 1974, creating the Budget Committee and requiring that the House adopt a total budget amount and "reconcile" individual appropriations to ensure their compliance with the budget resolution. Later reforms included the so-called Gramm-Rudman-Hollings bill of 1985, which originally pledged to balance the budget by 1991 and imposed new procedures to do so. The Budget Enforcement Act of 1990 (extended in 1993) included such procedures as "pay as you go," requiring new programs to be deficit neutral. Note that during the three reform years a Republican president faced a Democratic majority in the House.

The political-economic context for budgeting also changed. The two oil shocks of the 1970s slowed economic growth, generated inflation, and illustrated American interdependence with the world economy. Finally, beginning in the late 1970s, a series of tax limitation initiatives in various states, led by Proposition 13 in California in 1978, documented the unwillingness of the public to support new taxes to pay for government programs.

This convergence of partisan, institutional, and political-economic changes altered the politics of the Appropriations Committee. Scholars claimed that the president was now the guardian of the purse, the House the advocate for spending, and the Senate a check on House enthusiasms.[36] Others contended that the Appropriations Committee was an agent of the majority party.[37] Thus, different spending priorities would emerge depending on the party in power, especially under unified control. Conversely, other analysts argued that the full House was more important than the majority party.[38]

More recently, Aldrich, Brad T. Gomez, and Jennifer L. Merolla have examined the political and institutional factors that shaped appropriations from 1950 through 1998.[39] They asked whether annual appropriations changed as a result of changes in the makeup of the whole House, the Appropriations Committee, or the majority party (conditionally or unconditionally). They found the greatest support for the explanation offered by CPG. One possible reason for the difference between earlier analyses and theirs is that Aldrich, Gomez, and Merolla used a measure of CPG that varies as the levels of intraparty similarity in policy preferences and interparty polarization vary. Thus, the 1950s and 1960s were periods of relatively high conflict within the Democratic majority, whereas (as we noted above) the 1980s and 1990s had more intraparty homogeneity and interparty polarization. Perhaps as a result, they show that appropriations were expected to increase most dramatically from 1970 through 1994. There was little predicted increase in the 1950s and 1960s, primarily because the Democratic Party was internally divided. Finally, in the polarized Republican regime between 1995 and 1998, appropriations were expected to slow their increase dramatically. The evidence supported this account strongly. Overall, as the CPG measure increased during the last two decades of the Democratic House majority, appropriations increased by hundreds of billions of dollars, whereas the rate of increase slowed dramatically in the post–1994 period. Thus, Aldrich, Gomez, and Merolla concluded that not only does it matter which is the majority party, but it also matters how cohesive that majority is and how differentiated it is from the minority. Moreover, it appears to matter in a cumulative sense by approximately one to two trillion dollars.

Although the two uses of the Appropriations Committee discussed in this section may seem very different, they are not. It is no surprise that the Republican leadership would seek to use Appropriations for policymaking because one of its central policies is to reduce the size of government. In that context, legislating by means of riders to appropriations bills and legislating by approving smaller budgets are not different things.

Not Everything Is Partisan

To this point we have focused our attention on the increased partisanship in Congress and on the strengthening of the influence of the party structure relative to committees. In this section we want to emphasize that one should not overinterpret these patterns. Specifically, it is important to recognize that much of Congress's business does not involve party conflict, as Table 11-1 demonstrates.[40] It shows data from three Congresses on the proportion of bills that exhibited some conflict, either in committee or on the floor. The standard for conflict was very minimal: Was there even one roll call on the bill on which there was a minority larger than 10 percent? Despite this low threshold, however, only about one-third of the bills saw any conflict at all.

Why was there so seldom conflict on legislation, if Congress has become ever more partisan over the period covered by these data? The reason is that the agenda Congress deals with is multifaceted and diverse, and only a portion of it deals with the types of issues that provoke interparty disagreement. The parties care intensely about bills that relate to divisions among their members, their activists, and their electoral coalitions—things such as tax policy, the scope of government, regulation of business, and social issues such as abortion and gay rights. Most legislation, however, does not tap into these divisive subjects. Much legislation involves renewal of, or funding for, existing programs with wide support in the country or Congress, or proposals for new policies with many perceived benefits. This type of bill provides all members the chance to (in David Mayhew's words) "claim credit" or "take positions" and thereby enhance their chances for reelection.[41] Because members do not run directly against one another, there is not a zero-sum relationship among them, and all members can potentially benefit from the adoption of legislation.

This relationship is readily apparent in Table 11-1 when we consider different types of committees.[42] The prestige committees—most important to the party leadership—deal with more conflictual legislation in every Congress and

Table 11-1 Conflict on Legislation in the 96th, 100th, and 104th Congresses

	96th Congress (1979–1980)	100th Congress (1987–1988)	104th Congress (1995–1996)
Prestige committees	51.3% (150)	65.7% (67)	76.3% (93)
Policy committees	40.7% (317)	28.7% (394)	34.3% (376)
Constituency committees	20.8% (438)	17.8% (499)	23.8% (315)
All committees	32.8% (905)	25.6% (960)	35.1% (784)

Note: Numbers in each cell indicate the percentage of bills considered by those committees that exhibited some conflict, either in committee or on the floor, with the number of bills in that category in parentheses. See endnote 40.

also exhibit a systematic increase in conflict over time. The policy committees, which process most of the Congress's substantive legislation, reveal an intermediate level of conflict and no systematic increase. Finally, the constituency committees—those most involved with providing electoral benefits to members—show the least amount of conflict on legislation.

Not only does the propensity for partisan disagreement vary across types of committees and from bill to bill, but it also varies within a single piece of legislation. Consider the Freedom to Farm Act that we mentioned earlier, which in 1996 sought to reform federal farm policy. Table 11-2 shows the results of two roll calls on that bill.[43] The first vote involved an effort to cut the peanut price support program, a typical "distributive" policy issue had that offered electorally important benefits to some members from agricultural districts. In this instance, within both the Democratic and Republican parties, the members from the agriculture committees responded quite differently from other members, being much less inclined to support the abolition of peanut supports. Differences between the parties are small, and differences within them are large.

The second vote was on the Democrats' substitute proposal, which sought to keep farm policy closer to the status quo. Here the interparty differences are great. Only one Republican supported the Democrats' proposal, but 86 percent of the Democrats did. Moreover, the voting of committee members is virtually the same as that of members not on the committees. Thus some issues can provoke partisan responses while others do not, even within a single bill.

Senate Contrasts

Committees play a less-central role in the Senate than in the House because of a number of institutional differences between them. First, the Senate must deal with essentially the same legislative jurisdiction with less than one-fourth the membership. Senators are, therefore, spread more thinly and are less specialized. For example, in 2001 senators served on an average of 3.3 standing committees and 8.9 subcommittees; the corresponding numbers for representatives were 1.9 and 3.9. On the other hand, only about half of House members are the chair or

Table 11-2 Votes on the 1996 Freedom to Farm Act

	Phase Out Peanut Supports	Democratic Substitute
Republicans		
Agriculture committees	8.8% (34)	0.0% (34)
Others	61.3% (199)	0.5% (200)
All members	53.6% (233)	0.4% (234)
Democrats		
Agriculture committees	20.0% (25)	100.0% (23)
Others	48.5% (163)	84.8% (164)
All members	44.6% (188)	86.6% (187)
All members		
Agriculture committees	13.6% (59)	40.4% (57)
Others	55.5% (362)	38.5% (364)
All members	49.6% (421)	38.7% (421)

Note: Each cell gives the percentage of members voting "aye" on the two votes (the number of members is in parentheses). "Agriculture committees" means representatives who are on either the Committee on Agriculture or on the Appropriations Subcommittee on Agriculture and Rural Development. "Others" includes all other members.

ranking minority member of a committee or subcommittee, whereas most senators are, giving them an institutional power base on which to focus.[44]

The Senate's rules and traditions also vest more power in individuals and small groups than does the House. The most familiar manifestation of this is the ability of a minority to block passage of legislation through extended debate (a "filibuster"), but there are many other aspects of the institution that reinforce individual power to delay or block Senate action. The House is a "majoritarian" institution, in which the majority can work its will with even one more vote than the minority, but in the Senate the majority must usually pay attention to at least some minority views to achieve any results.

Another major difference, related to the preceding, is the role of the House Rules Committee that we discussed earlier. Through special rules, the majority party can decide which amendments may be considered on the floor, if any. Moreover, regular House rules require that amendments be "germane"—that is, they must deal with the same subject matter as the bill. In the Senate, neither of these conditions holds. Usually the only way to limit amendments is if senators *unanimously* consent to do so, and amendments need not be germane. Thus the Senate floor plays a much larger role in shaping the content of legislative outcomes than does the House floor, and it is much easier for senators who do not serve on the committee with jurisdiction to have an impact.

As a result of these differences, both Senate committees and Senate parties have been institutionally weaker than their House counterparts, and individual senators have been more consequential. Furthermore, because the majority party leadership usually has had to deal with some members of the minority, partisan conflict in the Senate has tended to be less frequent and less vitriolic. Nevertheless, over the last couple of decades party conflict has intensified in the Senate as well. For example, in 1995 the new GOP majority adopted some rules to enhance party influence. As in the House, six-year term limits were imposed on committee chairs. The selection of chairs was to be done by successive, secret-ballot votes, first among Republican committee members, then in the whole GOP Conference. Moreover, there were aspects of the Senate's business on which partisan conflict was as vigorous as any seen in the House. The prime example was confirmation of judicial nominations, in which only the Senate has a role. Democrats used the power of the filibuster to block Bush nominees they regarded as unacceptable, while frustrated Republicans railed against their actions.

The Present and the Future

We developed the theory of conditional party government to explain the ebb and flow of party influence in Congress over time. We have argued that as the policy preferences of party members become more homogeneous, and as their ideological centers of gravity become more divergent, rank-and-file members will be progressively more willing to delegate strong powers to their leaders to advance the party's program and to benefit it electorally. In this chapter we described how the relationship between the party organizations in Congress and the committee systems changed, arguing that the changes were in accord with the expectations of CPG, especially after the Republican takeover in 1994. Although most observers found the arguments and evidence persuasive with respect to the Gingrich Congress, some also raised the reasonable question of whether CPG would continue to account for congressional organization and policymaking.[45] In this concluding section, we address that issue by discussing developments in Congress in the last few years.

CPG theory has a number of key features that we have to account for to justify continued applicability: (1) Have intraparty homogeneity and interparty divergence remained high? (2) If so, has the majority party in particular continued to delegate strong powers to its leadership? and (3) Has the majority leadership continued to exercise its powers to facilitate achievement of the party's legislative and electoral goals?

With regard to the first question, the data are unequivocal. All research on the subject shows that the polarization of the parties continues.[46] The median positions of the parties on roll call measures are even a bit farther apart than they were in the 104th Congress. Moreover, the proportion of the Congress that takes positions in the middle of the ideological spectrum is smaller than ever. Thus the underlying "condition" for CPG is still well satisfied.

On the second point, the willingness of members to delegate power to party leaders persists as well. None of the significant authority granted to the Republican

House leadership has been rescinded. To the contrary, Speaker Dennis Hastert has sought and been granted additional power. For example, in late 2002 Hastert asked the GOP Conference to give him and the party even more influence over the Appropriations Committee by requiring that the chairs of its subcommittees be approved by the party Steering Committee.[47] (Remember that the Steering Committee is weighted toward leadership influence.) In addition, the Speaker arranged to give the Steering Committee the right to approve full committee chairs. In 2001 and 2003, under Hastert's leadership, the committee bypassed a number of more senior, moderate members to pick more junior and more conservative candidates for chairmanships. For example, Chris Shays of Connecticut, who had joined with Democrats against his party leaders in the successful fight for campaign finance reform legislation, was passed over for chair of the Government Reform Committee (where he was most senior) in favor of Tom Davis of Virginia, who had served on the committee only half as long.

Finally, regarding the continued exercise of leadership powers, Hastert and his colleagues have shown that they were more than willing to manipulate the legislative situation when it was needed. For example, Hastert and Senate Majority Leader Bill Frist presented a compromise that they had negotiated on the Medicare bill in late 2003, and Hastert pressured Ways and Means chair Bill Thomas of California to accept it against his will.[48] Around the same time, Majority Leader Tom DeLay of Texas gave the Armed Services Committee chair an ultimatum to pass the defense authorization bill within two days, or else the leadership would strip out a popular provision and send it to the floor alone.[49] And when Christopher Smith of New Jersey, chair of the Veterans' Affairs Committee, led a revolt over veterans legislation, the threats that the leadership used to bring recalcitrant members back in line included removal of members' pet projects from the bill and even removal of Smith as chair.[50]

Thus the leadership continues to pressure and influence committees' actions. They also continue to use the tools at their disposal to structure the floor agenda and actions taken after bills are passed. Despite statements by Hastert that under his regime the use of regular procedures would be restored, the GOP has continued to use restrictive special rules to block the Democrats from offering many of their preferred amendments. David Dreier of California, chair of the Rules Committee, noted that he used to complain about Democrats' use of special rules but that he learned "pretty quickly" that the majority party needed to use that device. " 'I had not known what it took to govern,' he acknowledged. Now 'our number one priority is to move our agenda.' "[51] Indeed, Don Wolfensberger, former head of the Republican staff on the Rules Committee, has concluded, "By the 107th Congress (2001–2003) . . . the Republicans had far exceeded the Democrats' worst excesses in restricting floor amendments."[52]

Another device that the GOP in both chambers has used in recent years has been restricting minority members from participating in the deliberations of conference committees, which are temporary panels set up to resolve differences in legislation after bills have been passed by both houses. For example, in 2003 only two moderate Democratic senators and no House Democrats were permitted to participate in the conference on the Medicare bill, and on the energy bill no Democrats at all were permitted in conference meetings. In using all of these techniques, the Republicans deny that they are being unfair to the Democrats. They contend that they are just doing what is necessary to enact their legislative agenda. As Speaker Hastert said in an interview in late 2003, "While a Speaker should strive to be fair, he is also judged by how he gets the job done. The job of the Speaker is to rule fairly, but ultimately to carry out the will of the majority." [53]

Thus all indications are that the theoretical account offered by CPG is as applicable in 2004 as it was in 1995. Partisan policy disagreement is just as strong, and partisan conflict just as intense. Indeed, these conditions continue to be reinforced by the close division of the two chambers. In every election since 1994, members of both parties have believed that they had a good chance to win majority control. That perception makes every decision on policy and legislative strategy potentially a high-stakes choice, giving the majority party strong incentive to use its institutional powers to the maximum. Therefore, as long as the legislative parties remain ideologically homogeneous and the ideological divergence between the two parties remains great, and as long as the partisan division of the chambers is close, we expect conditional party government theory to continue to provide a good explanation for congressional organization and activity.

Notes

Thanks to Jeremy Duff, of the Political Institutions and Public Choice Program at Michigan State University, for research assistance during the preparation of this chapter.

1. This interest in developing and sharing expertise is the central focus in the "informational" theory of legislative organization presented by Keith Krehbiel in *Information and Legislative Organization* (Chicago: University of Chicago Press, 1991).
2. Richard F. Fenno Jr., *Congressmen in Committees* (Boston: Little Brown, 1973), Chap. 1.
3. Indeed, David Mayhew contended that the institutional structure of the Congress was principally designed to foster members' reelection. See David R. Mayhew, *Congress: The Electoral Connection* (New Haven: Yale University Press, 1974). Also see E. Scott Adler, *Why Congressional Reforms Fail: Reelection and the House Committee System* (Chicago: University of Chicago Press, 2002).
4. See Richard L. Hall, *Participation in Congress* (New Haven: Yale University Press, 1996); and C. Lawrence Evans, *Leadership in Committee* (Ann Arbor: University of Michigan Press, 2001).
5. For more information on the history of the committee system, see Joseph Cooper, *The Origins of the Standing Committees and the Development of the Modern House* (Houston: Rice University Studies, 1970); and Christopher J. Deering and Steven S. Smith, *Committees in Congress*, 3rd ed. (Washington, D.C.: CQ Press, 1997).
6. For a detailed analysis of the growth of amending activity on the floors of both chambers see Steven S. Smith, *Call to Order: Floor Politics in the House and Senate* (Washington D.C.: Brookings Institution Press, 1989).
7. For more details, see David W. Rohde, *Parties and Leaders in the Postreform House* (Chicago: University of Chicago Press, 1991), Chap. 3.

8. See Rohde, *Parties and Leaders,* Chap. 2, and John H. Aldrich, *Why Parties? The Origin and Transformation of Political Parties in America* (Chicago: University of Chicago Press, 1995), Chaps. 6 and 7. An alternative (but compatible) theory of partisan organization of Congress is offered by Gary W. Cox and Mathew D. McCubbins, *Legislative Leviathan* (Berkeley: University of California Press, 1993).
9. Sara Brandes Crook and John R. Hibbing, "Congressional Reform and Party Discipline: The Effects of Changes in the Seniority System on Party Loyalty in the House of Representatives," *British Journal of Political Science* 15 (1985): 207–226. See also Fiona M. Wright, "The Caucus Reelection Requirement and the Transformation of Committee Chairs," *Legislative Studies Quarterly* 25 (2000): 469–480.
10. See Rohde, *Parties and Leaders,* 75–76.
11. Barbara Sinclair, *Legislators, Leaders, and Lawmaking: The U.S. House of Representatives in the Postreform Era* (Baltimore: Johns Hopkins University Press, 1995), 164.
12. For more details on this transformed relationship see Sinclair, *Legislators, Leaders, and Lawmaking,* Chap. 9, and Rohde, *Parties and Leaders,* Chap. 4.
13. Much has been written about the new role of the Rules Committee. See, for example, Bruce I. Oppenheimer, "The Rules Committee: New Arm of Leadership in a Decentralized House," in *Congress Reconsidered,* ed. Lawrence C. Dodd and Bruce I. Oppenheimer (New York: Praeger, 1977), 96–116; Stanley Bach and Steven S. Smith, *Managing Uncertainty in the House of Representatives* (Washington, D.C.: Brookings Institution Press, 1988); Sinclair, *Legislators, Leaders, and Lawmaking,* Chap. 8; and Rohde, *Parties and Leaders,* 98–118.
14. See Gary C. Jacobson, *The Politics of Congressional Elections,* 5th ed. (New York: Longman, 2001), 178–185.
15. The discussion in this section is drawn from John H. Aldrich and David W. Rohde, "The Transition to Republican Rule in the House: Implications for Theories of Congressional Politics," *Political Science Quarterly* 112 (1997–1998): 541–567; and C. Lawrence Evans and Walter J. Oleszek, *Congress Under Fire: Reform Politics and the Republican Majority* (Boston: Houghton Mifflin, 1997).
16. Quoted in Guy Gugliotta, "In New House, Barons Yield to the Boss," *Washington Post,* December 1, 1994, 1.
17. Recent research on the development of committee jurisdictions includes David C. King, *Turf Wars* (Chicago: University of Chicago Press, 1997); and Frank R. Baumgartner, Bryan D. Jones, and Michael C. MacLeod, "The Evolution of Legislative Jurisdictions," *Journal of Politics* 62 (May 2000): 321–349.
18. See Adler, *Why Congressional Reforms Fail.*
19. Sinclair, *Legislators, Leaders, and Lawmaking,* 163–197.
20. For more detail on the contract and Congress's actions on it, see James G. Gimpel, *Fulfilling the Contract: The First 100 Days* (Boston: Allyn and Bacon, 1996).
21. *Washington Post,* October 8, 1995, A5.
22. *Roll Call,* October 2, 1995, 20.
23. *Congressional Quarterly Weekly Report,* July 22, 1995, 2176.
24. *National Journal,* July 22, 1995, 1892.
25. *Washington Post,* March 26, 1996, A9.
26. Task forces had been used before the GOP majority took over. See Sinclair, *Legislators, Leaders, and Lawmaking.* For more recent details on task force use, see Barbara Sinclair, *Unorthodox Lawmaking: New Legislative Processes in the U.S. Congress,* 2nd ed. (Washington, D.C.: CQ Press, 2000).
27. See *Congressional Quarterly Weekly Report,* September 23, 1995, 2886; *Roll Call,* October 12, 1995, 3. For more systematic analysis of bypassing committees, see Charles J. Finocchiaro, "Setting the Stage: Party and Procedure in the Pre-Floor Agenda Setting of the U.S. House" (Ph.D. diss., Michigan State University, 2003); and Sinclair, *Unorthodox Lawmaking.*

28. Sinclair, *Unorthodox Lawmaking,* 94.
29. Ibid., 211 and 20, respectively.
30. *Roll Call,* March 20, 1995, 18.
31. *Roll Call,* November 28, 1994, 19.
32. *Congressional Quarterly Weekly Report,* October 21, 1995, 3207.
33. See Richard F. Fenno Jr., *The Power of the Purse* (Boston: Little, Brown, 1966); Fenno, *Congressmen in Committees*; and Joseph White, "The Functions and Power of the House Appropriations Committee" (Ph.D. diss., University of California, Berkeley, 1989).
34. This discussion is drawn mainly from John H. Aldrich and David W. Rohde, "The Republican Revolution and the House Appropriations Committee," *Journal of Politics* 62 (2000): 1–33; and Bryan W. Marshall, Brandon C. Prins, and David W. Rohde, "Majority Party Leadership, Strategic Choice, and Committee Power: Appropriations in the House, 1995–1998," in *Congress on Display, Congress at Work,* ed. William Bianco (Ann Arbor: University of Michigan Press, 2000), 69–99.
35. Elizabeth Drew, *Showdown: The Struggle between the Gingrich Congress and the Clinton White House* (New York: Simon and Schuster, 1996), 260.
36. See for example, Dennis Ippolito, *Congressional Spending* (Ithaca, N.Y.: Cornell University Press, 1981); Lance T. LeLoup, *The Fiscal Congress* (Westport, Conn.: Greenwood Press, 1980); Allen Schick, *Congress and Money* (Washington, D.C.: Urban Institute, 1980); and Aaron Wildavsky, *The New Politics of the Budgetary Process* (Glenview, Ill.: Scott, Foresman, 1988).
37. D. Roderick Kiewiet and Mathew D. McCubbins, *The Logic of Delegation* (Chicago: University of Chicago Press, 1991).
38. D. Roderick Kiewiet and Keith Krehbiel, "Here's the President. Where's the Party? U.S. Appropriations on Discretionary Domestic Spending, 1950–1999," *Leviathan* 30 (2002): 115–137.
39. John H. Aldrich, Brad T. Gomez, and Jennifer L. Merolla, "Follow the Money: Models of Congressional Governance and the Appropriations Process" (paper delivered at the annual meeting of the Midwest Political Science Association, Chicago, April 25–28, 2002). The discussion here is taken from unpublished revisions of that paper.
40. The data are adapted from Tables 1-4 in Jamie L. Carson, Charles J. Finocchiaro, and David W. Rohde, "Consensus and Conflict in House Decision Making: A Bill-Level Examination of Committee and Floor Behavior" (paper delivered at the annual meeting of the Midwest Political Science Association, Chicago, April 2001). The data include all public bills and joint resolutions referred to a committee and either reported by the committee or debated on the floor.
41. See Mayhew, *Congress: The Electoral Connection,* 52–73.
42. The classification was developed by Deering and Smith, *Committees in Congress,* 3rd ed., Chap. 3. The prestige committees are Appropriations and Ways and Means; the policy committees are Banking, Commerce, Education, Foreign Affairs, Government Operations, and Judiciary; the constituency committees are Agriculture, Armed Services, Interior, Merchant Marine, Science, Transportation, and Veterans' Affairs. (Committee names change over time. These are the names for the 96th Congress.) The committees that the authors term "unrequested" are omitted, as are Rules and Budget because they consider few bills. Note that bills referred to more than one committee are counted for each committee to which they were referred.
43. These data are taken from Mark S. Hurwitz, Roger J. Moiles, and David W. Rohde, "Distributive and Partisan Issues in Agriculture Policy in the 104th House," *American Political Science Review* 95 (2001): 915.
44. The dominant role of Senate subcommittee chairs is discussed in C. Lawrence Evans, *Leadership in Committee: A Comparative Analysis of Leadership Behavior in the U.S. Senate* (Ann Arbor: University of Michigan Press, 2001).

45. See, for example, Lawrence C. Dodd and Bruce I. Oppenheimer, "Congress and the Emerging Order: Conditional Party Government or Constructive Partisanship?" in *Congress Reconsidered,* 6th ed., ed. Lawrence C. Dodd and Bruce I. Oppenheimer (Washington, D.C.: CQ Press, 1997), 390–413.
46. See, for example, Richard Fleisher and Jon R. Bond, "The Shrinking Middle in the U.S. Congress," *British Journal of Political Science* 34 (July 2004): 429–451; and Sean Theriault, "The Case of the Vanishing Moderates: Party Polarization in the Modern Congress" (manuscript, University of Texas, 2004).
47. *Roll Call,* November 18, 2002, 1.
48. *Washington Post,* November 30, 2003, A8.
49. *CQ Weekly,* November 8, 2003, 2785.
50. *CQ Weekly,* July 26, 2003, 1910.
51. Jim VandeHei, "Using the Rules Committee to Block Democrats," *Washington Post,* June 16, 2003, A21.
52. Don Wolfensberger, "The Motion to Recommit in the House: The Creation, Evisceration, and Restoration of a Minority Right" (paper prepared for the Conference on the History of Congress, Stanford University, December 5–6, 2003), 31.
53. *Roll Call,* November 17, 2003, 4.

12. The (Dis)Integration of the House Appropriations Committee: Revisiting *The Power of the Purse* in a Partisan Era

Joshua B. Gordon

The historic foundation of congressional power is the control over the federal government's purse strings through the appropriations process. That power traces to the Constitution's stricture that only through congressional appropriations could money "be drawn from the Treasury," but it also rests on decades of policymaking tradition and repetition. However, congressional control has recently dwindled because of a broken appropriations process and increasing executive branch dominance.

The evidence is plentiful. In January 2004, the George W. Bush administration successfully struck language it opposed from an appropriations bill, despite its having been voted for by both houses of Congress. Just one year earlier, the appropriations process became so mangled that for the first time ever, one Congress (the 107th) punted the decisions necessary to operate the federal government to the next Congress (the 108th). In 2002, the House Appropriations Committee (HAC), the traditional anchor of the appropriations process, lost so much control over its agenda that committee leaders decided they were better off not even writing their largest social spending bill, lest they be on record supporting it.[1] All of this transpired during an unprecedented five consecutive years (and six out of the prior seven) in which Congress and the president had to agree six times or more to prevent the government from shutting down because they could not agree on how to spend its money. The only time during that period that Congress was able to enact individually all thirteen spending bills necessary to fund the government was during the wave of bipartisanship following the September 11, 2001, terrorist attacks.

Congressional staff members suggest that the appropriations process is in the worst shape anyone can remember. Budget beat writers have declared the process "broken" and claim that appropriators, at one time the most powerful members of Congress, have lost their power.[2] One fiscal policy expert has even said on the record, "It's horrible . . . but I think the only thing that would smooth the appropriations process is another terrorist event." [3]

This picture starkly contrasts with the one seen by congressional observers during much of the twentieth century. From the 1930s to the early 1990s the HAC possessed great policymaking power. In *The Power of the Purse* (1966), the most enduring and comprehensive picture political science has of the Appropriations Committee, Richard Fenno argued that the committee was the anchor for Congress's power over federal spending because it crafted masterly appropriations bills that smoothly garnered the support of Congress and the executive branch, while protecting the autonomous authority of the committee and the House itself.[4] Joseph White's (1989) excellent follow-up to Fenno, along with other examinations of the Appropriations Committee since, has shown that this power continued much as Fenno described right up until the early 1990s.[5] Then, after their 1994 Republican revolution, congressional Republican leaders decided to use this committee power to quickly and effectively achieve their far-reaching, conservative reform agenda rather than allow the committee to craft independent bills as it had done historically.

The House Republican Party leaders achieved minimal policy success with their efforts to dominate appropriations decisions, while leaving the appropriations process fraught with delay and gridlock. In doing so, they erred badly in 1995, engaging in a game of "chicken" with President Bill Clinton over fiscal priorities that led to a government shutdown and turned the public against the Republican Congress, in effect wiping out any momentum the Republicans had in national policy influence following their sweeping congressional victory less than two years before. Since then, House Republican leaders have repeatedly failed to find an effective strategy through which to control the appropriations process and yet have remained largely unwilling to let the committee perform its historic role in an independent manner. This impasse has led to further executive branch political and policy victories, regardless of whether the president was a Democrat or a Republican. In fact, many Republican committee members would argue that things have been worse since George W. Bush took office. During a discussion in 2003, House Appropriations Majority Staff Director James Dyer remembered that he had once told Clinton's director of the Office of Management and Budget (OMB), "One day you'll be gone and things will be better." Yet after two years of the Republican administration he realized that he "couldn't [have been] more wrong."[6]

The central problem for the congressional Republican Party is that the polarized partisanship within Congress since the early 1990s, combined with the institutional changes and interventionist party leaders brought in with the Republican revolution, has subverted the autonomy and fractured the internal unity of the House Appropriations Committee. As a result, the HAC is no longer able to write bills in the expert and dominant manner it did previously, leaving the appropriations process without its anchor. Rushing into the void, the Senate has tried to be more active in managing the process. Its Appropriations Committee decided in 1997 to start writing complete bills for the first time, rather than leaving the initial drafting of appropriations legislation to the House. This development has slowed the process and led to growing division between the House and Senate over core appropriations strategies. More troubling for Congress as a whole is that the executive branch has built on its successful micromanagement of appropriations details during the government shutdown and no longer feels the need to defer appropriations decisions to Congress, especially a Congress in which the House and Senate are increasingly divided. This is an important change in policy control for the country, as power has been lost by the branch of government and the House of Congress closest to the people, creating another area in which the executive branch is consolidating policy power. The purpose of this essay is to examine in detail the conditions that have led to this dramatic shift in appropriations power, starting with a look back at the reasons the House appropriations process proved so dominant in the mid-twentieth century, as detailed by Fenno, and then proceeding to assess why the process—and thus congressional control over the power of the purse—has deteriorated so greatly.

Fenno's House Appropriations Committee and Its Legacy

Richard Fenno's great insight from observing the HAC in the 1950s and 1960s was that the committee's internal unity—what he called "integration"—was the foundation for its dominance of the legislative process. The institutional structure he observed was one in which the committee members were so expert, efficient, balanced, and unanimous when writing their bills that the other members of the House, along with the members of the Senate and the executive branch, saw no reason to substantially alter the legislation or usurp the committee's power. This structure served the members of the committee because of the political and policy power that came when their recommendations and hard work were recognized, supported, and passed by the other actors. The structure served the House because the stability of its committee system and the broad reach of its domestic policy influence were anchored by the deference that the Senate and the president showed to the HAC. Additionally, by maintaining primary control over appropriations the House was able to level the playing field with the Senate—the generally more exclusive, prestigious, and powerful institution. Finally, the structure supported the power of the entire Congress vis-à-vis the executive branch because the ability to consistently and efficiently produce bills that ran the government reinforced congressional control over federal spending and because through that control Congress was best able to effectively oversee and direct the executive.

Appropriations Committee integration and unanimity, inherently including the norms of minimal partisanship and collegial social relations, were possible during Fenno's era because comity in Congress as a whole was the norm. Members tended to live and socialize together in Washington, D.C., within a community where partisan differences were de-emphasized.[7] In this environment, comity and collegiality were staples of the HAC more than any other committee in Congress. Members were picked to serve on the committee based on a specific set of characteristics that reinforced these behavioral norms.[8] Thus, HAC members were generally senior and represented safe districts because they were thought to have an easier time making sometimes tough and unpopular decisions. They also tended to be hard workers who were not known for their ideological dedication. Such members were selected for seats on the committee after "painstaking deliberation," to create a body composed of the most "responsible" legislators.[9] Furthermore, the committee had very low turnover, bolstering institutional memory and providing a continuity that increased the likelihood that committee norms would be passed on—a crucial support for integration. Additionally, Appropriations was an exclusive committee in the House (but not in the Senate), whose members were not allowed to serve on other committees—ensuring loyalty and the time and concentration required to become experts in an appropriations area. HAC members worked longer hours together than other committee members and did so within an environment hostile to hierarchical divisions. Even their committee room was understated and desegregated, with seating lacking the normal separation based on seniority. Overall, the effect of committee norms and membership characteristics was to make the committee a remarkably insular and unified group. One member at the time said, "You talk about the Senate being exclusive. It's a sideshow when you put it beside a subcommittee on appropriations. . . . they are a clan . . . a club." [10]

To aid in the development of collegiality, the committee avoided making members take partisan positions against each other, and roll call votes were avoided as often as possible—a delicate and strategic process under the direction of the subcommittee and full committee chairmen and ranking members. Members were encouraged to resolve differences in private, and were able to do so in part because markups were often held in sessions closed to the media. Overall, members achieved agreement by sharing a common belief in the decision-making process, practicing minimal partisanship when together, socializing new members into their norms, and recognizing common goals—the most critical goal being the drafting of well-crafted and balanced bills that could pass the House and the Senate and obtain a presidential signature.

The deck was stacked in favor of a well-integrated, collegial committee because of the need to counterbalance the fragmenting force of powerful subcommittees dominated by strong and autonomous chairmen, often called "cardinals." Such fragmentation was necessary to facilitate the sharp division of labor necessary to produce bills in the most expert and efficient manner possible. Appropriations subcommittees were considered the hardest-working institutions in Congress; they had to review the minute details of government agency justifications and then hold hearings in which they peppered executive branch policymakers with questions and warnings. Subcommittee members were personally selected by their chairmen, who often stayed with the same subcommittees for decades. This allowed each subcommittee to build up the institutional memory and expertise needed to challenge accurately the much larger resources of the bureaucracy over which they governed. The norm of reciprocity within the full committee encouraged members to respect and accept the work of all subcommittees with as little dissent and amendment as possible, thereby allowing the committee to present a unified face when taking its bills to the floor.

On the floor, committee leaders gave speeches stressing to the rest of the House how bipartisan and fair their committee process had been because they adhered to venerated norms and worked hard along the way. When it came time to vote, most House members from both parties had little reason to complain about the process or work product and were dependent on the HAC's expertise. They generally passed the bills with few amendments and by large margins.

Only then would the Senate Appropriations Committee act—always second because of tradition and because the House had the most time and knowledge to conduct hearings and grill the executive agencies. The Senate committee played the role of an "appeals court" for decisions made in the House, often not touching at least one-third of the House's bill and then only making small and incremental changes elsewhere. Quickly going to conference, the two sides split many differences on the bill, so that by the time the measure got to the president it still looked very similar to the original written by its HAC subcommittee. Because these measures had the bipartisan support of both houses of Congress, and because his executive agencies had been given fair and bipartisan hearings during the drafting process, the president almost always signed.

Appropriations after Fenno

In his 1966 book, Fenno recognized that the logic and effectiveness of the House appropriations process were not immutable. In fact, they rested on a variety of environmental conditions—the most important one being minimal partisanship. Fenno warned accordingly that "nothing would be more dysfunctional . . . than bitter and extended partisan controversy" for maintaining the norms that held the House Appropriations Committee together.[11] Ironically, the movement toward such a period in Congress was right around the corner.

The Vietnam and Watergate era saw congressional reforms and rules changes that fostered a more partisan congressional environment, while the southern realignment was about to change the political landscape more broadly. Yet in his comprehensive update of Fenno's research twenty years later, White concluded that the committee had proved highly stable and that by the late 1980s, "Appropriations arguably was at a peak of power and influence." [12] White found that it remained a "club," socializing its new members while still being led by autonomous and dominant subcommittee chairmen. The appropriations process remained "accommodative, compromising and moderate." Even the committee room remained "equivalent in style to, say, a meeting room at a Motel 6." White concluded, "Bipartisanship dominates because Appropriations feels it needs to accommodate as many members as possible, build as big a cushion against hard times or resentment or the President or any of the possible threats to its bills." [13] It was also the case that, because the Democratic Party maintained congressional control from 1966 to 1994, there were no abrupt shifts in leadership within the committee that might have undercut its stability and continuity.

The most important challenge for appropriators of the post-Watergate reform era was the coming of the modern congressional budget process in the Budget Act of 1974. The new mandate immediately injected partisanship into the normally bipartisan process of passing money bills:

> The production of a comprehensive budget plan . . . was simply impossible under the norms . . . that had dominated budget politics and decision-making in the pre-reform House. As suggested by a Republican staff member, "The macro focus . . . leads members to a broader debate based on what makes a Republican a Republican and a Democrat a Democrat." [14]

There is evidence that the partisanship in the budget process during the 1970s led to the increase in partisanship in the House as a whole over the following decades.[15] However, while controversy and bitterness reigned over the House floor during consideration of the budget resolutions, the HAC continued to receive support at "extraordinarily high levels." [16]

The specific rules of the budget process insulated the HAC from some degree of partisanship. The newly created Budget Committees were given the task of determining the total amount of spending by the federal government. That allowed the HAC to stay out of the divisive arguments over macroeconomic policy that were inflamed by the stagnant economy in the 1970s and the deficit crisis in the 1980s. Furthermore, rules changes now gave the HAC the "right to bind the floor to their allocational priorities. . . . probably the most significant formal change in how the committee does its work." [17] This allowed the committee to consolidate control over appropriations specifics, including the distribution of district benefits. The change reinforced bipartisanship and integration because it allowed the Democrats to keep their coalition together by widely dispersing benefits and spending liberally, and it kept the Republicans happy as long as their district interests were also served.[18]

As Fenno predicted, committee stability continued because the integrative norms and the still-exclusive atmosphere maintained membership contentment even in the face of challenge and loss brought on by the new rules and reforms. Thus, environmental and institutional changes did not immediately embroil the members in a crisis of power, even though they were under attack from external interests, whether from the budget committees, deficit hawks, or a president who disagreed with spending priorities. As Larry Dodd has suggested, under such fire power committees such as the HAC often become even more cohesive and strong internally.[19]

Even with the overwhelming similarities between the committee he observed and Fenno's, White nevertheless emphasized some changes in the HAC's institutional environment that, although not transformational during his observation period, were important because they would be amplified later, during the Republican revolution. Divisiveness and partisanship were slowly creeping into the appropriations arena, as amending activity increased on the House floor. White found that outside members challenged the committee more and won more often than they had in the past. The number of amendments on which the subcommittee chairmen and ranking members took opposite sides increased as well, showing unusual committee partisan division. The amendments, called "riders," came mostly in the form of limitation amendments to prohibit executive branch agencies from spending funds to perform a specific activity or enforce a specific regulation.[20] When proposed on the floor by non–committee members, these limits encroach upon appropriator terrain. However, even when sponsoring amendments against Appropriations, the Republican minority was careful about the extent of division. Looking back, a Democratic subcommittee chairman of the time recalled that during discussions with a Republican member who was against his bill, the member "told me how their floor plan would work and what amendments would be offered. . . . we didn't blindside one another." [21]

White reported that "there is some belief that the Committee is more subject to attack than it was in the olden days" and that the hostile floor was definitely "a source of uncertainty." [22] Overall, however,

> The Committee does succeed in winning House acceptance of the great bulk of the recommendations it brings to the floor. In the worst year, 1978, subcommittee chairmen were defeated on 17 amendments that they opposed, not much more than one per bill. In 1982, subcommittee chairmen lost only twice.[23]

In retrospect Congress and the HAC maintained much firmer control of appropriations decisions during the 1980s than one might assume given the popularity of President Reagan and his campaign to reduce government spending. The explanation often given for the ability of the HAC to survive Reagan's policy assault was his lack of interest in learning enough about appropriations to move beyond general calls for cutting government to fighting for specific spending reductions. When it came down to federal spending, "Reagan asked for so much less, compared to last year, than any other president, that a Congress that raised him substantially was still far more restrictive than in the heyday of Appropriations 'guardianship.'"[24] In this way, the Appropriations Committee resembled its conservative, Fenno-era counterpart, still acting in a bipartisan way to win the war over spending priorities, acting as district benefit claimants, and representing "Congress's preferences quite closely."[25] Similar processes occurred in the presidency of George H. W. Bush. However, his very public bipartisanship in negotiating fiscal issues on both the spending and the tax side enraged the more partisan elements of the Republican Party—especially when it involved tax increases. This situation ultimately cost Bush support from the right wing of his party, which contributed greatly to his loss of the 1992 election and perhaps doomed the future of bipartisan fiscal policy.

By the end of the 1980s and the early 1990s, the Appropriations Committee environment had changed under a new budget process and increased partisanship in ways that complicated Fenno's picture of appropriations of a quarter-century earlier. In White's perspective,

> The overall budgeting climate was not merely stormy; it was a persistent gale, uprooting institutions and behavior patterns throughout the political system. One might have expected these conditions to place House Appropriations under greater pressure.[26]

Instead, the fundamental logic of appropriations decision making remained remarkably similar to the one that Fenno documented, with the HAC remaining the central power in appropriations politics and Congress sustaining its control over the power of the purse. Then came the Republican revolution.

The Republican Revolution and Its Challenges

The Republican revolution, marked forcefully by the 1994 election of seventy-three new Republican House members in a sweeping takeover of majority party control in Congress, challenged the basic decision-making structure of the House and of Congress as a whole. Although partisanship had been increasing in Congress over the previous three decades, it achieved dominance only upon the Republican leadership's transformation of the institution's rules and social norms. Those changes were made as the most effective means to promote and enact the party's policy agenda. Yet they had consequences that made that agenda more difficult to achieve through the appropriations process, which was one of the main tools the Republicans chose to enact their policy preferences.

Republican Party leaders had made an implicit assumption based on their experience during the prior decades: that the House dominance of appropriations was essentially an inherent dominance, so that operating through the appropriations process would allow the party leadership to dominate national policymaking and spending. However, the power of the HAC and the House had actually rested not in a "constitutional inherency" but in the character of House appropriations politics that had evolved during the twentieth century, particularly in the fact that House appropriations bills were so much based on policy expertise, and so masterly in balancing the interests and demands of a wide range of groups and partisan interests, that they could withstand attack and shape the broad contours of the final policy agreed to by conference committees and signed by the president. While such bills had never secured all that a majority party ideally wanted, the majority party and its leaders did obtain, year in and year out, much of what they wanted, while also maintaining both control of the overall process and a working relationship with the minority party. The single-minded partisanship of House Republican leaders represented a major change in strategy, as the leaders intentionally undercut a wide range of committee norms, procedures, and political processes as a means to obtaining and consolidating political power. What they did not realize—because they were so focused on transforming the normal legislative process and committee system and because they did not have much experience with committee and legislative leadership—was that they were also undercutting the necessary conditions for a successful HAC-directed appropriations process.

Republican Government

The Republican ascent to majority control coincided with the takeover of the party by its younger, more partisan wing. The new party leaders, most visibly directed by Newt Gingrich of Georgia, were opposed to the type of bipartisan politics practiced during prior decades. During the 1980s alone, they saw their ideological godfather, Ronald Reagan, agree with Democrats to reverse some of his tax cuts, saw President Bush go back on his "read my lips" no-taxes pledge, and saw a bipartisan appropriations process continually increase government spending and build up huge deficits. The Republican leaders, many of whom had originally worked for or been conservative Democrats until the southern realignment (including Trent Lott, Phil Gramm, and Gingrich), began to realize that while conservative Republicanism was winning elections for the presidency by large margins, the congressional Republican party was still a substantial policy minority. They began to yearn for the institutional power they were used to having when they were a part of the majority. They decided dramatic change was necessary.

They crafted a political strategy that sought to take advantage of increased congressional partisanship while breaking the bonds of institutional norms. In the 1970s and 1980s, such norms reinforced Democratic control of Congress, even in the face of that party's increasingly liberal and partisan majority and despite the southern conservative split within the party. The norms allowed the Democrats to hold together; collegiality and consensual politics, especially on congressional committees, also worked to keep congressional Republicans from offering strong opposition to policies that went against their growing conservatism. The new Republicans decided to burn their bridges to the Democratic Party and set out to foster new bonds within the Republican Party to create an alternative set of norms, relationships, and socialization processes. Their plan was expansive. They encouraged the development of a whole host of supportive groups outside the House, such as fund-raising organizations, conservative think tanks, and farm teams in the states to encourage quality challengers to run for Congress.[27] They built intraparty caucuses to break up the power monopoly held by Republican Party leaders.[28] One such group, the Gingrich-led Conservative Opportunity Society,

> [b]egan guerrilla warfare against the Democratic leadership . . . interrupting House sessions, demanding roll calls on unpopular measures, engaging in uncivil discourse, and using special orders after the House adjourned to address a small but interested national audience on the cable network C-SPAN.[29]

They also attempted to sabotage committee legislation they disliked by amending and/or delaying it on the floor, whether they were involved in the subject matter or not—at the time an unusual affront to the norm of committee reciprocity.

Basically, they formed a new structure of power, influence, and institutional dominance supported by a new system for Republican social relations, not out of a misunderstanding of how social norms could be supportive, but precisely because they saw how such processes blocked their own rise. The disruptive offensive reached its greatest heights (and had its biggest opportunity) during the period of unified government under Democrats following Clinton's victory in 1992.

Challengers for congressional seats succeeded in making the majority party appear inept and corrupt. The networks of conservative groups succeeded in developing strong challengers at the local level, became adept at fund raising, and gained the ability to motivate their strongest grassroots supporters to go to the polls. All of these things helped elevate the party to a congressional majority.

Once in office, the Republicans turned their effort to remaking the internal operations of Congress to achieve their policy goals. The forefront of the effort was to enable tight party control by centralizing power within the office of the Speaker of the House. Gingrich was elected to the position and took over the right to assign committee chairmanships without regard to seniority. Committee chairmen were given greater power to appoint their subcommittee chairmen and hire staff. The Speaker was also given a greater say in committee membership. These changes made all committees more responsive to the party leadership, which could then centrally direct them to achieve the legislative goal of moving policy to the right.

The committee under the most focus was the House Appropriations Committee, both because of its apparent power in prior decades and because the rest of the House was tied up with passing the "Contract with America." The leadership knew the HAC was one of the last remaining bastions for consensual politics and knew it would require special focus to break through and gain control over its policymaking power. They tapped a chairman in violation of the seniority norm with whom they felt they could work closely. Robert Livingston, the man fifth in seniority on the committee at the time, got the job and then appointed subcommittee chairmen only upon their signing a loyalty pledge to the party leadership.

The HAC was particularly scorned by the new freshman class. They felt that the "old-guard" committee members "represented everything we were elected and served against"—an outdated politics in which career politicians with entrenched committee staff supported the bipartisan and irresponsible spending that stood in the way of good conservative policy and a balanced budget.[30] In some of their first acts, the Republican Conference voted to impose term limits on all appropriations subcommittee chairmen. After a wave of committee retirements—by Democrats who could not swallow minority status and Republicans who thought they would have greater control over the appropriations agenda—the freshmen made sure they were represented on the committee to infiltrate its culture and remake it from the inside. Of the eleven new members appointed to the HAC, seven were freshmen (the other four were sophomores). This represented a major change: over the prior forty years only 18 percent of Democratic appointees had been named to the committee in their first term. Thus, within a short time, the committee became much younger and less-connected to the consensual appropriations politics of old.

Additionally, the safe-seat norm for appointments was reversed: Some new members were selected for the committee because of their district's marginality, in an attempt by Republicans to solidify those members' holds on their districts. The ideological makeup of the committee accelerated on what had been a slow, twenty-five-year path of polarization. The gap between Democratic and Republican members of the committee grew as the gap between the parties in the House grew.[31] Committee Republicans, historically more liberal than their overall party in the House, also began to have ideologies more in line with their conference. Another important change was that the committee now saw less ideological diversity within each party's delegation, making bipartisanship more difficult because there were fewer members able to bridge the ideological gap to foster compromise and push must-pass legislation through the process.[32]

Committee socialization was hamstrung by new rules for dealing with the media and term limits on chairmen. During the Fenno era, one of the main factors that allowed the committee to socialize its members into committee norms was the ability to iron out differences away from the eyes of the public and the other House members. One element of the Republican revolution was a desire to open the legislative process to the public and the press, and the HAC began allowing the press into conference committee meetings and subcommittee markups (except defense and a few other national-security-related segments). This change brought opportunities for additional public grandstanding and reduced cover for compromise. Term limits forced chairmen to switch from committees that in some cases they had worked on for decades. In addition to contributing to overall loss of institutional memory, the change hamstrung the chairmen's ability to moderate disputes within the committee. One staff member explained,

> It really changes the dynamic . . . . you have the absence of the omnipotent, all-powerful subcommittee chair. Now, members aren't afraid to take a chairman on, in the old days they would never.[33]

With the tight leash on the handpicked committee chairman and the loyalty-oath-signing subcommittee chairmen, HAC autonomy shrunk greatly. The party leadership, over the objection of appropriators, pushed during committee markups for insertion of social-conservative legislative items into appropriations bills via controversial riders. This agitation disrupted the carefully nurtured bipartisan committee atmosphere by increasing partisan voting on amendments and, more consequential, the frequency of such votes.[34] Furthermore, there were major internal disagreements between the newest committee members and the old-guard cardinals, as the cardinals routinely voted for amendments supported by Democrats, whereas the newer members refused. The differences between the cardinals and the class of 1994 in votes on Republican-supported amendments increased consistently over the Congresses after the revolution.[35]

Appropriations outside the HAC

In prior eras, committee unanimity fostered by integration, along with procedural advantages and displays of unity on the floor, convinced the whole House to pass appropriations bills by wide margins and with little amendment. In just the first year after the revolution, overall partisan amending increased to at least three times the highest level seen during prior decades, and it continued at historically high rates in the years that followed.[36] Furthermore, appropriations subcommittee chairmen (representing the HAC's position) have been subject to much more frequent defeat on floor amendments.[37] Evidence also shows that "many of the cardinals were united and dissatisfied with a large number of the proposed changes to their bills that had the support of the GOP conference." [38]

The result of this conflict and activity was that although the committee was still able to pass legislation through the House, primarily because of the procedural and partisan prowess of the House leadership, its legislative success did not take the unanimous and consensual form it had in the past. This rougher road for the bills signaled to the other actors involved in appropriations—the president and Senate—that HAC legislation was no longer written in a consensual and inclusive manner. Even though the Senate was also under Republican control, its traditionally more moderate politics and liberal spending preferences put it so much at odds with the House that its Appropriations Committee felt the need, within three years of the Republican takeover, to write its own appropriations bills for the first time. The executive branch, with Democratic President Clinton at the helm, saw that the president could manipulate appropriations details through veto and government shutdown threats, since Republican positions on appropriations were now tailored to the conservative districts of the party members rather than being the result of a moderate and bipartisan process more in line with the national constituency. As a result of the new level of involvement of the Senate and the executive, final appropriations legislation now substantially diverged from the original, House-passed bills.

These developments can be seen more clearly by looking at some case studies showing the evolution of HAC politics over the past decade. While originally pushed along by the partisan animosity between the Republican Congress and Clinton, the appropriations split among the Senate, the House, and the executive branch actually increased in severity under the presidency of George W. Bush, with Bush and his agencies increasingly feeling free to follow their own policy perspectives and political needs, irrespective of congressional wishes.

The Contemporary Development of House Appropriations Policymaking

What is clear when one reviews some distinct stages that have emerged in the years since the Republican revolution is that, as Fenno suggested might happen, partisanship has undermined House power over the purse. The Senate and the executive branch have benefited in a trend that has continued regardless of the partisan makeup of the government. Furthermore, while the period of bipartisanship following the September 11 terrorist attacks shows that Congress and the HAC can still drive appropriations politics, the return to divisiveness and executive dominance shortly afterward suggests that the House loss of power might not be temporary or easily reversed.

The Clinton Era

The budget battles between Clinton and the Republican House, beginning with the 1995 government shutdown, fundamentally shaped all appropriations activity since. That opening battle was the first test of the House Republican leadership's partisan legislative strategy against the other branches of government, and it also gave Clinton an opening to reassert himself after his party's drubbing in the 1994 midterm elections. Ultimately, the House Republican failure in 1995 and in most of the battles afterward rewarded and reinforced Senate and executive branch assumption of appropriations control.

The Senate's move to write its own bills opened many new areas of spending, and by generally maintaining the tradition of working after the House the Senate was in a position to add large amounts to House spending totals. This placed House appropriators in the difficult position of trying to convince their chamber's members of a need to limit requests and awards in the name of fiscal discipline and budget cutting, while such discipline just allowed the Senate to increase spending and claim even more pork for themselves. Such a strategy was pushed, undoubtedly, by the two senators most identified with congressional pork barrel spending in recent congressional history, Ted Stevens, R-Alaska, and Robert Byrd, D-W.V., the Senate Appropriations Committee's chairman and ranking member.[39] Because the Democratic president's interest was also in increasing spending at the end of the process, the Senate committee could just blame Clinton for any ultimate increases. This abandonment of tight spending goals resulted in increased hostility between the House and Senate factions of the Republican Party. It also increased the willingness of the rank and file and leadership in the House to place even more limits on appropriators, out of anger, while simultaneously increasing mistrust between the HAC and the party.

President Clinton was convinced that he could benefit politically by vetoing bills written without Democratic input that included social-conservative legislative changes. His refusal to sign the must-pass bills surprised the House leaders, who had assumed that, like Reagan when he faced a Democratic Congress, Clinton would be forced to accept the bills regardless of distasteful provisions because the HAC and its bills inherently had momentum and power. Those leaders had failed to take into account, however, that even during the Reagan years the HAC, through its consensual process, incorporated Republicans in the decision making and that it followed much of Reagan's general budget direction. This time, the two parties reached a stalemate, and the federal government had to shut down its nonessential services on two different occasions until an agreement on appropriations could be reached. Clinton won the public relations war during the spectacle, as the public grew to believe that the Republicans were not capable of legislating maturely and had injected too much partisanship into the appropriations process.[40] This empowered Clinton to dictate the specific terms of the final agreement within a face-saving framework promoted by congressional leaders. Furthermore, it meant that Congress lost the future ability to negotiate using threats of government shutdowns because the public had linked blame for them to congressional, and not executive, failure.

After that first battle, the Republicans were forced to accept whatever changes Clinton demanded because they had no way to rewrite the appropriations bills in a bipartisan manner acceptable to the other actors in the process. The HAC had already been transformed into a partisan committee, and in ways that were not easily reversible given their foundation in the characteristics of the sitting committee members. Because the HAC's process was now annually directed by the partisan House leadership, dictates from the executive branch as to how to bring a bill in line with presidential preferences were the only way for the bill to be produced. Those with the knowledge and expertise to include and mold presidential desires, while maintaining House and congressional prerogatives—the Appropriations subcommittee chairmen—were not given the latitude or power to do so. Additionally, many in the Republican Conference, especially the 1994 freshman class, were uninterested in compromise and refused to support more bipartisan bills anyway, no matter what happened to their bills once they left the House floor. The minority Democrats had been so inflamed that they now resisted attempts at bipartisanship because, with electoral volatility, close seat margins, and a president behind them, they saw political gain in being obstructionist and fighting ideological fire with ideological fire.

Labor–Health and Human Services Subcommittee chairman John Porter, over whose bills many of the toughest battles were fought, suggests that had appropriators been allowed by their leadership to work with senators and Democrats from the beginning of the process, they might have been able ultimately to pass bills more conservative than the ones that actually passed:

> Before when we could work in a bipartisan manner, we would work together and things got done . . . at spending [levels] lower than the president, within our caps . . . . When we don't talk to the Dems we wind up with a bill well above [the president's] and more fiscally irresponsible, because things are just added on top to appease both parties.[41]

This problem, and the inability of party leaders to decide on a better appropriations strategy, haunted congressional Republicans. Furthermore, the transfer of power to the executive remained part of the appropriations landscape even after party control of the executive changed.

Legislative-Executive Relations under Bush before September 11

Republican appropriators expected major changes and a much easier working environment under President Bush. What occurred, however, was exactly the opposite—disagreement and presidential dictates at least as contentious as any before. That the problem can be tied to appropriations partisanship can be seen clearly when one looks at the appropriations process under Bush before and after the September 11 attacks.

In the beginning of 2001, Republican appropriators were looking forward to a unified government—a dream few of the older cardinals had ever imagined in their early days on the HAC.[42] Yet the cardinals were not in a strong position. Twelve of them were new to their positions because term limits had led to retirements and massive switching of subcommittee assignments. Clouding their legislative outlook were the huge amount of time and momentum being spent on passage of the first Bush tax cut and the fact that the downturn in the economy was rapidly eliminating the budget surplus. Rifts emerged within both parties over fiscal goals. Then the Democrats abruptly gained majority control of the Senate, following the Republican Party defection of Vermont senator Jim Jeffords, who was unhappy with the party's hyperpartisanship and spending policies. Congressional observers sounded doom-and-gloom predictions about the budget and appropriations process, suggesting, "No federal budget debate has ever been as chaotic as the one that will take place in Washington this fall." [43]

House appropriators did not know how final appropriations decisions were going to be made. One staff member reasoned that the "transition of revolving appropriations chairs . . . contributed to the lack of direction." [44] The cardinals were not getting signals from the leadership, and they were not empowered to take matters into their own hands. The leadership could not decide on the right spending level because it faced two very powerful factions within the Republican Conference—those who favored increased defense spending and those who put a higher priority on a balanced budget. The administration was not giving any direction either, hoping that at least some of the conflict could be resolved by Congress before its officials had to step into their first appropriations fire. Democrats, according to another staffer, were content to be unhelpful partisans for a while, to "sit back and see the administration find a solution." [45] A "train wreck" loomed, and it seemed that the only possible resolution on the radar screen was the unprecedented passage of all thirteen appropriations bills in one huge omnibus, in which defense and social spending could be dealt with together and the president could provide fiscal discipline through the veto pen.[46] Such a scenario was certainly never contemplated by Fenno and could not have made appropriators especially confident about their role in the fiscal process. Then came 9/11.

Bipartisanship after the Attacks

Immediately after September 11, the consensus was that everything about politics had changed, certainly with regard to the federal budget. Not only were "partisan divisions . . . out the window," but "legislators trying to reserve Social Security surpluses to pay down the national [debt] were apt to be crushed in a congressional stampede to go along with the president and throw money at the terrorist problem." [47] Both phenomena contributed greatly to a sudden return to a politics in which spending restraint was no longer an uncertain burden and bipartisanship was once again the norm—a politics with which appropriators could feel at home.

The HAC was immediately thrown into a position to lead Congress in its response to the attacks. An emergency supplemental appropriations bill was going to be needed as the primary vehicle through which Congress could act. Reports were that the "knee-jerk" reaction of some Republican appropriators was to give Bush "a blank check." [48] This reaction could be seen as demonstrating how partisan and institutionally weakened the HAC had become, although the initial shock and the wish to support the president were certainly motivators. Nevertheless, talks about the emergency money quickly began to stall, as appropriators and other members of Congress began to worry about losing their input in the country's response to terrorism.[49]

Democratic appropriators Byrd, in the Senate, and David Obey, Wis., the House committee's ranking member, began working behind the scenes to convince fellow appropriators of the need to cut through "their anger and sadness and think carefully about their next crucial actions." [50] Obey appealed to the members by explaining that "the types of armed conflict that the White House has the authority to engage in without Congress' approval have expanded dramatically, making it more important than ever that Congress maintain control over the federal budget." [51] Byrd, well known for his staunch defense of congressional prerogatives, reminded members simply, "We still have a Constitution." [52]

After spending numerous hours together in the aftermath of the attacks, Republicans and Democrats began to realize that they had to be completely unified both at the party leadership level and on the Appropriations Committees if they were to challenge even slightly a president with the complete support of the country to do whatever it took to get through the crisis. After "a rare bipartisan lunch meeting," their strategy to keep the power of the purse was set.[53] Congress and the Bush administration then "tangled for the better part of three days over control of the federal response to the most severe foreign assault ever on the United States." [54] Congress's delay clearly risked public contempt, yet members appeared willing to wait even longer because, according to bipartisan staff members, "White House officials had pressed for such sweeping, unfettered presidential power over the special purse that Reps and Dems alike were drawn together to rebuff them." [55] Congress's strategy paid off, and the White House caved to congressional demands, pressured by the symbolic deadline of the president's speech at the Washington National Cathedral memorial service for the attack victims on September 14.

Directly following the debate on the supplemental appropriation, conventional wisdom held that Congress would be in a hurry to wrap up its session in a flurry of bipartisanship and efficiency. The Republican chairman of the House Budget Committee quickly began pushing for sweeping legislation covering all the outstanding appropriations bills.[56] However, the now highly unified appropriators would not stand for the loss of traditional management, and senior appropriators slipped easily back into the mold of a bipartisan and autonomous committee. They also got together bicamerally, Senate and House appropriators joining forces to control the endgame in negotiations with the White House. The four leaders, Stevens, Young, Byrd, and Obey, decided to set an overall spending limit at a figure slightly higher than the administration had requested prior to September 11. For two weeks, the appropriators faced the administration and refused to budge on lowering the spending number. During that time, they were so unified that even "comments from the four expressing their frustration with the White House were nearly identical, with the always salty Stevens the most outspoken in his condemnation of his fellow Republicans at the other end of Pennsylvania Avenue."[57]

At the same time, in a display of appropriator unity that was possibly even more impressive, Obey had to square off against a fellow Democrat, Sen. Edward Kennedy, Mass., the chairman of the Senate's education authorizing committee. Kennedy tried to add an extra $8 billion for education, instead of the $4 billion increase that Obey had already fought for, "putting Obey in a far more difficult spot than any Republican could have." [58] Obey and the appropriators prevailed and the lower number stuck.

The key to the rest of the appropriations season was whether appropriators could maintain their internal unity when it came time to "grease the . . . process by avoiding squabbles over policy riders." [59] They again succeeded. On nearly every bill left for them to finish, they prevented controversial riders from impeding committee markups and passage. For example, for the first time since 1992, the House's District of Columbia spending bill did not bar the District from implementing its domestic partner health benefits law. The Labor–HHS bill, always one of the more contentious because of its emphasis on social programs and its large amount of money, was ushered through the HAC and to the floor after "painstaking work appropriators from both parties had done to keep the bill from sinking into its usual morass of ideological fights." [60] The result was that the Labor–HHS bill passed with an overwhelming and quite extraordinary margin of 373–43.[61] The House had finished eleven bills by the beginning of the fiscal year, and Labor–HHS by the second week of October.

The final appropriations measure, the defense bill, was delayed because of the beginning of the war in Afghanistan and the anthrax attack that shut down parts of the Senate for a month. It was finished toward the end of December, about the same time as the last bill had been finished a year earlier, during the final Clinton - Republican budget battle. Unlike what happened then, the appropriators were now unified and bipartisan, and even bicameral. House appropriators pushed each of the thirteen bills through the legislative process separately, without depending on omnibus legislation. They were able to restrain the contention and controversy that had previously polluted attempts at more traditional bipartisanship and order. More important, they won latitude from both the Republican leadership, and eventually the administration, to determine the details of their bills. Yet, according to many on the committees, there still prevailed the worst relationship ever between appropriators and the administration's budget director at least since the passage of the Budget Act in 1974.[62] The process clearly had the potential to break down again.

The Return of Conflict

After the end of 2001, appropriations reverted to a partisan, leadership-driven, and executive-branch-dominated process. Debate on an emergency supplemental bill in early 2002 was considered by one Hill staffer "the most partisan debate she had ever seen," after the leadership passed a rule for consideration of the bill that contained numerous "sticks in the eye" of the HAC, without consulting appropriators first.[63] Then, after four months of negotiations on the measure between the House and the Senate, appropriators agreed on a $30 billion package. Yet right before a final wrap-up meeting, the White House demanded last-minute cuts of $5 billion.

Appropriators were not happy. Byrd, on the Senate appropriators' behalf, said that "big mouth" OMB director Mitch Daniels, "who was not elected by the people of this country," had "mangled, mauled, and murdered the appropriations process." [64] Most upsetting to appropriators were last-minute, generally vague suggestions for cuts, combined with certain specific program cuts impossible for members of either party to make, including cuts to embassy security, the Transportation Security Administration, Pentagon renovations, and "most offensive of all—about $400 million in general defense spending." [65] Young went public, saying: "I'm convinced that the director of OMB is only concerned about numbers and has no concern about what those numbers do or do not do for the country, for our military, for our security." [66]

The eventual face-saving compromise, pushed by the Senate, moved the bill to the president's level and added $5 billion on a contingency basis that allowed the money to be spent if needed. After the bill passed, Bush rejected spending the extra money—a move many predicted would make fall 2002 "the ugliest appropriations season in a long, long, time." [67] The prediction was on the mark, as Congress and the president could not agree on any bill and, in an unprecedented step, punted the decisions to the next Congress—with new members of Congress and even two new appropriations chairmen. Committee members were left wondering whether they would ever again get appropriations on the right track. One conservative aide lamented the wounded state of appropriations: "We're really in uncharted territory right now and nobody knows how it is going to turn out." [68]

One of the first decisions made by the Republican Conference in the beginning of 2003, even before it approved the leftover appropriations bills, was to make Appropriations subcommittee chairmen subject to approval by the Republican leadership's Steering Committee. This procedure lessened the role that the committee chairman (who himself was selected by the Steering Committee) and seniority played in determining who became a cardinal. By singling out HAC subcommittee chairs, much as they had with term-limit rules, the conference members indicated their displeasure with the HAC and the desire to rein it in even further. Young felt that the initiative was "a mistake," and another appropriator felt the conference was just "piling on." [69] Nevertheless, the action seemed to add to the likelihood that the HAC would be responsive to partisan direction and allow the Republican model of appropriations to be tested further.

With Sen. Bill Frist, Tenn., taking over Republican leadership in the Senate, after Republican control returned following the 2002 elections, the Bush administration now had complete solidarity among the leadership of both chambers. This was going to make it even easier for the administration to orchestrate appropriations bills to its liking.

Full Bush Administration Control

The 2003 appropriations season presents an illuminating final model through which to understand the changes in distribution of appropriations power. Only a few months after the rocky conclusion of work on the prior year's bills, and almost a decade after the Republican takeover of Congress, it appeared that for the first time the stars were aligned for a smooth, HAC-led process. With unified control of the government, the Republican leadership in the House, Senate, and executive branch felt pressure to deliver a smooth legislative process from start to finish. They listened to appropriator pleas and set a realistic (larger) spending goal to grease the wheels of the legislative process. There also seemed to be a consensus to prevent contentious policy riders from hijacking the bills. When one of the cardinals pushed dramatic cuts in earmarks (the official term for pork) and Amtrak funding through his subcommittee, Young prevailed on him to remove those provisions from the bill before floor consideration.

However, the process did not go entirely according to plan. The House worked quickly and was able to approve all thirteen bills separately before the start of the fiscal year. The Senate, on the other hand, was tangled in partisan stalemate over other issues and worked much more slowly. Congress was able to pass to the president only three final bills in time for the start of the new fiscal year. More of a problem were the bipartisan policy riders attached to the remaining bills, which faced veto threats from the administration. Appropriations Democrats and a substantial number of Republicans—mainly in the Senate, but also in the House—joined to support amendments overturning administration overtime regulations favoring businesses, FCC media ownership rules favoring large broadcasting companies, greater allowances for government outsourcing, and tough restrictions on travel to Cuba. Opposition on these issues had been repeatedly expressed in Congress, and the rider votes came at a time when concerns about the Iraq war were building in Congress and the administration was on the defensive.[70]

As the end of the congressional session approached, the appropriators' strategy was to wrap the appropriations together in an omnibus bill and have conference negotiations proceed on the differences between the House and Senate versions. Although the administration's opposition worried appropriators, because the riders had passed in both houses they theoretically could not be revisited in conference. Furthermore, Bush had not vetoed a single bill since taking office. Appropriator conferees hoped that the administration would hesitate to veto the huge spending bill—containing billions of dollars for district projects and social spending for things such as the administration's highly touted African AIDS initiative—just to save a few regulations that were fairly unpopular with the people back home in congressional districts.

Nevertheless, the House Republican leadership, working with the White House to achieve what it called a "veto proof" bill (whether a veto was actually likely or not), threatened conferees on the section of the bill containing the overtime rule limitation that they must either drop it or face a long-term continuing resolution on their section—which would effectively eliminate any new spending and the member projects they had worked all year to pass. The Republican conferees dropped the limitation. Then the leadership announced that a compromise had been reached between conferees and the White House on media ownership rules, even though the parameters of the deal had not been discussed in conference. Finally, the other riders were stripped from the bill, and a few controversial new ones, including one to allow gun dealers to destroy purchase records after twenty-four hours, were added. Because omnibus legislation cannot be amended, there was nothing members of Congress could do to change the decisions.

These moves so inflamed Democrats that in the Senate they refused to agree to rules governing debate on the bill—effectively killing the measure for the rest of the year and pushing consideration into the next congressional session. In his announcement of the Democrats' decision, Minority Whip Harry Reid, Nev., said, " 'A legislator who would vote for [the bill] would have to have rocks in his head,' because the White House was trying to 'eliminate Congress.' "[71] Democratic appropriators felt that the actions violated agreements they had reached in conference, "undermining the entire process" because they had moved on to negotiate other provisions only because they were under the impression that the rider issues were closed.[72] The "breakdown" meant "they no longer had faith that future agreements with Republican colleagues would stand up." [73] Republican Stevens was angry because after working to achieve delicate compromises on many of the issues, he now doubted whether the bill could ever pass. "I told [the Administration and GOP leaders] not to screw around with this thing. I warned them this would happen," he said.[74]

But Stevens was wrong. When Congress came back in January, Democrats and the other members offered only symbolic protest before passing the omnibus. The fear of being blamed for a government shutdown, as they had been in the Clinton years, and the fear of losing earmarks and increased spending—as might have happened under a year-long continuing resolution—led them to give in.

The Republican leadership, working under unified government, had found an appropriations strategy that worked to get its policy preferences enacted. The leaders had learned that with a partisan HAC writing bills close to their preferences, they just had to offer a small degree of partisan restraint on riders and spending totals in order to move the legislation through the House. They had also learned that the Senate was going to proceed in its own way on appropriations but that with the support of the president, they could just change the bills to their liking once they went to conference, preferably in an omnibus. This learning was evident when the next appropriations year (2004) began with an acknowledgment by the HAC that it was aiming to put all thirteen bills together in an omnibus toward the end of the fiscal year. Such talk was normally postponed as long as possible because it was considered a committee concession of defeat. However, with still-simmering Democratic anger and the amplification of partisan hostility in an election year, committee leaders felt no need to disguise that the omnibus was their best option politically. Strategic learning could also be seen when the leadership and the administration did not vocally protest the resurrection of riders overturning the media and overtime regulations in both houses of Congress. They knew that they could again remove them when the time was right.

The practical effect of this refined House leadership strategy was to allow appropriators to pass their bills more smoothly, now that most subcommittee members and chairmen were no longer major threats to party preferences. It also gave the administration the power to circumvent appropriators and even majorities of Congress on any issue of interest. However, the strategy betrayed Congress's best interest as an institution because it solidified a transfer of the ultimate power over the purse to the executive branch. Furthermore, because the strategy depended on Republican unified government and an executive that shared almost completely the House leadership's devotion to Republican ideology, strategic success depended on a particular arrangement within government that could end with the next election, whereas the transfer of power was likely to last substantially longer. The many stages of appropriations development discussed in the above sections, showing the consistent gain of power by the executive through all combinations of government control, are good demonstrations of that likelihood.

Conclusion

The threats to House Appropriations Committee power will probably continue. Already the return to federal budget deficits is bringing calls for budget process reforms, some of which clearly target appropriators. In 2004 the House debated a bill that sought to enact discretionary spending caps which would allow the president to participate in setting binding appropriations spending totals. Although the bill had little chance of passage, appropriators took it very seriously and were highly organized in opposition. Even after winning negotiations to have the caps reduced from five years to two years, they still voted unanimously against the bill. The irony was that Congress had passed such caps in the past, including twice during the Clinton administration, without much organized opposition from the HAC.[75] However, under their own party's president, weary committee leaders felt they could not allow more usurpation and took to the floor proclaiming the bill a "step on the Constitution" and "a dire threat to Congress's . . . role as guardian of the federal treasury."[76]

Biennial budgeting and a new line-item veto (designed to pass constitutional muster) are also reforms that have been recently proposed to "fix" the appropriations process. Biennial budgeting would allow Congress to pass appropriations bills only once every two years. This option is attractive because it would limit the time Congress would have to spend debating the same controversial appropriations issues and would allow authorization committees more time to debate and pass their own legislation. The impetus behind a new line-item veto seems to be the explosion of pork projects inserted into appropriations bills. There are now well over ten thousand earmarks annually, an increase of over 640 percent in the ten years since the Republican revolution.[77] The line-item veto would allow the president to cut those projects from final bills.

These reform possibilities are mentioned here not because their passage is imminent (although two of them have passed during prior times of deficit fears) but because they all involve further limits on appropriator power, not a strengthening of appropriator control over the process. It is difficult to see a scenario in which appropriators and Congress regain the control they have lost. The period in Congress immediately after September 11 showed that if appropriators band together in a bicameral and bipartisan manner, they can bend policy toward their preferences. However, partisanship is so embedded within the contemporary Congress and its norms and committee processes that even momentum from national emergencies is incapable of supporting consensual appropriations policymaking for extended periods.

Notes

Much of the information in this chapter, including the congressional interviews, was collected while working in the office of House Appropriations Committee Chairman C. W. Bill Young and while working as a Budget Policy Analyst for The Concord Coalition. I am grateful for both opportunities and the guidance of Larry Dodd along the way. My initial research was supported by a Dirksen Center Congressional Fellowship.

1. The appropriation for the Departments of Labor, Health and Human Services, and Education, hereinafter Labor–HHS.
2. David Baumann, "On the Money: A Transfer of Power," *CongressDailyAM,* October 10, 2002.
3. Robert Bixby, executive director of The Concord Coalition, quoted in Daniel Parks, "Lawmakers' Keen Sense of Political Risk Trumps Avowed Goal of Budget Deal," *CQ Weekly,* August 3, 2001, 2106.
4. Richard F. Fenno Jr., *The Power of the Purse: Appropriations Politics in Congress* (Boston: Little, Brown, 1966).
5. Joseph White, "The Functions and Power of the House Appropriations Committee" (PhD diss., University of California, Berkeley, 1989). For more recent appropriations examinations see William Lehman, *Mr. Chairman: The Journal of a Congressional Appropriator* (Lanham, Md.: University Press of America, 2000); and Fiona Mary Wright, "Working Together While Growing Apart? The Causes and Consequences of the House Budget and Appropriations Committee Rivalry" (paper presented at the annual meeting of the Midwest Political Science Association, Chicago, 2000).
6. "The Final Word," *National Journal's CongressDaily,* March 25, 2002. The director of OMB is the president's main point person on the budget and negotiations with Congress over budget issues.

7. One reason for this environment was clearly the necessity within the majority Democratic Party to minimize the differences between its conservative southern wing and its more liberal members.
8. For a more detailed analysis of the characteristics of HAC members, see John H. Aldrich and David W. Rohde, "The Republican Revolution and the House Appropriations Committee," *Journal of Politics* 62 (February 2000): 1–33; Richard Fenno, *Congressmen in Committees* (Boston: Little, Brown, 1973); Joshua Gordon, "The Power of the Purse Reconsidered: Partisanship and Social Integration in the House Appropriations Committee" (PhD diss., University of Florida, 2002); Roderick Kiewiet and Mathew D. McCubbins, *The Logic of Delegation: Congressional Parties and the Appropriations Process* (Chicago: University of Chicago Press, 1991); and Fiona Wright, "Reform as Disruption: The Interaction of Political Pressure and Institutional Inertia on the 1974 Budget Act and Its Implications" (2002; article under review).
9. Fenno, *Power of the Purse,* 56.
10. Quoted in ibid., 38.
11. Ibid., 164.
12. White, "Functions and Power," 15.
13. Ibid., 15, 440, 317, 440.
14. Wright, "Reform as Disruption," 12–15.
15. See Wright, "Working Together" and "Congressional Reform and Its Institutional Consequences: The 1974 Budget Act in the U.S. House" (PhD diss., University of Florida, 2000).
16. Wright, "Working Together," 17.
17. White, "Functions and Power," 277.
18. Scott Adler describes this shift as one in which members went from being "guardians" to being "claimants" and provides evidence of the switch, including the postreform convergence of subcommittee assignments with constituency interests. E. Scott Adler, "Constituency Characteristics and the 'Guardian' Model of Appropriations Subcommittees, 1959–1998," *American Journal of Political Science* 44 (1): 104–114. See also Morris Fiorina, *Congress: Keystone of the Washington Establishment* (New Haven: Yale University Press, 1989); and Allen Schick, *Congress and Money* (Washington, D.C.: Urban Institute, 1980).
19. Lawrence C. Dodd, "The Cycles of Legislative Change: Building a Dynamic Theory," in *Political Science: The Science of Politics,* ed. Herbert Weisberg (New York: Agathon, 1986).
20. Riders are lines of legislative language attached to appropriations bills and technically violate the procedural prohibition against legislating on appropriations bills.
21. Lehman, *Mr. Chairman,* 214.
22. White, "Functions and Power," 413–414.
23. Ibid., 403.
24. Ibid., 424.
25. Ibid., 443.
26. Ibid., 124.
27. For a good discussion on the development of partisan think tanks and social networks, see David Ricci, *The Transformation of American Politics: The New Washington and the Rise of Think Tanks* (New Haven: Yale University Press, 1993).
28. Douglas Koopman, *Hostile Takeover: The House Republican Party 1980–1995* (Lanham, Md.: Rowman and Littlefield, 1996), 48.
29. Eric M. Uslaner, *The Decline of Comity in Congress* (Ann Arbor: University of Michigan Press, 1993), 23.
30. Author interview with freshman class member appointed to the HAC, July 13, 2000.
31. This can be shown by observing the Poole and Rosenthal DW-NOMINATE scores of committee members from 1975 to 2000. For more analysis see Gordon, "Power of

the Purse Reconsidered." The raw NOMINATE data set was provided by Fiona Wright from the University of Wisconsin.

32. Ibid.
33. Interview with author, August 9, 2000.
34. Aldrich and Rohde, "The Republican Revolution," 17.
35. Bryan Marshall, Brandon Prins, and David Rohde, "Majority Party Leadership, Strategic Choice and Committee Power: Appropriations in the House, 1995–1998," in *Congress on Display, Congress at Work,* ed. William Bianco (Ann Arbor: University of Michigan Press, 2000).
36. Ibid., 85.
37. See White, "Functions and Power," 403; and Marshall, Prins, and Rohde, "Majority Party Leadership," 87.
38. Marshall, Prins, and Rohde, "Majority Party Leadership," 86.
39. The number of Citizens Against Government Waste "Leading Oinker" awards won by the two well outdistances all other members of Congress.
40. One of the turning points was the media's caricaturing of Gingrich as a brat after his complaint about being snubbed by Clinton on Air Force One during travel to Yitzhak Rabin's funeral. For descriptions of the shutdown events see Richard Fenno, *Learning to Govern: An Institutional View of the 104th Congress* (Washington, D.C.: Brookings Institution Press, 1997); Linda Killian, *The Freshmen* (Boulder, Colo.: Westview, 1998); and David Maraniss and Michael Weisskopf, *Tell Newt to Shut Up!* (New York: Simon and Schuster, 1996).
41. John Edward Porter, interview with author, June 27, 2000.
42. The turn of events in the career of Chairman Bill Young as a Republican legislator, for example, is remarkable. When first elected to public office in 1960, Young was the first Republican state senator in Florida's history. He entered the House in 1971 and became a member of the HAC immediately following the Democratic success in the Watergate babies election. He won the chairmanship of the HAC in 1998 only after Livingston's shocking resignation from the House, having been passed over in 1994 by Gingrich's seniority violation. Needless to say, the excitement in his office was palpable even in summer 2000 because of the simple thought that such unified power was even possible.
43. Stan Collender, "Budget Battles," NationalJournal.com, September 4, 2001.
44. Interview with author, September 10, 2001.
45. Interview with author, September 10, 2001.
46. The Concord Coalition, "Appropriations Issue Brief," Washington, D.C., August 27, 2001.
47. First quote from Sen. Charles Schumer, D-N.Y., in "The Day After: Congress Returns," *CongressDaily,* September 12, 2001; second quote from *CongressDaily,* September 11, 2001, 3.
48. Daniel Parks, "Quiet Tension over Spending," *CQ Weekly,* September 15, 2001, 2130.
49. Ibid., 2129.
50. Quoted in Mary Dalrymple, "Obey Sounds a Solitary Warning," *CQ Weekly,* September 15, 2001, 2131.
51. Parks, "Quiet Tension," 2130.
52. Ibid.
53. Dalrymple, "Obey Sounds a Solitary Warning," 2131.
54. Parks, "Quiet Tension," 2126.
55. Quoted in Parks, "Quiet Tension," 2129.
56. Ibid., 2126. This would be an omnibus bill similar to the one mentioned earlier as a possible outcome prior to September 11.
57. Linda Caruso, "The Friday Buzz," *CongressDaily,* October 12, 2001.

58. Ibid.
59. Daniel Parks, "Spending Consensus Sought," *CQ Weekly,* September 22, 2001, 2208.
60. David Nather, "Carefully Balanced Bill Nearly Toppled," *CQ Weekly,* October 13, 2001, 2410.
61. In the previous year the bill passed with just 50.3 percent of the vote, and in 1998 and 1999 the House didn't even try to pass the bill on its own. See Fiona Wright, "Reform as Disruption," 39.
62. Daniel Parks, "Earmarks, Back with a Vengeance," *CQ Weekly,* December 1, 2001, 2929.
63. Quoted in Gallery Watch's "US Budget.com Articles," May 24, 2002. Term used by George Krumbhaar of US Budget.com, May 23, 2002.
64. Quoted in *CQ Daily Monitor Midday Update,* July 12, 2002, story 2; and in Bill Ghent and Keith Koffler, "Legislators Rip Daniels," *CongressDaily,* July 12, 2002.
65. Bill Ghent, "Appropriators also Criticize Administration," *CongressDaily,* July 12, 2002, 2.
66. Quoted in *CQ Daily Monitor Midday Update,* July 12, 2002, story 2.
67. Stan Collender, quoted in Bill Ghent, "Appropriations: Bush's Rejection," *Congress-Daily,* August 15, 2002.
68. Quoted in Bill Ghent, "The Friday Buzz," *CongressDaily,* September 27, 2002.
69. Quoted in Charlie Mitchell, "House GOP Subjects Cardinals to Steering Panel Review," *CongressDaily,* November 14, 2002.
70. Steven Pearlstein, "Sunday Briefing," *Washington Post,* September 14, 2003, E2.
71. Quoted in Peter Cohn and April Fulton, "Frist Hopes to Pass Omnibus," *Congress-Daily,* November 25, 2003.
72. Molly Peterson, "Appropriations: As Dems Deride GOP 'Compromise,'" *Congress-Daily,* November 25, 2003.
73. "Top Democrat," quoted in Joseph Schatz, "Contentious Fiscal '05 Looms," *CQ Weekly,* January 24, 2004, 209.
74. Quoted in Peter Cohn, "Appropriations: Senate Action Uncertain," *CongressDailyAM,* November 25, 2003.
75. Andrew Taylor, "Budget: House Soundly Defeats Conservatives' Bid," *CQ Today,* June 24, 2004.
76. Subcommittee Chairman Harold Rogers quoted in Taylor, "Budget"; Young, quoted in Peter Cohn, "Republican Leaders Still Planning Debate," *CongressDailyAM,* June 24, 2004.
77. The first appropriations passed under Republican control (fiscal 1996) showed a marked decrease (33 percent) in the number of projects from the last year of unified Democratic government, consistent with the budget-cutting rhetoric of the Republican revolution. However, the dollar amount dedicated to pork still increased and by 2004 had more than doubled from the last year of Democratic control, while overall discretionary spending only increased by 33 percent. These data come from Citizens against Government Waste (www.cagw.org). Sen. John McCain also catalogues earmarks and his numbers are very similar to CAGW's.

Part IV
Congress and Public Policy

13. Congress and the Politics of Judicial Appointments

Sarah A. Binder and Forrest Maltzman

Half a dozen computers and network servers seized, a renowned counterespionage and antiterrorism forensic expert hired, Secret Service investigators brought in, and scores of Senate staff interviewed by the Senate's sergeant-at-arms. Murder in the Capitol? Terrorist plot? No, it was just another skirmish in the battle over confirming federal judges. This time, in fall 2003, Republican staff pilfered computer files from Democrats, revealing the Democrats' collusion with organized interests to block controversial judicial nominees. Although Republicans cried foul, the stolen memos confirmed what seasoned observers of the Senate had come to expect: Selecting and confirming federal judges has become a no-holds-barred game among senators, presidents, and organized interests, each seeking to influence the ideological tenor of the federal bench.

In this chapter we explore the politics of judicial selection, focusing on partisan, institutional, and temporal forces that shape the fate of presidential appointments to the lower federal courts. Assessing patterns over the past fifty years, we depict broad trends in the process of judicial selection and pinpoint recent developments that have fueled conflict over the makeup of the federal bench. Although today's tactics in the battles over federal judges—from stolen memos to successful filibusters—are new, the underlying struggle to shape the federal bench is not. Both cooperation and competition are recurring themes in the politics of judicial selection, a politics strongly shaped not only by recent partisan pique but by enduring constitutional and institutional forces as well.

The Evolving Role of the Senate in Judicial Selection

Article II, Section 2 of the Constitution stipulates that presidential appointments must be made with the "Advice and Consent" of the Senate. Although Alexander Hamilton claimed in *Federalist* No. 76 that the Senate's role would be limited, this means that the president and the Senate share the appointment power.[1] The Senate's constitutionally prescribed role clearly grants senators opportunities to influence the fate of presidential appointees and thus the chance to shape the makeup of the federal bench.

The geographic design of the federal courts strongly shapes the nature of Senate involvement in selecting federal judges. Because federal trial and appellate-level courts are territorially defined, each federal judgeship is associated with a home state, and new judges are typically drawn from that state. As a result, senators attempt to influence the president's choice of appointees to federal courts in their states. There is considerable variation across the states in how senators handle their role in the selection process. In some states, the more senior senator recommends candidates for White House consideration; in most states, only senators or other elected officials from the president's party participate—a practice stemming from the treatment of judgeships as party patronage starting in the nineteenth century.[2] And in just a few states today—including California and Wisconsin—bipartisan selection commissions generate judicial candidates for White House review. However designed, the selection process affords senators the opportunity to influence the selection of judicial nominees from their states.[3]

Presidents are not obliged to heed senators' views in selecting nominees. Although the Constitution prescribes Senate "advice" as well as "consent," nothing in the Constitution requires the president to respect the views of interested senators from the state. In practice, however, judicial nominees must pass muster with the entire chamber, and thus presidents have an incentive to anticipate objections from home state and other interested senators in making appointments. In the past, federal judgeships rarely elicited the interest of senators outside the nominee's home state, and so the views of the home state senators from the president's party were typically sufficient to determine whether or not nominees would be confirmed. Other senators would defer to the views of the home state senator from the president's party, thus establishing the norm of *senatorial courtesy*.[4] Moreover, the Senate Judiciary Committee in the early twentieth century established the "blue slip" to solicit the views of home state senators—regardless of whether they were of the president's party—once nominees were referred to the committee.[5] By institutionalizing home state senators' role in the confirmation process, senators also gained some leverage over the president at the nomination stage. Threats to block a nominee during confirmation could theoretically be used to encourage the president to consider senators' views before making an appointment.

By the early twentieth century, the modern process for judicial selection had been shaped. Because in the past judicial selection has rarely elicited national attention, and because Senate nominations have only occasionally triggered open conflict, the received wisdom emphasizes the cooperative relationship between presidents and senators in shaping the federal bench. Senate observers have often said that the president merely defers to the views of the home state senators from his party when selecting judges for the nation's trial courts, the U.S. District Courts. Senators themselves fuel such perceptions of the process. As Sen. Phil Gramm, R-Texas, once boasted, "I'm given the power to make the appointment. . . . The people elected me to do that."[6] Presidents are said to be less likely to defer to senators over the selection of appellate judges for the U.S. Circuit

Figure 13-1 Length of Nomination Process for Judicial Nominees: Mean Number of Days, by Congress, between Vacancy and Nomination, 1947–1998

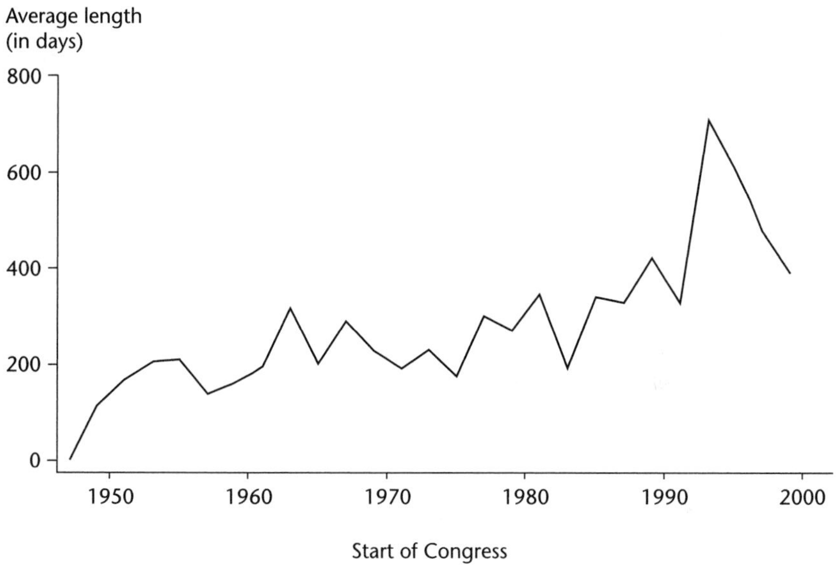

Source: Data compiled from Final Legislative and Executive Calendars, Senate Judiciary Committee, 80th–105th Congresses.

Courts of Appeals. Nevertheless, even here the process frequently reflects cooperation between home state senators and the White House.

Despite the conventional wisdom that cooperation is the rule, trends in the nomination and confirmation process suggest otherwise. Figure 13-1 shows the increasing length of time it takes a president to make a nomination for a vacant seat on the bench.[7] The amount of time it takes for the president to make a nomination surely reflects in large part the degree of disagreement over who should serve on the bench. The recent and marked increase in how long it takes to select nominees confirms recent charges that the process of advice and consent is newly politicized.

An examination of the confirmation process shows a similar pattern. The Senate took, on average, just one month to confirm judicial nominees during President Ronald Reagan's first term. By the end of President Bill Clinton's second term, the wait had increased on average fivefold for district court nominees and sevenfold for appellate court nominees. At least a fourth of Clinton's judicial nominees in the 106th Congress (1999–2000) waited more than six months to be confirmed, including U.S. District Court Judge Richard Paez, who had waited nearly four years to be confirmed to the U.S. Court of Appeals for the Ninth

Circuit. Confirmation delay continued to increase under President George W. Bush, reaching a record for appellate court nominees in the 107th Congress (2001–2002).

Still, delays weathered by recent presidents in securing confirmation of their nominees reflect more than Clinton's polarized relations with a Republican Senate or Bush's polarized relations with a Democratic Senate. Delays in the confirmation process were considerable in the mid-1980s, when Reagan saw Democratic Senates take, on average, nearly four months to confirm his judicial nominees. Even during a rare episode of unified Democratic control during 1993 and 1994, the Senate took an average of three months to confirm the majority party's nominees.

It would be a mistake to conclude that recent confirmation delays are entirely an aberration from the Senate's traditional mode of advice and consent. During Eisenhower's last term, for example, the Democratic Senate averaged four months to confirm the president's judicial nominees. Parallel to the foot-dragging that has occurred in recent years, it sometimes took the Democratic Senate led by Lyndon Johnson longer than seven months to conclude action on nominees slated by Eisenhower for vacancies on the federal bench. Although confirmation delay may be especially pronounced in recent years, disagreement between the president and Senate over federal judges has historical precedent.

The roots of today's impasse over federal judges are also visible in confirmation rates for judicial nominees. In Figure 13-2, a sharp decline in the rate of confirmation for district and appellate court appointees is quite striking. A perfect 100 percent of appellate court nominees were confirmed in the 1950s, but less than 40 percent were confirmed in the 107th Congress (2001–2002). Although confirmation rates for trial court nominees are quite variable, the fates of these lower court nominees roughly parallel the experience of appellate court nominees before the Senate. Overall, the data support the notion that the Senate confirmation process has markedly changed over the past ten years. Oddly enough, although the White House now spends longer than ever vetting potential federal judges, the chance of confirmation is at a fifty-year low. Still, it is important to remember that polarization of the process is not entirely new. Troubled waters for judicial nominees were pronounced as early as the early 1970s, no doubt reflecting partisan and ideological disagreements between President Richard Nixon and a Democratic Senate.

The Politics of Advice and Consent

How do we account for the Senate's uneven performance in confirming federal judges? Why were nominees of the past decade particularly likely to be denied a seat on the federal bench, and why does it take so long for the Senate to render its decision? Five forces are at the root of the difficulties presidents face in securing confirmation of judicial nominees. First and foremost are ideological forces: the array of policy views across the three branches affects the probability

Figure 13-2 Confirmation Rates for Judicial Nominees, 1947–2002

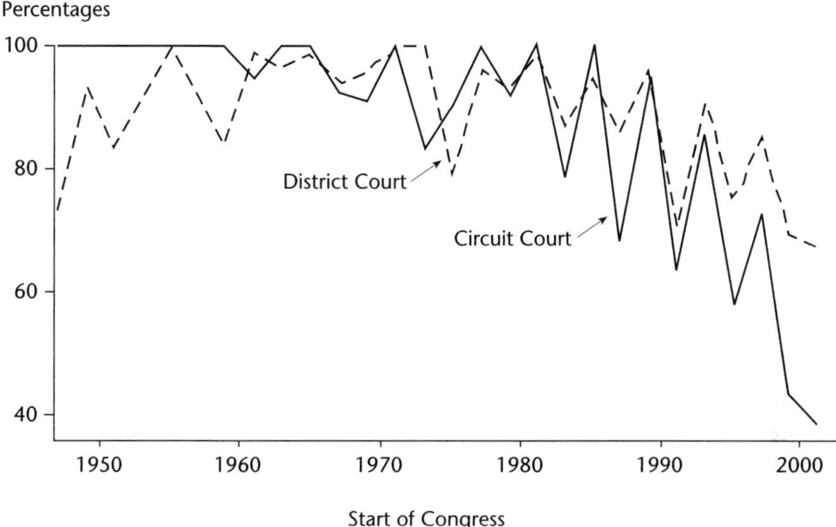

Sources: Data compiled from Final Legislative and Executive Calendars, Senate Judiciary Committee, 80th–105th Congresses. Data for 106th and 107th Congresses compiled from United States Senate Committee on the Judiciary Web site, http://judiciary.senate.gov.

of confirmation. Second, partisan forces matter: political contests between the president and the opposing Senate party help account for the Senate's treatment of judicial nominees. Third, institutional rules and practices in the Senate shape the likelihood of confirmation. Fourth, presidential capital and resources may matter. And finally, temporal forces shape the Senate's treatment of potential judges: the congressional calendar, electoral cycles, and historical changes in the importance of the federal bench combine to affect the fate of the president's nominees. We explore each of the forces in turn.

Partisan and Ideological Forces

Partisan and ideological forces are of course inextricably linked in the contemporary Congress as the two legislative parties have diverged ideologically in recent decades. Not surprisingly then, pundits assessing the Senate's treatment of Clinton's nominees have typically pointed to poisoned relations between conservative Republicans and Clinton. It was often suggested that personal, partisan, and ideological antagonisms between Clinton and far-right conservatives led Republican senators to delay even the most highly qualified nominees. Democrats' obstruction of several of Bush's nominees in the 108th Congress (2003–2004) was similarly attributed to partisan pique, as liberal Democrats criticized Bush's tendency to nominate extremely conservative (and presumably Republican) judges.

Partisan politics may affect the process of advice and consent more broadly in the guise of divided party government. Because judges have lifetime tenure and the capacity to make lasting decisions on the shape of public law, senators have good cause to scrutinize the views of all potential federal judges. Because presidents overwhelmingly seek to appoint judges of the president's party, Senate scrutiny of judicial nominees should be particularly intense when different parties control the White House and the Senate. It is not a surprise, then, that nominees considered during a period of divided control take significantly longer to be confirmed than those nominated during unified control. Judicial nominees are also less likely to be confirmed during divided government: Over the past fifty-five years, the Senate has confirmed an average of 94 percent of district and appellate court nominees considered during periods of unified control but roughly only 80 percent of nominees during divided government.

Partisan control of the branches is particularly likely to affect the course of nominations when presidents seek to fill vacancies on appellate courts whose judges are evenly balanced between the two parties. Because most appellate court cases are heard by randomly generated three-judge panels, nominations to courts that are evenly divided are likely to have a more significant impact on the law's development, compared with appointments to courts that lean decidedly in one ideological direction. Senate majorities are especially reluctant to confirm nominees to such courts when the appointment would tip the court balance in the favor of a president from the opposing party. One of the hardest hit courts is the Sixth Circuit Court of Appeals, straddling populous Midwest states such as Michigan and Ohio. In recent years, a quarter of the bench has been vacant, including one seat declared a judicial emergency after sitting empty for five years. Moreover, the Sixth Circuit has been precariously balanced between the parties, with the bench roughly half-filled by judges appointed by Democrats. The Senate slowdown on appointments to that circuit during the Clinton administration was likely motivated by its strategic importance, since confirming Clinton's nominees would have eliminated the opportunity for a future Republican president to move a balanced court into the conservative camp. Similarly, once Bush took office, the two Michigan senators (both Democrats) went to great lengths to prevent the Senate from taking action on Bush's conservative nominees for that court. In short, partisan dynamics—fueled in part by ideological conflict—strongly shape the Senate's conduct of advice and consent, making it difficult for presidents to stack the federal courts as they would prefer.

Institutional Forces

Partisan and ideological forces do not, of course, operate in a vacuum. The process of advice and consent is equally shaped by an array of Senate rules that distribute power in a unique way across the institution. Thus, to explain the fate of the president's judicial nominees, we need to know something about not only the partisan and ideological context, but also the institutional arena in which senators dispense their advice and consent. Senators are wise to the ways in which Senate rules and practices may be exploited in the confirmation process. Understanding how senators motivated by policy and political interests exploit pivotal rules and practices is essential for explaining the outcomes of advice and consent.

A prime institutional step for any nominee is securing approval from the Senate Judiciary Committee. Two significant hurdles await judicial nominees in that committee. First, by tradition, senators from the home state of each judicial nominee cast the first judgment on him or her. As suggested above, the veto power of home state senators is institutionalized in Judiciary panel procedures. Both of the state's senators are asked their views about judicial nominees from their home state pending before the committee. Senators can return the "blue slip," demarking their support of or objection to the nominee, or they can refuse to return the blue slip altogether—an action signaling opposition. One negative blue slip from a home state senator traditionally was sufficient to block further action on a nominee. As the process has become more polarized in recent years, committee chairs have been tempted to ignore objections from minority party senators. At a minimum, blue slips today weigh heavily in the committee chair's assessment concerning whether, when, and how to proceed on a nominee, but senators' objections do not necessarily prevent the committee from proceeding.

Historically, large ideological differences between the president and the home state senator have led to longer confirmation proceedings than normal for appellate court nominees, suggesting the power of home state senators to affect panel proceedings. Conversely, the strong support of one's home state senator is essential in navigating the committee successfully. Given the often fractured attention of the Senate and the willingness of senators to heed the preferences of the home state senator, having a strong advocate in the Senate with an interest in seeing the nomination proceed is critical in smoothing the way for nominees.

Second, the experience of judicial nominees in committee drives home the importance of Senate rules that grant considerable procedural powers to committee chairs. Because of the generally low salience of most judicial nominations, the Senate largely defers to the Judiciary Committee's judgment on whether and when to proceed with a nomination. Discretion over the fate of each nominee is held by the committee chair, who holds the power to convene hearings and to schedule a committee vote to report a nomination to the chamber. Not surprisingly, then, ideological differences between the panel chair and the president show a discernible effect on the course of judicial nominations. The greater the ideological differences between the president and the chair of the Judiciary panel, the longer it takes for the committee to act.

Once approved by committee, a nomination has a second broad institutional hurdle to clear: making it onto the Senate's crowded agenda. By rule and precedent, both majority and minority party coalitions can delay nominations after they clear committee. Because the presiding officer of the chamber gives the majority leader priority in being recognized to speak on the Senate floor, the majority leader has the upper hand in setting the chamber's agenda. This is especially so given his control of the executive session agenda, the arena in which nominations are called up for confirmation. When the president's party controls the Senate, this means that nominations are usually confirmed more quickly; under divided control, nominations can be kept off the floor by the majority leader. Such procedural advantages clearly enhance the importance of support from the majority leader in shaping the fate of presidential appointees.

The majority leader's discretion over the executive session agenda is not wielded without challenge, however: nominations can be filibustered. The chance that a nomination might be filibustered usually motivates the majority leader to seek unanimous consent of the full chamber before bringing a nomination before the Senate. Such consultation between the two parties means that nominations are unlikely to clear the Senate without the endorsement of the minority party.

The de facto requirement of minority party assent suggests that the party opposing the president retains significant power to affect the fate of nominees, even when the opposing party does not control the Senate. As policy differences increase between the president and the opposing party, that party is more likely to exercise its power to delay nominees. Given the high degree of polarization between the two parties today, it is not surprising that judicial nominations have become such a flash point for the parties. As we discuss below, when Democrats lost control of the Senate after the 2002 elections, they turned to a new tactic to block objectionable nominees: the filibuster. Although in the past Senate majorities have periodically had to fight to close debate on judicial nominees via cloture, successful filibusters are without modern precedent for nominees to lower courts. Such extreme tactics clearly result from the increased polarization between the two parties and the rising salience of the federal courts across the interest group community. Much of the variation in the fates of judicial nominees before the Senate is thus seemingly driven by ideologically motivated players and parties in both the executive and legislative branches who exploit the rules of the game in an effort to shape the makeup of the federal bench.

Presidential Forces

Presidents are not powerless in trying to shape the outcome of advice and consent. Although the president lacks a formal means of pushing nominations through to confirmation, presidents have a few tools that may affect the fates of their appointees. First, there is some support for the notion that better qualified nominees sail more quickly through the Senate, meaning that a higher rating from the American Bar Association (ABA) often cuts the time it takes to be confirmed and increases the probability of confirmation, at least in more recent decades. The type of nominee the president appoints, in other words, helps smooth the way to confirmation. The president's ability to encourage confirmation may also be shaped by his popularity with the public. Presidents who are highly regarded tend to store up political capital that can be used to increase the chances of confirmation for judicial nominees. All told, presidents have some influence over the speed of advice and consent, but their influence likely is exercised only at the margins of the legislative arena.

Temporal Forces

Finally, it is important to consider how secular or cyclical elements of the political calendar may shape the fate of judicial nominees. It is often suggested, for example, that extreme delays encountered by judicial nominees in recent years may be a natural consequence of an approaching presidential election. For example, with control of both the Senate and the White House up for grabs in November 2000, it was expected that Republican senators would approach their duties of advice and consent with extreme caution. Rather than confirming an outgoing Democratic president's last judicial nominees, pragmatic politics would dictate, Republicans should save these lifetime appointments for a president of their own party. Not surprisingly, in the run-up to the 2000 election, forty judicial nominees remained in limbo. Most of them had not even received a hearing before the Senate Judiciary panel.

There is certainly some truth to the idea that an approaching presidential election affects the politics of advice and consent. Over the past fifty years, Senate treatment of judicial nominations submitted or pending during a presidential election year has been significantly different than its treatment of other judicial nominations. First, the Senate has historically taken longer to confirm nominees pending before a presidential election than those submitted earlier in a president's term. Second, and more notably, presidential-election-year nominees are significantly less likely to be confirmed. For all judicial nominations submitted between 1947 and 2002, appointments pending in the Senate before a presidential election were 25 percent less likely to be confirmed than ones submitted earlier in a president's term.

All the same, presidents can also benefit from the political calendar. Strategically timing referral of a nomination is essential, as nominations made earlier in a president's term tend to move more swiftly. Nominations also move more swiftly when the Senate's confirmation load is lighter. The fewer nominees pending, the quicker a nominee will sail to confirmation.

Finally, and perhaps most important, the broad belief that the confirmation process has become more protracted over time is confirmed by the evidence in Figures 13-1 and 13-2, which shows the increasing amount of time it takes for presidents to select nominees and the declining rate of confirmation for both levels of the federal bench. As we explore below, such a secular increase in the length of the advice and consent process may result from the rising importance of the federal courts as policymaking players. Interest groups and politicians frequently and increasingly have used the federal courts as a means of resolving political disputes.[8] The result, we suspect, has been increased concern among political actors about the makeup of the federal bench and thus a heightened salience of the confirmation process beyond the affected court and state.

Explaining Trends in Advice and Consent

Recent conflict over judicial selection is not unprecedented in the Senate's past. Considerable variation occurs in how long it takes for the Senate to confirm nominees, and appointees are confirmed at different rates across courts and over time—even if recent trends are particularly striking. How do we account more systematically for the level of conflict in the process of advice and consent? The multiple forces outlined above are clearly at play. But for social scientists investigating general patterns over time, this raises a key question. Taking each of these forces, how well do the trends noted here hold up? Once they are subjected to multivariate controls, what can we conclude about the relative impact of partisan, ideological, institutional, and other forces on how long it takes the Senate to act on judicial nominees? How we answer this question will ultimately shape our evaluation of the state of advice and consent: How well do the president and the Senate discharge their constitutional duties?

In Table 13-1, we use a statistical technique known as duration analysis to model the forces that shape the Senate's treatment of appellate court nominees.[9] Duration analysis basically tells us the probability that the Senate will act on a nominee at a particular time.[10] The estimates generated by the analysis essentially indicate whether each independent variable increases or decreases the length of time it takes for the Senate to act. An independent variable whose coefficient has a positive sign means that increases in the value of the variable will speed up the probability of Senate action; negative-signed coefficients indicate that as the value of the independent variable increases, the likelihood of swift Senate confirmation goes down. In other words, to pinpoint the factors that typically drag out the confirmation process, we need to identify variables with negative and significant coefficients, as we indicate in Table 13-1. Once we know which forces are critical in shaping how long it takes for the Senate to act, we can then explore the substantive impact of those effects (see Table 13-2).[11]

The results shown in Table 13-1 can help us to disentangle the forces that shape the Senate's treatment of presidential appointees. Interestingly, ideological differences between the median senator and the president have no discernible impact on the timing of confirmation. Nor do ideological differences between the median senator and the nominee measurably affect the confirmation process. And the Senate does not generally treat nominations to evenly balanced, or "critical," circuits any differently than it does nominations to circuits with a notable partisan tilt. We can conclude from these initial results that delays in the confirmation process do not simply reflect competition between the branches over the makeup of the federal bench. Other forces must be at work in drawing out the confirmation process.

Table 13-1 Cox Regression of the Timing of Senate Confirmation Decisions, 1947–1998 (Nominations to U.S. Circuit Courts of Appeals)

Variable (Expected Direction)	Coefficient (Robust SE)
Ideological forces	
Ideological distance between Senate and president (−)	2.70 (.78)
Ideological distance between Senate and nominee (−)	.11 (.36)
Nomination to a closely balanced court (−)	.20 (.15)
Partisan forces	
Divided government (−)	−.33 (.20) *
Ideological distance between president and opposing party (−)	−3.14 (1.06) **
Nomination to a closely balanced court during divided government (−)	−.44 (.25) *
Institutional forces	
Ideological distance between Judiciary chair and president (−)	−.33 (.23)
Home state senator is ideologically distant from president (−)	.52 (.26)
Home state senator is ideologically distant from president during divided government (−)	−2.14 (1.19) *
Presidential forces	
Well-qualified nominee (+)	−.03 (.12)
Qualified nominee (+)	.98 (.76)
President's approval rating (+)	−.02 (.01)
Temporal forces	
Presidential election year (−)	−1.26 (.17) ***
Number of nominations pending (−)	−.02 (.00) ***
Time left in session (+)	−.00 (.00)
Congress # (−)	−.05 (.02) ***
Log likelihood	−1,786.13
χ^2	284.18***
N	413

Notes: The table reports results of a Cox regression model, based on Stata 8.0 *stcox* routine. Significance of coefficients is indicated as follows: $^{*}p < .05$, $^{**}p < .01$, $^{***}p < .001$ (all one-tailed t-tests). Details on measurement and estimation appear in Sarah A. Binder and Forrest Maltzman, "Senatorial Delay in Confirming Federal Judges, 1947–1998," *American Journal of Political Science* 46 (January 2002): 190–199.

We find much stronger effects for the partisan forces. Most notably, the confirmation process slows down in periods of divided control. As shown in Table 13-2, nomination of a potential judge during a period of divided government lowers his or her probability of swift confirmation by 29 percent. We can infer from the slowdown during divided control that the opposition party takes advantage of its scheduling power as the majority party to delay confirmation of nominees its members oppose. Divided government thus weakens the president's ability to shape the federal bench as he sees fit. Because the results show that the confirmation process generally goes more slowly during divided control, we can

Table 13-2 Magnitude of Effects on the Timing of Confirmation Decisions

Variable	Likelihood of Swift Confirmation (in percentages)
Nomination is made during divided government	−29
President and opposing party are ideologically opposed	−52
Nomination is made to a closely balanced circuit during divided government	−38
One home state senator is an ideological foe of the president	−88
Nomination is pending during a presidential election year	−72

Note: The calculation of substantive effects is explained in Sarah A. Binder and Forrest Maltzman, "Senatorial Delay in Confirming Federal Judges, 1947–1998," *American Journal of Political Science* 46 (January 2002): 190–199.

reject charges that conflict over judicial nominees is entirely new. Instead, partisan dynamics perennially shape the fate of judicial nominees before the Senate.

Divided government also shapes judicial selection politics in more specific ways. First, the Senate does not treat critical nominations differently than other nominations. But observe the fate of nominations to critical circuits during periods of divided government. The negative and significant coefficient means the following: If the president appoints someone to a critical circuit during unified government, the majority party typically confirms the nominee swiftly. That makes sense, since the nominee would tilt the balanced circuit in the majority party's favor. In contrast, if the president tries to appoint someone to a critical circuit during a period of divided control, confirmation of the nominee would tilt that circuit against the Senate majority party's views. Majority parties thus have an incentive during divided government to drag their heels on nominees to a critical circuit. As shown in Table 13-2, the magnitude of this effect is substantial: the risk of confirmation for critical nominations during divided control decreases 38 percent compared to periods of unified control.

That finding puts into perspective debates in the late 1990s over the makeup of the Sixth Circuit. In 1997 and 1998, the circuit was nearly evenly balanced between Democrats and Republicans, as Democrats made up roughly 45 percent of the bench.[12] That tight ideological balance led the parties to a stalemate over additional appointments, despite the fact that nearly a quarter of the bench was vacant during the period. Michigan's lone Republican senator blocked Clinton's nominees by exploiting the blue slip in the late 1990s, and the Republican chair of the Judiciary panel recognized his objections. Michigan's two Democratic senators after the 2000 elections then objected to Bush's appointments to the Sixth Circuit. General disagreement over the policy views of the nominees certainly motivated these senators, but their opposition was particularly intense because of the importance of appointments to those judgeships for the ideological balance of the regional bench.

Partisanship plays an especially important role if the parties are ideologically polarized. As the ideological distance increases between the president and the opposing party (regardless of whether it is the majority in the Senate), the probability of swift confirmation goes down. As shown in Table 13-2, a large ideological gap between the president and the opposing party can undermine the probability of a swift confirmation by more than 50 percent. Efforts by majority party Republicans on the Senate Judiciary Committee during Clinton's second term to delay hearings on his nominees are a prime example of how ideological disagreement between the parties can lead to long delays in the confirmation process. Ideological disagreement can also lead to long delays during periods of unified control, as it did when minority party Democrats faced off against Bush's conservative nominees in the 108th Congress (2003–2004). In this case, the opposing party exploited the need for a supermajority to impose cloture to prevent swift confirmation of presidential appointees. Even if a majority of the Senate wants to see a nominee swiftly confirmed, the ability of the opposing party to exploit institutional rules undercuts the power of the Senate majority.

The interplay among parties, their policy views, and the rules of the game is nicely illustrated by the impact that home state senators can have on the fate of nominees during a period of divided control. As shown in Table 13-1, when one of the home state senators is an ideological foe of the president, the likelihood of a nominee's swift confirmation deteriorates during a period of divided government. In fact, as suggested in Table 13-2, such a nominee would be nearly 90 percent less likely to see quick confirmation. How do home state foes of the president single-handedly drag out the process? The ability of home state senators to block nominees via the blue slip is instrumental here. Objections that home state senators convey to the Judiciary panel chair via the blue slip are simply much more likely to be honored by the chair in a period of divided government than otherwise, as such objections would undoubtedly come from senators of the chair's own party. Under divided government, the chair of the panel would be especially likely to use his scheduling powers against a nominee if objections arise from the ideological wing of the chair's own party.

We find little evidence that the quality of the nominee, as signaled by the American Bar Association, has much bearing on the fate of the typical appointment. One possibility is that the ABA might not be seen as a neutral evaluator of judicial nominees, and thus senators may systematically ignore its recommendations. Indeed, after Republicans became the Senate majority in 2001, they eliminated the ABA's privileged role in the vetting process. Alternatively, judicial qualifications may not be terribly important for most nominees. Politics, rather than a nominee's degree of qualification, may be paramount in shaping senators' evaluations.

Finally, temporal forces matter. First, the probability of swift confirmation goes down by some 72 percent when a nomination is pending during a presidential election year (Table 13-2). Second, and more important, it appears that the confirmation process has experienced a secular slowdown over the past half-century. Our variable that captures a gradual lengthening of the confirmation process (the Congress variable) shows a statistically significant and negative impact on the timing of Senate action. This means that in addition to the partisan, ideological, and institutional forces we have been discussing, there has also been a temporal slowdown in the confirmation process since the mid-twentieth century. That slowdown bears some further consideration, as battles over the makeup of the federal bench now occupy leaders and strategists for both major parties.

The Changing Face of Senate Obstruction

There is no doubt that the confirmation process has changed markedly in recent years. The news media now pay far more attention to these confirmation battles, and interest in the fate of presidential appointees now extends beyond the home state senators. Both parties—often spurred on by supportive groups outside the chamber—have made the plight of potential judges central to their campaigns for the White House and Congress.[13] The changing face of judicial selection can be seen most vividly in the introduction of new tactics by senators seeking to influence the outcome of advice and consent. Critics charge that these new tactics are unconstitutional and contrary to the intentions of the Framers of the Constitution. We believe, however, that far from being unconstitutional, these new tactics reflect adjustments by senators to the changing electoral and institutional context in which judicial selection takes place.

The key innovation in the confirmation process has been the successful use by the minority party of filibusters against controversial nominees. As of summer 2004, ten nominees for judgeships on the Circuit Courts of Appeals had been successfully filibustered by Senate Democrats, as a nearly united Democratic party prevented the Republican majority from invoking cloture via Rule 22 to end debate. In fact, Democrats had so frustrated the majority party after launching four filibusters that Republicans staged a forty-hour talkathon of their own to highlight Democrats' intransigence. But rather than convincing Democrats to give up their fight, the talkathon ended with Democrats blocking cloture on two more appellate court nominees. Citing the nominees' controversial views on issues including civil rights, environmental policy, and abortion rights of women, Democrats maintained that the Bush nominees held views too far from the mainstream to support confirmation.[14]

Critics charged that the filibusters were both unprecedented and unconstitutional, but there is little evidence to sustain such charges. Consider first the question of whether these were the first judicial nominees to be filibustered. Before the 108th Congress filibusters (2003–2004), debate on numerous judicial nominations had been subject to cloture votes. Granted, motions to invoke cloture may be filed even when no filibuster is under way. But given that most judicial nominees are confirmed by unanimous consent, it is reasonable to suspect that historical efforts to invoke cloture on judicial nominees were precipitated by threatened or actual filibusters on the Senate floor. Certainly the filibuster against the elevation of Abe Fortas to chief justice of the Supreme Court in 1968 falls in this category, as President Lyndon Johnson withdrew the nomination after the Senate rejected cloture, 45–53. Between the Fortas vote and the start of the Democratic filibusters in the 108th Congress, cloture was attempted fourteen times on district and circuit court nominations—including the appointments of Stephen Breyer to the Court of Appeals for the First Circuit and Richard Paez (after a four-year wait for confirmation) to the Ninth Circuit.[15] We can assume that the majority party was moved on those occasions to attempt cloture because of concerted opposition by minority party senators, even if none of the filibusters after Fortas was successful.

In contrast, all of the 108th Congress filibusters were successful. To be sure, successful obstruction of judicial nominations is not without precedent. Republicans successfully blocked scores of Clinton nominees when they controlled the Senate in the late 1990s. Republican floor and committee leaders simply refused to hold hearings or to call nominations up for a vote after they were reported from committee. Successful opposition to confirmation of new judges is not new, but the tactics of opposition—and their visibility to the public—certainly are.

Regardless of whether the Democratic filibusters were novel, Republicans also charged in the 108th Congress that they were unconstitutional: "The Constitution, fairly read, clearly calls for a majority vote on judicial nominees," argued Sen. Jeff Sessions, R-Ala.[16] If the Constitution is interpreted to require a simple majority vote for confirmation, then any rule or procedure that allows a minority of the body to block a majority from casting a vote on confirmation conflicts with the Constitution. This position led critics of the Democratic filibusters to charge that Rule 22 should not be applied to any executive nominations. Leaving aside the question of how debate would be conducted on judicial nominations in the absence of any Senate rule other than Rule 22 to limit debate, the plain face of Rule 22 seems to undermine that interpretation. According to the Senate rule book, a cloture petition can be filed "to bring to a close the debate upon any measure, motion, other matter pending before the Senate." Certainly nominations fall within the broad sweep of Rule 22.

Recognizing the limits of the constitutionality argument, Republican leaders in the 108th Congress advocated two reforms of the confirmation process. One reform would have implemented a sliding scale for cloture, successively reducing the number of votes needed to invoke cloture as debate goes on. Under the proposal, a simple majority could invoke cloture after two weeks of debate—thus eliminating the filibuster over judicial nominations. In theory, Senate rules can be changed by majority vote. But if the rule change were to be filibustered—which it surely would—then under Senate rules a two-thirds majority would be needed to break the filibuster. The slim Republican majority in the Senate thus made approval of this change extremely unlikely.

The Senate majority leader, Bill Frist, R-Tenn., also proposed in 2003 eliminating filibusters of judicial nominees through a more radical approach dubbed "the nuclear option." Under this approach, a simple majority of the Senate would seek through parliamentary appeals to establish the precedent that filibusters against nominations were unconstitutional. The history of cloture reform suggests that such a majority route to changing Senate rules might be possible.[17] But the approach was dubbed "the nuclear option" because of the consequences anticipated if the attempt were to succeed, namely that Democrats would exploit their remaining procedural advantages and shut down most Senate business. As Sen. Chuck Schumer, D-N.Y., remarked, the nuclear option would "vaporize every bridge in sight—bipartisan or otherwise." [18] Not surprisingly, given the anticipated fallout from the nuclear option, considerable dissent was apparent within Republican ranks—limiting the chances that it would be pursued. "Let's just see how that develops," remarked Sen. Robert Bennett, R-Utah, "because of the price you pay." [19]

The New Wars of Judicial Selection

Partisan conflict over advice and consent came to a head in March 2004 when the Senate Democratic Caucus vowed to block all executive and judicial nominations.[20] At issue were the president's decision to grant recess appointments to two of the judicial nominees filibustered by the Democrats and the White House's refusal to nominate Democratic choices for several bipartisan commissions. Such actions, Minority Leader Tom Daschle, D-S.D., charged on the Senate floor, "not only poison the nomination process, but they strike at the heart of the principle of checks and balances that is one of the pillars of the American democracy."[21] Democrats said they would lift the blockade after a couple of dozen Democrats had been appointed to bipartisan boards and commissions and after Bush had guaranteed that he would not make any more recess appointments.

Although that particular blockade was lifted two months later, the broader breakdown of the nomination process in 2004 suggests that the politics of judicial selection have changed markedly in recent years: the character of the process seems qualitatively different today than in the past. To be sure, not every nominee experiences intense opposition, as Democrats acquiesced to over a hundred of Bush's judicial appointees. But why has the process become so intensely polarized in recent years? The changing face of Senate obstruction in the battles over judges bears a deeper look.

Perhaps most striking about the new war over advice and consent is its visibility beyond the halls of the Senate. The rising salience of federal judgeships is visible on several fronts. First, intense interest in the selection of federal judges is no longer limited to the home state senators. Second, negative blue slips from home state senators no longer guarantee that a nomination will be killed, as recent Judiciary panel chairs have been hesitant to accord such influence to objections from the minority party. Third, recorded floor votes are now the norm for confirmation of appellate court judges, as nominations are of increased importance to groups outside the institution. And fourth, nominations now draw the attention of strategists within both political parties—as evidenced by the president's focus on judicial nominations in stumping for Republican Senate candidates in the 2002 midterm elections.

How do we account for the rising salience of federal judgeships to actors in and out of the Senate? It is tempting to claim that the activities of organized interests after the 1987 Supreme Court confirmation battle over Robert Bork are responsible. But interest groups have kept a close eye on judicial selection for quite some time. Both liberal and conservative groups were involved periodically from the late 1960s into the 1980s. And in 1984, liberal groups under the umbrella of the Alliance for Justice commenced systematic monitoring of judicial appointments, as had the conservative Judicial Reform Project of the Free Congress Foundation earlier in the decade. Although interest group tactics may have fanned the fires over judicial selection in recent years, the introduction of new blocking tactics in the Senate developed long after groups had become active in the process.[22] Outside groups may encourage senators to take more aggressive stands against judicial nominees, but by and large Senate opposition reflects senators' concerns about the policy impact of judges on the federal bench.

Rather than attribute the state of judicial selection to the lobbying of outside groups, we believe that the politics of judicial selection have been indelibly shaped by two concurrent trends. First, the two political parties are more ideologically opposed today than they have been for the past few decades. From the empirical analysis above, it appears plain that ideological differences between the parties encourage senators to exploit the rules of the game to their party's advantage.

Second, it is important to remember that if the courts were of little importance to the two parties, then polarized relations would matter little to senators and presidents in conducting advice and consent. However, the federal courts today are intricately involved in the interpretation and enforcement of federal law, particularly as the Supreme Court has limited its docket in recent years. The rising importance of the federal courts makes extremely important the second trend affecting judicial selection. When Democrats lost control of the Senate after the 2002 elections, the federal courts were nearly evenly balanced between Democratic and Republican appointees: the active judiciary was composed of 398 judges appointed by Republican presidents and 400 judges appointed by Democratic presidents.[23] Having lost control of the Senate, distrusting the ideological bent of Bush appointees, and finding the courts on the edge of partisan balance, the Democrats made scrutiny of judicial nominees a caucus priority in 2003 and achieved remarkable unity in blocking nominees they deemed particularly objectionable. Republicans responded in kind and found themselves embroiled in a staff memo scandal and threatening recalcitrant Democrats with the "nuclear option." Intense ideological disagreement, coupled with the rising importance of a closely balanced federal bench, has brought combatants in the wars of advice and consent to new tactics and new crises, as the two parties struggle to shape the future of the federal courts.

Table 13-3 Impact of Judicial Selection Delay on the Performance of the Circuit Courts of Appeals, 2002

Variable	Coefficient (SE)
Number of vacant judgeship months	.047 (.025)*
Number of appeals filed	.003 (.002)
Constant	6.781 (1.719) **
N	12
Prob. F.	.059
Adjusted R-squared	.346

Source: Data from *2002 Federal Court Management Statistics,* Administrative Office of the Courts (Washington, D.C.: Government Printing Office).

Note: Dependent variable is the time interval in months for the median case from filing of notice of appeal to disposition of the case, for each Circuit Court of Appeals in 2002. Includes only cases terminated on the merits of the case. For the explanatory variables, "Number of vacant judgeship months" is the number of months during the year that an authorized judgeship position was not filled, and "Number of appeals filed" is the total number of appeals filed with the court that year. Parameter estimates from regress routine in Stata 8.0.

$^{*}p = .05$, $^{**}p = .01$ (both one-tailed tests)

Does the Politics of Judicial Selection Matter?

Does it matter that the process of judicial selection has become so polarized in recent years? There are at least three ways in which the battles over advice and consent might matter to students of Congress and American politics. First, the performance of the federal courts might suffer. Second, the legitimacy of the courts as an institution might be harmed. And third, partisan battles might be harmful both for the Senate institutionally and for its members. Although not all of these consequences are amenable to empirical tests, we close by reviewing what is at stake in these conflicts over the federal bench.

Does it matter that federal judgeships now take, on average, far longer to fill? Preliminary evidence suggests that it does. Assessing the performance of the twelve circuit courts of appeal in 2002, we show in Table 13-3 that the longer more judgeships remained vacant on a circuit, the longer it took for the court to act on its docket of appeals. With data from a single year, our ability to generalize is limited. But the results suggest that the performance of the federal courts suffers when judgeships remain vacant, even after controlling for the size of each court's docket. The Sixth Circuit—handling appeals from the trial courts of Kentucky, Michigan, Ohio, and Tennessee—illustrates the dilemma starkly. With 25 percent of its bench vacant in 2002, the court was the slowest of all the circuit courts—even though its docket was the fourth smallest. As Michigan's attorney general remarked that year, "None of us is at our best when 25 percent of our colleagues are missing."[24] Granted, the duration of a vacancy reflects both presidential delay in choosing a nominee and senatorial delay in confirming her or him. But both delays can be attributed in large part to senators' willingness to exploit the rules of the game to influence the choice of federal judges.[25] Clearly, such delay has consequences for the federal bench, demonstrably limiting the performance of the appellate courts.

Does the conflict over the selection of federal judges have implications for the public's view of the courts? Given that judges receive lifetime appointments, ensuring the independence and legitimacy of the federal bench is essential for instilling and maintaining public confidence in the judiciary. We can conjecture that pronounced conflict over potential judges lessens public confidence in the courts. We know that the Supreme Court's *Bush v. Gore* (2000) decision, which awarded Bush the presidency, negatively affected Gore supporters' views of the Court as an institution.[26] Respondents to national surveys also seem receptive to the view that nominees' policy views should play a role in senators' confirmation decisions. When asked in 2002 about Senate consideration of Supreme Court nominees, over half of a Gallup poll's respondents agreed that senators should consider a nominee's policy views— even if the nominee is qualified legally and ethically for the bench.[27] Nearly 50 percent agreed that senators should vote to reject nominees if they have doubts about the president's choices.[28] Still, when queried about the Senate filibuster of Judge Charles Pickering's nomination to the U.S. Court of Appeals for the Fifth Circuit in 2002, nearly half of respondents believed that the debate was based more on "politics" than on "principle."[29] Such results suggest that even though the public sees ideology as relevant to the confirmation process, there is a considerable cost to such debates. Although it is difficult to establish that the public's broader view of the courts is shaped by the coverage of judicial selection, public confidence in federal judges is likely shaped by the politics of their selection.

Finally, the new wars of advice and consent likely will take a toll on the Senate itself. The events of the 108th Congress frayed the Senate's already wafer-thin veneer of comity. Given leaders' reliance on unanimous consent to make the Senate function, partisan disagreements always have the potential to make the Senate unmanageable. What makes the disputes over judicial nominees particularly troublesome for both parties is the sense that the process has spiraled out of control. To be sure, Democrats continued to confirm scores of Bush's nominees while holding up the few that they singled out for filibusters. But the developments of the 108th Congress created what one senator called a "breach of trust," and trust is an element typically deemed essential for securing bipartisan consent in that chamber.[30]

There are few signs that the wars of advice and consent will abate anytime soon. Reflecting on the Democrats' filibusters, Lindsay Graham, R-S.C., observed that "if you don't think down the road it will be answered in kind by the Republican Party, I think you are very naïve."[31] The new tactics, Graham warned, would become the norm. "Payback," Graham aptly summed up, "is hell." So long as ideological divisions lead senators to disagree over the makeup of the federal bench, and so long as the courts remain central in the interpretation of public law, battles over judicial selection are unlikely to go away. More likely, they will intensify—especially when the next vacancy on the Supreme Court occurs. Unless the president selects someone with moderate ideological stripes, past battles over confirming federal judges will pale in comparison. The stakes of who sits on the federal bench are simply too high for combatants in the battles of advice and consent to view the contest from the sidelines. Policy motivations and institutional opportunities will continue to shape the ideological character of the federal bench.

Notes

1. For a discussion of the Framers' intentions regarding "advice and consent," see John Ferling, "The Senate and Federal Judges: The Intent of the Founding Fathers," *Capitol Studies* 2 (winter 1974): 57–70.
2. On the emergence of federal judgeships as patronage, see Kermit Hall, *The Politics of Justice* (Lincoln: University of Nebraska Press, 1979).
3. The influence of home state senators in the selection of nominees is probed in Sarah A. Binder and Forrest Maltzman, "The Limits of Senatorial Courtesy," *Legislative Studies Quarterly* 24 (February 2004): 5–22; and Donald Songer, Thomas Hansford, and Tajuana Massie, "The Timing of Presidential Nominations to the Lower Federal Courts," *Political Research Quarterly* (March 2004): 145–154.
4. The logic of senatorial courtesy is explored in Tonja Jacobi, "The Senatorial Courtesy Game: Explaining the Norm of Informal Vetoes in 'Advice and Consent' Nominations," *Legislative Studies Quarterly* (forthcoming).
5. See Sarah A. Binder, "Origins of the Senate 'Blue Slip': The Creation of Senate Norms" (paper presented at the annual meeting of the Midwest Political Science Association, Chicago, April 2004).
6. As cited in Robert A. Carp and Ronald Stidham, *Judicial Process in America,* 2nd ed. (Washington, D.C.: CQ Press, 1993), 232.
7. The data include all nominees for the federal District Courts and Circuit Courts of Appeal eventually confirmed by the Senate.
8. See Robert Kagan, *Adversarial Legalism* (Cambridge: Harvard University Press, 2001); Thomas F. Burke, *Lawyers, Lawsuits, and Legal Rights: The Battle over Litigation in American Society* (Berkeley: University of California Press, 2004); and Gordon Silverstein, *How Law Kills Politics* (New York: Norton, forthcoming).
9. Details on measurement of the independent variables, the construction of the dependent variable, and the estimation strategy appear in Sarah A. Binder and Forrest Maltzman, "Senatorial Delay in Confirming Federal Judges, 1947–1998," *American Journal of Political Science* 46 (January 2002): 190–199. The model reported here differs slightly. Instead of including fixed effects to capture the impact of specific presidents on judicial selection, we include a time counter ("Congress") that allows one to gauge whether the process of advice and consent has changed significantly over time.
10. A duration model tells us the probability that the Senate will act on a nominee at a particular time, given that the Senate has not previously taken action on the nominee. Technically, the coefficients help us to understand whether a particular independent variable increases or decreases what is known as the "hazard" or "risk" of Senate action. The hazard of Senate action is thus roughly the probability of swift Senate action by the Senate to confirm a nominee. Duration analysis is particularly useful for understanding confirmation politics since the method incorporates information about whether, when, and how the Senate acts on any given nominee.
11. The statistical method for calculating substantive effects is detailed in Binder and Maltzman, "Senatorial Delay in Confirming Federal Judges."

12. We determine the partisan balance of the bench from Gary Zuk, Deborah Barrow, and Gerald S. Gryski, *A Multi-user Database on the Attributes of U.S. Appeals Court Judges, 1801–1994,* 1st ICPSR version (Ann Arbor, Mich.: Inter-University Consortium for Political and Social Research).
13. Involvement of interest groups in lower court judicial selection reaches back decades, but a marked increase in their organized involvement occurred in the early 1980s. See Gregory A. Caldeira and John R. Wright, "Lobbying for Justice: The Rise of Organized Conflict in the Politics of Federal Judgeships," in *Contemplating Courts,* ed. Lee Epstein (Washington, D.C.: CQ Press, 1995). See also Roy B. Flemming, Michael C. MacLeod, and Jeffery Talbert, "Witnesses at the Confirmations? The Appearances of Organized Interests at Senate Hearings of Federal Judicial Appointments, 1945–1992," *Political Research Quarterly* 51 (September 1998): 617–631; and Lauren Cohen Bell, *Warring Factions: Interest Groups, Money and the New Politics of Senate Confirmation* (Columbus: Ohio State University Press, 2002).
14. One nominee, Manuel Estrada, was opposed because the White House refused to grant Senate Democrats access to his writings from when he worked in the solicitor general's office; without those memos, Democrats charged that no paper trail existed with which to confirm Estrada's ideological views.
15. See Richard S. Beth, *Cloture Attempts on Nominations,* CRS Report for Congress RS20801, Congressional Research Service, updated December 11, 2002.
16. As cited in Jeffrey Toobin, "Advice and Dissent: The Fight over the President's Judicial Nominations," *The New Yorker,* May 26, 2003, 47.
17. See Sarah A. Binder and Steven S. Smith, *Politics or Principle? Filibustering in the United States Senate* (Washington, D.C.: Brookings Institution Press, 1997).
18. As cited in Helen Dewar, "GOP Votes to Break Nominee Filibusters: Democrats Appear Able to Block Plan," *Washington Post,* June 25, 2003, A21.
19. As cited in Paul Kane, "Rule Changes Unlikely," *Roll Call,* June 5, 2003.
20. See Paul Kane, "Nominations Put on Ice," *Roll Call,* March 29, 2004.
21. Sen. Tom Daschle, "Politicization of the Nomination Process," *Congressional Record,* March 26, 2004, S3200.
22. Recent tactics of two leading interest groups are detailed in Bob Davis and Robert S. Greenberger, "Two Old Foes Plot Tactics in Battle over Judgeships," *Wall Street Journal,* March 2, 2004.
23. See *Alliance for Justice Judicial Selection Project, 2001–2002 Biennial Report,* Appendix 3, 2002, available online at www.allianceforjustice.org/images/collection_images/2001-02_AFJ_Biennial_Report.pdf.
24. As cited in Terry Kinney, "Sixth Circuit Slowest of Appeals Courts," *Louisville Courier-Journal,* January 10, 2004.
25. On the sources of nomination delay, see Binder and Maltzman, "The Limits of Senatorial Courtesy," 5–22.
26. See Vincent Price and Anca Romantan, "Confidence in Institutions Before, During, and After 'Indecision 2000,'" *Journal of Politics* 66 (August 2004): 939–956.
27. See Gallup, CNN, *USA Today* Poll, June 12–23, 2002, Public Opinion Online, Roper Center at University of Connecticut, Accession number 0408132.
28. Hickman-Brown Research, July 10–16, 2001, as reported in *Poll Track,* July 30, 2001, www.nationaljournal.com.
29. Opinion Dynamics Poll, March 12, 2002, Public Opinion Online, Roper Center at University of Connecticut, Accession number 0399912.
30. Statement of Sen. Patrick Leahy, Senate Judiciary Committee, Executive Business Meeting, February 12, 2004.
31. As cited in Jennifer A. Dlouhy, "Judicial War far From Over," *CQ Weekly,* November 15, 2003, 2824.

14. The Politics of Taxing and Spending in Congress: Ideas, Strategy, and Policy

Catherine E. Rudder

In the initial years of the twenty-first century, congressional Republicans achieved a remarkable record of substantive and strategic success of historical proportions. Led by President George W. Bush, they enacted substantial tax cuts, even with extremely narrow party majorities, four years in a row without being deflected by other concerns and despite the demands of war. Upon assuming office in 2001, the new president successfully capitalized on the groundwork House Republicans had laid since their takeover of that body six years earlier. Shrugging aside worries about deficit spending and tax progressivity, the Republicans dramatically shifted the agenda toward reducing the tax burden on those who pay the most taxes in absolute terms and boosting incentives to save and invest.

More speculatively, a reasonable person could conclude that while tax reduction for the well-off is a primary goal of Republicans-in-government,[1] it is also a means to the larger goal of significantly diminishing the role of the federal government, outside of domestic and national security, in the lives of its citizens. In this view, the great size of the tax cuts, coupled with impending demands on the federal purse arising from the changing demographics of the population and the threat of the imposition of the Alternative Minimum Tax on the upper middle class, is likely to create a fiscal crisis that will force Congress to reconsider huge programs like Social Security and Medicare and to open wholesale reassessment of the tax code.[2]

The president and his antitax colleagues in Congress learned lessons from recent history about what works and what doesn't in reaching their goals. A new center of gravity in the Republican Party has reignited a strategy of "starving the beast" of government to compel reform of previously unassailable mandatory spending programs such as Social Security, Medicare, and Medicaid. Supply-side economic theory, popularized in the late 1970s and embraced by the Reagan administration, has provided some legitimacy, and political cover, for the huge deficits that have ensued.

The turnaround in policy has aroused deep concern within the professional tax policy community and otherwise-dissimilar think tanks ranging from the Center on Budget and Policy Priorities (CBPP), to the Committee for a Responsible Federal Budget, to the Concord Coalition. Critics variously assert that the nearly single-minded focus on tax reduction at all costs has come at the expense of the long-run health of the American economy, of the ability of the government to meet long-standing commitments to senior citizens and other Americans, and of the credibility and well-being of governing institutions. Congressional procedures to aid deliberation, fairness, transparency, and some measure of predictability and budget discipline have suffered under the tax-cutting regime, as has the fairness of the tax code. The path on which the tax cutters have put American government is, in the view of many knowledgeable observers, unsustainable and possibly dangerous.

Because this is also the view of many Democrats, this critique may look suspiciously partisan. In all likelihood, most Republicans and Democrats would agree that the stage is set for an action-forcing fiscal crisis. However, an alternative view is that rather than being dangerous, a crisis is needed to break the U.S. government out of its procrustean bed of entitlement spending, make it let go of the obsessive concern with progressive taxation, break through the myopic incrementalism characteristic of American politics, and liberate the economy to create new wealth.

The thesis of this chapter is that a major policy shift has occurred both between the Republicans- and Democrats-in-government and within each party. This policy realignment began with the election of Ronald Reagan and was completed with the election of President George W. Bush. The shift, reflected in the interpretations above, is important because the differences between the Democrats and Republicans are wide, and election outcomes—determining which party's ideas dominate—have and will have a powerful, long-term impact on the lives of Americans.

Democrats, chastened by huge deficits racked up in the 1980s but still desirous of maintaining a government-supported social safety net for citizens, support a fiscal conservatism that permits sustainable government and progressive taxation. The Democratic stance, led by former President Bill Clinton, was shaped largely in reaction to the Republican change in position and strategy over the past decade.

Once dominated by deficit hawks—those who oppose deficit spending—and parsimonious conservatives, the new Republican center has launched a sweeping reform of American national government. Deficits are of much less concern to these Republicans than are the goals of altering the tax structure to reward capital accumulation, forcing a reconsideration of entitlement spending, privatizing governmental functions, and reducing direct spending on social welfare programs. This program is more than simply a general disposition to cut taxes and constrain government. Rather, it is designed fundamentally to alter national politics-as-usual by means heretofore regarded as beyond the bounds of accepted political tactics.

The Fiscal Crisis: A Bleak Outlook or an Action-Forcing Strategy?

On February 3, 2004, in his testimony before Congress, Peter R. Orszag characterized the outlook for the federal budget as "unsustainable." Assuming current tax and spending policies over the next ten years, federal government revenues will fall short by $5 trillion, if the surpluses in Social Security are included, and by $8 trillion, excluding them.[3] Two months earlier, a report of the Congressional Budget Office similarly declared the budgetary situation "unsustainable," even taking into account discretionary budget cuts.[4]

The deterioration of the fiscal outlook, from a surplus of $1.3 trillion when the new administration arrived to a shortfall of $4.5 trillion, is hard to fathom.[5] Over the longer run, the picture worsens to an alarming degree. CBPP and its diverse collaborators predict "large, sustained deficits".[6] Auerbach and his colleagues expect the fiscal gap over the period from 2002 to 2075 to be 4.9 percent of the U.S. gross domestic product (GDP).[7]

The sources of the current deficits are several. On the simplest level, of course, expenditures exceed revenues. But why? Where did the projected surplus go? As with all budgetary matters, the answer depends on one's perspective and the assumptions underlying the analysis. Using data from the Urban Institute–Brookings Tax Policy Center and the Congressional Research Service, Isaac Shapiro and Joel Friedman present the view that the Republican tax cuts represent two-thirds of the fiscal 2004 deficit.[8]

The alternative explanation offered by the administration is that the recession of 2001–2003, fueled in large part by the enormous financial impact of the al Qaeda attacks on the United States on September 11, 2001, the wars in Afghanistan and Iraq, and new expenditures for homeland security account for the lion's share of the deficit.[9] Other calculations of the impact of the tax cuts range from about one-third[10] to one-half,[11] depending on the assumptions made. In any case, a very substantial portion of the deficit arose from the actions of Congress to cut taxes and does not stem from exogenous forces such as the weak economy or merely from new spending for defense and homeland security.[12]

Disappointing as they are, however, the immediate series of projected yearly deficits are not the most pressing concern. More important is that the effects of the Bush tax cuts will snowball, if they are made permanent, threatening an eventual fiscal avalanche.[13]

At the close of 2003, the Congressional Budget Office (CBO) reported that Congress was facing an "unsustainable budgetary situation" stemming from the impending retirements of the baby boom generation and their reliance on programs such as Social Security and Medicare that are automatically paid to recipients. The effects of this entirely predictable demographic change have been ignored by Congress and the president and have been made much worse by the huge loss of revenue from the Bush tax cuts in 2001, 2002, and 2003.[14] The demographic change coupled with the trillions in tax cuts will force Congress to make politically difficult choices, likely including large tax increases and substantial spending reductions.[15]

As Peter Orszag writes, the deficits "impose significant and growing economic costs over the medium term and potentially devastating effects over the longer term . . . [as] a self-reinforcing negative cycle" could develop.[16] Observers from Gokhale and Smetters[17] to Paul Krugman[18]—that is, those on different parts of the political spectrum—raise this problem. Certainly, policymakers will be confronted with an increasingly action-forcing state of affairs the longer the United States treads this path.[19]

The Evolution of Fiscal Policy

Following World War II, Congress and the president, regardless of party, found it relatively easy to reduce taxes and increase government spending as the economy grew. During this period of easy financing, as tax analyst Eugene Steuerle calls it, policymakers were more concerned with how to spend revenues than with how to raise them.[20]

Many observers mark President John Kennedy's 1962 investment tax credit and related policies that lowered the cost of capital as the first conscious attempt in recent times to use tax policy as a macroeconomic tool. Modest though this proposal was, it was seen by many observers to have worked as planned, and this success laid the groundwork for subsequent efforts to fashion policies that would bring about economic growth and low levels of unemployment without stimulating inflation.[21]

At first, Congress was not at the forefront of this effort. Its legislative machinery was ill-equipped to the task. Congress was at the mercy of the president's arsenal of experts and information centralized in the Office of Management and Budget (OMB). The theory followed by both congressional Republicans and Democrats was simple and straightforward: Budgets should be balanced. The center of gravity in the two congressional parties was different, but there was much overlap between the two, with the Democrats tending to favor more spending and more progressive and higher taxes than the Republicans.

The 1970s brought on two major changes, one political and one economic, that significantly altered the budgeting landscape. Just as James Madison had predicted in *The Federalist* No. 10, members of Congress proved jealous of their institutional prerogatives. In 1974 Congress was dominated by Democrats unwilling to respond to the dictates of the Republican president, Richard M. Nixon. Congress, wanting the independent expertise and structure necessary to assert the wishes of the majority in taxes and appropriations, passed the Budget and Impoundment Control Act. This legislation created the House and Senate Budget Committees, the Congressional Budget Office that would be able to go head-to-head with OMB, and procedures that forced Congress to take a comprehensive look at taxing and spending, including entitlements.[22] The ailing economy provided the second impetus. Starting in 1973, growth in productivity, the source of real economic growth, stalled.[23] With two serious recessions in this decade, the economy faltered. A neologism, "stagflation," was coined to characterize the situation of high inflation and low growth. An energy crisis, punctuated by two painful periods of gasoline shortages and price increases, persisted. The high inflation pushed people whose real incomes were not increasing into higher tax brackets. The economic times were out of joint.

Members of Congress now had the mechanisms in place and the need to try to respond. A minority of members from both parties, acutely aware both of the populist tax revolt at the state and national levels and of the need to reignite the economy in an increasingly competitive world, developed an intense interest in proposals to alter the tax structure.

A new phrase was creeping into the Beltway vocabulary, "supply-side economics," a theory that argued for tax cuts on the grounds that taxes create a disincentive to work and thus inhibit economic growth. Moreover, it was posited that cutting marginal tax rates, by encouraging people to work more, would actually generate revenue and hence cost the Treasury much less than the nominal size of the tax reduction. Supply-side theorists disagreed on how great this dynamic effect of tax cuts was. In the most extreme version, cutting taxes was said to lead to an increase in tax revenue.

Under the elixir of supply-side economics, endorsed by a few leading economists such as Harvard University's Martin Feldstein, who became an adviser in the Reagan administration, marginal tax rates could be cut, and such cuts would spark the economy. Economic growth would lead to increased wealth in the nation and increased revenues in the government's coffers.[24] Congress could respond to the growing opposition to rising taxes by cutting them and could erase deficits painlessly. Talk about taxation could move from one of fairness and progressivity—language that tended to benefit Democrats—to economic growth, creating incentives to invest and produce, and marginal rate cuts—language that appealed more to Republicans and their constituencies.

The Reagan Revolution

The 1980 election produced a landslide for the Republican Ronald Reagan and a Republican Senate majority for the first time in three decades, heralding an era of policy change. President Reagan had campaigned on reducing the size of government, cutting taxes, and strengthening national defense. He seemed to have a mandate, along with working majorities in the House and the Senate, to accomplish these goals.[25] Equally important, with his new OMB director, former representative David Stockman, Reagan had a knowledgeable, able strategist who understood the workings of the new congressional budget process and could use that process to accomplish the purposes of the president. While President Reagan was not a theorist, he felt that the high rate of taxes for those taxpayers who fell into the top tax bracket was wrong and should be changed. He was, in fact, driven by a normative conception of fairness, not economic theory, but many in his administration embraced supply-side theory, which was completely compatible with Reagan's wishes.[26]

Upon assuming office, President Reagan accomplished his key goals with a swiftness that was unparalleled. Turning the congressional budget process into a tool of the presidency, he obtained an unprecedented $750 billion reduction in taxes in his first year in office—much more than he originally asked for after a "bidding war" ensued in the House to add multiple tax advantages for various constituencies.[27] However, he obtained the goal closest to his heart, reducing marginal tax rates. The most significant element of this legislation was a reform in the tax code to eliminate the "bracket creep" caused by inflation. This change meant that the effects of inflation would not push taxpayers into higher tax brackets or reduce the value of the standard deduction and personal exemption. The change, however, also eliminated a lucrative way to increase government revenues without legislating tax increases. Indexing for inflation was to be more costly over the long term than all the other provisions in the 1981 act combined and was a major source of the subsequent deficits.[28]

After the passage of the Economic Recovery Tax Act in 1981, however, no more expensive tax cuts were in the offing for individuals in the subsequent seven years of Reagan's presidency.[29] Instead, in a congressional effort to limit the size of projected deficits, certain tax reductions enacted in 1981 were canceled. Nor could the president shrink domestic discretionary spending sufficiently to balance the tax cuts.[30] His Republicans in Congress had their own favorite programs that they were unwilling to pare. The defining characteristics of Congress—such as logrolling, clientelism, universalism, and credit-taking—had not been repealed.[31]

Nor did the magic of supply-side economics pan out: for a variety of reasons, tax cuts did not stimulate the economy sufficiently to pay for themselves in any discernible way.[32] Most important, concern over the swelling deficit swamped claims for the benefits of supply-side policies. Supply-side theory, however, lay dormant while the Congress attended to persistent deficits for the following two decades.

Notwithstanding his fierce desire to reduce the size of government (outside of defense), the Great Communicator ended his presidency with the major achievement of having reduced marginal tax rates on individuals but with a much larger government than he had started with in 1981 and a national debt triple that which existed when he entered office. Simply servicing the debt consumed 13 percent of the federal budget.[33]

Republicans learned that controlling the Senate and having a sometime working majority in the House were not enough to turn the direction of American politics around. Attracting House Democrats to Republican causes was not the same as controlling the levers of power by holding a party majority in the House. Moreover, despite some severe cuts to specific domestic discretionary programs, the payoff was relatively small as a proportion of government spending.[34] Popular programs and agencies such as the Education Department simply were not going to be eliminated, as Reagan had proposed, under the conditions that existed at that time. If significant inroads were to be made on the spending side of the ledger, Congress would have to be put in a position that would force members to accede to painful cuts in popular programs, especially politically impenetrable entitlements such as Social Security and Medicare.[35]

Reagan's own congressional partisans liked government programs that aided their constituents. In the end, too few Republicans were disposed to elevate tax cutting over deficit control or ready to restrict federal spending in their own district backyards. Enough Republicans either believed in balanced budgets or felt that they had to be responsive to their constituents' desires for spending.

Despite Reagan's limited success in concrete terms, something important was happening in American politics, something akin to the shifting of tectonic plates. The political parties were approaching parity within the American public. A realignment was occurring in the South with the Republicans ascendant. With the demise of the moderate-liberal wing of the Republican party and the gradual rise of conservative southern Republicans in positions of formal and informal party leadership, the parties in Congress were increasingly divided, party unity scores soared, and the middle where compromises could be forged was shrinking, trends that were to continue to the present time.[36] With Reagan's rout of the Democrats in 1980 and 1984, large majorities of American voters endorsed rhetorical themes that "government is the problem," government needs to be shrunk, and taxes need to be cut. A decade later, in declaring that the age of big government was over, President Bill Clinton, a Democrat, confirmed the Reagan revolution. Obviously, the age of big government was far from over, but an important psychological change and a shift in the balance of power had taken place that were to alter the possibilities in American politics, and the second President Bush was to capitalize on them in 2001.[37]

Like George Washington, Ronald Reagan managed to stay above the fray. Because of his success in leading the battle to cut marginal tax rates and largely to maintain those lower rates, he was a hero to the anti-taxers. That he was maneuvered by the Democrats and Republican deficit hawks in Congress into signing bills that raised taxes or reversed legislated tax cuts in order to narrow burgeoning deficits was insufficient to erase his tax-cutting reputation. His Republican successor, George H. W. Bush, had no such skill or luck.

As the heir apparent to President Reagan, Vice President Bush had cast his lot rhetorically with the tax cutters, or at least the stand-patters. The marginal rate cuts were to hold. "Read my lips," he said repeatedly on the campaign trail, "no new taxes." Bush's subsequent agreement in 1990 to raise marginal tax rates on individuals in order to avert a government shutdown was met with shock and disappointment in the Republican Party, especially among those who claimed the mantle of Ronald Reagan, the tax cutter, and was used by challenger Bill Clinton in 1992.[38] No explanation was adequate to excuse this betrayal to many hard-core, tax-cutting Republicans, even though the legislation placed the country back on the path to fiscal balance.[39]

The furor that the first President Bush's concession to the Democrats during the 1990 budget summit caused was a harbinger that the balance of power in the Republican Party was shifting from traditional Republican deficit hawks to tax cutters and a rising chorus in the House.[40] Still, for the tax-cutting supply-siders to triumph, gaining and maintaining formal control of the House and Senate took on an ever greater importance, as Republicans saw their policy gains evaporating. Patience and energy in pursuing a careful strategy would be required.

Clinton and the Deficit Hawks

Though the 1992 elections brought Democratic control to the House, Senate, and presidency, the victory was far from decisive. With less than a majority of the vote, challenger Bill Clinton nevertheless won the presidency, as third-party deficit hawk Ross Perot siphoned votes that likely would have gone to President Bush, who was running for a second term.[41] The Democrats' House majority was thin. Communism had collapsed in 1989–1991, and free market ideas were in ascendance. President Clinton was not going to succeed in adding large new government programs directly. Instead, he reverted to the tax code to reach arguably the two most important achievements of his initial two years in office and perhaps of his presidency. He employed the same legislative vehicle for both accomplishments.

Using congressional budget reconciliation procedures, as his predecessors Reagan and the first President Bush had, Clinton and his Democratic congressional allies strengthened the largest program to help poor families with children by moving a large swath of those earning the lowest income off the income tax rolls and by expanding the earned income tax credit for the working poor. Clinton's second major achievement was to increase the marginal tax rates on taxpayers with the highest incomes. The prized Reagan rate reductions for those with the highest incomes, slightly adjusted upward during his successor's term, were almost entirely reversed by Clinton and the Democratic Congress. The party divisions were sharp. The reconciliation bill squeaked through the House without one Republican vote, reflecting important differences in philosophy between the two congressional parties.

The Republicans immediately characterized this income tax increase on the top 2 percent of households (excluding a gas tax) as simply the largest tax increase in history, despite the fact that it was also a huge tax cut for many, with the middle class largely unaffected by the legislation.[42] This misleading but technically correct characterization seemed to take hold and to contribute to the Democrats' losing the House and Senate that year, an outcome unexpected by most observers.[43]

One thing the Democrats and Republicans could generally agree on in the 1980s and 1990s was the need to get deficits under control. While Republicans greatly preferred spending cuts to tax increases, the deficit hawks on both sides of the aisle exerted strong influence to make ends meet. Key mechanisms to accomplish this goal were the 1985 Gramm-Rudman-Hollings Deficit Reduction Act[44]—named for the principal sponsors of the legislation—and the 1990 Budget Enforcement Act and subsequent renewals in 1993 and 1997.[45] These rules worked over the 1990s to help erase the yearly deficits.[46]

However, procedural rules, like tax expenditures in the tax code, created distortions in policymaking. Despite the deficit, members of Congress still needed to serve constituents and still had policy preferences that they wanted to enact. Methods were developed to circumvent the rules. The 1990s could be seen as years of experimentation in how to game the system.

By 1999, however, rules to control deficits were beginning to seem silly, as surpluses, rather than deficits, were appearing on the horizon. After all, if the money is not needed, why not give it back to the people who are paying it? As Bush said in his first State of the Union address, "The people of America have been overcharged and on their behalf, I am here to ask for a refund."[47]

The ground had already been laid for tax cutting. Specific proposals, ranging from marginal rate cuts to reform of estate taxes, were crafted, publicized, and proposed in legislation by the Republican tax cutters after they took over the leadership of the House in 1995.

The Second Republican Revolution: A Successful Gingrich Strategy

With their victory in 1994, Republicans assumed control of the House for the first time in forty years and regained control of the Senate, which they had last held in 1986. With seventy-three new House Republicans, more conservative, more activist, more impatient, and fervently antitax, the balance within the party was shifting. They had been brought into the House thanks to the bold strategy, implemented over the previous decade and a half, of the new Speaker, Newt Gingrich. Gingrich had been a backbencher. He was not a gentleman in his approach to politics-as-usual, nor did he seem to respect the gentlemanly manner of his own House leadership as represented by Bob Michel, who had served as minority leader for fourteen years before Gingrich engineered his retirement in 1995.

For Gingrich, cooperating in any way with the Democrats meant losing.[48] He had successfully led the charge to depose Democratic Speaker Jim Wright (a precursor to the successful approach House Republicans would take toward President Bill Clinton a decade later). He disparaged Congress and then identified the Democrats with that "corrupt" institution. He recruited and trained the cadre of quality congressional challengers who entered office in 1995.[49] He was brash and hard-hitting; his language was inundated with superlatives and exaggerations and was sometimes misleading, as in the example earlier concerning "the largest tax increase in history."[50] The strategy he followed was one of no-holds-barred, and it worked. Earlier generations had followed the maxim, "To get along, go along." Gingrich was not interested in getting along; he was yearning to change American politics. He did. And he set the example for his followers and for others. A minority party mindset would have to be recalibrated to one of controlling the levers of power in the House, and it was.[51] Gingrich forged a new agenda for his Republican revolution that, while not enacted into law in the end, laid the groundwork for future years, as did much of the tax activity of the House Republicans in the second half of the 1990s.[52] For Gingrich, ideological goals trumped institutional maintenance.

Though Gingrich met an early demise as Speaker in an ethics irregularity, the revolution that he had launched did not. Newt Gingrich made four significant contributions to the Republican Party that are important in understanding the politics of taxing and spending over the last ten years. First, he brought into the House a new cadre of troops who were impatient for change in politics-as-usual, who admired Gingrich's bold strategy and tactics, and who provided the numbers necessary to create a Republican majority in the House and to support a new brand of leadership as represented by Republican Whip Tom "the Hammer" DeLay and Majority Leader Dick Armey, both fierce adversaries of the Democrats and opponents of the income tax. The differences between the Republican House and Senate on tax and spending policy became somewhat more pronounced as the House came to be dominated by the tax cutters and the Senate by the deficit hawks. This difference, however, was not as apparent under surplus conditions or in the initial delirium of united Republican government at the turn of the century.

Second, the Speaker centralized power in the House, and he and other members learned to use it.[53] Subcommittees were weakened. Committee chairmen took up the slack but were beholden to a combination of the Republican Conference and the leadership for their positions, which were term limited. Because of the Republicans' astounding electoral victory in 1994, which Gingrich received the lion's share of the credit for masterminding, House Republicans were willing to endorse much of what Gingrich proposed. And, because they were handpicked, the committee chairs not only were loyal to the leaders, but they tended to have similar ideas about policy. Anti-taxer Bill Archer, for example, was named chairman of the Committee on Ways and Means in 1995. Having supported the repeal of the Sixteenth Amendment, which authorized the income tax, he was on the far side of the antitax faction.

Third, Gingrich brought renewed hope to the Republicans. Breaking the half-century stronghold the Democrats had had on the House of Representatives opened the doors for the future. House Republicans had no intention of relinquishing their newfound control, or of slowing down, notwithstanding Clinton's reelection in 1996. The Republicans, led by Majority Whip DeLay, stepped up efforts to use reapportionment to create safe Republican seats. The aim was to abolish electoral advantage that Democrats had held because of the drawing of district lines.[54] With more safe seats, House Republicans would be freer to cast votes that fit a Republican ideology.

Fourth, and of supreme importance in understanding current congressional politics, the Gingrich tactics, somewhat akin to Lee Atwater's on the electoral side of the house, were vindicated.[55] The attitude of "All's fair in love and war" was adopted. Not only did such tactics at last bring the victories that Republicans in the recent past could only dream of, but also the political situation was looking increasingly like war, to adopt some language from Gingrich. Parties were increasingly divided. The Republican tax cutters were surer than ever of the righteousness of their cause. The stakes were huge. Even Ronald Reagan, affable and dedicated to less government and lower taxes, could not for long penetrate the fortress of taxes and spending, especially entitlement spending, that the Democrats had built. Sharper tactics were needed. The Gingrich beam lit the way.

Republicans pressed for the elimination of the income tax and for a variety of tax cuts. A series of trial balloons were launched, including a national sales tax to do away with the income tax, proposed by Ways and Means chairman Archer and Sen. Dick Lugar, and different versions of flat taxes that were first floated in the late 1970s and early 1980s. Republicans sparred with Clinton, sometimes successfully in that legislation was enacted, although not entirely to their liking, as with the Taxpayer Relief Act of 1997 and the IRS Restructuring and Reform Act of 1998. Other unsuccessful efforts, such as those aimed at reducing (not yet eliminating) estate and gift taxes, laid the foundation for much more substantial changes in the coming George W. Bush administration. While deficits had not yet been obliterated as a concern among Republicans, especially a few key Senate Republicans who held the balance, tax cutting was the top priority. As Jim Nussle, chairman of the House Budget Committee, and Vice President Dick Cheney both said in 2004, deficits don't matter.[56]

Hence, tax cutting, not deficit reduction, became the center of gravity within the Republican Party, with the Senate Republicans providing a slight centrifugal pull from this consensus. Unlike the last Republican revolution, ushered in by Ronald Reagan, this revolution lacked a president, but the Republicans controlled both the Senate and the House. House leaders were now experienced in using the institutional levers of power to accomplish their goals, and they could whip bare majorities into disciplined ones. A cadre of dedicated, uncompromising tax cutters were well prepared and had primed the engine for giving money back to people before the Democrats could spend it. A stark, Gingrich-esque vocabulary, such as calling estate taxes "death taxes," had taken hold. An ideology was in place.[57] The congressional Republicans were ready for a Republican president.

The Ideology, the Strategy, and the Tactics: Ready to Go

This overview of the budget and tax battles over two decades provides the background necessary to answer the questions, Why might the Republicans intentionally precipitate a budget crisis of historic proportions? and How would they go about it? The beliefs of the party-in-government and the political lessons of recent congressional history point to plausible answers.

The past two decades have demonstrated the seeming impossibility of making a significant dent on the size of government or of cutting marginal tax rates permanently. David Stockman, Reagan's director of the Office of Management and Budget, first articulated the strategy, "Starve the beast," meaning cut taxes so that insufficient money is available for spending programs.[58] As discussed earlier, despite spending restraint in domestic discretionary programs and even some reform in the Social Security program, this strategy was unsuccessful in the 1980s when the Republicans controlled the presidency and the Senate. Too many people were concerned about deficits (including Republicans, investors, and Wall Street), and mandatory and discretionary spending programs were too popular with the public, including Republicans, to achieve significant spending cuts. For "starve the beast" to work, a no-way-out situation must be created. A crisis must be precipitated that leads elected leaders and the public to conclude that certain actions, in this case severely cutting mandatory social spending, are absolutely necessary. To hasten a state of affairs that is dire before anything can be done to avert it and allow spending-as-usual, as was the case in the 1980s, certain tactics and modi operandi were adopted.

Gingrich taught the Republicans to keep their eyes on the goal. Thus, if being concerned about deficits in the short run would undermine fundamental change, then deficits should be downplayed. Windows of opportunity have limited time spans.[59] A recession can be used to justify a tax cut that was actually devised for entirely different reasons prior to onset of the downturn. A terrorist attack on American soil provides a new justification for more tax cuts.[60]

While Republicans in Congress pursued the tax-cutting agenda, the larger Republican coalition had to hold. For Main Street Republicans and the deficit hawks, fiscal responsibility and deficit reduction would be discussed, if not vigorously pursued. For social conservatives, the tax code could be used, following Clinton's example, for family policy by reducing the "marriage penalty," increasing the child care tax credit[61] and creating new tax-assisted savings accounts. When there was broad popular support, for example, for prescription drug coverage under Medicare, a detour would be necessary. That neither the public nor the media go for the mind-numbing details of tax policymaking and budgetary matters, no matter how important they are, provides considerable leeway for legislation.

The noncooperating Democrats would have to be excluded from negotiations wherever possible. Legislation would be proposed and voted on within twenty-four hours in the House Committee on Ways and Means, leaving little or no time for serious deliberation. Liberal House Democrats would be excluded from conference committees. Votes on the floor of the House would be kept for extended periods of time when necessary to ensure victory.

Finally, technical information issued by official government agencies needed to be controlled, especially information that would provide ammunition for one's opponents or that would sound an alarm bell. Nonpartisan analytical agencies within Treasury and Congress would be quelled, and analytical studies revealing the distributional elements of tax cuts or reasonable projections of the long-term effects of policy choices, for example, discouraged.[62]

Implementation of the Strategy: A Unified Republican Government at Last

The 2000 elections produced the first unified Republican government in more than a half-century, but Bush's margins were extraordinarily narrow, with a 50–50 tie in the Senate and a House majority trimmed to a fragile 221–212, down from 1998. Senate Finance Committee chair William Roth, proud author of the Kemp-Roth tax cut proposal, from which Reagan was to borrow, and the Roth IRA, was defeated, and fellow tax cutter Charles Grassley replaced him.

Grassley certainly wanted to help the new president succeed. At the same time, several of his moderate Republican colleagues on the Finance Committee were very concerned about deficits and were more concerned than some about the impact of tax cuts on people of different incomes, as were a few other Senate moderates and most of the Democrats. The close party balance in the Senate meant that even one senator could make all the difference in the success of the president and the congressional tax cutters.[63]

When Sen. James Jeffords, a member of the Finance Committee, left the Republican Party to become an independent (after casting his vote for the 2001 tax cut as he had promised), the Democrats assumed control of the Senate for a brief period until the Republicans took it back. Even this setback did not stop the president and the congressional tax cutters. Nothing got in their way of reducing income taxes.

In the House, new Ways and Means chairman Bill Thomas, who replaced the retiring Bill Archer, was a reliable ally of the new president and did not hide his partisanship. Another opponent of the income tax, he used his position forcefully and effectively. He did not hesitate to exclude Democrats or to issue chairman's substitutes to major tax bills hours before a scheduled vote.[64] The House leadership was staunchly antitax and pushed the envelope every step of the way.

In fact, on March 1, 2001, the House played the first card, not the president, who had wanted to start with his education proposals before moving to tax cuts.[65] Before a House budget resolution could be passed for fiscal 2002 and before the president provided any budget details to his first sketchy outline,[66] the House Committee on Ways and Means approved, on a party-line vote, H.R. 3, the Economic Growth and Tax Relief Act of 2001, a $958 billion tax cut package. Only one week later, on March 8, the House passed the bill, with the Republicans unanimous and a few Democratic votes in favor, 230–198. The race to cut taxes was on.

The Democratic leadership—Senate and House minority leaders Tom Daschle and Richard Gephardt, along with Charles Rangel, ranking Democrat of Ways and Means—together proposed an alternative tax cut bill of about $900 billion, larger than the one Clinton had vetoed in 1998. The ground continued to shift toward more, higher tax cuts, propelled by House tax-cutting enthusiasts. Republican House leaders Armey and DeLay called and raised the Democrats with a $2.2 trillion tax decrease proposal. Then, on a 23–19 party-line vote, the House Budget Committee made room in its fiscal 2002 budget resolution for a $1.6 trillion tax cut over ten years and a 4 percent increase in discretionary spending.[67]

The more cautious Senate, concerned about the reappearance of deficits and with a 50–50 party split, was less enthusiastic about tax cutting and wanted twice the discretionary spending increase of the House. Passed on April 6, the Senate budget resolution called for a $1.187 trillion tax cut for ten years, plus an extra $85 trillion for 2001 to stimulate the economy.[68]

During this period the work of the Committee on Ways and Means had continued apace on such matters as the elimination of estate and gift taxes. However, because of the urgency of moving a tax bill before Jeffords's departure from the party—and hence the Republicans' loss of their majority and control in the Senate—and because the Senate was the more reluctant body when it came to tax cuts, action now centered in the Senate. The chairman and ranking member of the Senate Finance Committee worked well together, unlike the House.

Ranking Finance Committee member Max Baucus, a conservative Democrat, was well inclined toward tax cuts. He and Chairman Grassley forged a compromise designed to garner more than a bare majority of votes in the committee and on the floor. On May 23, the Senate approved the Grassley-Baucus bill, 62–38. Prior to the vote, Democrats offered a number of amendments, all of which failed, to alter the balance of benefits away from the wealthiest taxpayers and toward the working poor and middle income taxpayers.[69]

Meeting within two days of Senate passage, the conference committee excluded House Democrats. It was composed of the two tax committee chairs and two Democrats, Baucus and John Breaux, from the Senate Finance Committee. Large and complicated, the conference report made over 400 alterations in the tax code and generally followed the Senate bill.[70]

To accomplish this feat, the tax cutters had to use almost every manipulation of congressional budget rules imaginable. To circumvent the Byrd rule in the Senate, which requires sixty votes for legislation to incur revenue loss beyond the ten-year budget window of the budget resolution, and to limit the estimated cost of the bill, some provisions were set to expire at the end of 2010, after which time taxes would revert to former levels. To hide the cost, the elimination of the estate tax would occur gradually, and then the tax would be instantly restored in the tenth year. Within the ten-year time frame, some cuts would start immediately but would be phased out to allow other cuts to be put in place.[71]

On the following day, May 26, in an unusual Saturday session, both houses approved the conference report. On June 7, the president signed the Economic Growth and Tax Relief Reconciliation Act of 2001. Within two months of the president's providing details on his budget, a huge tax bill was enacted into law. The speed of this feat was breathtaking. The discipline was remarkable. Bush had insisted that business tax cuts, on the whole, would not be included in the legislation, and they were not.

The content of the bill, both in its manipulation of budget rules and in its impact, was historic. As Eugene Steuerle observed, "It had become clear that the winners in budgetary politics were those who promised easy gratification now but left financing to future policymakers." [72] Now the built-in entitlement spending increases that had been championed by the Democrats would be advancing toward a head-on collision with tax cuts built into the future. Moreover, the distribution of the cuts greatly favored the very rich, that is, taxpayers at the top 1 percent of income, the very people who experienced large income gains in the 1990s when others did not.

The anti-taxers had successfully repositioned the choices that were going to face policymakers in the future. The work was far from complete, however.

Barely one month after passage of the tax cut, House majority leader Dick Armey forcefully nudged his compatriots in an editorial in the *Washington Times,* calling the tax code "the enemy at the gate"; it was "choking innovation and growth while it grows more complex and unfair." [73] Much more was to come.

Spurred on by the tragic events of September 11, 2001, the House and Senate had each passed its own version of another tax cut bill. A compromise in the form of the Job Creation and Worker Assistance Act of 2002 was signed by the president on March 9, costing $94 billion over five years. This legislation was a disappointment compared with the high, but different, hopes the Republicans and Democrats had had for this legislative vehicle.[74] Within the span of one year, however, Republicans had enacted two large tax cuts.

Even as revenue estimates continued to fall and spending rose for the wars in Afghanistan and Iraq and for new programs, Congress and the president plowed forward with yet another tax cut, the Jobs Growth Tax Relief Reconciliation Act of 2003. This time, however, budget hawks were beginning to get nervous. Chairman Grassley and the Senate Republicans insisted on their budget figure, and President Bush ended up with about half of what he had originally wanted. Nevertheless, the tax cut (including refundable credits), totaling $330 billion over eleven years, was the third-largest in U.S. history.[75] Following the manipulative techniques of 2001, most of these breaks were slated to expire in one year, to make the cost seem lower, and then would evaporate if not subsequently extended in new legislation. Indeed, much of the $330 billion cost of the 2003 legislation derived from its accelerating provisions enacted in 2001 and 2002 that were not established permanently in law so as to avoid the necessity of recording the full impact of the tax cuts.[76]

Congress enacted yet another costly measure, the Medicare Prescription Drug, Improvement, and Modernization Act of 2003, that was slated to cost $395 billion but will likely cost between $450 billion and $500 billion over ten years and $1 trillion over the following ten years. The administration had suppressed the much higher estimates by the leading governmental Medicare actuary, Richard Foster, of the cost of the legislation, and in so doing accelerated the date that this program is projected to become insolvent.[77]

In 2004 two additional tax proposals were in the offing, again with Senate budget hawks skittish about mounting deficits.[78] One was a bill, the Jumpstart Our Business Strength (JOBS) Act, the impetus of which was to replace the tax break for Foreign Sales Corporations that has been outlawed by the World Trade Organization.[79] The second bill, the fourth tax cut for certain individuals in as many years, extended expiring provisions of previous tax bills, provided a temporary reprieve from the Alternative Minimum Tax for taxpayers it was never intended to tap,[80] and extended the $1,000 child credit provision so that it would not revert to $800. The desirability and perhaps inevitability of the passage of each of these provisions could have been anticipated, and they could have been included in previous legislation. They were not included so as to avoid showing the actual cost of the provisions over time. This tax cut passed with large margins in the House and Senate and was signed by President Bush less than two months before the 2004 elections.

If the impact of all federal taxes on taxpayers in different income categories is assessed, the Republican tax cuts have primarily benefited the rich. Though billed as middle-class tax relief, Republican tax legislation largely aided the 20 percent of households with the highest incomes. The bottom quintile received less than 0.1 percent.[81] The 2001 and 2003 "tax cuts" are not net tax cuts for 75–80 percent of the population, if the eventual need to pay for them—by benefit cuts and tax increases—is taken into account. If one incorporates the need to finance the tax cuts into the analysis, low-income households could lose up to 21 percent of their income, according to one plausible estimate.[82] Because the Bush Treasury and the Joint Tax Committee have quit performing traditional distributional analyses, outside organizations must be relied upon for these assessments.[83]

Conclusion

Consistent with the ideas, strategy, and tactics explicated here, Bush and the Republican tax cutters have publicly ignored the unsustainable budgetary path on which they appear to have intentionally and hurriedly set the country. Aided by effective leadership, by the shift in the center of gravity in the Republican Party toward tax cutting, by the existence of an advance guard in the House, and by unified, disciplined Republican government, tax-cutting Republicans have successfully pursued their agenda. This agenda is driven by an ideology that is bold and unproven. It is shaped by past experience, political interests, economic and political beliefs, and hopes for the future. The successful pursuit of this agenda was made possible by a party realignment in the country—as Republicans became dominant in the South—and a related policy realignment in Congress and the parties-in-government.

The centerpiece of the Republican agenda, following supply-side theory, is to reduce and eliminate taxes to benefit primarily very-high-income households, holders of capital, and business. Such tax cutting has been pursued simultaneously as a tactic, a strategy, and an end in itself. With the shift away from deficit reduction to tax cuts, Republicans have deftly maneuvered congressional Democrats into a politically untenable and defensive position. Even when tax cuts largely advantage the very well-off, Democrats are pressed to explain why they oppose tax cuts. Enough of the public indiscriminately supports tax cuts—or sufficiently misunderstands their effect—to make opposing Republican proposals a losing proposition for Democrats in competitive districts and states.

Predictably, many Democrats and budget hawks in both parties, seeing the unpopularity and futility of opposing tax cuts, have supported them. Still, the center of gravity among congressional Democrats is Clintonesque: balance the budget, keep financial markets happy, create a fiscal situation that covers governmental programs and past promises made in entitlement legislation, and pay attention to distributing benefits progressively.

The Republicans seem to be taking an enormous gamble on America's future by working to create an action-forcing crisis of the large dimensions described at the outset of this chapter. If they win their apparent bet, and entitlement spending is greatly restricted, Republicans will have achieved their goal of fundamentally reducing the size of government and its role in people's lives, both as benefactor and tax collector. If the theory on which the Republican strategy is based is correct, the economy should thrive, even if everyone does not. If the Republicans' strategy is miscast, the economic consequences are anybody's guess. The effect of this strategy on the credibility and functioning of governmental institutions is similarly unclear. Like the professional budget and tax analysts, however, institutionalists have good reason to be wary.

Notes

I am indebted to Larry Dodd, Cynthia Harrison, John Gist, Lee Fritschler, and James Pfiffner for their many helpful suggestions to improve this chapter and to Philip Magness, Lindsey Poulin, and Emily Hymowitz for their able research assistance.

1. Paul Allen Beck and Frank J. Sorauf, *Party Politics in America,* 7th ed. (New York: HarperCollins, 1992).
2. For a provocative assessment of the antitax strategy, see Daniel Altman, *Neoconomy: George Bush's Revolutionary Gamble with America's Future* (New York: Public Affairs, Perseus Books, 2004). The alternative minimum tax was designed to ensure that more very high income earners actually will pay income tax, despite their eligibility for tax deductions and other preferences that otherwise reduce tax liability. Because the alternative tax is not indexed for inflation, an estimated 30 million families are likely to be hit by this tax by 2010. See Leonard E. Burman, William G. Gale, and Jeffrey Rohaly, "The AMT: Projections and Problems," *Tax Notes,* July 7, 2003, 105–117; and Edmund L. Andrews, "Initiative by Bush on the Income Tax Has Innate Conflicts: Potential Reforms Shift Burden from Wealthy to Middle Class," *New York Times,* October 6, 2004, C1, C3.
3. Peter R. Orszag, "The Federal Budget Outlook," testimony before the House Committee on the Budget, February 3, 2004, www.brookings.edu/views/testimony/orszag/20040203.pdf (accessed June 10, 2004). Using adjusted CBO figures, the Center on Budget and Policy Priorities (CBPP), in conjunction with a number of other budget groups across the political spectrum, estimates that the budget outlook in the ten-year period ending in 2011 has deteriorated by $8.8 trillion. See David Kamin and Richard Kogan, "Deficit Picture Grimmer Than CBO's March Projections Suggest" (Washington, D.C.: Center on Budget and Policy Priorities, 2004).
4. Congressional Budget Office (CBO), *The Long-Term Budget Outlook* (Washington, D.C.: U.S. Government Printing Office, 2003).
5. These figures deviate substantially from those of CBO in order to eliminate the bias in CBO baseline estimates (see previous note). CBO projected a ten-year surplus of $5.6 trillion, exceeding 4 percent of GDP, at that time. However, that figure was unrealistic in that a substantial deficit in the out-years could be anticipated. See Alan J.

Auerbach, William G. Gale, Peter R. Orszag, and Samara R. Potter, "Budget Blues: The Fiscal Outlook and Options for Reform," in *Discussion Paper No. 10* (Washington, D.C.: Urban-Brookings Tax Policy Center, 2003); William Gale and Peter R. Orszag, "Perspectives on the Budget Outlook," *Tax Notes* 98 (2003): 1005–1117, for details.

6. Kamin and Kogan, "Deficit Picture Grimmer."
7. Similar concerns are amplified by Jagadeesh Gokhale and Kent Smetters, *Fiscal and Generational Imbalances: New Budget Measures for New Budget Priorities* (Washington, D.C.: AEI Press, 2003), a book that arose from a Bush Treasury–sponsored study. Gokhale and Smetters estimate that the combined effect of current spending and tax policies, coupled with the need to finance them, will eventually result in a fiscal imbalance of a staggering $44.2 trillion. Despite the apparent severity of the situation, President Bush chose in his annual budget in February 2003 to ignore the Treasury report on which these dire predictions are based.
8. Specifically, the projected 2004 deficit, which according to the OMB stood at 4.2 percent of GDP, would be 1.6 percent of GDP, had the succession of Republican tax cuts not been enacted in 2001, 2002, and 2003. Isaac Shapiro and Joel Friedman, "Tax Returns: A Comprehensive Assessment of the Bush Administration's Record on Cutting Taxes" (Washington, D.C.: Center on Budget and Policy Priorities, 2004), www.cbpp.org/4-14-04tax-sum.htm (accessed July 20, 2004).
9. Office of Management and Budget, *Analytical Perspectives, Budget of the United States Government, Fiscal Year 2005* (Washington, D.C.: U.S. Government Printing Office, 2004).
10. Office of Management and Budget, *Fiscal Year 2005 Mid-Session Review, Budget of the U.S. Government* (Washington, D.C.: U.S. Government Printing Office, 2004).
11. Kamin and Kogan, "Deficit Picture Grimmer."
12. Congressional Budget Office, *Where Did the Revenues Go?* (Washington, D.C.: U.S. Government Printing Office, 2002).
13. The Bush administration counters that the United States will grow its way out of this predicament. See Eduardo Porter, "Does the Economy Have Cement Shoes?" *New York Times,* August 1, 2004, 4. This argument is a variation of supply-side economics, a theory created by interested think tanks, not the academy. The basic assertion of this theory is that marginal tax rate reductions will generate sufficient economic activity and, hence, new tax revenue, to more than make up for the cost of the tax cuts. Based on empirical evidence and careful analysis by an agency possibly sympathetic to this idea, such an eventuality is highly unlikely. See Congressional Budget Office, *The Long-Term Budget Outlook.* The administration, though it may disagree, is surely well aware of such contrary studies.
14. Note that the reports assessing the effects of the Bush tax cuts do not include the added impact of the reductions of 2004.
15. Congressional Budget Office, *The Long-Term Budget Outlook*; Alice M. Rivlin and Isabel Sawhill, *Restoring Fiscal Sanity: How to Balance the Budget* (Washington, D.C.: Brookings Institution Press, 2004).
16. Orszag, "The Federal Budget Outlook."
17. Gokhale and Smetters, *Fiscal and Generational Imbalances.*
18. Paul Krugman, "The Tax-Cut Con," *New York Times,* September 14, 2003, 54.
19. Not reversing the direction toward which the economy has been set could lead to an economic crisis characterized by loss of confidence of foreign investors in the U.S. economy, a decline in the value of the dollar, rapid increases in interest rates and prices, and a collapse of the stock market. In short, a fiscal time bomb has been set, one that seems calculated to force a fundamental change in tax and spending policy (Altman, *Neoconomy*).

20. C. Eugene Steuerle, *The Tax Decade: How Taxes Came to Dominate the Public Agenda* (Washington, D.C.: Urban Institute Press, 1992).
21. Joint Economic Committee, U.S. Congress, *Taxes and Long-Term Economic Growth* (Washington, D.C.: U.S. Government Printing Office, 1997).
22. Allen Schick and Felix LoStracco, *The Federal Budget: Politics, Policy, Process,* rev. ed. (Washington, D.C.: Brookings Institution Press, 2000).
23. Edwin Dean and Kent Kunze. "Recent Changes in the Growth of U.S. Multifactor Productivity," *Monthly Labor Review,* May 1988, Vol. 111, no. 5, 14–18.
24. Martin Feldstein, "Supply Side Economics: Old Truths and New Claims," in "Supply-Side Economics: What Remains?" Papers and Proceedings of the Ninety-Eighth Annual Meeting of the American Economic Association, *American Economic Review* 76 (2; 1986): 26–30.
25. Though the Democrats controlled the House, so-called Blue Dog Democrats held the balance and frequently voted with the Republicans.
26. Steuerle, *The Tax Decade.*
27. Catherine E. Rudder, "Fiscal Responsibility and the Revenue Committees," in *Congress Reconsidered,* 3rd ed., ed. Lawrence C. Dodd and Bruce I. Oppenheimer (Washington, D.C.: CQ Press, 1985).
28. C. Eugene Steuerle, *Contemporary U.S. Tax Policy* (Washington, D.C.: Urban Institute Press, 2004).
29. The 1986 Tax Reform Act was revenue-neutral, meaning that any tax decreases had to be paid for by increasing taxes somewhere else in the tax code. As a result, marginal rates for businesses were decreased in exchange for removing certain tax expenditures that had been available to many businesses.
30. Congress did manage to improve the financing of Social Security in 1983 with a combination of payroll tax increases and benefit cuts phased in over many years.
31. David R. Mayhew, *Congress: The Electoral Connection* (New Haven: Yale University Press, 1974).
32. Feldstein, "Supply-Side Economics."
33. Office of Management and Budget, *Analytical Perspectives.* At its height, the interest on the debt was 15 percent of the budget.
34. For example, domestic discretionary spending in 1988 constituted 14.8 percent of outlays, slightly more than interest on the national debt. See Congressional Budget Office, *The Budget and Economic Outlook: Fiscal Years 2005–2014,* released on January 26, 2004; Appendix F, "Historical Budget Data."
35. Congress did succeed in 1983 in a bipartisan effort to avert a funding crisis in the largest entitlement program, Social Security. Cutting such mandatory spending in a way that would redefine government's role in people's lives, however, proved impossible. Even to mention reductions in benefits caused a firestorm, although a short-term financing crisis propelled a reduction of benefits. R. Douglas Arnold, "The Politics of Reforming Social Security," *Political Science Quarterly* 113 (1998): 213–240.
36. David W. Rohde, *Parties and Leaders in the Postreform House* (Chicago: University of Chicago Press, 1991).
37. The statement, "The era of big government is over" was made in a radio speech delivered on January 27, 1996. The exact text can be found at www.cnn.com/US/9601/budget/01-27/clinton_radio/.
38. Candidate Bush first used the phrase, "Read my lips: No new taxes" in the New Hampshire primary, and it became a central element in his acceptance speech at the 1988 Republican National Convention in New Orleans. The text read as follows: "I'm the one who will not raise taxes. My opponent says he'll raise them as a last resort, or a third resort. But when a politician talks like that, you know that's one resort he'll be checking into. My opponent won't rule out raising taxes. But I will. And the Congress will push me to raise taxes and I'll say no. And they'll push, and I'll say no, and they'll

push again, and all I can say to them is "Read my lips: No new taxes" (accessible at www.4president.org/speeches/georgebush1988convention.htm).

39. Eugene Steuerle ranked the Omnibus Budget Reconciliation Act of 1990 "among the largest and most successful acts in the entire deficit-reduction period of 1982–1997" (*Contemporary U.S. Tax Policy,* 157).
40. Catherine E. Rudder, "Fiscal Responsibility, Fairness, and the Revenue Committees," in *Congress Reconsidered,* 4th ed., ed. Lawrence C. Dodd and Bruce I. Oppenheimer (Washington, D.C.: CQ Press, 1989); and Steuerle, *The Tax Decade.* Subsequently, Sen. Domenici has moved from the budget hawk camp toward the tax cutters. Dole did become the 1994 Republican nominee for president, running on a ticket with tax cutter Jack Kemp. Dole's candidacy represented the past, not the future of the Republican Party. As chairman of the Senate Finance Committee and then as majority leader, he was considered a responsible legislator in that he was willing to negotiate with the Democrats to get deficits under control. From the point of view of the tax cutters of the 1990s, this was no way to win the battle to alter the role of government in people's lives.
41. Jonathan Nagler and R. Michael Alvarez, "Economics, Issues and the Perot Candidacy: Voter Choice in the 1992 Presidential Election," *American Journal of Political Science* 39 (1995): 714–744.
42. Steuerle, *Contemporary U.S. Tax Policy.*
43. David W. Brady, John F. Cogan, and Douglas Rivers, "How the Republicans Captured the House: An Assessment of the 1994 Midterm Elections," Essays in Public Policy No. 57 (Stanford: Hoover Institution on War, Revolution, and Peace, Stanford University, 1995).
44. The formal name of the statute is the Balanced Budget and Emergency Deficit Control Act of 1985.
45. Together, they provided for (1) sequestration, or forced across-the-board spending cuts for all nonexempt discretionary spending in one of three categories (domestic, international, and military), if the established spending cap on that category of legislation is exceeded; and (2) revenue and spending neutrality, a pay-as-you-go (PayGo) rule, borrowed from the successful Tax Reform Act of 1986, that requires that every spending increase and every tax decrease be matched by an equivalent spending decrease or tax increase. See Bill Heniff Jr., "Pay-As-You-Go Rules in the Federal Budget Process," Congressional Research Service, December 28, 1998, www.house.gov/rules/98-20006.htm (accessed July 22, 2004).
46. Real discretionary spending was less than 1 percent higher in 1998 than it was in 1994. See Allen Schick, "Bush's Budget Problem," in *The George W. Bush Presidency: An Early Assessment,* ed. F. I. Greenstein (Baltimore: Johns Hopkins University Press, 2003), 87. Discretionary domestic spending as a percent of GDP between fiscal years 1992 and 1999 fell from 3.4 percent to 3.0 percent. See Congressional Budget Office, *The Budget and Economic Outlook: Fiscal Years 2005–2014* (Washington, D.C.: U.S. Government Printing Office, 2004). New entitlements were not added, presumably because no sources to fund them could be found. Deficit reduction was also aided by increased tax collections, caused by the booming economy, as people both made more money and graduated into higher marginal brackets. The 1990 and 1993 tax increases on those benefiting most from the economic expansion increased government revenues. The tax increases on the well-off were dwarfed by the increase in income this group experienced in the economic expansion of the 1990s. That there was no groundswell of support among high-income earners to reduce their taxes supports the argument, offered here, that the Republican tax-cutting agenda was a top-down, ideologically based enterprise.
47. Quoted in Sheldon David Pollack, *Refinancing America: The Republican Antitax Agenda* (Albany: State University of New York Press, 2003), 121.

48. Deborah A. Stone, *Policy Paradox: The Art of Political Decision Making* rev. ed. (New York: Norton, 2002).
49. A major identifier of a quality candidate is the degree of prior governing experience of that candidate. See Gary C. Jacobson, *The Politics of Congressional Elections,* 6th ed. (New York: Pearson Longman, 2004).
50. Fifty percent of taxpayers erroneously thought their taxes had been raised. Steuerle, *Contemporary U.S. Tax Policy,* 174.
51. Richard F. Fenno, *Learning to Govern: An Institutional View of the 104th Congress* (Washington, D.C.: Brookings Institution Press, 1997).
52. For example, many of the items that were later to be found in the more muscular tax cuts of 2001 and 2003 first saw the practical light of day in the American Dream Restoration Act (H.R. 1215), which grew out of the Contract with America and was vetoed by President Clinton. These included estate and gift tax reform (rather than elimination), a child tax credit, marriage "penalty" reform, new medical spending accounts, and cuts in the capital gains rate. This failed effort was followed by what one observer described as a "full-scale assault on the federal tax laws" (Pollack, *Refinancing America,* 81) and on the Internal Revenue Service. The ground was shifting as the 1990s progressed. The IRS attack "worked," but this success was greatly to the detriment of the country. See Pollack, *Refinancing America,* 93–95; Albert B. Crenshaw, "A Shackled IRS," *Washington Post,* October 3, 2004, B1; R. Sam Garrett, James A. Thurber, A. Lee Fritschler, and David H. Rosenbloom, "Assessing the Impact of Bureaucracy-Bashing from Electoral Campaigns," *Public Administration Review,* forthcoming. The attack followed the slash-and-burn tactics previously advocated by Gingrich, who worked as if an institution like Congress or the IRS must be shaken to its roots for consequential change to occur, notwithstanding collateral damage to these bodies.
53. Fenno, *Learning to Govern.*
54. James E. Campbell, *Cheap Seats: The Democratic Party's Advantage in U.S. House Elections* (Columbus: Ohio State University Press, 1996).
55. South Carolinian Lee Atwater was an extremely effective political operative for the Republican Party. He sometimes used tactics that were criticized as outside the bounds of acceptability. On his deathbed, he apologized. See "Atwater Apologizes for '88 Remark about Dukakis; Bush Campaign Chief Linked Convicted Murderer Willie Horton, Democratic Candidate" (Associated Press), *Washington Post,* January 13, 1991.
56. See Ron Suskind, *The Price of Loyalty: George W. Bush, the White House, and the Education of Paul O'Neill* (New York: Simon and Schuster, 2004), for the Cheney quote. Chairman Nussle was quoted in the *BNA Daily Tax Report* on March 17, 2004. Richard Kogan, David Kamin, and Joel Friedman, "Too Good to Be True," CBPP: Washington, D.C., revised March 22, 2004, www.cbpp.org/3-19-04tax.htm.
57. "While the Republicans have all but completed their transformation into an ideological party in the classic European sense, the Democrats have remained, in essence, an old fashioned non-ideological party," observes Nils Gilman. "In the last decades, however, the Republicans have adopted a new and very different tack. Instead of just pandering to local interest groups, they have decided that they want to recast the country in a radically different mold, according to a well-articulated ideological vision." See Nils Gilman, "What the Rise of the Republicans as America's First Ideological Party Means for the Democrats," *The Forum,* Vol. 2, 2004, no. 1, article 2, www.bepress.com/forum/vol2/iss1/art2 (accessed October 7, 2004).
58. David Alan Stockman, *The Triumph of Politics: How the Reagan Revolution Failed* (New York: Harper and Row, 1986).
59. John W. Kingdon, *Agendas, Alternatives, and Public Policies,* 2nd ed. (New York: Longman, 2003).

60. For an extensive review of the claims of the Bush administration for the tax cuts in comparison to the actual impact of the cuts, see Isaac Shapiro and Joel Friedman, "Tax Returns: A Comprehensive Assessment of the Bush Administration's Record on Cutting Taxes," Center on Budget and Policy Priorities, 2004, www.cbpp.org/4-14-04tax-sum.htm (accessed July 20, 2004).
61. In 2003 this group was intentionally excluded in the final negotiations with the Senate on the bill, but it was included upon the insistence of Senate Democrats in the 2004 individual tax cut bill.
62. Tax Analysts goes so far as to suggest that Treasury's Office of Tax Policy might be renamed Office of Tax Propaganda. See "The Decline and Fall of Distribution Analysis," www.taxanalysts.com/www/readingsintaxpolicy.nsf/WebSubjects/C8A4AE46E85, page 6 (accessed December 10, 2003). The two main governmental bodies to produce neutral distribution analysis were the Joint Committee on Taxation and Treasury's Office of Tax Analysis. Both have sharply curtailed this work. What is produced by the joint committee presents "a distorted picture" (Tax Analysts, p. 3), while Treasury's limited analyses limit their distribution analysis to the income tax, excluding all other taxes, such as Social Security, a "questionable and misleading" practice, according to Tax Analysts (p. 5). For additional information on misleading analyses, see Joel Friedman, Robert Greenstein, and Isaac Shapiro, "Are Taxes Exceptionally Concentrated at the Top? Treasury Department Release Creates Misleading Impression about Taxes that High-Income Taxpayers Pay," Center on Budget and Policy Priorities, www.cbpp.org/4-15-04tax.htm (accessed July 20, 2004). Their analysis concludes that Treasury uses statistics "selectively to create questionable impressions about the nature of the nation's tax burden and the impact of the tax cuts enacted since 2001" (p. 6).
63. Pollack, *Refinancing America,* 117; *CQ Weekly,* "Profile: Charles E. Grassley," January 17, 2004, 147.
64. Chairman's marks (that is, substitutes replacing the entire bill) have been used in all major tax legislation since 2001. These are usually offered within twenty-four hours of final committee votes, most of which have been divided along party lines.
65. Pollack, *Refinancing America,* 126.
66. The administration did not offer details on President Bush's tax plan until April 9, 2001.
67. Pollack, *Refinancing America,* 126–129.
68. All Republican senators and fifteen Democrats voted for this plan, which moved $450 billion into deficit reduction and education. By May 1, Bush acknowledged that the $1.6 trillion tax cut on which he had finally settled would have to be trimmed. The budget resolutions settled on a $1.35 trillion tax cut, $1.25 trillion over ten years plus a special "stimulus" of $100 billion to be effective in 2001, prior to the beginning of fiscal year 2002.
69. Pollack, *Refinancing America,* 127–130.
70. Key items included marginal rate tax cuts, elimination of the estate tax, a large reduction in the gift tax, a lessening of the "marriage penalty," a doubling of the child care tax credit to $1,000, increases in contribution limits on tax-advantaged retirement accounts, tax breaks for education (a concession to attract Democratic votes in the Senate), and a new, retroactive, 10 percent tax bracket that meant immediate tax rebates of $300, $500, or $600 for most households in 2001. See *CQ Weekly,* "2001 Legislative Summary: Tax Cut Reconciliation," December 22, 2001, 3049–3050.
71. William Gale and Peter R. Orszag, *Sunsets in the Tax Code* (Washington, D.C.: The Urban Institute and the Brookings Institution, 2003); *CQ Weekly,* "What Happens If Tax Cuts Are Allowed to Expire," January 24, 2004, 201.
72. Steuerle, *Contemporary U.S. Tax Policy,* 210–211.
73. July 23, 2001, A19, cited in Pollack, *Refinancing America,* 131–132.

74. Despite its title, the largest share of the bill went to accelerating the depreciation schedule for certain capital expenditures of businesses at a cost to the Treasury of almost $60 billion and a benefit to qualifying expenses worth about a 22 percent reduction in the cost of the capital expense (Steuerle, *Contemporary U.S. Tax Policy,* n. 13, 233). In addition to the direct cost, this kind of provision distorts investment decisions in a way detrimental to encouraging capital investment in the future (Steuerle, *Contemporary U.S. Tax Policy,* 221).
75. Reductions for individuals and business included lower dividend and capital gains rates (at a maximum rate of 15 percent and as low as 5 percent for some taxpayers), expanded depreciation for capital investment for business, temporary relief for the alternative minimum tax, lower rates of depreciation for "small business," an increased child tax credit, more "marriage penalty" relief, and a widening of the 10 percent bracket. Predictably, most of these provisions aided upper-income households (*CQ Weekly,* "2003 Legislative Summary: Tax Reconciliation," December 13, 2003, 3133). For example, half of all stock dividends went to the households with incomes exceeding $200,000 (the highest 3.8 percent), according to Leonard E. Burman of the Urban Institute (Andrews, "Initiative by Bush on the Income Tax," C3).
76. One estimate of the cost of the 2001 and 2003 tax cuts without the sunsets and related likely changes is as much as 3 percent of GDP (Steuerle, *Contemporary U.S. Tax Policy,* 228).
77. Mark Sherman, "Report Says Medicare to Go Broke by 2019," Associated Press Wire Service, March 23, 2004. Advertised as a method to lower the prescription drug costs of Medicare recipients, this legislation will hasten the fiscal crisis in Medicare caused by an aging population, has encouraged employers to drop prescription drug coverage for their retirees, and has provided a windfall for businesses and HMOs. It prevents the government from negotiating with pharmaceutical companies to lower drug costs, outlaws individuals from purchasing lower-cost drugs from Canada, and works to redirect seniors away from the Medicare program and toward private providers. Despite the help of $600 per year for the least-well-off seniors and the goading of Democrats to expand the prescription drug benefit, overall the legislation serves as the poster child for the intentions of the administration and the Republicans in Congress who supported the bill. See Joint Committee on Taxation, U.S. Congress, "Estimated Revenue Effect of Certain Provisions Contained in the Conference Agreement for H.R.1, the 'Medicare Prescription Drug, Improvement, and Modernization Act of 2003'" (Washington, D.C.: U.S. Government Printing Office, 2003).
78. Joseph J. Schatz, "Tax Cuts, Spending Limits Divide Deficit-Conscious Republicans," *CQ Weekly,* January 31, 2004, 278.
79. The replacement would cost much more than the original export provision. Greatly influenced by large multinationals' lobbying, this fix, in one incarnation, would provide corporations such as General Electric a windfall in the billions of dollars. See Jeffrey H. Birnbaum and Jonathan Weisman, "GE Lobbyists Mold Tax Bill," *Washington Post,* July 18, 2004. According to an analysis by the Tax Policy Center, "the main impact of the legislation will be to make the corporate income tax system more complex, less efficient, and less fair." See Kimberly A. Clausing, 2004. *The FSC/ETI Bills: Manufacturing Tax Loopholes and International Tax Problems* (Washington, D.C.: Tax Policy Center, Urban Institute-Brookings Institution, 2004), 1.
80. Leonard E. Burman, William G. Gale, and Jeffrey Rohaly, "The AMT: Projections and Problems," *Tax Notes,* July 7, 2003, 105–117.
81. Leonard E. Burman, "An Analysis of the 2004 House Tax Cuts," Tax Policy Center, www.urban.org/UploadedPDF/1000661_2004TaxCuts.pdf (accessed July 22, 2004).
82. William G. Gale, Peter R. Orszag, and Isaac Shapiro, "Distributional Effects of the 2001 and 2003 Tax Cuts and their Financing," Tax Policy Center, www.urban.org/UploadedPDF/411018_tax_cuts.pdf (accessed July 22, 2004).

83. The groups most interested in distributional analyses, such as the Center for Tax Justice and CBPP, are seen as liberal, and thus their analyses, no matter how accurate, can be questioned for bias. Fortunately, the Brookings Institution and the Urban Institute have teamed up to create the Tax Policy Center, which works to provide the kind of sophisticated distributional analyses formerly provided by the government. The formerly relatively evenhanded governmental institutions' abrupt end of performing these assessments is an indication of their politicization by the Republicans.

15. Congress and Policymaking in an Age of Terrorism

Donald R. Wolfensberger

> *It is the nature of war to increase the executive at the expense of the legislative authority.*
>
> —Alexander Hamilton, *The Federalist,* No. 8

> *The President is at liberty, both in law and conscience, to be as big a man as he can. His capacity will set the limit; and if Congress be overborne by him, it will be no fault of the makers of the Constitution—it will be from no lack of constitutional powers on its part, but only because the President has the nation behind him, and Congress has not. He has no means of compelling Congress except through public opinion. . . . The Constitution bids him speak, and times of stress and change must more and more thrust upon him the attitude of originator of policies.*
>
> —Woodrow Wilson, *Constitutional Government,* 1908

Some have marked the September 11, 2001, terrorist attacks on the United States as the real beginning of George W. Bush's presidency—a presidency characterized in the immediate aftermath of the event by strength, resolve, purpose, and overwhelming public support and approval. When the nation is under attack, it draws together with a strong sense of national unity and patriotism. Even the federal government, which traditionally suffers from low levels of public confidence and trust, assumes the mantle of national security blanket—indispensable, comforting, and protective.

In any national crisis, Congress tends to reflect the mood and will of the people by rallying behind the president and his policies. Immediately after President Bush's September 20, 2001, antiterrorism address to a joint session of Congress, presidential historian Michael Beschloss enthused on national television that "the imperial presidency is back. We just saw it." Beschloss went on to explain that just as Congress deferred to presidential requests on foreign, defense, and domestic policy matters during World War II and the Cold War, "Now, George Bush is the center of the American solar system; that was not true ten days ago."[1]

There is little question that the modern presidency that so dominated our system of government during most of the twentieth century is still very much the dominant force in domestic and foreign policymaking at the outset of the twenty-first century. Moreover, few would dispute that in times of international crises and domestic emergencies the powers of the presidency are enhanced and exercised at the expense of what is often seen as an acquiescent and deferential Congress.

However, such superficial conclusions do not do justice to what actually happens in the tug-and-pull between the branches, even in times of crisis and stress.

It is the thesis of this chapter that although the post–September 11 environment at least temporarily elevated presidential power and prestige to levels not known since the height of the Cold War, Congress is not as acquiescent and deferential as some would have it be or have us believe it is. Just as talk of a resurgent Congress in the wake of Vietnam and Watergate in the seventies was premature and exaggerated, so, too, is talk today of a submissive or irrelevant Congress.

I will examine three policy issues in the 107th Congress arising out of the September 11 attacks and how Congress dealt with them: the authorization for the use of force against terrorists and those harboring them; internal security and civil liberties, as reflected in the passage of the USA Patriot Act; and homeland security as captured in the battle over aviation security and over the creation of a new cabinet department.

Congress and the Policy Process

During the 107th Congress (2001–2002), President George W. Bush enjoyed at least nominal unified party government for less than five months (with Vice President Dick Cheney making the difference in the 50–50 Senate) before Sen. James Jeffords, Vt., switched from Republican to independent and put control of the Senate under the Democrats. During that brief period, though, the president managed to sign into law two of his top priorities—his massive tax-cutting bill and the No Child Left Behind education initiative. The former bill passed on a near-party-line vote while the latter was a bipartisan effort. How the policy process might have played out thereafter absent the 9/11 attacks cannot be fully known, though it is likely that on issues of importance to the president's party, the tax bill model of partisan—not bipartisan—lawmaking would have been the norm. Indeed, after the rush of post–9/11 emergency legislation, things settled back into that pattern, as both parties in Congress resumed their battle for chamber control by opposing each other rather than compromising on key legislative issues.

However, regardless of whether the government is under unified or split party control, Congress still asserts its prerogatives and influence on the policy process, both institutionally and as a body of individual district and state representatives. It does so occasionally in the form of bold policy initiatives that originate in Congress rather than at the White House. More often it does so in less-dramatic yet important ways: through oversight and investigations; through the use of creative, structural and procedural innovations inside Congress; through new structures, processes, and reporting requirements imposed on the executive; and through experimental, pilot projects.[2] It is sometimes said that Congress only tinkers with the details in the policy process (the pejorative term for which is "micromanagement"). But the devil in such details is often what keeps the executive responsive and accountable to Congress and the people.

In addition to institutional prerogatives, Congress is driven by partisan and individual forces, motives, and interests. These vary in their intensity depending on the public mood, as the Wilson epigraph to this chapter makes clear. When the president is perceived as strong and decisive in the wake of a traumatic event, Congress and its members are less likely to challenge the president directly. But the further away from the event in time, the more public moods, attention, and support shift and fade, and the more congressional scrutiny and criticisms of executive policies increase.

This may occur through formal legislative actions by Congress as a whole or oversight actions by its committees and subcommittees. Or it may occur more informally, through opposition party criticisms or on the initiative of individual member "policy entrepreneurs," building coalitions for policy change both within and outside the institution. Taken together, these forces point to a Congress that can still have significant policy influence in a variety of ways, even during a period of national trauma and presidential ascendancy.

To fully understand this, one must recognize that the policy process is not a neat, linear progression of stages, running sequentially from agenda setting and discussion to decision and implementation. Nor is it always a formal process. Instead, it involves a more circular motion of feedback loops that double back on each other to inform and reinform policymakers at all stages in the process. This in turn produces an ever-evolving process of thinking and rethinking, adjustments and improvements, based on new information derived from experience and evaluation.

Congress is critical because it supplies the funds for policy execution. If left out of the feedback loop (whether at the conceptualization or implementation stages), Congress can be a swift policy executioner in the terminal sense.[3] The rejection of the Clinton health care initiative in the 103rd Congress (1993–1994) paints this reality in stark relief. No members of Congress participated in the first lady's health care task force that developed the legislation, and therefore Congress had little understanding or sense of ownership of the proposal when it was sent to the Hill.

This chapter depicts the initial stages of the policy process, when a host of new issues were thrust onto the policy agenda by the September 2001 terrorist attacks. Such time-limited and abbreviated studies cannot begin to project how the issues, their solutions, or implementation will play out over time, as they evolve and are adjusted by Congress and the executive in their policy process interactions. But they do begin to highlight and pinpoint some of the forces and complexities at work, ones that will continue to influence these policy issues for years to come.

The Use of Force and Emergency Spending

In response to the terrorist attacks on the United States, President George W. Bush asked Congress for a broad grant of authority and flexibility to use force against those responsible for the attacks and spend billions of dollars on the emergency. Conventional wisdom might have us expect complete congressional acquiescence in such requests in the immediate aftermath of such a horrific event. Indeed, Congress did act with uncharacteristic dispatch, bypassing its committee process and forgoing extended floor deliberations to complete action within three days of the attacks. However, despite a public display of unity and support for the president's efforts, Congress still left its own distinct imprint on both measures as a result of lengthy, behind-the-scenes negotiations between the White House and a small, bipartisan and bicameral group of party and committee leaders headed by House Speaker J. Dennis Hastert, R-Ill.

In drafting the Constitution, the Framers agreed that the president would have inherent authority to repel foreign invasion and respond to direct attacks on the United States without a declaration of war or statutory authorization from Congress. The 1973 War Powers Resolution, enacted over President Nixon's veto, reflects this understanding in the "purpose and policy" section. The president's constitutional powers as commander in chief, it reads, may only be exercised pursuant to a declaration of war, specific statutory authority from Congress, or "a national emergency created by attack upon the United States, its territories or possessions, or its armed forces."[4]

The September 11 attack on the United States certainly fit the latter category, for which the president did not need prior authorization to respond. However, even under the terms of the War Powers Resolution, unless a declaration of war has been passed, the president must withdraw U.S. troops from hostilities (or imminent hostilities) within sixty days after reporting to Congress on their deployment (or within ninety days if the president certifies more time is needed for safe withdrawal), or unless Congress by law extends the sixty-day withdrawal deadline. In the case of the terrorist attacks, however, the president and Congress agreed that prior approval of military action was an important way to show the world the country's unity and resolve in the face of the new threat.

On the evening of Wednesday, September 12, the day after the attacks, Vice President Cheney delivered to House Speaker Hastert a White House draft resolution authorizing the president to use force against those responsible for the terrorist attacks. The White House draft authorized the president not only "to use all necessary force against those nations, organizations or persons he determines planned, authorized, harbored, committed or aided in the planning or commission of the attacks," but also "to deter and preempt any future acts of terrorism or aggression against the United States."[5]

The latter clause was dropped after it met with bipartisan resistance from some of the congressional negotiators, who remembered how President Johnson had used the broadly worded, 1964 Gulf of Tonkin Resolution to escalate and prolong American involvement in Vietnam. There is little question, in retrospect, that had the language been retained in the enacted version, the president could have used it a year later to launch the preemptive war against Iraq, without having to prove any link to the September 11 attacks and without having to seek additional authority from Congress.[6]

Another compromise, that received no mention in the popular press, related to the War Powers Resolution. A new subsection, titled "War Powers Resolution Requirements," was added after the paragraph authorizing the president to use force against the terrorists. It stated that "consistent with section 8(a)(1) of the War Powers Resolution, the Congress declares that this section is intended to constitute specific statutory authorization within the meaning of section 5(b) of the War Powers Resolution" and that nothing in the resolution "supersedes any requirements of the War Powers Resolution." As a trade-off, however, congressional negotiators accepted a new "whereas" clause in the preamble, proposed by White House negotiators, saying that "the President has authority under the Constitution to take action to deter and prevent acts of international terrorism against the United States."[7]

These seemingly contradictory assertions of constitutional prerogatives by the president and Congress may seem to cancel each other out, except for the fact that the congressional language is in the operative, resolving clause of the resolution, whereas the White House language on the inherent powers of the president is in the nonbinding preamble. Nevertheless, President Bush had the last word on the matter, in his statement on signing the resolution into law, when he asserted, "In signing the resolution, I maintain the longstanding position of the executive branch regarding the President's constitutional authority to use force . . . and regarding the constitutionality of the War Powers Resolution."[8]

Senate Foreign Relations Committee Chairman Joe Biden, D-Del., who participated in drafting the final compromise, said it struck a balance by demonstrating that both branches should have a say over military action. "We gave the president all the authority he needed," Biden said, "without giving up our constitutional right to decide whether force should be used."[9] Senate Minority Leader Trent Lott, R-Miss., concurred, saying the final compromise was broad enough for the president "to deal with this terrorist attack and threat" yet "tight enough that the constitutional requirements and limitations are protected."[10]

With negotiations over the use-of-force resolution and the $40 billion emergency supplemental appropriations bill wrapped up late Thursday evening, both houses proceeded to consider the use-of-force resolution on Friday, September 14. The Senate, usually considered the body with greater foreign policy powers and expertise, approved the use-of-force resolution 98 to 0 and the supplemental appropriations bill by unanimous consent, without debate. Only the majority and minority leaders, Tom Daschle, D-S.D., and Lott, spoke briefly as other senators hurried to buses waiting to take them to the National Cathedral to attend the memorial service for the attack victims.

The House, on the other hand, passed the emergency supplemental, 422 to 0, after an hour of debate Friday morning and returned after the memorial service for five hours of debate on the use-of-force measure before passing it 420 to 1. Rep. Barbara Lee, D-Calif., cast the only dissenting vote. The record shows that some two hundred House members spoke on the use-of-force resolution, for an average of one minute each—hardly the stuff of a great debate but still shaming the Senate (notwithstanding its self-characterization as "the world's greatest deliberative body").

As with the use-of-force resolution, the overwhelming public display of support by Congress for the emergency supplemental funds belied sharp differences between the branches over the issue of flexibility, which played out behind the scenes. The president had originally asked for $20 billion, with full discretion to determine the appropriate mix between domestic recovery and national security purposes. As the ranking Democrat on the House Appropriations Committee, Rep. David Obey, Wis., explained during debate on the bill, "The first package presented to us was, frankly a blank check; and to the credit of the people involved, that approach was rejected." He went on to say that even though the bill still gave the president unprecedented authority, "it does retain reasonable congressional ability to make its own judgments."[11]

Specifically, one-fourth of the $40 billion would be available immediately upon the signature of the president, to be spent in areas of government he deemed appropriate after consultation with Congress. A second $10 billion would become available after he had published his plans for its use, and Congress had fifteen days to review those plans. The other $20 billion, however, would be spent based on a presidential budget request and action on it by Congress, and at least half must be spent on responding to domestic cleanup, reconstruction, and humanitarian needs, with the rest going for tightening security and military operations.

Obey noted in his statement that Congress has only two powers that mean anything, the war power and the power of the purse. While Congress's power to determine when we go to war has substantially eroded over the last thirty years, and it is the president who decides whether we will pull the trigger, he went on, "Congress has a double obligation under the oath that we all took to maintain the power of the purse. . . . because that is the fundamental power that Congress has to preserve liberty for every American."[12] Congress did take that obligation seriously in the weeks and months following September 11 in carefully exercising its own judgment in the allocation of resources.

The USA Patriot Act and Civil Liberties

The administration's request for additional law enforcement tools to combat terrorism is another example of how the policy process can be short-circuited during a crisis to respond to perceived emergency needs and how the president during wartime gets most of what he asks for. Nevertheless, the prospect of increasing federal investigative authority at the expense of civil liberties touches a sensitive nerve with many members of Congress, conservatives and liberals alike. Passing the USA PATRIOT Act[13] involved long and difficult negotiations between House and Senate party and committee leaders and White House and Justice Department representatives. As with the use-of-force resolution, the result was less than the president requested and bore the clear imprint of congressional concern about potential abuse of the new powers granted.

The process began on September 19, 2001, when administration officials met in a Capitol office with House and Senate party and committee leaders. Among those present were Attorney General John Ashcroft; White House Counsel Alberto Gonzalez; Senate Judiciary Committee Chairman Patrick Leahy, D-Vt., and his ranking minority member, Orrin Hatch, R-Utah; House Majority Leader Richard Armey, R-Texas; and ranking House Judiciary Committee member John Conyers Jr., D-Mich. At the meeting, Leahy distributed a 165-page proposal he had developed called the "Uniting and Strengthening America Act." Ashcroft's lieutenant, Viet Dinh, handed out the department's forty-page proposal—a crash drafting effort that was "the fruit of several all-nighters at Justice." Ashcroft had earlier called on Congress to pass the administration's plan within a week's time—something that did not sit well with Leahy or Armey. Armey told Ashcroft during the meeting that it might take a few weeks to adopt a bill.[14]

Following the meeting, Ashcroft told reporters, "We need every tool available to us to curtail the potential of additional terrorist attacks" and that there was a need to pass the bill as quickly as possible. Leahy sounded a more cautious note: "The worst thing that could happen is we damage our Constitution. If the Constitution is shredded, the terrorists win." And Armey, who was already urging a sunset provision for parts of the bill, sided with Leahy's concerns: "What we are trying to save are our civil liberties, and they're very precious."[15]

The two proposals had much in common, including clarification of how "trap and trace" laws applied to e-mail and the Internet, bolstering the money-laundering and wiretap laws, and making it easier for authorities to get approval for wiretaps in spying and counterintelligence cases. However, the administration proposal went much farther than Leahy had in mind, calling for the indefinite detention of noncitizens suspected of involvement with terrorism, allowing Internet service providers or employers to permit the FBI to tap e-mail, and allowing foreign intelligence to be used in U.S. criminal proceedings.

To those familiar with such things, the administration package was a grab bag of recycled proposals that the Justice Department had previously tried unsuccessfully to get Congress to enact. House Judiciary Committee member Bob Barr, R-Ga., for instance, a former U.S. attorney, asked Justice Department officials at a September 24 hearing why it was necessary to "cast such a wide net" by proposing changes to criminal law and procedure generally. "Does it have anything to do with the fact that the department has sought many of these authorities on numerous other occasions, has been unsuccessful in obtaining them and now seeks to take advantage of what is obviously an emergency situation to obtain authorities that it has been unable to obtain previously?"[16]

The House and Senate Judiciary Committees held just one day of hearings each, in late September, taking testimony only from Attorney General Ashcroft and other Justice Department officials and not from opponents of the legislation. Although both committee chairmen had the same aim of developing a consensus bill that would have broad bipartisan support, their means of arriving at that end differed considerably. Leahy was interested in moving expeditiously through private, bipartisan negotiations with the administration, avoiding the more prolonged and public process of formal committee deliberations. He and other Democrats feared they would be hammered for being "soft on terrorism" if they delayed or opposed action on the measure.[17]

House Judiciary Committee Chairman James F. Sensenbrenner Jr., R-Wis., on the other hand, was insistent on formally developing and approving a bipartisan package in his committee, without the assistance or pressure of the leadership or the administration. However, House Speaker Hastert had originally announced plans to consider the legislation in two stages: First, the relatively noncontroversial provisions, such as tougher penalties on terrorists, would be considered under an expedited floor process without committee clearance; a second bill, containing the more controversial provisions, would be considered under the "regular order" of committee hearings and deliberation.[18]

Sensenbrenner's committee-centered approach stemmed from a concern that his own party leadership might hijack and draft the bill for floor consideration: "I am very fearful that if this bill is put on a slow roll, all of a sudden we will lose as a committee our right to make improvements and to attempt to reach a bipartisan process to present to the House of Representatives." As one GOP leadership aide reacted, the leaders were not interested in "bipartisanship for the sake of bipartisanship. We're not trying to do this to make the nation feel better. We're doing this to get things done."[19]

Leahy's strategy involved long and hard negotiations with the administration, with the inevitable setbacks, frustrations, and disappointments. But the resulting compromise had the hoped-for bipartisan leadership blessing that paid off well for Leahy's personal investment of time and effort. As a result, the measure was brought to the floor by the leadership under an expedited unanimous consent agreement that bypassed committee consideration altogether. The Senate bill was introduced on October 4 by Majority Leader Daschle, along with twenty-five cosponsors, two days after Sensenbrenner introduced his version with a bipartisan group of about two dozen House cosponsors.[20]

Although both bills contained most of what the administration had requested, neither included Ashcroft's request for authority to use information obtained from foreign wiretaps against American citizens or authority to detain noncitizens indefinitely. But whereas the House bill dropped authority for "black bag" searches of suspects' homes without their knowledge, the Senate allowed such searches if the government showed "reasonable cause to believe" that notification would produce an "adverse result." Moreover, the House version had a two-year sunset provision for many of the enforcement authorities, while the Senate's had none.

The Senate began consideration of its bill on October 11, under a unanimous consent agreement that called for four hours of general debate, divided equally between the parties, plus forty minutes each on four amendments—three of them offered by Sen. Russ Feingold, D-Wis., chairman of the Judiciary Subcommittee on the Constitution. All three of Feingold's amendments were tabled by overwhelming votes, and the Senate proceeded to pass the bill as introduced, 96 to 1, with Feingold casting the lone dissenting vote.

The House bill was ordered reported from the Judiciary Committee on October 3 on a 36 to 0 vote, to a standing ovation from committee members—a rare display of bipartisanship in a committee that had been badly riven by presidential impeachment proceedings just three years earlier. The committee adopted all nine amendments offered in markup, eight by voice vote.

The spirit of bipartisanship came crashing down in the Rules Committee and on the House floor on October 12, when the fears of leadership intervention that Sensenbrenner had expressed earlier became a self-fulfilling prophecy. The special rule that was reported jettisoned the work of the Judiciary Committee in favor of a new version that Sensenbrenner had introduced after negotiations with the majority leadership. It was closer to the bill adopted by the Senate and supported by the administration. One of the main differences was that the two-year sunset provision in the original House-reported bill became three years, plus two additional years if the president thought an extension was in the national interest. Specifically, the rule provided that instead of the substitute reported by the Judiciary Committee, the text of the new bill, introduced that same day by Sensenbrenner, would be considered as adopted.[21]

This is what is called a "self-executing rule" because, upon the adoption of the rule, the amendment specified in the rule is automatically injected into the bill before it is even called up in the House, thereby avoiding a separate debate and vote on the amendment. Political scientist Barbara Sinclair calls this an example of a "post-committee adjustment," one of many tools available to the majority leadership to solve collective action problems in passing legislation important to the party.[22] Moreover, under the terms of the special rule, the new version would be debatable for just one hour and would not be subject to amendment (unless offered in a minority party motion to recommit with instructions).[23]

When the rule was called up on the House floor later that same day, it was narrowly adopted after heated debate, 214 to 208, with only three Democrats voting for it and three Republicans against. Interestingly, the Democrats' failed attempt to change the rule (by defeating the previous question) would not have altered the terms of consideration of the USA Patriot Act. Instead, it would have made in order consideration of an aviation security bill that was still stuck in the Transportation and Infrastructure Committee over the issue of federalizing airport security screeners.

Although Sensenbrenner had gone along with the leadership in introducing the new version of the bill, and had voted for the rule, the prospect that the bill might subsequently be defeated led to a leadership-supported unanimous consent request by Sensenbrenner to modify the substitute by striking from it three sections dealing with money laundering. This also assured further negotiations with the Senate, since Majority Leader Daschle said the bill would never pass the Senate without the money-laundering provisions in it.

Despite the furor raised over the rule, the bill as modified went on to pass the House, 337 to 79. The minority's motion to recommit the bill was not offered by ranking Judiciary Committee Democrat Conyers, but instead by Rep. Jerrold Nadler, D-N.Y., whose amendment would have confined the enforcement provisions to terrorist investigations and not extended them to such other crimes as those relating to firearms dealing and drugs. The Nadler motion garnered a mere 73 votes, while 375 members voted against it.

Differences between the House and Senate versions were still substantial and significant, but the House and Senate leadership were under intense pressure from the administration to complete work on the bill as soon as possible, especially after an anthrax-laced letter, opened in Daschle's office on October 17, forced a temporary shutdown of the Capitol complex and renewed fears of a terrorist attack.

This new sense of urgency led to another short-circuiting of the normal process of either going to conference or sending amended versions of a bill back and forth between the two houses until agreement is reached. The final negotiations between the administration and House and Senate committee and party leaders were held in Speaker Hastert's office. The most significant change was a shortening of the sunset provisions from what amounted to five years to four years and retention of some court oversight provisions that Leahy and Armey felt especially strongly about (though it was not as much as they had wanted). House passage of a separate money-laundering bill on October 17, 412 to 1, enabled negotiators to restore that component to the antiterrorism package—a piece critical to the support of Daschle and Senate Democrats.[24]

On October 23, Sensenbrenner introduced the final compromise as a new bill and called it up in the House under the suspension of the rules procedure, which allows for just forty minutes of debate and no amendments (or motion to recommit) and requires a two-thirds vote for passage. The vote on passage, postponed until the following day, was 357 to 66. All 21 Judiciary Committee Republicans voted for the bill, but committee Democrats were split, with seven voting for and nine, including ranking member Conyers, voting against. The next day the Senate took up the bill and passed it, 98 to 1, without amendment. On October 26 President Bush signed the measure into law at a White House ceremony.

The measure as finally enacted did not have the benefit of a House or Senate committee report or a conference report. This could not only cause problems when it came to interpreting and implementing the act but could also lead to serious legal challenges. The account of the bill's odyssey carried by the respected and nonpartisan *CQ Weekly* captured "the legislation's strange path" with such terms as, "a variety of incarnations," "the secretive, expedited process," "days of closed-door negotiations," and "convoluted process."[25] In short, the legislative process for the antiterrorism bill did not measure up to Speaker Hastert's promise of "the regular order." But then, as Barbara Sinclair makes clear in her studies of the contemporary legislative process, "Unorthodox lawmaking has become standard operating procedure in the U.S. Congress."[26]

To their credit, Sensenbrenner and Conyers in the House and Senate Judiciary Committee members Leahy, Arlen Specter, and Charles Grassley, took their oversight responsibilities seriously and pressed the administration for answers to numerous questions about the implementation of the Patriot Act and such related matters as military tribunals. Sensenbrenner threatened to subpoena the attorney general prior to the August 2002 recess. After considerable stonewalling, Justice began to provide answers and more cooperation with its oversight panels in Congress.[27]

The portrayal of the Patriot Act as a possible threat to individual liberties began to penetrate the American consciousness in 2003 and became a common theme among Democratic presidential primary candidates, who denounced the administration's actions. Attorney General Ashcroft attempted to counter the criticisms with a national publicity tour, but it only heightened public awareness of the issues involved. Calls for amending the Patriot Act received positive responses from Democratic audiences during the 2004 presidential primaries but were not a significant issue in the general election campaign.

Homeland Security

Although the administration got most of what it wanted on the use of force, emergency supplemental, and antiterrorism legislation, it found itself playing catch-up ball and even changing sides when it came to two important domestic security issues in the 107th Congress—aviation security and a cabinet department of homeland security.

The financial health and safety of airlines was a matter of grave concern in many minds after the terrorists commandeered four airplanes on September 11 and crashed three into the World Trade Center and the Pentagon. On September 21, after negotiations between administration officials and congressional party and committee leaders, Congress cleared a $15 billion aid package for the airlines, without committee consideration or floor amendments in either body. In briefing reporters on the bill that same day, White House press spokesman Ari Fleischer was adamant that the aid package did not contemplate federalizing security workers: "Under this agreement there will not be a federal takeover of security," Fleischer insisted. "There will be a stepped-up federal role in increasing security." The administration did plan to use $3 billion of the $40 billion emergency supplemental to strengthen airline security, including putting more air marshals on planes.[28]

The administration's aviation security proposals, outlined by the president on September 12, called for grants and matching funds to help airlines provide more secure cockpits, installation of new security cameras in cockpits, development of modern technology to allow a hijacked plane to be landed from ground controls, and expansion of the air marshal program. However, many Democrats and some Republicans were already discussing the need to do even more, including federalizing the jobs of thousands of airport security screeners.

Sen. Ernest "Fritz" Hollings, D-S.C., chairman of the Senate Commerce, Science and Transportation Committee, had been trying for years to federalize security workers. "No one would think of a private corporation running the FBI," Hollings said on September 27. "We're going to insist on progress in airline and airport security through federalization." Transportation Secretary Norman Y. Mineta estimated that the cost of making airport screeners federal employees would be $1.8 billion. As the stalemate over the issue stretched into early October, Mineta suggested to Republican leaders in Congress a willingness to bring screeners onto the federal payroll if they would be prohibited from striking and exempt from civil service job protection. The leadership turned the offer down flat.[29]

The logjam was partially broken when the Senate passed the Hollings aviation security bill on October 11, 100 to 0. The bill included a provision to make all aviation screeners federal employees. House Republicans and the administration, however, still resisted the federalization of airport security workers. White House spokesman Fleischer reiterated the administration's belief "that there may be better ways to accomplish the same goal without making everybody a federal employee."[30]

Republicans on the House Transportation and Infrastructure Committee introduced their own proposal on October 17 that would leave it to the president to decide whether to federalize security workers or continue them as contract employees, and impose a $2.50 per passenger surcharge to help cover the costs. Committee Democrats, led by ranking minority member James L. Oberstar, D-Minn., countered with their own bill to federalize the screeners and impose a $3.50 per passenger fee. Committee Chairman Don Young, R-Alaska, indicated that he wanted to take his bill directly to the Rules Committee and then to the House floor, bypassing consideration by his own committee.

On October 31 the Rules Committee obliged with a modified closed rule, allowing for consideration of just two further amendments to the bill—one by Young (a manager's amendment) and a substitute by Oberstar. Eighteen other members who had requested amendments from the Rules Committee were turned down. On November 1, after a further change in Young's amendment during consideration of the rule, the rule was adopted by voice vote. On the key vote, Oberstar's substitute lost, 214 to 218, after the president personally intervened to persuade wavering Republicans to support the bill. The bill went on to pass, 286 to 139. Bush later indicated he would work with members of both houses in settling their differences which he said were "small" and "can be reconciled quickly."[31]

The conference report resolving differences between the houses was adopted by the House 410 to 9, and by the Senate by voice vote, on November 16, 2001. The measure, signed into law by the president on November 19, made security screeners employees of a new Transportation Security Administration in the Department of Transportation (the Senate bill would have put them in the Justice Department). Following a one-year transition period, the screeners would be federal employees for two years, after which airport authorities could replace them with private contract employees subject to the same standards as federal screeners, with the approval of the Transportation Department. The measure also included other important new airport and airline security standards contained in both versions and the administration's proposal.

What had finally helped dislodge the measure from conference was an airline crash in New York on November 12. Senate Minority Leader Lott was in the city at the time and saw the smoke from the crash, some fifteen miles away. That was an attention getter, according to a Lott aide, and he realized "a terrorist action could happen anywhere." Lott returned to the Capitol and began to broker a compromise between Hollings and House Majority Whip Tom DeLay that became the centerpiece of the final deal.[32]

The issue of organizing the government for homeland security took a somewhat similar path, with the president eventually taking a 180-degree turn from opposition to support of a cabinet department. On October 8, 2001, the president issued an executive order establishing an Office of Homeland Security in the Executive Office of the President and appointed former Pennsylvania governor Tom Ridge as assistant to the president for homeland security. The mission of the new office would be to "develop and coordinate the implementation of a comprehensive national strategy to secure the United States from terrorist threats or attacks."[33]

Many members in Congress from both parties expressed skepticism about how effective such an office in the White House could be in redirecting the energies and efforts of numerous federal agencies. Without statutory authority or budgetary control, they argued, the new adviser to the president could not begin to get his arms around the problem.

Since March 2001, six months before the 9/11 attacks, Rep. Mac Thornberry, R-Texas, had been trying to obtain action on his bill to create a national homeland security agency. The bill was based on one of the recommendations in the report of the U.S. Commission on National Security/21st Century, chaired by former senators Gary Hart, D-Colo., and Warren Rudman, R-N.H., released in February. On October 11, Sen. Joe Lieberman, D-Conn., introduced the first Senate bill to establish a national department on homeland security. As chairman of the Governmental Affairs Committee, Lieberman was in a position to propel his bill onto the national agenda and the Senate calendar, and indeed that's what he did. After holding fourteen hearings in fall 2001 and into the next spring on various aspects of the homeland security problem, Lieberman introduced a new bill on May 2, 2002. On May 22 it was ordered favorably reported from the Governmental Affairs Committee on a 7 to 3 vote.[34]

On June 6, 2002, in a televised address to the nation, President Bush announced a change of course on the need for a cabinet department. "As Governor Ridge has worked with all levels of government to prepare a national strategy," the president explained, "and as we have learned more about the plans and capabilities of the terrorist network, we have concluded that our government must be reorganized to deal more effectively with the new threats of the 21st century." And he continued, "Right now, as many as a hundred different government agencies have some responsibilities for homeland security, and no one has final accountability."[35] The proposed new department would combine twenty-two federal agencies, with 170,000 employees, at an annual budget of $37 billion. The newly formed Transportation Security Administration, with over 41,000 employees, was moved by the act from the Department of Transportation to Homeland Security.

In the House, Speaker Dennis Hastert moved quickly to organize that body for action on the president's proposal. After careful consultations with the minority leadership, the Speaker unveiled a resolution to create a House Select Committee on Homeland Security to be composed of nine members, five from the majority party and four from the minority, for the purpose of pulling together the recommendations of the various committees of jurisdiction over components of the proposed department. The resolution was careful to state that the select committee would cease to exist after final disposition of the bill, and that "Upon the dissolution of the Select Committee, this resolution shall not be construed to alter the jurisdiction of any standing committee."[36]

As Rules Committee Chairman David Dreier, R-Calif., explained it during the June 19 floor consideration of the resolution, "It establishes a process for considering the President's initiative similar to one that was used a quarter of a century ago by Speaker Tom O'Neill in addressing the energy crisis."[37] As with the Ad Hoc Select Committee on Energy in 1977, the committees of jurisdiction would have a deadline for reporting their recommendations. Majority Leader Dick Armey indicated during debate that the deadline would be July 12—a twenty-three-day time frame, compared with the sixty days O'Neill had given on the energy policy bill. Instead of reporting to the House by amendments to the bill, the committees were directed by the resolution to transmit their recommendations directly to the select committee (meaning only the select committee would issue a formal report on the bill).

Finally, unlike the forty-member ad hoc energy committee in 1977, which was broadly representative of the standing committees of jurisdiction (including five standing committee chairmen), the nine member homeland security committee would be composed exclusively of members of the Republican and Democratic leadership. Majority Leader Armey was tapped by Hastert to chair the committee, and Minority Leader Richard Gephardt, D-Mo., designated Minority Whip Nancy Pelosi, D-Calif., as the ranking minority member.[38] Although one member of the 1977 select energy committee had referred to it as a "super Rules Committee," the 2002 panel more aptly fit that description as an arm of the leadership, given its makeup and powers.

Just as the resolution creating the select committee had been reported from the Rules Committee by voice vote, the spirit of "bipartisanship" (probably the most overused word during debate on the resolution) carried the measure to adoption in the House by voice vote as well. The only expressions of concern from the minority side were over what type of amendment process would be established for consideration of the bill. Ranking Rules Committee member Martin Frost, D-Texas, said he hoped it would be brought to the floor under an open amendment process. Minority Whip Pelosi, on the other hand, while not using the term "open rule," asked Armey whether "the rule will preserve minority rights protected by the House and will be a fair process." Armey responded that "it is the Speaker's intention that he and Democrat Leader Gephardt [will] propose to the Committee on Rules a resolution governing the consideration of the select committee's product and jointly recommend that it be adopted."[39]

It might be asked why the Speaker did not simply leave it to the existing Rules Committee to pull the pieces together after the other committees had reported their recommendations. It may be that the Speaker wanted to avoid the usual partisan skirmishing that takes place in the highly charged Rules Committee and instead invest the responsibility in a panel having a clean slate and a spirit of goodwill and bipartisanship. As will be seen, that spirit did not last long. The select committee became the focal point for a partisan split and for spats over a number of issues, large and small.

The president's bill, introduced by Armey on June 24 "by request," was referred to twelve committees, seven of which formally reported recommendations to the select committee by the July 12 deadline; the other five did not report.[40] Not surprisingly, several committees differed with the administration's plans to transfer all or parts of agencies under their jurisdiction. The Committee on Transportation and Infrastructure recommended against folding the Coast Guard and Federal Emergency Management Agency into the new department. Ways and Means voted to keep the revenue and trade functions of Customs out. Judiciary voted to transfer only the law enforcement functions of the Immigration and Naturalization Service (INS). And Science objected to the transfer of the Computer Security Division of the National Institute of Standards and Technology to a department of homeland security. In addition, Appropriations objected to giving the president flexibility to transfer up to 5 percent of the funds appropriated among agencies transferred to the department. And the Government Reform Committee voted 21 to 19 to allow workers transferred to the department to retain their union rights.[41]

The select committee then held three days of hearings on the bill in mid-July. On July 19, Armey offered an amendment in the nature of a substitute combining the recommendations of the various committees, and a marathon markup session ensued at which 29 amendments were offered, 10 by Republicans and 19 by Democrats. All the Republican amendments were adopted; six of the Democratic amendments were adopted by voice vote, and the other thirteen were rejected on party-line, roll call votes.

Most of the standing committee recommendations that departed from the administration's plan were reversed by the select committee in its final package, which was ordered reported on a 5 to 4, party-line vote. The exceptions were an agreement to include only the enforcement and border protection activities of INS in the new department and an International Relations Committee recommendation to leave visa authority with the State Department. The 5 percent intradepartmental fund transfer authority was reduced to 2 percent for two years.

On the personnel issue, a compromise was adopted in the select committee, affirming the bargaining rights of employees transferred to the department but allowing the secretary to exempt those involved in national security matters and allowing the department to establish its own rules for hiring, firing, pay scales, and performance reviews.[42]

In their minority views appended to the report, filed on July 24, the four Democrats on the select committee made clear that while they were united with the president and committee Republicans in their determination to win the war on terrorism, they did not think the bill reported by the select committee "sufficiently meets the test of making the American people safer." In their six-page critique, they noted that the majority members had attempted to postpone indefinitely the installation of explosive detection devices at airports, had rejected the sharing of intelligence information, had rejected an attempt to deny homeland security contracts to U.S. subsidiaries located in offshore tax havens, and had turned back the clock on civil service protections for workers in the new department. The minority views concluded that "the majority missed an historic opportunity to approve a homeland security bill worthy of the American people by opposing Democratic initiatives "to reduce risk and respond to terrorist attacks."[43]

On July 25, the day the committee filed its report, the House began consideration of the bill under a structured special rule. Minority Leader Gephardt had originally pressed for an open rule, but when 103 amendments were filed with the Rules Committee, a bipartisan compromise was negotiated that allowed for the consideration of 27 amendments (14 by Republicans and 13 by Democrats). The rule was adopted by voice vote.[44]

The House passed the bill on the evening of July 26, 295 to 132. Prior to final passage, however, the House took the surprising and rare action of adopting, by an overwhelming margin of 318 to 110, a minority party motion offered by Rep. Rosa DeLauro, D-Conn., to recommit with instructions. The further amendment contained in the instructions would prohibit the secretary of the Department of Homeland Security from contracting with any subsidiary of a U.S. corporation located in a tax haven country—an amendment that had been rejected in the select committee and denied by the Rules Committee.

For the most part, the select committee's product was upheld on a series of amendments to reverse decisions on agency transfers and personnel matters. All of the Democratic leadership and minority members of the select committee, except Frost, voted against the bill on final passage.

The Senate, with nothing comparable to the House Rules Committee and its authority to limit the amendment process (other than by unanimous consent), took from July 31 to November 19, 2002, to complete action on the bill, mainly because of a filibuster over the treatment of civil service employees. The measure was finally adopted 90 to 9, after an 83 to 16 vote to invoke cloture. The president signed the measure into law on November 25.

It is ironic that House and Senate Democrats attempted to politicize the issue of homeland organization by charging that the administration was doing too little, too late, or was slighting the rights of federal employees being absorbed by the new department. The ploy seemed to backfire in November 2002, when Republican television ads were used against certain vulnerable Democratic members for delaying enactment of the cabinet bill. Two of those targeted, Sen. Jean Carnahan, D-Mo., and Sen. Max Cleland, D-Ga., were defeated.

Conclusions

This chapter has explored whether anything has changed in the policymaking process in Congress since September 2001. The answer, as we have seen, even when looking at major new issues spawned by the crisis, is "not much." After the initial rush and blush of bipartisanship on emergency measures in the immediate aftermath of the attacks, things settled back into pre-9/11 patterns and practices, albeit with an expanded agenda and more things competing for resources (especially after the Iraq war began in 2003).

The war on terrorism is probably more analogous to the Cold War than to World War II, given the absence of distinct enemy states, clearly drawn battle fronts, or any agreed-upon idea of what might constitute victory. Contrary to Michael Beschloss's assertion, quoted at the beginning of this chapter, during the Cold War Congress did not completely acquiesce in the president's foreign policies, let alone in his major domestic policy requests. Nor, for that matter, did partisan politics stop at the water's edge.

That said, the terrorist attacks have been compared to Pearl Harbor because of the surprise assault on home territory and the large number of lives lost. The very nature of the September 11 attacks, hitting at the heart of the nation's government and financial centers, literally brought everything home. And, as former House Speaker Tip O'Neill continues to remind us from the grave, "All politics is local."

Some have used the term "intermestic" to describe the blurring of lines between international and domestic issues in this new age of globalization. More and more today, much, if not all, of foreign politics and policies has a local dimension. That is as true of terrorism as it is of trade. Transnational terrorism is the dark side of globalization, involving as it does the free flow of extremist ideas, fanatical people, and violent acts across international borders. And it is now not only at our doorstep but inside the house.

When such threats of foreign origin hover so close to home, it is understandable that people will be more concerned and attentive to them than to other foreign policy questions and that differences over appropriate responses will develop between the parties and branches, as they do among individual citizens. Those who naïvely thought that 9/11 would usher in a new era of political unity and harmony, and that old lines of party, power, and authority would simply melt away, fail to understand the historical roots and conditioning of our constitutional and party systems. These remain both a strength and a weakness during times of high danger and stress.

The creative tensions between the two major parties, between the president and Congress, and even between the House and Senate, play out in a variety of ways depending on the issue and the public mood. But overall, we are better off having such tensions and differences than we would be if policy solutions were devised and dictated by a government in which all power was concentrated in a single authority. That continues to be the genius and vulnerability of our system. It is as the Founders intended it to be.

Notes

1. For more on the question of whether the September 11 attacks mark the return of an imperial presidency see Donald R. Wolfensberger, "The Return of the Imperial Presidency?" *Wilson Quarterly,* spring 2002, 36–41.
2. See, for instance, James M. Lindsay and Randall B. Ripley, "How Congress Influences Foreign and Defense Policy," in *Congress Resurgent: Foreign and Defense Policy on Capitol Hill,* ed. Randall B. Ripley and James M. Lindsay (Ann Arbor: University of Michigan Press, 1993), for an excellent discussion of the ways in which Congress influences foreign and defense policies indirectly by (a) generating anticipated reactions in the executive branch; (b) identifying or changing executive policymakers through procedural legislation to influence their decisions; and (c) changing the climate of opinions held by the public and by political elites surrounding policies for the purpose of changing the policies. These same tactics can be seen at work on domestic policymaking as well.
3. See, for example, *Who Makes Public Policy?: The Struggle for Control between Congress and the Executive,* ed. Robert S. Gilmour and Alexis A. Halley (Chatham, N.J.: Chatham House Publishers, 1994), for an excellent discussion and case studies of the dynamics of policymaking between Congress and the executive branch.
4. H.J. Res. 542, *Joint resolution concerning the war powers of Congress and the President,* Public Law 93-148, November 7, 1973, sec. 2(c).
5. "Text of Bush Proposal," *CQ Daily Monitor,* Friday, September 14, 2001, 2.
6. Attacking Iraq was already under consideration according to Bob Woodward's book *Bush at War* (New York: Simon and Schuster, 2002). At a September 12, 2001, NSC meeting in the White House, "Rumsfeld raised the question of Iraq. Why shouldn't we go against Iraq, not just al Qaeda? He asked. Rumsfeld was speaking not only for himself when he raised the question. His deputy, Paul D. Wolfowitz, was committed to a policy that would make Iraq a principal target of the first round in the war on terrorism. . . . Bush made clear it was not the time to resolve the issue" (49).
7. S.J. Res. 23, *To authorize the use of United States Armed Forces against those responsible for the recent attacks against the United States,* Public Law 107-40, September 18, 2001, sec. 2.
8. "Statement on Signing the Authorization for Use of Military Force" (S.J. Res. 23, approved September 18, 2001, Public Law 107-40), *Weekly Compilation of Presidential Documents,* for the week ending September 21, 2001, 1334. President George H. W. Bush used nearly identical language in signing into law the joint resolution authorizing the use of force to expel Iraq from Kuwait in 1991 (*Weekly Compilation of Presidential Documents for the Week Ending January 19, 1991,* 48). The 1991 use of force resolution did have the same references to the War Powers Resolution but not the language on the president's inherent constitutional authority to use force (H.J. Res. 77; Public Law 102-1). Every president since Nixon has asserted that the War Powers Resolution is unconstitutional.

9. Miles A. Pomper, "In for the Long Haul," *CQ Weekly,* September 15, 2001, 2119.
10. John Lancaster and Helen Dewar, "Congress Clears Use of Force, $40 Billion in Emergency Aid," *Washington Post,* September 15, 2001, A4.
11. *Congressional Record,* September 14, 2001, H5621.
12. Ibid.
13. The bill's title is written in capital letters because it is an acronym that stands for "Uniting and Strengthening America by Providing Appropriate Tools Required to Intercept and Obstruct Terrorism." It is now more commonly referred to as the "Patriot Act."
14. Robert O'Harrow Jr., "Six Weeks in Autumn," *Washington Post Magazine,* October 27, 2002, 17–18.
15. Adriel Bettelheim and Elizabeth Palmer, "Balancing Liberty and Security," *CQ Weekly,* September 22, 2001, 2210, 2212.
16. Elizabeth A. Palmer, "Committees Taking a Critical Look at Ashcroft's Request for Broad New Powers," *CQ Weekly,* September 29, 2001, 2263.
17. O'Harrow, "Six Weeks in Autumn," 17.
18. Bettelheim and Palmer, "Balancing Liberty and Security."
19. Palmer, "Committees Taking a Critical Look," 2265.
20. S. 1510, 107th Congress, introduced by Sen. Thomas A. Daschle, October 4, 2001; and, H.R. 2975, 107th Congress, introduced by Rep. James F. Sensenbrenner Jr., October 2, 2001. The House bill was also referred to the committees on Intelligence, International Relations, Resources, and Ways and Means, but they took no action and were discharged of consideration on October 11.
21. H.R. 3108, 107th Congress, introduced by Rep. Sensenbrenner, October 12, 2001.
22. Barbara Sinclair, *Unorthodox Lawmaking: New Legislative Processes in the U.S. Congress,* 2nd ed. (Washington: CQ Press, 2000). The other new processes or procedural innovations she documents are bill referrals to multiple committees, bypassing committees, complex and restrictive special rules, omnibus bills, and executive-legislative summits.
23. H. Res. 264, 107th Congress, introduced by Rep. Lincoln Diaz-Balart, providing for the consideration of H.R. 2975.
24. H.R. 3162, 107th Congress, introduced by Rep. Sensenbrenner, October 23, 2001.
25. Elizabeth A. Palmer, "Terrorism Bill's Sparse Paper Trail May Cause Legal Vulnerabilities," *CQ Weekly,* October 27, 2001, 2533, 2534.
26. Sinclair, *Unorthodox Lawmaking,* 218.
27. See, for instance, Jackie Koszczuk, "Lawmakers Struggle to Keep An Eye on Patriot Act," *CQ Weekly,* September 7, 2002, 2284–2288,
28. James C. Benton, "Pressure to Secure the Skies," *CQ Weekly,* September 22, 2001, 2215.
29. James C. Benton, "Bush Wants Joint Federal-Private Effort to Increase Airport Security," *CQ Weekly,* September 29, 2001, 2267.
30. James C. Benton, "Senate-Passed Aviation Security Bill Declared a No-Go by House GOP," *CQ Weekly,* October 13, 2001, 2402.
31. James C. Benton, "Bush's Appeal Gives GOP Victory on Airline Security Bill," *CQ Weekly,* November 3, 2001, 2603. The Democrats tried unsuccessfully to defeat the previous question on the rule to make in order an additional bill (H.R. 2955) to provide assistance to employees who lost their jobs due to the shutdown of airports and the discontinuance of flights resulting from the terrorist attacks or security measures. The previous question was adopted, 218 to 207.
32. James C. Benton, "Cleared Aviation Security Bill Is Crippled Industry's Best Hope," *CQ Weekly,* November 17, 2001, 2729–2730.
33. Executive Order 13228, "Establishing an Office of Homeland Security and the Homeland Security Council," October 8, 2001, *Weekly Compilation of Presidential Documents,* October 15, 2001, 1434–1435.

34. The Thornberry bill was H.R. 1158; the first Lieberman bill was S. 1148. And the Lieberman bill reported from the Governmental Affairs Committee was S. 2452, the National Homeland Security and Combating Terrorism Act of 2002. Senate Rpt. 107-175, report to accompany S. 2452, June 24, 2002.
35. George W. Bush, "Address to the Nation on the Proposed Department of Homeland Security, June 6, 2002," *Weekly Compilation of Presidential Documents,* June 10, 2002, 964.
36. H. Res. 449, 107th Congress, 2nd session, sec. 7.
37. *Congressional Record,* June 19, 2002, H3694.
38. The other Republican members were: Majority Whip Tom DeLay, Texas, conference chairman J. C. Watts, Okla., conference vice chairman Deborah Pryce, Ohio, and leadership chairman Rob Portman, Ohio. The other Democratic members were Caucus chairman Martin Frost, Texas, Caucus vice chairman Robert Menendez, N.J., and Rosa DeLauro, Conn., assistant to the Democratic Leader.
39. *Congressional Record,* June 19, 2002, H3696.
40. H.R. 5005, 107th Congress, introduced by Rep. Armey, June 24, 2002, and referred to twelve committees in addition to the select committee. The seven committees formally reporting recommendations to the select committee were Agriculture, Energy and Commerce, International Relations, Judiciary, Science, Transportation and Infrastructure, and Ways and Means. Those not reporting recommendations were Appropriations, Armed Services, Financial Services, Government Reform, and Intelligence, though some chairmen transmitted their own views instead.
41. Charles R. Wise, "Reorganizing the Federal Government for Homeland Security: Congress Attempts to Create a New Department," *Extensions,* fall 2002, 16.
42. Ibid.
43. U.S. House of Representatives, Select Committee on Homeland Security, "Homeland Security Act of 2002," report to accompany H.R. 5005, July 24, 2002 (H. Rpt. 107-609, Part 1), 217, 223.
44. H. Res. 502, 107th Congress, introduced by Rep. Pryce, July 25, 2002.

Part V
Congress and Political Change

16. From Congressional to Presidential Preeminence: Power and Politics in Late Nineteenth-Century America and Today

Joseph Cooper

In a classic work published in 1885, Woodrow Wilson accurately portrayed American government at the national level as congressional government.[1] No such portrait could be drawn today. The prestige and power of the president have grown so substantially since the late nineteenth century that his role in leading our nation is now taken simply as a given. As a result, public controversy focuses on the president's wisdom and skill in solving current problems, not on the vastly expanded dimensions of his role. Absorption in the present is, of course, to be expected. In every age we must deal with the world as we find it. Nonetheless, historical perspective always deepens our understanding. Looking back can help us to understand how and why the roles of Congress and the president have changed and what past trends suggest for the future. This chapter therefore compares and contrasts the balance of power between the Congress and presidency in the late nineteenth and late twentieth centuries. My aim is to highlight the magnitude and assess the significance of the shift from congressional preeminence in late nineteenth-century America to presidential preeminence today.

The analysis examines the roles of the president and Congress in three primary arenas of national decision making—the electoral system, the legislative system, and the administrative system. My premise is that change in the balance of congressional and presidential power reflects change in their positions in these systems and that leverage in one system reinforces leverage in the others. The analysis also touches on the courts and the states to include aspects of the topic tied to the roles of these units. Finally, it traces changes in doctrine, in widely accepted notions of proper behavior and operation, as well as changes in practice, in actual behavior and operation. Since doctrine frames our understanding of the way the world works and should work, of what is appropriate and what should be expected and desired, the story of institutional change is necessarily a story of doctrinal as well as behavioral change.

Congressional Preeminence, 1869–1910

In analyzing congressional preeminence in the late nineteenth century, I focus on the years between 1869, the year Ulysses Grant became president, and 1910, the year of the revolt against Speaker Cannon. The story, however, is not only a story of preeminence, but also one of decline. I will therefore be attentive to the varying rhythms of change in the three primary arenas of national decision making as well as to their defining features.

The Electoral System

In 1869, as in the preceding decades, the electoral system was controlled by, and primarily responsive to, state and local party organizations and leaders.[2] Nominations for local, state, and national offices were determined by party caucuses or conventions with party leaders at state and local levels often exercising hierarchical power. Though there was considerable regional variation, the era was one in which party machines and bosses were common and integral parts of the overall pattern of politics. The parties also ran the elections and the campaigns. Voting eligibility was in the hands of partisan officials—present-day registration laws did not exist. Ballots were printed by the parties as partisan documents with no provision for split-ticket voting, distinctively colored, and handed to voters when they came to the polls. Similarly, political campaigns were conducted and directed by the parties. In these campaigns the primary strategy was the mobilization of partisans, not persuasion on the basis of issues. The main techniques relied upon were parades to heighten feelings of solidarity and the use of party workers to maximize turnout, supplemented by partisan leaflets and pamphlets and by articles in newspapers that were entirely committed to one party or the other.

Both ideal and material rewards were important. On the one hand, jobs at all levels of government were distributed on the basis of patronage and provided incentives for party work and for careers in politics. On the other, there were sharp divisions between the parties with respect to the tariff, financial policy, civil rights, and national development. These incentives, together with emotional attachment to the parties, inherited from the past and powerfully reinforced by the Civil War, made partisan identification very widespread and very strong. As for the funding of parties and campaigns, practice dovetailed with the pattern of politics. Aside from contributions from groups and individuals motivated by a desire for favorable legislation or treatment, patronage employees were expected to contribute a portion of their salaries to aid in election campaigns, and party newspapers received government printing contracts from fellow partisans when in office.

Organizationally, then, the national parties were little more than loose coalitions of state and local party organizations that gathered every four years to choose a candidate for the presidency whose views were acceptable to partisans in the various regions of the nation and whose candidacy maximized the chances of gaining or maintaining control of federal patronage. In such an electoral system congressmen, not presidents, were preeminent. Presidents might head the ticket, but they did not head the party. The party as a whole and its organized units had their own highly independent basis of support in party identification and in state patronage, as well as in hallowed conventions of the Congress, such as senatorial courtesy, that placed federal patronage in congressional hands. The president's party was thus not a creature of the president nor subservient to him. Rather, he was highly dependent on the support of party units and their leaders for nomination and election. Similarly, congressmen were tied tightly to local party organizations and leaders for nomination and electoral success, and senators, chosen in this period by state legislatures, were tied to state party organizations and leaders. Interest groups in the modern sense of entities organized on a mass basis across the nation and operating at all levels of government, as opposed to lobbies representing private or personalized interests and focused at the legislative level, were only beginning to appear, and before the 1890s, with only a few exceptions, were not powerful enough to pressure parties. Political parties were, in short, the primary engines of politics at the electoral level and as organizations were more powerful than individual candidates, lobbies, or interest groups.

Equally important, prevailing doctrine legitimated and reinforced the role and power of party, as did the limited role of the federal government. Representative government was equated with party government. Parties, through the policies presented to the public in their platforms, were seen as the primary vehicles of popular rule. Such a view in itself made presidents and all elected officials creatures of their parties and subservient to a corporate whole. Underlying this conceptualization of the role of party was a notion of the existence of a common or collective good that the parties could be seen to embody and represent. In contrast, lobbies and interest groups remained illegitimate since they presumably were motivated by partial or special interests. Ironically, Madisonian distaste for factions retained its hold but not with respect to parties. The subordination of presidents to parties was also powerfully reinforced by traditional norms that disdained any open or public pursuit of office or favor. Nineteenth-century candidates for the presidency refrained from pursuing nomination or election through public appeals for support, did not attend the nominating convention, and when formally notified of their nomination by a committee, their first act in accepting the nomination was to embrace the party platform, initially in a letter and later in the century in a speech. Thus, both theoretical and pragmatic factors led presidential candidates to run and present themselves as representatives of their parties and to rely on their parties to do the campaigning. Finally, as we shall see shortly in greater detail, the doctrine of dual federalism prevailed in theory and practice and reserved most major functions of government to the states. The result was to make politics more local than national in terms of both issues and jobs.

In sum, then, a variety of factors combined to create an election system that raised state and local parties above any competitors for power and made congressmen, and especially senators, who were often the key party leaders in their states, more powerful than the president. An electoral system organized and run by state and local party units and premised on belief in party government, regard for patronage, disdain for interest groups, and a limited federal role was an electoral system that was party centered, not president centered. It was an electoral system in which senators and congressmen were highly independent of the president in their states and localities and far more influential over party policies and nominations at the national level.

Nonetheless, this party-centered electoral system was not immune to challenges that eroded the contours of party power. After 1880 discontent with the domination party organizations exercised over elections sparked discontent in a nation that was growing and changing dramatically in response to a variety of forces—industrialization, urbanization, expanding immigration, changes in technology, the emergence of universities and professional disciplines in a variety of fields, the end of the frontier, and the transformation of the United States into a world power. These forces combined to define a political world whose growing complexity increasingly constrained the ability of parties to represent and satisfy discontented elements of the population. Concomitantly, the growth of large corporate enterprises with political needs led to alliances between party leaders and business leaders that easily aroused the anger and distrust of groups who could not move the political system to respond to their needs. Such discontent, combined with the ability of party organizations and leaders to dominate the electoral process, spawned doctrinal change and efforts at reform. Older traditions of individualism and notions of popular sovereignty were resurrected and combined to challenge notions of party discipline and power, to depict the parties as corrupt handmaidens of the trusts, and to provide a rationale for reform based on rule of the people.

The result was a number of important reforms that diminished the power of party in the three decades that followed 1880. Partisan control of elections was undermined by the adoption of the Australian ballot in the 1890s and the growth of personal registration requirements after 1900. Partisan control of nominations was undermined by the widespread adoption of the direct primary between 1900 and 1910 for both congressional and presidential candidates, and in 1913 by the passage of a constitutional amendment providing for the direct election of senators. Last but not least, a civil service system was adopted for federal employees in the 1880s. Although crafted to constrain growth in the number of important positions in the system and to preserve loopholes for campaign contributions by patronage employees, in the decade after 1900 civil service reform in both these regards became substantial and significant. Equally important, civil service reform also enveloped the states and localities.

The conduct of campaigns changed as well. In response to the growth of a mass public, increased income from advertising, and new canons of professionalism, the press severed its dependence on parties and became an independent entity. At the same time, the modes of campaigning altered, with less emphasis on mobilization and parades and more emphasis on persuasion through pamphlets, mailings, speeches, and planted news stories. The result, it should be noted, was not to convert American politics into an academic seminar, but rather to enhance dependence on advertising and awareness of the important contributions that new professionals in this field could make. All these changes, in turn, affected and were accompanied by changes that increased the importance of the president in national politics.

Beginning in the 1880s, building on the model set by the Tilden campaign in 1876, presidential candidates began to take firmer control of national campaigns through increased reliance on national party campaign units controlled by their agents. In the 1890s they began to make public speeches to increasingly larger audiences when accepting party nominations and in so doing gave more emphasis to their own policy positions, while still pledging fealty to the party platform. Candidates also began to travel around the country by train to publicize themselves and their positions. By 1910 it had become common for presidents to see the presidency as a "bully pulpit" and no longer hesitate to make public speeches and appearances to promote their policy views. Finally, as a consequence of organizational learning, as well as doctrinal change that deprived the parties of exclusive identification with the common interest, between 1890 and 1920 a large variety of mass interest groups were organized across a wide range of economic and professional areas. The age of mass politics and mass democracy had begun.

All these changes were associated with changing expectations regarding the role of the federal government that served as both cause and effect of the growth of presidential power in the party system. Nonetheless, the decline of party should not be exaggerated. Despite the direct primary and civil service reform, in many, if not most, localities parties remained strong enough to control the outcomes of primaries. Despite the rise of a public presidency, state and local party leaders still controlled presidential selection, as Teddy Roosevelt found out to his chagrin in 1912. Despite the decreased emphasis on mobilization and the increased reliance on persuasion and advertising strategies, party workers remained critical both in bringing voters to the polls and in disseminating the party message. Despite the greater importance and independence of the president in the party system, he did not become the personal embodiment of his party but only the chief partisan. Despite the growth in the role of the federal government and the emergence of an interest group system, state and local spending still substantially outstripped federal spending, and parties by far remained the more powerful entities. In sum, many of the distinctive characteristics of the nineteenth century remained in place, albeit weakened and on a road to further attenuation and even disappearance. The emergence of the modern electoral system had only begun.

The Legislative System

The rhythms of change in the legislative system of the late nineteenth century were quite different than those that prevailed in the election system. In both the House and Senate the story is not one of erosion after 1880, but of the emergence of centralized rule in the 1890s and then substantial decline in the decade after 1910.[3]

The House by the 1870s had evolved into a body that bestowed substantial organizational power on its standing committees and its elected leader, the Speaker. The standing committees, in practice before 1880 and by rule thereafter, had monopoly control over bills in their jurisdictions and great deference on the floor. The Speaker had the authority to appoint the standing committees and treated seniority as a secondary consideration. Other facets of the rules secured these dual bases of leadership of the House—a germaneness rule that protected committee control of the agenda, a previous question rule for limiting debate on the floor, and the Speaker's power over recognition.

Nonetheless, the House remained difficult to control. The Speaker shared power with the committee chairs, especially the chair of the Appropriations Committee, and was highly vulnerable to minority delaying tactics. These limitations were eliminated after 1880. In the 1880s a series of precedents transformed the Rules Committee, chaired and controlled by the Speaker, into an instrument for setting the floor agenda and controlling debate and amendment in committee of the whole. These precedents were formalized in the Reed Rules of 1890, which also gave the Speaker the authority to overcome minority obstruction through nonparticipation in quorum calls or dilatory motions. Finally, the power of the Speaker's chief rival, the Appropriations Committee chair, was trimmed back in the 1880s by stripping the committee of most major appropriations bills. The result, after some initial resistance by the Democrats in the two Congresses that followed the first Reed Congress, was to transform the Speaker into a "czar" by making the committee chairs his servants and forcing individual members to court his favor both to secure desired committee assignments and to bring vital constituency bills to the floor. It should be noted, however, that czar rule rested as much on high levels of party unity and belief in the doctrines of party government as on increases in the formal powers of the Speaker. Indeed, it was these factors that motivated and legitimated centralization, and in the end the exercise of the Speaker's formal powers rested on his ability to mobilize majorities on the floor.

The development of centralized rule in the Senate was more delayed and emerged in a manner that was consistent with the traditional reluctance of the Senate to limit the power and discretion of the individual senator. Thus, the nineteenth-century Senate, in contrast to the House, refused to limit debate in any but very minor ways, did not adopt a germaneness rule, vested committee appointment in party units, and resisted the appointment of party leaders or steering committees to give direction to the party caucuses. Under these conditions the standing committees had no rivals, and the Senate relied on its committee chairs to direct and move its business. The passage of important legislation in the post–Civil War Senate thus had to be based—far more than in the House—on high levels of policy agreement in the majority party, the support of committee chairs (who had achieved seniority rights to their positions by the 1870s), and reliance on unanimous consent as a mechanism for agenda setting.

As in the House, partisan agreement in the Senate increased in the late 1880s and 1890s and, combined with mounting dissatisfaction over the highly chaotic character of the conduct of business, led to a centralization of power. The form it took, however, was quite different than in the House. Whereas czar rule in the House rested on the intersection of the Speaker's power under the rules and his power as leader of his party, centralization in the Senate rested on the ability of a small and unified clique of majority partisans to take control of and use the caucus, the newly created party steering committee, and the party committee on committees to direct committee and floor business and to reward and punish fellow partisans. A form of centralized rule, based on interlocking positions on key party and Senate committees, thus emerged in the Senate after 1897, though one far more dependent on party unity and somewhat less able consistently to control outcomes than in the House.

The drive for centralization in both houses was tied to a Congress-centered view of what was required to enhance the character and performance of representative government in the United States. Presidents were not prime leaders, or even active participants, in the lawmaking process before 1890. Though Jacksonian claims that the president was the tribune of the people played a role in winning the fight for a discretionary presidential veto, their relevance and strength waned after the issue was settled in the 1840s. Thus, in mid and late nineteenth-century America, standards and expectations in all areas of legislative practice were defined by Whig doctrine. This doctrine saw Congress as the prime representative of the American people because of its ability to capture the complexities of interest and opinion in the public through the host of local and state constituencies it represented. An integral and related component was that the separation of powers principle, implicit in the Constitution, should be interpreted strictly to mean that the president had no proper role in lawmaking other than to identify problems at the start of a Congress and to veto laws that were against the public interest. As for lesser executive officers, their proper role was to provide Congress, and especially its committees, with information and proposals when requested—to serve as instruments of the Congress. It is thus no accident that bills drafted by executive officers, though not entirely absent, were seen as illegitimate and provided in a covert fashion; that cabinet officers were denied the right to participate in floor debate; and that presidential involvement was sporadic, covert, and often in response to the requests of congressional party leaders. The simple fact was that Whig doctrine provided a far better fit to the character of the election system and the power of state and local party leaders than Jacksonian doctrine. Thus, for example, Senator George Hoar could note that in the 1870s, if senators went to the White House it was to give advice, not to take it, and that they would regard efforts to influence them as an affront.[4] To cite another example, in 1888 Senator John Sherman responded to President-elect Benjamin Harrison's request for advice by reminding him that a president should have no policy distinct from that of his party and that party policy was better determined in Congress than in the executive.[5]

Still, changes in the character of the party system and the responsibilities of the federal government after 1880 had their effects. Ironically, the rise of centralized rule in Congress was accompanied by an expansion of the president's role in the legislative process. One can see the signs of change in Cleveland's open advocacy of tariff and monetary reform and McKinley's increased and substantial influence, albeit still covert, over legislative decision making. Yet the clearest signposts of change came with the presidency of Teddy Roosevelt, who boldly proclaimed the stewardship of the presidency, openly and actively sought to influence members to pass major pieces of legislation, gave the press quarters in the White House and began to meet with selected reporters, sought to mobilize public support for legislation he favored, and invented a slogan, "the Square Deal," to symbolize an entire policy program. His successor as president, W. H. Taft, though not as dramatic or energetic, continued to act as legislative leader in these same regards. A page had clearly been turned in the evolution of the president's role in the legislative process. Nonetheless, the centralization of power in the Congress, rooted in a party system that was strong organizationally at the state and local levels, substantially constrained presidential leadership. Roosevelt and Taft had no choice but to work with Speaker Cannon and Sen. Nelson Aldrich, the foremost Senate Republican leader, and these men were not the lieutenants of the president that congressional leaders are today, but far closer to coequals.

Centralized party rule in the House and Senate, however, did not endure. The same forces that weakened the hold of party over the electoral system undermined centralization in the Congress under the auspices of party. If the notion of party government began to be seriously challenged at the electoral level by Progressives who saw the power of party bosses as illegitimate and exploitive, such doctrines began to be asserted in Congress after 1903 on behalf of the right of individual members to resist party discipline and vote their consciences and/or constituencies. When the size of the Republican majority declined, as it did in the election of 1908 in the House and 1910 in the Senate, the number of Progressive Republicans, though a small minority in the party, was sufficient in combination with the minority Democrats to challenge party rule in both houses. In the House a series of rules changes from 1909 through 1911 deprived the Speaker of his historic power to appoint the standing committees, removed him from the Rules Committee, and created a number of mechanisms, from the Consent Calendar to discharge, designed to make the floor more accessible to cross-party majorities and individual members. In the Senate no rules changes were needed to end the oligarchic rule of a clique of party leaders because the formal rules contributed little to their power. Rather, by the beginning of the 62nd Congress (1911–1913) a cross-partisan coalition of Progressive Republicans and minority party Democrats had gained sufficient strength to cripple oligarchic rule on behalf of a majority of the majority party. Aldrich retired in 1911, at the end of the 61st Congress (1909–1911)—his day as well as Cannon's had passed.

The immediate outcome proved to be a disappointment for Progressive reformers as well as a boon for the presidency. In the House the leaders of the highly united and disciplined Democratic majority that took control in the 62nd Congress nullified the effects of the rules changes they had supported by running the House as tightly through the party caucus as it had been run through the power of the Speaker. Their takeover of the House was soon accompanied by the accession of Woodrow Wilson to the presidency in 1913. The result was to define the outlines of a very different system of party rule, one that was quite new for the period after 1867 and a precursor of later developments. In terms of doctrine, Woodrow Wilson gave the claim that the president served as the representative of the people a broader, firmer, and very modern definition. He extended the traditional concept of the president as tribune or steward of the people to embrace the notion that to attain the public interest the nation needed a leader to sense and educate the will of the people, a task only the president could perform. In practice, Wilson turned the caucus and the partisan loyalties of the House into instruments of his policy desires and programs. The potential of partisan organization in Congress to serve as an instrument not of congressional power but of presidential power was thus revealed. The immediate impact in the Senate was similar. When the Democrats took control of the Senate in 1913, party became the fulcrum of Wilson's leadership there as well. The position of majority party leader was formally established, matching what the House had done a decade earlier, and in contrast to Republican practice, the chairmanships of the key party committees were concentrated in his hands. Clearly, the motivation was to foster programmatic presidential leadership in a body far harder to organize and run than the House.

Nonetheless, this new form of party rule proved to be only an interlude. High levels of party unity on policy goals were essential to the viability of this system of governance in both the House and Senate. In neither body could they be sustained after the passage of the Wilsonian program in his first term, although the advent of World War I bolstered Wilson's influence for a brief period. In 1919, when the Republicans regained control of the House and Senate, a very different legislative system was in place. In the House, the Speaker and majority party leader had far less power and control than in 1908, but far more than would be present at midcentury after several decades of further, albeit irregular, decentralization. In a more factionalized Senate, the dispersal of power, as might be expected, was more pronounced, and committee chairs again emerged as the primary leaders. Last but not least, although the nation and his party now expected the president to provide leadership and participate actively in the legislative process, Congress's continuing strength in the party and administrative systems, as well as residues of belief in Whig doctrine, led to restrained leadership on the part of Republican presidents. In sum, if after 1910, late nineteenth-century expectations regarding congressional power and autonomy no longer prevailed, we are still far from the theory and practice of presidential leadership that would emerge in the 1930s and continue to evolve thereafter.

The Administrative System

The rhythms of change in the administrative system responded to the same forces that prompted change in the party and legislative systems.[6] In the 1870s Congress was clearly dominant in the administrative system, just as it was in the legislative system. Here too, conceptions of the president's role were defined by Whig doctrine. Policy was conceived as properly determined by law and the president's role as simply to ensure, as the Constitution literally interpreted provided, that statutory provisions were faithfully executed by the department heads. Hence, Wilson's depiction of the president as a clerk in the mid-1880s, if somewhat exaggerated, still captured the essence of doctrine and practice before 1890. Congress expected to define public policy, regarded the departments as its instruments, and saw the president as more of an overseer of the executive branch than its director. Indeed, even in areas of foreign and defense policy, where it was acknowledged that the president had greater authority than in domestic affairs, Congress believed it had a major, if not definitive, role on the basis of its statutory and appropriations power over military organization, resources, and deployments and its constitutional powers over war making, treaties, and appointments.

These conceptions and expectations were strongly rooted in the politics of the party and legislative systems. Even after the defeat of the Johnson impeachment in 1868, the president's removal power remained under attack. The Senate continued to insist that the power to consent to appointments necessarily implied the power to consent to removals. What was at issue was not only the authority of the president to remove executive officers, but also his role in the party system. Despite the fact that presidents lacked the political and staff resources to control appointments in any comprehensive fashion, the power to remove key officials, such as the heads of the Custom Houses, who in turn controlled large numbers of patronage employees, gave him the ability to favor certain state and local party leaders and factions over others and constituted an important basis of presidential power in the party system of the time.

Presidents Hayes, Garfield, and Cleveland won this fight. They defeated a number of attempted incursions on the president's removal power. Still, the result was only to preserve a basic component of the president's constitutional authority—not to give him control of the administrative process. The department heads, though chosen by the president, were allied with major components of the president's party and not infrequently important state party leaders themselves. They thus had independent bases of action and support that presidents had to respect. Equally, if not more important, the department heads interacted on a far closer and continuing basis with the appropriate congressional committees than with the president. After all, it was these committees that controlled their authority and funds, whereas the president had only a few staff secretaries, limited involvement in the legislative process, and no budget power. Rather, the annual estimates of departmental funding needs were prepared by the departments, collected by the secretary of the Treasury, and sent to Congress without review or comment. As a result, departmental legislation and appropriations were far more attuned to the will of congressional committees than the will of the president. Indeed, even in foreign and military affairs, where presidents retained substantial initiative and discretion in treaty making and handling disputes with foreign powers, the committees of Congress were powerful and intimately involved.

Underlying this system of administration were not only practice and doctrine regarding the Congress and presidency, but also practice and doctrine with respect to the role of the states and the federal courts. In the 1870s and 1880s the traditional doctrine of "dual federalism" prevailed and reserved health, education, welfare, and police functions to the states. As a result, the amount of funds expended by states and localities was substantially larger than the amount spent by the federal government, and the federal government's expenditures were largely in the areas of national defense, the post office, and veterans' benefits. As for the federal courts, they acted as the guarantors of dual federalism. Equally important, judicial proceedings were regarded as the preferred and legitimate mode of implementing the law when the exercise of executive authority under law affected private interests or rights. Major legislation of this type was sparse before 1880, but the point remains that doctrine conceded little to the need for judicial restraint in deciding cases involving the exercise of executive discretion.

As in the case of the party system, events in the 1880s signaled that substantial change both in doctrine and practice was under way. One impetus for change derived from the forces that were changing the party system. The passage of civil service reform in 1883 had profound effects on the administrative system as well as the party system, although these effects were incremental over time, not immediate. The cumulative impact of this reform helped to free the presidency from the web of constraints and time-consuming tasks imposed by the traditional patronage system. The growth of a professional civil service was thus much to his advantage. On the one hand, reform constrained a prime basis of congressional influence and involvement. On the other, it redefined the context of administration in ways favorable to presidential power. Although it also contributed to bureaucratic power and autonomy, a professional civil service had an equal, if not greater, effect in promoting increased presidential control of the personnel and management of the executive branch, in advancing the notion that the president was, and needed to be, a chief executive—not a mere clerk.

However, the emergence of the president as a chief executive rested primarily on the further expansion of the responsibilities of the federal government. Once again a signal event took place in the 1880s—the passage of the Interstate Commerce Act of 1887, which authorized federal regulation of the railroads. Although the federal courts initially took advantage of ambiguities in the statute to act on the basis of traditional notions of their role and cripple the authority of the Interstate Commerce Commission (ICC), the forces promoting an expanded federal role could not be contained. In the decades that followed 1887, new legislation was passed in a variety of areas that established the foundations of an administrative state by the advent of World War I. In business and financial areas, legislation was passed that, combined with some retreat on the part of the courts, endowed the ICC with ample power to regulate the railroads. Other legislation established the Federal Trade Commission (FTC) to regulate unfair trade practices, authorized Justice Department antitrust investigations and prosecutions, and created a Department of Commerce and the Federal Reserve System. In agricultural areas, the extension activities of the Department of Agriculture, also initiated in 1887, increased in every decade, and legislation for safeguarding the purity of food and drugs, controlling insecticides, monitoring cotton futures, and underwriting farm loans was passed. In health and welfare, a Department of Labor was created, an eight-hour day for workers on common carriers established, a Children's Bureau provided for in statute, and legislation limiting child labor passed. Finally, in a milestone event in the evolution of federalism, a grant-in-aid program for highway construction in the states was passed. These developments in domestic policy were accompanied by expansion of the responsibilities of the federal government in foreign affairs. The Spanish American War heightened and combined with the nationalizing effects of rapid industrialization and continental expansion to prompt the United States to see itself, and to act, as a world power with global interests, rather than an insular power whose interests were largely confined to the defense of its territorial boundaries.

The result of expanded federal responsibilities was an expansion in presidential roles and power both in theory and in practice. Though bureaucratic power and autonomy also increased, presidents began to direct the executive branch in a far more active and comprehensive manner in domestic affairs. Roosevelt spurred the Justice Department into momentous antitrust prosecutions and on his own authority initiated a program for conserving land and forests, setting aside millions of acres of public land. Taft continued to spur antitrust prosecutions, and he intervened strongly to protect the policies of his secretary of interior from attack by the politically powerful head of the Forestry Service and Congress. Wilson induced Congress not only to create a number of new programs and agencies, but also to give him extraordinary power over the economy during World War I. Presidents also became more active and assertive in international affairs. Teddy Roosevelt took initiative in ending the Russo-Japanese War, sent the fleet around the world, and played a major role in creating Panama and building the Panama Canal. Wilson continued the practices of Roosevelt and Taft of intervening militarily in the affairs of Central American nations, played a more open and forceful role in leading the country into World War I than McKinley had played in 1898, and after the war was the chief architect of the League of Nations as well as the chief proponent of the view that the United States should join without reservations. Nor did these changes in activity occur without changes in process. Driven by the huge spike in expenditures that accompanied World War I, a historic change was made in the budget process in 1921. The president, aided by a new agency, the Bureau of the Budget, was vested with the power to coordinate departmental budget requests and present them in a single and unified document to the Congress.

These expansions in presidential initiative and activity were accompanied and legitimated by powerful challenges to Whig doctrine. Theodore Roosevelt resurrected the Hamiltonian notion that the grant of executive power to the president in Article II was a broad grant of inherent power and argued that the president had the authority to act without congressional authorization as long as he did not violate statute or the Constitution. In combination with Wilson's view of administration as a science, advanced long before his presidency but highly influential in putting a premium on neutral competence in the minds of reformers, the effect was to provide a powerful rationale for presidential management. Indeed, the change in the budget process could not have occurred without changes in doctrine as well as demands. In addition, both Roosevelt and Wilson vigorously promoted the concept of an active and positive federal role, which soon led to a new doctrine of "cooperative federalism" to challenge traditional notions of "dual federalism," and they sought as well to expand the boundaries of the president's war power.

Despite these changes, the initial decades of the twentieth century had more in common with the last decades of the nineteenth century than with the last decades of the twentieth. If the role of the federal government expanded in theory and practice, the range of its regulatory and welfare responsibilities remained limited. As late as 1920 all governmental expenditures remained below 10 percent of GNP, and state and local expenditures were more than double federal expenditures. If the president's assertiveness increased in the administrative process and his power was augmented by the creation of an executive budget process in 1921, Congress's relationships with departments through its committees was still strongly rooted in the party system and its authorization and funding prerogatives. It is no accident that the creation of the Budget Bureau was accompanied by the reconsolidation of all appropriations bills in a single committee in both House and Senate or that the new unit was placed in the Treasury Department, which Congress from 1789 on had regarded as its agency as much as the president's. Finally, if expansion in the role of the federal government was an effect as well as a cause of the growth in bureaucratic autonomy, bureaucratic power and politics remained far less formidable than they would become after the New Deal.

In terms of doctrine, if Whig doctrine regarding presidential power in the administrative process was under attack from several directions, the belief that policy discretion properly resided in Congress remained strong, as did its corollary that laws should be written in detail. Similarly, if the courts retreated somewhat to accommodate the rise of new regulatory agencies, they did not embrace deference to administrative expertise, as they would later in the century, and the notion that administrative action that invaded private interests was properly a matter for some form of judicial decision making continued to have an impact. Thus, for example, the FTC and the secretary of agriculture, in exercising their regulatory authority, had to proceed through issuing "cease and desist" orders and enforcing them through court prosecutions. It is true as well that claims of inherent presidential power continued to be countered by the claim that the president had no more power than what was clearly and explicitly conferred by statute or the Constitution, and belief in neutral competence by continuing belief in the necessary primacy of congressional policy control. As for foreign affairs, the Senate's fight with Wilson over the League of Nations was in effect a fight over Congress's ability to control the initiation of major conflicts. The Senate's victory testified not only to the continuing strength of isolationism, but also to the continuing strength of traditional doctrine regarding the war power. In sum, then, though the foundations of the modern state and the modern presidency had emerged, they remained pale shadows of what was to come.

Conclusion

The late nineteenth century was, as is often claimed, an era of congressional preeminence. It was, however, not one that was immune to change. Congress's power and position in the party, legislative, and administrative systems combined with the supremacy of Whig doctrine to make the political system congressionally centered. Nonetheless, in all three systems congressional power began to decline after 1880, and the pace of decline accelerated after 1900. By 1910 Congress had lost the preeminence it had in 1880, but the presidency did not immediately gain the role and ascendance it would later assume. It is to the impacts of the continuing development of presidential power in fashioning the modern presidency that I now wish to turn.

Presidential Preeminence, 1969–2004

In analyzing presidential preeminence in the late twentieth century, I focus on the years between 1969, the year Richard Nixon became president, and the present. This is not to deny that the presidency gained preeminence well before the 1960s. The Great Depression and World War II raised public expectations regarding the role of the federal government and the stakes of politics to new and far higher levels. And once again the president was the main beneficiary. He assumed prime responsibility for economic prosperity and national security in the eyes of the public, and that in turn provided a lever for substantial changes in practice and in doctrine. The president emerged as the best or true representative of the public interest and undisputed leader of his party, as well as chief legislator and chief executive. In contrast, all the pillars of the late nineteenth-century polity that restrained presidential power declined in strength. Congress lost power and position in all arenas of decision making; cooperative federalism in the form of grant-in-aid programs overcame traditional attachment to dual federalism; and the federal courts, after some initial resistance to the New Deal in the mid-1930s, transformed the commerce clause into a plenary grant of federal power and embraced judicial deference to administrative expertise. Nonetheless, the polity of the 1960s is not the polity of today. What the late 1960s mark is not an end point in the growth of presidential power, but a critical point of transition from the New

Deal era to the modern one. Let me turn, then, to the emergence in recent decades of the current balance of power between the president and Congress.

The Electoral System

As late as the early 1960s, the national party system could still be seen in traditional terms as a coalition of state and local party organizations. These organizations, to be sure, had less control over nomination and campaigns than at the turn of the century. The direct primary, civil service, and the expansion of federal welfare programs had weakened their power, and the number of local parties that still qualified as "machines" had dwindled. Nonetheless, in the 1950s and 1960s state and local party leaders continued to be of major importance in determining the presidential nominee, and many state and local party organizations still controlled nominations for federal, state, and local offices. As for campaigns, party organizations continued to play a major role in contacting voters and bringing them to the polls, and party identification remained strong. Finally, though interest groups increased in number, resources, and influence after 1920, and several major ones were now intimately allied with one or the other of the major parties, they remained junior partners in the coalitions who were consulted, but expected to participate in campaigns under the direction of party leaders.

In the decades that followed the 1960s, the electoral system was transformed in ways that left few, if any, traces of the traditional party system.[7] The system changed from one in which presidential elections provided the glue that united strong state and local party organizations into one in which such elections became personalized vehicles for presidential control of the party system. One dimension of change was organizational. By the late 1960s, continuing decline in the power of state and local party machines, marked by successful attacks in the 1950s and early 1960s on most of the few such organizations that still qualified as machines, created the conditions for radical change. The strife-ridden Democratic Convention of 1968 sparked a wholesale assault on the power of state and local party leaders to control the selection of presidential nominees. Within a short period, presidential primaries multiplied in number in both parties and became the mechanism for choosing delegates in the great majority of states. The convention system for choosing presidential nominees, a system that had endured since the 1830s, was no more—replaced by a convention that was now simply a TV event scripted to promote a party nominee chosen through primaries.

The decline of state and local party control of the presidential nominations process was matched by a similar decline in party control of presidential campaigns. In 1972 President Nixon extended practices that had been developing since the 1950s. He built his own campaign organization and used it both to displace and to control the regular party organization, especially at the national level. Subsequent presidents adopted and further refined this mode of operation with the result that the presidential campaign organization became a personal instrument of the presidential candidate at both national and state levels. Thus, in the

2004 election President Bush recruited thousands of individuals across the nation to staff campaign and fund raising units created in his name and to fill key positions in national and state party units. As for Senator Kerry, his mode of operation was quite similar, though initially more dependent on independent groups for mobilizing voters and issue ads because of his party's lag in developing a broad donor base.

The emergence of a personalized party system centered on the president was, however, not simply a product of organizational change. It was also the product of a number of other developments that interacted with organizational change and with one another to cap a presidential takeover of the party system that had been proceeding for decades. One was the growth of plebiscitary politics. The advent of TV, jet airplanes, highly professionalized polling and media advertising, and new forms of grassroots politics transformed presidential campaigns. The result was a mode of campaigning that emphasized direct and immediate communication with the public at large through TV, multiple personal appearances across the country, standardized messages, and heavy use of volunteers. A second was a substantial increase in the degree to which politics was nationalized. In the late 1990s the national policy agenda included not only broader and more demanding forms of the core economic, social, and national security issues of the 1960s, but also a new set of controversial issues from abortion, to gay rights, to tort reform, to the privacy of medical records. A third was an increase in political polarization. A secular realignment of the components of the two major parties occurred after 1969. The result was to redefine the composition of the parties in more consistent ways ideologically as the New Deal coalition broke down, and to produce far more unified and coherent parties in the 1990s than had existed in the 1960s. Fourth and last, turn-of-the-century Progressive doctrines that equated popular rule with the rule of a coherent public will and sanctified the claims of individual conscience as opposed to party loyalty gained increasing acceptance. The result in recent decades has been to blur, if not obliterate, the distinctions between representative government and pure democracy that were articles of faith for the Framers and to reduce the force of party to voluntary agreement on ideal goals to the detriment of party identification and loyalty.

All these factors reinforced one another. Plebiscitary politics was well suited to a politics that was dependent on policy goals, not patronage, and media, not party machines. It also substantially increased the costs of campaigns, which severely stressed another key function of traditional party organizations. The nationalization of politics combined with political polarization to resuscitate levels of baseline party voting and reduce switch-ticket voting, despite the decline in the strength of state and local party organizations. Purist notions of democracy legitimated plebiscitary politics, encouraged the dismantling of state and local party organizations, and privileged ideology as a basis for party allegiance. Equally if not more important, all these factors contributed to the president's dominance of the party system. A party system in which president far outranks state and party leaders in organizational resources and fund-raising ability and in which the nationalization of politics, plebiscitary politics, and polarized parties combine to make the president his party's prime symbol and spokesman is a party system that is subject to his initiative and direction.

As might be expected, the impacts of these forces were not confined to presidential elections. Congressional elections also became candidate centered, more poll and media driven, more responsive to national issues and polarized politics, and more costly. However, the effects went beyond mere mirroring of the features of presidential elections. Organizationally, the roles of national party committees and congressional party units expanded to fill the void created by the decline of state and local parties. Such units have become heavily involved in recruiting and training candidates, voter turnout, fund raising, coordinating campaigns across the nation and within the states, and recommending media specialists and pollsters. The decline in traditional party organizational activity has thus given rise to new forms of party involvement in service to local candidates—but through national units controlled by or responsive to agents of the president or the party nominee. Moreover, it is not only national party units, but the presidency itself that has become more directly involved in congressional elections. This can be seen in the larger role the White House now plays in candidate recruitment and fund raising in Senate races and in the substantial increase in presidential appearances on behalf of party candidates in both houses. Finally, plebiscitary politics has led to the emergence of a "permanent campaign," to a merger of the processes of campaigning and governing in which the mobilizing of support through intense and continuing interaction with the public has become a prime ingredient in governing as well as elections. In a presidentially led and polarized party system, such a form of politics advantages presidential power. Members of Congress must coordinate and even subordinate their policy positions to the more general messages of their parties, messages that the president defines for his party not only in election campaigns but in policy struggles between elections in anticipation of upcoming elections.

Nonetheless, if presidential power in the electoral system has increased, this does not mean that congressional elections do not retain a substantial amount of independence in their determinants and effects. The expansion of the role of the federal government has enlarged, not diminished, the personal electoral advantages that members can derive from delivering program benefits to their states and districts. In addition, neither the nationalization of politics nor partisan polarization has destroyed regional variation in policy orientations and attitudes. As a result, localism continues to play a greater role in determining the outcomes of congressional than presidential elections. Nor do results at the individual level necessarily translate in a consistent fashion to the aggregate level. Safety at the individual level has increased because the service component of the incumbency effect has remained strong and been reinforced by the impacts of increased partisan coherence and redistricting in reducing the heterogeneity of districts. Increased safety for members, however, does not mean that majority margins in Congress cannot diminish, as the regional compositions of the parties change and the ranks of the former majority are thinned not only by replacement but, more importantly, by retirement, party switching, and redistricting. This is what happened in the 1990s after several decades of growing Republican strength in the South. Nor does it mean that a single party coalition will dominate elections to all the branches of government, as the Republican and New Deal coalitions did in the first half of the twentieth century. Indeed, since the 1960s presidential elections overall have been more volatile and competitive than congressional elections, and coattail effects that once were strong have been inconsistent and marginal. After a long hiatus, divided government has thus become a recurrent feature of American politics, just as it was between 1867 and 1896. In important regards, then, the presidentialization of the election system has been restrained by features of our political system that are rooted in constitutionally designed differences in the character of constituencies and terms of office within and between the branches.

It is true as well that a plebiscitary and polarized party system led by the president involves weaknesses not present in the traditional party system. In part, this is due to the greater volatility of a party system that is hinged on personalized, presidential leadership and ideological coherence rather than party organization and identification. In part, it is due to the greater power of interest groups. As the stakes of politics increased, the costs of campaigns exploded, and party was transformed into an entity that was more dependent on policy agreement than allegiance and patronage, interest groups both proliferated and gained increased power through their ability to mobilize the votes of their members and to fund campaigns through PACs. They ceased being junior partners in electoral coalitions and became allies that presidential and congressional candidates had to accommodate and feared to disappoint. In part, however, it is also due to changes in campaign finance law since the 1970s. Initially, "hard money" contributions in direct support of candidates, whether individual or through PACs, were limited, but "soft money" contributions for voter mobilization and issue ads were not. The result was not only that the national parties assumed a substantial role in raising and spending "soft money," but also that independent "527" groups (labeled for the section of the tax code that frees them from taxation) began to be created for similar purposes. The most recent changes in campaign finance law banning "soft money" contributions to national parties have greatly enhanced the importance of such groups to the detriment of the role of parties in campaigns.

In sum, then, the election system that emerged in the last decades of the twentieth century is a very different one than the traditional party system, even in its attenuated midcentury form. Practice and doctrine in the modern election system have both liberated the president from the constraints of the traditional party system and transformed the party system into a bastion of presidential power, not congressional power. It is true that the disconnects that continue to exist between congressional and presidential elections preserve a basis for congressional autonomy. It is true as well that a party system tied to a personalized presidency is a party system with greater potential for functional displacement than a party system tied to strong state and local party organizations. Nonetheless, the fundamental reality of the modern election system is the high degree to which the president is now the focal point of the party system.

The Legislative System

The late 1960s also mark a turning point in the development of the modern legislative system.[8] This is the period of the breakdown of the "Textbook Congress," a distinctive type of Congress that was the successor to the Congresses of the 1920s and 1930s and far more stable, even though it involved lower levels of leadership power and party voting. The Textbook Congress thus marks not only an end point in the transition from the Congresses of the turn of the twentieth century but also the departure point in the transition to the Congresses of the twenty-first century.

The catalyst for the emergence of the Textbook Congress was a deep and continuing split that developed in the late 1930s between the southern and northern wings of the Democratic Party at a time when southern Democrats in both houses constituted roughly half of the majority party and included its most senior members. The result was to make the Textbook Congress one in which party leaders were weak, committees strong, and majority party rule quite vulnerable to challenge by a conservative, cross-partisan coalition. In the House, the Speaker was reduced to functioning as a mediator or broker between divergent wings of the party, who deferred to the committee chairs and avoided violations of seniority or use of party mechanisms, so as not to exacerbate internal divisions. In the Senate, committees and committee chairs were even stronger and the party leadership even weaker. The rules and customs of the Senate combined with a divided majority party to deliver the Senate into the hands of a clique of senior senators, largely southern in composition. These senators dominated the key Senate committees, used the party committee on committees as well as their committee positions to enforce a set of norms that bolstered their power, and in alliance with conservative Republicans could defeat any legislation they opposed. The Senate thus assumed the aura of a "club" in which northern Democrats were excluded from power.

However, it was not only decentralization and cross-partisan rule that defined the Congresses of the mid-twentieth century. It was presidential leadership as well. In the Textbook Congress, even more than in the 1930s, congressional party leaders, with little internal organizational power and more divided parties, had little choice but to rely on the president to set policy goals and provide political muscle. Such reliance dovetailed with a dramatic and parallel enhancement of the organizational resources of the president. In 1939 an Executive Office of the President (EOP) was created that included among other units a White House Office and the Bureau of the Budget. These two units, and others added in the 1940s, institutionalized and extended the president's ability to define and coordinate policy initiatives, control agency legislative requests, and apply pressure in the legislative process. Finally, as is not surprising, doctrinal change joined with political and organizational factors to entrench presidential leadership. The dynamic leadership of President Franklin Roosevelt in responding to the depression obliterated the remnants of Whig theory that had continued to play a role in the restraint shown by his Republican predecessors. By the 1950s prominent theorists of the presidency, such as Richard Neustadt, simply assumed that an active and skilled president was the key to the attainment of the public interest and saw the primary problem of American politics as the successful exercise of presidential power.

Despite its longevity, the Textbook Congress was not immutable. In both the House and the Senate the election of 1958 increased the number of northern, liberal Democrats to roughly two-thirds of the majority party. In the Senate, the decline in the prevailing structure of power was swift. By the mid-1960s the passage of the Civil Rights Acts and the appointment of substantial numbers of liberal Democrats to the party unit that controlled committee assignments demonstrated that the oligarchic power of a clique of southern Senators had substantially eroded. By the early 1970s the number of positions on important committees had been increased to accommodate northern Democrats. In addition, TV and the increasing nationalization of politics led Senators to see themselves as actors on a national stage who should function as generalists, not specialists, across a variety of issues and be guided by their own policy views and political ambitions. As a result, during the 1970s the number of votes on the floor substantially increased as did the number and range of filibusters. At the same time party voting declined to levels even lower than in the Textbook Congress, and the traditional norms of specialization, apprenticeship, and reciprocity that had buttressed oligarchic rule substantially eroded. The ordered and "clubby" Senate of the Textbook Congress was no more, replaced by a Senate marked by individualism and disarray.

In the House the election of a partisan Republican president, Richard Nixon, in 1968 ignited northern Democratic discontent that had been damped down for a decade by the opposition of the Speaker and the accomplishments of Democratic presidents. The result was a series of reforms in caucus rules in the first half of the 1970s that substantially increased the power of northern Democrats and junior members. The most important changes concerned secret ballot election in caucus of all standing committee chairs and appropriations subcommittee chairs, Speaker control of Democratic appointments to the Rules Committee, and subcommittee reforms to limit the power of chairs. In addition, changes in House rules and in law imposed additional limits on the power of chairs and eliminated the historic ban on recorded roll call votes in committee of the whole. As in the Senate, however, party voting declined to historically low levels due to the emergence of new issues and the continuing presence of the southern Democratic–Republican coalition. Neither could the caucus, though now resuscitated, nor a newly created policy or steering committee compensate for the destruction of the old system of power. Thus, in the House as well as the

Senate, a key immediate result of the demise of the Textbook Congress was unanticipated—the majority leadership lost much of its ability to control proceedings on the floor.

Nonetheless, the Congresses of the 1970s proved to be just an interlude. Congress was subject to the same forces that were changing the electoral system, albeit in a less immediate manner. If initially levels of party voting declined as the New Deal party system broke down, they began to climb as a new party system emerged and gained strength. Over the course of several decades the Republican electoral coalition became more consistently conservative, as increased strength in the South was added to traditional support in the Midwest and Great Plains, and strength in the Northeast and sections of the Mid-Atlantic and Pacific Coast declined. The flip side of these changes was just as important—the Democratic Party became more consistently liberal. The result at the legislative level was to make the House and Senate parties more consistently liberal or conservative and, by heightening party unity, to generate increases in party voting that by the mid-1980s signaled the onset of a new era and by the mid-1990s approached pre-1910 levels.

The effects of change in the election system on the legislative system were, however, not limited to increased partisan polarization, nor was this result tied only to increasing internal coherence within the electoral coalitions of the two parties. The secular, rolling realignment that destroyed the New Deal party system and manifested itself first in presidential elections, then Senate elections, and finally House elections also enhanced the difficulty of a single party controlling election results in all three sets of constituencies that underpin the House, Senate, and presidency. Thus, despite an increase in the number and salience of national issues, the years after 1970 were marked by recurrent instances of divided government, which in turn reinforced party polarization, increased congressional resistance to the president, and gave new strategic importance to the president's veto power. A final aspect of change was a factor, also discussed earlier, that developed in tandem with polarized politics and divided government—the growth of plebiscitary politics. The blurring of the distinction between campaigning and governing increased the centrality of the president in the legislative process, though not necessarily his success. Given both message politics and party polarization, the need for congressional parties to frame policies in relation to their support or opposition to the president intensified. In the end, then, whether government was unified or divided, the incentives for party members to unite and engage in blame-game politics in relation to the positions of the president substantially increased.

As a result, a new type of Congress came into existence in the latter half of the 1980s that was quite different from the Textbook Congress. Houses and Senates that were more partisan, more message driven, and more politicized in their relationships to the president and the electorate emerged and became increasingly defined by these features. In the House, the leadership regained control of the floor in the 1980s due to the cumulative effects of a variety of new mechanisms that added to leadership power, such as multiple referral, restrictive rules, and the streamlining of suspension, as well as heightened party discipline and the continuing effects of the 1970s reforms in committee appointments. The Democratic Houses from 1985 to 1993 were thus characterized by higher levels of party voting, more powerful party leaders, and an adversarial relationship to Republican presidents. The transition to a Republican House in 1995 did not diminish these features but strengthened them. The Republicans adopted the mechanisms of leadership power they inherited from the Democrats and extended them by establishing a new committee on committees controlled by the Speaker and further downgrading the role of seniority. In addition, the smaller majority margins that accompanied this transition, combined with increases in levels of party voting, resulted in even firmer leadership direction of committee outcomes and floor proceedings both to attain party policy goals and to protect the clarity of party messages. Indeed, when narrow margins were combined with unified government, as they were in the 108th Congress, they induced even more aggressive use of leadership power—prolonging floor votes until a majority could be cobbled together, denying minority members a role in conferences, and denying projects to Democrats who voted against the funding bill. An inevitable result has been an increase in partisan hostility to levels that have severely diminished traditional practices of disagreeing without being disagreeable and forming friendships across party lines.

The modern Senate has also been marked by high levels of partisanship, divided government, and plebiscitary politics. Nonetheless, the Senate remains a very different body than the House. The Senate did act to rein in the filibuster by decreasing the number of votes required for cloture to sixty and by adopting majority cloture in limited areas, for example, budget votes. Nonetheless, the Senate's refusal to abandon unanimous consent as its preferred method of conducting business, to impose majority cloture, or even to adopt a germaneness rule made it far less able than the House to regain control of its proceedings. Rather, in an age in which the touchstone of party is ideology, the Senate could grow more partisan while still remaining highly individualistic. The modern Senate is thus a body in which sixty votes are key to passing major measures, but very difficult to achieve both because of partisan conflict and because party margins narrowed even earlier than in the House. It is a body in which action on the floor often supersedes action in committee and in which the role of party leaders focuses on parliamentary maneuver and oscillates between seeking partisan advantage to gain public favor and seeking bipartisan support to elicit the sixty votes needed to pass legislation. There has thus been less difference in the operation of Democratic Senates before 1995 and Republican Senates after 1995 than in the case of the House. Nonetheless, partisan maneuvering has increased as the stakes of politics have increased. So too has partisan hostility as a consequence of the manner in which the supermajoritarian features of the Senate pit the majority against the minority on issues in which feelings are intense. The extension of the filibuster to judicial nominations illustrates both. Yet, ironically enough, the difficulty of passing legislation in the Senate has given the Senate the whip hand in resolving conflicts between the bodies. Moreover, if the disjunction between partisanship and action that exists in the Senate does not exist in the House, the result is to force the House majority leadership, especially when government is unified, to be even more rigidly partisan than it might otherwise be.

In sum, the fact that the modern Congress is once again highly partisan does not mean that the modern legislative system operates in much the same way as in the days of Cannon and Aldrich. Heightened partisanship in the modern Congress no longer means greater congressional power and effectiveness. What it means in divided government is inaction and plebiscitary politics. What it means in unified government is use of party and party leaders as instruments of the president, especially in the House, as well as plebiscitary politics.[9] As a result, congressional power in the legislative process now rests far more on divided government, slim majority margins, and the filibuster and far less on leadership structures and electoral linkages that are independent of the president.

The Administrative System

Once again the late 1960s mark the beginnings of dramatic change in the character of presidential power.[10] Although the dangers of the post–World War II era allowed the president to exercise unprecedented power in national security affairs without a declaration of war, his power in domestic affairs was far less affected. Rather, he continued to be constrained by the character of the party system, weakened as it might be from the late nineteenth century, and by the compartmentalized issues and decentralized politics of the Textbook Congress. After 1970, however, a sizable expansion in welfare and regulatory programs under Presidents Johnson and Nixon, the growth of a plebiscitary and personalized party system, and recurrent periods of divided government provided the incentives and conditions for narrowing the gap between the president's power as chief executive and his power as commander-in-chief.

In both regards, doctrinal changes played an important role. In national security affairs, a consensus in favor of the president's authority to act unilaterally to deploy troops abroad and to initiate hostilities emerged in the early 1950s in response to communist threats in Europe and Korea and, though shaken by the Vietnam War, still prevails. In domestic affairs, proponents of presidential power embraced past doctrines regarding the inherent executive power of the president and his primacy as a representative of the people and integrated them with more recent claims from the public administration literature regarding the need for central coordination and management. The result was a rationale for presidential power that made presidential control of the executive branch the governing standard in all areas of policy and, as in the case of the legislative process, transformed previously accepted constraints on presidential power into problems to be combated and overcome. Equally important, presidents increasingly began to see themselves as peculiarly, if not exclusively, responsible for the public interest, not only in matters of national security but in matters of domestic policy as well.

The changes in doctrine regarding the president's role and power as chief executive, combined with changes in the character of national politics after 1970, propelled the rise of an administrative presidency to accompany a growing administrative state. Four strategies were pursued to increase presidential power in domestic policy that mimicked prior strategies in foreign and defense policy. The first was to take firmer control of the selection of political appointments to top policymaking positions in the executive branch. In national security affairs important steps in this direction had been taken in the 1940s and 1950s by creating a Department of Defense and tightening presidential control of top officials in the State and Defense Departments. However, it was the Nixon administration that first understood that the traditional White House posture of deferring to the desires of department heads and national party officials would no longer suffice in any area of policy. After some retrogression under President Carter, the White House Personnel Office became an instrument for imposing routinized and comprehensive control of all political nominees to ensure that they were loyal to the policies of the administration and strong enough not to become the captives of career bureaucrats.

A second strategy was to increase overhead or central control of executive policymaking. As in the case of reliance on the National Security Council in foreign and defense policy, this strategy involved reliance on an institutionalized presidency, expanded in size and function, and particularly on key staff in the White House Office and the Office of Management and Budget (OMB; as the Budget Bureau was renamed in 1970). As a result, and in line with their reduced status and importance in the party system, cabinet officers became far more subject, both in terms of policy decisions and public pronouncements, to White House direction and far more dispensable when they resisted White House control.[11] In addition, in the 1980s departmental and agency rule making, a prime mechanism of executive policymaking, was subjected to control through OMB review, and since the mid-1990s such control has involved presidential direction in setting policy goals prior to the formulation and review of specific proposed rules. The president and his lieutenants thus now supervise the exercise of rule making power in a host of areas that have direct and immediate effects on the lives of citizens—for example, carbon dioxide emissions, food labeling, the privacy of medical records, and auto safety standards.

A third strategy mimicked another prime strategy for expanding presidential power in national security affairs—unilateral action to define and control policy. In national security affairs, a variety of ways of exercising presidential authority exist, but reliance is often placed on national security directives prepared by the National Security Council and signed by the president. In domestic affairs, executive orders have long been the principal mechanism because the constitutional basis for action is tied to presidential authority over the implementation of law. In recent decades, however, presidents have increasingly begun to use such orders for purposes that are far from closely related to the statutory provisions on which they are ostensibly based. They have rather become an instrument for advancing presidential policy goals; for example, the executive orders establishing OMB rule-making review, authorizing $40 billion in loan guarantees to stabilize Mexican currency, creating and empowering a faith-based initiatives agency, and promoting affirmative action through government contracting. A fourth and final strategy, increasingly prevalent in areas of domestic policy as well as defense and foreign policy, is an expansion in assertions of executive privilege, in refusals to provide information on the content, grounds, or processes of executive decision making requested by Congress. Such claims have broadened since the late 1960s, particularly under Clinton and Bush.

All these strategies have enhanced presidential power. Nonetheless, the effects of the increases in presidential power that have occurred should not be exaggerated. In national security policy, Vietnam broke the bipartisan agreement and habits of deference that were the heritage of World War II. Thus, although Congress's attempt through the War Powers Resolution to control unilateral presidential action failed, presidents have in cases of major conflict "voluntarily" sought congressional approval. In addition, they can encounter difficulty and even, as in the cases of Vietnam and Nicaragua, defeat in attempting to secure the congressional support they require to sustain and fund their policies. Finally, though the treaty provisions of the Constitution have largely been bypassed through the use of executive agreements, presidents continue to rely on treaties or legislation in important areas of foreign and trade policy that are highly controversial.

In domestic policy the increased power of an administrative presidency has been checked by growth in the power of federal courts and interest groups. The federal courts since the 1970s have both subjected administrative rule making to more stringent procedural review and interpreted the authorizing statutes far more expansively in terms of their own sense of what the broad purposes of these statutes require. The result has been a judicialization of the administrative system in which statutory interpretation and procedural review have provided a broad platform for judicial intervention, and by so doing increased opportunities for interest groups to use the courts to contest administrative decisions. The most formidable challenges to departmental and agency rules now come more often from interest groups acting through the courts, not from Congress. The irony is that the power of the federal courts has been resurrected to a position closer to that occupied in the late nineteenth century, but with less restraint in the actual language of statutes or respect for congressional prerogatives

As for the Congress, the emergence of an administrative presidency has redefined but not destroyed the balance of power between the branches. Congress's traditional prerogatives over legislation and appropriations continue to provide important sources of leverage in controlling executive decision making. Congress's ability to define clear standards in legislation is variable but not absent. It can also compensate for deficiencies in such standards by specifying decision rules and procedural restrictions in statutes. In both cases Congress "loads the dice" in favor of its policy desires by enhancing the ability of courts and interest groups to serve as guardians of its intent. In addition, Congress has a variety of oversight mechanisms available. Short-term authorizations that require agencies to secure congressional approval of their programs periodically and annual appropriations review, combined with the selective use of "riders," provide leverage for forcing concessions and bolstering informal committee influence. Nor has bureaucratic power disappeared. The scope and complexity of modern policy problems sustain patterns of bureaucratic politics that the White House cannot eliminate and may at times simply have to endure. Similarly, individual bureaucrats retain considerable power, grounded in their longevity, the barriers to monitoring, and the president's need for proactive support, not simply grudging acquiescence. Finally, though the nationalization of politics has reduced the power of the states, the anchoring of the national government in federalism provides a basis for reassertions of state power, as does the federal government's need to win the cooperation of the states by accommodating the substantial regional differences that exist.

Yet, if the impacts of expanded presidential power should not be exaggerated, neither should they be denied. Though the days of bipartisan agreement and deference to presidential leadership in national security affairs are long gone, by the 1990s the presidency had regained most of the ground it lost after Vietnam. Presidential power remains strongly rooted in the harsh demands of providing for national security under modern conditions and has been bolstered both by changes in practice that have become hard precedents and by the growth of plebiscitary politics. That the War Powers Resolution has been ignored by presidents is thus no surprise. Nor is the fact that presidents do not often lose when they ask Congress for support. As events from World War II to Iraq demonstrate, national security crises augment presidential power, and the true limits are political and highly dependent on policy difficulties or failures.

In domestic policy congressional control of executive policymaking has also declined, despite Congress's legislative and appropriations powers and despite its efforts to reform the budget process, enhance its staff resources, and increase the number of oversight hearings.[12] Congress rarely succeeds in reversing executive orders or rules in legislation it originates, and it cannot easily or routinely force major concessions from the executive in reauthorizing legislation or the appropriations process. Nor can the basic weaknesses of post hoc control be remedied by seeking to load the dice in favor of the policies congressional legislation is intended to serve. The ambiguities that are now often present in legislation grant executive officials wide latitude and allow the courts and interest groups to pursue their own goals as much, if not more, than to safeguard Congress's goals. The barriers that limit congressional power thus derive from integral features of contemporary politics—the substantive complexities that force broad delegations of discretion, the president's enhanced capacity for overhead control, the difficulties of assembling majorities without fudging key provisions, and the harsh constraints imposed on Congress's ability to act against the executive when majorities are slim, party loyalty is equated with presidential support, and the president can veto all matters not backed by supermajorities in both houses.

As for the bureaucracy, though bureaucratic power and politics remain far from negligible, the president is now clearly in charge. He can use White House and OMB staff to control major policy decisions. The infighting that occurs is thus largely to gain his favor. Similarly, the president can use his staff resources as well as executive orders to outflank or neutralize foot-dragging. The situation with respect to the states is similar, though more uneven. Recently, federal power and control have declined, as illustrated by the increased flexibility accorded the states in student testing and welfare and increased political and judicial opposition to federal mandates that stretch state financial resources. Still, federal control of state policymaking expanded so substantially after 1960 that the retracement that has occurred has recovered only a part of what was lost.

In sum, then, once again profound changes in the society, economy, and international position of the United States during the second half of the twentieth century generated profound change in the political system. In the case of the administrative system a huge expansion in executive responsibility and discretion could not be deterred and was accompanied by a corresponding increase in the stakes of politics and significant changes in the character of politics and doctrine. The result was to magnify the inducements and opportunities for presidents to expand their prerogatives and control in all areas of executive decision making and to lead Congress to provide the institutional mechanisms and accept the basic practices of presidential power. That an administrative presidency in domestic affairs and a presidency with even greater ability to act unilaterally in national security affairs has arisen is thus no accident but a response to the underlying realities of the twentieth century.

Conclusion

If the late nineteenth century was the age of Congress, it is the presidency, not Congress, that has become the driving force in modern politics. The dynamics of this reversal are powered by the altered positions of the president and Congress in our basic systems of governance. Just as congressional preeminence in the late nineteenth century derived from Congress's position in the electoral, legislative, and administrative systems, presidential preeminence in the modern political system derives from the president's position in these systems and the ways in which power in one system translates into power in the others. Nonetheless, care must still be taken not to transform the results of complex patterns of change into a caricature. Although the configurations of power have been altered in all three systems, the American political system continues to involve all the traditional units, and all retain significant roles in a complex and variable pattern of relationships. The constitutional design, though buffeted and frayed by the winds of change, remains in place and continues to constrain the modern presidency, despite its increased stature and power.

Future Prospects

The new baselines that have been set in the operation of representative government in the United States are both challenging and dangerous. Presidential power and plebiscitary politics, in themselves and in combination with partisan polarization, threaten the deliberative and accommodative qualities that are the hallmarks of representative government. One can argue that such patterns of politics are nonetheless apt responses to the needs to expand the capacity for governmental action and to make government more "democratic." Yet even aside from the stark departures from Madisonian notions of representative government these patterns involve, there are immense practical costs. The price of the advantages conferred on the president is constant attention to public and group opinion, constant success in leading them, and constant engagement in taking credit or avoiding blame. Given the inability to dictate events, as well as the difficulties that stem from the hard choices modern politics in America involves, the irony is that in the end plebiscitary politics provides only a fickle and trying basis for presidential power. Even worse, in combination with the high stakes of modern politics and polarized parties, the degree of venom and rigidity it breeds poisons the processes of democratic politics. Both majority and minority partisans, in their ideological zeal, are tempted to believe that the only thing that matters is political victory, no matter what the damage done to the national interest and to the levels of mutual trust, tolerance, and self-discipline that are so necessary for the viability of democratic politics.

Thus, what is most worrisome about the state of the union as we enter the twenty-first century is not that the balance of power now favors the president. It is rather the long-term trend in the direction of presidential power and the precariousness of representative government in a politics that is as highly personalized, media dominated, and event driven as ours has become. Certainly, the reappearance of a majority party coalition able to dominate both houses of Congress would further enhance presidential power. But even if that does not occur, the forces that have driven presidential power in the twentieth century remain strong and will be intensified by crises as well as by prolonged inability to solve pressing national problems legislatively. The growth of presidential power is thus not likely to abate unless the demands on government diminish and/or the president's preeminence in the party system declines. However, in this new age of terrorism such demands are likely to increase, to further blur the distinctions between national security and domestic policy, and to enhance the preeminence of the presidency in all arenas of politics. Yet if the presidency becomes more powerful, it will nonetheless remain insecure. The breadth and depth of the expectations concentrated in the presidency, combined with the difficulty of the problems, produce a situation in which the president is continually on trial. If history is any guide, a political system in which executive leadership is powerful and capable of growing more powerful, and at the same time personal, plebiscitary, and beset by difficult problems, is one that poses a harsh test for the future of republican government.

In the nineteenth century, leaders who were principled, humane, and politically gifted and a people capable of rising above their political biases and immediate self-interest were critical necessities only occasionally. In the twenty-first century, the bar for the preservation of liberty will be much higher.

Notes

1. Woodrow Wilson, *Congressional Government* (Baltimore: Johns Hopkins University Press, 1981).
2. For material on the election system in the late nineteenth and early twentieth centuries see James Bryce, *The American Commonwealth* (New York: Macmillan, 1901), Vol. 2; Michael McGerr, *The Decline of Popular Politics* (New York: Oxford University Press, 1986); Jeffrey Tulis, *The Rhetorical Presidency* (Princeton: Princeton University Press, 1987); Everett C. Ladd, *American Political Parties* (New York: Norton, 1970); Morton Keller, *Affairs of State* (Cambridge: Harvard University Press, 1977). See also Richard Ellis, "Accepting the Nomination," in *Speaking to the People: The Rhetorical Presidency in Historical Perspective,* ed. Richard Ellis (Amherst: University of Massachusetts Press, 1998), 112–134, and Daniel Tichenor and Richard Harris, "Organized Interests and American Political Development," *Political Science Quarterly* 117 (winter 2002–2003): 587–612.
3. For material on the legislative system in the late nineteenth and early twentieth centuries see Wilson, *Congressional Government;* Bryce, *American Commonwealth,* Vol. 1; Leonard White, *The Republican Era* (New York: Free Press, 1958); Lauros McConachie, *Congressional Committees* (Boston: Crowell, 1898); David Rothman, *Power and Politics* (New York: Athenaeum, 1969); and Sarah Binder, *Minority Rights, Majority Rule* (Cambridge: Cambridge University Press, 1997). See also Joseph Cooper and Elizabeth Rybicki, "Analyzing Institutional Change" and Gerald Gamm and Steven Smith, "Emergence of Senate Party Leadership," in *U.S. Senate Exceptionalism,* ed. Bruce I. Oppenheimer (Columbus: Ohio State University Press, 2002), 182–211 and 212–241; Joseph Cooper and David Brady, "Institutional Context and Leadership Style: The House from Cannon to Rayburn," *American Political Science Review* 75 (June 1981): 411–425; and David Brady and David Epstein, "Intraparty Preferences, Heterogeneity, and the Origins of the Modern Congress," *Journal of Law, Economics, and Organization* 13 (April 1997): 26–48. For evidence on congressional party voting see Joseph Cooper and Garry Young, "Party and Preference in Congressional Decision Making," in *Party, Process, and Political Change in Congress,* ed. David Brady and Mathew McCubbins (Stanford: Stanford University Press, 2002), 64–107; and Steven Smith and Gerald Gamm, "The Dynamics of Party Government in Congress," in *Congress Reconsidered,* 7th ed., ed. Lawrence C. Dodd and Bruce I. Oppenheimer (Washington, D.C.: CQ Press, 2001), 245–269.
4. George Hoar, *Autobiography of Seventy Years* (New York: Scribner's, 1903), Vol. 2, 46.
5. Wilfred Binkley, *President and Congress* (New York: Knopf, 1947), 181.
6. For material on the administrative system in the late nineteenth and early twentieth centuries, see Wilson, *Congressional Government*; Ballard Campbell, *The Growth of American Government* (Bloomington: Indiana University Press, 1995); Stephen Skowronek, *Building a New American State* (Cambridge: Cambridge University Press, 1982); White, *The Republican Era;* Bryce, *American Commonwealth,* Vol. 1; Daniel Carpenter, *The Forging of Bureaucratic Autonomy* (Princeton: Princeton University Press, 2001); and Arthur Schlesinger, *The Imperial Presidency* (Boston: Houghton Mifflin, 1973).

7. For material on the modern electoral system see Paul Abramson, John Aldrich, and David Rohde, *Change and Continuity in the 2000 and 2002 Elections* (Washington, D.C.: CQ Press, 2003); Jeffrey Stonecash, Mark Brewer, and Mack Mariani, *Diverging Parties* (Boulder: Westview Press, 2003); Allen Cigler and Burdett Loomis, *Interest Group Politics* (Washington, D.C.: CQ Press, 2002); Samuel Kernell, *Going Public* (Washington, D.C.: CQ Press, 1997); and Michael Malbin, *Life after Reform* (Lanham, Md.: Rowman and Littlefield, 2003). See also Hugh Heclo, "Campaigning and Governing: A Conspectus," in *The Permanent Campaign,* ed. Norman Ornstein and Thomas Mann (Washington, D.C.: American Enterprise Institute, 2000), 1–38; and Gary Jacobson, "Partisan Polarization in Presidential Support: The Electoral Connection," *Congress and the Presidency* 30 (spring 2003): 1–37. For material on the electoral system at midcentury and the transition to the modern electoral system see V. O. Key Jr., *Politics, Parties, and Interest Groups* (New York: Crowell, 1964); E. C. Ladd and Charles Hadley, *Transformations of the American Party System* (New York: Norton, 1975); Jack Walker, *Mobilizing Interest Groups in America* (Ann Arbor: University of Michigan Press, 1991); and Theodore Lowi, *The Personal President* (Ithaca: Cornell University Press, 1985).
8. For material on the modern legislative system see Barbara Sinclair, *Unorthodox Lawmaking* (Washington, D.C.: CQ Press, 2000); Jon Bond and Richard Fleisher, eds., *Polarized Politics* (Washington, D.C.: CQ Press, 2000); and Burdett Loomis and Wendy Schiller, *The Contemporary Congress* (Belmont: Wadsworth, 2004). See also Gary Jacobson, "Reversal of Fortune," in *Continuity and Change in House Elections,* ed. David Brady, John Cogan, and Morris Fiorina (Stanford: Stanford University Press, 2000), 10–39; and C. Lawrence Evans, "Committees, Leaders, and Message Politics," in *Congress Reconsidered,* 7th ed., ed. Lawrence C. Dodd and Bruce I. Oppenheimer (Washington, D.C.: CQ Press, 2001), 217–245. For material on the legislative system at midcentury and the transition to the modern legislative system see Barbara Sinclair, *The Transformation of the U.S. Senate* (Baltimore: Johns Hopkins University Press, 1989); Nelson Polsby, *How Congress Evolves* (New York: Oxford, 2004); and Gary Gregg, *The Presidential Republic* (Lanham, Md.: Rowman and Littlefield, 1997). See also Joseph Cooper, "The Twentieth Century Congress," in *Congress Reconsidered,* 7th ed., ed. Lawrence C. Dodd and Bruce I. Oppenheimer (Washington, D.C.: CQ Press, 2001), 335–367. For evidence on congressional party voting see Cooper and Young, "Party and Preference in Congressional Decision Making," and Smith and Gamm, "Dynamics of Party Government."
9. Indeed, in the modern Congress even the presence of cabinet members on the floor to aid party leaders in passing a presidential program seems acceptable. See David Broder, "Time Was GOP's Ally," *Washington Post,* November 23, 2003, A1.
10. For material on the modern administrative system see Thomas Weko, *The Politicizing Presidency* (Lawrence: University Press of Kansas, 1995); Kenneth Mayer, *With the Stroke of a Pen* (Princeton: Princeton University Press, 2001); Phillip Cooper, *By Order of the President* (Lawrence: University Press of Kansas, 2002); William Howell, *Power without Persuasion* (Princeton: Princeton University Press, 2003); R. Shep Melnick, *Between the Lines* (Washington, D.C.: Brookings Institution Press, 1994); and Martha Derthick, *Keeping the Compound Republic* (Washington, D.C.: Brookings Institution Press, 2002). See also Elena Kagan, "Presidential Administration," *Harvard Law Review* 114 (June 2001): 2246–2385; Joel Aberbach, "What Happened to the Watchful Eye," *Congress and the Presidency* 29 (spring 2002): 3–25; Jeffrey Hill and James Brazier, "Constraining Administrative Decisions," *Journal of Law, Economics, and Organization* 7 (fall 1991): 373–400; William West, "Searching for a Theory of Bureaucratic Structure," *Journal of Public Administration Research and Theory* 7 (October 1997): 591–613; and I. M. Destler, "Congress and Foreign Policy at Century's End," in *Congress Reconsidered,* 7th ed., ed. Lawrence C. Dodd and Bruce I. Oppen-

heimer (Washington, D.C.: CQ Press, 2001), 315–335. For material on the administrative system at midcentury and the transition to the modern administrative system see James Sundquist, *The Decline and Resurgence of Congress* (Washington, D.C.: Brookings Institution Press, 1981); Sidney Milkis, *The President and the Parties* (New York: Oxford University Press, 1993); Mark Rozell, *Executive Privilege* (Baltimore: Johns Hopkins University Press, 1994); and Gordon Silverstein, *Imbalance of Power* (New York: Oxford University Press, 1997).

11. For illustrative evidence note the travails of Paul O'Neill in Ron Suskind, *The Price of Loyalty* (New York: Simon and Schuster, 2004). Note also Interior Secretary Bruce Babbitt's boast that 80 percent of Clinton's policy goals regarding the public lands were accomplished by executive order, despite congressional opposition, and Tommy Thompson's wry comment that as a Bush cabinet member he reported to the White House and OMB. See Matt Kelley, "Babbitt, Changing Rules Will Hurt GOP," *Washington Post,* January 8, 2001, and Alexandra Starr, "Muzzling 'King Tommy'," *Business Week,* May 7, 2001, 76.
12. The legislative veto, the most promising device that Congress developed for countering the growth in executive power, was vitiated by a Supreme Court decision in 1983 that, in effect, made it contingent on a two-thirds vote instead of a simple majority vote. See Joseph Cooper, "The Legislative Veto in the 1980s," in *Congress Reconsidered,* 3rd ed., ed. Lawrence C. Dodd and Bruce I. Oppenheimer, (Washington, D.C.: CQ Press, 1985), 364–389.

17. African Americans and the New Politics of Inclusion: A Representational Dilemma?

Kerry L. Haynie

By the end of the 1970s, it was readily apparent that African Americans were no longer excluded from representation in Congress. African American representatives have now become firmly rooted fixtures on the congressional landscape. For example, in each of the last five congresses (104th–108th), they have made up at least 9 percent of the total membership of the House of Representatives. Notwithstanding the fact that their representation in the House falls well short of being proportionate to their presence in the population, and although they have never made up more than 1 percent of the membership in any one session of the U.S. Senate, their recent levels of representation in the House denote a tremendous gain in the access that African Americans as a group have to an important deliberative and policymaking institution.

From the time that they were first elected to Congress in the 1870s to the present, African American representatives collectively have been the leading proponents of a legislative agenda that seeks to address the particular and sometimes distinctive needs of African Americans and other disadvantaged minorities. Historically, these legislators have attempted, first and foremost, to be the agents or conduits of minority economic, political, and social advancement. In other words, over the years African Americans in Congress by and large have played the role of race representative, advocating a targeted, race-conscious agenda that, if fully enacted, would likely have resulted in noticeable changes in the social and economic policy status quo.[1]

Race representatives emerged and became prominent when there was a rigid system of separation in American society in general and a firm wall of segregation between blacks and whites in housing, education, and in particular, political power.[2] Coming from racially isolated and segregated environments, in which the majority of the inhabitants were economically and socially distressed, race representatives tended to practice a politics that almost always put matters of race above all others. Race representatives frequently adopted or were cast in the role of "outsiders"—meaning politicians who often do not conform to the norms and traditions of the institutions in which they operate.[3] This race representative role was clearly well suited for African Americans in Congress during periods when they were few in number and lacked sufficient allies to help them advance their agenda. For example, Richard Champagne and Leroy Rieselbach argue that at the time of the founding of the Congressional Black Caucus in 1971, black legislators "had few incentives or opportunities to engage in conventional legislative politics . . . . they lacked the ability to bargain from positions of strength and instead were forced to make their views known outside the normal legislative process."[4]

Thus, as has become increasingly clear over the past twenty years, physical presence (that is, descriptive representation) and symbolic-outsider or protest politics are not enough to guarantee a group meaningful inclusion in deliberations or measurable influence over policy decisions. Several scholars, most notably, Rufus P. Browning, Dale R. Marshall and, David H. Tabb, have persuasively argued that African American officeholders must achieve *political incorporation* as a precondition to having a significant effect on government policies and programs. The term "political incorporation" refers to the extent to which a group is represented in important coalitions in policymaking institutions and the degree to which the group has been able to achieve positions from which it can exercise sustained influence over policy agendas.[5] Relative to race and representation in governing institutions, Browning, Marshall, and Tabb's landmark study precipitated among academics, activists, and politicians what can rightly be called a "new politics of inclusion." This new politics of inclusion shifted attention away from an almost exclusive concern with the number or percentage of a cohesive political subgroup, such as African Americans, present in a legislative body toward an interest in how well such groups are strategically placed in formal institutional positions of power. This new politics of inclusion explicitly recognizes that political incorporation is an important factor in the linkages between descriptive and substantive representation.

African Americans in the U.S. House of Representatives have greatly improved their status in terms of seniority, party leadership positions, and overall institutional power over the past three decades.[6] During this period, there has also been significant growth in the numbers of Hispanics and white women in the Democratic legislative caucus who are potential coalition partners in pressing a progressive legislative agenda. With rising levels of incorporation, black members of the House increasingly find themselves in positions to have a more effectual voice in policymaking debates, within both the Democratic Party and the House as a whole. According to Champagne and Rieselbach, as a result of an increase in their institutional power, African American members "have increasingly been drawn into the maelstrom of bargaining, compromising, and coalition-building politics that characterizes an individualistic House of Representatives."[7] They proclaim that African American members can now be viewed as "skilled 'insiders' in ordinary, Washington-based legislative politics." [8]

This transformation of African American members of Congress from political outsiders to insiders gives rise to an important question for students of congressional politics: Have the gains in black political incorporation come at the expense of the representation of black interests? One of the many ironies of racial group politics in the United States is that in seeking to advance or enact public policies that serve the interest of racial minorities, minority group representatives must operate in a political system and within institutions—such as the U.S. Congress—that are biased against quick or drastic change and in which the advocacy of minority interests may be incongruent with professional advancement and policy successes.[9] This chapter explores this potential representation dilemma. Using data mostly from the 107th Congress (2001–2002), I examine whether the new politics of inclusion, which is concerned primarily with increased African American institutional incorporation, is associated with changes in the behavior of African American members of Congress relative to their advocacy and support of black interests.

African American Incorporation in the 107th House

When the 107th Congress was gaveled to order in 2001, there were thirty-eight African American members. All were members of the House. Thirty-seven were Democrats, fourteen were women, and they represented twenty-one states plus the District of Columbia (see Table 17-1). The twenty-one states include a state from most of the geographic regions in the country, with only the Mountain West and the Pacific Northwest not represented. Sixteen of the thirty-eight representatives (42 percent) were from the South. The districts from which the black Democrats were elected were both urban and rural and on average had populations in which African Americans made up slightly more than 50 percent of the total. Surprisingly, ten of the members represented districts that were not majority-black. Eight of those, however, had majority-minority populations. Sanford Bishop, 2nd District, Ga., and Julia Carson, 7th District, Ind., were the only African American House Democrats elected from majority-white districts.[10]

In an earlier study, I developed an African American political incorporation index especially for legislatures.[11] The index includes measures for the number of African Americans in the legislature, whether or not African Americans are in the majority party, the percentage of the Democratic Party that they constitute, the number of prestige or power committee assignments they hold, their average seniority, and the number of African Americans in leadership positions. Descriptive representation is accounted for in this conceptualization of incorporation, but the scale relies most heavily on variables that are directly associated with power and influence in legislatures. It recognizes that to achieve the capacity to exert strong and substantial influence in legislatures, African Americans not only need a continuous descriptive presence, but they also must obtain leadership positions and strategic committee assignments.

The data in Table 17-2 substantiate the assertion of increased African American incorporation in the House of Representatives. For comparison, along with data from the 107th Congress the table includes data from the 103rd and 104th. The 103rd House (1993–1994) is the last session in which African American Democrats were in the majority party. The 104th (1995–1996) marks the first session of the current era of Republican control of the House. The 107th (2001–2002) is the most recent Congress for which complete data are available.

When the Congressional Black Caucus was formed in 1971, there were just thirteen African Americans in the House. Only one of the thirteen held a leadership position, and none had an assignment on a prestige committee. As the data in Table 17-2 make clear, this situation changed dramatically in the ensuing thirty years. For example, in the 103rd Congress, the last session in which their

Table 17-1 African Americans in the 107th Congress (2001–2002)

State	District	Member	% Blacks in District	% Minorities in District
Alabama	7	Earl Hilliard	62.0	64.0
California	9	Barbara Lee	26.4	58.0
	32	Diane Watson	30.5	68.5
	35	Maxine Waters	34.7	74.0
	37	Juanita Millender-McDonald	22.5	54.7
Florida	3	Corrine Brown	49.9	57.6
	17	Carrie Meek	56.9	67.1
	23	Alcee Hastings	52.0	62.5
Georgia	2	Sanford Bishop Jr.	44.8	48.5
	4	Cynthia McKinney	53.5	64.2
	5	John Lewis	56.1	63.0
Illinois	1	Bobby Rush	65.5	70.5
	2	Jesse Jackson Jr.	62.4	70.3
	7	Danny Davis	62.0	70.2
Indiana	10	Julia Carson	29.5	35.2
Louisiana	2	William Jefferson	64.1	69.8
Maryland	4	Albert Wynn	57.3	69.7
	7	Elijah Cummings	59.1	65.1
Michigan	14	John Conyers Jr.	61.4	67.0
	15	Carolyn Cheeks Kilpatrick	60.8	68.2
Mississippi	2	Bennie Thompson	63.5	65.0
Missouri	1	William Clay	49.8	53.5
New Jersey	10	Donald Payne	57.7	71.6
New York	6	Gregory Meeks	53.9	81.1
	10	Edolphus Towns	63.0	79.0
	11	Major Owens	61.2	75.1
	15	Charles Rangel	34.6	71.8
North Carolina	1	Eva Clayton	50.7	54.6
	12	Melvin Watt	45.0	52.8
Ohio	11	Stephanie Tubbs Jones	55.9	60.3
Oklahoma	4	J. C. Watts Jr. (R)	6.7	30.3
Pennsylvania	2	Chaka Fattah	61.3	69.2
South Carolina	6	James Clyburn	57.0	59.2
Tennessee	9	Harold Ford Jr.	59.7	63.9
Texas	18	Sheila Jackson-Lee	42.5	62.9
	30	Eddie Bernice Johnson	40.8	61.1
Virginia	3	Robert Scott	56.4	61.4
D.C.	NA	Eleanor Holmes Norton	NA	NA

party was in the majority, black Democrats held nine prestigious committee assignments and thirty-two leadership positions. They included John Lewis, Ga., one of four chief deputy whips, and John Conyers Jr., Mich., and William Clay, Mo., chairs respectively of the Government Operations and the Post Office and Civil Service Committees. Although the Republican takeover in 1995 resulted in Democrats' surrendering their institutional leadership positions, the African

Table 17-2 Elements of African American Incorporation, 103rd, 104th, and 107th Congresses

	103rd (1993–1994)	104th (1995–1996)	107th (2001–2002)
Number of African Americans in House	39	38	36
% of total House membership	8.9	8.7	8.3
% of Democratic Caucus	15.1	18.1	17.6
Number leadership positions[a]	32	19	22
Number of prestige committee assignments[b]	9	6	10
Average seniority (in years)	6.0	7.9	8.8

Notes: Table includes data for African American Democrats only. There was 1 African American Republican in the 103rd Congress; there were 2 in the 104th, and 1 in the 107th House.

[a]Leadership positions include standing committee and subcommittee chairs, party whips, and membership on the Democratic Steering and Policy Committee and the Democratic Congressional Campaign Committee.

[b]Prestige Committees are Appropriations, Budget, Rules, and Ways and Means.

American legislators were able to maintain some important strategic standing in the House by virtue of maintaining power and influence within the Democratic Party's organizational hierarchy. After the change in party control, they became a larger proportion of the Democratic caucus, gained more party whip positions, and they increased their presence on the Democratic Steering and Policy Committee. In the 107th Congress, for example, John Lewis and Maxine Waters, Calif., were two of the Democrats' four chief deputy whips, and African Americans were represented on the Steering and Policy Committee in proportion to their presence in the Democratic caucus (17 percent). Thus while their overall institutional power was noticeably diminished, they remained important and invested players in the bargaining and coalition politics of the House.

Regardless of which party is in control, it is likely that future increases in African American influence in Congress will come more from increased political incorporation than from increases in the numbers of African Americans elected. That is, given the current political and legal climate regarding the creation of majority-minority legislative districts and the fact that, even under the best of circumstances, there is a finite number of such districts that can be drawn, it is likely that the number of African Americans receiving prestige committee assignments or acquiring leadership positions will increase faster than the number of additional African Americans elected to the House. Greater incorporation may be the most efficient and effective short-term strategy for ensuring the substantive representation of black interests in Congress. Yet, as mentioned above, an increased reliance on political incorporation may present African American legislators with a profound dilemma.

One cost of achieving higher levels of incorporation might be that these African Americans will be required to behave less like race men and women and display a more overt commitment to the values of the larger institution. For example, to increase their power and influence, black representatives might prioritize assignments on prestige committees over assignments on committees whose jurisdictions include traditional black interest areas. Similarly, Lucius Barker and Mack Jones argue that seeking more institutional incorporation may lead African American legislators to deracialize their agendas.[12] They define *deracialization* as "the practice of blacks articulating political demands in terms that are not racially specific so that they appeal to a broader group and presumably do not alienate those who are predisposed to oppose black efforts."[13] Because it is often linked with attempts at coalition building, deracialization is advocated by many as a useful means of integrating African Americans into political institutions and advancing black interests.[14] However, Barker and Jones persuasively argue that deracialization may contribute to what they call the "routinization" of black politics, in which the behavior of African Americans becomes more "system supporting" and less "system challenging."[15] If such tradeoffs become necessary, greater incorporation of African American legislators may be inconsistent with efforts to articulate and promote the interests of African American constituents. I address this potential tradeoff dilemma by examining the committee assignment patterns and roll call voting behavior of African Americans in Congress during a portion of the outsider-to-insider transition period.

Committee Assignments and Interest Representation

The literature on legislatures has long recognized the importance of standing committees in the policymaking process.[16] Legislative scholars routinely use a typology developed by Steven Smith and Christopher Deering to categorize committees into what have become four well-known committee types—prestige, policy, constituency, and unrequested.[17] Prestige committees are considered the most powerful or most influential. The Appropriations, Budget, Rules, and Ways and Means Committees are in this group. Committees that address important policy domains, such as education, national security, or transportation, make up the policy committee category. Constituency committees are those that provide members with the opportunity to be directly responsive to the particular needs of their constituents and districts. Agriculture, Science, and Veterans' Affairs are examples of constituency committees. Committees that are not generally coveted by members are labeled "unrequested," or undesirable.

Committees perform vital agenda-setting and gate-keeping functions. That is, committees control the substantive content of bills, as well as determine if and when a piece of legislation will reach the full House. They have the capacity to prevent legislation—even that which might enjoy the support of the majority of the legislature—from ever being considered. Committees thus can substantially control the set of issues and policy initiatives that are debated in and decided by Congress.[18] Committee assignments also have instrumental importance. It is through participation in committees that legislators have their greatest direct effect on public policy. Standing committees can place members of Congress in important strategic positions from which they are able to promote and advance their policy agendas. From the perspective of the representative, however, all committee assignments are not the same. Committees have varying jurisdictions and unique responsibilities, and legislators are better able to advance their agendas and the interests of their constituents if they receive certain committee assignments rather than others. Members of Congress tend to rank committees whose jurisdiction is relevant to the interests found in their district high on their committee assignment request list. Such assignments allow representatives to act, or appear to act, in a manner that is responsive to their constituents.[19]

Kenneth Shepsle has suggested that because standing committees are jurisdictionally based, their members acquire a stake in their respective jurisdictions. This results in committees that consist primarily of what he calls "interesteds" or "preference outliers." Shepsle argues that this is agreeable to legislators "because this arrangement permits them to specialize and accumulate power in just those areas of special interest to those who must renew their contracts every other year."[20] Because they consist mainly of "interesteds" and "preference outliers", standing committees are an excellent venue from which to explore the degree to which African American members of Congress advocate for or seek to protect black interests and whether or not increased political incorporation comes at the expense of black interest representation.[21] Given that the overwhelming majority of these legislators are elected from majority-black districts with distinctive economic and social needs, it is reasonable to expect them to be significantly represented on those committees whose jurisdictions include traditional minority interest areas, such as civil rights, education, health care, social welfare, and employment opportunities.

Influence potential is a measure commonly used to estimate the significance and instrumental value of particular committee assignments to groups in a legislature. It is the percentage of a committee's members who come from a particular legislative subgroup. Because committees enable their members to specialize and acquire power in the policy areas within their jurisdiction, the degree to which a cohesive, well-organized group is represented on a committee reflects that group's potential influence over particular policy areas. Table 17-3 contains data on African American representation on House standing committees. The committees are listed according to their percentage of black members, from highest to lowest percentage, using 107th House data. Committee assignment information from the 104th Congress is included for comparison purposes.

At first glance it may appear that the African American members have forsaken the traditional black interest committees in favor of constituency and policy committees that have broader jurisdictions. While it is true that black representatives are increasingly becoming involved and identified with issues that have no overt or direct race-specific content, they have not necessarily turned away from the long-standing black interest issues such as civil rights, education, equal employment opportunities, social welfare, and urban development. Changes in

Table 17-3 African American Representation on House Standing Committees, 107th and 104th Congresses

Committee	Committee Type[a]	107th % Black[b]	107th Equity Ratio	104th % Black	104th Equity Ratio
Government Reform	Policy	16.7	8.4	12.0	3.5
International Relations	Policy	12.2	3.9	9.3	0.8
Financial Services	Policy	11.7	3.4	12.0	3.5
Judiciary	Policy	10.8	2.5	11.4	2.9
Official Conduct	Unrequested	10.0	1.7	0.0	−8.5
Small Business	Constituency	8.6	0.3	17.0	8.5
Education and Workforce	Policy	8.3	0.0	11.6	3.1
Agriculture	Constituency	8.3	0.0	10.0	1.5
Rules	Prestige	7.7	−0.6	0.0	−8.5
Ways and Means	Prestige	7.3	−1.0	8.3	−0.2
Veterans' Affairs	Constituency	6.9	−1.4	12.1	3.6
Transportation	Policy	6.7	−1.6	6.6	−1.9
Appropriations	Prestige	6.2	−2.1	3.6	−4.9
Select Intelligence	Unrequested	5.3	−3.0	6.3	−2.2
Energy and Commerce	Policy	5.3	−3.0	4.3	−4.2
Budget	Prestige	4.7	−3.6	2.4	−6.1
Science	Constituency	2.1	−6.2	6.0	−2.5
Resources	Constituency	2.0	−6.3	0.0	−8.5
Armed Services	Constituency	1.7	−6.6	3.6	−4.9

[a]Committee Type is taken from Steven S. Smith and Christopher J. Deering, *Committees in Congress*, 2nd ed. (Washington, D.C.: CQ Press, 1990), 87.

[b]% Black and % Hispanic are percentages of the total committee membership African American or Hispanic. The one African American Republican who served in the 107th House is excluded from % Black data.

committee jurisdictions that the Republicans made upon taking control of the House in 1995 mask some of the subtleties in the distribution of committee assignments shown in Table 17-3. For example, the Committee on Government Reform deals with matters pertaining to the District of Columbia, criminal justice, drug policy, and human resources. Housing, community development, and consumer credit are issues that figure prominently on the agenda of the Financial Services Committee. The Small Business Committee's jurisdiction covers workforce matters and government programs. Among the issues that the International Relations Committee considers is legislation related to U.S. policy toward Africa. All of these issues are included in most conceptualizations of black interests.

The data in Table 17-3 show that African Americans expanded their representation on committees from a presence on sixteen of the nineteen committees in the 104th House, to having at least one member on every committee in the 107th. In other words, by 2001, African Americans had a seat at the table and a voice in the deliberations over all the legislation on the congressional agenda. This had been a goal of the Congressional Black Caucus from its inception. Four committees whose jurisdictions include many traditional black interests issues, Government Reform, International Relations, Financial Services, and Judiciary, ranked among the top five for African American representation and influence potential. By comparison, in the 104th House, each of the top five committees can be classified as a black interest committee.

The fourth and sixth columns of Table 17-3 contain an equity ratio for each committee. The equity ratio assesses the proportionality of African American representation. Specifically, it is the percentage of African Americans on a committee, minus the overall percentage of African Americans in the House. For example, in the 107th House, African Americans constituted 16.7 percent of the Government Reform Committee, and they made up 8.3 percent of the entire House, which yields an equity ratio of 8.4 for this committee. An equity ratio of zero equals perfect proportional committee representation. A positive score indicates that African Americans are overrepresented on the committee, and a negative ratio means that they are underrepresented.

African Americans were either proportionately represented or overrepresented on eight of the nineteen House standing committees in both the 104th and 107th Congresses. Of the eight, only two are not clearly or directly identified with black interest issues, the Agriculture Committee in both the 104th and 107th and the Official Conduct Committee in the 107th. Given that assignments on prestige committees are among the factors associated with increased institutional incorporation, it is interesting that the African Americans were underrepresented on all four of the prestige committees in both the 104th and 107th Congresses. From this examination of their standing committee assignment choices, it appears that African American representatives have not exchanged their concern for, and advocacy of, black interests for increased power and broader institutional influence. However, to get a more complete picture of their committee assignment behavior, it is important to consider African Americans' presence on House subcommittees.

Table 17-4 contains data on subcommittee saliency. *Saliency* is the percentage of all African American committee assignments devoted to a particular type of committee. This measure provides a more nuanced assessment of the relative importance to African American legislators of the various committee types and the policy areas within their jurisdiction. For example, if African American members as a group hold a total of ten subcommittee assignments, and four of those assignments are on policy subcommittees, then policy subcommittees would have a saliency score of 40 percent. If two of those assignments are on constituency committees, constituency committees would have a saliency score of 20 percent; and we could say that, based on their subcommittee service, policy matters seem to resonate more with African American legislators than do constituency issues.

In both the 104th and 107th sessions of the House, policy subcommittees with broad jurisdictions were the most salient subcommittees to the African American members. The Aviation; the Domestic Monetary Policy, Technology,

Table 17-4 Saliency and African American Membership on House Subcommittees, by Committee Type, 104th and 107th Congresses

	Saliency[a]	
Subcommittee Type	104th	107th
Black interest[b]	20.8	28.9
Constituency	17.9	26.7
Policy	44.3	38.9
Prestige	16.0	4.4

[a]Saliency is the percentage of the total number of black subcommittee assignments to that particular committee type.

[b]Black interest subcommittees are those whose jurisdiction includes the policy areas that are of special concern to black citizens. See Kerry L. Haynie, *African American Legislators in the American States* (New York: Columbia University Press, 2001), 116.

and Economic Growth; the Financial Institutions and Consumer Credit; and the International Monetary Policy and Trade Subcommittees were among the most popular policy subcommittee assignments for these legislators. Black interest was the second-most-salient committee type. The Education Reform, the Housing and Community Opportunity, and the Civil Service and Census Subcommittees were among the most popular black interest subcommittees. It is interesting to note that whereas the saliency of policy subcommittees declined between the two Congresses, the saliency of black interest subcommittees increased. Relative to the other subcommittee types, prestige subcommittees were the least salient to the African Americans in both sessions. Moreover, the saliency of prestige committees declined dramatically from one Congress to the next.

The committee and subcommittee assignment data presented here indicate that African American legislators now, perhaps more than at any other time in the past, place a more varied array of irons in the public policy fire. These data also suggest that it is not the case that these representatives have turned away from black interests while achieving higher levels of institutional incorporation. Instead, it appears that the African American members of Congress have attempted to balance their concern for issues that may be beneficial to their districts, their legislative careers, or both, with concern and advocacy for traditional black interest issues.[22] That is, while they were well positioned on committees to advance or protect interests in a broad array of policy areas, they were also well positioned to exert influence in support of a more particularized black interest agenda.

Roll Call Votes and Black Interests

The roll call voting behavior of black legislators provides us with an additional opportunity to assess whether or not acquiring more institutional clout is associated with a decrease in the attention that these legislators give to black interests. As discussed above, African American members of Congress have long played the role of race representative. They view themselves as the primary advocates for and protectors of black people and their interests. Related to this, several studies have found that African American representatives are more likely than nonblack representatives to seek to ensure that a black-interest perspective is articulated, understood, and advanced.[23] Below, I use roll call ratings compiled by three interest groups, the American Conservative Union (ACU), Americans for Democratic Action (ADA), and the Leadership Conference on Civil Rights (LCCR), to assess whether African American representatives are less inclined to support the interests of blacks as they acquire more institutional power. The ACU is a conservative, umbrella lobbying organization that seeks to promote the ideals and advance the causes of conservatism in government and public affairs. The ACU rates each member of Congress on a scale of zero to 100, based on their votes on a group of bills that are deemed relevant to the core mission of the organization. The higher a member's rating, the more conservative he or she is judged to be. Similarly, the ADA is a liberal lobbying organization that champions progressive ideals and values in the public policy arena. After each legislative session, ADA evaluates members of the House and Senate based on their votes on twenty bills that it considers the most important in advancing the group's interests. Legislators are awarded five points, up to a maximum of 100, for each roll call vote that is in agreement with ADA's position. The Leadership Conference on Civil Rights is a coalition of more than 180 liberal progressive organizations that advocate for civil rights and economic equity and opportunity for racial and ethnic minorities, women, senior citizens, and the disabled. The LCCR index, which also ranges from zero to 100, measures the proportion of a legislator's roll call votes that support the stated position of the coalition.

Each of these three indices includes some bills that do not directly correspond to, or are peripheral to, black interests. However, they are reliable indicators of liberal (or conservative) voting in Congress.[24] Because public opinion polls and surveys routinely show that, collectively, African Americans are one of the most cohesive and consistent liberal political groups in the country, the scales are reasonable proxies for assessing support for black interests.[25]

Table 17-5 presents the ACU, ADA, and LCCR roll call ratings for black and nonblack Democrats who served in the House in the 104th and 107th Congresses. These data show that African American Democrats are decidedly more liberal than nonblack Democrats. Regardless of whether we rely on the ratings of the liberal-leaning ADA and LCCR, or those of the conservative oriented ACU, the results are the same. African American representatives are easily the most liberal politically relevant subgroup in the House. More important for our purposes here, the three sets of interest group ratings together suggest that between the 104th and 107th sessions of Congress, a period in which they increased their institutional power, African Americans did not, as a group, become noticeably more conservative in their voting behavior. In fact, two of the three indices, the ACU and the LCCR, indicate that the black legislators might have become slightly more liberal. As was the case with their committee assignment behavior,

Table 17-5 Ideology and Roll Call Voting in the House, 104th and 107th Congresses

	Black Democrats	Other Democrats
104th ACU ratings	8.0	20.7
107th ACU ratings	7.6	19.7
104th ADA ratings	90.0	69.5
107th ADA ratings	87.5	77.8
104th LCCR ratings	93.8	76.2
107th LCCR ratings	96.7	68.0

Sources: ACU and ADA ratings are from summaries found in the *Congressional Quarterly Weekly Report* and *CQ Weekly*. LCCR ratings were constructed by the author using data found on the LCCR Web site.

Note: ACU is the American Conservative Union; ADA is Americans for Democratic Action; LCCR is the Leadership Conference on Civil Rights. Ratings indicate percentage of major votes in which members voted in agreement with the organization's position.

we find little evidence here that higher levels of political incorporation are achieved at the expense of providing significant, substantive representation to African American citizens.

Conclusions

In representative democracies like the United States, legitimacy and trust in the political system are dependent to a significant degree on the system's ability to ensure that the substantive interests that exist among the citizenry are represented through deliberation and aggregation.[26] Deliberation, according to Jane Mansbridge, functions to transform interests and create commonality. Aggregation, she argues, aims at "producing some form of relatively legitimate decision in the context of fundamentally conflicting interests."[27] Political institutions are the primary conduits for ensuring that this ideal is met. In the United States, legislatures, more than any other political institution, embody these important principles of democracy. For example, William Keefe and Morris Ogul have argued that legislatures provide the government with legitimacy by

> being responsive and accountable to the people. In the process of representing the people, the legislature helps to illuminate and resolve conflict and to build consensus. It listens to grievances, addresses public problems, explores alternatives, protects or alters past decisions and policies, considers future requirements, and does what the people are not organized to do for themselves.[28]

In short, legislatures are what Alan Rosenthal calls "the guts of democracy."[29] As such, they have a profound effect on how various groups and their interests are included and integrated into the political process and into the society at large. Legislatures are especially important to political subgroups such as African Americans, who once were prevented from participating equally in policymaking and governance and whose interests and views often have not been represented in deliberative and aggregative processes. As the national legislature, the U.S. Congress is the most significant and the most far-reaching legislature in the country, and it is thus especially important to such groups.

After decades of struggle, African American members of Congress appear to be meeting the challenges of the new politics of inclusion. African Americans now are represented in Congress not only by having seats at the table. By virtue of increasing levels of political incorporation, they now also have a significant voice in deliberations over national policy. They have indeed made the transition from political outsider to consummate insider. In the process of this transition, they have not, as the analysis above indicates, turned away from their traditional role of race representative. African Americans in the House or Representatives remain the primary advocates for, and strongest supporters of, the interests of black citizens. Although this may change in the future, to date it appears that being a race representative and a political insider is not necessarily an either-or proposition. African American members of Congress have found ways to make it both-and, rather than either-or.

Notes

1. For a discussion of the race representative concept, see Kerry L. Haynie, *African American Legislators in the American States* (New York: Columbia University Press, 2001), 4.
2. Elijah Anderson, "The Precarious Balance: Race Man or Sellout?" in *The Darden Dilemma,* ed. Ellis Cose (New York: Harper-Perennial), 117.
3. Ralph K. Huitt, "The Outsider in the Senate," *American Political Science Review* 55 (1957): 566–575.
4. Richard A. Champagne and Leroy N. Rieselbach, "The Evolving Congressional Black Caucus: The Reagan-Bush Years," in *Blacks and the American Political System,* ed. H. L. Perry and Wayne Parent (Gainesville: University of Florida Press, 1995), 134.
5. Rufus P. Browning, Dale Rogers Marshall, and David H. Tabb, *Protest Is Not Enough: The Struggle of Blacks and Hispanics for Equality in Urban Politics* (Berkeley: University of California Press, 1984).
6. See Champagne and Rieselbach, "The Evolving Congressional Black Caucus"; David T. Canon, *Race, Redistricting, and Representation: The Unintended Consequences of Black Majority Districts* (Chicago: University of Chicago Press, 1999); Katherine Tate, *Black Faces in the Mirror: African Americans and Their Representatives in the U.S. Congress* (Princeton: Princeton University Press, 2003); Kenneth J. Whitby, *The Color of Representation: Congressional Behavior and Black Constituents* (Ann Arbor: University of Michigan Press, 1998).
7. Champagne and Rieselbach, "The Evolving Congressional Black Caucus," 133.
8. Ibid., 134.
9. Lerone Bennett Jr., "The Politics of the Outsider," *Negro Digest* 17 (1963): 5–8; Mervyn M. Dymally, ed., *The Black Politician: His Struggle for Power* (Belmont, Calif.: Duxbury Press, 1971); Sally Friedman, "Committee Advancement of Women and

Blacks in Congress: A Test of the Responsible Legislator Thesis," *Women and Politics* 13 (1993): 27–52.

10. J. C. Watts, an African American Republican, also represented a district that had a majority-white population.
11. Haynie, *African American Legislators,* 65–68.
12. Lucius Barker and Mack Jones, *African Americans and the American Political System,* 4th ed. (Englewood Cliffs, N.J.: Prentice Hall, 1994).
13. Ibid., 321.
14. Charles V. Hamilton, "Deracialization: Examination of a Political Strategy," *First World* 1: 3–5; Theda Skocpol, "Targeting within Universalism: Politically Viable Politics to Combat Poverty in the United States," in *The Urban Underclass,* ed. Christopher Jencks and Paul E. Peterson (Washington, D.C.: Brookings Institution Press, 1991); Carol M. Swain, *Black Faces, Black Interests: The Representation of African Americans in Congress* (Cambridge: Harvard University Press, 1993); William J. Wilson, "Race-Neutral Programs and the Democratic Coalition," *The American Prospect* 1: 74–81.
15. Barker and Jones, *African Americans and the American Political System,* 322.
16. The following discussion makes extensive use of Haynie, *African American Legislators,* 39–50.
17. See Steven S. Smith and Christopher J. Deering, *Committees in Congress,* 2nd ed. (Washington, D.C.: CQ Press, 1990), 87.
18. See, for example, Charles L. Clapp, *The Congressman: His Job as He Sees It* (Washington, D.C.: Brookings Institution Press, 1963); Wayne L. Francis, *The Legislative Committee Game: A Comparative Analysis of the Fifty States* (Columbus: Ohio State University Press, 1989); George Goodwin, *The Little Legislatures: Committees of Congress* (Boston: University of Massachusetts Press, 1970); Kevin B. Grier and Michael C. Munger, "Committee Assignments, Constituent Preferences, and Campaign Contributions," *Economic Inquiry* 29 (1991): 24–43; Richard L. Hall, "Participation and Purpose in Committee Decision-Making," *American Political Science Review* 81 (1987): 105–128; Kenneth A. Shepsle, "Congressional Committee Assignments: An Optimization Model with Institutional Constraints," *Public Choice* 21 (1975): 55–78; Kenneth A. Shepsle, "Representation and Governance: The Great Trade-off," *Political Science Quarterly* 103 (1988): 461–483; Smith and Deering, *Committees in Congress*; and Charles Stewart, "Committee Hierarchies in the Modernizing House, 1875–1947," *American Journal of Political Science* 36 (1992): 835–856.
19. Heinz Eulau and Paul D. Karps, "The Puzzle of Representation: Specifying Components of Responsiveness," *Legislative Studies Quarterly* 2 (1977): 233–254; Richard Fenno, *Congressmen in Committees* (Boston: Little, Brown, 1973); David W. Rohde and Kenneth A. Shepsle, "Democratic Committee Assignments in the House of Representatives: Strategic Aspects of a Social Choice Process," *American Political Science Review* 67 (1973): 889–905; Stewart, "Committee Hierarchies in the Modernizing House."
20. Shepsle, "Representation and Governance," 471–472.
21. Unless otherwise specified, "minority group," as used here refers to African Americans and Hispanics.
22. See Canon, *Race, Redistricting, and Representation,* 159–164; and Haynie, *African American Legislators,* 39–62, for similar findings.
23. Kathleen A. Bratton and Kerry L. Haynie, "Agenda-Setting and Legislative Success in State Legislatures: The Effects of Gender and Race," *Journal of Politics* 61 (1999): 658–679; Haynie, *African American Legislators*; Tate, *Black Faces in the Mirror*; and Whitby, *The Color of Representation.*
24. Richard J. Fleisher, "Explaining the Change in Roll-Call Voting Behavior of Southern Democrats," *Journal of Politics* 55 (1993): 327–341; James A. Stimson, Michael B.

MacKuen, and Robert Erikson, "Dynamic Representation," *American Political Science Review* 89 (1995): 543–565.

25. See Charles S. Bullock III, "Congressional Voting and the Mobilization of a Black Electorate in the South," *Journal of Politics* 43 (1981): 662–682; and Kenneth J. Whitby, "Measuring Congressional Responsiveness to the Policy Interest of Black Constituents," *Social Science Quarterly* 68 (1987): 367–377 for works that examine correlations among the various interest group scales.
26. Joseph M. Bessette, *The Mild Voice of Reason: Deliberative Democracy and American National Government* (Chicago: University of Chicago Press, 1994); Bernard Manin, *The Principles of Representative Government* (Cambridge: Cambridge University Press, 1997); Jane Mansbridge, "Should Blacks Represent Blacks and Women Represent Women? A Contingent 'Yes,'" *Journal of Politics* 61 (1999): 628–657.
27. Mansbridge, "Should Blacks Represent Blacks," 634.
28. William L. Keefe and Morris S. Ogul, *The American Legislative Process* (Englewood Cliffs, N.J.: Prentice Hall, 1993), 446.
29. Alan Rosenthal, "The Legislative Institution—In Transition and at Risk," in *The State of the States,* 2nd ed., ed. Carl E. Van Horn (Washington, D.C.: CQ Press, 1993).

18. Re-Envisioning Congress: Theoretical Perspectives on Congressional Change—2004

Lawrence C. Dodd

The early twenty-first century has coincided with a time of remarkable change in the U.S. Congress. For much of the twentieth century, from the Great Depression onward, the Democrats were the majority party in Congress, steering the country toward an activist social agenda and generating a remarkable amount of institutional and policy innovation. The party's core agenda issues such as Social Security were so popular, and Democratic incumbents paid such close attention to constituents' service needs and to interest groups' programmatic concerns, that the party appeared to have a permanent lock on Congress, particularly the House of Representatives. Thus as Congress entered the 1990s most observers expected Democratic control to continue,[1] despite public opinion polls demonstrating widespread unhappiness with Congress as an institution.[2] Instead, the decade witnessed a dramatic Republican assault on the Democrats and on Congress itself, which culminated in the "Republican revolution" in the 1994 elections.

Once in control of Congress, the Republicans engaged in an aggressive push toward majority party dominance of national government. During the first four years in power they pursued a political and policy struggle of historic proportions with the Democratic president and his congressional party. This struggle included two government shutdowns, the enactment of welfare reform over the objections of most congressional Democrats, and the impeachment of President Clinton. As the struggle went forward, the Republicans maintained control of the House and Senate by slim margins in the 1996 and 1998 elections. The 2000 elections, again generating narrow Republican majorities, extended the Republicans' control into a fourth Congress, delivered the presidency to their nominee, George W. Bush, and gave the party unified control of national government. The 2004 elections then solidified united party control, with expanded Republican majorities in the House and Senate and a popular vote majority for their president. This victory positioned the party to consolidate its long-term dominance of Congress and the presidency and possibly to reshape the Supreme Court for decades to come.

How could this have happened? What does it tell us about Congress as an institution? And what might it tell us about American politics in the first decade of the new century?

In this chapter I address these questions by presenting three theoretical perspectives that, taken together, help us to understand such periods of unexpected change and to clarify the placement and meaning of such changes in contemporary politics. These theories argue that such upheavals, illustrated forcefully by the Republican revolution, can best be understood not as aberrations in our politics but as the natural, long-term outgrowth of three factors: the goals and strategies that politicians bring to congressional politics, the shifting societal contexts that they confront, and the changing ideas about politics that they experiment with as they pursue their goals and address societal problems. To better understand these three theories and their significance for Congress, we will start by considering why the Republican revolution was so puzzling and how the three theories can help us address that puzzle. Then we will examine the three theories, the sense they make out of contemporary politics, and what they together can tell us about the current state of Congress and the nation.

The Puzzle and Explanatory Strategy

What is so puzzling about the Republican revolution is that it occurred at all, given the hold on Congress that the Democrats appeared to enjoy, and that it followed the path it did once the Republicans assumed control of Congress. Three aspects of this overall puzzle require particular attention.

First, the Republican victory came at a time when members of Congress possessed more resources than at any other time in history for conducting constituent service, contacting constituents personally, addressing specific programmatic needs, and traveling home to meet with constituents. The incumbent advantage in congressional elections seemed assured, and there appeared little role for national policy agendas or national election forces in congressional elections. These factors seemed to tilt Congress decisively toward Democratic control and to make a serious Republican challenge almost inconceivable, short of conditions such as a major economic crisis. Republican takeover of the House of Representatives seemed particularly unlikely because localized constituent service and targeted federal programs appeared to provide a very special incumbent advantage in the relatively small congressional districts that compose the House. Despite these expectations, in 1994 the Republican Party produced one of the most massive vote swings against an incumbent congressional party in American history.[3] The Republicans captured both the House and Senate and even defeated powerful House committee chairs and the Democratic Speaker, Tom Foley. They accomplished all of this, moreover, in a time of good economic conditions. They did so by stressing a common policy agenda and nationalizing the congressional elections.

Second, as they maneuvered for control of Congress in the decade prior to the 1994 election, and during the 1994 campaign itself, the Republicans systematically attacked the legitimacy of Congress as a governing institution. After gaining control of the Congress that they had worked so hard to capture, Republicans then found themselves constrained by the public distrust of Congress they had helped inflame. Unable to put in place a strong leadership structure, they found themselves blamed for two government shutdowns, embroiled in factional fights, and subjected to three straight elections in which they lost seats in the House and stumbled precariously in the Senate, barely holding on to control of Congress. Their remarkable surge forward in 1994 thus was followed not by the rapid consolidation of a new Republican era that it seemed to portend but by stalemate. This sense of stalemate and tenuousness in the party's hold on power was reinforced by the electoral college controversy surrounding George W. Bush's 2000 presidential victory, which cast a cloud of illegitimacy over the party's claim to unified party control of government once it arrived.

Third, despite the difficulties the Republicans faced as they sought to solidify control of Congress and assert unified party government, their support at the polls did not collapse. They rebounded from the government shutdowns and maintained control of both houses in the 1996, 1998, and 2000 elections, despite a Democratic resurgence. Along the way, the party enacted major new legislation, from reform of welfare laws to trade normalization with China. The Republicans momentarily lost control of the Senate in summer 2001 when Sen. Jim Jeffords, R-Vt., switched to independent status and gave the Democrats chamber control, but the party re-won control at the polls in 2002, while expanding its margin in the House. Then came the major move forward in control of the House and Senate in the 2004 elections, as discussed in the prologue, including the defeat of the Democrats' most visible national spokesperson, Senate Minority Leader Tom Daschle of South Dakota. The Republicans' decade-long hold on power, combined with the impressive congressional victories of 2002 and 2004, made clear that the 1994 victory was not a fluke. The Republican revolution had been real, not a momentary electoral anomaly, positioning the party for sustained pursuit of unified and consolidated control of the national government.

In response to these developments, analysts have presented an interpretation of the Republican revolution that stresses its uniqueness and attributes it almost entirely to the hard work and brilliance of one man, Rep. Newt Gingrich of Georgia.[4] The general image conveyed by the coverage of events of 1994 and thereafter emphasized the overarching role of Gingrich in orienting congressional Republicans toward a systematic assault on the Democrats in the 1980s and early 1990s, in creating a strategy of attacking Congress in order to discredit the governing Democrats, in aggressively using GOPAC to build a Republican base, in building a "farm team" of Republican challengers, and in creating the thematic focus on a Conservative Opportunity Society and on the Contract with America.

The result has been a kind of "great man" theory of revolution that seems to imply that if only Gingrich had been defeated in 1990, when he faced an extremely close election, the Democrats would have maintained control of Congress and New Deal–Great Society hegemony would have gone unchallenged. This perspective further implies that the Republicans faltered midway through the 104th Congress because Gingrich became overwhelmed with hubris; they recovered in summer 1996 because he recovered; they struggled thereafter because of his ethical struggles and loss of nerve; and they suffered grievously with his miscalculation in relying on impeachment of Clinton to save the Republican Party. Their rebound in the 106th Congress then could be attributed to Gingrich's sagacity in maneuvering Dennis Hastert, Ill., into the speakership as he resigned from the House, putting in place a soft-spoken Gingrich ally who could continue the revolution without generating the negative vibes associated with Gingrich himself. Well served by this leadership transition, congressional Republicans were then positioned to take advantage of the political skills that another great man, George W. Bush, would bring to the head of their national ticket in 2000 and thereafter.

Certainly there is some truth in the emphasis on Gingrich's critical role in the revolution, and on George W. Bush's role in helping realize its longer-term potential. Individuals do matter in politics and history. A gifted politician may see historical dynamics more clearly than others and act in ways that accentuate them. Yet how can an individual overcome "scientific" truths, such as the argument by congressional scholars that citizens' preoccupation with casework politics and public lack of interest in sweeping policy agendas had frozen the Republicans out of contention in the House and limited their future in the Senate? And even if Gingrich, and later Bush, were remarkably adept at sensing the underlying dynamics of history, what was it that they had sensed? What were the historical dynamics that had suggested opportunities to exploit and strategies to pursue?[5]

In contrast to the great man or personalistic perspective, this chapter argues that developments such as the Republican revolution reflect broader dynamics in institutions and societies, and that it is through our identification of such dynamics that we make systematic sense out of critical events.[6] In the short run there are always advantages—city machines in the late nineteenth century, constituent service in the late twentieth century—that benefit one party or group and appear to contemporary observers to make it impregnable to political challenge. But in the long run there are historical processes at work that erode such advantages and subject legislators, their parties, and Congress to new political circumstances. As we understand these dynamic processes, thinking about Congress not by focusing on short-term and static partisan advantages but by assessing long-term dynamic processes, we gain a general sense of how and why surprising upheavals such as the Republican revolution occur. We also learn to focus less on great men and more on the underlying dynamics that help generate and constrain great leadership and in the process change the structure of politics.

To understand the historical processes shaping contemporary politics, I look at Congress through three theoretical perspectives: First, we will employ a *social choice* or microeconomic perspective, which sees the revolution as a predictable stage in a natural and ongoing cycle of organizational and partisan change in Congress, a cycle generated by the strategic ways in which politicians and parties pursue governing power. Second, we will employ a *social structure* or historical-sociological perspective, which sees the revolution as a product of postindustrial societal tensions and public frustrations that overwhelmed a Congress and governing party still oriented toward industrial-era politics. Third, we will employ a cognitive or *social learning* perspective, which sees the revolution as an experimental phase in the effort of politicians and citizens to discover principles and strategies by which to resolve postindustrial policy problems and legitimize a new governing regime.

By looking at congressional politics through these distinct theoretical lenses, we can understand Congress in much the same way as we understand sporting events such as basketball. To some degree we explain which team wins and which loses by focusing on the nature or logic of basketball as a game and the skills, training, personal goals, and team commitment that players bring to it. Invariably, as we do so, we find that one team initially prepares well and works hard to win, but then with success and time it becomes lax and self-indulgent, while another grows strong, leading winners to lose and losers to win. A concentrated focus on the preparation, strategies, and psychology of teams serves us well as we try to explain a basketball game, but few of us rely solely on these "foreground" issues to fully understand teams' successes and failures. We also look at the background context within which games are played: who has the home-court advantage and has best cultivated such advantage; who has the most at stake in a game and may be most willing to take unusual risks or to break normal conventions, as in "talking trash" to gain psychological advantage over another team. Finally, as great teams meet on the court, we invariably consider the philosophies of the game held by the different coaches, schools, and regions of the country: Which philosophy is better, a strong defense or an aggressive running offense? Which philosophy is outmoded and no longer reflects the realities of a new basketball era? Which is innovative and in touch with new strategies and understandings?

In explaining college basketball, or some other sport, we consider each of these factors—the foreground game, the background context, and the overarching philosophies—and then we also look across these dimensions, thinking about their interaction. To what extent, for example, can contextual factors like home-court advantage, or a new and innovative basketball philosophy, make a winner out of a sure loser? As we talk about these issues, each of us has our favorite set of arguments or theories that we debate with others. We do so partly to explain who has won or to predict who will win. But we do so also to understand the essence of the game, to gain perspective on how that essence is changing, and to see how and why the game may change again in the future.

We are following a similar strategy in using a multitheoretical perspective to understand the congressional game and how it changes. Thus the social choice theory is an argument about the foreground of politics—how partisan teams play the game of congressional politics and how maneuvering and jockeying for power lead first one party to succeed and then another. The social structure theory is an argument about the background of contemporary politics, about how societal and institutional contexts influence the way citizens feel about congressional politics and thus shape the strategies and opportunities available to parties as they seek power. Finally, the social learning theory is an argument about how the ideas that politicians bring to the game shape their ability to play effectively, create enthusiasm in their fans, and not only generate victory but make their victory worthwhile.

The remainder of this chapter presents these three theories, one by one, and then concludes with a short assessment of what the theories, taken together, tell us about congressional politics early in the twenty-first century. In particular, we consider several factors that could shape and constrain Republicans' long-term consolidation of their hold on unified national government. In presenting these theories and arguments, I ask the reader not simply to respond to them in terms of partisan or ideological preference but to step back, look beyond which team you prefer, and consider the lessons to be learned about Congress and contemporary politics as we bring into clearer focus the dynamic processes that shape the congressional game. With this understanding, let us turn first to our social choice theory and see how far it goes in explaining the broad patterning of the events of the past decade, and then turn to the social structure and social learning theories, in turn, building a more layered and intertwined perspective as we go.

The Social Choice Theory

The social choice theory is designed to clarify how the political game normally proceeds in the foreground of congressional life, irrespective of historical context.[7] Our concern is with identifying the central goal that drives legislators' behavior, much as the desire to win inspires a basketball team, and with examining how legislators' goal-oriented behavior shapes and alters congressional politics across time. A range of motives exists among legislators, any one of which, separately or in combination with others, could form the basis of a theory of congressional change. These include the reelection motive stressed by Morris Fiorina and David Mayhew,[8] the dual goals of reelection and policy stressed by John Aldrich and David Rohde,[9] and the multiple goals of reelection, policymaking, and influence examined by Richard Fenno and Barbara Sinclair.[10] Yet the goal that most universally runs through the discussion of politics, from Machiavelli onward, and that would seem to encompass the other goals, is personal power. Thus it is the concern for governing power around which Anthony Downs builds his classic study of the ways that politicians' goals shape legislative elections and democratic government.[11] It is the concern for personal power that Barry Weingast sees as the basis for reelection activities and norm behavior in Congress.[12] The work of Roger Davidson and Walter Oleszek; C. Lawrence Evans and Oleszek; Glenn Parker; and Raymond Wolfinger and Joan Hollinger provides further evidence that members' concern for personal power or autonomy shapes and constrains party loyalty, resource distribution, and reform on Capitol Hill.[13] Thus the central goal around which we will build our social choice theory of Congress is the quest for personal power.

Our strategy is to specify the logical ways in which legislators' pursuit of power shapes the organizational politics of Congress. Microeconomic theorists argue that the pursuit of profit by individuals and firms ultimately leads to national economic cycles of boom and bust. Does the pursuit of power by legislators and their parties likewise lead to predictable patterns of congressional change? Do such patterns provide a plausible explanation of the contemporary upheavals in Congress? Social choice theory argues that the pursuit of power by members and their parties generates recurring cycles of partisan alternation in Congress. We will look at how well the theory explains contemporary developments.

Congress and the Quest for Power

The foundation of our social choice theory is that the quest for personal power by individual legislators leads them to seek power positions and resources within Congress that provide influence over national policymaking.[14] In the pursuit of personal power, members organize into partisan teams composed of like-minded members who would use power to serve similar policy objectives. The majority party will control the major power positions within the legislature, such as committee or subcommittee chairs and the speakership. It will also oversee the organizational resources of the assembly, such as office assignments and staff, and it will largely determine congressional rules and procedures. For these reasons, and in ways discussed more fully by John Aldrich and David Rohde in Chapter 11, the majority's dominance of institutional power and resources gives it the upper hand in policymaking and governance.

Being in the majority gives members the chance to exercise personal power by becoming committee or party leaders, by skillfully using resources distributed by the party, and by benefiting from rules and procedures that aid majority party policymaking. To attain personal power, members thus must work together to develop political strategies and legislative successes that enable the party and its members to gain public support and consolidate control of the assembly.

The efforts of legislators to gain personal power through service in the majority party involve a special paradox. Members' ability to work together in pursuit of majority party status requires a centralized party leadership that can coordinate their activities. Such coordination helps the party to develop a coherent campaign strategy designed to win a legislative majority, address the central policy problems preoccupying its members and supporters, and demonstrate its effective governing capacities in order to retain power. To ensure effective coordination, a party may want to limit the number of "power positions" and powerful legislators, so that undue resistance to party policy and electoral strategies does not emerge among autonomous power-wielders within the party. Yet the rank-and-file party members will push for the creation of numerous power positions, such as committee or subcommittee chairs, and for special resources such as staff, so that they can have real influence on policy. Such influence renders service in the majority a rewarding experience and also allows members to stress significant personal accomplishments in reelection campaigns. Moreover, the majority party itself will need to spread organizational positions and resources somewhat widely in order to draw on the expertise and energy of members in crafting the details of its policy programs and communicating the programs to constituents. The party also will have incentive to distribute positions and resources widely, so that the resulting incumbent advantage helps the party reelect its members and maintain its hold on power. Doing so, however, carries great risks for the party.

The success of individual members in gaining power positions and resources brings policymaking and electoral benefits to the party but also some considerable detriments. For example, the success of members in gaining extensive staff allotments not only helps them perform constituent service, potentially aiding both their reelection and the party's retention of power, but also can enable them to prepare and push bills that party leaders might find objectionable. Similarly, gaining a committee or subcommittee chair may provide a member special advantage when running for reelection, aiding the party's hold on majority status, but it also gives him or her an opportunity to push constituent interests that could undermine the party's program. As members gain such power positions and resources, and the autonomy such success can bring, their personal policy preferences and distinctive pressures of their constituents may push them away from the party's policy stances, thereby undermining party coordination and limiting the ability of the party to campaign or govern as an effective team.

The pronounced tension between centralized party power and autonomous personal power generates long-term cycles of organizational and partisan change in Congress. These cycles result from the contrasting personal calculus and political strategies of majority and minority party members.[15]

The Cycles of Congressional Change

After cooperating to win majority status and consolidate party control of the legislature, members of the majority party naturally push to divide up significant power resources among themselves so that all can benefit from the fruits of victory. They will thus support the creation of increasing numbers of formal and informal power positions within the legislature. They will lobby for greater personal resources such as office staff and travel allotments. And they will seek to establish rules within the party caucus and legislative chamber that respect the personal prerogatives of members. In pursuing these various efforts, they in turn fragment the structure of centralized party authority and undermine the majority party's capacity for internal coordination. These developments weaken their party's ability to respond to new policy problems or political circumstances and can thereby undermine public satisfaction with the party's governing success. Yet the decline in enthusiasm for the party itself will appear to be offset by the growing security of party incumbents, who use their increased autonomy and resources to build incumbent advantage in home districts.[16]

In contrast, members of the minority party have far fewer power resources to divide among themselves and significant incentive to support centralized coordination in order to battle with the majority over control of the assembly. Of course, their party may have suffered such a large reduction when it lost control that a rapid return to majority status appears unrealistic. This can constrain minority party members from an immediate focus on cooperation and party loyalty. But as their sojourn in the political wilderness lengthens, minority party members are far more likely than members of the majority to constrain their desire for immediate autonomy and focus on how best to cooperate in gaining majority party status, since that is their only real avenue to meaningful personal power. They will thus increasingly accept some degree of centralized party coordination.

As the minority party challenges the majority, the latter will appear invulnerable owing to the success of its members in winning reelection, but appearances will be deceptive.[17] The fragmented and uncoordinated nature of majority party governance, which helps generate incumbent advantage, also generates festering policy problems in the nation and a growing sense of governing crisis. The electorate, in response, increasingly focuses on assessing the governing capacity of the majority party rather than the personalized benefits received from its members. It is, after all, a party's ability to use institutional power to respond to policy problems and govern effectively that justifies its hold on majority status. Citizens thus will not indefinitely support majority party legislators simply because they ensure the delivery of benefits from programs that address "old problems." Rather, they will consider punishing majority party legislators for current policy failures.[18] This reaction against the majority party will then be assisted by the strategies and actions of the minority.

The out party, sensing the vulnerability of the majority, will use its centralized capacities to coordinate a national election campaign and to focus its candidates on a clear, unified, and coherent party agenda designed to address governing crises and emphasize its capacity to govern. It also will seek to highlight and magnify particular policy problems and perceived crises, even to the point of ensuring policy immobilism that helps to foster such problems. Meanwhile, the majority party will look to the incumbent advantage enjoyed by its members in order to assure itself that the minority party challenge will be fruitless. Its overconfidence will be reinforced by the vested interests that party members have in maintaining the fragmented status quo within Congress, so that they ignore growing public hostility to their party.

Faced with these circumstances, frustrated voters will revolt against the majority party and install the minority in power, doing so in a manner that appears sudden and unexpected but that is in fact a natural consequence of the ways in which members and parties pursue legislative power across time. The old minority party then will have its opportunity to address societal problems and consolidate institutional control. Buoyed by its momentum and the initial loyalty of members, it will almost certainly experience early policy successes. But the underlying issue is whether the new majority party can reform the legislature in ways that reduce the internal fragmentation that the old majority party had built into organizational rules and arrangements. If the new majority party can implement centralizing reforms appropriate to its governing tasks, it may be able to sustain majority status and operate as a powerful congressional party for some time, perhaps several decades, before the power quests of its members erode its centralized structure. If it fails, it may squander its opportunity and allow the opposing party to regain institutional control. Should the minority party itself remain weak and unable to rally, a cross-party coalition of factions may dominate Congress. The resurgent party, or factional coalition, then would face its own challenge in developing a governing structure that could address societal problems and sustain it in power. In time, any successful governing party or coalition would face magnified tensions between its need for centralized power and the desire of its members for autonomy, experience debilitating organizational fragmentation, and confront an unexpected and surprising minority party challenge.

The success of majority party legislators in fragmenting congressional power, combined with the willingness of minority party legislators to accept centralized party guidance, builds long-term cycles of partisan or factional alternation into the organizational life of Congress, according to our social choice theory. How well does this argument account for the upheavals of the 1990s, particularly the coming of the Republican revolution?

The Revolution as a Cyclical Stage

Seen through the lens of social choice theory, the Republican revolution can be explained as a classic product of the recurring cycles of organizational change. The current organizational cycle of Congress began with electoral upheavals of the 1960s and centralizing reforms of the 1970s that solidified liberal Democratic control. The 1980s and early 1990s were a period of fragmentation and growing immobilism, when the popularity of Democratic incumbents as constituent servants masked growing disenchantment with the party's governing capacities. The sudden and surprising defeat of the Democrats in 1994 was a result of the public's long-term unhappiness with the party. This unhappiness came forth in full fury and produced the defeat of the party's most visible and vulnerable incumbents, at a time when the Democrats had proved unable to address the critical governing items that they had promised the nation in the 1992 elections, such as changing the welfare system and implementing national health care, even when joined by a Democratic president. The defeat was unexpected because politicians and political analysts alike had focused on the incumbent advantages the Democrats enjoyed and discounted the public's growing frustration with political gridlock. The defeat was aided by the efforts of the Republicans to pursue a coordinated campaign strategy that used party resources effectively and presented a compelling image of a party prepared to govern cohesively in pursuit of an agenda widely supported by its candidates.

From the perspective of social choice theory, the brilliant electoral strategies of Republican leaders such as Gingrich were a skillful response to the opportunities afforded them by career ambitions, organizational fragmentation, and policy immobilism within the majority Democratic Party, rather than the machinations of a rare political genius. The early organizational innovations and policy successes of the Republican Party were natural consequences of the internal cohesion it had developed in its pursuit of majority status and of members' concerns to act on its governing mandate. Subsequent factional conflict among Republicans resulted, in part, from the natural reemergence of personal ambitions and power pursuits within a majority party and from frustrations with the realities of governing in a complex policymaking environment.

But the factional conflict was also a consequence of the failure of the party, particularly in the House, to enact reforms that would institutionalize a centralized authority structure. Leaders granted such centralized authority could manage conflict and pursue strategies that would sustain and consolidate the revolution. Rather than decisively strengthening the speakership, the Republicans enacted limits on service as Speaker that substantially weakened party leadership during the Gingrich era, retracting the term limit mandate only in December 2002, long after Gingrich had left the scene. Instead, they relied on the personal power of Gingrich, the good will of members, and debts owed him by members and committee chairs during his speakership. In addition, rather than streamlining the committee system in ways that might make it a more effective policymaking instrument and less a vehicle of member ambitions, for example by strengthening the budget committees and expanding their capacity to constrain and prioritize spending across the federal budget, the Republicans largely kept the old system in place, making changes that were mainly cosmetic and that did little to aid decisive action on their new agenda. The Republicans thus would face a difficult task in consolidating their control, particularly given the electorate's close division between Republicans and Democrats.

The social choice theory of organizational cycles seems to go a long way in accounting for the Republicans' sudden and surprising defeat of a long-term majority party, yet it also has its limits. Why, at their moment of victory, did the Republicans not follow through and implement real reform, choosing instead to undercut the very centralized leadership that had "brought them to the dance"? Why did they maneuver, moreover, for constitutional changes such as term limits and budget constraints that would seem to limit their own power as a majority party?[19] Why did the Republicans themselves so rapidly become the object of public scorn? And why did factional problems emerge so rapidly at the highest levels of leadership activity, so that the Republicans' governing capacities were thrown into serious question despite their great electoral victory?

The social choice theory, focused as it is on the general patterning of congressional change irrespective of historical context, cannot satisfactorily account for these distinctive characteristics and problems of the 1994 revolution. To do so, for reasons illustrated powerfully by Steven Smith and Gerald Gamm in Chapter 8 and Joseph Cooper in Chapter 16, we need to shift our conceptual focus to background factors and examine the social context and historical conditions within which it occurred.

The Social Structure Theory

As we shift from the foreground of congressional politics to the background, we will consider how Congress's power struggles and organizational cycles are shaped and altered by the societal conditions within which they occur. In doing so, we will be taking a sociological approach to Congress.

A strong sociological tradition exists in studies of the historical development of Congress. It is exemplified notably by Nelson Polsby's argument that societal modernization generates growing demands on legislatures and induces organizational specialization and institutionalization as they respond, a pattern he demonstrates for the U.S. House of Representatives.[20] We also have insightful sociological analyses of congressional politics during specific eras.[21] Thus James Sterling Young demonstrates how agrarianism, regionalism, and popular suspicion of government generated a passive, factionalized, and constrained early Congress. Woodrow Wilson argues that social changes after the Civil War strengthened the governing role of a centralized, party-driven Congress and pushed the nation toward congressional government. Joseph Cooper and David Brady highlight the ways industrialization and growing careerist politics produced a crisis of adaptation in the early-twentieth-century Congress that undermined strong parties and crippled congressional government. And Theodore Lowi charts the ways that advanced industrialization in midcentury helped create a bureaucratized and clientelist politics that he called "interest group liberalism," solidifying committee government and subsystem politics within a weakened Congress.

Our concern is to assess whether changes in social structure during the contemporary period are having an equally profound impact on Congress and its party politics and whether this shift in context can thereby help us better understand the Republican revolution. This issue requires us first to identify the fundamental changes occurring in the contemporary era and then to consider their potential significance.

The Postindustrial Transition

Historical sociologists have argued that the most critical change among advanced industrial democracies from the 1950s onward has been the move to a postindustrial society driven by a high-tech economy dependent on technological innovation and dominated by service-based employment.[22] The issue facing such nations is whether the policy programs and governing arrangements created to manage industrial-era problems can adapt to this new world.

During the advanced industrial era of the early twentieth century, as the workforce was employed in blue-collar, mass production industry and subject to periods of severe economic dislocations, democracies such as the United States created extensive social service programs. These programs were designed to supplement the health and retirement benefits that blue-collar workers received through union contracts with employers and to aid unemployed workers hurt by the ebbs and flows of the economic cycles associated with modern capitalism. Severe downturns such as the Great Depression not only caused great harm to large groups of individuals (with as many as a quarter of adult Americans unemployed at critical points during the 1930s) but put the stability of the nation and the sustainability of capitalist democracy at risk, thereby reinforcing the need for social programs. Governments also created "safety net" programs such as price supports for the industries. Governments created these programs because large numbers of specialized workers, along with stable manufacturing and agricultural sectors, were essential to the industrial production that generated strong national economies. Such nations also created large bureaucracies to implement the programs and generated political processes such as interest group liberalism and subsystem politics that sustained support for the programs. They also solidified class-based party systems that designed and oversaw the operation of the service programs.

According to social structure theory, the move to a postindustrial society introduces policy problems and political pressures that the governing arrangements inherited from the industrial era cannot address.[23] Although the postindustrialist economy creates high-tech jobs that employ a highly educated and specialized workforce, it also erodes the security of citizens as the new postindustrial employment sectors reduce or eliminate the social benefits provided workers by the union contracts of the industrial era. These citizens turn to government, which is already committed to providing safety nets, and expect it to replace and expand the lost benefits.

In addition, the educated citizens of the postindustrial era expect the national government to address a broadening array of quality-of-life issues overlooked in the industrial era—from racial and gender equality, to consumer protection, to environmental regulation, to quality education, and the list goes on. These "postmaterialist" demands[24] put enormous fiscal pressure on the government, pressures not fully offset by growing economic productivity. They also push government into cultural controversies over the values that an activist government should support. These pressures are illustrated by division within the nation over whether abortion should be legal and receive the same kinds of government recognition and funding as other medical procedures, or whether gay couples should have access to benefits and protections the government provides to heterosexuals.[25]

Two political arrangements inherited from the advanced industrial era exacerbate these problems. First, government reliance on expensive and impersonal bureaucracies to implement postindustrial programs further magnifies their cost, while their impersonal nature and intrusiveness accentuate perceptions of cultural insensitivity. Second, electoral rules and interest group politics entrench preexisting political parties in power, despite their preoccupation with programmatic positions adopted in the industrial era, inhibiting the rise of new parties that might address the new economic and cultural issues.

Social structure theory suggests that citizens faced with such circumstances will question the legitimacy of their government. In particular, they will turn against the democratic institutions most responsible for making public policy and against the traditional parties. Although the severity of public hostility will vary with the boom and bust cycles of national economies, declining somewhat in good times, the public's growing disenchantment with governing institutions eventually should produce a breakdown in democratic government.

This breakdown will occur not because postindustrial citizens are antidemocratic but because the institutional and political arrangements inherited from the industrial era do not provide them with adequate mechanisms with which to generate and legitimate new policy directions and governing regimes. The antiquated structures and procedures of a passing era are instead likely to cripple the capacity of citizens to convey their genuine policy preferences and political loyalties to their elected representatives, leading them to question such democratic procedures. No more vivid illustration of this argument is needed than the crisis over the selection of the new president in the weeks following the 2000 elections. This crisis gave dramatic demonstration of just how debilitated twenty-first-century politics may be when regulated by antiquated procedures, from an eighteenth-century electoral college to nineteenth-century judicial procedures to twentieth-century punch cards, with such procedures throwing the legitimacy of the new president into doubt. The election controversy created issues of legitimacy around the presidency of George W. Bush and Republican control of national government that shadowed the party throughout Bush's first term.

Congress and the Crisis of Legitimation

The social structure argument suggests that disenchantment with the legitimacy of governing institutions should be an integral part of contemporary American politics and that such disenchantment should focus, in particular, on Congress and its two parties.[26] The public would be concerned with Congress because of its powerful role in national policymaking, a role greater than that of national legislatures elsewhere. In addition, as Morris Fiorina argued eloquently in *Congress: Keystone of the Washington Establishment,* the electoral and organizational politics of Congress—including the rise of careerist politicians, the prevalence of constituent service activities, engrained norms of seniority, the limited governing capacity of congressional parties, and the veto power of committees—have made it the institution most constrained by industrial-era clientelist and casework politics and by safe incumbents who benefit from such politics.[27] These developments make Congress the national institution most pressured to continue industrial-era policy strategies and reinforce the inclination of citizens to turn their fury against it.

Most important, Congress suffers because it is controlled by parties still rooted in industrial-era politics. Because the Democratic Party created the service state, and thus is the party most constrained by interest group liberalism, public hostility focuses first and foremost on it. This hostility provides strategic opportunities for short-term Republican challenges. But social structure theory questions the long-term capacities of the Republican Party, or any industrial-era party, to solidify public support. Each party will be too beholden to its own industrial-era clientele groups, too blinded by industrial-era programmatic positions, and too compromised by the behavior of its own incumbents to address the problems of postindustrialism in innovative ways.

As we look at the contemporary Congress from a critical sociological perspective, we see an institution out of sync with the emerging postindustrial society and prone to a severe crisis of institutional legitimacy. Power struggles and partisan shifts may be proceeding in the foreground according to normal cyclical patterns predicted by social choice theory. Looking at Congress solely through social choice lenses, we might conclude that nothing truly serious was occurring on Capitol Hill, other than the normal alternation of partisan elites that we occasionally expect. But historical sociologists, looking through the lens of social structure theory, see the Republican revolution as a more momentous development.

The Revolution as a Product of Postindustrial Tensions

The Republican revolution that engulfed Congress in the mid-1990s, as seen from a critical sociological perspective, was a consequence of the growing societal tensions associated with postindustrialism and the legitimation crisis those tensions necessarily generate. In the preceding decades the Democratic Party had held firmly to its orthodox programmatic orientation, the protection and expansion of Social Security, while otherwise failing to provide innovative leadership, when seen against proposals for massive, rapid, and fundamental change. This failure was demonstrated in soaring deficits and in the continuance of festering problems with the environment, poverty, crime, and other quality-of-life concerns. With it came the public's growing disillusionment with Congress and its governing party and the attendant doubts about their governing legitimacy. As a party pursuing power and seeking electoral support, the Republicans embraced the public frustration, gave it public voice, and rode it to power.

The Republican attack began in the 1970s, when President Richard Nixon chided the "credit card Congress" and wasteful Democrats and impounded funds that had been enacted by the Democrats in a constitutionally prescribed manner. Nixon's actions threatened to upend the balance of constitutional power between Congress and the president, before the courts forced him to retreat.[28] The election of Ronald Reagan in 1980 then renewed the Republican assault. Reagan challenged the Democrats' support for "big government" and pushed massive tax cuts, derided their "permissive" stance on cultural issues such as abortion, and scorned their support for "welfare dependency." Reagan also questioned the Democratic commitment to forceful assertion of American interests and power on the international stage and pushed an increase in military spending. His outreach to "Reagan Democrats" in the South and Midwest seemed to portend an imminent Republican takeover of Congress, but the 1982 recession ended such momentum. The Iran-contra controversy in his second term then raised constitutional issues that weakened Reagan's governing authority.

In the end, the concerted and sustained challenge to the Democrats came to the fore in the 1980s within Congress itself, led by young Republicans such as Newt Gingrich and Trent Lott. Convinced that the constituent service activities of incumbent Democrats gave them an unfair advantage that could lock their party in power permanently unless dire measures were taken, Gingrich and his allies engaged in a furious attack that violated the most fundamental norms of comity and decorum within the Congress.[29] In doing so, they highlighted the misdeeds of the Democrats, from Speaker Jim Wright's questionable use of book royalties to members' bounced checks in the House bank, as a way to underscore the sense of a governing party and Congress that were corrupt and illegitimate at the core. To address the problems, they proposed term limits on members, constitutional constraints on Congress's budgetary power, and strengthening the presidency (the institution Republicans had dominated for most of the previous forty years) by granting presidents the line-item veto. And they also questioned the policy positions of the governing Democrats, along the lines of Nixon and Reagan, and proposed the Democrats' removal from power.

These tactics and proposals, attacking not just the policy positions of Democrats but the constitutional authority and governing legitimacy of Congress itself, struck a chord with the public, to a large extent reflecting and magnifying rather than creating public opinion. Coming at a time when the Democrats were vulnerable because of their internal fragmentation, the Republican attack swept the majority party from power in dramatic fashion, appearing to shake the foundations of congressional politics and to mandate dramatic change.

Ironically, and as social structure theory would suggest, once in power the Republicans became victims of the legitimation crisis they had helped to fuel. Early on, as they sought to organize Congress, the party's call for term limits on members (which lost momentum once it became the majority party) became transformed into pressure within the party for imposing term limits on the Republican Speaker and committee chairs in the House, as a way of demonstrating to the public the party's sincerity about reform. Thus did their attack on the institution boomerang, limiting their own capacity to put in place a governing structure that would help them pursue broad-scale governmental change.[30] Meanwhile, as discussed by John Hibbing and Christopher Larimer in Chapter 3, the public continued to be suspicious of Congress and politicians in general following the Republican takeover. In part this suspicion extended to the Republicans because their earlier investigation of the ethical problems of Democrats (as in the scandal over bounced checks) had also tarnished many of their own colleagues. But the public's wariness of the Republicans had been magnified by the doubts the party had cast on Congress as a governing institution. If Congress was truly as corrupt and outmoded as the Republicans had suggested, it was not clear that they could really improve matters. Citizens thus granted little leeway to the new congressional majority party.

When the Republican Party shut down the government in a budgetary struggle with the president in late 1995, and then proved unable to negotiate with the president because of the weak authority granted to its leadership, the public saw the fiasco as an illustration of the Republicans' own governing incompetence, and the momentum of the revolution stalled. Thereafter, ethical problems associated with Speaker Gingrich, combined with the move of House Republicans to impeach President Clinton despite his public support, deepened citizen disenchantment with Republican governance. It was only the absence of a viable alternative party capable of forcefully moving Congress beyond the Democratic era that kept the Republicans in control during the 1990s. The long-term security of this control then seemed even less certain after the 2000 crisis surrounding Bush's election, particularly when the tax cuts he championed at the beginning of his presidency failed to generate sustained job growth following a cyclical downturn in the economy. Rather, their size and tilt to the wealthy, together with energy and environmental policies favorable to industry, seemed to reinforce the sense that the Republican Party was dominated by its industrial-era clientele groups, just as was the case with the Democrats when they were in power.

From a critical sociological perspective, then, the Republican revolution and its aftermath serve both as a demonstration of the powerful tensions emerging with postindustrialism and as proof of the inability of Congress and the existing congressional parties to address the tensions. This perspective, articulated strongly by Ralph Nader during his 2000 presidential bid, sees the parties and Congress as illegitimate governing instruments destined to lead the nation further astray. Social choice theory then adds the prediction that Republicans' consolidation of their majority will generate renewed pressures toward organizational fragmentation and increased governing problems. The interaction of internal congressional dynamics and external societal tensions seems likely to generate a magnified legitimation crisis, increasing the threat to representative democracy.

These concerns raise serious questions. Is there any model for understanding contemporary politics that might suggest a way to avoid institutional collapse? Is there some ameliorative process at work across the foreground and background of congressional politics that we are simply missing as we look through the lenses of social choice and social structure theories? Moreover, might the Republican revolution be a part of this process, its role helping us to explain the party's continued success in renewing and expanding control of Congress and unified national government in the 2004 elections? These questions suggest that we step back and consider whether there is a broader integrative pattern linking these foreground and background worlds, a shift in which might transform the outcome. Let us now look at Congress through the lens of social learning theory.

The Social Learning Theory

Our goal in turning to social learning theory is to examine how the ideas of citizens and politicians help shape congressional politics and to consider whether new ideas can facilitate the adjustment to a new political era. A cognitive perspective asks that we study Congress by becoming aware of the belief systems and learning processes that characterize society across time and by seeing Congress and its parties as participants in societal learning.

Central to the dominant scholarly conceptions of social learning, particularly as developed by Gregory Bateson and Geoffrey Vickers, is the perception that individuals and groups develop understandings of the world that they share with one another in order to operate effectively.[31] Each generation must develop a realistic understanding of how best to balance personal and collective well-being within its particular historical conditions. Insofar as it does so, its members can compete effectively in pursuit of personal interests at the same time as they address collective social problems and construct viable societies. As the world changes and ideas become outmoded, the ability to accomplish such personal goals and public purposes declines. The solution, from a social learning perspective, is for a new generation to engage in experimental learning of new ideas appropriate to new circumstances. As they discover such ideas and integrate them with orthodox perspectives essential to societal continuity, a more viable social paradigm emerges that can facilitate societal well-being and effective governance.

What might a learning perspective tell us about the capacity of Congress to respond to postindustrialism and the role of the Republican revolution in that process? This requires us first to consider more closely the nature of social learning.

The Process of Social Learning: Crisis, Experimentation, and Paradigm Shift

All of us have experienced the process of social learning in our lives. As an example, think back to sports as a metaphor for understanding politics. Occasionally we see teams that fail to adjust to new circumstances, such as the adoption of the three-point shot in college basketball, and thus lose regularly. The team's coaching staff understands the school's social culture and recruiting strengths, but the coaches learned the game before the new rules were envisioned, so they are committed to an older, more conservative philosophy of basketball. Frustrated after several losing seasons, anxious fans demand change, and college administrators search for a new coaching staff. The college may have to experiment with several coaching arrangements, introducing new members who embrace a more aggressive basketball philosophy while keeping some existing coaches, before it discovers a staff whose approach effectively balances a respect for the program's historic strengths with new ideas about how best to play the game. Once the school finds such a staff, the players learn new strategies of play, and excited fans learn to appreciate the three-point shot. Such a process of social learning, undertaken across several years by administrators, staff, players, and fans, can rejuvenate support for basketball on a campus.

Social learning theory argues that the significant role that ideas and learning play in our private lives, as illustrated here by basketball, also can be seen in politics.[32] An institution such as Congress may have governing problems, not just because of debilitating power struggles or entrenched interests, but because of outmoded thinking. The ideas or social paradigms that dominate congressional politics may once have worked, but times change. Those who learned about politics in the previous era may be so accustomed to thinking within the old paradigm that they fail to comprehend that society is changing and oppose efforts to experiment with new ideas. A social crisis would then lead groups of citizens to demand action and to support ambitious politicians who are willing to experiment and change.

As with finding a successful coaching staff, it may take time, a series of experimental shifts in leaders and programs, and the creative combination of new ideas and orthodox perspectives to find a viable paradigm. It also may take a new generation of politicians and social activists, drawn to service in Congress because of its great constitutional power, who challenge existing arrangements and push new policy perspectives.[33] As the new generation experiments with innovative ideas and constructs a new approach that appears to work, Congress and the nation experience a paradigm shift that can reshape politics and society as powerfully as a new philosophy of basketball can reshape campus sports.

Extensive change in governing paradigms is necessarily slow, in part because of the difficulty of restructuring politics in the midst of complex structures, anachronistic rules, and entrenched alliances but also because social learning itself is a slow process. It requires moments of crisis and recognition of problems, both of which can focus attention on the critical issues, and also incremental processes of experimentation and assimilation.[34] The reliance of Congress on popular elections to select its members helps to make it sensitive to social problems and to the occasional upheavals in the public's partisan loyalties that signal deep societal tensions and crises. The deliberative nature of the committee system and the institution's overall decision-making processes facilitates the informed and methodical reconstruction of paradigmatic understanding in response to crises.

Actual paradigmatic shift comes in phases of innovation followed by assimilative retrenchment, as new ideas break forth amid crisis and then are integrated into preexisting understandings. These phases bring with them segmented and partial paradigm shifts: Congress and the nation experiment with some ideas central to a new era, see their value and limits when institutionalized in governing strategies, and move on to new problems and paradigmatic adjustment. This pattern of phased and segmented transformation of paradigms can be seen in the response of Congress and its parties to postindustrialism, with the Republican revolution being one such phase of experimental learning.

Congress and the Politics of Renewal: Responding to Postindustrialism

Starting in the 1950s, when the postindustrial transition first began to emerge, we see incremental phases of a paradigm shift across decades of experimentation and assimilation. During the 1950s Congress was still dominated by southern Democrats elected in a segregated political world and was characterized, as it had been since the late 1930s, by a deep resistance to social activism, with the exception of Social Security and occasional increases in the minimum wage. There were few signs of the strong partisan leadership necessary for broad-scale policy innovation. Congressional policymaking depended, instead, on a conservative coalition of southern Democrats and northern Republicans committed to the status quo. Congress truly seemed immune to new ideas, social learning, or a transformative response to postindustrialism.[35] But in fact it did change and respond.

In the 1960s, activated by the influx of a new generation of northern Democratic liberals and presidential leadership from two former members, John Kennedy and Lyndon Johnson, Congress broke its policy immobilism and implemented a broad range of programs designed to address postmaterialist policy concerns—including affirmative action for racial and ethnic minorities and women, health care for retired and displaced citizens, environmental and consumer reforms to protect our quality of life, and federal aid to education. This response came amid a growing sense of disorder and crisis over the nation's inability to address vital issues such as civil rights. It also came amid increased belief within the Democratic Party that its traditional commitment to social justice entailed not just the righting of economic wrongs and insecurities induce by modern capitalism, which continued to concern it with respect to fate of the elderly. It also entailed response to such injustices as racial, ethnic, and gender inequality, the inequality in educational opportunities of the young, or the undue social costs accompanying environmental degradation or consumer fraud. This period of expanded activism, highlighted in Sarah Binder's statistical analysis of postwar growth in policy agendas in Chapter 13 of the 7th edition of *Congress Reconsidered*,[36] laid the foundations for a postmaterialist paradigm that moved the nation beyond issues of Social Security and responded broadly to social movements and citizen protests of early postindustrialism. It also moved the Democratic Party beyond attention to, and electoral reliance on, organized labor and connected it to new social movements transforming the face of the nation.

These developments broadened the base of the party and created substantial demands that it fulfill its new postmaterialist agenda. At the same time, such Great Society activism enlarged government bureaucracy and expanded its fiscal commitments in ways that fostered concern about the size, reach, and costs of the national government. It also involved the national government—and thus the governing Democrats in Congress—ever more deeply in cultural and moral conundrums embedded in American society. Such conundrums revolved particularly around the tension between collective responsibility of the nation to ensure social justice and equal opportunity for its citizens, as espoused by the Democrats, and concern that individuals assume primary responsibility for personal well-being, long a foundation principle of the Republican Party.

Growing cultural divisions were augmented by the intrusion of cold war politics into American society, as the Vietnam War led many citizens, particularly liberals and young people within the Democratic Party, to question the extent of their personal obligation to support or be involved with an unjust and costly war. The conflict over the war, combined with the growing concern about the power and reach of the federal government in civil rights and social policy, increased the intransigence of southern conservative Democrats in Congress, who were a minority of the party but held many positions of committee leadership vital to the passage of the party's social agenda. With the loss of the White House in 1968, leadership in behalf of the party's agenda depended on effective action by its majorities in the House and Senate.

In the 1970s the Democrats enacted a wide range of reforms designed to reconstruct their congressional party so as to limit the power of entrenched southern Democrats and ensure the party's sustained commitment to, and effective enactment of, its postmaterialist agenda. These reforms created a new "incentive structure" for career-minded Democratic legislators, in which movement to power and influence in committees and the party rested less on seniority and more on members' commitment to fostering the party's broad policy agenda. By extension, these reforms created disincentives for ambitious politicians to build careers as congressional Democrats in regions such as the South, where constituents were substantially at odds with large elements of the party's new programmatic image. Simultaneously, Democrats joined with reformist Republicans to experiment with new congressional rules and structures that would protect the policymaking authority of Congress in the new era. In doing so they created an innovative new congressional budget process to help Congress maintain fiscal integrity as it pursued its new agenda. This process introduced annual votes on budget resolutions that specified taxing and spending targets for the government, thereby pushing members and the parties to be clearer than in the past about broad priorities and principles. Overall, the reforms of the 1970s encouraged the congressional parties to become more responsible in their articulation of and pursuit of clearly etched policy agendas, a move long espoused by such congressional reformers as Richard Bolling and by academic political scientists.[37]

The Reagan revolution during the 1980s pushed Congress to reassess and reaffirm the extent of its postmaterialist commitments, to experiment with new revenue strategies aimed at ending the economic stagnation that had arisen in a time of expanded spending, and to consider a more muscular approach to foreign policy. It also brought a new generation of southern Republicans into Congress and reinforced ideological shifts within the party toward a more socially conservative stance.[38] This growth of Republicanism in the South had begun in response to the Democrats' paradigmatic shift away from tolerance of southern segregation, a shift counterbalanced by the growing states' rights rhetoric among southwestern and western Republicans such as John Tower of Texas, Barry Goldwater of Arizona, and Ronald Reagan of California. The Democrats' embrace of civil rights and voting rights legislation in the mid-1960s, against the opposition of powerful southern congressional Democrats, led many white southerners to begin abandoning the party, voting for southern Republicans and thus slowly shifting southern House and Senate seats to Republican control. This shift was aided over time by the switch of southern Democrats such as Strom Thurmond of South Carolina to the Republican Party and the decisions of young southern white politicians such as Newt Gingrich to build their careers in the Republican Party.

With growing Republicanism in the South, congressional Republicans became more attuned to cultural concerns dominant in the South. This involved not just concerns about the role of the federal government in affirmative action, but also concerns about traditional moral issues and family values associated with fundamentalist Protestant churches of the South. Simultaneously, newly enfranchised southern blacks moved to the Democratic Party, reinforcing its focus on social justice and ensuring that Democrats would continue to hold onto House seats in areas of the South dominated by African Americans. These parallel developments created the sort of deep red Anglo districts and deep blue African American districts in the South that Bruce Oppenheimer discusses in Chapter 6, a process somewhat mirrored outside the South as different groups in New England, the Midwest, and the West responded in distinct ways to the repositioning of the parties' policy agendas.

As Congress entered the 1990s it had in many ways become a new institution, which had responded to postindustrialism in ways that would have seemed inconceivable in the mid-1950s. Although it had not embraced a postindustrial paradigm that addressed the full range of problems that the new era posed, Congress had moved the nation in incremental and segmented phases toward new ideas about what government could do. It had also moved to a new vision of how Congress might organize itself and pursue policy implementation, relying more on party discipline and strong party leadership and somewhat less on norms of seniority, specialized policy expertise, and committee government.

As these processes went forward, the parties demonstrated that they were not as entrenched in industrial-era alignments and policy perspectives as social structure theorists had surmised. The Democrats had moved beyond their labor base of the Rooseveltian era and beyond reliance on the safe but segregated South to ensure their national dominance. The party had moved toward a more inclusive stance that reached out to minorities and women and pursued policies, such as environmental protection or consumer safety, that alienated parts of its old labor base. Republicans had moved beyond their benign acceptance of New Deal social activism, beyond their acceptance of permanent minority status that seemed to come with inability to compete in the South, and toward their own version of expanded inclusiveness. Republican inclusiveness entailed an openness to southern social and cultural concerns and to the realignment of political forces inside the party as well as between the two parties.

As additional proof of the adaptive capacities of the parties and Congress, in the early 1990s congressional Democrats abandoned a long-term fascination with deficit spending and embraced a commitment to balanced budgets. While this move had been facilitated by the growing attentiveness to fiscal policy that came with the new budget process put in place in the 1970s and the struggles with deficits in the 1980s, it was given momentum by the new Democratic president, Bill Clinton. He sought to combine the pursuit of postmaterialist programs with fiscal policies that could sustain economic growth and the available revenue for such programs. This move, together with Clinton's repositioning of the party in support of stronger law enforcement, went some distance in addressing fiscal and cultural problems associated with the postmaterialist Democratic agenda that alienated key voters. Yet left unaddressed by congressional Democrats was their undue reliance on the federal bureaucracy to implement activist programs.

During the 1980s and early 1990s, many state and local governments—Democrat and Republican alike—had experimented with new ideas about how to "reinvent government" and avoid excessive bureaucracy. Bill Clinton and Vice President Al Gore brought this new perspective to the national government in 1993, with the new Democratic administration focused particularly on new "entrepreneurial strategies" for recrafting government programs.[39] These entrepreneurial strategies involved continued government commitment to activist programs such as welfare and public health, but they utilized the private sector to run some aspects of such programs and implemented incentive systems taken from private industry to redesign the government bureaucracies that would oversee them. They also included devolving to states and localities responsibility for the implementation of key social programs and requiring that citizens take significant responsibility for their own personal well-being. The movement to such entrepreneurial strategies thus would reduce the cost of specific social programs to the federal government and had the added benefit of providing ways to limit federal government intrusion into private lives, thereby addressing the cultural issues that concerned voters.

Congressional Democrats, who had done much to address key postindustrial issues, approached these new ideas cautiously and stymied efforts by the Clinton administration to experiment with them in areas such as health care and welfare. These "old" Democratic reformers, elected in the 1960s and 1970s and now heading key committees and subcommittees, continued to support more traditional, bureaucratized approaches to social policy. They were often locked into such commitments by the need to maintain support from groups benefiting from the traditional design of programs and by the need to sustain the personal influence and expertise they had developed within the existing bureaucratic structure and the congressional committee system that regulated it. Yet most also believed that existing arrangements provided a more reliable and equitable way to address policy concerns than a rushed transformation of government, as seen in the Clinton health reforms, with a more gradualist and expertise-informed experimentation being called for. Their strong support for traditional programmatic strategies and gradualism came, however, at a time when citizens were increasingly frustrated by the inability of the government to rein in its bureaucracy. It also occurred at the point where Republicans were mounting their strong assault on the legitimacy of Congress, questioning whether it and the governing Democrats were truly responsive to the interests and values of citizens. At this critical moment, the

Democrats' failure to support Clinton's experiments with entrepreneurial reforms provided the congressional Republican Party a historic opportunity to push new entrepreneurial strategies of its own and become a major player in this next phase of postindustrial experimentation and paradigm shift.[40]

The Revolution as a Phase in Experimental Learning

Characterized by greater generational turnover than the governing Democrats, and thus more distant from New Deal and Great Society ideas about government, the congressional Republican Party had by the early to mid-1990s come to contain a growing number of new members willing to challenge existing assumptions about government.[41] With backgrounds in private industry and state legislatures, these young Republicans had their own ideas about reinventing government, accepting the need for social programs but often supporting more radical entrepreneurial strategies than had Clinton and Gore and showing more attentiveness to the ways such strategies helped address cultural and family-value issues salient to regional constituencies. They also tended to be a "post-Vietnam" generation of politicians, often too young to have served in the war or cushioned from it by draft deferments or National Guard service, and thus generally untouched by the personal conflicts and suspicion of militarism associated with it. Rather, as the political heirs of Ronald Reagan, their attention was on limiting national government involvement in domestic life through the reinvention of its social programs, with foreign policy seen more nearly as the area of the national government's legitimate power.

Although the Republican Party continued to be attached to traditional policies, including support for business and low taxes, these new perspectives on reinventing and limiting government in the domestic sphere came to the fore of the party's policy agenda. They provided ways to reframe such traditional party commitments, so that low taxes and the restructuring of the tax system became not just a business-related policy but a by-product of government restructuring to make it more responsive to cultural concerns about government intrusiveness and individual responsibility. Most critically, the party balanced its attack on Congress and the congressional Democrats with innovative proposals for policy reform, so that its candidates did not simply oppose existing programs but had constructive strategies to propose for improving them. As congressional Republicans mounted their 1994 campaign, issues such as welfare reform became core elements of the Contract with America and constituted much of what made it innovative, defining the differences between the congressional parties in some distinctly new ways.

Seen through the lens of social learning theory, what is important about the 1994 election is that it presented a choice between the Democrats' bureaucratized approach to social programs and the new, entrepreneurial approach of congressional Republicans. The Republican victory can be seen as signaling the electorate's frustration with the congressional Democrats' traditionalist perspectives and its willingness to risk experimenting with the Republicans' new direction. The election thus was not just a stage in the normal, cyclical alternation in parties, nor just a product of postindustrial tensions, though both helped make it possible; it was also a phase in the process of experimental learning whereby the nation was incrementally recrafting its governing regime. It was the opportunity to experiment with new ideas and programmatic strategies—with new philosophies of the game—that galvanized the Republican activists, particularly Newt Gingrich, and constituted their contribution to national governance.

Once in power, the Republicans faced the difficulty of learning to govern after forty years as the minority party, while simultaneously pursuing their vision of governmental change.[42] Undermined by a weak leadership structure, by inexperience with the responsibilities of majority party status, and by internal divisions, the Republicans made critical missteps early on that squandered their opportunity to institute fundamental alterations in national government. Yet when the party sought common ground with the president and some Democrats, as on welfare reform, telecommunications restructuring, and the revamping of agricultural policy, congressional Republicans achieved victories that served to actualize their entrepreneurial agenda. Such accomplishments helped the party to demonstrate the promise of its paradigmatic shift and to provide citizens with a reason to maintain it in power, despite a concerted Democratic counterattack in the 1996, 1998, and 2000 elections.

Simultaneously, though less evident to much of the public at the time, congressional Republicans pushed for more forceful assertion of American power on the world scene. In particular, in 1998 they passed the Iraqi Liberation Act at a time when President Clinton could not afford politically to veto it. Asserting that "it should be the policy of the U.S. to remove the Iraqi regime," the act "institutionalized the idea of regime change in Iraq" as U.S. policy and thereby established a justification for its subsequent invasion well before the 2000 elections.[43] The great difficulty for the Republicans, both in pursuing their more assertive ideas about foreign policy and in expanding on their domestic policy successes, lay in the veto power and political skill of the Democratic president and the obstructionist successes of his minority congressional party. To truly pursue their paradigm shift, they needed united control of national government and expanded margins in the House and Senate.

The 2000 and 2004 elections gave the Republicans their great chance to push toward unified control of government and seek consolidation of their national majority status. In George W. Bush they had a gifted politician at the head of the ticket articulating the policy perspectives that had emerged within the congressional party over the previous two decades and representing its conservative southern base. Yet the election also provided Democrats their opportunity for a comeback. The victory of neither party was foreordained in 2000, as the popular vote majority of the Democratic candidate, Al Gore, demonstrated. Moreover, congressional Democrats were sufficiently close to the Republicans in the number of seats they controlled in the House and Senate, particularly through the 2002 elections, that their reassertion of congressional control was not unrealistic.

What was historically determinative with respect to the elections, rather than their prestructured outcomes, was that they pitted two closely competitive parties that had adapted in different ways to postindustrialism. Much of that adaptation had come from within the Congress itself over the previous several decades, rather than being driven by the presidency. Thus, much of the continuing competitiveness of the Democrats resulted from their adjustment in their support base and congressional rules in the 1960s and 1970s, which created a more modern, postsegregationist and postindustrial party, in touch with new forms of progressivism. Similarly, the foundation for the victories of George W. Bush and the growing consolidation of Republican power had been laid by congressional Republicans, as they solidified their competitive stance in the South, challenged Democratic hegemony through aggressive campaigns nationwide, and pushed their entrepreneurial and cultural agendas. Members of Congress responded to and exploited opportunities created by the historical forces at work in the contemporary era, crafting a substantially new party system and new patterns of congressional government as they went.

The elections then provided citizens with critical moments of choice and potential self-correction, as they considered which party could best move the nation forward. Their choice in 2000 was complicated by the cross-pressure citizens felt between the strong economy they attributed to the leadership of the Democratic president and their qualms about the cultural and moral values pursued by his party, qualms his private behavior reinforced. The choice in 2004 was made difficult by the tension between the strong performance of the Republican president and Congress in response to the 9/11 terrorist strikes, as Donald Wolfensberger discusses in Chapter 15, and questions about the competence of the president and his party with respect to stewardship of the economy and the invasion of Iraq. And across the elections the hold of Republicans on Congress was made questionable by their seeming inability to make the appropriations process work, as Joshua Gordon discusses in Chapter 12, and by verbal and ethical missteps by leaders such as Trent Lott and Tom DeLay. Yet, impressed by Republicans' resolute response to the terrorist strikes and by their stance on cultural values, the citizens increasingly tilted across the four years toward solidification of Republican control of national government, reinforced in the trend by savvy Republican moves such as the redistricting of House seats by the Republican legislature in Texas. Most fundamentally, the tilt appeared to owe to the desire of citizens for clarity of direction and accountability in performance of the national government, with a majority finally willing in 2004 to give Republicans their clear shot at governing.

This moment of clear choice came slowly and erratically, from the perspective of social learning theory, because reassessment of existing paradigms and experimentation with new ideas is an inherently difficult, lengthy, conflictual, and problematic process. Yet with the 2004 elections, the Republican revolution seems fully realized, and concern turns to how effectively the party can govern, so as to consolidate long-term national majority status. As this transition occurs, and however it may turn out, the essential contributions of the revolution, particularly from the standpoint of the Congress and its institutional legitimacy, need to be recognized.

With the defeat of a long-term governing party in 1994 and the decade-long move to new governing strategies, the Republicans helped to break the sense of paralysis that existed in American politics in the early 1990s and focus the nation on vital issues of deep concern to the citizenry. In doing so, they greatly spurred the process of paradigm reassessment and reconstruction, to such an extent that in the 2000 elections congressional Democrats touted welfare reform, and in 2004 serious proposals for reform of Social Security, long unmentionable in American politics, were commonplace in national debates.

Most critically, as the congressional Republicans faced the opportunity and responsibilities of governing on a sustained basis, which they had not held, in truth, since the 1920s, they came to see more clearly the strengths and contributions of Congress to national governance and even came to defend its prerogatives. They asserted the constitutional role of Congress in annual negotiations with the president, and they asserted their right to impeach a president, drawing on powers that a generation earlier they had denounced when they were used against a Republican president, Richard Nixon. Calls for congressional term limits vanished from party platforms, and the push for constraints on congressional authority decreased. Although Republicans were still struggling to find a vision of Congress that could mesh with their entrepreneurial policy agenda, they were now less prone to emphasize its flaws as justification for reducing its institutional power and constitutional prerogatives.

The Republican revolution thus demonstrates just how critical it is to representative democracy for political parties to alternate in power in legislative assemblies, so that they all will appreciate the complexities and contributions of representative government and will testify in behalf of such assemblies to their diverse supporters. With this testimony from Republicans, American elections have focused less on the legitimacy of Congress as a policymaking institution and more on the principles and strategies that should govern the nation's policy response. This shift surely constitutes a further step toward a viable postindustrial paradigm and the relegitimation of Congress as a governing institution.

Conclusion

Congress is a dynamic institution continually being reshaped by cycles of partisan learning and regime change. For a time it may be dominated by one party or factional coalition, by entrenched societal interests and institutional arrangements, and by an overarching philosophy or governing paradigm. But across time governing groups become overconfident of their mastery of electoral and organizational politics, societal change upends the support bases of the entrenched regime, and innovative ideas and experimental learning allow a new generation of partisans to open pathways to policy responsiveness and institutional renewal. The Republican revolution is a classic instance of these processes at work, as was the rise of liberal Democratic reformers a generation earlier. As Congress and its parties respond to these processes in the contemporary era, they adapt the nation to postindustrialism and incrementally address the issues of governing legitimacy that confront them.

With the 2004 elections, the adaptive processes in Congress and national politics moved the country into a new phase—an effort by Republicans to consolidate their hold on national power through effective performance in governance and skillful crafting of reliable long-term citizen support. The party would now appear to have clear advantages in this effort. With solid majorities in the House and Senate and popular majority support for their president, lingering questions about Republicans' legitimate hold on power are dissipating and they have more room for maneuver as they seek to build policy majorities on Capitol Hill. In doing so, the party has strengthened its dominance in the South, now its core electoral base, while remaining competitive nationally, particularly in the Midwest and West. And it has a message that resonates with voters, that a majority has embraced amid a highly engaged and contested election, signaling some considerable commitment to the party and its principles that may sustain it through difficult times.[44] Moreover, Republicans are poised to exploit potential weaknesses within the Democratic Party. These include the possibility that popular longtime Democratic incumbents in Congress may choose to retire in the face of the Republicans' strength on the Hill, giving the Republican Party an opportunity to expand its majority through capturing contests for open seats previously held by Democrats; the deepening difficulties Democrats have in competing in much of the South, particularly for Senate seats; and the Democrats' ongoing failure to develop a compelling approach to citizen concerns about cultural values and individual responsibility.

The momentary strength of congressional Republicans and the weakness of Democrats, however, should not blind observers to the potential pitfalls that the majority party now faces. Within Congress Republicans continue to struggle with the creation of a policy process that generates responsible and timely decisions and that does so in a way that engages its policy experts within the standing committees. A critical task before Republicans in Congress now is to craft a process that provides members with satisfying and meaningful input into policy decisions and also protects the powers of the institution vis-à-vis the executive. In the short run, in their push to majority status the Republicans in Congress increasingly accepted considerable assertion of policymaking power by party leaders and the Republican president. But with majority status more clearly in hand, members now may come to demand greater personal payoff within the Congress and greater presidential respect for Congress in congressional-executive negotiations. Ensuring that service in Congress is rewarding to members in a Republican era is critical to maintaining quality candidates for office and encouraging them to take seriously the policymaking responsibilities of the institution. Yet should Republicans go too far in spreading power and autonomy among members, that can weaken the party's cohesion and governing capacities. All of this is to say that Republicans now must confront the tensions between individual autonomy and collective governance that come as the rewards and responsibilities of majority party status become increasingly evident.

Within the nation and world at large, Republicans must recognize that societal and international changes continue unabated, so that many of the forces that created opportunities for them to exploit over the past several decades may prove transient and even countervailing in their longer-term consequences. As but one example, the southern realignment could be complicated by a growing Latino population in the South and by movement to the South of the descendants of the African Americans who left it for the North during the era of southern segregation. Both developments could provide Democrats with renewed opportunities in some southern states, including the two largest, Florida and Texas. These opportunities could be magnified by the growing experience and clout of minority members within Congress, as Kerry Haynie discusses in Chapter 17 with respect to African Americans. Moreover, insofar as the southern realignment solidifies and southerners dominate the Republican Party, the result could be such a strongly conservative party that more moderate electorates elsewhere in the nation could become alienated from the party's policy stances.[45] As a second example, the forces of globalization could generate growing economic dislocations in the nation that give greater salience and resonance to the Democrats' stress on economic issues. As a third, unpopular or destructive policy actions by Republicans in controversial areas such as judicial appointments, as Sarah Binder and Forrest Maltzman discuss in Chapter 13, could reignite concerns about institutional legitimacy, this time perhaps coming forcefully from the left. And as a fourth, the ongoing restructuring of post–cold war power dynamics, including the rise of nonstate terrorism, may continue to pose unforeseen challenges that could test the party in new ways.

Finally, looking to the world of ideas, what ultimately matters with respect to party principles, congressional programs, and paradigm shifts is not just how well they resonate with citizens in the abstract, but how well a party delivers on promises and how effective its programs and principles prove to be in practice. A critical issue in this respect is how accurately a party gauges the true nature of social reality, the viability of programs within that reality, and their long-term side effects. Such concerns, raised forcefully by Catherine Rudder in her discussion of fiscal policy and reform of social programs in Chapter 14, pose perhaps the greatest threat to long-term Republican consolidation of power.

Democrats were sustained in power for decades not just because of constituent service prowess or safe southern seats but because their broad principles of social justice seemed appropriate to the Depression era and post–Depression world, and their programs, such as Social Security and price supports, appeared to work in protecting workers and fostering a sound economy. Similarly, their early adjustment to postindustrialism gained broad acceptance, as an increasingly educated, affluent, and informed nation could not tolerate segregation, poverty among the elderly, second-class status for women, and other injustices inherited from industrial-era social relations.

The party's majority collapsed in the face of cultural dilemmas and fiscal pressures that emerged with the longer-term side effects of postindustrialism and Democrats' progressive response to it. The cultural dilemmas are best illustrated by the growing sense that some social programs enacted by Democrats induced an ethic of dependency among recipients of government support and by the moral concerns raised as the party championed women's right to choice with respect to abortion, even including government financing of some such procedures. The longer-term fiscal pressures are illustrated by the anticipation of systemic crises in the maintenance of entitlement programs, such as Social Security and Medicare, as the nation's population ages and by concerns that the tax structure necessary to meet entitlement obligations could undermine the sustenance of an innovative, productive, and growing economy.

Republicans now propose to restructure much that Democrats put in place that appeared to work for considerable periods of time—Social Security, the progressive tax system, Medicare for the elderly, social programs for the poor, privacy in lifestyle choices, and so forth. The restructuring is justified as a response to cultural concerns and family values and also as an attempt to address projected fiscal crises generated by social programs. Republicans also appear prepared to continue the pursuit of a more interventionist approach to international relations than the multilateral strategy long associated with Democratic administrations, with this response justified by the unique threats posed by modern terrorism. The question is how well these initiatives will work in practice, attending to economic and international realities while generating a more moral and fiscally sound nation, and at what social as well as economic price to individual citizens. Additional questions include the price of the Republicans' efforts in terms of constitutional power arrangements, particularly for the sustainability of a strong Congress in the face of growing reliance on party discipline within Congress in support of presidential policy and power.[46] Also of concern is the effect that a muscular foreign policy may have on citizens' personal liberties, particularly insofar as terrorism continues to blur the boundaries between domestic and international security.[47]

As I conclude this analysis in the week following the 2004 elections, it is far too early to know how successful the Republican majority will prove to be in its efforts and how well Congress will serve the nation as these policy struggles proceed. The challenges facing the party and the Congress are substantial. Moreover, as the events of 9/11 demonstrate, history will have its surprises just around the bend, testing the nation's resolve, creativity, and learning capacities anew. Problems with debilitating ambitions, antiquated procedures, and entrenched interests also continue—moderated by waves of reform and change but still capable of inserting themselves destructively into congressional politics and national life. In the face of these concerns, we cannot be sure that our policy experiments and institutional adjustments are adequate to the challenge.

What we know at this point is that we have already adjusted our governing perspectives across a forty-year process of experimentation and governing innovation within Congress, with these adjustments sustaining the nation in past challenges and generating this moment of concentrated attention to new ones. We also know one other thing: that Congress, the parties, and the electorate are capable of rising to the occasion, restructuring political alignments, and learning to address societal problems anew.

To appreciate this capacity, we must attend to the conceptual lenses through which we examine Congress and craft multiple theoretical perspectives that help us envision it more completely. Such perspectives should enable us to look beyond momentary partisan controversies and see the dynamic, historical processes at play in congressional politics. In crafting such lenses, we must bring to the endeavor the commonsense judgment we demonstrate in daily life, taking care to focus on the motives and strategic behavior of participants in the foreground, on the shifting background contexts, and then ultimately on the ideas that participants hold about politics and society.

As we do so, crafting social choice theories to analyze the foreground, social structure theories to interpret the background, and social learning theories to comprehend the role of ideas, we see an overall pattern that no one of our theories could fully illuminate that helps us understand how Congress can constructively respond to societal problems. Through these multiple lenses, we see the contest for governing power that ensures that partisans will highlight societal problems as they challenge for control of Congress. We see the dynamic societal changes that generate new citizen demands, policy challenges, and electoral coalitions. And we see the coming of a new generation of legislators, social activists, and engaged citizens, who push Congress to experiment with fresh ideas, address the pressing policy challenges, and solve societal problems.

Examining the contemporary Congress through these multiple lenses, we see an institution responding to the problems and opportunities of postindustrialism—gradually, incrementally, and partially, but also in sustained and consequential ways. The concerns to which Congress has responded, though perhaps too limited in number and imperfect in their resolution, are significant ones, and they include such seemingly intransigent problems as racial segregation, gender inequality, poverty among the elderly, urban pollution, budget deficits, economic restructuring, welfare dependency, and international terrorism. Although Congress has not tackled these issues alone, and at times has exacerbated them, it ultimately has contributed to the experimental learning that helped to address them. This capacity of a political institution to contribute to social learning in a sustained and consequential fashion and in a manner ultimately controlled and shaped by a nation's citizens is no small accomplishment.

Time will tell whether the new Republican Congress now helps us learn enough of the right things, and adequately assimilate them with the enduring truths inherited from past generations, to redress the continuing problems associated with postindustrialism. Insofar as it does, it can consolidate a new partisan regime that could conceivably set the direction of the nation for decades to come. And insofar as its experiments fail, we should recall that the essence of policy experimentation within our democracy is the ability of our nation's citizens to learn from error and try again, a lesson Democrats have experienced with growing force over the past decade, to their regret, and that Republicans should keep firmly in mind. This is, after all, the great promise of representative government and electoral democracy—both the ability of a citizenry to find firm footing through the iterative crafting of responsive and responsible new regimes and the ability to hold regimes accountable for their performance. Moreover, Congress is the great stage on which so much of this regime crafting and sustained accountability proceeds. Perhaps this realization will encourage us to embrace the possibilities that this era of Republican experimentation presents and to recognize the vital and legitimate roles that Congress can play—as an arena of majority policy crafting and minority policy challenge—as we approach the challenges ahead.

Notes

1. William F. Connelly and John J. Pitney Jr., *Congress' Permanent Minority? Republicans in the U.S. House* (Lanham, Md.: Rowman and Littlefield, 1994).
2. Joseph Cooper, ed., *Congress and the Decline of Public Trust* (Boulder, Colo.: Westview, 1999), and John R. Hibbing and Elizabeth Theiss-Morse, *Congress as Public Enemy: Public Attitudes toward American Political Institutions* (Cambridge: Cambridge University Press, 1995).
3. Walter Dean Burnham, "Realignment Lives," in *The Clinton Presidency,* ed. Bert Rockman (Pittsburgh: University of Pittsburgh Press, 1995).
4. For an overview of the Republican revolution and Gingrich's perceived role in it, see Dan Balz and Ronald Brownstein, *Storming the Gates: Protest Politics and the Republican Revival* (Boston: Little, Brown, 1996).
5. For a revealing look at Gingrich's own take on these matters, see Newt Gingrich and Marianne Gingrich, "Postindustrial Politics: The Leader as Learner," *The Futurist,* December 1981, 30–32.
6. Walter Dean Burnham, "Pattern Recognition and 'Doing' Political History: Art, Science, or Bootless Enterprise?" and Hugh Heclo, "Ideas, Interests, and Institutions," both in *The Dynamics of American Politics,* ed. Lawrence C. Dodd and Calvin Jillson (Boulder, Colo.: Westview, 1994).
7. On social choice theory, see William H. Riker, *Liberalism vs. Populism* (San Francisco: W. H. Freeman, 1982); and Kenneth A. Shepsle and Mark S. Bonchek, *Analyzing Politics: Rationality, Behavior, and Institutions* (New York: Norton, 1997).
8. Morris P. Fiorina, *Representatives, Roll Calls, and Constituencies* (Lexington, Mass.: Lexington Books, 1974); Morris Fiorina, *Congress: Keystone of the Washington Establishment* (New Haven: Yale University Press, 1977); and David R. Mayhew, *Congress: The Electoral Connection* (New Haven: Yale University Press, 1974).
9. See, for example, their essay "The Logic of Conditional Party Government: Revisiting the Electoral Connection," in *Congress Reconsidered,* 7th ed., ed. Lawrence C. Dodd and Bruce I. Oppenheimer (Washington, D.C.: CQ Press, 2001).
10. Richard F. Fenno Jr., *Congressmen in Committees* (Boston: Little, Brown, 1973); and Barbara Sinclair, *Legislators, Leaders, and Lawmaking: The U.S. House of Representatives in the Postreform Era* (Baltimore: Johns Hopkins University Press, 1995).

11. Anthony Downs, *An Economic Theory of Democracy* (New York: Harper and Row, 1957).
12. Barry R. Weingast, "A Rational Choice Perspective on Congressional Norms," *American Journal of Political Science* 23 (1979): 249.
13. Roger H. Davidson and Walter Oleszek, *Congress against Itself* (Bloomington: Indiana University Press, 1977); C. Lawrence Evans and Walter J. Oleszek, *Congress Under Fire* (Boston: Houghton Mifflin, 1997); Glenn R. Parker, *Institutional Change, Discretion, and the Making of Modern Congress: An Economic Interpretation* (Ann Arbor: University of Michigan Press, 1992); and Raymond E. Wolfinger and Joan Heifetz Hollinger, "Safe Seats, Seniority, and Power in Congress," *American Political Science Review* 80 (1965): 337–349.
14. Lawrence C. Dodd, "Congress and the Quest for Power," in *Congress Reconsidered,* ed. Lawrence C. Dodd and Bruce I. Oppenheimer (New York: Praeger, 1977).
15. Lawrence C. Dodd, "The Cycles of Legislative Change," in *Political Science: The Science of Politics,* ed. Herbert Weisberg (New York: Agathon, 1986).
16. Fiorina, *Congress: Keystone of the Washington Establishment.*
17. Gary Jacobson, "The Marginals Never Vanished," *American Journal of Political Science* 31 (1987): 126–141; and Thomas E. Mann, *Unsafe at Any Margin* (Washington, D.C.: American Enterprise Institute, 1978).
18. This argument reflects the "retrospective voting perspective" developed by Key and Fiorina in their study of presidential elections. See V. O. Key, *The Responsible Electorate* (New York: Vintage, 1966); and Morris Fiorina, *Retrospective Voting in American National Elections* (New Haven: Yale University Press, 1981).
19. For a more extensive discussion of this paradox, see Bruce I. Oppenheimer, "Abdicating Congressional Power," in *Congress Reconsidered,* 6th ed., ed. Lawrence C. Dodd and Bruce I. Oppenheimer (Washington, D.C.: CQ Press, 1997).
20. Nelson Polsby, "The Institutionalization of the U.S. House of Representatives," *American Political Science Review* 62 (1968): 144–168. See also Nelson Polsby, *How Congress Evolves* (New York: Oxford, 2004).
21. See James Sterling Young, *The Washington Community, 1800–1828* (New York: Columbia University Press, 1966); Woodrow Wilson, *Congressional Government* (Gloucester, Mass.: Peter Smith, reissued 1973); Joseph Cooper and David W. Brady, "Toward a Diachronic Analysis of Change," *American Political Science Review* 75 (1981): 988–1006; and Theodore J. Lowi, *The End of Liberalism* (New York: Norton, 1979). Other important historical analyses that reflect the influence of social context include Elaine Swift, *The Making of the American Senate* (Ann Arbor: University of Michigan Press, 1996); and Eric Schickler, *Disjointed Pluralism: Institutional Innovation and the Development of the U.S. Congress* (Princeton: Princeton University Press, 2001).
22. For discussion of the "legitimation crisis paradigm" within sociology, see Edward W. Lehman, *The Viable Polity* (Philadelphia: Temple University Press, 1992); for a forceful statement, see Jürgen Habermas, *Legitimation Crisis* (Boston: Beacon, 1973).
23. For a general statement of the powerful influence that antiquated institutions may have on new historical eras, see Karen Oren and Stephen Skowronek, "Beyond the Iconography of Order: Notes for a 'New Institutionalism,'" in *The Dynamics of American Politics,* ed. Dodd and Jillson.
24. On the nature of postmaterialism in the contemporary era, see Ronald Inglehart, *Culture Shift in Advanced Industrial Democracies* (Princeton: Princeton University Press, 1994).
25. On the development of such cultural concerns as salient election issues, see David C. Leege, Kenneth Wald, Paul Mueller, and Brian Krueger, *The Politics of Cultural Differences: Social Change and Voter Mobilization Strategies in the Post–New Deal Period* (Princeton: Princeton University Press, 2002). For an analysis of congressional

response to the rise of cultural issues, see Elizabeth A. Oldmixon, *Making Moral Decisions: God, Sex and the U.S. House of Representatives* (Washington, D.C.: Georgetown University Press, 2005).

26. Lawrence C. Dodd, "Congress, the Constitution, and the Crisis of Legitimation," in *Congress Reconsidered,* 2nd ed., ed. Lawrence C. Dodd and Bruce I. Oppenheimer (Washington, D.C.: CQ Press, 1981). For a broad-gauged historical discussion of the ways in which the organization of Congress (focused on the House) can influence its legitimacy as a policymaking institution, see Joseph Cooper, "The Origins of the Standing Committees and the Development of the Modern House," *Rice University Studies* 56 (3): 111–130.
27. Morris Fiorina, *Congress: Keystone of the Washington Establishment,* 2nd ed. (New Haven: Yale University Press, 1989).
28. For an insightful and thorough discussion of the subsequent quarter-century struggle within Congress over how best to deal with budget policymaking and deficit spending, see Jasmine Farrier, *Passing the Buck: Congress, the Budget, and Deficits* (Lexington: University Press of Kentucky, 2004).
29. Eric M. Uslaner, *The Decline of Comity in Congress* (Ann Arbor: University of Michigan Press, 1993).
30. For a discussion of the ways in which term limits on the Speaker, and related factors, helped create a weakened leadership structure, see Ronald M. Peters Jr., "Institutional Context and Leadership Style," in *New Majority or Old Minority?* ed. Nicol C. Rae and Colton Campbell (Lanham, Md.: Rowman and Littlefield, 1999); see also Dodd and Oppenheimer, "Revolution in the House: Testing the Limits of Party Government," in *Congress Reconsidered,* 6th ed., 1997.
31. Gregory Bateson, *Steps to an Ecology of Mind* (New York: Ballantine, 1972); and Geoffrey Vickers, *Value Systems and Social Process* (London: Tavistock, 1968). For a useful application of social learning theory to political science, see Peter Hall, "Policy Paradigms, Social Learning and the State," *Comparative Politics* 25 (1993): 75–96. My application of social learning theory to politics here, following Hall's lead, restates it in the language of philosopher of science Thomas Kuhn. See Thomas Kuhn, *The Structure of Scientific Revolutions* (Chicago: University of Chicago Press, 1970).
32. For my earlier application of social learning theory to American politics, see Lawrence C. Dodd, "Congress, the Presidency, and the American Experience," in *Divided Democracy,* ed. James A. Thurber (Washington, D.C.: CQ Press, 1991); and Lawrence C. Dodd, "Political Learning and Political Change," in *The Dynamics of American Politics,* ed. Dodd and Jillson.
33. Lawrence C. Dodd, "A Theory of Congressional Cycles," in *Congress and Policy Change,* ed. Gerald Wright, Leroy Rieselbach, and Lawrence C. Dodd (New York: Agathon, 1986).
34. John W. Kingdon, *Agendas, Alternatives, and Public Policy* (Boston: Little, Brown, 1984); and David R. Mayhew, *America's Congress* (New Haven: Yale University Press, 2000).
35. See James MacGregor Burns, *The Deadlock of Democracy* (Englewood Cliffs, N.J.: Prentice Hall, 1963); and Samuel P. Huntington, "Congressional Responses to the Twentieth Century," in *The Congress and America's Future,* ed. David B. Truman (Englewood Cliffs, N.J.: Prentice Hall, 1965).
36. See also Sarah A. Binder, *Stalemate: Causes and Consequences of Legislative Gridlock* (Washington, D.C.: Brookings Institution Press, 2003).
37. Richard Bolling, *House Out of Order* (New York: Dutton, 1965); and *Power in the House* (New York: Dutton, 1965). See also the discussion in David W. Rohde, *Parties and Leaders in the Postreform House* (Chicago: University of Chicago Press, 1991), chap. 1. For an innovative theoretical explanation for the long-term historical transition from

party government in the late nineteenth century, to committee government in the mid-twentieth century, and now back to party government, see Thomas Raven, "Institutional Development in the House of Representatives, 1890–2000," paper presented at the 100th Annual Meeting of the American Political Science Association, Chicago, Illinois, September 4, 2004.

38. Earl Black and Merle Black, *The Rise of Southern Republicans* (Cambridge, Mass.: Harvard University Press, 2002).
39. On the emergence of this entrepreneurial perspective and its importance for Congress, see Lawrence C. Dodd, "Congress and the Politics of Renewal," in *Congress Reconsidered,* 5th ed., ed. Lawrence C. Dodd and Bruce I. Oppenheimer (Washington, D.C.: CQ Press, 1993).
40. See, for supportive analysis, Haynes Johnson and David Broder, *The System* (Boston: Little, Brown, 1996); see also President Clinton's assessment of this period in Joe Klein, "Eight Years: Bill Clinton and the Politics of Persistence," in *The New Yorker,* October 16–23, 2000, 206–209.
41. Michael B. Berkman, *The State Roots of National Policy* (Pittsburgh: University of Pittsburgh Press, 1991); and Douglas L. Koopman, *Hostile Takeover: The House Republican Party, 1980–1995* (Lanham, Md.: Rowman and Littlefield, 1996).
42. Richard F. Fenno Jr., *Learning to Govern* (Washington, D.C.: Brookings Institution Press, 1997); and David Price, *The Congressional Experience,* 3rd edition (Boulder, Colo.: Westview, 2004), particularly chaps. 7, 8, and 9.
43. See Manar El Shorbagy, "The Congressional Dilemma over Iraqi Policy," an unpublished working paper discussed at the Woodrow Wilson International Center for Scholars in November 2003. The quotes are from page three of the discussion paper. El Shorbagy is the Academic Director of the Al Waleed Center for American Studies at the American University in Cairo, Egypt.
44. For an extended discussion of how intense, highly contested and engaged elections can generate strong voter support for parties and regimes, see Leslie E. Anderson and Lawrence C. Dodd, *Learning Democracy: Citizen Engagement and Electoral Choice in Nicaragua, 1990–2001* (Chicago: University of Chicago Press, 2005).
45. Theodore Lowi, *The End of the Republican Era* (Norman: University of Oklahoma Press, 1995).
46. For an insightful and prescient discussion of the potential threat that a strengthening of party government in the House could pose for its autonomy from the presidency, see Cooper, "The Origins of the Standing Committees and the Development of the Modern House," 128–130.
47. For relevant discussions, see the chapters in *Transforming the American Polity: The Presidency of George W. Bush and the War on Terrorism,* ed. Richard Conley (Upper Saddle River, N.J.: Prentice Hall, 2005).

Suggested Readings

✧ ✧ ✧

Aberbach, Joel D. *Keeping a Watchful Eye.* Washington, D.C.: Brookings, 1990.

Abramowitz, Alan I. "Incumbency, Campaign Spending, and the Decline of Competition in U.S. House Elections." *Journal of Politics* 53 (1991): 34–56.

Abramowitz, Alan I., and Jeffrey A. Segal. *Senate Elections.* Ann Arbor: University of Michigan Press, 1992.

Abramson, Paul, John H. Aldrich, and David W. Rohde. "Progressive Ambition among United States Senators: 1972–1988." *Journal of Politics* 49 (1987): 3–35.

Adler, E. Scott. *Why Congressional Reforms Fail.* Chicago: University of Chicago Press, 2002.

Adler, E. Scott, and John S. Lipinski. "Demand - Side Theory and Congressional Committee Composition: A Constituency Characteristics Approach." *American Journal of Political Science* 41 (1997): 895–918.

Aldrich, John H. *Why Parties? The Origin and Transformation of Political Parties in America.* Chicago: University of Chicago Press, 1995.

Aldrich, John H., and David W. Rohde. "The Republican Revolution and the House Appropriations Committee." *Journal of Politics* 62 (February 2000): 1–33.

Alesina, Alberto, and Howard Rosenthal. "Partisan Cycles in Congressional Elections and the Macroeconomy." *American Political Science Review* 83 (1989): 373–398.

Anderson, Thorton. *Creating the Constitution: The Convention of 1787 and the First Congress.* University Park: Pennsylvania State University Press, 1993.

Ansolabehere, Stephen, and Alan Gerber. "The Effects of Filing Fees and Petition Requirements in U.S. House Elections." *Legislative Studies Quarterly* 21 (1996): 249–264.

Ansolabehere, Stephen, James M. Snyder Jr., and Charles Stewart III. "Candidate Positioning in U.S. House Elections." *American Journal of Political Science* 45 (2001): 136–159.

Ansolabehere, Stephen, James M. Snyder Jr., and Michael M. Ting. "Bargaining in Bicameral Legislatures: When and Why Does Malapportionment Matter?" *American Political Science Review* 97 (2003): 471–481.

Arnold, Laura W. "The Distribution of Senate Committee Positions: Change or More of the Same?" *Legislative Studies Quarterly* 26 (2001): 227–249.

Arnold, R. Douglas. *Congress and the Bureaucracy.* New Haven: Yale University Press, 1979.

———. *The Logic of Congressional Action.* New Haven: Yale University Press, 1990.

Asher, Herbert B. "The Learning of Legislative Norms." *American Political Science Review* 67 (1973): 499–513.

Bach, Stanley, and Steven S. Smith. *Managing Uncertainty in the House: Adaptation and Innovation in Special Rules.* Washington, D.C.: Brookings, 1988.

Baker, Ross K. *House and Senate.* New York: Norton, 1989.

Balla, Steven J., and John R. Wright. "Interest Groups, Advisory Committees, and Congressional Control of the Bureaucracy." *American Journal of Political Science* 45 (2001): 799–812.

Bauer, Raymond A., Ithiel de Sola Pool, and Lewis A. Dexter. *American Business and Public Policy.* New York: Atherton, 1963.

Baumgartner, Frank R., and Bryan D. Jones. "Agenda Dynamics and Policy Subsystems." *Journal of Politics* 53 (November 1991): 1044–1074.

Baumgartner, Frank R., Bryan D. Jones, and Michael C. MacLeod. "The Evolution of Legislative Jurisdictions." *Journal of Politics* 62 (2000): 321–349.

Bell, Lauren Cohen. *Warring Factions: Interest Groups, Money, and the New Politics of Senate Confirmation.* Columbus: Ohio State University Press, 2002.

Benjamin, Gerald, and Michael Malbin, eds. *Limiting Legislative Terms.* Washington, D.C.: CQ Press, 1992.

Berkman, Michael B. "State Legislators in Congress: Strategic Politicians, Professional Legislatures, and the Party Nexus." *American Journal of Political Science* 38 (1994): 1025–1055.

___. *The State Roots of National Politics: Congress and the Tax Agenda, 1978–1986.* Pittsburgh: University of Pittsburgh Press, 1993.

Bianco, William T. *Trust: Representatives and Constituents.* Ann Arbor: University of Michigan Press, 1994.

Bibby, John F., and Roger H. Davidson. *On Capitol Hill.* 2nd ed. Hinsdale, Ill.: Dryden Press, 1972.

Binder, Sarah A. "The Dynamics of Legislative Gridlock, 1947–96." *American Political Science Review* 93 (1999): 519–534.

___. *Minority Rights, Majority Rule.* New York: Cambridge University Press, 1997.

___. "The Partisan Basis of Procedural Choice: Allocating Parliamentary Rights in the House, 1789–1900." *American Political Science Review* 90 (1996): 8–20.

___. *Stalemate: Causes and Consequences of Legislative Gridlock.* Washington, D.C.: Brookings, 2003.

Binder, Sarah A., and Forrest Maltzman. "The Limits of Senatorial Courtesy." *Legislative Studies Quarterly* 24 (2004): 5–22.

Binder, Sarah A., and Steven S. Smith. *Politics or Principle? Filibustering in the United States Senate.* Washington, D.C.: Brookings, 1997.

Black, Earl, and Merle Black. *The Rise of Southern Republicans.* Cambridge, Mass.: Harvard University Press, 2002.

Bolling, Richard. *House Out of Order.* New York: Dutton, 1965.

___. *Power in the House.* New York: Dutton, 1965.

Bond, Jon R., and Richard Fleisher. *Polarized Politics: The President and the Congress in a Partisan Era.* Washington, D.C.: CQ Press, 2000.

———. *The President in the Legislative Arena.* Chicago: University of Chicago Press, 1990.

Born, Richard. "Changes in the Competitiveness of House Primary Elections, 1956–1976." *American Politics Quarterly* 8 (1980): 495–506.

Bosso, Christopher. *Pesticides and Politics: The Life Cycle of a Public Issue.* Pittsburgh: University of Pittsburgh Press, 1988.

Brady, David W. *Congressional Voting in a Partisan Era: A Study of the McKinley Houses.* Lawrence: University Press of Kansas, 1973.

———. *Critical Elections and Congressional Policy Making.* Stanford: Stanford University Press, 1988.

Brady, David W., and Mathew McCubbins, eds. *Party, Process, and Political Change in Congress.* Stanford: Stanford University Press, 2002.

Brady, David W., and Craig Volden. *Revolving Gridlock: Politics and Policy from Carter to Clinton.* Boulder, Colo.: Westview, 1998.

Brady, David W., Joseph Cooper, and Patricia A. Hurley. "The Decline of Party in the U.S. House of Representatives, 1887–1968." *Legislative Studies Quarterly* 4 (1979): 381–407.

Bullock, Charles S., III. "House Committee Assignments." In *The Congressional System: Notes and Readings.* 2nd ed. Ed. Leroy N. Rieselbach. North Scituate, Mass.: Duxbury Press, 1979.

Burrell, Barbara C. *A Woman's Place Is in the House.* Ann Arbor: University of Michigan Press, 1994.

Cain, Bruce, John Ferejohn, and Morris Fiorina. *The Personal Vote: Constituency Service and Electoral Independence.* Cambridge: Harvard University Press, 1967.

Campbell, James E. *The Presidential Pulse of Congressional Elections.* Lexington: University Press of Kentucky, 1993.

Canes-Wrone, Brandice, David W. Brady, and John F. Cogan. "Out of Step, Out of Office: Electoral Accountability and House Members' Voting." *American Political Science Review* 96 (2002): 127–140.

Canon, David T. *Actors, Athletes, and Astronauts: Political Amateurs in the United States Congress.* Chicago: University of Chicago Press, 1990.

———. *Race, Redistricting, and Representation: The Unintended Consequences of Black Majority Districts.* Chicago: University of Chicago Press, 1999.

Canon, David T., and Kenneth R. Mayer. *The Dysfunctional Congress? The Individual Roots of an Institutional Dilemma.* Boulder, Colo.: Westview, 1999.

Canon, David T., Matthew Schousen, and Patrick Sellers. "The Supply Side of Congressional Redistricting: Race and Strategic Politicians, 1972–1992." *Journal of Politics* 58 (1996): 846–862.

Clausen, Aage R. *How Congressmen Decide.* New York: St. Martin's, 1973.

Clem, Alan L., ed. *The Making of Congressmen: Seven Campaigns of 1974.* North Scituate, Mass.: Duxbury Press, 1976.

Collie, Melissa, and Brian E. Roberts. "Trading Places: Choice and Committee Chairs in the U.S. Senate, 1950–1986." *Journal of Politics* 54 (1992): 231–245.

Cook, Elizabeth Adell, Sue Thomas, and Clyde Wilcox, eds. *The Year of the Woman: Myths and Reality.* Boulder, Colo.: Westview, 1994.

Cooper, Joseph. *The Origins of the Standing Committees and the Development of the Modern House.* Houston: Rice University Studies, 1971.

___, ed. *Congress and the Decline of Public Trust.* Boulder, Colo.: Westview, 1999.

Cooper, Joseph, and David W. Brady. "Institutional Context and Leadership Style: The House from Cannon to Rayburn." *American Political Science Review* 75 (1981): 411–425.

___. "Toward a Diachronic Analysis of Congress." *American Political Science Review* 75 (1981): 988–1006.

Cooper, Joseph, and G. Calvin Mackenzie. *The House at Work.* Austin: University of Texas Press, 1981.

Cooper, Joseph, and Garry Young. "Partisanship, Bipartisanship, and Crosspartisanship in Congress since the New Deal." In *Congress Reconsidered.* 6th ed. Ed. Lawrence C. Dodd and Bruce I. Oppenheimer. Washington, D.C.: CQ Press, 1997.

Cover, Albert D. "Contacting Congressional Constituents: Some Patterns of Perquisite Use." *American Journal of Political Science* 24 (1980): 125–134.

Cover, Albert D., and David R. Mayhew. "Congressional Dynamics and the Decline of Competitive Congressional Elections." In *Congress Reconsidered.* 2nd ed. Ed. Lawrence C. Dodd and Bruce I. Oppenheimer. Washington, D.C.: CQ Press, 1981.

Cox, Gary, and Jonathan Katz. *Elbridge Gerry's Salamander.* Cambridge: Cambridge University Press, 2002.

Cox, Gary, and Mathew McCubbins. *Legislative Leviathan: Party Government in the House.* Berkeley: University of California Press, 1993.

___. *Parties and Committees in the U.S. House of Representatives.* Berkeley: University of California Press, 1990.

Cox, Gary W., and Keith T. Poole. "On Measuring Partisanship in Roll-Call Voting: The U.S. House of Representatives, 1877–1999." *American Journal of Political Science* 46 (2002): 477–489.

Cox, James, Gregory Hager, and David Lowery. "Regime Change in Presidential and Congressional Budgeting: Role Discontinuity or Role Evolution?" *American Journal of Political Science* 37 (1993): 88–118.

Davidson, Roger H., ed. *The Postreform Congress.* New York: St. Martin's, 1992.

Davidson, Roger H., and Walter J. Oleszek. *Congress against Itself.* Bloomington: Indiana University Press, 1977.

___. *Congress and Its Members.* 5th ed. Washington, D.C.: CQ Press, 1996.

De Boef, Suzanna, and James A. Stimson. "The Dynamic Structure of Congressional Elections." *Journal of Politics* 55 (1993): 630–648.

Deering, Christopher J., and Steven S. Smith. *Committees in Congress.* 3rd ed. Washington, D.C.: CQ Press, 1997.

DeGregorio, Christine, and Kevin Snider. "Leadership Appeal in the U.S. House of Representatives: Comparing Officeholders and Aides." *Legislative Studies Quarterly* 20 (1995): 491–511.

Destler, I. M. *Renewing Fast-Track Legislation.* Washington, D.C.: Institute for International Economics and Policy Analysis, no. 50, September 1997.

Dexter, Lewis A. *How Organizations Are Represented in Washington.* Indianapolis: Bobbs-Merrill, 1969.

___. *The Sociology and Politics of Congress.* Chicago: Rand McNally, 1969.

Dion, Douglas. *Turning the Legislative Thumbscrew: Minority Rights and Procedural Change in Legislative Politics.* Ann Arbor: University of Michigan Press, 1997.

Dion, Douglas, and John Huber. "Procedural Choice and the House Committee on Rules." *Journal of Politics* 58 (1996): 25–53.

Dodd, Lawrence C. "Coalition-Building by Party Leaders: A Case Study of House Democrats." *Congress and the Presidency Journal* 10 (fall 1983): 145–168.

___. "Congress and the Quest for Power." In *Congress Reconsidered.* 1st ed. Ed. Lawrence C. Dodd and Bruce I. Oppenheimer. New York: Praeger, 1977.

___. "Congress, the Constitution, and the Crisis of Legitimation." In *Congress Reconsidered.* 2nd ed. Ed. Lawrence C. Dodd and Bruce I. Oppenheimer. Washington, D.C.: CQ Press, 1981.

___. "The Cycles of Legislative Change." In *Political Science: The Science of Politics.* Ed. Herbert F. Weisberg. New York: Agathon Press, 1986.

___. "Making Sense Out of Our Exceptional Senate: Perspectives and Commentary." In *U.S. Senate Exceptionalism.* Ed. Bruce I. Oppenheimer. Columbus: Ohio State University Press, 2002, 350–363.

Dodd, Lawrence C., and Richard L. Schott. *Congress and the Administrative State.* 2nd ed. Boulder, Colo.: Westview, 1994.

Eckhardt, Bob, and Charles L. Black Jr. *The Titles of Power: Conversations on the American Constitution.* New Haven: Yale University Press, 1976.

Endersby, James W., and Karen M. McCurdy. "Committee Assignments in the U.S. Senate." *Legislative Studies Quarterly* 21 (1996): 219–234.

Epstein, David, and Peter Zemsky. "Money Talks: Deterring Quality Challengers in Congressional Elections." *American Political Science Review* 89 (1995): 295–308.

Erikson, Robert S. "The Advantage of Incumbency in Congressional Elections." *Polity* 3 (1971): 395–405.

___. "Is There Such a Thing as a Safe Seat?" *Polity* 8 (1976): 623–632.

___. "The Puzzle of Midterm Loss." *Journal of Politics* 50 (1988): 1011–1029.

Eulau, Heinz, and Paul Karps. "The Puzzle of Representation." *Legislative Studies Quarterly* 2 (1977): 233–254.

Evans, C. Lawrence. *Leadership in Committee.* Ann Arbor: University of Michigan Press, 1991.

Evans, C. Lawrence, and Walter J. Oleszek. *Congress Under Fire.* Boston: Houghton Mifflin, 1997.

Evans, Diana. *Greasing the Wheels: Using Pork Barrel Projects to Build Majority Coalitions in Congress.* Cambridge: Cambridge University Press, 2004.

___. "Policy and Pork: The Use of Pork Barrel Projects to Build Policy Coalitions in the House of Representatives." *American Journal of Political Science* 38 (1994): 894–917.

Fenno, Richard F., Jr. *Congressmen in Committees.* Boston: Little, Brown, 1973.

___. *Going Home: Black Representatives and Their Constituents.* Chicago: University of Chicago Press, 2003.

___. *Home Style: House Members in Their Districts.* Boston: Little, Brown, 1978.

___. *Learning to Govern: An Institutional View of the 104th Congress.* Washington, D.C.: Brookings, 1997.

___. *The Power of the Purse.* Boston: Little, Brown, 1966.

___. *Senators on the Campaign Trail: The Politics of Representation.* Norman: University of Oklahoma Press, 1996.

___. *The United States Senate: A Bicameral Perspective.* Washington, D.C.: American Enterprise Institute, 1982.

Ferejohn, John A. *Pork Barrel Politics.* Stanford: Stanford University Press, 1974.

Fiorina, Morris P. *Congress: Keystone of the Washington Establishment.* New Haven: Yale University Press, 1977.

___. *Divided Government.* New York: Allyn and Bacon, 1995.

___. *Representatives, Roll Calls, and Constituencies.* Lexington, Mass.: Lexington Books, 1974.

Fiorina, Morris P., David W. Rohde, and Peter Wissel. "Historical Change in House Turnover." In *Congress in Change.* Ed. Norman J. Ornstein. New York: Praeger, 1975.

Fishel, Jeff. *Party and Opposition.* New York: David McKay, 1973.

Fisher, Louis. *The Constitution between Friends: Congress, the President, and the Law.* New York: St. Martin's, 1978.

Fleisher, Richard, and Jon R. Bond. "The Shrinking Middle in the U.S. Congress." *British Journal of Political Science* 34 (July 2004): 429–451.

Flemming, Gregory N. "Presidential Coattails in Open-Seat Elections." *Legislative Studies Quarterly* 20 (1995): 197–211.

Fowler, Linda L. *Candidates, Congress, and American Democracy.* Ann Arbor: University of Michigan Press, 1993.

Fowler, Linda L., and Robert D. McClure. *Political Ambition: Who Decides to Run for Congress?* New Haven: Yale University Press, 1989.

Fox, Harrison W., Jr., and Susan Webb Hammond. *Congressional Staffs: The Invisible Force in American Lawmaking.* New York: Free Press, 1977.

Franklin, Daniel P. *Making Ends Meet.* Washington, D.C.: CQ Press, 1993.

Frantzich, Stephen E. "Computerized Information Technology in the U.S. House of Representatives." *Legislative Studies Quarterly* 4 (1979): 255–280.

Freeman, J. Leiper. *The Political Process.* New York: Random House, 1955.

Friedman, Sally. "House Committee Assignments of Women and Minority Newcomers." *Legislative Studies Quarterly* 21 (1996): 73–82.

Froman, Lewis A., Jr. *The Congressional Process: Strategies, Rules, and Procedures.* Boston: Little, Brown, 1967.

Gamm, Gerald, and Kenneth Shepsle. "The Emergence of Legislative Institutions: Standing Committees in the House and Senate, 1810–1825." *Legislative Studies Quarterly* 14 (1989): 39–66.

Gibson, Martha L. *Conflict amid Consensus in American Trade Policy.* Washington, D.C.: Georgetown University Press, 2000.

___. "Issues, Coalitions, and Divided Government." *Congress and the Presidency* 22 (1995): 155–166.

Gilmour, John B. *Reconcilable Differences.* Berkeley: University of California Press, 1990.

Gilmour, John B., and Paul Rothstein. "A Dynamic Model of Loss, Retirement, and Tenure in the U.S. House." *Journal of Politics* 58 (1996): 54–68.

Glazer, Amihai, and Bernard Grofman. "Two Plus Two Plus Two Equals Six: Tenure of Office of Senators and Representatives, 1953–1983." *Legislative Studies Quarterly* 12 (1987): 555–563.

Goehlert, Robert U., and John R. Sayre. *The United States Congress: A Bibliography.* New York: Free Press, 1982.

Goodwin, George, Jr. *The Little Legislatures.* Amherst: University of Massachusetts Press, 1970.

Groseclose, Timothy. "The Committee Outlier Debate: A Review and a Reexamination of Some of the Evidence." *Public Choice* 80 (1994): 265–273.

Groseclose, Timothy, and Keith Krehbiel. "Golden Parachutes, Rubber Checks, and Strategic Retirements from the 102nd House." *American Journal of Political Science* 38 (February 1994): 75–99.

Hager, Gregory, and Jeffery Talbert. "Look for the Party Label: Party Influences on Voting in the U.S. House." *Legislative Studies Quarterly* 25 (2000): 75–99.

Hall, Richard L. "Participation and Purpose in Committee Decision Making." *American Political Science Review* 81 (1987): 105–127.

___. *Participation in Congress.* New Haven: Yale University Press, 1993.

Hammond, Susan Webb. *Congressional Caucuses in National Policymaking.* Baltimore: Johns Hopkins University Press, 1997.

Harris, Joseph. *Congressional Control of Administration.* Washington, D.C.: Brookings, 1964.

Hawkesworth, Mary. "Congressional Enactments of Race-Gender: Toward a Theory of Raced-Gendered Institutions." *American Political Science Review* 97 (2003): 529–550.

Hechler, Kenneth W. *Insurgency: Personalities and Politics in the Taft Era.* New York: Columbia University Press, 1940.

Heitshusen, Valerie. "The Allocation of Federal Money to House Committee Members: Distributive Theory and Policy Jurisdictions." *American Politics Research* (formerly *American Politics Quarterly*) 29 (January 2001): 80–98.

___. "Interest Group Lobbying and U.S. House Decentralization: Linking Information Type to Committee Hearing Appearances." *Political Research Quarterly* 53 (March 2000): 151–176.

Henry, Charles P. "Legitimizing Race in Congressional Politics." *American Politics Quarterly* 5 (1977): 149–176.

Herrnson, Paul S. *Congressional Elections: Campaigning at Home and in Washington.* Washington, D.C.: CQ Press, 1995.

___. *Party Campaigning in the 1980s.* Cambridge: Harvard University Press, 1988.

Hershey, Marjorie R. *The Making of Campaign Strategy.* Lexington, Mass.: Lexington Books, 1974.

Hibbing, John R. *Congressional Careers.* Chapel Hill: University of North Carolina Press, 1991.

Hibbing, John R., and Elizabeth Theiss-Morse. *Congress as Public Enemy: Public Attitudes toward American Political Institutions.* Cambridge: Cambridge University Press, 1995.

Hinckley, Barbara. *The Seniority System in Congress.* Bloomington: Indiana University Press, 1971.

Hoadly, John F. "The Emergence of Political Parties in Congress, 1789–1803." *American Political Science Review* 74 (1980): 757–779.

Holtzman, Abraham. *Legislative Liaison.* Chicago: Rand McNally, 1970.

Huitt, Ralph K., and Robert L. Peabody. *Congress: Two Decades of Analysis.* New York: Harper, 1969.

Huntington, Samuel P. "Congressional Responses to the Twentieth Century." In *The Congress and America's Future.* 2nd ed. Ed. David B. Truman. Englewood Cliffs, N.J.: Prentice Hall, 1973.

Hurley, Patricia, and Kim Quaile Hill. "Beyond the Demand-Input Model: A Theory of Representational Linkages." *Journal of Politics* 65 (2003): 304–326.

___. "The Prospects for Issue-Voting in Contemporary Congressional Elections." *American Politics Quarterly* 8 (1980): 425–448.

Hurwitz, Mark S., Roger J. Moiles, and David W. Rohde. "Distributive and Partisan Issues in Agriculture Policy in the 104th House." *American Political Science Review* 95 (2001): 911–922.

Jackson, John. *Constituencies and Leaders in Congress.* Cambridge: Harvard University Press, 1974.

Jacobson, Gary C. *The Electoral Origins of Divided Government.* Boulder, Colo.: Westview, 1990.

___. "The Marginals Never Vanished: Incumbency and Competition in Elections to the U.S. House of Representatives, 1952–81." *American Journal of Political Science* 31 (1987): 126–141.

———. *Money in Congressional Elections.* New Haven: Yale University Press, 1980.

———. *The Politics of Congressional Elections.* 6th ed. New York: Pearson Longman, 2004.

Jacobson, Gary C., and Samuel Kernell. *Strategy and Choice in Congressional Elections.* New Haven: Yale University Press, 1983.

Jewell, Malcolm E. *Senatorial Politics and Foreign Policy.* Lexington: University Press of Kentucky, 1962.

Jewell, Malcolm E., and Samuel C. Patterson. *The Legislative Process in the United States.* 3rd ed. New York: Random House, 1977.

Jillson, Calvin, and Rick K. Wilson. *Congressional Dynamics: Structure, Coordination, and Choice in the First American Congress, 1774–1789.* Stanford: Stanford University Press, 1994.

Johannes, John R. *Policy Innovation in Congress.* Morristown, N.J.: General Learning Press, 1972.

Jones, Bryan D., Frank R. Baumgartner, and Jeffrey C. Talbert. "The Destruction of Issue Monopolies in Congress." *American Political Science Review* 87 (1993): 657–671.

Jones, Bryan D., Frank R. Baumgartner, and James L. True. "Policy Punctuations: U.S. Budget Authority, 1947–1995." *Journal of Politics* 60 (1998): 1–33.

Jones, Charles O. *The Minority Party in Congress.* Boston: Little, Brown, 1970.

———. "Will Reform Change Congress?" In *Congress Reconsidered.* 1st ed. Ed. Lawrence C. Dodd and Bruce I. Oppenheimer. New York: Praeger, 1977.

Kahn, Kim Fridkin, and Patrick J. Kenney. *The Spectacle of U.S. Senate Campaigns.* Princeton: Princeton University Press, 1999.

Katz, Jonathan, and Brian Sala. "Careerism, Committee Assignments, and the Electoral Connection." *American Political Science Review* 90 (1996): 21–33.

Kazee, Thomas, ed. *Who Runs for Congress? Ambition, Context, and Candidate Emergence.* Washington, D.C.: CQ Press, 1994.

Kelly, Sean Q. "Democratic Leadership in the Modern Senate: The Emerging Roles of the Democratic Policy Committee." *Congress and the Presidency* 22 (1995): 113–140.

Kiewiet, Roderick, and Mathew D. McCubbins. *The Spending Power.* Berkeley: University of California Press, 1991.

King, David C. *Turf Wars: How Congressional Committees Claim Jurisdiction.* Chicago: University of Chicago Press, 1997.

Kingdon, John W. *Candidates for Office.* New York: Random House, 1968.

———. *Congressmen's Voting Decisions.* New York: Harper, 1973.

Krasno, Jonathan S. *Challengers, Competition, and Reelection: Comparing Senate and House Elections.* New Haven: Yale University Press, 1994.

Krehbiel, Keith. "Are Congressional Committees Composed of Preference Outliers?" *American Political Science Review* 84 (1990): 149–164.

———. *Information and Legislative Organization.* Ann Arbor: University of Michigan Press, 1990.

___. *Pivotal Politics: A Theory of U.S. Lawmaking.* Chicago: University of Chicago Press, 1998.

Krehbiel, Keith, Kenneth A. Shepsle, and Barry R. Weingast. "Why Are Congressional Committees Powerful?" *American Political Science Review* 81 (1987): 929–948.

Kuklinski, James H. "District Competitiveness and Legislative Roll Call Behavior: A Reassessment of the Marginality Hypothesis." *American Journal of Political Science* 21 (1977): 627–638.

Lau, Richard R., and Gerald M. Pomper. "Effectiveness of Negative Campaigning in U.S. Senate Elections." *American Journal of Political Science* 46 (2002): 47–66.

Lawrence, Eric D., Forrest Maltzman, and Paul J. Wahlbeck. "The Politics of Speaker Cannon's Committee Assignments." *American Journal of Political Science* 45 (2001): 551–562.

Lee, Frances E. "Senate Representation and Coalition Building in Distributive Politics." *American Political Science Review* 94 (2000): 50–72.

Lee, Frances E., and Bruce I. Oppenheimer. *Sizing Up the Senate.* Chicago: University of Chicago Press, 1999.

LeLoup, Lance T., and Steven Shull. "Congress versus the Executive: The 'Two Presidencies' Reconsidered." *Social Science Quarterly* 59 (1979): 704–719.

Lindsay, James M. *Congress and the Politics of U.S. Foreign Policy.* Baltimore: Johns Hopkins University Press, 1994.

Lipinski, Daniel. *Congressional Communication.* Ann Arbor: University of Michigan Press, 2004.

Loewenberg, Gerhard, and Samuel Patterson. *Comparing Legislatures.* Boston: Little, Brown, 1979.

Longley, Lawrence D., and Walter J. Oleszek. *Bicameral Politics: Conference Committees in Congress.* New Haven: Yale University Press, 1989.

Loomis, Burdette A. *The New American Politician: Ambition, Entrepreneurship, and the Changing Face of Political Life.* New York: Basic Books, 1988.

___, ed. *Esteemed Colleagues: Civility and Deliberation in the U.S. Senate.* Washington, D.C.: Brookings, 2000.

Lowi, Theodore J. *The End of Liberalism.* New York: Norton, 1969, 1979.

___. *The End of the Republican Era.* Norman: University of Oklahoma Press, 1995.

Maass, Arthur. *Congress and the Common Good.* New York: Basic Books, 1983.

Maisel, Louis S. *From Obscurity to Oblivion: Running in the Congressional Primary.* Knoxville: University of Tennessee Press, 1982.

Malbin, Michael. *Life after Reform.* Lanham, Md.: Rowman and Littlefield, 2003.

Maltzman, Forrest. "Meeting Competing Demands: Committee Performance in the Post-Reform House." *American Journal of Political Science* 39 (1995): 653–682.

Manley, John F. *The Politics of Finance.* Boston: Little, Brown, 1970.

Mann, Thomas E. *Unsafe at Any Margin: Interpreting Congressional Elections.* Washington, D.C.: American Enterprise Institute, 1978.

———, ed. *A Question of Balance: The President, the Congress, and Foreign Policy.* Washington, D.C.: Brookings, 1990.

Mann, Thomas E., and Raymond E. Wolfinger. "Candidates and Parties in Congressional Elections." *American Political Science Review* 74 (1980): 616–632.

Matthews, Donald R. *U.S. Senators and Their World.* New York: Vintage Books, 1960.

Mayhew, David R. *America's Congress: Actions in the Public Sphere, James Madison through Newt Gingrich.* New Haven: Yale University Press, 2000.

———. *Congress: The Electoral Connection.* New Haven: Yale University Press, 1974.

———. *Divided We Govern.* New Haven: Yale University Press, 1991.

———. *Party Loyalty among Congressmen.* Cambridge: Harvard University Press, 1966.

McAdams, John C., and John R. Johannes. "Congressmen, Perquisites, and Elections." *Journal of Politics* 50 (1988): 412–439.

Meernik, James. "Presidential Support in Congress: Conflict and Consensus in Foreign and Defense Policy." *Journal of Politics* 55 (1993): 569–587.

Mezey, Michael L. *Congress, the President, and Public Policy.* Boulder, Colo.: Westview, 1989.

Moe, Terry M. "An Assessment of the Positive Theory of Congressional Dominance." *Legislative Studies Quarterly* 12 (1987): 475–520.

Mondak, Jeffrey. "Competence, Integrity, and Electoral Success of Congressional Incumbents." *Journal of Politics* 57 (1995): 1043–1069.

Nelson, Garrison. "Partisan Patterns of House Leadership Change, 1789–1977." *American Political Science Review* 71 (1977): 918–939.

Niemi, Richard, and Laura Winsky. "The Persistence of Partisan Redistricting Effects in Congressional Elections in the 1970s and 1980s." *Journal of Politics* 54 (1992): 563–572.

Norpoth, Helmut. "Explaining Party Cohesion in Congress: The Case of Shared Party Attributes." *American Political Science Review* 70 (1976): 1157–1171.

Ogul, Morris S. *Congress Oversees the Bureaucracy.* Pittsburgh: University of Pittsburgh Press, 1976.

Oldmixon, Elizabeth A. *Making Moral Decisions: God, Sex and the U.S. House of Representatives.* Washington, D.C.: Georgetown University Press, 2005.

Oleszek, Walter J. *Congressional Procedures and the Policy Process.* 5th ed. Washington, D.C.: CQ Press, 2001.

Oppenheimer, Bruce I. *Oil and the Congressional Process: The Limits of Symbolic Politics.* Lexington, Mass.: Lexington Books, 1974.

———. "The Representational Experience: The Effect of State Population on Senator-Constituency Linkages." *American Journal of Political Science* 40 (1996): 1280–1299.

———. "The Rules Committee: New Arm of Leadership in a Decentralized House." In *Congress Reconsidered.* 1st ed. Ed. Lawrence C. Dodd and Bruce I. Oppenheimer. New York: Praeger, 1977.

___. "Split-Party Control of Congress, 1981–1986: Exploring Electoral and Apportionment Explanations." *American Journal of Political Science* 33 (1989): 653–669.

___, ed. *U.S. Senate Exceptionalism.* Columbus: Ohio State University Press, 2002.

Orfield, Gary. *Congressional Power: Congress and Social Change.* New York: Harcourt, 1975.

Ornstein, Norman J. *Congress in Change: Evolution and Reform.* New York: Praeger, 1975.

Ornstein, Norman J., and Shirley Elder. *Interest Groups, Lobbying, and Policymaking.* Washington, D.C.: CQ Press, 1978.

Ornstein, Norman J., Thomas E. Mann, and Michael J. Malbin. *Vital Statistics on Congress, 1995–1996.* Washington, D.C.: Congressional Quarterly, 1995.

Owens, John E. "Curbing the Fiefdoms: Party-Committee Relations in the Contemporary U.S. House of Representatives." In *The Changing Roles of Parliamentary Committees.* Ed. Lawrence D. Longley and Attila Agh. Appleton, Wis.: Research Committee of Legislative Specialists, 1997.

Parker, Glenn R. *Homeward Bound: Explaining Changes in Congressional Behavior.* Pittsburgh: University of Pittsburgh Press, 1986.

___. *Institutional Change, Discretion, and the Making of the Modern Congress.* Ann Arbor: University of Michigan Press, 1992.

Parker, Glenn R., and S. L. Parker. "Factions in Committees: The U.S. House of Representatives." *American Political Science Review* 73 (1979): 85–102.

Patterson, James T. *Congressional Conservatism and the New Deal.* Lexington: University Press of Kentucky, 1967.

Payne, James L. "The Personal Electoral Advantage of House Incumbents, 1936–1976." *American Politics Quarterly* 8 (1980): 465–482.

Peabody, Robert L. *Leadership in Congress: Stability, Succession, and Change.* Boston: Little, Brown, 1976.

Peabody, Robert L., and Nelson W. Polsby, eds. *New Perspectives on the House of Representatives.* 3rd ed. Chicago: Rand McNally, 1977.

Peters, Ronald M., Jr. *The American Speakership.* Baltimore: Johns Hopkins University Press, 1990.

Peterson, Mark A. *Legislating Together: The White House and Capitol Hill from Eisenhower to Reagan.* Cambridge: Harvard University Press, 1990.

Polsby, Nelson W. *Congress and the Presidency.* 3rd ed. Englewood Cliffs, N.J.: Prentice Hall, 1976.

___. *How Congress Evolves.* New York: Oxford, 2004.

___. "Institutionalization in the U.S. House of Representatives." *American Political Science Review* 62 (1968): 144–168.

Polsby, Nelson W., Miriam Gallagher, and Barry Rundquist. "The Growth of the Seniority System in the House of Representatives." *American Political Science Review* 63 (1969): 787–807.

Poole, Keith T., and Howard Rosenthal. *Congress: A Political-Economic History of Roll Call Voting.* New York: Oxford University Press, 1997.

Powell, Lynda W. "Issue Representation in Congress." *Journal of Politics* 44 (1982): 658–678.

Price, David E. *The Congressional Experience.* Boulder, Colo.: Westview, 2000.

___. *Who Makes the Laws?* Cambridge, Mass.: Schenkman, 1972.

Price, H. Douglas. "Congress and the Evolution of Legislative Professionalism." In *Congress in Change.* Ed. Norman J. Ornstein. New York: Praeger, 1975.

Ragsdale, Lyn, and Timothy E. Cook. "Representatives' Actions and Challengers' Reactions: Limits to Candidate Connections in the House." *American Journal of Political Science* 31 (1987): 45–81.

Ragsdale, Lyn, and Jerrold G. Rusk. "Candidates, Issues, and Participation in Senate Elections." *Legislative Studies Quarterly* 20 (1995): 305–328.

Rieselbach, Leroy N. *Congressional Politics: The Evolving Legislative System.* 2nd ed. Boulder, Colo.: Westview, 1995.

___. *Congressional Reform: The Changing Modern Congress.* Washington, D.C.: CQ Press, 1994.

Ripley, Randall B., and Grace N. Franklin. *Congress, the Bureaucracy, and Public Policy.* 5th ed. Belmont, Calif.: Wadsworth, 1991.

Ripley, Randall B., and James M. Lindsay, eds. *Congress Resurgent: Foreign and Defense Policy on Capitol Hill.* Ann Arbor: University of Michigan Press, 1993.

Roberts, Jason M., and Steven S. Smith. "Procedural Contexts, Party Strategy, and Conditional Party Voting in the U.S. House of Representatives, 1971–2000." *American Journal of Political Science* 47 (2003): 305–317.

Rohde, David W. *Parties and Leaders in the Postreform House.* Chicago: University of Chicago Press, 1991.

Rohde, David W., and Kenneth A. Shepsle. "Democratic Committee Assignments in the U.S. House of Representatives." *American Political Science Review* 67 (1973): 889–905.

Rothman, David J. *Politics and Power.* New York: Athenaeum, 1969.

Rudder, Catherine E. "Committee Reform and the Revenue Process." In *Congress Reconsidered.* 1st ed. Ed. Lawrence C. Dodd and Bruce I. Oppenheimer. New York: Praeger, 1977.

Saloma, John S., III. *Congress and the New Politics.* Boston: Little, Brown, 1969.

Schick, Allen. *Making Economic Policy in Congress.* Washington, D.C.: American Enterprise Institute, 1983.

Schickler, Eric. *Disjointed Pluralism.* Princeton: Princeton University Press, 2001.

___. "Institutional Change in the House of Representatives, 1867–1998: A Test of Partisan and Ideological Power Balance Models." *American Political Science Review* 94 (2000): 269–288.

Schickler, Eric, and Andrew Rich. "Party Government in the House Reconsidered: A Response to Cox and McCubbins." *American Journal of Political Science* 41 (1997): 1387–1394.

Schiller, Wendy J. *Partners and Rivals: Representation in U.S. Senate Delegations.* Princeton: Princeton University Press, 2000.

___. "Senators as Political Entrepreneurs: Using Bill Sponsorship to Shape Legislative Agendas." *American Journal of Political Science* 39 (1995): 186–203.

Schneider, Jerrold E. *Ideological Coalitions in Congress.* Greenwood, Conn.: Greenwood Press, 1979.

Schwarz, John E., and L. Earl Shaw. *The United States Congress in Comparative Perspective.* Hinsdale, Ill.: Dryden Press, 1976.

Seidman, Harold. *Politics, Position, and Power.* 2nd ed. London: Oxford University Press, 1975.

Sellers, Patrick J. "Winning Media Coverage in the U.S. Congress." In *U.S. Senate Exceptionalism.* Ed. Bruce I. Oppenheimer. Columbus: Ohio State University Press, 2002, 132–156.

Shepsle, Kenneth A. "The Changing Textbook Congress: Equilibrium in Congressional Institutions and Behavior." In *American Political Institutions and the Problems of Our Time.* Ed. John E. Chubb and Paul E. Peterson. Washington: Brookings, 1990.

___. *The Giant Jigsaw Puzzle.* Chicago: University of Chicago Press, 1978.

Shepsle, Kenneth A., and Barry R. Weingast, eds. *Positive Theories of Congressional Institutions.* Ann Arbor: University of Michigan Press, 1995.

Shipan, Charles R. "Regulatory Regimes, Agency Actions, and the Conditional Nature of Congressional Influence." *American Political Science Review* 98 (2003): 467–480.

Sinclair, Barbara. *Legislators, Leaders, and Lawmaking: The U.S. House of Representatives in the Postreform Era.* Baltimore: Johns Hopkins University Press, 1995.

___. *Majority Leadership in the U.S. House.* Baltimore: Johns Hopkins University Press, 1983.

___. *The Transformation of the U.S. Senate.* Baltimore: Johns Hopkins University Press, 1989.

___. *Unorthodox Lawmaking: New Legislative Processes in the U.S. Congress.* 2nd ed. Washington, D.C.: CQ Press, 1997.

Smith, Steven S. *The American Congress.* Boston: Houghton Mifflin, 1995.

___. *Call to Order: Floor Politics in the House and Senate.* Washington, D.C.: Brookings, 1989.

Snyder, James, and Tim Groseclose. "Estimating Party Influence in Congressional Roll-Call Voting." *American Journal of Political Science* 44 (2000): 193–211.

Stein, Robert M., and Kenneth N. Bickers. *Perpetuating the Pork: Policy Subsystems and American Democracy.* New York: Cambridge University Press, 1995.

Stimson, James A., Michael B. MacKuen, and Robert S. Erikson. "Dynamic Representation." *American Political Science Review* 89 (1995): 543–565.

Stone, Walter J. "The Dynamics of Constituency: Electoral Control in the House." *American Politics Quarterly* 8 (1980): 399–424.

Strahan, Randall. *New Ways and Means: Reform and Change in a Congressional Committee.* Chapel Hill: University of North Carolina Press, 1990.

Sundquist, James L. *The Decline and Resurgence of Congress.* Washington, D.C.: Brookings, 1981.

___. *Politics and Policy.* Washington, D.C.: Brookings, 1968.

Swain, Carol M. *Black Faces, Black Interests: The Representation of African Americans in Congress.* Cambridge: Harvard University Press, 1993.

Swift, Elaine K. *The Making of an American Senate: Reconstitutive Change in Congress, 1787–1841.* Ann Arbor: University of Michigan Press, 1996.

Talbert, Jeffrey, Bryan D. Jones, and Frank R. Baumgartner. "Nonlegislative Hearings and Policy Change in Congress." *American Journal of Political Science* 39 (1995): 383–405.

Tate, Katherine. *Black Faces in the Mirror: African Americans and Their Representatives in the U.S. Congress.* Princeton: Princeton University Press, 2003.

Thomas, Sue. *How Women Legislate.* New York: Oxford University Press, 1994.

Thurber, James A., ed. *Rivals for Power: Presidential-Congressional Relations.* Washington, D.C.: CQ Press, 1996.

Thurber, James A., and Roger H. Davidson. *Remaking Congress: Change and Stability in the 1990s.* Washington, D.C.: CQ Press, 1995.

Truman, David B. *The Governmental Process.* New York: Knopf, 1951.

Turner, Julius. *Party and Constituency: Pressures on Congress.* Rev. ed. by Edward V. Schneier Jr. Baltimore: Johns Hopkins University Press, 1970.

Unekis, Joseph, and Leroy N. Rieselbach. *Congressional Committee Politics: Continuity and Change.* New York: Praeger, 1984.

Uslaner, Eric M. *The Decline of Comity in Congress.* Ann Arbor: University of Michigan Press, 1993.

Vogler, David J. *The Politics of Congress.* 6th ed. Madison, Wis.: Brown and Benchmark, 1993.

___. *The Third House.* Evanston, Ill.: Northwestern University Press, 1971.

Wahlke, John C., Heinz H. Eulau, W. Buchanan, and L. C. Ferguson. *The Legislative System: Explorations in Legislative Behavior.* New York: Wiley, 1962.

Wawro, Gregory. *Legislative Entrepreneurship in the U.S. House of Representatives.* Ann Arbor: University of Michigan Press, 2000.

Wayne, S. J. *The Legislative Presidency.* New York: Harper, 1978.

Weingast, Barry. "Floor Behavior in the U.S. Congress: Committee Power under the Open Rule." *American Political Science Review* 83 (1989): 795–815.

Weisberg, Herbert F. "Evaluating Theories of Congressional Roll Call Voting." *American Journal of Political Science* 22 (1978): 554–577.

Weisberg, Herbert F., Eric S. Heberlig, and Lisa M. Campoli. *Classics in Congressional Politics.* New York: Longman, 1999.

Westefield, L. P. "Majority Party Leadership and the Committee System in the House of Representatives." *American Political Science Review* 68 (1974): 1593–1604.

Wildavsky, Aaron. *The Politics of the Budgetary Process.* Boston: Little, Brown, 1964.

Wilson, Rick. "Forward and Backward Agenda Procedures: Committee Experience and Structurally Induced Equilibrium." *Journal of Politics* 48 (1986): 390–409.

Wilson, Woodrow. *Congressional Government.* 1885. Reprint, Gloucester, Mass.: Peter Smith, 1973.

Wolfensberger, Donald R. *Congress and the People: Deliberative Democracy on Trial.* Baltimore: Johns Hopkins University Press, 2000.

Wolfinger, Raymond E., and Joan Heifetz Hollinger. "Safe Seats, Seniority, and Power in Congress." *American Political Science Review* 59 (1965): 337–349.

Wright, Fiona A. "The Caucus Reelection Requirement and the Transformation of House Committee Chairs, 1959–94." *Legislative Studies Quarterly* 25 (August 2000): 469–480.

Wright, Gerald C., and Michael B. Berkman. "Candidates and Policy in United States Senate Elections." *American Political Science Review* 80 (1986): 567–588.

Wright, Gerald C., Leroy Rieselbach, and Lawrence C. Dodd, eds. *Congress and Policy Change.* New York: Agathon, 1986.

Wright, John. "PACs, Contributions, and Roll Calls: An Organizational Perspective." *American Political Science Review* 75 (1985): 400–414.

Young, Garry. "Committee Gatekeeping and Proposal Power under Single and Multiple Referral." *Journal of Theoretical Politics* 8 (1996): 65–78.

Young, James S. *The Washington Community, 1800–1828.* New York: Columbia University Press, 1966.

Index of Scholars

(Cited in chapter endnotes)

Subject Index